OXFORD JUNIOR ENCYCLOPAEDIA

GENERAL EDITORS

LAURA E. SALT AND ROBERT SINCLAIR

ILLUSTRATIONS EDITOR: HELEN MARY PETTER

VOLUME XII

THE ARTS

OXFORD UNIVERSITY PRESS

Oxford University Press, Amen House, London E.C.4

GLASGOW NEW YORK TORONTO MELBOURNE WELLINGTON
BOMBAY CALCUTTA MADRAS KARACHI
CAPE TOWN IBADAN NAIROBI ACCRA SINGAPORE

FIRST PUBLISHED 1954
REPRINTED WITH CORRECTIONS 1956, 1957

PRINTED IN GREAT BRITAIN
AT THE UNIVERSITY PRESS, OXFORD
BY CHARLES BATEY, PRINTER TO THE UNIVERSITY

PREFACE

IN authorizing the preparation of this work the Delegates of the Oxford University Press had foremost in mind the need to provide a basic book of reference for school libraries. In form it was to be a genuine encyclopaedia, in treatment and vocabulary suitable for the young reader. To many children (and indeed to many adults) reading is not a natural activity: they do not turn to books for their own sake. But they can be trained to go to books for information which they want for some particular purpose—and thus, very often, to form a habit which will be of lifelong value. Their capacity to read continuously for any length of time being limited, they can absorb knowledge better if they get it in small quantities: therefore they will often read reference books when they may reject the reading of more extended matter. Again, it is probably true to say of such readers that their approach is from the particular to the general, and from the application to the principle, rather than the reverse, that their main interest is in the modern world around them, and that since they are not very good at conceiving things outside their own experience, their capacity for grasping abstract ideas is limited. On the other hand, once their interest is aroused, they will often pursue a subject to remarkable lengths, so long as its development is logical and the treatment avoids dullness.

But such generalizations can easily be overdone: many children using the books will not be of this type. Moreover, it was evident from the first that a project involving so great an amount of work, however exactly it might meet its principal mark, would be fully justified only if it could be of service to a far wider circle of readers. Even for the age-group first in mind, anything like 'writing-down to children' must plainly be taboo—but clear exposition and simple language are no bad qualities in writing for any audience. Here, then, it seemed, was the opportunity to provide a work of reference suitable for many readers to whom the large, standard encyclopaedias are too heavy and technical, and the popular alternatives for the most part neither sufficiently complete nor authoritative. The fact that the plan allowed for an exceptionally large proportion of illustrations to text (between one-quarter and one-third of the total space) is an advantage to any reader, since pictures may, in many instances, save whole paragraphs of involved explanation. With these secondary aims well in mind, therefore, the General

Editors have ventured to hope that the encyclopaedia may find usefulness not only among certain younger children, but also among older students in clubs, libraries, and Young People's Colleges, and even to no small extent among their parents and other adults who may wish for a simple approach to some unfamiliar or forgotten subject.

SCOPE AND EMPHASIS. Within certain limits the OXFORD JUNIOR ENCY-CLOPAEDIA purports to be reasonably comprehensive, though (in common with all general encyclopaedias) not exhaustive. Chief among these limits is that matter already easily available in school textbooks is included only so far as its presence is necessary for the proper understanding of the subject under discussion. Thus, although an immense field of history is surveyed, it will be found mainly under headings dealing with its effects, or in the biographies of those who lived to make it. Purely technical or scientific subjects, also, are omitted except when they have some general interest. In natural history and kindred studies the immense variety of forms necessarily led at times either to their treatment by groups or to their omission on purely arbitrary decisions as to which species would, in all probability, never be looked for, or because there was nothing particularly interesting to say of them. In point of general balance the stress is laid rather on the modern world, though due space is given to the factors which have shaped it, no less than to those which are changing it.

ARRANGEMENT. The encyclopaedia is planned to consist of twelve volumes. Each is arranged alphabetically within itself, and each deals with a particular range of related subjects. Within its terms of reference, then, each volume is virtually self-contained, and, owing to the great number of single-line cross-references, can well be used alone. This arrangement, which has several incidental advantages (as of production, in difficult times, and of prompt revision later), arose mainly from one consideration. If articles were to be kept really short—and, in fact, few approach and almost none exceeds 2,000 words—many subjects could be dealt with comprehensively only by referring the reader to other relevant articles—itself a desirable thing to do. It was clearly preferable for these to be under his hand, rather than be dispersed through any of the twelve volumes at the caprice of the alphabet. This the present arrangement achieves to a great extent. If it has led to a small amount of overlapping, that again is not without its advantages.

The cross-references play an indispensable part in the make-up of the encyclopaedia. They are of two kinds: references in the text to further articles amplifying the particular point under review, and references at the end of an article to others taking the whole subject farther. Therefore, a reader looking up any wide subject, such as ARCHITECTURE, and following up its cross-references either in the text or at the end of the article, can discover under what main headwords the subject is treated. These, again, will refer him to any subsidiary articles, as also, in many cases, to those of a complementary nature. Thus he may be guided either from the general to the particular or vice versa. It is believed that the titles of the twelve volumes (see p. xiii), in conjunction with their sub-titles, will usually lead the reader straight to the volume containing the information he wants. In selecting headwords, the rules generally followed have been to prefer the familiar, or even the colloquial, reserving the technical alternative for a single-line entry, and to group narrow subjects under a headword of wider scope. Thus, for CUBISM, *see* MODERN ART; COUNTERPOINT, *see* HARMONY; TEMPERA, *see* PAINTING METHODS; FUGUE, *see* MUSICAL FORM; METAPHOR, *see* FIGURES OF SPEECH.

L. E. S., R. S.

OXFORD, 1954

LIST OF CONTRIBUTORS

VOLUME EDITOR

HELEN MARY PETTER

PRINCIPAL CONTRIBUTORS

W. K. DAVIN (*Literature*).

CECIL GOULD, Assistant Keeper, National Gallery (*Art*).

J. M. RICHARDS, A.R.I.B.A. (*Architecture*).

ERIC TAYLOR, M.A., B.Mus. (*Music*).

OTHER CONTRIBUTORS

CYRIL ALDRED, B.A., F.S.A. (Scot.), Assistant Keeper in the Department of Art and Ethnography, Royal Scottish Museum, Edinburgh.

THOMAS ARMSTRONG, D.Mus., F.R.C.O., F.R.C.M., Lecturer in Music in the University of Oxford.

AUDREY M. BAKER, Ph.D.

PHILIP BARLOW, Assistant Keeper of Art, National Museum of Wales, Cardiff.

JOHN R. BIGGS, M.S.I.A., A.T.D., F.R.S.A., Head of the Department of Commercial and Industrial Design, Brighton College of Art.

JAMES BOSWELL, F.S.I.A.

MANFRED H. BRÄUDE.

H. J. BRAUNHOLTZ, C.B.E., M.A., formerly Keeper of the Department of Ethnography, British Museum; Past President of the Royal Anthropological Institute.

D. S. BREWER, M.A., Lecturer in English in the University of Birmingham.

D. H. BURDEN, M.A. (Oxon).

REV. G. W. BUTTERWORTH, Litt.D.

JOAN CHISSELL, Assistant Music Critic of *The Times*; Extra-Mural Lecturer in Music in the Universities of Oxford and London.

ALEC CLIFTON-TAYLOR, M.A. (Oxon), B.A. (Lond.), Extra-Mural Lecturer in the History of Art in the University of London.

A. O. J. COCKSHUT.

WILLIAM COHN, M.A.

D. P. COSTELLO.

HEBE COX.

J. A. DAVISON, T.D., M.A. (Oxon), Professor of Greek Language and Literature in the University of Leeds.

A. DOREEN D. DUNBABIN.

THOMAS EVANS.

J. C. GHOSH.

CECIL GRAYSON, M.A.

BARBARA HARE.

PETER HATCH, M.S.I.A., Art Director and Typographer, Council of Industrial Design.

DAVID HAWKES, M.A., Lecturer in Chinese in the University of Oxford.

SYBILLE EDITH HAYNES, Ph.D. (Frankfurt).

R. A. HIGGINS, B.A., Assistant Keeper of Greek and Roman Antiquities, British Museum.

RICHARD WYATT HUTCHINSON, M.A. (Cantab.), F.S.A., F.R.A.I.

G. L. LEWIS, M.A., D.Phil., Lecturer in Turkish in the University of Oxford.

MARGARET S. MACDONALD-TAYLOR, A.R.C.A., Hon. A.R.I.B.A., formerly Lecturer, Royal College of Art.

E. G. MIDGLEY, B.Litt., M.A.

D. E. MILLS, M.A. (Cantab.), B.A. (Lond.), Lecturer in Japanese in the School of Oriental and African Studies, University of London.

CLIFFORD MUSGRAVE, Director, Brighton Art Gallery and Museum.

IONA OPIE.

PETER OPIE.

MARGARET PENNING-ROWSELL.

STUART PIGGOTT, Abercromby Professor of Prehistoric Archaeology in the University of Edinburgh.

R. H. PINDER-WILSON, Assistant Keeper in the Department of Oriental Antiquities, British Museum.

DAVID PIPER.

ANNE RIDLER.

NEVILLE ROGERS.

GEORGE P. SCHMIDT, JR., B.A.

SHEILA SHANNON.

E. L. STAHL.

D. R. SUTHERLAND.

TAMARA TALBOT RICE.

R. C. TAYLOR.

CECIL THOMAS, O.B.E., F.R.B.S., Past Master of the Art Workers' Guild.

MERLIN THOMAS.

J. C. TREWIN.

REX WARNER.

M. I. WEBB.

WILLIAM WELLS, M.A., A.M.A., Deputy Director, Manchester City Art Galleries.

CHARLES WHEELER.

MARGARET WHINNEY, D.Litt., F.S.A., Reader in the History of Art in the University of London.

JOHN WHITE.

CYRIL WINN, M.A. (Oxon), Fellow and Professor, Trinity College of Music, London.

D. J. WISEMAN, O.B.E., M.A., Assistant Keeper in the Department of Egyptian and Assyrian Antiquities, British Museum.

JOHN WOODWARD.

PAMELA WYNN REEVES, B.A. (Lond.), Ph.D.

Assistant General Editor—A. T. G. POCOCK.

Assistant Illustrations Editor—GILLIAN AVERY.

COLOUR PLATES

BLACK AND WHITE PLATES

PLAN OF VOLUMES

HOW TO USE THIS BOOK

THIS VOLUME is one of twelve, each on a separate subject, the whole set forming what is called an encyclopaedia, or work from which you can find out almost anything you want to know. (The word comes originally from the Greek *enkuklios*, circular or complete, and *paideia*, education.) Each of the twelve volumes is arranged alphabetically within itself, as twelve dictionaries would be.

The difference between a dictionary and an encyclopaedia is that, while the first gives you no more than the meanings and derivations of words, the second tells you a very great deal more about their subjects. For instance, from a dictionary you could find that an ALLEGORY is a literary work describing one thing under the guise of another and you would find little more; but an encyclopaedia will tell you that ALLEGORY is primarily a way of conveying ideas by representing the ideas as persons; that it was most popular in the Middle Ages; and it will tell you which are the most famous allegories in literature and what they are about. Then a dictionary contains nearly every word in the language; but an encyclopaedia deals only with words and subjects about which there is something interesting to be said, beyond their bare meanings. So you should not expect to find every word in an encyclopaedia —every subject is there, but not every word.

To find any subject, you have first to decide in which of the twelve volumes it comes. Each of these has a title as well as a number, and also a list of general subjects to make the title clearer. All these are set out in the Plan of Volumes on the previous page. Very often you will be able to tell from the title alone which volume contains the information you need; but if not, the list of sub-headings on the plan on p. xiii will help to direct you. For example, if you want to read about people, the way they have lived at different times and places, and the things they have believed and worshipped, you would turn to Volume I. If, however, you want to find out about an animal or plant, you would look it up in Volume II, Natural History; but if you wanted to know how that animal or plant is used in something like farming, fishing, or trapping, you would find it in Volume VI. If your subject were something in nature that does not have life—such as the sun, or a particular country or river, or a kind of stone—you would find it in Volume III, with tides, earthquakes, the weather, and many other things.

Matters connected with communication of any kind—of people, or goods, or even of ideas—are in Volume IV. So you would look there for languages and printing and broadcasting, as well as for ships and trains and roads. But if it is the engineering side of any of these things that interests you, Volume VIII, Engineering, is the place to try. Business and trade are in Volume VII. Recreations are in Volume IX, which includes games and sports, entertainment, clubs, animal pets, and sporting animals. How we are governed and protected by the State, the law, and the armed forces is told in Volume X. Volume XI deals with almost everything connected with our homes, from the building and furnishing of the house to the clothes and health of those who live in it. The title of Volume V, Great Lives, explains itself; and a rather fuller account of the volume you are now reading, on the Arts, is given on page xvi.

To find your subject in the volume, think of its ordinary name and then look it up just as though you were using a dictionary—the As on the first page and the Zs (if there are any) on the last. If you cannot find it, try a more general word. For instance, if you want to read about Saxon Churches, and cannot find it under that name (as you cannot), try CHURCH ARCHITECTURE, ENGLISH—which will lead you to it. As you read any article, you will probably come across the titles of other articles in some way connected with what you are reading. You will know that they are titles of other articles because they will be printed in capital letters. Either they will be followed by (q.v.) in brackets (this is short for the Latin *quod vide*, and means 'which see'), or else they themselves will be in brackets, with the word *see* in front of them. You can look up these other articles at once if you want to know more about the particular point dealt with, or you can save them up until you have finished the article you are reading. At the end of any article you may find the words 'See also', followed by one or more titles in small capital letters. If you look these titles up, they will tell you still more about the subject that interests you. These last 'cross-references' are very useful if you want to look up a particularly wide subject (such as POETRY or ITALIAN ART), because they show you at once the titles of all the main articles dealing with it. You can then decide for yourself which to read.

WHAT YOU WILL FIND IN THIS VOLUME

THIS VOLUME IS ABOUT THE FINE ARTS: ARCHITECTURE, PAINTING,
AND SCULPTURE, MUSIC, POETRY, PROSE, AND DRAMA

MAN AND THE ARTS. At all times and in all places men have not been content with producing merely the bare necessities of life but have sought also to beautify what they have done and made. They have recorded their thoughts and feelings in POETRY, in MUSIC, in works of ARCHITECTURE and SCULPTURE, and in pictures. Art has been used to enrich religious ceremonies and express men's profoundest ideas, as well as to decorate with ORNAMENT the simplest objects in daily use.

VISUAL ARTS. In this volume you can read about the history of art at different times and places, from SUMERIAN ART to MODERN ART and from CHINESE ART to AMERICAN ART. Articles such as PAINTING METHODS and STONE CARVING describe the way artists work, and others, such as PORTRAITS and LANDSCAPE PAINTING, describe the subjects they depict. Special techniques are described in articles on ETCHING AND ENGRAVING, STAINED GLASS, MOSAICS, and other articles. ST. PAUL'S CATHEDRAL, the ELGIN MARBLES, and other outstanding works of art are described, as well as styles of architecture, such as GEORGIAN ARCHITECTURE and the SKYSCRAPER.

MUSIC. This volume gives accounts of different types of music such as PLAINSONG, SACRED MUSIC, DANCE MUSIC, and ORIENTAL MUSIC. It explains the elements of music in articles on MELODY AND RHYTHM, HARMONY, and SCALES, and other technical aspects in MUSICAL FORM and ORCHESTRATION. Various kinds of composition are described, both choral and orchestral, such as SONGS and OPERA, CHAMBER MUSIC and SYMPHONY.

LITERATURE. The history of the literature of different peoples is described in articles on LATIN LITERATURE, ENGLISH LITERATURE, and so on. Poetic forms, such as BALLAD, ODE, and SONNET, are described, as are prose forms such as HISTORIES, ESSAYS, and the NOVEL, and the dramatic forms of COMEDY and TRAGEDY. Accounts of outstanding periods of dramatic art are given in such articles as GREEK DRAMA and SHAKESPEARIAN DRAMA. Various literary devices, such as FIGURES OF SPEECH and ALLEGORY, are described, and also various types of literature, such as NATURE WRITING and NURSERY RHYMES. The CANTERBURY TALES, the DIVINE COMEDY, PARADISE LOST, and a few other outstanding works of literature are described in separate articles.

The words in capitals are the titles of some of the articles

A

ABSTRACT ART, *see* MODERN ART, Section 5.

ACADEMIES. **1.** Important institutions devoted to learning are frequently called academies. In England these include the British Academy, the Royal Academy of Arts, and the Royal Academy of Music. There are also the Royal Irish and Cambrian (Welsh) Academies and the Scottish Academy. Many other countries have national academies of art, literature, and science.

The word 'Academy' is derived from the name of an olive grove near ancient Athens where PLATO (q.v. Vol. V) and his pupils met to discuss philosophy. At the RENAISSANCE (q.v. Vol. I) men of learning and fashion in the Italian cities set up informal debating clubs to discuss the new ideas of that exciting age. These academies, as they came to be called, gradually became organized societies of scholars with definite rules and programmes of study, under the control of the rulers of the various States. An academy at Rome was founded by the Pope, chiefly for the study of Latin; one at Florence, encouraged by Cosimo de MEDICI (q.v. Vol. V), the Grand Duke of Tuscany, was devoted to the Italian language. By the 17th century the movement had spread to France; a private literary society in Paris was brought under the control of the State by the King's Minister, RICHELIEU (q.v. Vol. V), who desired to make France supreme in the arts of peace as well as in war. The Académie Française received a royal charter in 1635. It has published an official dictionary and grammar, and, though not conspicuous for fostering genius and originality, it is recognized today as the body chiefly responsible for preserving the strength and purity of the French language. Today the members of the Académie Française are known as the 'Forty Immortals'.

By contrast with academies which fostered the arts, literature, and philosophy, scientific academies had stormy beginnings in 16th-century Italy, for scientific discoveries, such as those of GALILEO (q.v. Vol. V), which contradicted the accepted ideas of the time, were frowned on by the Church. The existence of scientific academies was recognized by about 1650, but their main development was in England and France. The Royal Society, which received its charter from Charles II in 1662, had originated privately among followers of Francis BACON, and numbered many famous scientists, such as NEWTON, BOYLE, and WREN (qq.v. Vol. V). In 1666 the Académie des Sciences was founded in France by the Minister Colbert, who wished to marshal all the arts and sciences in the service of the State; State pensions were organized for deserving artists and scientists. The academies of science, literature, fine arts, and political philosophy are now associated to form the Institut de France.

Academies modelled on the French pattern and under State control sprang up all over Europe during the 18th century. Britain was an exception, for the Royal Society (which is still devoted to science) is independent of State control, nor is it now affiliated to the British Academy (a body mainly concerned with literature) which received a charter only in 1902. All modern academies publish their 'proceedings' and works of scholarship, and many award prizes and organize lectures. International exchange of ideas is provided for the humanities by the Union Académique Internationale (U.A.I), and for science by the International Council of Scientific Unions.

2. ART ACADEMIES. In the Middle Ages artists were regarded as mere craftsmen and as such belonged to CRAFT GUILDS (q.v. Vol. VII). But

By gracious permission of H.M. the Queen

THE LIFE SCHOOL AT THE ROYAL ACADEMY

Painting by Johann Zoffany (1733–1810). The model to be drawn is being posed before the Royal Academicians

in Renaissance Italy artists became more and more esteemed, many of them enjoying the friendship of princes and popes. Artistic societies of a new kind were founded in Florence and in Rome, and to stress their superiority over the guilds the fashionable name 'academy' was applied to them. They were intended to draw together the leading artists into a body which should be the supreme authority in art, while retaining something of the function of the craft guilds. In addition to this, and unlike other academies, they were to provide education in art for the young artist.

France went a step farther: all privileged painters of the Court were compelled to join an academy which was founded in Paris in 1648; this ensured that they painted in the style approved by the King and the Court. By means of the academy classes the Court style was imposed on the rising generation of painters.

During the 18th century, art academies were established under State control all over Europe, England's Royal Academy, founded under the presidency of Sir Joshua REYNOLDS (q.v.

Vol. V) in 1768, being exceptional in its independence of State support and control. The Royal Academy derives its income from its annual exhibitions, and its teaching is given free to selected students. This teaching, like that of all the other early art academies, was at first confined to drawing live models or from plaster casts of antique sculpture. Oil painting was not taught in academies until the 19th century, the basis of what was known as 'academic' art being that of the draughtsman rather than of the painter. The academy art schools demanded almost mathematical accuracy and gave little scope for originality; consequently a reaction against academic art began in the later 18th century and has continued, on and off, ever since (*see* ROMANTIC MOVEMENT and MODERN ART). So rigid were the ideas of the Royal Academy that the great landscape-painter, John CONSTABLE (q.v. Vol. V), was not elected to it until he was over 50, and even then it was stressed that a great honour was being conferred on a mere landscape-painter. Not only was a style of painting rigidly imposed but only those subjects which had noble or moral themes were considered by the academies to be worthy of art.

The academies continued with little change until the revival of industrial art, originated in England by William MORRIS (q.v. Vol. V), brought new ideas. The academic movement had done much to destroy the fusion of art and craft; Morris worked for their reunion, believing that art, to be truly alive and of value in the modern world, has an important task to carry out in industry and in the day-to-day business of living.

ACROPOLIS, ATHENS. This word, meaning 'Upper City', was the name for the citadel or fortress of Greek cities. The best known is the Acropolis of ATHENS (q.v. Vol. III), built on an isolated rock rising steeply from the plain of Attica.

The earliest remains of fortifications on the Acropolis are MYCENAEAN (q.v. Vol. I). By the 6th century B.C. it had become the religious centre of Attica, but in 480–479 B.C. all its buildings were destroyed by the Persians. Shortly after, the walls were restored by THEMISTOCLES and Cimon, and PERICLES (qq.v. Vol. V) carried out a splendid new building programme which included the Parthenon, a new temple for the city's patron-goddess Athena. The fragments of statues and architecture remaining from the

Persian destruction were used as a filling for the south terrace of the Acropolis. When these were excavated in modern times our knowledge of early Greek art was very much increased.

The sculptor Phidias was responsible for supervising the rebuilding of the Acropolis. The Parthenon, which was built by the architect Ictinus between 447 and 432 B.C. to contain Phidias' colossal statue of Athena, is the finest example of a temple in the Doric ORDER OF ARCHITECTURE (q.v.). Round the outside walls of the temple-chamber ran a frieze of relief-sculpture, and the gables of the building were filled with statues (*see* ELGIN MARBLES).

Between 437 and 432 B.C. the Propylaea, a monumental gate, was built at the west end of the Acropolis to the plans of Mnesicles. The Erechtheum, which dates from the time of the Peloponnesian war (431–404 B.C.), was a temple in the Ionic order with a complicated plan designed to include shrines of the hero Erechtheus, and the deities Poseidon and Athena (*see* Vol. I, p. 203). At the same period was built the small Ionic temple of Athena Nike (Victory), which stood within a low carved balustrade on a bastion flanking the approach to the Propylaea on the south.

On the south slope of the Acropolis are situated the theatre of Dionysus (Greek in origin, but reconstructed in Roman times) and the Odeum or

THE ACROPOLIS, ATHENS

P. E. Corbett

music-hall built for the Athenians by their bene-factor, Herodes Atticus (c. A.D. 102–78).

See also GREEK ART.
See also Vol. I: GREEK CIVILIZATION.

ACTING, see DRAMA. *See also* Vol. IX: ACTING, HISTORY OF.

AENEID, THE, by Virgil, *see* EPIC POETRY. *See also* Vol. V: VIRGIL.

AFRICAN ART. The art of the NEGRO AFRI-CANS (q.v. Vol. I) living south of the Sahara may be divided into two classes: the decora-tion of utilitarian objects, which is mainly non-religious, and the representation of living figures, which is mainly religious in character. The former is universal throughout Africa, and its purpose is simply to please the eye. The latter, on the other hand, is closely connected with spiritual beliefs, and plays an important part in ceremonial life. It is found, with few exceptions, only in the western side of the continent, extend-ing from the Sudan and the Guinea coast in the north to Angola in the south, and including the Cameroons and the great central region of the Congo. In these regions the mode of life is chiefly agricultural, with settled villages, while east of the great lakes and in South Africa nomad cattle-keeping tribes predominate.

In the east and south the people for the most part decorate the surfaces of objects of daily use, such as wooden dishes and spoons, calabashes (gourds), and pottery vessels, with geometric patterns applied by painting, carving, or burn-ing; or they work designs into the texture of baskets and beadwork ornaments. These patterns

British Museum
WOODEN CUP CARVED WITH A DECORATIVE PATTERN. FROM THE BELGIAN CONGO

are simple but show a strong feeling for sym-metrical composition. The MASAI (q.v. Vol. I) of East Africa paint skin shields (*see* Vol. I, p. 299); in Kenya wooden stools are often inlaid with beads or wire; finely burnished pottery with impressed patterns is made in Uganda; black and white patterned basketwork comes from Ruanda-Urundi, Tan-ganyika, and Northern

British Museum
BASKET WITH GEOMETRIC AND ANIMAL ORNAMENT FROM NORTHERN RHODESIA

Rhodesia; several Rhodesian tribes make grace-fully carved headrests; and the Zulus have grooved wooden milk-pails. There are other decorative crafts in these regions, including well-designed coloured beadwork.

The figure carvings and masks of West Africa and the Congo are now recognized as impor-tant works of art. They represented supernatural beings, and their purpose was religious—to be used in religious ceremonies and dances. Their makers never thought of them as isolated from this context, to be looked at simply as works of art.

Wood is the favourite medium of the African sculptor, though ivory and horn are also used. The figures are always hewn out of a single block of wood with adze, knife, and chisel; this helps to explain the stiff shape of some carvings, since they have to fit the shape of the tree trunk. Sometimes the tool marks are left visible, break-ing up the surface into many small facets; some-times the surface is scraped smooth and polished. Some of the carvings are blackened, while several Nigerian tribes paint them in bright colours. Others cover their masks with tightly stretched skin to give them a lifelike appearance.

The art of modelling figures in clay is also widespread in West Africa, and pottery vases representing the dead are made in the upper Congo region. Modelling in clay is perhaps most highly developed by the Ibos of Nigeria, who fill their 'Mbari' houses with vigorous figure scenes for special religious occasions. In parts of West Africa, bronze objects are cast from

LEFT: SKIN-COVERED MASK IN NATURALISTIC STYLE FROM S.E. NIGERIA. The mask, worn on the top of the head, is part of an elaborate costume. CENTRE: WOODEN FIGURE FROM THE BELGIAN CONGO. The markings on the body represent decorations made by cutting the skin. RIGHT: POTTERY FIGURE FROM N. NIGERIA

British Museum

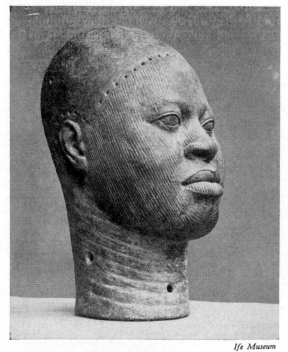

Ife Museum

ANCIENT BRONZE HEAD FROM IFE, S. NIGERIA

British Museum

16TH-CENTURY RELIEF OF THE KING OF BENIN WITH ATTENDANTS

wax models. Wonderfully realistic portrait heads used to be made at Ife in southern Nigeria, and more stylized heads, figures, and reliefs portray the Court life of Benin City as it was in the 15th and 16th centuries. In the Gold Coast the ASHANTI (q.v. Vol. I) made miniature brass figures and groups to use as gold weights; these give a vivid picture of their daily occupations. There is no stone sculpture today, but old soapstone carvings from Sierra Leone and Rhodesia and stone figures in southern Nigeria show that it was practised locally in ancient times.

In addition to sculpture in the round, there are many interesting examples of carving in relief on large wooden doors and house-posts, and on ivory tusks, bowls, and armlets in Nigeria. In northern Nigeria intricate geometric patterns are modelled in relief on the walls of mud houses, and the Ashanti used to practise a similar art. Carved surface decoration is seen at its best in the beautiful wooden cups, boxes, pipes, and other domestic objects found in the central Congo region. There is little pictorial art, but some tribes paint figures on the walls of their huts and compounds. Some Nigerian women paint elaborate scroll patterns on their bodies for special occasions, while body decoration by a sort of TATTOOING (q.v. Vol. XI) was highly developed in the Congo.

Both the figures and masks generally serve religious and magical purposes. The figures are often believed to contain the souls of ancestors or other protective spirits, and offerings are made to them (*see* Vol. I, p. 19). Sometimes, however, they are merely symbols of gods, memorials of the dead, or naturalistic portrait figures of chiefs. The small fetish figures of the Congo are believed, when treated with 'medicine', to bring good luck or avert disease, and they were sometimes used for DIVINATION (q.v. Vol. I).

Masks are chiefly used by secret societies, and the wearers impersonate spirits of good or evil in religious rites, which are held in honour of the dead, to promote fertility of crops, or at the INITIATION CEREMONIES (q.v. Vol. I). Masks are of different kinds; those worn over the head like helmets or on top of the head, with a costume concealing the wearer's body, resemble sculpture in the round, while the face masks are carved chiefly to be seen from the front. Many masks represent animals, and in some there is a combination of human and animal features.

Broadly speaking, African sculpture does not aim at complete realism in the sense of accurate reproduction of natural form. At times the artist does, in fact, achieve realistic effects, as in some masks and figures from southern Nigeria and the lower Congo, though none of these is comparable with the bronzes of Ife for fidelity to nature. In general the treatment of the human figure is governed not by the scientific study of anatomy but by traditional formulae of a more or less fanciful kind, which differ from tribe to tribe. The natural shapes and proportions of the bodily features are modified, simplified, and distorted in an endless variety of styles, which in extreme cases develop into unrecognizable abstract forms. The head, hands, and feet are often exaggerated, and the features of the face reduced to symmetrical patterns. The face may be shown as a sunk or concave surface; the eyes may protrude like tubes, the nose may appear as a narrow ridge prolonged over the forehead, and the mouth as a circle, oval, or rectangular projection, or it may be omitted altogether. The effect of these arbitrary changes may seem grotesque to our eyes; but to the people who used them they had familiar meanings. Though the tribal conventions were followed fairly closely by the artist, he felt free to express his individuality in matters of detail, and no two carvings are exactly alike. The result is that African art as a whole shows an amazing richness of invention in its treatment of the human form.

A completely different kind of art was produced by the BUSHMEN (q.v. Vol. I) and their forerunners in East and South Africa. This consisted of paintings on the walls of caves and rock-shelters. The most frequent subjects are game animals such as eland, springbok, zebra, and

BUSHMAN CAVE PAINTING OF ELANDS

rhinoceros, which are shown either singly, or in groups illustrating hunting scenes. Many of these are believed to have been made in order to obtain success in the chase by the process known as 'imitative MAGIC' (q.v. Vol. I). Other pictures show lively dances, ceremonies, or battles between Bushmen and Negroes. The animals are generally drawn with remarkable accuracy, but the human figures are less realistic, and there is a tendency to draw the body and limbs in long thin lines. These paintings date from different periods, and are often superimposed on each other, giving us an idea of the succession of styles. In addition to the paintings, many figures of animals were engraved on hard rocks in the open veldt of SOUTH AFRICA (q.v. Vol. III), some of them seeming to be of great antiquity. Various symbolic and geometric designs are also found in the pictures and the engravings.

See also PRIMITIVE ART.
See also Vol. I: NEGRO AFRICANS.

ALLEGORY. This is primarily a way of conveying ideas by representing them as persons; and of describing and discussing these ideas through the adventures and speech of the persons who represent them. But persons or institutions, as well as ideas, may be thus represented. Some prose works and many poems are completely allegorical in character, and the allegory is sometimes complex.

The two best-known allegories in English are the 16th-century poem *The Faerie Queene* (1589–96) by Edmund SPENSER (q.v. Vol. V) and the 17th-century prose work the PILGRIM'S PROGRESS (q.v.) by John Bunyan. The first of these is a complex allegory; the Faerie Queene herself, for example, represents both Glory and Queen Elizabeth; and Duessa, another character, represents Falsehood, Mary, Queen of Scots, and the Roman Catholic Church. Thus in this allegory a character may represent an idea, a person, an institution, or even all three; and the story the characters enact is capable of more than one interpretation. But the allegories of contemporary and political events are always subservient to, though interwoven with, the strong central spiritual allegory. The story of the first book recounts how Una, protected by the Red Cross Knight, overcomes the wiles of Duessa and other enemies, or to give it its spiritual meaning, how truth, guided by holiness, overcomes the powers of darkness. But Spenser also used the same story to represent the struggle of the English Church against the Roman. Bunyan's allegory, too, is a spiritual one. The enchanting journey of Pilgrim, with its dangers and its pleasant sojourns, typifies the inner life—the soul's voyage 'from this world to that which is to come'.

Spiritual conflict, always one of the main themes of allegorical poets, is the theme of the first fully allegorical poem we know of—the late Latin poem *Psychomachia* (the Battle for the Soul) by Prudentius (born A.D. 348)—which describes the Virtues and Vices engaged in a battle for the soul.

Another very popular theme of allegory is love, and in particular the courtly love of the Middle Ages (*see* ROMANCE LITERATURE). When the French poet Chrétien de Troyes, who wrote stories based on the ARTHURIAN LEGEND (q.v. Vol. I), wished to describe the inner emotional life of Lancelot in his love for the Queen Guinevere, he used allegorical terms. Lancelot, for example, in seeking to serve the Queen, hesitates to get into a tumbril—a cart that criminals were carried in. Lancelot's conflict is represented as a debate in which Reason forbids him to mount, while Love urges him to.

Many medieval poets wrote allegories of love where the allegory was not introduced incidentally, but was the basic structure of the poem. The most important of these is the first part of the *Romance of the Rose* by Guillaume de Lorris, an allegorical poem in the form of a dream—a favourite allegorical device. The Dreamer, walking aimlessly by the river of Life, comes to the garden of Delight, which he enters at the invitation of Idleness (*see* p. 383). The god of Love follows him, unseen. The Dreamer sees reflected in a fountain all the garden of Delight, and the one unopened rosebud of the garden captures his desire. He tries to pluck the Rose, but is struck by an arrow shot by the god of Love. The Rose is a symbol of his lady's love. The lady never appears in the poem, but different aspects of her personality appear as characters in the story—for instance, Bialacoil ('Fairwelcome'), Pity, Fear, Shame. The Dreamer's attempts to win the Rose are aided by some of these characters, and foiled by others. He is aided, too, by outside allies, such as Venus; and is prevented by others, such as Jealousy, who symbolizes the Lady's guardians. Jealousy builds a castle about the Rose, and the Dreamer weeps outside and appeals to the sweetness of his lady—that is, to Bialacoil. In the second part of the poem, which is by a later writer, the allegory is interrupted by long satirical and instructive digressions; but the story ends with the Dreamer, by Venus's intervention, winning the Rose.

This poem had a great influence on poets for centuries: CHAUCER's love-poems (q.v. Vol. V) were its direct descendants. His allegorical lament for Blanche, John of Gaunt's first wife —*The Book of the Duchess* (1369)—is also in the form of a dream. *The Parliament of Fowls*, a joyful allegory full of comedy and beauty, is set in a garden like the garden of the Rose—though much of the allegory in it resembles that of the Italian Renaissance poets, in particular of BOCCACCIO (q.v. Vol. V).

Apart from Chaucer's work, the most important English poem of the late 14th century is another allegory, *Piers Plowman*, the greater part of which, at any rate, is by William Langland. It is written in alliterative verse (*see* VERSIFICATION, Section 2). The poet has a vision of a high tower (Truth), a deep dungeon (Wrong), and between, 'a fair field full of folk all going about their business—monks, beggars, labourers, cooks with 'hot pies, hot', winedealers with 'white wine of Osney'. Conscience preaches to the people, Repentance moves their hearts, they wish to seek 'St. Truth'. Piers Plowman offers to guide them if they will help him plough. Some are willing, some are lazy— which leads the poet to digress in order to discuss the labour problems of the age. There are other digressions on corruption in the Church, in praise of poverty and love, and on narratives of Christ's life. There are descriptions of the attacks of Antichrist and Pride upon the house 'Unity', and of Death's attack upon Mankind. In the 14th century the moral tone of the poem and its allegorical form were both familiar and popular; now the work is valued rather for its superb poetry and for the fascinating picture it presents of the life of 14th-century England.

Pearl is another exquisite 14th-century alliterative poem of unkown authorship. Pearl is the author's daughter, who died when she was two. In the garden where she was buried the author has a vision of a river, beyond which is Paradise. He recognizes his daughter, now grown-up, seated in Paradise, and she tells him of her happiness and reproaches him for mourning. He plunges into the river to join her, and awakens comforted and resigned. Another allegory of the same period is the *Confessio Amantis* (A Lover's Confession) by John Gower (1330–1408)—'moral Gower', as Chaucer called him. In this, Gower tries to fuse love interest, moral teaching, and general instruction. The *Testament of Love* by Thomas Usk (died 1388) is important for being written in prose, not verse, as was customary for a love allegory.

In the 15th century, though allegories were the favourite literary form, they were in general more numerous than noteworthy. In style and form John Lydgate imitated but never equalled Chaucer. The Scottish poet, William Dunbar, wrote several allegories, among them a marriagesong, *The Thistle and the Rose*, in which the Thistle symbolizes James IV, and the Rose his bride, Margaret Tudor.

Although *The Faerie Queene* and *The Pilgrim's Progress* were written later, allegory has never been a main literary form since the 15th century. Today readers as well as writers are out of practice in keeping in mind at the same time both the appearance and the imaginative likeness behind that appearance—both the literal and the allegorical sense.

See also Plate I, opp. p. 16.

ALLITERATION, *see* BEOWULF; VERSIFICATION, Section 2.

ALTAR. In ancient religions the altar was the place on which offerings to the gods were laid and sacrifices performed; in a Christian church it is the table at which Holy Communion is celebrated. It is placed at the east end of the chancel or sanctuary and provides the climax to the whole interior of the church. Large churches often have subsidiary chapels with their own altars, and then the principal one is called the High Altar. In the first Christian churches the altar was of wood; but stone altars soon became common, partly because the tombs of the martyrs in the catacombs at Rome were used as altars and, later, relics of the martyrs were placed under the altars in churches. After the Reformation Protestant countries again used movable wooden altars, shaped like tables, and altars in English parish churches are still required by law to have this form. Stone altars are more usual in cathedrals. An altar cloth covers the top, and a frontal is draped round the sides.

The altar is generally raised on steps above

National Buildings Record

THE REREDOS, WINCHESTER CATHEDRAL
EARLY 15TH CENTURY

The original figures were destroyed at the Reformation,
and new ones added in the 19th century

the floor of the chancel. At the back is a raised shelf, called the 'retable', on which can be placed a crucifix, candlesticks, and vases of flowers. Behind this are curtains or a carved or painted panel called a 'reredos' or altar-piece. In medieval churches, and still in Roman Catholic churches, the reredos is the most important artistic feature of the altar; at Winchester and Durham, for example, there are large elaborate ones with carved figures in niches. If there is an ambulatory or passage round the east end behind the High Altar, the reredos serves as a screen closing the east end of the chancel. Many of these reredoses, however, were destroyed during the Puritan rule in the 17th century.

A large proportion of the pictures painted in Italy up to the 15th century were altar-pieces. These were sometimes a single panel on which was depicted a scene from the life of Christ or a saint; sometimes they were built up of a number of separate paintings, with smaller panels beneath the main panels depicting scenes from the lives of the figures above. In northern Europe the altar-pieces were often triptychs, consisting of a centre panel bearing a painted scene, and two painted wing-panels at the sides, hinged

to fold over the centre panel. In Germany the centre panel was often carved in relief and coloured. A large and elaborately decorated altar-piece is often one of the richest features in Spanish churches.

In the 14th and 15th centuries a large number of retables were carved in alabaster from Staffordshire and Derbyshire. These consisted of a series of panels, each carved with a figure or scene from the life of Christ, the Virgin, or the saints. These retables were not only sent all over England but were exported to places as far away as Spain and Russia.

The High Altar sometimes has over it a canopy supported on columns, as at St. Peter's, Rome (*see* Vol. V, p. 43). This is called a 'ciborium' or 'baldachino'. The latter name strictly refers only to a canopy of cloth, since the word comes from a corruption of Baghdad, where the cloth for this purpose originally came from.

In the Middle Ages people often had small private altars in their homes, and they carried these about with them on their travels. Ivory was a favourite material for such altars and for the altar-pieces with which they were decorated. Ivory panels, often hinged together to form diptychs (two-panel pictures) and triptychs, were minutely carved with a large number of holy scenes (*see* IVORY CARVING).

See also CHURCH ARCHITECTURE, ENGLISH.

AMERICAN ART. More than 300 years ago, civilized Europeans began to leave homelands already rich in history and artistic tradition to found colonies in a New World where everything had to be created. While they remained European in many ways, the settlers had to solve many problems for survival in the wilderness, and the struggle altered their way of thinking. Solitude made them self-reliant, poverty made them practical. Simple and useful things were valued more than elegant and decorative frills; luxury was an evil, and laziness a vice. Consequently in the United States, architecture, painting, and sculpture have been most original when they were concerned with practical things for everyday use.

Since shelter is a basic need, architecture in America has always been the leading art. Painting and sculpture began as useful crafts and developed into important arts under the influence of England and France.

Between 1700 and 1800 each colonist was

his own craftsman, architect, and handyman. He built everything himself, either alone, or with the help of his neighbour. He used local materials, wood, brick, or stone, whichever was more easily obtained, though in America wood was the chief building material. To furnish their homes, the settlers usually made their own tables, chairs, and cooking utensils, though in the towns where trade flourished, a few wealthy inhabitants sometimes imported these articles from Europe. Local artists painted sign-boards for wayside inns, they decorated stage-coaches, and were occasionally commissioned to paint a family portrait.

Sculpture, for the most part, consisted of wood carving. Cabinet-makers and joiners frequently decorated their handiwork by carving and whittling patterns on doors or upon overhanging eaves.

In the 18th century in the eastern colonies, as the settlements became more established and wealthier, the arts became more formal and European styles grew popular. About 1750, books containing measured drawings of rediscovered Greek and Roman structures were brought to America from Europe, where they had already greatly influenced architects. They were soon purchased by groups of Americans, and the designs in them, which were intended for stone buildings, were copied in wood and simplified for economy's sake.

Europe influenced American painting too. In the 1770's the American painters Benjamin West and John Singleton Copley were in Italy studying with some of the finest artists in Europe.

National Gallery of Art, Washington, D.C.

GEORGE WASHINGTON BY GILBERT STUART (1755–1828)
Stuart had studied under Benjamin West in London. His portraits, though simpler, were like those of the English painters

Parker Gallery

ABRAHAM LINCOLN'S HOUSE, SPRINGFIELD, ILLINOIS
Classical proportions and details have been adapted to building in wood. Coloured lithograph, 1860

They soon became famous, and taught their skill to younger Americans who followed them to Europe. These students brought back to America the traditional European style.

By the end of the century art schools had been established, and the artists became known outside America. European artists, such as Houdon, the French sculptor, and L'Enfant, a French architect and city-planner, went to America, thus forging even closer links between the continents. Houdon carved many portrait busts of George Washington, while L'Enfant, one of the planners of Paris, made plans for the new capital city of Washington, D.C.

America in the early 19th century entered a period of rapid growth, increasing trade, and sudden wealth. With this new wealth Americans began to travel, first in the states of the Union and then overseas to Europe. While the pioneers continued to push westward, carrying with them the traditions of home-made craftsmanship, the cities in the East were fast becoming more and more cosmopolitan. From Britain came the railway and industry. From the Continent came new styles of architecture.

Many of the newly-rich began to look for luxurious pleasures at a time when seaport cities such as Boston, New York, and Philadelphia were growing in size. Industrial towns sprang up, with their smoke-blackened houses and crowded slums; mansions were constructed for the display of riches, the owners often imitating European fashions without thought for good taste or usefulness.

Only in painting was there any sign of artistic progress, for painters continued to look for native beauty around them. They became the news-reporters of the westward pioneer movement: they painted landscapes with pioneer settlements and covered wagons, and they tried to capture the mood of local, everyday scenes.

The greatest of these 'reporter-painters' was Winslow Homer. Homer never studied abroad but, on the contrary, was himself studied by European painters. He began his career as an illustrator for an American magazine, for, in this period when the camera was not yet used widely, papers depended upon artists to provide their pictures. In an age of magazines and calendar pictures, paintings of everyday life in town and country were popular.

Sculptors now began to find work in carving portrait busts or statues of famous Americans. A few wealthy city-dwellers would sometimes import large numbers of Italian and French masterpieces for private collections; but, though these collections often served to fill museums, there were not enough of them seriously to affect native American painting and sculpture until much later.

In 1885 the city of Chicago built the first SKYSCRAPER [q.v.]. The introduction of steel-frame construction made it possible to build higher than ever before, and this had a startling effect on the development of American cities. Where a city such as London continued to expand in area, Chicago, New York, and other American cities grew in height. The skyscraper became the chief American contribution to the art of building.

In the Chicago Fair of 1893, a small group of architects, in revolt against the ornamental style of the period, began to erect their buildings in a purely functional manner. They held that beauty meant simplicity and usefulness, and that useless decoration represented something foreign to the pioneer spirit. The result of their work was to redirect American architecture towards the practical point of view of the early settlers. In the 20th century, architects such as Frank Lloyd Wright in America, as well as others in Europe, have been concerned with simple and economical designs.

These changes of taste and outlook also affected painting. Among the best of those who followed Winslow Homer was Thomas Eakins, who studied in France at a time when the French Impressionist painters were starting to show their work. Eakins returned to his Philadelphia home to paint with intense realism the people and country he knew. The best-known sculptor of the century was Augustus Saint-Gaudens, who made sculptures of famous men, including Abraham Lincoln.

The First World War made Americans intensely aware of their strength and new responsibilities in a changing world. The United States had emerged as one of the most powerful countries in the world, and American artists began to look to their own land for inspiration rather than to Europe, and to create an

Cleveland Museum of Art, Ohio

'TURNING STAKE BOAT' BY THOMAS EAKINS (1844–1916)

This is not only a sincere record of the scene, but is skilfully composed so that the upright and horizontal lines make an interesting pattern (*Hinman B. Hurlbut Collection*)

Art Institute of Chicago

'THE CAUDILLO ZAPATA, 1930' BY JOSÉ CLEMENTE OROZCO
(1883–1949)

The Mexican people appeal to their leader, Zapata, to fight for them

'American School' of architecture, painting, and sculpture.

The great depression between 1930 and 1940 forced people everywhere to consider economy. In America, the Government became a sponsor for the arts, giving artists employment through vast building projects in the south and west. Artists from Latin America worked in the United States, among the most important of whom were the two Mexican mural painters, Diego Rivera and José Clemente Orozco. Mexican art derives from the colourful, religious pageantry of the Latin countries, and this tradition was strong in the work of Orozco. Rivera chose subjects that reflected the revolutionary changes in modern Mexican history, especially the rise of the peasant. In their wall paintings both Orozco and Rivera experimented with different tech-

niques, and adapted their powerful sense of design to subjects drawn from the life around them.

Since the Second World War, the destinies of Europe and America have been linked together. Architecture, painting, and sculpture have become not American nor European but an art common to both continents.

See also Vol. I: AMERICANS.

AMERICAN-INDIAN ART. Before the coming of Europeans to America, the whole of North and South America was populated by various branches of AMERICAN INDIANS (q.v. Vol. I), with the exception of the ESKIMOES (q.v. Vol. I) in the extreme north. While different modes of life had developed in response to varying kinds of environment, life was still primitive, except in Mexico, Peru, and parts of Central America, where culture and art had risen above the primitive level long before the discovery of America (*see* Vol. I: MEXICAN ANCIENT CIVILIZATIONS, and PERU, ANCIENT). Since the beginning of colonization in America, tribal arts have been affected in varying degrees by contact with the white man; but in many regions, particularly the west, their native vigour and individuality persisted until quite recently and are not wholly extinguished even today. Rock-paintings and engravings, and the stone and pottery relics from ancient burials show that American-Indian art was flourishing many centuries ago.

The Eskimoes, who live by hunting and fishing under difficult conditions, are not only ingenious craftsmen but gifted artists. Useful objects, such as ivory bow-drills and pipes, are decorated with miniature blackened engravings of lively hunting scenes and other events in their life. Their best work appears in the small ivory carvings in the round on bag handles, arrow-straighteners, and so on (*see* Vol. I, p. 162), which represent animals such as seal, polar bear, and duck most realistically. In Alaska, where they have been influenced by their Indian neighbours, the Eskimoes also have carved and

British Museum

ESKIMO IVORY BOWS AND ARROW STRAIGHTENERS ENGRAVED WITH ANIMALS AND FIGURES painted ritual masks of spirits with curiously distorted features, which show imagination and a keen sense of humour.

The art of the American Indians varies according to the region in which they live. Wood-carving is the supreme art in the forest region of the north-west coast from Alaska to Vancouver Island. It is here that the splendid totem poles,

British Museum

SHALE TOBACCO PIPE WITH TOTEMIC CARVINGS OF ANIMALS. FROM BRITISH COLUMBIA

sometimes more than 60 feet high (*see* Colour Plate, Vol. I, opp. p. 464), and the carved and painted house-posts have been produced. These were carved from top to bottom with heraldic figures of animals (bears, beavers, frogs, or eagles) and men in a conventional style, representing the ancestors or legendary heroes of the owner's clan (*see* TOTEMISM, Vol. I). The animals are so stylized that they can often only be identified by some special feature, such as the claws of the bear, the teeth or tail of the beaver, or the dorsal fin of the killer whale. The carvings were not religious but made for display at their feasts, and were intended to enhance the social prestige of their owners by their size and quality and by the cost and labour involved in producing them. Greater diversity of style was shown in their painted wooden masks, worn in dramatic ceremonies, some of which were realistic, and others quite grotesque or furnished with movable eyes and jaws. The same style is used to decorate many kinds of useful objects, including boxes, rattles, dishes, horn spoons, and slate tobacco pipes. The carvings are often intricate, and parts of animals, such as eyes, are used separately to make up formal designs.

British Museum

WOODEN DANCE RATTLE REPRESENTING A BEAR. FROM BRITISH COLUMBIA

Among the agricultural Pueblo Indians of Arizona and New Mexico, where water was precious, the women's craft of pottery was most highly developed both in shape and in the painted decoration, which was admirably adapted to the curved surfaces of the vessels (*see* p. 362). The designs, in red, brown, and black on a white or orange surface, are mainly geometric—zigzags, triangles, and step and scroll meanders—with which bird and animal figures, and even insects, were sometimes combined. The elements of the designs were probably symbolic in origin, and some of them are still recognized as symbols of rain and clouds. The cliff-dwellers in this region more than 1,000 years ago used to decorate their vases with superb black and white patterns derived from basket-work; in another unique style the coils of clay from which the pots were built up were made to overlap so as to produce ornamental wavy lines in relief.

British Museum

DOLL FROM THE PUEBLOS OF ARIZONA AND NEW MEXICO

The painted wooden masks, representing deities and spirits, of the Pueblo Indians were richly varied; they also reproduced these types in the form of gaily-coloured little dolls. Both here and in California, basketwork of a high degree of skill was decorated with inwoven patterns, often radiating from the centre and giving the impression of whirling motion (*see* Colour Plate, Vol. I, opp. p. 10). Some of the basketwork was adorned with shell beads or feathers. The Pueblo Indians also made beautiful woven and embroidered cloths, and silver and turquoise jewellery.

A peculiar form of art found among the Pueblo Indians is seen in the 'sandpaintings', made by sprinkling coloured powders on a bed of sand. The complicated designs showing stylized figures of supernatural spirits are used by medicine men in the ritual healing of the sick.

The art of the hunting Indians of the central plains and eastern forests is chiefly expressed in the decoration of animal skins, used for making tepees (tents), robes, moccasins, bags, and

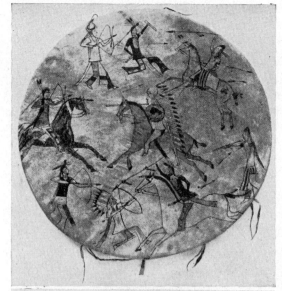

Museum of Modern Art, New York

ABOVE: BATTLE SCENE PAINTED ON A PLAINS INDIAN SKIN
SHIELD COVER

BELOW: STONE FIGURE IN REALISTIC STYLE, FROM AN OLD
BURIAL IN TENNESSEE

From F. H. Douglas and René d'Harnoncourt, *Indian Art
of the United States*

shields. Buffalo-skin robes were often impressed and painted in colours with historical scenes of battle or the chase. The galloping horsemen, though rather flatly drawn, are full of life and movement, but there is not much feeling for orderly composition. This work was done by men, while geometric decoration with triangular and circular patterns was women's work. In the old days skins were embroidered with dyed porcupine quills, feathers, and shells, but more recently coloured glass beadwork has taken their place, and colonial influence is evident in many of the floral designs.

Among the finest arts of America were the small sculptures in stone and the pottery portraits made by the ancient people of Ohio and the Mississippi Valley. Figures of birds and animals carved on stone pipes and bowls are remarkable for their refinement and realism. Some of the art of this south-eastern region reveals the influence of ancient Mexican culture.

Art in South America, except in the ancient Peruvian and Inca civilizations of the Andes, was more localized and less highly developed than in the north. Most noteworthy are the painted decoration of pottery, the geometrically patterned beadwork, and the feather ornaments of the upper Amazon region. In the basketwork of British Guiana the patterns include stylized angular figures of animals, and among some tribes of the Paraguayan Chaco symbolical designs are woven by the women into woollen blankets and marriage belts.

See also PRIMITIVE ART.

See also Vol. I: AMERICAN INDIANS, CENTRAL AND SOUTH; AMERICAN INDIANS, NORTH; ESKIMOES.

AMERICAN LITERATURE. The growth of American literature is bound up with the growth of America as a nation. The early settlers in America went there for various reasons: to escape religious persecution in their own country or lured by promise of quick wealth from the country's gold and tobacco. In the 19th century further emigrants went, driven by poverty and hardship from their own over-populated countries—Irish, Scandinavian, Italians, Poles, and others.

These historical factors influenced the growth of American literature in various ways. In the first place the early settlements were 'separate': that is, there were many colonies or settlements rather than one nation. Secondly, all these

Metropolitan Museum of Art, New York

'THE GULF STREAM' BY WINSLOW HOMER (1836–1910)

The lonely figure in the damaged boat, at the mercy of waves, sharks, and storms, is symbolic of America's fight with nature as the resources of the continent were developed. This subject is found in the literature and the art of the 19th century

people had their roots in a European tradition: America had no folk-lore of its own; it had no epic, such as the *Iliad* in Greece or *Beowulf* in England, which related an heroic and vanished past. Thirdly, there was no wide American reading public; indeed in the very early days there was not even the means of printing books in the country. Thus the earliest American writers were really European writers living in America; and even though they might have left Europe for some long time, their writing was clearly influenced by and for the most part merely an imitation of European, and in particular English, literature. Even this sort of literature was confined to those parts of America where a civilized society existed: there were many parts where settlers were too isolated or too fully engaged in the struggle for survival to concern themselves with putting down their impressions or thoughts in writing. American writing in the 18th and early 19th century wholly reflects these conditions. The writers were gathered chiefly around New York or in Massachusetts.

Of these early writers Washington Irving (1783–1859) and James Fenimore Cooper (1789–1851) are the most important, though neither has sufficient seriousness or originality to rank as a first-rate writer. Both, however, are concerned with American subjects. Washington Irving, a humorist and essayist in the style of ADDISON (q.v. Vol. V), gives in his *Sketch-Book* a record of his impressions of America and England. *The Legend of Sleepy Hollow* and *Rip Van Winkle*, his best-known sketches, are about local American subjects treated almost like fairy-tales. Fenimore Cooper's rousing 'leatherstocking' stories, *The Deerslayer*, *The Last of the Mohicans*, and others, are stories of American history—the life of adventure on the western frontier and the settlement of those areas. The hero of these tales is Natty Bumppo, and the stories tell of his adventures on the prairie and against the Indians.

During the 19th century American literature really began to emerge. Firstly, there was the group of New England writers. To New England had come the Puritan settlers, determined to set up a government according to the Word of

God, and with hearts stirred to anger and grief by the problems of sin and evil and damnation. Nathaniel Hawthorne (1804–64) is above all the novelist of these people: in *The Scarlet Letter* and *The House of the Seven Gables* he shows how a dark and sinful past can act like a curse on the present. There is little humour in Hawthorne, but within his limited range his writing is powerful and intense. Herman Melville's novel *Moby Dick* (1851), one of the greatest American novels, tells how a whaling ship commanded by Captain Ahab goes in search of Moby Dick, a white whale which he had pursued and which had mauled him in the past. Melville writes passionately of the human fight with the destructive power of evil. There is madness and strangeness in the book, and its impact on the imagination is unforgettable.

Lastly, bridging the gap between the 19th and 20th centuries, Henry James (1843–1916) deals with the problems of corruption and betrayal in such novels as *The Portrait of a Lady* and *The Wings of the Dove*. James, the son of wealthy and cultured parents, lived in England for many years and mixed with aristocratic society; as a writer he differs from his New England predecessors in that he had a grasp of the surface of civilized society which they lacked; he had a stylishness, a power of wit, and sense of comedy of his own, as well as great intelligence and subtlety. Furthermore, he was more concerned than they with the NOVEL (q.v.) as an art form, and his themes and settings are as much European as American. James is often a difficult and even exasperating writer, but his influence on the novelists of his time has been great—the modern novel in America and England, in particular, owes much to him. Another writer whose influence has spread far beyond his own country is Edgar Allan Poe (1809–49), whose strange short stories, such as *The Fall of the House of Usher*, have the quality of nightmare (*see* DETECTIVE STORIES), and whose poetry exerted considerable influence on 19th-century French poetry.

The New England novelists deal with a background that is American and also has tradition and a sense of the past. But a more specific and distinctively American way of writing can be seen in the work of Mark TWAIN (q.v. Vol. V). In his greatest work, *Huckleberry Finn* (1884), he writes of the valley of the Mississippi, and of the adventures of Huckleberry, the lad who has run away down river. At the end of the book he is brought back to live with and be taught manners by Aunt Sally. Huckleberry is one of the most significant figures of American literature. When, in the last words of the book, he says: 'But I reckon I got to light out for the Territory ahead of the rest, because Aunt Sally she's going to adopt me and sivilise me, and I can't stand it. I been there before', we have a statement of a dominant American theme, a gay, confident turning away from Europe and from a tired civilization, and a setting out for an undiscovered and romantic West. This deeply American attitude of Huckleberry's, together with the simple and tough humorous style, makes *Huckleberry Finn* a very American book. Another writer who insists on and emphasizes the American nature of his work is the poet Walt WHITMAN (q.v. Vol. V), the most remarkable prophet of American optimism, whose poetic style broke sharply with the established manner of poetry and helped to introduce modern 'free verse'. Whitman's poetry at its worst is slapdash and bumptious; at its best it strongly affirms the poet's acceptance of life in all its variety.

By the end of the 19th century American literature was no longer a mere offshoot of English literature, but was producing its own traditions of writing. Its writers and critics were beginning to insist that America was their proper theme, and that to express America and to interpret America to the Americans was their chief duty as writers. The aim of 20th-century American writing became concentrated on the essential task of welding together all the various groups of settlers, different in race and background, and creating from them one race, a new nation. The age of the national EPIC (q.v.) came late in America.

Ernest Hemingway—perhaps the third American writer to exert a deep influence on European writing—with his direct and un-ornate style, writes of man in the simple heroic setting of struggle and war. Other writers have taken special parts of America as their background: realistic novelists such as Theodore Dreiser write of the life in cities and show the corrupting influences of wealth and power; Sinclair Lewis in *Main Street* writes satirically of life in a small mid-western town, and in *Babbitt* has drawn one of the most memorable American types, the prosperous business man; William Faulkner is a powerful novelist of the dark South. It is in the

PRIMAVERA
PAINTING BY BOTTICELLI, 1477–8
This allegory of Spring was probably painted for the 14-year-old nephew of Lorenzo de Medici, the Magnificent. The central figure is Venus, who represents the virtues that the young man should choose, just as Paris, who is picking the apple, chooses the goddess

WORK. PAINTING BY FORD MADOX BROWN, 1852–63
This is an allegory on the nobility of labour. The workmen are in bright sunlight, and in the shadows are the thinkers, the idle and rich, and those who supply the latter's needs

CLASSICAL: THE PARTHENON, ATHENS, BUILT 447–432 B.C.

GOTHIC: SALISBURY CATHEDRAL BUILT IN THE 13TH CENTURY

novel that America has chiefly succeeded in expressing itself, though poetry, too, has flourished. At the present day American literature is rich and varied, and takes its place among the great literatures of the time.

See also NOVEL.
See also Vol. I: AMERICANS.

ANGLICAN CHANT, *see* SACRED MUSIC.

ANTHEM. This is a choral composition sung in services in the Church of England. It was originally based on the motet of the pre-Reformation Church, and serves the function in Anglican services which the motet does in Roman Catholic services. The motet is an independent composition for voices; in the Mass it is usually sung at the Offertory, but it is not an indispensable part of the service as are, for example, the Gloria and the Gradual. It is frequently based on PLAINSONG (q.v.) melodies; indeed, it grew up as an elaboration of these. The art of the motet reached its highest point in the compositions of the Catholic composers of the 16th century, such as Palestrina, Vittoria, Byrd, and others. A motet is invariably unaccompanied, and retains to this day the form perfected in the 16th century. Anthems are usually now accompanied by the organ.

After the Reformation, anthems were at first similar to motets with English words, though they were rarely based on plainsong themes. With the changes of musical style, however, their character altered. William Byrd (*c.* 1542–1623), although he remained a Catholic composer and wrote many motets and Masses for the old Latin rite, made many important contributions to the new liturgy of the English Church, and his works showed some of the ways in which the anthem was to develop. He introduced for the first time passages for solo voice with viol accompaniment. Orlando Gibbons (1583–1625) extended these so that they formed whole sections of the anthem, and came to be known as verse anthems.

In the Restoration period Pelham Humphrey, a chorister of the Chapel Royal, was sent by Charles II to study music in France, where he learnt the Italian methods used at the French Court. On his return he wrote much longer anthems, consisting of several movements and interspersed with choruses and arias, duets, trios, and so on for solo voices. A special feature of these anthems are the interludes for string orchestra, of which King Charles II was very fond. PURCELL developed this type of anthem, and when HANDEL (qq.v. Vol. V) came to England shortly afterwards, he wrote large-scale anthems, such as the Chandos series, written for performance in the private chapel of the Duke of Chandos. These, however, resemble rather the CANTATAS (q.v.) of J. S. Bach than the usual type of English anthem. Their length and complexity make them unsuitable for performance in the normal church services. In the English Prayer Book of 1662 provision was made for the singing of an anthem at Morning and Evening Prayer towards the end of the Service by the following direction: 'in quires and places where they sing here followeth the anthem'. This clearly refers to cathedrals and collegiate churches where there was a professional choir of men, and also, probably, a choir school.

The anthems of Greene and Boyce in the 18th century were built upon Purcell's models, but without the instrumental interludes and not too lengthy for use in church services. In the 19th century S. S. Wesley brought a new spirit to the anthems which he wrote, especially to the organ accompaniments, which now became independent of the voice parts instead of merely doubling them as they had hitherto done. In the 20th century the rapid development of the art of music had its effect also on the music of the Church and especially on the anthem. This was reflected most notably, perhaps, in the anthems of C. V. Stanford and Charles Wood. Since then most leading musicians have contributed anthems for use in church.

See also SACRED MUSIC.

ANTHOLOGIES. The word 'Anthology', which literally means a collection of flowers, is used as title for a selection of writings, usually by many authors—generally short poems, but also sometimes short extracts from longer prose or verse works. Such volumes—as in the case of the *Greek Anthology*—have often preserved works which would otherwise have been lost.

The *Greek Anthology* was compiled under the Emperor Constantine VII (10th century A.D.) by Cephalas. He drew largely on three previous anthologies: the *Garland* of Meleager (*c.* 90 B.C.), the *Garland* of Philippus (A.D. 40), and Agathias's *Circle* (A.D. 570). Cephalas rearranged poems from these collections and added others. The only known manuscript of this anthology was discovered in 1607 by the French scholar Salmasius, when he was 19 years old, in the Palatine Library at Heidelberg. It ranges from the 7th century B.C. to the 10th century A.D. and contains about 6,000 poems of very unequal merit by more than 300 writers. In this bouquet the fairest flowers of poetry shine out from a tangle of weeds and artificial flowers.

There was also a *Latin Anthology*, compiled in the 6th century and very popular in the Middle Ages, but no complete copy of it has survived. Since the 16th century many collections of both Greek and Latin poems have been arranged, some containing selections from poets not otherwise easily accessible, others aiming at giving a selection of the best poetry.

One of the most famous collections of English lyric poetry is commonly known as *Tottel's Miscellany* (1557). When Slender, in *The Merry Wives of Windsor*, about to court Ann Page says, 'I had rather than forty shillings I had my Book of Songs and Sonnets here', it is to *Tottel's Miscellany* that he is referring. There were many other contemporary collections, often with delightful names: *A Handful of Pleasant Delights* (1584), *The Paradyse of Daynty Devises* (1576), *A Gorgeous Gallery of Gallant Inventions* (1578), *The Phoenix Nest* (1593), and *England's Helicon* (1600). This last, *England's Helicon*, is an anthology of PASTORAL poetry (q.v.) including poems by Sidney, Greene, Lodge, and Drayton. The editor, probably Nicholas Ling, frequently made small changes in the title or text of a poem to make it conform more nearly to the pastoral pattern. Nevertheless, this very attractive collection is the most important anthology of English lyrics between *Tottel's Miscellany* and Palgrave's *Golden Treasury*.

In the 17th century Tonson, the publisher who bought Milton's *Paradise Lost*, published a well-known series of miscellanies between 1684 and 1708, edited by Dryden. These collections of contemporary verse are less lyrical in character. The lyrists of the 17th century—Donne, Crashaw, Herrick, for example—were scarcely represented in these or other anthologies till the 19th century. A very important anthology, published in 1765, is Percy's *Reliques of Ancient English Poetry: Consisting of Old Heroic Ballads, Songs, and other pieces of our earlier poets (Chiefly of the Lyric kind)*. This had a great influence in reviving interest in early English poetry (*see* BALLADS).

The best known of all English anthologies, Palgrave's *Golden Treasury of Songs and Lyrics* (1861, 2nd series 1896), presented Palgrave's selection of the best lyrics from all English literature. It is but one of many anthologies published during the 19th and 20th centuries. Some, like *An Anthology of World Poetry* (edited by Mark van Doren, 1929) have presented poems from all ages and all languages, in English translation. Some have confined themselves to one language and one period—perhaps, like Grierson's *Metaphysical Lyrics and Poems of the Seventeenth Century* (1921), to a rather neglected period. This book has had a considerable influence on contemporary poets. Others, such as the *Oxford Book of French Verse*, confine themselves to one language but select from all periods of its literature.

Some modern anthologies are personal, both in their selection and in their arrangement. Aldous Huxley, for example, in *Texts and Pretexts*, arranges in juxtaposition texts on the same subject selected from Latin, French, English, and other literatures. The results are often very interesting, and afford—as the title suggests—pretext for comment. What an anthologist selects reveals his own taste and often that of his age. It helps to form or develop the taste of his readers, and it serves to illustrate or chart literary movements.

See also LYRIC POETRY.

AQUATINT, *see* ETCHING AND ENGRAVING, Section 5.

ARABIAN NIGHTS. This is the best known of the many collections of fairy-tales that have circulated for centuries in Arabic-speaking lands. This particular collection, the Arabic title being *Alf layla wa-layla* ('The Thousand Nights and a Night'), originated in India and came into Arabic through Persian at the beginning of the 11th century. We have a clue to its origin in the way in which the individual tales are strung together: Scheherazade, the wife of the blood-thirsty King Shahriyar, saves herself from death at his hands by telling him wonderful tales, night after night, and stopping always at an exciting point. This device of a 'framework-story', within which other stories are fitted, is common in INDIAN LITERATURE (q.v.).

Evidence for the *Arabian Nights* having come by way of Persia is seen in the fact that not a few of the characters, including Scheherazade and Shahriyar themselves, have Persian names.

No one writer was responsible for all the stories, and story-tellers of every period have altered the old tales and added new ones of their own. *Aladdin* and *Ali Baba*, which are two of the best-known stories in the English version, were incorporated in the collection comparatively recently. In at least one case an ancient Greek theme is recognizable: the cannibal of Sindbad's fifth voyage is clearly a reminiscence of the Cyclops from whom Odysseus had such a narrow escape (*see* HOMERIC LITERATURE).

All the stories, whatever their origin, were given an Arab colouring by the Arab story-tellers, so that the *Arabian Nights* show us countless glimpses of medieval Moslem life. It is noticeable that magic and the Jinn play a smaller part in the tales set in Baghdad than in those set in Cairo, such as the stories of Judar, Ali of Cairo, and Ma'aruf. This accords with an observation of Ibn Khaldun that the people of Egypt have, from the time of the Pharaohs, been addicted to sorcery.

See also ARABIC LITERATURE.
See also Vol. I: FAIRY TALES.

ARABIC ART, *see* ISLAMIC ART.

ARABIC LITERATURE. Arabic, the tongue in which the Koran, the sacred book of ISLAM (q.v. Vol. I), was revealed, is the common written language of all those who accept MOHAMMED (q.v. Vol. V) as the messenger of God, in much the same way as Latin is the common language of the Roman Catholic Church all over the world (*see* ARABIC LANGUAGE, Vol. IV). Consequently, only a part of all the vast literature in Arabic is the work of ARABS (q.v. Vol. I). The Moslem peoples of Turkey, Persia, India, and the Far East have all produced considerable literatures in their own languages, yet, because of this international quality of Arabic, the terms 'Islamic' literature and 'Arabic' literature are often used interchangeably.

Apart from the Koran, pride of place in Arabic literature has always been given to the *Mu'allaqat*, seven poems of the 6th century A.D., which, like most other pre-Islamic poems, each present a series of scenes from BEDOUIN life (q.v. Vol. I). In this style of composition the poet's aim is not novelty of theme but the demonstration of his artistry in the treatment of familiar subjects: descriptions of a deserted encampment, a lost love, a swift camel.

Soon after the death of Mohammed (A.D. 632), in order to preserve the correct pronunciation of the text of the Koran and to establish its meaning, people began to collect and study the old poetry and examples of Bedouin speech; it was thought that the purest Arabic survived in the desert long after it had become corrupted by non-Arab influences in the towns. At the same time, out of a desire to find rules for conduct in matters where the Koran offered no guidance, reminiscences of the daily life of the Prophet were collected from those who had known him. For some time literary men concerned themselves mainly with these two subjects and with the writing of history; poetry was out of favour because Mohammed had disapproved of it. In the beginning of the 8th century, however, there was a poetic revival, the finest products of which were the love-poems of Omar ibn Abi Rabi's.

Under the Caliph al-Ma'mun (813–33) many Greek philosophical and scientific works were translated into Arabic, and were later translated from Arabic into Latin by the European scholars who came to study at Cordova in Moorish Spain and other centres of Moslem civilization. Thus Europe is indebted to the Arabs for the preservation of many of the treasures of Greek learning.

Many Arabs regard al-Mutanabbi (died 965) as their greatest poet. Particularly vivid are his descriptions of battles in which he fought at the side of his patron, the Prince of Aleppo. Many of al-Mutanabbi's lines have become proverbs.

The most perfectly developed literary form in Arabic is the *maqama*, a witty tale told partly in rhymed prose. Its creator was al-Hamadhani (969–1008), and the most polished *maqamat* were written by al-Hariri (1054–1122), who aimed not merely at entertaining but also at showing off the enormous wealth of the Arabic vocabulary and his own mastery of it (*see* Vol. IV, p. 31).

In the 14th century the great historian Ibn Khaldun of Tunis is equally authoritative and readable when describing the rise and fall of civilizations or the methods used by professional sorcerers to extract money from their dupes. There are many other great names; geographers, story-tellers, philosophers, and scientists. Only a minute fraction of all the vast store of Arabic literature has been translated into English.

See also ARABIAN NIGHTS.
See also Vol. IV: ARABIC LANGUAGE.

ARCH. This bridges an opening by means of stones or bricks arranged in a curve so that each supports the others and the wall above it. The arch was first fully used by the Romans (Fig. 1*a*). Semicircular arches are a dominating feature of many Roman buildings, distinguishing them sharply from Greek buildings, in which the 'post-and-beam' construction was always used.

An arch can span a wide opening with comparatively small stones. The Romans were thus able to achieve great engineering feats such as their cross-country aqueducts (*see* Vol. I, p. 412). From the arch they evolved the VAULT and DOME (qq.v.) with which they roofed their enormous public buildings.

European builders up to the middle of the 12th century used the round arch, sometimes copying Roman examples where these were visible, as in the south of France, sometimes showing little skill or understanding of the structure, as in Anglo-Saxon buildings (Fig. 1*b*). In the latter the span of the arch was narrow, and sometimes, instead of a round head made of small stones, two long stones were leant together to make a triangular shaped arch (Fig. 1*c*). The Romanesque builders of the 11th and 12th centuries showed great skill and inventiveness in the use of the round-headed arch (Fig. 1*d*) (*see* ROMANESQUE ART); but its rigid shape had serious drawbacks when used in connexion with

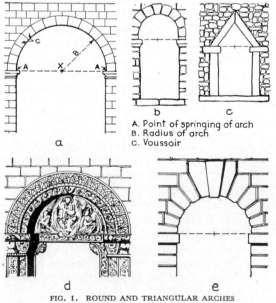

A. Point of springing of arch
B. Radius of arch
C. Voussoir

FIG. 1. ROUND AND TRIANGULAR ARCHES

a, Roman; *b*. Saxon; *c*. Saxon triangular; *d*. Norman;
e, Renaissance

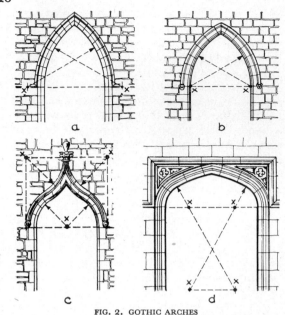

FIG. 2. GOTHIC ARCHES

a. Lancet; *b*. Equilateral; *c*. Ogee; *d*. Four-centred

vaulting, since, a round arch being semicircular, its height is always half its width. Gothic builders used the pointed arch, which permitted different widths of opening to be spanned by arches of the same height. This made possible a much greater range of structural forms, especially in the building of large vaults.

The chief difference structurally between round and pointed arches is that the round arch has a wedge-shaped stone (called the keystone) at the top, which is often enlarged and decorated (Fig. 1*e*), whereas the top of the pointed arch is simply the vertical joint between two stones (Fig. 2*a*). The individual stones forming an arch are called 'voussoirs'.

Pointed arches of various shapes were used in GOTHIC ARCHITECTURE (q.v.) for door and window openings and for arcades, niches, and all kinds of decorative features. The sides of a pointed arch are arcs of circles, the centres of which are at different points for different kinds of arches. In the late 12th and early 13th centuries the characteristic Early English arch was a narrow lancet (Fig. 2*a*); in the Decorated period which followed, a rather wider equilateral arch (Fig. 2*b*) was used and sometimes an 'ogee' arch, composed of two double (or S) curves (Fig. 2*c*). In the Perpendicular period, when arches were required to be wide and often **had a horizontal moulding or 'dripstone' over** them, the four-centred arch was introduced (Fig. 2d). On the Continent the equilateral arch was chiefly used in the 13th century and later the ogee arch, which was especially popular in Italy.

In Islamic architecture the arch was used from early times and derived from Roman and Eastern Mediterranean forms. The builders used a variety of shapes, the pointed arch (Fig. 3a), an arch in which the centre portion consists of a single flat curve (Fig. 3b), and in MOORISH ART (q.v.) the horse-shoe arch, a rounded arch of more than a semicircle (Fig. 3c).

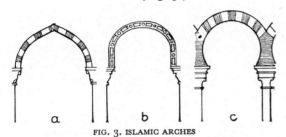

FIG. 3. ISLAMIC ARCHES
a. Pointed; b. Round; c. Horseshoe

In Renaissance architecture, though arched construction was not elaborated into ambitious forms of vaulting, the round arch was used in a great variety of ways for door and window openings and arcading of all kinds. In modern architecture the arch is little used because stone construction has largely given way to steel and concrete, which do not normally lend themselves to curved forms.

ARCHITECTURE. An architect is a man who not only provides people with the buildings they need for various purposes but who aims at making those buildings works of art. In the best architecture the artistic and practical aspects are not kept separate, but are closely connected. For example, in the medieval cathedrals the means used to obtain artistic effects—the soaring arches and pinnacles, flying buttresses, and intricate vaulting—were a direct result of the medieval stone-masons' engineering experiments, and the masons' efforts were prompted by their desire to make each new building an improvement on the last from the point of view of serving its purpose efficiently as well as nobly.

On the other hand, there have been periods—such as the Georgian—when very little development has taken place either in the way buildings served their practical purposes or in their con-

struction. The artistic qualities of GEORGIAN ARCHITECTURE (q.v.) did not depend directly on either of these, but on the skill, originality, and good judgement with which certain agreed rules of proportion, decoration, and so on were applied—and these rules were applicable to any kind of building. The rules on which the architecture of any period are based depend on the way of life of the people of that period, and remain unchanged only so long as the way of life remains settled. Sooner or later social or political upheavals occur, and the style of architecture is also upset and changed. The Industrial Revolution, for example, brought the Georgian period to an end, as the fall of the Roman Empire had, many centuries earlier, ended the Classical period. After such social upheavals architecture again enters an experimental phase.

The kind of life people are living also, of course, determines the kinds of building that they want, and therefore the direction in which their architects and engineers choose to experiment. But once more, it is not always possible to tell whether demand inspires the experiment or whether it is successful experiments that stimulate demand. For example, the ancient Romans, who were remarkable engineers, discovered the use of the ARCH and the VAULT (qq.v.) and were therefore able to build for themselves vast halls and arenas of a kind that the Greeks, with their simple post-and-beam construction, could never have built. But it would be equally true to say that the Romans' need for covered spaces where great crowds could assemble led them to use the arch and vault, whereas the Greeks had been content with the limitations of the beam construction of their temples because these buildings were closed shrines, to be viewed by the general public from the outside only. Similarly, with medieval houses, one cannot say whether the gradual increase in the size of the windows was due to the sense of security which people felt when houses ceased to be liable to attack, or to the technical skill and knowledge that made it possible to pierce larger holes in the walls.

Whichever way round we put it, however, the purpose which a building is meant to serve is the first thing that determines the form it will take. In earlier days, purposes were few and simple: there were houses big and small for living in, halls of various kinds for meetings (public baths in Roman times, guild-halls in medieval times, parliament buildings and assembly halls later, and so on), churches and temples for worshipping in, and castles for defence; but there was very little else. Even buying, selling, and the manufacture of goods was carried on mostly in people's houses or in the open market-place. But as scientific invention and discovery made life more complex, many new kinds of buildings were needed: banks, railway stations, factories and department stores, cinemas, and airports, with the result that architecture became a much more complicated business. Previously the architect could have the look of a building in his mind's eye from the beginning; the general shape of a church or a town hall was always much the same, and the architect did not have the problem of working it out afresh on each occasion. But nowadays that is what he has to do, after studying the particular manufacturing processes if his building is a factory, after studying the routine followed by the doctors, nurses, and patients if it is a hospital, and so on. He must not start with a ready-made idea of what the building will look like. That is why today buildings are said to be designed from within outwards, as opposed to the 19th-century habit of designing buildings first as a shell, and then fitting in the complicated internal arrangements afterwards—a method which often resulted in buildings which were unsuitable for their purpose, and therefore unsatisfactory from an artistic standpoint.

Another factor, besides its purpose, which determines the appearance of a building is the method of construction. It is only in comparatively recent times that the range of materials and methods available to the architect has allowed for fundamental differences in construction. The Greeks used flat beams resting on pillars or solid walls, mostly in stone or marble (see GREEK ART). The Romans did the same, but introduced the round arch, which enabled them to build more varied and ambitious structures and to cover in large vaulted halls (see ROMAN ART). The Romans used a certain amount of brick and concrete as well as stone. The Normans used methods similar to those of the Romans for large stone buildings like churches, and simple timber construction for houses. (see ROMANESQUE ART). The Gothic builders, using smaller stones, devised the pointed arch, and developed their knowledge of building mechanics to a high degree. They were able to build huge stone structures in which arches and buttresses transferred the weight of high stone vaults safely to the ground, making the whole building one large system of thrusts and counter-thrusts in which each portion played its part (see GOTHIC ART). The method of construction used in each period is clearly seen in the buildings belonging to it, so that to describe the way a building is constructed is also to describe its style of architecture (see Plate 2).

In more modern times, however, this is less clearly so, as some of the new methods of construction that have been introduced into architecture—cast iron at the end of the 18th century, steel towards the end of the 19th, and reinforced concrete early in the 20th—have been used by architects either to imitate buildings constructed by older methods or to build structures to be hidden later by brick or stone façades. Yet new structural materials have had a marked effect on the architecture of recent times. They have been responsible, for example, for the prevalence of flat roofs and large windows and for buildings with a large, uninterrupted floor-space. In the most modern buildings the materials are allowed largely to determine the appearance (see MODERN ARCHITECTURE).

Other modern inventions have also affected architectural design. Not only the large spans of steel or concrete beams but also the large sheets of plate glass which can now be manufactured have made the huge window areas of modern buildings technically possible. But rooms with such large windows would not be practicable were it not for the improvement in methods of heating. Similarly, flat roofs have only become practicable since improved methods of keeping out water were invented.

The influence of materials on architecture is not solely a matter of the invention or introduction of new materials. Materials have at all times varied according to locality, according to economic circumstances, and (to a lesser extent) according to fashion. Though improvement in transport has largely done away with the need for using only local materials, these are still often preferable, as they blend better with the landscape and with existing buildings. In earlier times every region had its prevalent materials on which the form and colour of its architecture depended: marble in Greece, stone in Italy and many parts of northern Europe, brick in the Low Countries and East Anglia, and timber in

PRESTBURY OLD HALL, CHESHIRE: A TIMBER-FRAME HOUSE

The steep roof, and windows as large as the construction will allow,
are typical of northern buildings

COURTYARD OF A HOSPITAL IN TOLEDO

The rooms are protected from the heat by
small windows and deep balconies

A SCHOOL AT WELWYN GARDEN CITY

Light steel frame construction makes possible large windows and a flat roof

Scandinavia. Sometimes, when economic circumstances allowed, stone—which permitted the most ambitious structures and could be enriched by carving—was imported into districts lacking stone, as happened when many of the great medieval cathedrals were built, as well as the most important buildings in London. And when fashion demanded it, buildings were, at certain times, deliberately given an appearance and finish foreign to those of the natural local materials, as in the case of the stucco (painted plaster) with which brick buildings were almost invariably covered during the first half of the 19th century (see REGENCY ARCHITECTURE). The structural material underneath the artificial surface, however, still dictated the general type of the building, the arrangement of the walls, the shape of the roofs, and the size and spacing of the windows.

The purpose of the buildings and the means at the architect's disposal (that is, the available materials and methods of construction) are thus the two practical influences that have always shaped the development of architecture. The demands of the climate must also be considered —shady porches and small windows, for example, in sunny countries; large windows facing south in sunless ones; and steep-pitched roofs in wet and snowy ones. The opportunities presented or limitations imposed by the site are also important. The shapes of many buildings, indeed, are largely determined by the lie of the land, its slopes or level areas, how it is best approached, and how best protected from the prevailing wind.

Finally, the development of architecture through the successive periods of history is influenced by changes in fashions and ideals. The reasons which determine whether emphasis shall be laid on vertical or horizontal lines, on symmetry or absence of symmetry, and which cause systems of ornament and decoration to be established and discarded are partly, as we have seen, the product of the lives people live, their knowledge of the science of building, and the materials they build in; but they are also closely bound up with the whole cultural and artistic development of their times. This can be seen very clearly at the time of the Renaissance, when the Gothic style no longer satisfied people's needs, and architects turned to classical styles for inspiration, finding not only the solution to practical problems but a style of building and decoration which was pleasing to men imbued with a love of CLASSICAL ART (q.v.).

See also CHURCH ARCHITECTURE, ENGLISH; ORDERS OF ARCHITECTURE.
See also Vol. VII: BUILDING INDUSTRY.
See also Vol. VIII: BUILDING.

ARCHITECTURE, MODERN, see MODERN ARCHITECTURE.

ARIA, see SONG, HISTORY OF, Section 4.

ART. Although this is a universal human activity, art is one of the hardest things in the world to define. Learned men and artists, who have for centuries argued about it, can agree on one thing only—that anyone who tried to lay down a rigid law to decide what was art and what was not would be wrong. The Latin word *ars* meant 'skill', whether of mind or body, and particularly human skill in contrast to the marvels of nature. In the Middle Ages the 'liberal arts' were the subjects studied by scholars—grammar, logic, rhetoric, arithmetic, geometry, music, and astronomy; hence the degrees of Master and Bachelor of Arts granted by universities. In modern times the arts or the fine arts are held to consist of literature (including drama), music, drawing and painting, sculpture, and architecture. Today the word 'art', if used alone, usually means the visual arts only—painting, drawing, sculpture, and engraving. But in this article art is discussed in its wider meaning.

The study of 'aesthetics', which is concerned with the principles of fine art, has never succeeded in framing any practical rules of taste. For example, men have long debated whether the subject-matter of art or the skill with which the artist expressed himself was the more important. Which is the nearer to a work of art —a noble landscape painted by a second-class artist or a sketch of a daisy made by a first-class one? Most experts agree that above a certain level of merit both the artist's manner and his subject-matter—often called 'form' and 'content'—influence one another so deeply that they can hardly be separated and analysed.

Ever since the Golden Age of ancient Greece men have discussed whether art had anything to do with beauty; but as everyone tends to use that word in a different and private sense, such discussion often leads only to confusion. For instance, a young girl or a view of a mountain may be called beautiful, yet neither is a work of art,

Alinari

GUIDO RICCIO DA FOGLIANO ON HORSEBACK

The brilliantly caparisoned horse and rider are set against a simplified decorative landscape. The detail shows the realistic portrait of the soldier-adventurer. Fresco by Simone Martini (c. 1285–c. 1357) in the Palazzo Comunale, Siena

for art is man-made. Again, a portrait of an ugly old woman may be considered a beautifully sensitive and harmonious painting.

Many of the world's most famous works of art are fundamentally tragic. The poems and plays of Greece; medieval church architecture, sculpture, and music; early Italian painting; much of the art of Shakespeare; much modern writing, such as the novels and poetry of Thomas Hardy—all these reflect the tragic situation of men, surrounded by stupendous forces which may destroy them. So the subject-matter of art is often heroic, awesome, or sad. For this reason it has sometimes been suggested that the test of great art is passionate feeling. Yet much good music and painting is without passion in the ordinary sense.

At the other extreme comes the test of pleasure; yet this also cannot be consistently applied: much art is pleasing, but art which has no other quality but that it is pleasing is rarely great.

Perhaps the only thing common to most works of art is a feeling that the artist is sincerely trying to pass on to those around him ideas which he considers worth while expressing. Yet even this definition fails if it makes all art seem serious or pompous. Many great artists have expressed their sense of fun: the music of Beethoven and Haydn contains light-hearted musical 'jokes', while in all the arts there are countless examples of gay, even frivolous moods.

Art, indeed, is none the less excellent when it shows itself in small and even trivial things. A countryman who makes a gay knot of straw in his horse's mane or adds a shining brass stud to its harness is expressing the artistic instinct which all men have to some degree and have had since the days when prehistoric man painted pictures of animals on the walls of caves or carved them on their tools and weapons (*see* PREHISTORIC ART).

In its simple forms, art is often linked with some useful purpose or limited by a usable shape (*see* PRIMITIVE ART). Thus the pre-Roman inhabitants of Britain applied their art to such objects as pins and shields. Yet a Celtic decorated and jewelled shield from the grave of a barbarous British tribesman can show a creative splendour as great in its own class as the magnificent painted walls and ceilings of the VATICAN (q.v.).

In most times art has served a social need. The cathedrals and abbeys of the Middle Ages were built to allow for the complicated requirements of religious ceremonies. These were seldom the design of a single architect, but grew slowly over several generations. Here is another contradiction in the history of art. Fine creative work need not be the product of a single great artist, but can be the work of a group following a sound tradition.

At all times the patron of art has played an important part. Artists have always had to work for their living, and consequently have had to carry out the commissions of those who paid them. In the Middle Ages artists and craftsmen made churches for bishops and abbots, castles and palaces for kings and barons, and great halls for town guilds. Later, when the nobility and merchant classes were the chief sources of wealth, painters, sculptors, musicians, and playwrights were in a sense the upper domestic servants of rich private patrons. The great composers, Bach, Haydn, and others, wrote their music under these conditions; Shakespeare is believed to have been attached as a writer to the Lord Chamberlain's company of players; Holbein, Van Dyck, Boucher, David, Velazquez, and Goya were court painters in England, France, and Spain.

In the late 18th and 19th centuries, painters, writers, and composers became largely independent of patrons, risking great poverty if they were unsuccessful in selling their work to publishers, theatres, orchestras, or private buyers of pictures. Commercial entertainment, catering for the public, took the place of private entertainment reserved for noblemen's houses, and the more successful artists reaped the profit, and sometimes riches and fame. As Britain's population and prosperity increased, artists of small talent were encouraged to produce second-rate books, pictures, and music in the hope of making a living from people of less educated taste. Such conditions encourage artists to imitate closely the standards of art favoured by the largest number of customers.

During the present century another change has come; the painter and sculptor, the composer and dramatist all receive commissions from government departments, educational institutions, the B.B.C., and great industrial corporations rather than from private people.

What makes the taste of one period differ from that of another, and why a period of elegant taste is sometimes followed by the reverse, are mysteries impossible to explain fully. Certain factors give partial explanations. For example, when railways were able to carry cheap bricks to all parts of England, traditional building with handsome local stone began to die out. The Industrial Revolution, which made people concentrate on making money quickly, gave rise to much ugly and shoddy work. Yet obviously the new railways, machines, and factories in themselves were not entirely responsible for changing the taste and judgement of the British public. Good art and good taste are as often a matter of morality and education as of machinery and money.

In all the fine arts, though there may be certain definite standards of artistic merit, the opinion of respected judges undoubtedly changes with every generation. It is true, for instance, that many accepted combinations of sound in modern music would have been thought wrong or unmusical 50 years ago, while at many periods painters have been admired who would have been considered unskilful or even mad a century earlier. The best literary critics of Dr. Johnson's day thought the METAPHYSICAL POETRY (q.v.) of the 17th century inartistic, and admired poetry which 50 or 60 years later was looked down on. Such changes of taste are born of the spirit of creative experiment in countless artists, generally led by a few pioneers. But at all periods there are obviously many more merely competent painters, composers, and writers than there are creative ones, and the work of the second-rate always tends to confuse the achievements of the pioneers in the eyes of the public of their day.

People as a whole are brought up on the artistic standards of the previous generation, and cannot appreciate the pioneers who break new ground in their own time. The appreciation is left to their children or grandchildren, who, in turn, develop prejudices which prevent their understanding the new trends of their day. But artists themselves do not easily produce new ideas without outside stimulus, so the whole process is greatly affected by social change or its absence. When a country is protected from warfare, immigration, and other economic and social changes, artistic standards may remain the same for generations. But change causes new ideas to be discussed, and encourages the arts and customs of one country or region to spread to others, where artists are stimulated to seek new forms.

There is no such thing as a 'natural' appreciation of works of art, whether literary, musical, or visual. People have to be educated by experience to master the enjoyment of a fine art, just as much as they have to train to be able to compete in a bicycle or swimming race. In many cases a natural aptitude and love of an art will shorten the period of apprenticeship. But someone seeing his tenth opera will understand its pattern more easily than someone seeing his first, and the more poetry a person reads or pictures he looks at, the more will he appreciate and enjoy the work of the poet or painter.

In the last hundred years the development of photography, the press, the cinema, the radio, the increasing speed of travel by land, sea, and air, the great growth of education, and the building of museums, theatres, and art galleries in many countries, have led to a more widespread diffusion of the arts than ever before. Thus local forms of art, crafts, architecture, costume, and house decoration have been swept away wholesale, and artists in many countries are producing music, painting, and drama which have little relation to their local traditions.

See also MODERN ART.

ART GALLERIES. Most of the great picture galleries and museums of antiquities on the continent of Europe, such as those at Paris, Madrid, Vienna, Florence, and Dresden, began as the private collections of kings. At some stage during the 19th or 20th century these were made over to the State and became public museums.

The galleries of Great Britain, however, like its MUSEUMS (q.v. Vol. X), started in another way, and the large royal collection has remained private. The most important galleries were established at various times by a special Act of Parliament, and private collections or single objects were purchased for them by the

British Museum

THE PORTLAND VASE

Greek vase of black and white glass carved in relief, 1st century A.D. In 1845 it was smashed by a madman

AN 18TH-CENTURY EXHIBITION

The Royal Academy in 1787. The crowded walls contrast with modern galleries where the pictures are hung so that each one can be clearly seen. Engraving after J. H. Ramburg

Government. Later, fine collections, such as the Wallace Collection, have been bequeathed to the nation by private persons. Municipal galleries and museums have also been established.

The British Museum, which is housed in a huge building in Bloomsbury, London, is the largest collection of antiquities in the world. It contains examples of the art of primitive peoples all over the world and of the great ancient civilizations. The most famous of its very many treasures are the ELGIN MARBLES (q.v.), the Rosetta Stone (*see* HIEROGLYPHICS, Vol. IV), the Codex Sinaiticus (*see* BIBLE, Vol. I), the Portland Vase, a Greek vase of the 1st century A.D., and the Lindisfarne Gospels, an illuminated manuscript which was made in Northumbria in the 7th century. There is also an immense library of printed books (*see* BRITISH MUSEUM LIBRARY, Vol. IV), a Print Room which contains a huge collection of drawings by the Old Masters, and the Department of Manuscripts containing many of the greatest medieval ILLUMINATED MANUSCRIPTS (q.v.), as well as others of historical and literary interest.

The National Gallery in Trafalgar Square consisted, when it was founded in 1824, of the collection of thirty-eight pictures formed by a wealthy Russian merchant, J. J. Angerstein, who had settled in England. Throughout the 19th century, and particularly during the time of Sir Charles Eastlake, its first director, many Old Masters, some of the highest quality, were added. Today it consists of over 2,000 pictures —a few Graeco-Roman portraits and works by almost every great European painter from the 12th to the 19th century.

The neighbouring National Portrait Gallery is concerned only with portraits of distinguished British men and women.

The Tate Gallery (Millbank, London), the gift of Sir Henry Tate, in 1897, now consists of a collection of British pictures together with a section of modern painting and sculpture of most European countries.

The Victoria and Albert Museum (South Kensington) was founded as a result of the Great Exhibition of 1851. It is devoted chiefly to European sculpture (medieval and Renaissance)

and to the so-called 'minor arts'—such as tapestry, ironwork, furniture, porcelain, glass, and costume. It has also a considerable number of water-colours, some oils, and the largest art library in Britain. For many years the Sovereign has lent to it the Raphael Cartoons, a very important example of Italian High Renaissance art (*see* Vol. I, p. 320).

The Wallace Collection (Manchester Square, London), bequeathed to the nation by Lady Wallace in 1897, contains a large collection of armour, some notable Dutch and English paintings, and the finest general collection of French 18th-century paintings, furniture, porcelain, and sculpture.

The National Gallery of Scotland (Edinburgh) was first opened in 1859. It consists of about 2,000 pictures of most of the European schools, and a small collection of sculpture, drawings, and prints.

The National Museum of Wales at Cardiff was incorporated by Royal Charter in 1907, but not opened until 1927. In addition to departments of geology, botany, zoology, archaeology, and folk-life, it has a department of art which is not confined to the work of Welsh artists.

The National Maritime Museum at Greenwich, the newest of the great national museums, was founded in 1934, and although it is not first and foremost an art museum, for it was established for the 'illustration and study of the maritime history of Great Britain', it has what is probably the most representative collection of British painting in the country.

See also Vol. X: MUSEUMS.

ARTHURIAN LITERATURE.

Until the end of the 16th century King Arthur was thought to have really existed, and to have been the greatest king of Britain. This is because he was mentioned in a popular 12th-century history of Britain, written in Latin by Geoffrey of Monmouth, which was translated into French and became a favourite subject of ROMANCE LITERATURE (q.v.). The first appearance of the story in English is a remarkable 13th-century historical poem called the *Brut*, written by Layamon. Here Arthur is depicted as a primitive and heroic king of Britain, who defends his country against the invader. In later writings Arthur and his knights came to represent the highest ideals of CHIVALRY (q.v. Vol. X), and the many stories about them were called the

'matter of Britain'. A number of these stories, mostly in French, were translated and adapted by Sir Thomas Malory, whose *Morte D'Arthur* was printed by Caxton in 1485. Caxton's was the only text known until recently, when a manuscript was discovered at Winchester, which gives a rather longer text free from Caxton's alterations; this was printed in 1947. Malory

Laroussa

THE FIRST KISS OF LAUNCELOT AND GUINEVERE

Illumination from a 14th-century French Romance.
(*Bibl. Nat. MS. Fr. 118*)

tells of Arthur's wondrous birth, his obscure boyhood, and how he proved his right to the throne. Then he tells of his successful wars, his marriage to Guinevere, and the establishment of the Knights of the Round Table, among whom are Launcelot the greatest of them all, Gawain, Tristram, Kay, and Gareth. Many adventures of the knights follow, in which they overcome evil and succour the weak. Then comes the legend of the Holy Grail, the cup our Lord used at the Last Supper. According to the legend all the knights had to search for the Holy Grail, but only those who were perfect would succeed. Many died in the search, and only Sir Galahad and two others proved worthy. Sir Launcelot failed because of his love for Queen Guinevere. When Launcelot's love finally brought about war between Arthur and Launcelot, Arthur's son Mordred tried to capture the kingdom. He failed, but all was brought to destruction.

The *Morte D'Arthur* is full of excellent stories of knights rescuing oppressed ladies and undergoing strange adventures. A knight's duty was to be brave, honourable, loyal, merciful, to help ladies in distress, and never to fight in a bad cause. The characters are simple, passionate, violent, aristocratic. Their adventures are told with lively sympathy and realistic detail, in a straightforward style at times capable of great power, particularly in dialogue, which is everywhere magnificently alive. It is their speech, especially, which makes the final drama of Launcelot's love for the Queen and its disastrous result so interesting, noble, and pathetic. Malory is a great story-teller, but his sources were so varied and contradictory that the *Morte D'Arthur* itself is occasionally confusing and inconsistent.

The Arthurian legend has frequently been a subject for literature since the time of Malory. Spenser's *The Faerie Queene* is influenced by the *Morte D'Arthur*, while Milton and Dryden each thought of writing Arthurian epics. Swinburne and Morris both wrote Arthurian tales; but the most famous of later versions is Tennyson's *Idylls of the King*. These simplify and refine the tales. Arthur becomes 'the blameless King', a rather priggish character. The fighting is unreal and the love-stories colourless. The whole is overshadowed by the faithlessness of Launcelot and Guinevere, and the sadness of their betrayal of Arthur is the most powerful part of the poem. The whole story is meant to suggest the Soul's war with the Body, Arthur representing the Soul. The poem is pleasant to read; the verse carries the story unweariedly, and there are many beauties of description.

See also Vol. I: ARTHURIAN LEGEND.

ASSYRIAN ART.

The beginnings of the ASSYRIAN CIVILIZATION (q.v. Vol. I), in the lands between the rivers Tigris and Euphrates, may go back to about 3500 B.C.; but during their early history the Assyrians seem to have been dominated by the more powerful SUMERIAN and BABYLONIAN CIVILIZATIONS (qq.v. Vol. I). We know little of their art before the rise of the Assyrian Empire in the 10th century B.C., when their widespread wars of conquest no doubt brought them in contact with the art of their neighbours, even as far afield as Egypt. Among the spoils brought back by the conquerors were many craftsmen and objects of art.

The Assyrians were not only great warriors but were themselves great artists. Each victorious king built or remodelled a palace, and even a whole city, as a permanent record of his skill at arms and of his religious fervour. When King Ashur-nazir-pal II built the city of Nimrud in 879 B.C., he lined the public rooms and adjacent corridors of his palace with stone slabs on which were sculptured in low relief accounts of his conquests, religious ceremonies, and occasionally also scenes from domestic life. The figures, which are drawn larger than life, appear rather stiff, bulky, and unbending. There was no real attempt at portraiture, the King and his courtiers all looking much alike. The King looks very much as he does in his statue found in a temple (*see* Vol. I, p. 41). The details in the carving of animals, trees, and plants or the patterns on the royal garments are executed with great care. The subject-matter and style in all the sculptures is much the same—warlike scenes of sieges, lines of prisoners (some being tortured), displays of booty, and animals, especially lions, being hunted with bows, spears, daggers, and nets. An inscription in CUNEIFORM WRITING (q.v. Vol. IV) was often cut across the face of the sculptures, showing that they were propaganda pieces, intended not only to illustrate the royal records but also to impress both visiting ambassadors and the local people. Some of the carvings still bear traces of black, red, and white paint. Above them were highly coloured glazed friezes, similar in subject and style to the sculptures beneath them. Parts of the ceiling were covered with plaster painted in geometric patterns.

Assyrian palaces were built on a regular plan which changed very little. On each side of the inner courtyards ranged a series of long, narrow rooms, each decorated with sculptures appropriate to their use: around the throne room were scenes of battles, and in the wings used for administrative and religious purposes were scenes in which the King figures in a civil or religious role, and also unsculptured but inscribed walls. The façade and gateways were dominated by huge carvings of men or winged lions and bulls, sometimes 15 or more feet high, carved from blocks of gypsum weighing more than 20 tons. These figures were the guardians of the palace, set there to prevent the entrance of evil.

Later reliefs, such as those made for Sennacherib (705–681 B.C.), show so much detail and perspective that the scenes sometimes look overcrowded. The distinctive costume of foreigners

KING ASHUR-NAZIR-PAL

Relief from the wall of his palace at Nimrud
(879 B.C.)

COLOSSAL WINGED BULL WITH HUMAN HEAD AND WINGED
FIGURE

Doorpost in the Palace of Sargon at Khorsabad,
722–705 B.C.

KING ASHUR-BANI-PAL POURING LIBATIONS OVER CORPSES OF LIONS KILLED IN THE HUNT

Musicians play before the altar. The inscription reads, 'I am Ashur-bani-pal, the king of the world, the king of Assyria
Relief from the Palace of Nineveh, 7th century B.C.

BRONZE RELIEFS FROM GATES MADE FOR SHALMANESER III, ILLUSTRATING HIS CAMPAIGNS OF 860 to 849 B.C.
Above, the king with his bodyguard and chariot; below, chariots crossing a river by a bridge of boats

is faithfully portrayed, as is the type of country through which the troops were passing. Sennacherib, who was a great builder, took a delight in carvings depicting his irrigation works and slaves moving the massive blocks of stone with which he rebuilt Nineveh. He claimed to be the first to make large figures by casting them in moulds 'as when one makes a half-shekel piece'—a technique used by the Assyrians for making small figures, jewellery, and objects such as arrow-heads (see BRONZE SCULPTURE).

The Assyrians used stone for the reliefs on the palace walls, free-standing statues, obelisks, and other monuments. But they also worked with the same care and love of intimate detail in bronze, making bronzes for decorating the palace gate (such as the gates of Shalmaneser III, made in 848 B.C.) and fine vessels for the banquet table. They decorated furniture with delicately carved ivories, and engraved small scenes on precious stone for use as cylinder seals. They made finely moulded pottery of a very high quality.

The last great Assyrian monarch and the most artistic, Ashur-bani-pal (668–626 B.C.), had carved for his palace a famous series of lion-hunt scenes (see Vol. I, p. 43). These are the largest and perhaps the finest of all carvings before the time of Greece, and surpass all the many Assyrian wall sculptures which have been excavated.

The development of Assyrian art was rudely interrupted by the capture and destruction of the Assyrian capital, Nineveh, by the Babylonians in 612 B.C. Their conquerors, however, copied the Assyrian art and it was through their influence that this art passed to Greece.

See also BABYLONIAN ART.
See also Vol. I: ASSYRIAN CIVILIZATION.

AUGUSTAN AGE. Goldsmith was perhaps the first to give to the reign of Queen Anne the title 'Augustan Age', calling it a period 'when language and learning arrived at its highest perfection'. We generally apply the term to that period of our culture which fills the last 40 years of the 17th and the first 40 years of the 18th century. Like the Golden Age of Rome under Augustus, this period seemed to its contemporaries the age of supreme achievement in the arts, towards which previous ages had but shown the way. It had a sense of security and self-certainty because it had at last obtained control over its passions, its ideas, and its language. Above all, it delighted in control and reason, polish and elegance, imposing the dignity and simplicity of order on the world and its emotions. It distrusted the abnormal, the freakish, the enthusiastic, and the 'romantick', seeking to remove these blemishes from nature and to present the shapely, well-mannered world it held as its ideal.

The artist was no lone exile from society, but a member of it, a man speaking to men of things all had in common; for the audience was small —in effect London was the audience, and that part of London only which had a common educational background and interests. The art produced in such an age may lack something of the sublime and the mysterious, but it is never vague or silly. It has a strong backbone of common sense and sharpness of thought, coupled with its elegance and dignified simplicity.

The age's literature is its greatest glory, beginning as it does with the poetry of DRYDEN (q.v. Vol. V). In his poetry of argument and SATIRE (q.v.), written in powerful heroic couplets, he set the direction for the poetry of succeeding years. We find such strong yet simple eloquence as these lines from Dryden's *Religio Laici*:

Dim as the borrowed beams of moon and stars
To lonely, weary, wandering travellers
Is Reason to the soul: and as on high
Those rolling fires discover but the sky,
Not light us here; so Reason's glimmering ray
Was lent, not to assure our doubtful way,
But guide us upward to a better day.
And as those nightly tapers disappear
When day's bright lord ascends our hemisphere,
So pale grows Reason at Religion's sight,
So dies, and so dissolves in supernatural light.

In *Absalom and Achitophel* there are powerful satirical lines where every word adds to the force of the attack, as in this account of Dryden's enemy, the Duke of Buckingham:

Railing and praising were his usual themes,
And both, to show his judgment, in extremes:
So over violent, or over civil
That every man with him was God or Devil.
In squandering wealth was his peculiar art;
Nothing went unrewarded but desert.
Beggared by fools, whom still he found too late,
He had his jest, and they had his estate.

POPE (q.v. Vol. V) brought this kind of poetry to perfection in his superbly finished and controlled verse. He replaced the subtleties and delicacies of the Elizabethans and the witty fantastic complexities of METAPHYSICAL POETRY (q.v.) with a new clarity of expression and normality of thought. The opening of the Second Epistle of his *Essay on Man* shows his poetry at its finest, every line full of meaning, the rhythms and rhymes, the images, the balancing of sounds and phrases, all contributing to the strength and beauty of the verse:

Know then thyself, presume not God to scan,
The proper study of mankind is man.
Placed on this isthmus of a middle state,
A being darkly wise, and rudely great:
With too much knowledge for the sceptic side,
With too much weakness for the stoic's pride,
He hangs between; in doubt to act, or rest;
In doubt to deem himself a god, or beast;
In doubt his mind or body to prefer;
Born but to die, and reasoning but to err;
Alike in ignorance, his reason such,
Whether he thinks too little, or too much:
Chaos of thought and passion, all confused;
Still by himself abused or disabused;
Created half to rise, and half to fall;
Great Lord of all things, yet a prey to all;
Sole judge of truth, in endless error hurled;
The glory, jest, and riddle of the world!

In prose, too, the new desire for simplicity and clarity conquered, and Dryden, Addison, and Steele established its critical standards by their examples.

'The reign of Queen Anne', in the words of Horace Walpole, 'so illustrated by heroes, poets, and authors, was not equally fortunate in artists. Except Kneller scarce a painter of note'. Indeed, the period is filled with a host of forgotten portrait and landscape painters, until the genius of William HOGARTH (q.v. Vol. V), with his satirical pictures of social scenes, added a visual counterpart to the great satirical literature of the time. In music, the English tradition culminated in the operas and orchestral music of PURCELL at the end of the 17th century. When HANDEL (qq.v. Vol. V) came to England, his oratorios, operas, and orchestral pieces introduced the new German style. Then the Italian opera conquered the theatres of London.

Significantly enough in this age of elegance and dignified living, the most social art, that of architecture, flourished. Architecture was no longer a mere part of the builder's trade, but was

HOUGHTON HALL, NORFOLK
An example of Palladian architecture built by Colin Campbell between 1722 and 1727 for Sir Robert Walpole

considered an art worthy of the attention of the finest and noblest minds. It is significant that in 1715, under the guidance of the Earl of Burlington, a young nobleman who had spent several years in Italy studying architecture, there was published a volume of drawings by PALLADIO (q.v. Vol. V) of Roman and classical buildings. This Italian architect had studied the buildings of ancient Rome and modelled his own buildings upon them. Palladio's drawings and Burlington's practical building popularized the so-called 'Palladian' architecture in England. As in the literature of the time, the move was away from the elaborate and ornate style of BAROQUE ART (q.v.) to a simple and grand 'Roman' architecture. Augustan architecture lays great stress on classical perfection of proportion, based on rules and standards worked out from observations and measurements of Roman buildings and those by Palladio, on the carefully balanced distribution of windows and doors, and on the use of classical decoration such as pillars and pediments. Burlington House in Piccadilly and many great country houses such as Walpole's at Houghton and Viscount Cobham's at Stowe were built in this style.

The art of designing the great gardens and parks which surrounded these houses followed a curiously different development. Instead of the nobly severe symmetry of the formal gardens such as those at VERSAILLES (q.v.), there was a break away to a freer 'natural' garden. Geometrical flower-beds and walks gave way to sweeps of lawn broken by trees providing prospects and variety; rectangular canals and ponds are changed to winding rivulets and serpentine-edged lakes (*see* LANDSCAPE ART). It is in these fine houses and gardens that the conscious greatness of the age is to be seen. It is of them that Pope speaks in his *Epistle to Burlington*,

You show us, Rome was glorious, not profuse,
And pompous buildings once were things of Use.

And his poem, reviewing these achievements, concludes with words which consciously accept this as the Golden Age, the Augustan Age,

These Honours, Peace to happy Britain brings,
These are Imperial Works, and worthy Kings.

See also CLASSICAL ART; GEORGIAN ARCHITECTURE.

AUTOBIOGRAPHY, *see* BIOGRAPHY.

B

BABYLON, HANGING GARDENS OF, *see* WONDERS OF THE WORLD.

BABYLONIAN ART. It is not possible to draw a clear dividing line between the two ancient civilizations of Iraq, the BABYLONIAN and the ASSYRIAN (qq.v. Vol. I). Any difference is one of geography and detail. The Babylonians dominated ancient Iraq at two widely separated periods, the first (Hammurabi) Babylonian Dynasty lasting from about 1950 to 1650 B.C. and the second lasting for some 70 years after the Assyrian downfall in 612 B.C.

The early Babylonians were the direct inheritors of the SUMERIAN CIVILIZATION (q.v. Vol. I) in southern Iraq; therefore it is not surprising to find that the few stone statues, plaques, and reliefs found in that stoneless land during the first Babylonian Dynasty closely resemble SUMERIAN ART (q.v.). One distinct mark of the period was the use of the dark red-black stone, haematite (an iron ore), for making cylindrical seals, on which were engraved small scenes, mostly depicting the owner of the seal approaching his god in worship. The Babylonians made great advances in cast and hammered bronze figures, but otherwise the few large objects yet found do not show great originality.

The vividly coloured wall-paintings found in the ruins of a palace excavated by the French at Mari on the northern borders of Babylonia are so far a unique discovery. On the white plastered walls leading to the main palace apartments were painted scenes of the royal investiture and of sacrifices offered to the goddess Ishtar. They were drawn in heavy black lines and filled in with deep or opaque red, blue, and black. There is a free and frank spirit about much of this work found at Mari, which is un-like other Babylonian art. The people in the pictures really appear to be leading the animals to the slaughter or entering the royal presence with dignity; even the palm-trees up which the slaves are climbing are shown in their true proportion and in faithful detail. Some aspects of this painting are strikingly reminiscent of wall-paintings in Egypt and in KNOSSOS (q.v.) in Crete, though no relationship has been proved. The dress and deportment of many of the Mari figures is the same as on the Babylonian cylinder seals. As no paintings like these have been found elsewhere in Babylonia, we cannot know whether these are unique or whether they are characteristic of Babylonian painting as a whole.

The second Babylonian Empire (612 to 539 B.C.) became very rich and powerful under the great King Nebuchadnezzar II. Babylon was

British Museum

SUN GOD TABLET, *c.* 870 B.C.
The relief shows Nabu-pal-iddina, King of Babylon, coming to worship at the temple

rebuilt and the main gateway and sacred processional way decorated with glazed bricks on which animals were carved in relief or painted in bright colours (*see* Vol. I, p. 60). In the palaces the walls were painted with repetitive floral designs. But apart from the massive size of its solid brick structures, the late Babylonian architecture is not remarkable, its styles and even materials being borrowed from the Assyrians or from the still earlier Sumerians. With the conquest of Babylon by the Persians in 539 B.C. and later by the Greeks, the art of Babylonia, like its civilization, soon died out.

See also ASSYRIAN ART; SUMERIAN ART.
See also Vol. I: BABYLONIAN CIVILIZATION.

BALLAD. A traditional ballad is a FOLK-SONG (q.v.) which tells a story. The origins of such ballads are obscure, and their authors unknown. They were sung or recited, sometimes with the accompaniment of a dance, to small groups of people. The first ballads appeared in the 12th century, and gained such popularity that by the early 16th century ballads were being made and sung all over Europe. They were not written down, but lived in the memories and speech of people for many hundreds of years. It is probable but not certain that at first they were rendered by professional MINSTRELS (q.v. Vol. IX), and that later they were known and enjoyed by people of all social classes. But after the knowledge and habit of reading spread, the educated classes lost interest in ballads, and this heritage passed to the peasants. Already in the 16th century they were quite out of fashion in courtly circles; Sir Philip SIDNEY (q.v. Vol. V), for instance, said: 'Certainly I must confess mine own barbarousness, I never heard the old song of Percy and Douglas that I found not my heart moved more than with a trumpet.' But ballads retained their popularity in more lowly circles, as Addison witnessed when, in the *Spectator* in 1711, he described ballads as 'the darling songs of the common people'.

Today, even in England, there are a few people who remember the old ballads. But only in isolated and remote communities is ballad-singing and ballad-making a regular practice; such communities have been found in northern Russia, in the east Baltic states, and in the mountains of North Carolina (U.S.A.). Educated people know ballads only from the printed collections which have been made in many languages—particularly in Danish, Russian, Spanish, German, and English—by ballad-scholars who searched for them in old manuscripts and among the people who still know and say them. The most important collection of English ballads was made by Professor Child of Harvard University (published 1883–98). It contains every known version of the 305 ballads which he collected; and some of these ballads have ten, a few as many as twenty, versions. These different versions came about because the words of a ballad that is passed on orally from one person to another and never written down are sometimes misunderstood, or changed deliberately, or slurred and altered in the course of a few generations.

The stories ballads tell are historical, or quasi-historical, like the Scottish ballads that relate the feuds of the Border; adventurous, like the cycle of Robin Hood ballads; romantic, like the beautiful 'Helen of Kirkconnell'. This opens and closes with the lover's passionate longing for his dead love, Helen, and in the middle stanzas, in two flash-backs, tells how Helen died to succour him, and the revenge he took on her murderer. Other ballads have domestic, religious, or magical themes. Some, like 'Thomas the Rhymer', recount a visit to fairyland. In this ballad the Queen of Elfland takes Thomas on her milk-white steed—

> Oh they rode on, and farther on,
>   And they waded rivers abune the knee;
> And they saw neither sun nor moon,
>   But they heard the roaring of the sea.

Some ballads are native to England and Scotland, but some have probably come from Denmark or other lands, variants of these being found in many countries of Europe.

Ballads vary in length from a few lines to several hundreds. Their forms differ from country to country, and even within the same country. English ballads are written in stanzas (or verses), and one type of stanza has been used so often that we call it 'ballad-stanza'. Originally a couplet with two equal lines of 14 syllables or 7 feet, it broke down into a 4-line stanza (quatrain) whose 1st and 3rd lines have 4 feet, and whose 2nd and 4th have 3. Many ballads have refrains, some relevant to the story, but most mere nonsense jingles, like 'Down a down a down a down', or 'Fa la la la, fa la la la ra re'. These may be substitutes for musical accompaniments.

A common form is to tell the story in the 1st and 3rd lines of the stanza, and repeat a refrain to create atmosphere in the 2nd and 4th. The stanzas of 'Hynd Horn', for example, go like this:

> In good greenwood, there I was born,
> *With a hey lillelu and a how lo lan;*
> And all my forbears me beforn.
> *And the birk and the broom blows bonnie.*

and the tragic ballad 'Babylon' runs:

> There were three ladies live in a bower—
> *Eh, wow, bonnie!*
> And they went out to pull a flower
> *On the bonnie banks o' Fordie.*

Besides refrain, there is much repetition of phrases in the ballads, often for dramatic effect; and some descriptions and phrases recur in ballad after ballad in a formalized way, almost as a formula. For instance, if a lady must ride, a stanza like this often appears:

> 'Go saddle to me the black, the black,
> Go saddle to me the brown,
> Go saddle to me the swiftest steed
> That e'er rid to Wallington!'
>
> ('Fair Mary of Wallington')

And when the sons of 'The Wife of Usher's Well' become restless,

> Up then crew the red, red cock,
> And up and crew the gray;
> The eldest to the youngest said,
> ''Tis time we were away'.

Phrases such as,

> She hadna pu'd a rose, a rose,
> A rose but barely ane,
>
> ('Tam Lin')

or

> She hadna sail'd a league, a league,
> A league but barely twa,
>
> ('The Daemon Lover')

are very common; and 'milk-white steed', 'blude-red wine', or 'red, red rose' occur frequently.

The ballad tells a story, but it tells it in a special way. Just as in a drama, there is one action. The whole interest is focused on a situation and its outcome. If a series of events is revealed, it is only as these events relate to this central situation or its outcome. The story unfolds swiftly and dramatically, and is revealed

Country Life

PAGE FROM SCOTT'S MANUSCRIPT OF HIS BALLAD OF LOCHIN-VAR FROM 'MARMION', ILLUSTRATED BY DANIEL TERRY

In the possession of Sir Fergus Graham, Bt., M.P.

not only by narration, but by dialogue (sometimes, as in 'Edward, Edward' and 'Lord Randal', entirely by dialogue). Sudden transitions from one time to another, or from one person to another, focus the central situation from different angles, and forward the action dramatically. The most famous of all English ballads, 'The Ballad of Sir Patrick Spens', has many of these formal characteristics—it tells a story, focusing on Sir Patrick Spens and his fate; it tells it in narrative and dialogue dramatically, with no explicit comment from the author. It uses ballad-stanza, and apt repetitions.

> O lang, lang may the ladies sit,
> Wi' their fans into their hand,

and again

> And lang, lang may the maidens sit
> Wi' their gowd kames in their hair.

In the last quarter of the 18th century, European poets of the ROMANTIC MOVEMENT (q.v.), admiring the traditional ballad's simplicity of theme and form, emulated it. Of these literary ballads, especially successful are *Erlkönig* (The Erl-King) by Goethe (1749–1832);

'Proud Maisie' by Sir Walter Scott (1771–1832); and the ballads of Wordsworth and Coleridge published in the volume *Lyrical Ballads* (1798), outstanding among which is Coleridge's *Rime of the Ancient Mariner*. Since this resurgence, the most notable English ballads are Rudyard Kipling's (1865–1936) *Barrack-Room Ballads* (1892), and *The Ballad of Reading Gaol* (1898) by Oscar Wilde.

See also FOLK-SONG.

BALLET MUSIC. Music is essential in BALLET (q.v. Vol. IX) to provide a rhythmic background for the dancers, and to heighten the atmosphere of the story enacted through the medium of dancing. The music, written in accordance with the demands of the stage action, is usually in the form of short pieces of contrasting rhythms and moods, which follow each other without discernible break, and collectively form a 'suite'.

Apart from Lully (1632–87), who was employed at the court of LOUIS XIV (q.v. Vol. V) where all kinds of dancing were very popular, very few important composers wrote ballet music in its early days (apart from short ballet interludes in the course of an OPERA (q.v.)). In independent ballets the *maîtres de ballet* cared only about the dancing and liked the music to be as unobtrusive as possible. It was not till the 19th century that a reform began, with France in the lead. *Giselle* (1841) with music by Adolphe Adam, and *Coppelia* (1870) and *Sylvia* (1876) with music by Delibes, are the earliest ballets to survive, largely because of the quality of the music. Delibes was accused by his contemporaries of being too 'symphonic', which shows what very slender, barren kind of music had satisfied dancers previously.

The Russian, TCHAIKOVSKY (q.v. Vol. V), is generally considered to be the first important composer to write ballet music, which, though irresistible for dancing because of its enchanting tunes and lilting rhythms, can yet hold its own as music, when played independently in the concert hall. *Swan Lake* was not a success at its first performance in 1877, as it was too subtle for dancers accustomed only to banal music; but Tchaikovsky subsequently triumphed with *The Sleeping Princess* (1890) and *Nutcracker* (1892).

When DIAGHILEFF (q.v. Vol. V) became associated with the Russian ballet early in the 20th century, ballet music came into its own, for this cultured impresario had studied both music and art and realized that dance, décor, and music should all contribute equally to ballet if it was to become a really great art-form. Stravinsky was the first composer of renown to benefit fully from this enlightened attitude, and his *Petrouchka* (1911) and *Rite of Spring* (1913), though very difficult rhythmically for the dancers to master, raised the status of ballet music to its present position of honour. Ever since then, nearly all the greatest composers throughout the world have written ballet music. Ravel's *Daphnis and Chloe* (1909), Falla's *The Three-Cornered Hat* (1919), and Vaughan Williams's *Job* (1931) are but three of numerous distinguished examples.

In spite of the increasing tendency for composers to write new music for each important new production, a considerable number of ballets in the present-day repertory make use of existing music not originally intended for dancing. Sometimes an arranger is called in to orchestrate, adapt, and string together a number of small pieces, as was the case with CHOPIN's music in *Les Sylphides*, Scarlatti's in *The Good Humoured Ladies*, or LISZT's in *Apparitions*; sometimes a complete symphony, concerto, or tone-poem is appropriated as it stands, for instance, BRAHMS's Fourth Symphony for Massine's *Choreatium*, Tchaikovsky's Second Piano Concerto for Balanchine's *Ballet Imperial*, or DEBUSSY's *Prélude à l'après-midi d'un faune* for NIJINSKY's ballet of the same name (qq.v. Vol. V). Such ballets are successful if the arranger on the one hand treats the original music with respect, and if the choreographer on the other is musician enough to consider the music's design when devising his décor. Balanchine is outstandingly scrupulous in this latter respect.

See also DANCE MUSIC.
See also Vol. IX: BALLET.

BAPTISTERY, *see* FONT.

BAROQUE ART. The word 'baroque', originally a term of contempt, is now used seriously for the style of art which developed on the Continent in the 17th century. The word comes from the Portuguese for an odd-shaped pearl, and was applied by the French to the profuse decoration which is characteristic of the style.

The term is used both for the baroque art of the 17th century and also for the characteristics which are typical of the art of that period but

Alinari

THE TREVI FOUNTAIN, ROME, BUILT BY NICCOLO SALVI, 1762

The colossal pillars reach the whole height of the building, and the windows and central niche are framed by smaller ones. The fountain and building are designed as one grand composition in the Baroque manner.

which sometimes occur at other times. For instance, some late Roman art has baroque features, and in the height of the Renaissance Correggio painted an almost fully developed baroque decoration in Parma Cathedral.

The principles of the baroque style are quite unlike those of the CLASSICAL ART (q.v.) of the Italian Renaissance. Its chief characteristics are an exuberance and richness of form and decoration which disregard strict classical rules and give a sense of movement and excitement. The effect of a baroque building is of overwhelming magnificence and grandeur, in which the architecture, sculpture, and painting all merge into a single composition.

The importance of the whole at the expense of the details runs through all baroque art. In the paintings the figures are as closely knit together as the pieces of a jig-saw puzzle, each one taking its place as part of a big overall design which usually recedes in depth from the front of the picture and conveys a feeling of movement. A single figure isolated from a painting of this kind would look ridiculous. In a typical painting of the Renaissance, on the other hand, each figure is so designed that it is not only a part of the general composition, but it is also a complete entity in itself, the reason for this being that each figure is less closely connected with the one next to it, and the figures are usually placed side by side rather than leading into the distance (*see* Vol. I, p. 402).

Similar principles apply in architecture. In a Renaissance building each storey is considered as a separate entity, with its own pillars or pilasters; if the building is in three storeys there are three rows of pillars or pilasters, one above the other. In baroque architecture, on the other hand, a three-storeyed building has only one row of colossal pillars or pilasters which start on the ground floor, or first floor, and run right to the top of the building.

Baroque art was developed and used by the Roman Catholic Church in Italy and in Austria,

Alinari

CEILING PAINTED BY PIETRO DA CORTONA (1596–1669) IN THE BARBERINI PALACE, ROME

The subject is the triumph of Divine Providence aided by the Papacy in the time of Urban VIII. The painting gives the illusion of the ceiling opening to the sky with the figures flying to Heaven

Germany, and Flanders. The Reformation had weakened the power of the Church, and it was not until about 100 years after Luther had broken away that it was able to reorganize itself. Then it started a campaign, called the Counter-Reformation, to regain its position as the spiritual ruler of the whole of Europe. A religious society, the Jesuits, were particularly active. They realized that art could very effectively be made to have what would now be called 'propaganda value', and the churches were skilfully designed with this aim in view.

The leading artist of the period, Lorenzo BERNINI (q.v. Vol. V), was deeply affected by Jesuit teaching. His main art was sculpture, but he was also an architect and painter—indeed it is often difficult in a baroque church to draw a dividing line between the three arts. The first baroque work of art—Bernini's *baldachino*, or canopy, over the High Altar at ST. PETER'S CATHEDRAL, Rome (q.v.), which was made about 1630—is neither architecture nor sculpture but something between the two (*see* Vol. V, p. 43). A typical baroque church is in itself conceived like a work of sculpture: the walls curve in and out, and sculptured figures blend with the painted figures on the ceiling in such a way that one cannot always be certain which is which. The purpose of the artists is to stimulate religious feeling. The spectator is swept off his feet by the overwhelming emotional effect of the three arts so cunningly blended, and by the dramatic treatment of the subject. Whereas the figures in classical paintings of the High Renaissance are aloof and appear to disregard the spectator, baroque decorative schemes seem to sweep the spectator up in the movement of the sacred figures, which appear to fill the whole church. It was thought that a man's faith would be strengthened in this way.

One method of achieving this emotional effect was to make the sculpture and painting give the illusion of reality and life. In sculpture, effects were achieved which were technically beyond anything which had been done before. Bernini, for example, could make marble convey the textures of flesh, clouds, and draperies, and in his latest sculptures he even made the marble suggest the effect of light. The ceiling decorations appear to reveal vistas leading up into limitless space. These effects were achieved by using the kind of false perspective and trick painting which had been developed for paint-

ing theatrical scenery. Indeed, baroque art is essentially theatrical, particularly in its use of light for dramatic effect. Bernini went so far in one case as to install a special hidden light above one of his statues to make it look more effective, and windows were often placed so that they cast light on a statue while remaining invisible themselves.

Although baroque art was especially developed for religious purposes, powerful leaders of the Church, and later kings, saw that it was also suitable for palaces or for almost any building which required magnificence of general effect. In Rome baroque FOUNTAINS (q.v.) proved most effective, the restless quality of the style admirably suiting the effect of the moving water. Starting in Rome early in the 17th century, the style spread rapidly to the north and took root in Turin and then in VIENNA and PRAGUE (qq.v. Vol. III). In Flanders RUBENS (q.v. Vol. V) evolved independently a northern type of baroque painting, though the sculpture and architecture and above all the blending of the three were inferior. The style reached what is perhaps its culmination of magnificence in Bavaria in the first half of the 18th century, where the grandeur of the palaces, such as those of the Prince-Bishops, have never been surpassed (*see* GERMAN ART). The style also exercised great influence in other parts of Catholic Europe, though in France the prevailing taste was always too classical for baroque to establish a real hold. In Protestant countries, such as England, where the taste in art was more restrained, it never had more than an indirect and partial influence. The works of Sir John VANBRUGH (q.v. Vol. V), such as Blenheim Palace, have a theatrical quality akin to the baroque, and Thomas Archer, the architect of Birmingham Cathedral, alone among English architects, used curved surfaces effectively. But the fully baroque church as built in Italy, Austria, and Germany, in which the architecture, sculpture, and painted decoration are welded completely together and conceived as a whole, has no counterpart in England.

See also ITALIAN ART; ROCOCO ART.

BAYEUX TAPESTRY. This is one of the earliest and most important pieces of medieval embroidery in existence. It is not really a TAPESTRY (q.v. Vol. VII), since the design is embroidered on to the material and not woven

Victoria and Albert Museum

EDWARD THE CONFESSOR GIVING INSTRUCTIONS TO TWO
PERSONS, ONE OF THEM HAROLD
Detail from the Bayeux Tapestry

into it. It is made of coarse linen and worked in woollen thread, partly in stem stitch and partly in laid work, in blues, greens, yellows, and greys. The strip of linen is about 80 yards long by 19 inches wide. It is not definitely known when it was made or for whom, but it seems probable that Bishop Odo of Bayeux commissioned it and that it was worked about 1070 or 1080, probably in Kent. The subject is the events leading up to the Norman Conquest of England. The scenes start with Edward the Confessor addressing Harold, Duke of the English; they go on to show Harold visiting Normandy and taking an oath to William of Normandy; then the death of King Edward, the crowning of Harold, Duke William embarking and crossing the sea with his men and horses, and his landing at Pevensey; and then the Battle of Hastings with the death of Harold in the fighting (*see* Vol. X, p. 182).

The tapestry belongs to the town of Bayeux in Normandy, and was originally hung round the nave of the cathedral during festivals. A full-sized photographic replica can be seen at the Victoria and Albert Museum in London.

See also Vol. XI: EMBROIDERY.

BEGGAR'S OPERA, THE, by John Gay, *see* OPERA, HISTORY OF.

BEOWULF. This long EPIC poem (q.v.), written in the 8th century at the height of Anglo-Saxon culture, is by an unknown author. The first part tells how Hrothgar, the wise old king of the Danes, built a famous gold-roofed hall for himself and his warriors, but could not enjoy it because it was haunted at night by a fierce monster. The 'joyless' Grendel, 'grim and greedy', came each night from the dark fens to kill the warriors who slept in the hall. Beowulf, a young and mighty prince of the Geats from south Sweden, came to Hrothgar's rescue. He fought Grendel single-handed in the hall at night, and after a fearful battle tore off his arm. Grendel fled, fatally wounded. The next night, after the rejoicing, Grendel's mother came unexpectedly for revenge, and snatched away a warrior. Beowulf sought her out in her cave beneath a deep, gloomy lake and slew her also. He returned home with great honour and rich rewards.

The second part of the poem tells how Beowulf, having ruled his people wisely and bravely for 50 years, heard that a fire-breathing dragon was laying his country waste. The dragon was the guardian of a great and ancient treasure-hoard, which a thief had disturbed. Beowulf went out to attack the dragon and save his people, although he knew he would die in the attempt. In the fight he was deserted by all his men save his young relative Wiglaf. These two alone killed the dragon, though Beowulf afterwards died of his wounds.

This is a story of man's fight against the powers of darkness, evil, and death, and of the beauty of heroic courage and honour. Its setting is Anglo-Saxon court life, and the story gives us many glimpses of 'the joys of the hall', feasting and song, stately manners and speeches, ancient weapons, golden ornaments. Although there was never actually such a person as Beowulf, his story is fitted into real events which happened in the 6th century in Scandinavia. The author often turns aside to mention other heroic tales or events from history which illustrate his main story; or he pauses for a description, whether of beauty or mystery. He comments on the sadness and strangeness of life, and emphasizes man's duty to be brave, generous, and honourable. God will not desert the man with these virtues.

The style is elaborate and remote from ordinary life; ships are 'foamy-necked', the sun is 'God's bright sign', the sea is 'the whale's road'.

The poem has just over 3,000 lines, and the verse-pattern is composed of two heavy or stressed syllables and an irregular number of light syllables in each half-line. As with much Anglo-Saxon poetry, alliteration is very often used—that is, certain stressed syllables in each line start with the same sound, as, for example:

the cúrrents éddied,
The séa against the sánd; séamen cárried
Into the bélly of the shíp the bríght tréasure.

Anglo-Saxon, or Old English, although it is the ancestor of modern English, is so different from it that, unless we have studied it, we cannot read *Beowulf* except in translation. In the original the two and a half lines quoted above run like this:

stréamas wúndon,
Súnd wið sánde; sécgas bæron
On béarm nácan béorhte Frætwe.

See also ENGLISH LITERATURE; EPIC POETRY; VERSI-FICATION.
See also Vol. IV: ENGLISH LANGUAGE.

BIBLE, *see* TRANSLATIONS, Section 2. *See also* Vol. I: BIBLE.

BIOGRAPHY. Biography is the art of writing, in a literary form, the history of the life of an individual man or woman. Biography often has an historical interest, giving a picture of bygone ages through the lives of individuals. Its chief concern, however, is the growth and development of a man's character, and its bearing on the course of his whole life. The biographer must take into consideration all the facts of his subject's life, without suppressing or distorting any aspects of personality which may seem to him discreditable or inconsistent. An unwillingness to reveal any aspect of the subject's character or life for fear, perhaps, of giving offence, or a distortion of facts to suit some theory, makes an unconvincing biography. The biographer must also have the literary skill to be able to bring his subject to life in the imagination of the reader.

Autobiography, which is the portrayal of a person's life and character by the person himself, is closely allied to the writing of memoirs, LETTERS, and DIARIES (qq.v.), such as those of John Evelyn and Samuel Pepys. The author who writes about himself has naturally the fullest possible knowledge of all the facts, and can speak of them with genuine feeling; but he cannot write with real objectivity, and he lacks the advantage which even a slight distance in time usually gives the biographer in seeing his subject in true perspective. Autobiography, therefore, rarely conveys a man's whole history so satisfactorily as does biography, though it may give the reader a vivid sense of reality. Cowley, a 17th-century writer, expresses the autobiographer's dilemma when he says: 'It is a hard and nice subject for a man to write of himself; it grates his own heart to say anything of disparagement, and the reader's ears to hear anything of praise from him.'

The lives of the great have been recorded since ancient times, but in these old histories of the deeds of heroes and saints it is often impossible to separate truth from legend. The most famous biographical writer of classical times is the Greek PLUTARCH (q.v. Vol. V), of the 1st century A.D., whose *Parallel Lives* of Greeks and Romans provided the plots of some of Shakespeare's plays. There were forty-six of these *Lives*, all of them being essentially portraits of characters, the facts of their lives being recorded only where they illustrate character. A 16th-century artist, Vasari, a contemporary of Michaelangelo in Renaissance Italy, wrote a series of *Lives of the Most Excellent Architects, Painters and Sculptors*. Though he mingled fact and legend, much of our knowledge of Italian painters is based on his work.

The earliest English biographer of literary importance is George Cavendish (1500–61), who in his *Life of Wolsey* portrays Cardinal Wolsey's worldly magnificence, the grandeur of his position at Court, and the depths of his subsequent disgrace. Although the writer has a moral theme in mind (the ever-changing fortunes of men) he does not distort facts to make them fit his theory (*see* WOLSEY, Vol. V). Unlike previous chroniclers, Cavendish and his contemporary William Roper, who wrote a life of Sir Thomas MORE (q.v. Vol. V), centred their attention on individual character rather than on external action.

During the 17th century historical writing, the writing of memoirs, letters, and diaries, and accounts of travels were all popular; but biography was side-tracked into brief character-sketches or eulogistic memoirs. The most famous collector of biographical information in this century was John Aubrey (1626–97) who, if he had only been more industrious and methodical, would have made a supremely good biographer: he was insatiably curious about the oddities of individual character, had a feeling for truth as well as a love of gossip, and could catch in a phrase the appearance as well as the nature of his victims. Of Sir John Birkenhead, for example, he writes: 'He was exceedingly confident, witty, not very grateful to his benefactors, would lye damnably. He was of midaling stature, great goggli eies. Not of a sweet aspect . . .'. Aubrey himself, however, was described by a friend as 'a shiftless person, roving and magotie-headed', and his *Lives* are a collection of brilliantly entertaining notes, often tantalising in their incompleteness, rather than full-length biographies.

Dr. Samuel JOHNSON (q.v. Vol. V) dominated 18th-century biography both as a biographer himself in his *Lives of the Poets* and as the subject for Boswell's famous biographical study. Dr. Johnson was the first to proclaim that biography was a distinct branch of literature. The interest of a biography lies, he says, in 'the parallel circumstances and kindred images to which we readily conform our minds'— that is to say, the truth which biography reveals is close enough to the reader's own experience for him to be able to absorb it readily and profit by it. Truth, Dr. Johnson emphasizes, is essential to the art of biography: 'There are many', he writes, 'who think it an act of piety to hide the faults or failings of their friends, even when they can no longer suffer by their detection . . . If we owe regard to the memory of the dead, there is yet more respect to be laid to knowledge, to virtue, and to truth.'

Boswell's *Life of Johnson*, as Boswell himself remarked, is 'the most entertaining book that ever appeared'. The interesting nature of Dr. Johnson's character and the opportunities which Boswell had for close study of it would not have made the book the masterpiece it is without Boswell's own alertness, powers of observation, and taste for vivid detail. Boswell arranged with great skill the 'prodigious multiplicity of materials' after Johnson's death, shaping the confusion of details into a closely constructed narrative which does not flag in interest throughout its whole length. 'It appears to me', he wrote, 'that mine is the best plan of biography that can be conceived; for my readers will as near as may be accompany Johnson in his progress, and, as it were, see each scene as it happened.' Boswell, in fact, invented and perfected a method of putting a living person on paper.

The 19th century was fruitful in biography, as in other kinds of literature. Lockhart in his *Life of Sir Walter Scott* (1838) writes, 'It was my wish to let the character develop itself', and in his long book, with its mass of details and extensive use of Scott's own letters and diaries, the biographer refrains from any direct comment but allows the material to build up the character. Lockhart's biography was hotly attacked, for by the 1840's the early Victorians were already valuing respectability and discretion higher than uncensored truth. In consequence, the many biographies of this period do not now seem to us very interesting. They created, however, so wide a demand for biography that in 1882 the *Dictionary of National Biography* was started under Sir Leslie Stephen. The great *Life of Carlyle* by Froude, published in nine volumes between 1881 and 1884, is a completely convincing full-length portrait of every side of a curious and not altogether pleasant character. CARLYLE (q.v. Vol. V), revered as a thinker and historian, had personal characteristics such as conceit and egoism which a less honest biographer than Froude might have suppressed. Froude suppressed nothing, and consequently like Lockhart's book, the biography met with a great deal of disapproval.

Two writers who have helped to form the modern outlook on biography are Edmund Gosse and Lytton Strachey. Gosse's *Father and Son* is autobiographical, the interest being focussed upon the character of the writer's father and the clash between his narrow religious fanaticism and the temperament of his son. This personal tragedy is developed with great literary skill and presented truthfully and convincingly. Lytton Strachey's *Eminent Victorians* (1918) and *Queen Victoria* (1921) treat their famous subjects with sceptical detachment, which in the hands of inferior imitators has degenerated into cynical 'debunking'. Strachey solved the problem of selection among the overwhelming mass of material by developing certain aspects of his subject, and leaving others untouched.

A biographer who decides to present all the facts about his subject's life in as scientific and objective a way as possible has to decide what of all the material he has collected is important enough to include, and how far he needs to describe and explain the historical background. The American tendency to include a great deal may leave the central character obscured. Some biographers attempt to analyse and describe the psychological processes underlying the facts of a life; others leave the reader to draw his own conclusions from these facts. Some biographers decide that they cannot give a convincing portrait of their subject without using their literary skill in setting scenes and reconstructing conversations for which there is little or no historical warrant. James Barke, for example, has written a five-volume novel round the life of Robert Burns (q.v. Vol. V), which is not, he claims, strictly a biography, but yet is created with scrupulous historical accuracy and may well give a more vivid and readable account of the poet's life than a pure biography could do. Autobiography, too, lends itself to this subjective literary method, a notable example being the three-volume account of his early life by the Russian writer Maxim Gorki. In France there is a tradition of popular biographies that are both scholarly and readable, but in England the claims of fact and fiction are only reconciled with difficulty.

See also Diaries; Letters; Histories.

BLANK VERSE, see Versification, Section 3.

BLUES, see Jazz.

BOOKBINDING, see Vol. VII: Bookbinding.

BRASSES. Memorial brasses —flat metal plates fixed to the floor or, in later times to the

Surrey Archaeological Soc.

BRASS OF SIR JOHN DAUBERNON, 1277, STOKE D'ABERNON, SURREY

wall of a church—were used in Britain and on the Continent from the 12th century onwards as an alternative to carved stone Tombs (q.v.) and effigies. The earliest surviving brass in England dates from 1277 and commemorates Sir John Daubernon at Stoke d'Abernon, Surrey.

Brasses were made of 'latten', a copper-zinc alloy, not true brass. The design was engraved on the latten, and the lines were sometimes filled with coloured enamel. The entire brass was then let into a shallow depression or 'matrix' cut in a stone laid in the floor of the church: often these matrices can be seen in churches, though the brasses have disappeared. Many brasses were destroyed at the Reformation, and more by the Puritans in the 17th century. Some were stolen and the brasses used again, either by altering the engraving or reversing the sheet and making a new engraving on the back. These are called 'palimpsests' (from a Greek word applied to twice-used parchments). Numerous brasses have been lost by neglect, or removed when the churches were restored.

Brasses were made in imitation of the stone effigies which were commonly placed on top of tombs. Not only was the pose of the figures similar— knights with crossed legs or handling their swords, ladies with their hands in prayer or holding the string of their cloaks—but they also copied the canopies over their heads and the animals which supported their feet. Round the figures there was often an inscription giving the name of the person and the date of death.

During the Middle Ages the brasses, usually life-size or half life-size, were laid flat on the floor of the church. In the 16th century wall memorials were more often used, and

National Buildings Record

BRASS OF GEORGE COLES, DIED 1640, AND HIS WIVES AND
CHILDREN IN ST. SEPULCHRE'S CHURCH, NORTHAMPTON

small brasses were engraved with portraits of husband and wife, often kneeling facing each other, with their diminutive family also on their knees, the sons behind the father, the daughters behind their mother. From about this time the faces were often portraits; earlier the faces were generally of a standard pattern.

Records can be made of brasses by taking rubbings of them. This is done by covering them with white paper and rubbing over the paper with heel-ball (a hard, black wax used by cobblers). The result is a tracing of the brass as a black or dark grey pattern, with the black lines of the brass showing white. The dark parts may be painted over afterwards with Indian ink to which ox-gall has been added, to make it settle on the waxy surface.

See also TOMBS.

BRITISH ART. The early history of the British Isles is marked by a series of invasions from the mainland of Europe. In many cases the invaders settled down and mixed with the natives, and from this mixture evolved the British peoples —something distinct from the various races

from which they have come. In art a similar process took place, though it continued to a later date. British art has constantly been changed and enriched by contact with European art, but it has almost always assimilated these foreign influences and sometimes in turn has influenced the art of the Continent.

The earliest art in Britain—stone monuments such as STONEHENGE or AVEBURY (qq.v. Vol. I), or figures cut in chalk hills, such as the Giant at Cerne Abbas in Dorset—dates from prehistoric times, about which we still know little. We know more about the Celts, a central European people, tribes of whom settled in Britain in the last centuries B.C. (*see* CELTIC CIVILIZATION, Vol. I). They have left works of art in metal such as bronze mirrors and weapons chased with fine flowing patterns, and in some cases decorated with brightly coloured enamel (*see* PREHISTORIC ART, Section 4).

The Romans brought an art to Britain which was quite unlike the native art. During the four centuries of their stay they, and British craftsmen under their direction, built stone temples, market places, and villas; they carved figures of gods for shrines and decorated their floors with MOSAICS (q.v.), making skilful decorative use of the human figure—a thing which Celtic art had avoided. After the Roman occupation the country was the victim of attacks by marauding Angles and Saxons, and conditions were too unstable for the arts to flourish. After the new invaders had settled, however, and before the Danish invasions of the 9th century an English school of art grew up, particularly in Northumbria, which for a time was the most important centre of culture in northern Europe. The Northumbrian monks were in touch with the Christian church at Byzantium, and borrowed ideas from them. For example, they took the Byzantine patterns of leaves and birds and mixed them successfully with the Celtic flowing patterns. They produced a series of magnificent manuscripts, the most famous being the Lindisfarne Gospels, and they carved a number of tall stone crosses (*see* CROSSES, STONE, and Plate 6). In Ireland, to which Christianity had been brought from Celtic Britain, the Celtic tradition long flourished, and richly decorated manuscripts and metal objects were produced. The monks who carried Christianity from Northumbria and Ireland to other parts of northern Europe took with them a knowledge of their arts.

THE CHICHESTER ROUNDEL, *c.* 1260
Wall-painting in the Bishop's Palace, Chichester

LEFT: SCULPTURED ANGEL, *c.* 1225, IN THE SOUTH TRANSEPT,
WESTMINSTER ABBEY
The figure is designed to fit the shape of the spandrel above
the arch

THE SYON COPE, LATE 13TH CENTURY
Scenes from the life of Christ and the Virgin, the Apostles, angels, and heraldic devices are very finely embroidered on
linen with gilt and silver thread and coloured silks

In the 9th century, during the Danish invasions, little art was produced, except for weapons and personal ornaments for warrior chiefs. Finally ALFRED made peace with the Danes, and encouraged art and learning. He brought books from Europe where there had been a revival of learning under CHARLEMAGNE (qq.v. Vol. V), and from these the Saxon artists drew new inspiration. In their manuscript paintings and their stone and ivory carving they depict human figures with great feeling and enrich their work with magnificent patterns (*see* MEDIEVAL ART, EARLY).

For some time after the Norman Conquest nothing was produced to equal the delicate grace of the Anglo-Saxon manuscripts; but the Normans made a great contribution to architecture by introducing the ROMANESQUE ART (q.v.) of building, which in England is called 'Norman'. Cathedrals and abbeys built at this time, such as Durham, Norwich, and Peterborough, were among the largest and most splendid in Europe. Decoration, often in the form of zig-zag ornament cut in the arches, was crude, but sturdy and very effective in relation to the architecture. Paintings in rich colours added to the grand effect of the heavy round piers and decorated arches.

Though the Normans began to use the pointed arch in the vault at Durham the fully developed GOTHIC ART (q.v.) was introduced by the French architect, William of Sens, who built the choir of Canterbury Cathedral in 1174. Gothic buildings in England were not so accomplished as those in France, but they were also less exaggerated. Instead of concentrating, as the French did, on overwhelming height, the English cathedrals expand in length. There were sometimes double transepts, and beyond the choir, instead of chapels radiating from an apse as in France, a square-ended Lady Chapel was built. The various styles of English Gothic in the 13th, 14th, and 15th centuries are described under the heading CHURCH ARCHITECTURE, ENGLISH. Most of the cathedrals were built in the 12th and 13th centuries, but they were continually added to in the following centuries so that, with few exceptions, they are composed of styles of all periods. As the wool trade increased the wealth of the country in the 14th and 15th centuries many parish churches, especially in the wool districts, were completely rebuilt.

The churches were decorated with figure sculpture. This was not concentrated in the portals, as in the French cathedrals, but spread over the West Front, as in Wells and Exeter, or enriched the triangular space between arches, as in Westminster Abbey or the Angel Choir at Lincoln. Carved foliage decorated the capitals of columns and the bosses of vaults; and wooden choir stalls and roofs were richly carved. Much of this medieval sculpture was destroyed both at the Reformation and again by Cromwell's soldiers in the Civil War, the chief remaining examples being the effigies on TOMBS (q.v.). The paintings and STAINED GLASS (q.v.) which enriched the churches have also been largely destroyed, and little is left of the glowing colour which used to decorate medieval churches. The SHRINES (q.v.) of saints such as those of Edward the Confessor at Westminster and Thomas à Becket at Canterbury were once magnificently decorated with gold and precious stones, and the embroidered vestments of the priests added more colour. English embroidery, called *opus Anglicanum*, was famous throughout Europe.

The most important medieval domestic architecture that survives is fortified, notably the magnificent series of Edwardian castles in Wales, such as Caernarvon and Harlech (*see* Vol. V, p. 193) and the beautiful manor houses with their magnificent halls (*see* HOUSES, Vol. XI).

The quality of English medieval painting can best be seen in the ILLUMINATED MANUSCRIPTS (q.v.). In the 12th century large, brilliantly decorated books were made, but later books became smaller and the illuminations more graceful and delicate. In the 14th century a school of illumination in East Anglia produced Bibles and Psalters with richly decorated borders and charming drawings of contemporary life (*see* p. 202).

The Renaissance in British art starts in the 16th century with a fresh wave of continental influence—mainly Flemish and German. The brilliant portraiture of the German Hans HOLBEIN the Younger (q.v. Vol. V) has illumined for us the Court of Henry VIII. After his day a fine tradition of MINIATURE painting (q.v.), a typically English form of art, sprang up in Elizabethan England. Though buildings were decorated with classical ornaments, the nature of the Renaissance was not understood until the 17th century when the architect Inigo JONES (q.v. Vol. V) visited Italy. His buildings, which showed a perfect understanding of the more

SIR JEREMIAH SMITH, ADMIRAL OF THE BLUE
PAINTING BY SIR PETER LELY (1618–80)

GEORGINA, COUNTESS BATHURST
PAINTING BY SIR THOMAS LAWRENCE (1769–1830)

THE DUCHESS OF DEVONSHIRE AND HER DAUGHTER
PAINTING BY SIR JOSHUA REYNOLDS 1784

PLATE 4   BRITISH ART

TABLEY HOUSE
PAINTING BY RICHARD
WILSON (1714–82)

BELOW:

LEFT: THE VALE OF
DEDHAM. PAINTING BY JOHN
CONSTABLE (1776–1837)

RIGHT: THE OLD BEDFORD
MUSIC HALL. PAINTING BY
W. R. SICKERT (1860–1942)

restrained type of classical architecture, exercised a lasting effect on English architecture. Sir Christopher WREN (q.v. Vol. V), the architect of St. PAUL's (q.v.) and numerous City churches, evolved a particularly personal and English form of the classical style. His splendid designs were ably carried out by the English master-craftsmen at his disposal, notably the wood-carver, Grinling GIBBONS (q.v. Vol. V). The BAROQUE ART (q.v.) which Wren introduced with restraint was carried to much greater extremes by his followers VANBRUGH (q.v. Vol. V) and Hawksmoor—extremes so little suited to English taste that a return to a stricter style was started in the second quarter of the 18th century by Lord Burlington (*see* AUGUSTAN AGE). At this period English architecture and sculpture became more and more classical, culminating in the Greek revival in the early 19th century (*see* CLASSICAL ART). The revived Greek style in architecture was followed by the GOTHIC REVIVAL (q.v.), which still survives in many modern church designs.

The chief interest in painting of the Protestant English in the 16th and 17th centuries was in portraits, and most of the painters were Flemish or Dutch who modified their styles to suit their patrons, thus producing a typically English school. The Fleming VAN DYCK (q.v. Vol. V) reflects the sumptuous style of the Court of Charles I, and after the Restoration the Dutch artist Lely painted portraits of admirals which depict the character of the men who were responsible for building up British sea-power, and of the beautiful women who made the Court of Charles II notorious.

In the 18th century English painters at last came into their own. The demand for their work came chiefly from wealthy private patrons. These, having built themselves splendid houses, wished to decorate them in fitting style, chiefly with portraits of themselves and of their families. The houses were normally very large, and in consequence many of the portraits are 7 or 8 feet high, and show the sitter at full length, often with a view of his property in the background. REYNOLDS and GAINSBOROUGH (qq.v. Vol. V) were but the most gifted of many native British portraitists whose work reflects the polish and elegance of upper-class life in the British Isles in the second half of the 18th century. Other painters specialized in small portrait groups (*see* CONVERSATION PIECE) while one great artist, William HOGARTH (q.v. Vol. V), set himself to reform the morals of society by painting and engraving scenes showing the ill effects of common vices (see p. 405).

The British tradition of fine craftsmanship, which has contributed so much to British art at every stage of its long history, reached perhaps its highest level in the minor arts of the 18th century. Furniture such as Chippendale's, porcelain such as that made by WEDGWOOD (q.v. Vol. V) or at Chelsea, Worcester, or Derby, (*see* PORCELAIN, Vol. VII), and magnificent wrought ironwork represented a combination of elegance and usefulness which was in keeping with the spirit of the time.

By the end of the 18th century a school of LANDSCAPE PAINTING (q.v.) was firmly established—notably by Wilson and Gainsborough in oils, and Alexander and J. R. Cozens in water-colours. This reached its culmination in the early 19th century in the works of TURNER, CONSTABLE (qq.v. Vol. V), Crome, Cotman, Girtin, and others. Wilson, working in Italy, followed the style of CLAUDE (q.v. Vol. V), but his paintings are often portraits of actual places rather than the idealized landscapes of Claude. This attitude to landscape painting was a particularly English contribution, and the work of Constable, Turner, and the water-colour painters greatly influenced the French painters of the 19th century (*see* WATER-COLOURS).

British art in the hundred years from the mid-19th century to the present day has followed a varied course. The PRE-RAPHAELITES (q.v.) tried to recapture the spirit of early Italian art, and William MORRIS (q.v. Vol. V) attempted to revive the traditional glories of British craftsmanship. The New English Art Club was founded in 1886 as a progressive rival of the Royal Academy by painters who had studied IMPRESSIONIST PAINTING (q.v.). British art came increasingly under the influence of various movements in Europe, the Parisian school of painters, the German and French architects, and Scandinavian decorators (*see* MODERN ART).

BRONZE SCULPTURE. Bronze is an alloy mainly consisting of copper, to which a small percentage of hardening metal is added. The usual mixture consists of nine parts of copper and one part of tin, but varying proportions are used according to the hardness required. Zinc, lead, or brass—itself an alloy of copper and zinc—have at times been used instead of tin.

The most usual method of working bronze for sculpture is by casting from a model made in clay or wax, though, especially in early times, it was also hammered. Objects can be cast solid or hollow, the latter being most usual for all but the smallest figures. There are three stages: (1) a full-size model of clay or wax is made; (2) a mould accurately reproducing every detail of the model is made; (3) the model is cast in bronze in the mould (hollow cast), or the mould is cast without the model (solid cast).

1. Clay has to be modelled while wet; this and its pliable character make it necessary for all but very small models to have some internal support, or 'armature'. This consists of one or more iron braces supporting an arrangement of stiff but flexible wires, which are made to correspond with the pose of the torso, head, and limbs of the model. The clay is then built up around the armature. The model may be completed in clay, or the incomplete model may be covered with a layer of wax the thickness desired for the metal (usually not more than $\frac{3}{8}$ in.) and the final modelling done in the wax.

2. A mould is then made round the model. If the model was completed in clay, a plaster of

Victoria and Albert Museum
THE GLOUCESTER CANDLESTICK
This is about 2 ft. high, cast in bronze by the *cire perdue* method

paris cast is made from the mould and another cast made from this consisting of a layer of wax with a fire-resisting core. For larger works the mould is made in several sections (piece mould) which are held in position by another, outer, envelope. To make sure that the molten metal can reach every corner of the mould, runners or 'gates' made of wax rods run through the mould to the base and at all downward-pointing projections on the model. Gases formed by the molten metal might cause bubbles which would make hollows on the surface of the cast, so wax rods or pieces of string, called 'vents', are run through the mould at the head and all upward-pointing projections of the figure to allow the gases to escape.

3. All the wax is melted out, and the molten bronze is poured in to replace it—a method known as the 'lost wax' (*cire perdue*) process. Mould and core are then removed. Vents and gates, which were melted or burnt away, form bronze rods on the figure, and the joints of the piece mould leave the surface uneven in places. The surface is, therefore, worked over to produce the desired amount of smoothness and sharpness of detail. This final work in particular reveals the hand of the master.

Dean and Chapter, Westminster Abbey
GILT BRONZE EFFIGY OF QUEEN ELEANOR IN WESTMINSTER ABBEY
This was the first full-size medieval bronze figure, made about 1290 by William Torel

Anderson

PANEL FROM THE BRONZE DOOR OF THE BAPTISTERY, FLORENCE, BY
LORENZO GHIBERTI

The subject is the story of Joseph with, in the foreground, the vessels being
found in Benjamin's sack

RIGHT: MERCURY. BRONZE FIGURE BY GIOVANNI DA BOLOGNA

Alinari

A new bronze sculpture is bright, but the metal is soon darkened by corrosion which forms an incrustation of brown, green, or red shades, called the 'patina'. The patina can be produced artificially with acid and lacquer. Sculpture has frequently been given a patina in this way since the Renaissance, and occasionally before that time.

From the time of the Bronze Age, when PRE-HISTORIC TOOLS AND WEAPONS (q.v. Vol. I) were first made of metal, bronze was also used for sculpture. The Bronze Age occurred at different times in different parts of the world—in Egypt before 3000 B.C.; in Mesopotamia by 2000 B.C.; in China early in the second millennium B.C.; thereafter its use spread through Asia Minor to Europe and reached Scandinavia and the West by about 1500 B.C. The early reliefs and statues in EGYPTIAN and SUMERIAN ART (qq.v.) were made by carving a core of wood and bitumen roughly into shape, and hammering a sheet of bronze over it to fit the core. The finer details were presumably worked in the metal only. Some of the heads were cast, and so were figures of smaller animals, deities, demons, and others found in Mesopotamia.

The Greeks evolved a style particularly their own. From the 6th century B.C., all great artists created much of their best works in bronze (*see* GREEK ART). We know most of it only from marble copies and from literary references, for most of the early work was melted down because of the high value of the metal. There remain, however, enough magnificent pieces to show that by the 5th century B.C. the Greeks had mastered the technique. Sculpture in stone or wood is made by cutting away the material, and the work is limited by the size of the block. There is no such limitation with bronze, and the design of the sculpture can therefore be far freer. Limbs and drapery can be made to move with ease. The strength of the material allows a great deal of undercutting, and the finish of the casting will reproduce the finest details.

The best and most important Roman bronze sculpture belongs to the later days of the Roman Empire when portrait sculpture was produced with great freedom of design and accuracy of detail (*see* ROMAN ART). The tensile strength of bronze was taxed to the limit in vast compositions such as the equestrian statue of Marcus Aurelius at Rome (*see* p. 381).

In the early Middle Ages there was little large-scale bronze sculpture in the round, but large works were made in relief. A notable example are the bronze doors made for Bishop

Tate Gallery

JOHN THE BAPTIST BY AUGUSTE RODIN

Bernward of Hildesheim (Germany) in 1015, which has reliefs of the Creation and Fall of Man and of the Passion of Christ in sixteen panels. A smaller work of great intricacy is the Gloucester Candlestick (about 1110) which has a design of intertwining figures, monsters, and animals. Bronze was used for effigies on TOMBS (q.v.); the full-scale figures in Westminster Abbey of Eleanor of Castile, Edward I's queen, and of Henry III, both made in the late 13th century by a London goldsmith, William Torel, show that the technique of casting had been completely mastered.

In Italy many large churches preserve their medieval bronze doors from the early 12th century onwards. The design of these doors, with reliefs arranged in panels, continued into the 15th century, when the new spirit of the Renaissance brought to ITALIAN ART (q.v.) fresh forms and ideas. Lorenzo Ghiberti (1378–1455) made two pairs of doors for the Baptistery at Florence in which he shows an understanding of the new science of perspective in the landscape backgrounds to the figures, which are modelled almost in the round. DONATELLO (q.v. Vol. V)

used perspective to give astonishing effects of space in very low relief, and he also revived the tradition of the late Roman equestrian statue to celebrate the Italian soldier-adventurer of the day (*see* Vol. I, p. 400).

In the centuries following the Renaissance the technical possibilities of bronze casting were carried to their limit. Giovanni da Bologna (1524–1608), for example, modelled a statue of Mercury in which he attempted the impossible, trying to overcome the weight of matter by making the sensation of flying the main theme of his work. Bronze sculpture was used throughout Europe for TOMBS and MONUMENTS, ornamental figures, and FOUNTAINS (qq.v.), especially in Germany and France. Gilt bronze (ormolu) was used particularly in the 17th and 18th centuries for furniture mounts (see p. 99).

By the early 19th century, the industrial process of sand CASTING (q.v. Vol. VIII) was successfully adapted to the casting of models in bronze. The method is mechanically so precise that no working-over is necessary after casting. In consequence, the technique was used for producing life-size monumental statues which, lacking artistic quality, were altogether lifeless. Later, Rodin (1840–1917) and Epstein made delicate bronze heads, exploiting the capacity of the technique for reproducing the smallest detail. Rodin was particularly successful in making the lights and shades play on the surface.

See also SCULPTURE; STONE CARVING; WOOD CARVING.

BYZANTINE ART. The people of the BYZANTINE EMPIRE (q.v. Vol. I) belonged to various races and cultures. They were Roman in outlook, mainly Greek in blood and temperament, but in many ways much influenced by the peoples of Syria and Mesopotamia. They were, however, closely united by their faith, for their absorption in Christianity formed the basis of their life. By the 4th century A.D. their passionately religious outlook had produced a Christian art that was completely different from the Roman art, which it soon superseded. This new style formed very quickly, and it established itself so firmly that it flourished with only minor changes for 1,000 years, and deeply affected the art of most of the Christian world. It took so strong a hold in the countries of the ORTHODOX EASTERN CHURCH (q.v. Vol. I)—Russia, Greece, and the Balkans—that even today much of their

Photo Sabah

CHURCH OF THE VIRGIN PAMMAKARISTOS, CONSTANTINOPLE, 1315
A cruciform Church of the late Byzantine period

religious art continues to conform to the Byzantine manner.

Under the Emperors CONSTANTINE (q.v. Vol. V) and Theodosius the Great (379–95) the new trends evolved gradually; but under JUSTINIAN (q.v. Vol. V) they crystallized into a finished style, producing so spectacular a flow of highly accomplished works that this reign is now known as the First Golden Age. The 7th century saw little change, but early in the 8th century a dynasty came into power which forbade the representation of the Divine form and even that of saints in religious art. This ban was imposed for more than a century. When it was lifted in 843 a marvellous period of productivity followed, a period now called the Second Golden Age. At this time Byzantium was at the height of its wealth and power; and as its love of luxury was boundless, the finest materials were used for the production of beautiful objects. Much of the best Byzantine work that survives to our day belongs to this age. This prosperity was shattered in 1204 when Constantinople was conquered by the armies of the Fourth Crusade

(*see* CRUSADES, Vol. I). The Byzantine Emperors who returned to power in 1261, thus ruled over an ever-diminishing territory until they were finally overcome by the Turks in 1453. During this last phase rare and expensive materials were beyond the reach even of the Imperial family; yet the intrinsic merit of late Byzantine work is so great that the absence of precious adornments passes unnoticed. A pure beauty of form and craftsmanship was achieved, notably in such inexpensive material as paint, and it was at this period that most of the finest Byzantine paintings were produced.

The Byzantines excelled in every field of art. In architecture they evolved a new style for churches from two types of Roman building: the three-aisled, flat-roofed basilica and the domed and vaulted buildings such as the circular Pantheon and the great imperial baths (*see* ROMAN ART). The Byzantines produced a cruciform plan, and then placed a DOME (q.v.) above the central crossing. They completed the transformation by rounding the east end to form either a single apse or, more often, three apses,

Victoria and Albert Museum

THE BERESFORD HOPE ENAMEL, 6TH–7TH CENTURY

This enamel Cross probably held a relic

Bibl. Nat., Paris

DAVID COMPOSING THE PSALMS

Illumination from the Paris Psalter, 9th century

Victoria and Albert Museum

Schlossmuseum, Berlin

SILK TEXTILE WITH WOVEN PATTERN OF CONFRONTED
ANIMALS, *c.* 1000

From the reliquary of Charlemagne in Aachen Cathedral

LEFT: ST. JOHN THE BAPTIST SURROUNDED BY FOUR APOSTLES

Ivory relief, perhaps from a book cover. 11th or 12th century

The result was admirably suited to the needs of Christian worship. Innumerable churches throughout the empire, many of them of great loveliness, were built in this style. Most are comparatively small, but the finest of them all—the great cathedral of St. SOPHIA (q.v.), erected by Justinian in Constantinople in the 6th century—is vast.

In addition to their churches, the Byzantines built many spectacular monasteries, some of which still exist. Their palaces were the most sumptuous of their day. Their baths, libraries, hospitals, and guest-houses were of great distinction. In the early days they carried on the splendid Roman traditions of building; but apart from their churches, their most important later constructions were immense subterranean cisterns and defence works designed to withstand fierce sieges. The cisterns were vaulted and domed, the roofs supported by great columns surmounted by splendid capitals. During a siege Constantinople depended upon them for its water supply, and many are still in use today. The walls of Constantinople (*see* ISTANBUL, Vol. III), though they are now crumbling, still appear formidable in places, their round and square towers breaking the skyline in a seemingly endless succession, and culminating in the final grandeur of the Seven Towers and the Golden Gate. Through this gate of gleaming white marble the Emperors used to make their official entries into the capital.

The Byzantines lavished rich decoration on their buildings. The interiors of the churches were particularly sumptuous: the lower parts of the walls were panelled with rare marbles, and the upper parts were covered with MOSAICS (q.v.) and wall paintings, unfolding the story of the Scriptures in a marvellous succession of scenes. The general effect is most impressive and exciting.

Byzantine religious painting was governed by clearly defined rules, each scene being allotted its own particular place in the decorative scheme. The actual way in which each personage was represented—the pose and gesture, and even the colour of the vestments and robes—was also exactly prescribed. The artists, who were generally monks working for the glory of God, not for individual fame, were expected to remain anonymous. Because innovation was forbidden, they concentrated all their genius upon the delicacy and firmness of their lines, upon the

Photo Lykides

A PROPHET
Detail of an 11th-century mosaic in the Church of St. Sophia, Salonika

emotional and symbolic as well as the decorative use of colour, and upon the intensity of feeling expressed in the works. The artists were allowed some latitude in the painting of the backgrounds, but even here the deviations were very slight.

A great many religious paintings survive, both upon the interior walls of the churches and also on panels called ICONS (q.v.), which were used throughout the Orthodox Eastern world for devotional purposes. The style of these was much the same as in the wall paintings—indeed, both were often the work of one artist, and as in both the subjects were controlled by the same rules, the icon painter was as little concerned as the wall painter with problems of perspective. The icons form an extremely important branch of early Christian painting, and their religious power was so intense that the icon painters' rendering of the subjects was often accepted by Italian painters of the 14th century.

Much fine painting is also to be found in Byzantine ILLUMINATED MANUSCRIPTS (q.v.). Skilled calligraphers embellished their pages with ornamental lettering, chapter headings,

T. Talbot Rice

THE PROPHET MELCHIZEDEK
14th-century Byzantine painting from the Brontocheion
Monastery, Mistra, Greece

associated with Roman portraiture. In the 8th century very elaborate decorative and symbolic motifs were the fashion, but these later gave place to religious scenes of deep sensitivity. In these the delicate, elongated, deeply emotional figures were carved with a sculptor's skill, and even tiny objects had all the force of a major work of art.

Metal work varied from vast metal doors set up in the sanctuaries to innumerable crosses in every conceivable size, metal, and technique. Precious reliquaries, often adorned with jewels, metal icons, book bindings, whether in repoussé or filigree, ecclesiastical plate, and a great variety of secular jewellery are all of the highest order. The Byzantines excelled in that most difficult technique—cloisonné enamel. The design was outlined by tiny gold wire threads fixed to a gold base, and the partitions which these formed were then filled in with pigments and fired. The work needed the utmost delicacy of craftsmanship, and even in plaques measuring no more than an inch or two across the pigments remained translucent, the drawing clear and masterly.

Every aspect of Byzantine life was marked by the artistry of its craftsmanship. The woven silks and brocades, bearing fiercely vital animals facing each other in stylized designs, intricate geometric patterns, or exuberant floral motifs, rank with the finest of the medieval world. The splendid embroideries in gold thread and coloured silks added a sumptuous note to their church interiors. Their ceramics and glass, their coinage and lead seals, and other minor arts carry the vivid stamp of their genius, revealing their deep understanding of art and their unerring, sensitive feeling for the materials in which they worked.

See also ICONS; MOSAICS; ST. SOPHIA.
See also Vol. I: BYZANTINE EMPIRE.
See also Vol. III: ISTANBUL.

and marginal designs of superb quality. The illuminations, which provide these volumes with their main glory, were generally the work of painters, and they are in the same style as the wall paintings and icons. The books were sumptuously bound, either in tooled leather, carved boards, or ivory panels, or in worked metal ornamented by jewels, cloisonné ENAMEL (q.v. Vol. VII), or carved ivory plaques.

IVORY CARVING (q.v.) was used for a great many purposes in Byzantium. Caskets, plaques, handles, and mounts of various sorts were all elaborately and finely carved. The earlier examples were Roman in style, the foreshortened, majestic, and dignified figures retaining the directness and somewhat solid appearance

C

CADENZA, *see* CONCERTO.

CANON, *see* MUSICAL FORM, Section 8.

CANTATA. This word was first used about the year 1600 to describe vocal music, in contrast to the sonata (sounded) or instrumental music. At this time the *cantata da camera* (chamber cantata) consisted of the musical recitation of a short drama or story in verse by one voice, with slender accompaniment by a single instrument; this form of singing was known as recitative. Later, in order to impart some variety, an air or aria was introduced and repeated at different points in the course of the recitative (*see* SONG, HISTORY OF). Indeed the cantata differed very little in its layout from OPERA (q.v.), which had recently made its first appearance, except that it required neither scenery nor acting. This style of cantata was brought to perfection by the Italian composer, Carissimi (1605–74), who was also the first to adopt it for use in church under the title of *cantata da chiesa*. In the early 18th century the cantata grew in popularity, and not only sections for chorus but orchestral accompaniment as well came to be added. J. S. BACH and HANDEL (qq.v. Vol. V) developed the secular or non-religious cantata by the introduction of solos for different voices, choruses, and orchestral accompaniment, as, for instance, in Bach's *Peasant Cantata* and Handel's *Acis and Galatea*. In the modern cantata, as sung in the concert hall, the recitative is entirely dispensed with.

The Church cantata reached its zenith in the hands of Bach, who composed no fewer than five series for use throughout the Church's year. The words were chosen with great care, sometimes from the Bible and sometimes from hymns, and were so selected and arranged that they formed a complete whole. The musical form was infinitely variable. Usually, however, the cantata opened with a chorus, and was followed by a series of recitatives, arias, and duets, often ending with a simple chorale or hymn; but the distribution of these was never the same in any two cantatas. Indeed it is clear that Bach had to compose to suit the vocal and instrumental resources which were available to him at the time, for the personnel of both soloists and orchestral players seemed to be continually changing. Sometimes the organ was joined by strings alone, at others by an orchestra of strings, wood-wind, and brass. The cantata in this form proved to be an important feature of the church services in Germany, and was usually performed before the sermon. One of the best known of Bach's works is the *Christmas Oratorio*, which is really a series of short cantatas for separate performance on six days of that festival. After his time the popularity of the Church cantata waned, and his cantatas were temporarily left on one side, only to be revived about 100 years later by the enthusiastic efforts of such admirers as Mendelssohn in Germany and Samuel Wesley in England.

Since that time innumerable cantatas have been written, but mainly with secular words; this is especially true of those composed by British musicians, which are popular with the many choral societies in this country.

See also ANTHEM; SACRED MUSIC; ORATORIO.

CANTERBURY TALES. These stories, some in verse and some in prose, were written by Geoffrey CHAUCER (q.v. Vol. V) in the 14th century. Most of them are written in the heroic couplet (*see* VERSIFICATION), the first important English poems to be written in this very popular metre.

Chaucer starts by describing how a group of pilgrims journeying together from London to Canterbury agree to beguile the journey by each telling stories, two on the way there and two on the return journey. Hardly any of the later stories were written. Chaucer, in 'The General Prologue', gives a series of brilliant sketches of the pilgrims, a very varied company of people. He makes fun of many of them, though some, such as the 'verray parfit gentil knight' and the simple Ploughman, he idealizes. Some of the sketches almost certainly refer to real people.

The Knight tells the first story, a noble if rather far-fetched romance about two young knights who fall in love with the same lady. It is

British Museum

THE WIFE OF BATH
Woodcut from Caxton's *Canterbury Tales*, printed in 1484

rich with description, adventure, and poetic thought. The 'Miller's Tale' and 'Reeve's Tale', by contrast, are realistic in setting, coarse and fantastic in plot, and very funny. The 'Man of Law's Tale' of Constance, twice betrayed and set adrift on the sea but preserved by the Blessed Virgin, is in contrast to the Shipman's worldly comic tales about a merchant, his wife, and a monk. The Prioress follows with a short, beautifully told miracle of the Virgin and a martyred child. Then Chaucer himself, as a pilgrim, begins to tell the absurd 'Tale of Sir Thopas'—a good example of his self-mocking humour—but eventually tells quite seriously a long prose 'Tale of Melibeus', about prudence. The Monk then relates several short 'tragedies'; after which the Nun's Priest tells the delightful tale of the

Cock and the Fox, where all Chaucer's learning and serious thought are turned to the use of comedy. The 'Physician's Tale' is rather uninspired, but the 'Pardoner's Tale' is a striking story of how three men sought Death and found it. In a remarkable prologue to his tale the Pardoner reveals all his own shameful tricks. The 'Wife of Bath' begins with a prologue about her five successive husbands, and then tells a charming fairy-story about who should have 'mastery' in marriage. A quarrel between the Friar and Summoner leads each to tell a scandalous tale against the other. 'A Clerk ther was of Oxenford also', one of Chaucer's idealized characters, who tells the story of patient Griselda, whose husband tested her love by making her suffer. The Merchant follows with a powerful, bitter, and joyless tale about marriage, which is relieved by the pleasant 'Squire's Tale', an unfinished courtly romance with a magic horse and ring. The Franklin tells a story about courtesy, love, and honour in marriage. The other tales are less connected. The last tale is the Parson's sermon on penitence and the Seven Deadly Sins. It is followed by a short list of all Chaucer's writings, and a condemnation of anything which may be thought sinful in them, which are probably the last words he wrote.

Many of the Tales are connected by 'links' in which the pilgrims talk, argue, and interrupt in a most lively way. This delightful work was mainly written after 1387, but Chaucer did not complete it, and the order of some of the tales is uncertain.

See also ENGLISH LITERATURE.
See also Vol. V: CHAUCER.

CARICATURE. An Italian, Annibale Carracci (1560–1609), was, as far as we know, the first artist deliberately to make comic portraits of living people, and from his name has come the word caricature. The practice of using distortion or exaggeration of the features to emphasize character is, of course, much older and can be seen in some Egyptian and Greek drawings and carvings. Such works were probably not usually based on individuals but were comic generalizations, poking fun at human failings rather than at particular persons. Later Italian artists developed the caricature into a popular form of light entertainment, seen at its best in the work of Pietro Ghezzi (1674–1755), whose touch was light and not too unkind to his sitters.

British Museum

THE KNIGHT
Woodcut from Caxton's *Canterbury Tales*, printed in 1484

The first famous English caricaturist, George (later Marquis) Townshend, used personal caricature as a political weapon, probably for the first time. His work, however, was far surpassed by that of William HOGARTH (q.v. Vol. V), who, being a deeply serious and gifted painter, resented being called a caricaturist, which carried a suggestion of triviality. He believed, rightly, that his work was far superior to that of the Italian caricaturists, though he probably borrowed some of their ideas. With his great genius he changed the whole nature of the art and gave it a new vitality and purpose. His paintings show without mercy the face of a period of England's history when coarseness and culture rubbed elbows. The new contribution he made to European art was in his unerring eye for a moral weakness in society and in his powerfully expressed disapproval of folly or corruption (*see* p. 405).

Hogarth's work led to the development of an English school of satire, of which the leading artists were Thomas Rowlandson (1756–1827) and James Gillray (1757–1815). These artists used caricature as a direct political weapon to attack the opponents of the parties for which they were working (*see* Vol. X, pp. 311, 445). They evolved a free, lively, but bitter and often grotesque manner, using ETCHING (q.v.) and aquatint as their method of reproduction. Their plates were printed in black, coloured by hand, and then sold in printsellers' shops. They performed much the same function as the modern newspaper cartoon, and folios of these prints were often in great demand to entertain guests at a party. The development of cheap printed periodicals and the spread of literacy put an end to this English school of satire early in the 19th century.

In France, however, a young artist, Charles Philipon (1806–62), began the publication of illustrated papers with a weekly, *La Caricature*, in 1830 and a daily, *Le Charivari*, in 1832. Both these journals, being strongly opposed to the government of the day, had stormy beginnings under a strict but clumsy censorship. They survived all attempts to suppress them, and though they published some work of poor quality, they gradually evolved a vigorous school of caricaturists which included Daumier, Gavarni, Grandville, and Monnier. From the beginning the talent of Honoré Daumier (1808–79) outshone all other contributors, and all modern caricature

'EQUILIBRE EUROPÉEN.'   CARICATURE BY DAUMIER
The figure represents Europe balanced precariously on a smoking bomb. From *Le Charivari*, 1867

has drawn its inspiration from his work. In 1832 he was sent to prison for a caricature of King Louis-Philippe, but on his release he returned undaunted to attack the government in *Le Charivari*'s pages.

The process of printing by LITHOGRAPHY (q.v.), which had recently been developed, gave Daumier a great advantage over earlier caricaturists, for it allowed him to draw with the utmost freedom and vigour. He contributed caricatures to Philipon's publications for the whole of his working life, and his last cartoons show a vitality of touch which has never since been equalled, although the quality of the printing fell off in the later numbers.

Caricature in England developed along less vigorous lines. *Punch*, describing itself as 'The London Charivari', appeared first in 1841. It was less sharp in its criticism than Philipon's paper, and gave more space to comic topical comment. England was moving into a period of commercial prosperity and political stability, and no artist arose with satiric powers to match the writing of Dickens or Thackeray. But a number of draughtsmen such as John Leech, Richard Doyle, George Cruikshank, and, later, Charles Keene laid the foundations of a new

Ashmolean Museum

ROBERT BROWNING TAKING TEA WITH THE BROWNING SOCIETY
Caricature by Max Beerbohm. The artist is making fun of the reverent admiration accorded to Browning

type of comic art in which caricature played a minor and genial part. In 1862, when the periodical *Vanity Fair* first appeared, it published somewhat genteel caricatures of eminent people. The best of the early contributors were J. J. Tissot, 'Ape' (Carlo Pellegrini), and 'Spy' (Leslie Ward) whose work for *Vanity Fair* had more affinity with the 18th-century Italians than with either English or French cartoons (*see* Vol. V, pp. 436, 457). A later contributor in the true tradition of caricature was Sir Max Beerbohm, whose drawings are flavoured with a wit that does not fade with time. He had a light style, and his success was due more to the humorous perception of his subject's character than to the quality of his drawing.

Practising caricaturists today are almost all political cartoonists working for daily newspapers, and normally their drawings are expected to reflect the editorial policy of the paper. Drawing for a far wider public than earlier caricaturists, these newspaper cartoonists have gradually ceased to draw only real personalities but have also invented characters whose behaviour can be used as social or political comment—for instance, Low's 'Colonel Blimp', and Strube's 'Little Man'. The work of Carl Giles shows a new development in caricature by its preoccupation with the total background of the social scene. Giles has widened the range of caricature to include in the artist's target the whole population and activity of the modern State.

See also SATIRE.

CAROLS. The carol is primarily a traditional song commemorating the birth of Christ, but it has come to include also songs for other great festivals of the Church, as well as for the seasons of the year. Carols, unlike HYMNS (q.v.), were never part of the church services. They were popular in origin, usually simple in form, and often had choruses in which all might join. The word is derived from the Old French *caroler*, which meant to 'dance in a ring'. In the Middle Ages carols were danced as well as sung, mainly in the open air, the singers being called WAITS (q.v. Vol. IX). Some of the oldest of these, like 'The Holly and the Ivy', were originally pagan, but were adapted by the Christian Church for use at its festivals. It is said that, when in the 13th century St. Francis of Assisi first made a 'crib' (a miniature tableau of the stable at Bethlehem on the first Christmas Day), the practice of singing and dancing round it became common, and many of the Christmas carols of Europe can be traced to this practice. Others are to be found in some of the MIRACLE PLAYS (q.v.) of the 15th century, of which the 'Coventry Carol' from the Coventry Mystery Play is a good example. These are similar to folk-songs and include songs such as 'I saw three ships' and 'The Cherry Tree Carol'. As Miracle Plays dealt with Gospel stories other than those concerning the birth of Christ, carols drawn from them were suitable for use at other festivals of the Church. There are other carols, even more like folk-songs, which tell a quaint story, having only the remotest connexion with the biblical version— 'Dives and Lazarus', for example, and 'King Herod and the Cock'. A manuscript in Balliol College Library, Oxford, contains an interesting collection of carols including some early 15th-century ones which were written down from memory by an alderman grocer of London between 1500 and 1536.

During the 17th century the Puritans in England and Scotland discouraged carol singing because of its association with the festivals of the Church of which they disapproved, but many carols were preserved in folk-songs and on broadsheets. Such collections of these as were published from time to time were called 'printed matter suitable for Christmas'. In 1871 the first serious collection of Christmas carols was made, of which less than half proved to be genuine traditional ones, and the rest new tunes, written by church musicians of the time; these latter for the most part lacked inspiration. By the turn of the century many more of the traditional carols had been recovered. Modern composers had written carols which they hoped 'would give voice to the common emotions of healthy people in language that can be understood'.

Carols are found all over Europe. In France they are called Noëls (Noël meaning Christmas), a word which appears in English carols as 'Nowell'. One of the earliest of the French carols is that sung in commemoration of Christ's flight into Egypt; a version of this tune is preserved in the hymn 'Soldiers, who are Christ's below'. France has a wealth of fine carols, many of which were set to tunes of a dance-like character; in-deed, the chief characteristic of most of these carols is their sparkling gaiety.

The carols of Germany are for the most part more dignified and restrained than those of other European countries. They are, in fact, cradle songs rather than true carols. Many of them are to be found in English collections, notably 'In Dulci Jubilo' and 'A Great and Mighty Wonder'. German musicians were among the first to harmonize these carol tunes when elsewhere they were being sung in unison, and J. S. BACH (q.v. Vol. V) treated many of them in this way.

See also FOLK-SONG; HYMNS.

CARTOON, see CARICATURE; DRAWING.

CATACOMBS, see EARLY CHRISTIAN ART.

CELTIC ART, see PREHISTORIC ART, Section 4.

CHAMBER MUSIC. In early days this term was used to describe the most intimate of all kinds of music, involving only a handful of performers, and commonly performed at home instead of in public places such as a church or theatre. Now that there are public concert halls where chamber music is frequently played, the term can no longer be understood literally; but it still implies an intimate kind of music for a small number of performers only, in contrast to the massed forces required by ORATORIO, OPERA, or SYMPHONY, for example (qq.v.). Most typical is the string quartet. Provided there is no more than one player to a part, however, a composer can write for five, six, seven, or eight players (or even more), and still call his composition chamber music. Instrumental duets and trios also rank as chamber music, but works for a solo instrument, or for a solo singer with piano accompaniment, by tacit agreement, do not.

Larouss·

LA CAROLE, A MEDIEVAL DANCE
13th-century French illumination from the *Romance of the Rose* (*Bibl. de l'Arsenal MS. 5209*)

THE GRILLER STRING QUARTET
Left to right: 1st violin, cello, viola, and 2nd violin

B.B.C.

The string quartet is but one of many different combinations of instruments found in the chamber music repertory, though stringed instruments have nearly always provided the 'foundation tone' for most chamber music. The piano has always been popular in trios and quartets, and SCHUBERT and SCHUMANN (qq.v. Vol. V), following the example of that tireless experimentalist, Boccherini (1743–1805), wrote delightful quintets for piano and strings; Schubert's 'Trout' Quintet (called after one of his best-known songs, the tune of which is quoted in the course of the quintet) is one of the most loved of all chamber works involving piano. WOOD-WIND INSTRUMENTS (q.v. Vol. IX) have also made regular appearances in chamber music; Mozart wrote for them with particular affection, and Beethoven and Schubert contributed a magnificent septet and octet respectively for wind and strings. Some 20th-century composers have explored various other new combinations of sounds, such as the flute, harp, clarinet, and string quartet used by Ravel for his beautiful Septet, or the flute, clarinet, and two each of bassoons, trumpets, and trombones in Stravinsky's stark Octet.

In Elizabethan times most cultured homes possessed a 'chest of viols', that is, a set of VIOLS (q.v. Vol. IX) of different pitches, and composers wrote chamber works, which they called 'fancies', for these gentle, golden-toned instruments. When viols were superseded by the instruments of the violin family (*see* STRING INSTRUMENTS, Vol. IX), sonatas for two violins with a 'cello 'continuo' (accompaniment) and a simple chordal accompaniment for the harpsichord became a particularly popular form of chamber music. It was not, however, till the arrival of HAYDN and MOZART (qq.v. Vol. V) in the 18th century that chamber music first began to assume the definite traits by which we recognize it today—notably in the equal importance of all the instruments involved. To Haydn goes the credit for establishing the string quartet. He dispensed with the harpsichord, and recognizing the distinctive character of the viola, he allowed both it and the 'cello to provide just as important melodic contributions to the general theme as the first and second violins. BEETHOVEN (q.v. Vol. V) recognized the worth of Haydn's achievement, and himself composed sixteen quartets which contain some of the most searching music he ever wrote. BARTÓK's six masterly string quartets (q.v. Vol. V) show that he, too, found just as much satisfaction in the medium as his predecessors.

Generally speaking, chamber music has adopted the current forms and idioms and reflected the general tendencies of each successive century—PROGRAMME MUSIC (q.v.), for example, occasionally came to the fore in the 19th century, (as in Smetana's string quartet *Aus meinem Leben* (*From my life*), and preoccupation with colour rather than with design marked the style of the French composers a little later. Nevertheless it is true to say that at all times chamber music has remained the most 'pure' of all forms of music, and, because its intimate character makes it unsuitable for large-scale concert performance, it does not have a great popular appeal.

See also MUSIC, HISTORY OF.

CHANSON DE ROLAND. The 12th-century French EPIC poem (q.v.), the Song of Roland, is preserved in its finest form in a manuscript now in the Bodleian Library at Oxford. Its author, a Norman poet, Turold, was not the first to tell the story; the minstrel Taillefer, according to a 12th-century writer, sang to Duke William before the battle of Hastings a song of 'Charlemagne and Roland and Oliver, and those other knights who died at Roncevaux'. Turold seems to have written his version to spur on knights and barons of the early 12th century to go on crusade, and to devote themselves single-mindedly, as the Emperor CHARLEMAGNE (q.v. Vol. V) does in the poem, to the cause of Christianity.

The poem describes how the great warrior, Roland, nephew of Charlemagne, was left to guard the passes of the Pyrenees while the Emperor, with the main body of the crusading army, returned to France after receiving the submission of the Saracens of Spain. With Roland were Oliver, his brother-in-arms, and a small force of knights. But Roland's stepfather, Ganelon, who hated his stepson, betrayed him and his men to the Saracens. As soon as Charlemagne's army was well on its way over the Pyrenees, a vast army of pagans attacked the rearguard. If Roland had sounded his famous horn, the Olifant, before the battle began, Charlemagne could have turned back to save him; but Roland was too proud to summon help until nearly all his small force was slain. Then, in order to secure Christian burial for himself and his men, he blew three mighty blasts on the horn. Though Charlemagne hurried back as soon as he heard the sound of the horn, he was too late; Roland and all the rear-guard were dead. The Emperor avenged them not only by defeating the remainder of the Spanish Saracens, but also by slaying the ruler of all the pagans, Baligant, and annihilating his great army. Then he returned sorrowfully to France to give honourable burial to Roland and Oliver. The traitor, Ganelon, after a trial by combat, was condemned and put to death. The poem ends with an exhortation to the Emperor by the Archangel Gabriel in a vision once again to take up arms for his faith.

The poem is a stirring call to the feudal lords of the early 12th century to lay aside personal feuds which hinder the work of God, and to take the Cross and fight for their faith against the Saracens (see CRUSADES, Vol. I). Ganelon was jeopardizing the cause of Christianity when he caused the death of knights who were on crusade. Even Roland, the great warrior, has to suffer because he sacrificed himself and his knights rather than his pride. It is Charlemagne, the champion of Christianity, for whom God performs miracles, and who never flags in God's service, who is the real hero.

The story of Roncevaux was one of the most famous of the French epic tales. It inspired poets in many countries for three centuries, and then again, in the 19th century, with the revival of interest in medieval literature, the story fired writers, for example, Victor Hugo, to try to recapture something of the spirit of the medieval epic. How deeply the story has sunk into the European tradition is shown by the way it has served as a continuing inspiration to artists and poets right down to modern times.

See also EPIC POETRY.
See also Vol. V: CHARLEMAGNE.

CHANTRY. In the Middle Ages people often gave money to churches, especially abbeys and cathedrals, to pay for a chapel in which Masses were chanted for their souls after their death—

National Buildings Record

THE WARWICK CHANTRY, TEWKESBURY ABBEY, ERECTED IN 1422

hence they were called chantry chapels. These were sometimes erected within the body of the church or were built out from one of the aisles or the chancel. They generally contained the tomb of the founder and an altar, and were separated from the main body of the church by wooden or some openwork screens. The tombs and screens are often richly carved and decorated; Worcester Cathedral has a fine example, erected in 1504 to Arthur, son of Henry VII. Tewkesbury Abbey is famous for its chantry chapels.

See also TOMBS.

CHAPTER HOUSE. A cathedral is governed by the chapter, consisting of the canons presided over by the dean. The chapter house, where the chapter meets, is usually an independent structure attached to the cathedral by a passage and a flight of stairs, the passage often being an extension of the cloister. It is usually a vaulted chamber with high windows and stone seats round the walls on which the members of the chapter sit. Most English Gothic chapter houses are octagonal (eight-sided), with the vaulting supported by a central pillar. The 13th-century chapter houses at Westminster Abbey (restored

H. Felton

THE CHAPTER HOUSE, WELLS CATHEDRAL

1865), Wells, and Salisbury (*see* Vol. I, p. 127) are outstanding examples. Wells chapter house is approached by an especially picturesque stone staircase. The 12th-century chapter house at Worcester is round; those at Canterbury, Chester, Exeter, and Gloucester are oblong, as are nearly all chapter houses on the Continent. That at Southwell (14th century), which is octagonal but without a central pillar, is famous for the naturalistic carving of leaves on the capitals of the columns.

See also CHURCH ARCHITECTURE, ENGLISH.

CHARTRES CATHEDRAL. This cathedral, one of the most magnificent Gothic cathedrals in the world, has looked much as it does now since about 1220. It is the successor of earlier churches, and beneath it is a well at which miracles of healing were supposed to have taken place, and which was probably already a centre of worship when the first Christian missionaries came to Chartres.

The only part of the 11th-century church which remains is the simple vaulted crypt. Its plan was followed by the present choir which was built above it. The lower part of the present west front, and the towers flanking it, were built in the 1140's. The three west doors are richly sculptured with figures at the sides of the entrance, over the doors, and in the arches round them. Their style shows the first stage of Gothic sculpture, still with some of the stiffness of Romanesque figures. The figures of the Ancestors of Christ at the sides are imprisoned in the shape of the columns, the drapery being arranged in patterns rather than natural folds (*see* p. 410). The sculptors were experimenting with carving single, almost free-standing figures, and in the reliefs above the doors there is an attempt to portray solid beings in natural proportions. Above the central door is the Last Judgement, on the north the Ascension of Christ, and on the south the Virgin of Chartres. Round the arches are small groups and figures: the twenty-four Elders and twelve Angels in the centre, the Signs of the Zodiac and various occupations of the month round the Ascension, and round the south door the Seven Liberal Arts. Lastly, the capitals of the columns supporting these arches have a series of scenes from the early life of Christ.

In 1194 a large part of the cathedral was burnt again, and by about 1220 the last rebuilding

THE NORTH PORTAL OF CHARTRES CATHEDRAL AND NORTH-WEST TOWER

was nearly finished. The interior has been little changed, except that the choir was recased at the time of the French Revolution. Tall, sturdy piers with slender shafts carry pointed arches. Above a narrow triforium (the arcade above the piers of the nave) are great windows, each a pair of lancets with a rose window above. The weight of the Gothic roof (*see* VAULT) is partly borne by massive buttresses and flying buttresses.

At the ends of the transepts are triple doorways sculptured as magnificently as the older west front and with similar subjects. The inner doorways were made about 1200, and in this rather more developed Gothic sculpture the figures are no longer stiff and elongated like columns, but turn more freely to each other, their draperies falling into natural folds. A little later porticoes were added to the doorways; on these are carved saints and personifications of virtues and vices, in which delicacy and charm have replaced the dignity and solemnity of the earlier figures.

The crowning splendour of Chartres is its glass. With the exception of a few windows of the late 12th century, which in richness of colour rival anything done later, all the glass dates from the years 1215–40. The windows of the choir were mostly given by nobles, or by the ecclesiastics who alone would often see them, and the windows in the nave, the part which the congregation used, were given by the craft guilds of the city. The great rose window of the north transept was the gift of the French royal family. In the tall clerestory windows above the nave are gigantic figures of the prophets and apostles, resplendent in crimson and azure robes. Closer to the eye, the windows of the aisles are broken up into geometric shapes, containing scenes from the Bible and the lives of saints.

In the 15th century a chapel was added between two nave buttresses, and in the early 16th century a daring filigree stone spire was added to the old north tower which was only meant to support a spire of wood. In 1516 a new choir screen was begun; it progressed so slowly that

National Gallery

'CHRIST AT EMMAUS' BY CARAVAGGIO
Strong light and shade are used to add reality and intensity to this scene

Art Gallery, Derby

'THE ORRERY' BY JOSEPH WRIGHT OF DERBY
An orrery is a model of the solar system with a light at the centre to represent the sun

by the time it was finished it had incorporated examples of 17th- and 18th-century sculpture.

See also Gothic Art; Sculpture.

CHIAROSCURO. The word, which refers to contrasts of light and shade in paintings and drawings, is made up of two Italian adjectives, *chiaro* (light) and *oscuro* (dark), the 'ch' being pronounced like 'k'. In any picture where the artist is trying to suggest the effects of nature—that is, in nearly all European painting except the primitive and some 20th-century art—there must be some degree of chiaroscuro. The side of an object nearest the light will reflect the light brightly, while the side away from it will be in shadow. This arrangement of the light and shade gives the appearance of solidity because, if an object interrupts the beam of light and so throws a shadow, it must have bulk. But even in nature the amount of contrast which there may be between light and shade varies. In strong sunlight there is also strong shadow; but on a cloudy day the light is diffused and we

do not see the source of it—consequently the shadows are weak.

The term chiaroscuro is particularly associated with a small number of 17th-century painters who used light and shade in an extreme form, with very bright light (almost always artificial) and correspondingly inky shadows. Of these the most famous was the Italian painter, Michelangelo da Caravaggio (1573–1610), who used stronger contrasts of light and shade in his paintings than anyone had done before. The figures are depicted nearly always indoors rather than in the open air, brightly lit from one angle and almost always against a dark background. The source of light, though it is not shown, is clearly artificial.

Caravaggio himself developed this extreme form of chiaroscuro to make his pictures more vivid and also more dramatic. When the human body is very brightly lit, the contrasts between the projecting parts and the hollows are stressed and, in consequence, the painted figure appears more solid and therefore more real than under other lighting conditions. When, as in Caravaggio's paintings, brightly lit figures are seen against inky darkness the effect is dramatic, as one sees in the frequent use of such devices on the stage. The Italian followers of Caravaggio sometimes became so obsessed with the striking results which his methods made possible that they exaggerated it, and some of their pictures are ludicrously over-dramatic. But in other European countries, Caravaggio's work led to more satisfactory results. Three of the greatest painters—REMBRANDT, VELAZQUEZ, and VERMEER (qq.v. Vol. V)—could hardly have painted quite as they did without his example. In England an 18th-century painter, Joseph Wright (usually known as Wright of Derby), developed a gentler type of chiaroscuro painting, with figures lit sometimes by a single candle, in which the extremes of Caravaggio's style have been modified to suit English taste.

Shadows are not entirely without colour for, though no direct light may fall on them, there is always light reflected from other surfaces, which lightens their tone and reveals their colours. Artists have always observed this fact, but in the 19th century they studied it more carefully. In IMPRESSIONIST PAINTING (q.v.) an attempt was made to reproduce the brilliance of light, and in order to achieve this, painters sought to depict the reflected lights and subtle colours in shadows, rather than their dark tones.

CHILDREN'S BOOKS. In the present day children's books form one of the largest branches of the book trade. In 1950, for instance, 1,141 new books for children were published in Britain, and 907 in the U.S.A.—more than a tenth of all the books produced being specially designed for children's reading, exclusive of books for use in school.

Until Charles II's time almost all books were scarce and valuable, and few, if any, were specially printed for the young, except Primers and Books of Courtesy which instructed a child in his behaviour. The most interesting stories a child was given to read, other than those in the Bible, were stories of martyrs and saints, and FABLES (q.v.), particularly the fables of Aesop. He might also come across the legendary stories: tales of King Arthur (see ARTHURIAN LITERATURE), BALLADS (q.v.) about Robin Hood, and romantic histories of champions such as St. George, Guy, Earl of Warwick, and Sir Bevis of

THE

HISTORY

O. F.

Sir Richard Whittington, THRICE

Lord Mayor of LONDON.

London: Printed by C. SYMPSON, in Stonecutter Street, Fleet Market.

Opie Collection

THE COVER OF A CHAP BOOK

Southampton, whose heroic exploits included fights with 'Giants, Monsters, Wild Beasts and Armies'. These stories were printed on cheap paper, were profusely illustrated with fierce and vivid woodcuts, and were published in pamphlet form. They were the stock-in-trade of the wandering pedlars, known as 'chapmen', and held a place equivalent to the popular bookstall magazines of our own time. We know that they were sought after and enjoyed by many a schoolboy in the 16th, 17th, and 18th centuries.

The first stories written especially for children were of very different calibre. James Janeway's *A Token for Children; being an Exact Account of the Conversion, Holy and Exemplary Lives, and Joyful Deaths of Several Young Children*, which was in print by 1676, is an example. It is true that shortly after this, in 1678, one of the best stories of all time, Bunyan's PILGRIM'S PROGRESS (q.v.), was published; and that the beginning of the 18th century saw the writing of *Robinson Crusoe* (see DEFOE, Vol. V) and *Gulliver's Travels* (see SWIFT, Vol. V); but it must be remembered that, however much these stories are now looked upon as 'Children's Classics', they were not originally written for children.

The most important book of the early 18th century, actually advertised as 'very entertaining and instructive for children', was the translation in 1729 of Perrault's fairy-tales (Cinderella, Blue Beard, and six others) by Robert Samber. Before this there had also appeared two notable books of verse: John Bunyan's *A Book for Boys and Girls; or, Country Rhimes for Children* (1686), and *Divine Songs attempted in Easy Language for the Use of Children* (1715) by Isaac Watts. These two books were openly instructive, but the verses were so kindly and diverting that generations of our forefathers took pleasure in learning them by heart. For a long period there was hardly a well-brought-up child who could not repeat, with Watts,

> Let Dogs delight to bark and bite,
> For God has made them so;
> Let Bears and Lions growl and fight,
> For 'tis their Nature, too.
>
> But Children, you should never let
> Such angry passions rise;
> Your little hands were never made
> To tear each other's Eyes.

When, therefore, publishers began regularly producing books for children towards the middle of the 18th century, there was already a good foundation laid for the stories which were to come. The old fables were universally admired and recommended; the ARABIAN NIGHTS (q.v.) had been translated by 1708; the French fairy-tales, and also the old English ones such as 'Jack the Giant Killer', were constantly being reprinted; there were innumerable riddle books and books of jests; and NURSERY RHYMES (q.v.) were alive in the language.

The first pleasure

books for children, designed for 'Cheating Children into Learning Without any Beating', made use of all this material. Such a volume was *A Little Pretty Pocket-Book, Intended for the Instruction and Amusement of Little Master Tommy, and Pretty Miss Polly. With Two Letters from Jack the Giant-Killer*, published by John Newbery in 1744. It was a little book, so small, like many others of the period, that it literally could be fitted into a waistcoat pocket; yet it had 122 pages, sturdy binding, and pleasing illustrations not much bigger than postage stamps. It contained descriptions of thirty-two games, a rhyming alphabet, several fables in verse, and rules for behaviour ('Go not Singing, Whistling nor Hollowing along the Street'). This was the first of John Newbery's books for children, and marks the beginning of a firm of publishers which specialized in children's literature for more than 140 years.

Most writers up to the early 19th century were didactic, writers with a lesson to teach as well as a tale to tell. The first important book with no object but fun and fantasy, *The Butterfly's Ball, and the Grasshopper's Feast* (1807), was written by William Roscoe, historian and member of Parliament:

The Times

FRONTISPIECE AND TITLE-PAGE TO 'THE HISTORY OF LITTLE GOODY TWO-SHOES'
Published by J. Newbery, 1766 (*Opie Collection*)

ILLUSTRATION TO CATHERINE SINCLAIR'S 'HOLIDAY HOUSE'

Come take up your Hats, and away let us haste
To the Butterfly's Ball, and the Grasshopper's
  Feast.
The Trumpeter, Gad-Fly, has summon'd the Crew,
And the Revels are now only waiting for you.

There followed a rush of similar verse, preparing
the way for the master of nonsense—

.... old Derry down Derry
Who loved to see little folks merry—

Edward Lear, author and illustrator of the
limericks in *A Book of Nonsense* (1846) and in
More Nonsense (1872), and of verses such as 'The
Owl and the Pussy-Cat' and 'The Jumblies' (*see*
COMIC VERSE).

After the accession of Queen Victoria, children's books took much the shape they have
today, and we can still read and enjoy many of
the stories which our grandmothers and great-
grandmothers loved—for example, Catherine
Sinclair's *Holiday House*, written in 1839, ('Now
children! I have only one piece of serious important advice to give you all, so attend to me!
—Never crack nuts with your teeth!'). Others
are Captain Marryat's *The Children of the New
Forest* (1847), a tale set in the days of the Round-
heads, and Charlotte M. Yonge's historical tales,
such as *The Little Duke* (1854) and *The Lances of
Lynwood* (1855).

In 1865 appeared *Alice's Adventures in Wonderland* by Lewis CARROLL (q.v. Vol. V), a book
appreciated equally by old and young; followed
in 1871 by *Through the Looking-Glass and What
Alice Found There*, one of the rare instances in
which a sequel is as good as or better than the
original story. Children's books during the 19th
century showed an increasing breadth of understanding. The beauty of Lewis Carroll (a
mathematical lecturer at Oxford whose real
name was the Rev. C. L. Dodgson) is that in
the *Alice* books he makes absurdity sound like
sense, so that we begin to wonder whether some
of our own certainties are not nonsense.

It's a poor sort of memory that only works backwards,' the Queen remarked.

'What sort of things do you remember best?' Alice
ventured to ask.

'Oh, things that happened the week after next,' the
Queen replied in a careless tone. 'For instance . . .
there's the King's Messenger. He's in prison now
being punished, and the trial doesn't even begin until
next Wednesday; and of course the crime comes last
of all.'

It is a good thing, Lewis Carroll is saying in
effect, for a person to be able to feel other
possibilities than those he might ordinarily
expect; and to be able to view them from other
ways round than those which he ordinarily sees.

The second half of the 19th century was rich
in the literature which in one way or another
stretches the imagination. Charles KINGSLEY
(q.v. Vol. V) turned a dirty little chimney-sweep
into a water-baby in the *Water Babies* (1863),
and in so doing hastened the end of the practice
in which young boys were forced to climb up
inside chimneys to clean them. Anna Sewell
in *Black Beauty* (1877) gave her readers a fresh
vision of the lives of animals, and of human
callousness, by telling her story from the horse's
point of view. George MacDonald's *At the Back
of the North Wind* (1871) and Mrs. Molesworth's
The Cuckoo Clock (1877) give us a feeling of other-
worldliness. The two styles of writing—the
practical (and usually adventurous), and the
poetic and other-worldly—have constantly com-
peted with each other in the history of children's
literature; and sometimes one type of story and
sometimes the other appeals to our changing
inclinations. In the present day the two kinds
of writing can be seen in the books of Arthur
Ransome on the one hand and of Walter de la
Mare on the other.

See also BALLAD; COMIC VERSE; NURSERY RHYMES.
See also VOL. I: FAIRY-TALES.

CHINESE ART. This is the oldest still-flourish-
ing art in the world, with a continuous history of
more than 3,000 years. The art of Mesopotamia
and Egypt is far older than that of China, but

in these countries it is no longer living. Just as much Western art springs from Greek art, Chinese art has inspired that of the entire Far East—Japan, Korea, central Asia, Tibet, Mongolia, and even Annam. Europe, too, owes many an artistic impulse to China, as well as the introduction of various techniques, particularly in the arts of pottery, textiles, and lacquer (*see* CHINOISERIE).

Chinese art includes the building of temples, palaces, and public buildings, as well as painting and sculpture, and the making of vessels, textiles, and implements of all kinds. In some ways it follows along the same lines as Western art and uses the same techniques. But there are a number of essential differences. In architecture, wood is a more important material in China than stone. Houses are often of only one storey and spread over large areas, with gardens and courts between the various wings (*see* PEKING, FORBIDDEN CITY), though palaces, temples, and PAGODAS (q.v.) are higher. Roofs do not cover houses alone; they are also put over gateways, bridges, walls, and monuments (*see* Vol. I, p. 109). Several roofs are often piled one on top of the other and the edges bent up in graceful curves.

A very important difference between the Eastern and the Western conception of art is that in China the art of handwriting (calligraphy) has always been regarded as the noblest

Private Collection
CARVED JADE DRAGON PENDANTS, 5TH–3RD CENTURY B.C.

form of art. The Chinese developed the art of writing very early. Their written language consists, not of letters which make up words, but of characters, each representing an idea or thing (*see* CHINESE LANGUAGE, Vol. IV). Each character is a symbolic picture which suggests its meaning as well as having a beautiful shape, and it is this double beauty and significance which gives calligraphy its importance. Painting only comes second to it—in fact it was more or less a development of calligraphy—and even today it has never lost its relationship to calligraphy. Painting and calligraphy alone are regarded by the Chinese as fine arts—everything else is craftsmanship. The painter, instead of painting his pictures on canvas or wood in oil colours, paints on silk or paper in watercolours, often only in the varying tones of black Indian ink. The long pictures, unframed though mounted with silk, are sometimes hung on the wall (usually called by the Japanese word *Kakemono*), or are kept in horizontal rolls which must be unrolled bit by bit to be seen. The Chinese painter has never been much interested in drawing the nude human figure or in exact geometric perspective. Naturalism is rarely the sole aim; it is far more important to give full effect to the rhythm and inner vitality of the individual strokes of the brush, which are never blurred but always clearly defined, though they are often dissolved into washes.

The sculptor not only worked in stone, wood, or bronze, but also sometimes modelled his statues entirely in LACQUER (q.v.), or at least coated them with lacquer. The Chinese invented

Private Collection
BRONZE SACRIFICIAL VESSEL
The pattern represents a monster head and dragons.
Shang Dynasty (16th–11th century B.C.)

AN EMPEROR DEFENDED FROM A WILD BEAR BY HIS WIFE AND GUARDS
Part of a long handscroll, probably after an original of the 4th century A.D.

the technique of lacquer as early as the 2nd millennium B.C., and it has always played a far more important role in China than in the West, where it only became known in the 17th century. PORCELAIN (q.v. Vol. VII), also, was first made in China perhaps as early as the 4th or 5th century A.D.; in the 7th or 8th centuries porcelain was to all intents and purposes perfected, whereas in the West it was only rediscovered in the 18th century. So fully is the debt to China recognized that English-speaking peoples use the word 'china' to mean porcelain. JADE (q.v. Vol. III) is another specifically Chinese material. From about the 2nd millennium B.C. carved jade was very popular for ritual objects, ceremonial weapons, jewellery, and small sculptures, and it was valued very highly owing to its agreeable surface, its colour, and its hardness. It even had a religious significance.

Chinese art was possibly influenced to a certain extent by the much older arts of Mesopotamia (*see* SUMERIAN and BABYLONIAN ART), and the technique of casting in bronze and of glazing pottery may have come from there. Certain features of Chinese mythology and astronomy also point in the same direction.

At different periods Chinese art has also been influenced by the civilizations of Greece, Persia, India, and Islam.

As everywhere else in the world, so too in China, a prehistoric period (Early and Later Stone Ages) precedes the historic one, in which painted and unpainted pottery, often of great beauty, was produced. The evolution of Chinese art can be divided into five long periods, for which, however, there are no very distinct boundary lines. China's art never remained stationary but, like all creative art, strove continually for new forms. It changed, however, less rapidly than in the West; what was often achieved in the West in a matter of decades was not infrequently the work of centuries in the East.

The first period includes the dynasties of Hsia, Shang Yin, and Chou, ending in the 3rd century B.C. (*see* CHINESE CIVILIZATION, Vol. I). Little is known historically of the Hsia dynasty, and definite records only date back to the second part of the Shang dynasty. The most important examples of Shang art are widely varied bronze sacrificial vessels of severe form, decorated chiefly with animal motives which have a religious significance. The Chinese themselves value these vessels above all for the inscriptions they bear, for these are amongst the oldest records of Chinese script and history.

The second period begins when China was united in the year 221 B.C. under the Emperor Shih Huang Ti. Shih Huang Ti was the builder of the GREAT WALL OF CHINA (q.v. Vol. III), erected to protect the country against the attacks of the restless nomad tribes on its frontiers. Objects of bronze and jade are the most important examples of the art of the period; in addition glazed earthenware vessels and tomb-figures of clay have been found. It is from the two Han dynasties (2nd century B.C.–2nd century A.D.) that the first examples of silk textiles, lacquer, and painting, as well as of sculpture in stone, have been preserved in any substantial quantity.

One of the most important events of the Han period was the introduction of BUDDHISM (q.v. Vol. I) from India and central Asia during the first centuries A.D., and with it a Buddhist art which took its place alongside the native art and influenced it. Buddhist temples and monasteries were built and decorated with sculpture and frescoes, the best-preserved being those which, following Indian prototypes, were hewn into the rocks. These belong to the third period of Chinese art, beginning in the 5th century A.D. Their walls are covered with sculpture.

The climax of the third period is reached in the Sui (589–618) and T'ang dynasties (618–906). After centuries of invasions and civil war, China was again united, and at that time was probably the mightiest empire in the world. All branches of art flourished, and much has remained intact or is recorded in books. The art came closer to nature than before, had a greater richness in colour, a more varied ornamentation, and larger dimensions. Side by side with Buddhist painting, which had lost its former religious severity, there was a completely non-religious painting treating chiefly historical subjects and scenes of Court life. Funerary objects of glazed and unglazed pottery which have been found in tombs give an astonishingly vivid picture of the life and activity of the people of the time (see Vol. I, p. 106). A large number of painters achieved such fame that even today their names are as familiar to the educated Chinese as are those of the great poets.

The 10th century marks the beginning of the fourth period which culminated in the Sung dynasty (960–1279), when Chinese art reached its climax as European art did in the Renaissance period. The greatest achievement of these centuries was the evolution of pure landscape painting long before Europe conceived of such a possibility. No less important are the new types of pottery. Their beauty depends on the nobility of the forms and on the great luminosity of the single-coloured glazes—that is to say, on the perfection of the potters' materials rather than on their decoration (see Colour Plate, opp. p. 224).

The last great period of Chinese art covers the reign of the Ming Emperors (1369–1644), and the last Chinese dynasty of the Manchu (1645–1912). Painting was still regarded as the most important art, and there were a large number of excellent painters, who sometimes achieved works of outstanding originality (see Vol. I, Colour Plate, opp. p. 112). Again, though here was much artistic production in architecture and in the crafts of porcelain, lacquer, and textiles, and though the quality was high, art was striving rather for superficial decorative effects and technical perfection. New porcelain techniques

National Museum, Stockholm

A BODHISATTVA (FUTURE BUDDHA)
Limestone figure, 6th century A.D.

Museum, Peking

SUNG LANDSCAPE PAINTED IN INK AND LIGHT COLOURS
ON SILK
Attributed to Ma Yüan (active *c.* A.D. 1190–1224)

were evolved, notably blue under-glaze painting and the use of enamel colours over the glazing. European porcelain factories copied to a greater or lesser degree the Chinese designs and methods of this period. Great technical perfection was also attained in ivory and jade carving, and in cloisonné ENAMEL (q.v. Vol. VII and Colour Plate, opp. p. 176). The majority of the older Chinese buildings still standing today belong to the 18th century, though some date back to the Ming period. There are very few buildings older than that.

See also PEKING, FORBIDDEN CITY; LACQUER; CHINOISERIE.
See also Vol. I: CHINESE CIVILIZATION; CHINESE PEOPLES.

CHINESE LITERATURE. The earliest Chinese document of real literary interest is the *Book of Songs* (*Shih Ching*), a collection of rather more than 300 songs, hymns, choruses, and poems, mostly composed between the 11th and 6th centuries B.C., but perhaps written down rather later. Some of these are songs used in religious ceremonies or solemn choruses to be sung at such occasions as royal banquets; but the great majority are folk-songs—many of them songs of love and courtship which give us a delightful picture of the life of those early peasants and a strong impression of their deep love of nature and of beauty. A knowledge of the 'Three Hundred Songs', as they were called, was considered an indispensable part of the education of a gentleman in the Chou dynasty, and later they became one of the 'classics' of Confucianism (*see* SACRED BOOKS, Section 4, Vol. I), when the flowers, birds, and lovers of the songs were given an allegorical meaning with so strongly moralistic an interpretation that the original meaning was lost.

The period of primitive simplicity which the *Book of Songs* represents was followed by a time of great social change and upheaval, producing a ferment of new ideas (*see* CHINESE CIVILIZATION, Vol. I)—a revolution in thought comparable to the wave of philosophy and speculation which swept through Greece in the West at much the same time. In China sophists, philosophers, and thinkers travelled from state to state looking for a ruler who would employ them and put their theories into practice. Sometimes a philosopher would gather a group of disciples about him to form a 'school', and each school generally had its book in which the Master's teaching was written, sometimes partly by the Master himself, but more often entirely by his disciples. CONFUCIUS (q.v. Vol. V) is the earliest and best-known of these teachers, though of the others whose books have come down to us perhaps the most beautiful and well-loved is that of the Taoist mystic Chuang Tzu, who hid his mystical teachings in a fund of delightful parables and stories.

The poetry of the *Book of Songs* has a solid, 'four-square' rhythm, in which the commonest form is a line containing four single-syllable words. Most of the poems are very short. Towards the end of the Chou era a new kind of poetry began to appear in the southernmost part of the Chinese world, the kingdom of Ch'u in the Yangtze Valley. These people believed in wizards and priestesses who could draw the gods down from heaven or call back the wandering souls of the sick and the dead by their songs and dances. Some of these songs are preserved in a collection called *Ch'u Tz'u* (*The Songs of Ch'u*). They are much longer than any of the poems in the *Book of Songs*, and the rhythms, too, are quite different: there is a longer, freer line, and much use is made of alliteration. The language is rich and heavy and full of wild, splendid imagery. The longest of the poems, the *Li Sao* (*Sorrows*), containing more than 370 lines, describes in allegory the disappointments and sufferings of the poet, and tells how he flies off in a chariot drawn by dragons and travels through all the marvels of the earth and the heavens and the fairy mountains in search of lovely women of legend, and how, meeting with nothing but disappointment, he finally turns back to earth in despair. The following lines are translated from *Li Sao*:

> In the morning I drove my chariot from Ts'ang-wu;
> In the evening I came to the Hanging Garden of
>   K'un-lun.
> I wanted to stay a while in those fairy precincts,
> But the evening sun was hurrying to his setting:
> So I bade the sun's charioteer to stay his passage
> And stop by the Yen-tzu mountain and not go down.

During the Han dynasty (206 B.C.–A.D. 220) Court poetry continued to be written mostly in the Ch'u style. A sort of prose-poem based on the Ch'u style, called a *fu*, also became fashionable, and writers composed essays on a wide range of subjects, some serious, some frivolous, but all conspicuous for elegance and richness of language. Indeed, some *fu* are merely an excuse for piling up lists of rare and exotic words.

The dreadful sufferings and disorders which followed the collapse of the Han dynasty made people revolt against the artificial *fu*, and poets tended to return to the extreme simplicity of the past, using a form called 'Five Word Poetry', in which each line consists of five single-syllable words, a form which was also used in folk-songs. One of the Han emperors had founded a special government department charged with the collection and preservation of folk-songs, the best-known of which, 'A Peacock in the Southeast flies', is a long ballad telling of the tragic love of a young couple who were separated by a cruel mother-in-law and killed themselves rather than submit to remarriage to another partner.

During this troubled period (A.D. 220–618) before the coming of the T'ang dynasty, the most important influence in art and literature was BUDDHISM (q.v. Vol. I), the Indian religion which swept like a flood over China. To translate the Buddhist scriptures from SANSKRIT (q.v. Vol. IV), the Chinese were obliged, for the first time in their history, to make a scholarly study of a foreign language, and the result was a whole series of discoveries about language in general and their own language in particular (*see* CHINESE LANGUAGE, Vol. IV). For instance, the discovery of the tonal differences of Chinese words led to the invention of new kinds of 'Five Word' and 'Seven Word' poetry, in which not only did the lines rhyme (as always in Chinese poetry), but also, inside the line, words were so chosen and arranged that their tones made patterns, and one line balanced musically with another.

Although this period was such an inventive one, the unsettled political situation made most

THE POET IN HIS DRAGON CHARIOT
Chinese woodcut illustrating the poem quoted from *Li Sao*

men of letters try to escape from reality and seek refuge in mysticism. Their poetry was full of philosophizings and a gloomy preoccupation with death and decay. T'ao Ch'ien, a delightful poet of this period, wrote a poem which is a sort of escapist parable. It tells of a fisherman who followed a tiny stream between orchards of peach blossom until it took him through a cleft in the mountains into a hidden valley where men had lived for hundreds of years cut off from the troubles of the outside world. Later, after his return home, when he wanted to go back to the Happy Valley he could never find the way there again.

The T'ang dynasty (618–906) was a Golden Age in art and literature as well as in wealth and power. Poetry was a compulsory subject in the civil service examinations, and all educated Chinese wrote verses. Of the huge galaxy of T'ang poets perhaps the best-known are Tu Fu, Li Po, and Po Chü-i, much of whose poetry has been translated by Dr. A. Waley. The tone-pattern poetry reached its peak during this period, and poets such as Tu Fu used this highly complicated medium so skilfully that the result has a deceptive appearance of great simplicity. The following little poem by the painter-poet Wang Wei in the original contains only forty words. Not only is there perfect balance in the rhythm of the lines, but the thoughts are balanced as well—for instance, 'bright moon' and 'clear stream'; 'bamboos rustle' and 'lotuses shake'.

> In the silent mountains, fresh from the rain,
> Evening brings the autumn air.
> A bright moon shines through the pine-tree tops;
> The clear stream bubbles over the stones.
> Bamboos rustle as a wash-girl goes by homewards;
> Lotuses shake as a fisherman pushes his boat off.
> Gently the sweets of summer die.
> Princeling, here you may stay.

In China cultured people wrote poetry and pursued classical studies, but such literary occupations as that of the novelist or of the playwright were considered ungentlemanly. During the 13th and 14th centuries, however, when China was under foreign occupation, Chinese educated people, being often unable to obtain government posts, turned their attention to these popular kinds of literature and began to write verse dramas or stories. All Chinese drama until recently was meant to be sung and acted to music, and should more properly be called opera. The music, however, has often been lost, and we can now only guess what the plays were like when performed. Most plays of this period which have survived are very short and sometimes describe only a single episode. The later, longer plays are mostly love-stories with few characters besides the hero and heroine and the emphasis placed on the exquisite beauty of the words rather than on the action.

The novel developed from the art of the professional story-teller. Such story-tellers generally ended a session at some important point in the story with the request to 'come again if you want to know what happened next'. Until comparatively recently novelists still called each chapter a *hui* or 'time', and ended each chapter with 'Next time we shall learn what happened after that'. The earlier novels were usually full of marvels and adventures; but the famous 18th-century novel, *The Dream of the Red Chamber*, is an extremely realistic account of life in a big, wealthy family. The characters are portrayed so vividly that Chinese often argue about their respective merits as warmly as though they were living people.

Except for drama and the novel, all writing was until recently in an archaic 'written language' which only the educated could understand. In 1917, some years after the revolution of SUN YAT-SEN (q.v. Vol. V), a movement was started to replace the written language by the language of everyday speech, and today newspapers, novels, plays, and poems are all written in colloquial language. The greatest writer so far in this new style has been Lu Hsün (1881–1936), a short-story writer whose best-known story, *The True History of Ah Q*, is a favourite with the Chinese. The peasant hero, Ah Q, is an old scamp who endears himself to us by his patient, droll resignation in the face of every conceivable rebuff and humiliation. Some say that Lu Hsün meant to portray in him the China of his own day.

See also Vol. I: CHINESE CIVILIZATION.
See also Vol. IV: CHINESE LANGUAGE.

CHINESE MUSIC, *see* ORIENTAL MUSIC, Section 1.

CHINOISERIE. In the 18th and early 19th centuries Oriental art and decoration—particularly Chinese—were fashionable in Europe. Not only were many things imported from China but

European craftsmen made furniture, pottery, and even buildings in imitation of the Chinese style. Such familiar though outlandish things were produced as the Pagoda in Kew Gardens near London, the Chinese rooms of the Pavilion at Brighton, and the willow-pattern on domestic china. The name 'chinoiserie', which the French gave to these articles and schemes of decoration, was used also in England to describe the things made in imitation of Oriental styles.

Even as early as the days of Queen Elizabeth I people had been excited by the novelty and beauty of Chinese porcelain, silks, and LACQUER cabinets (q.v.); but it was not until late in the 17th century that such articles were brought to Europe in large enough quantities to influence the design of European works of art. A great deal of Chinese lacquer, porcelain, and fabrics came to the West at this time through Dutch merchants. In the reign of William and Mary the 'Chinese Taste' became so popular that English craftsmen made furniture with doors and panels painted in the Chinese fashion with Chinese scenes and landscapes in gold and colours on backgrounds of scarlet, green, and black.

Chinese fashions were given encouragement by the Architect and Surveyor-General to King George III, Sir William Chambers, when he published in 1757 his book *Designs of Chinese Buildings, Furniture, etc.* Chambers had been to China as a young man, and it was he who built the Pagoda at Kew. In 1772 he followed up his book with another on Oriental Gardening, and all over England Chinese bridges and summer-houses appeared in the parks of great houses. Even the flower-beds and crooked paths were laid out in the irregular Chinese fashion, which was carefully planned from the very first to look accidental and casual. In France, Germany, and Scandinavia, Chinese gardens were even more popular than in England. The gay and playful Chinese style was a relief from the stiff, formal gardening which had been in vogue, with straight paths set between clipped hedges, and mathematically designed flower-beds (*see* LAND-SCAPE ART).

Not only the art but also the philosophy and literature of China appealed to Europeans, for Chinese thought had a civilized politeness that was in accord with the ceremonious manners of the 18th century. There was, too, a sense of tolerance for differing points of view, and a

Victoria and Albert Museum

BEDSTEAD DECORATED WITH BLACK AND GOLD LACQUER
Probably made by Chippendale (1718–79) for the Duke of Beaufort

tendency to rely upon common sense rather than upon superstition. In France thinkers such as ROUSSEAU and VOLTAIRE (qq.v. Vol. V), who were planning new forms of society based upon science instead of upon the ideas of the Middle Ages, found inspiration in Chinese philosophy. Thus China became a kind of Utopia to many writers and artists of the time, just as it had been in earlier times a land of wealth and romance to travellers and poets—the legendary Cathay (*see* MARCO POLO, Vol. V).

By the middle of the 18th century people were decorating their rooms with gay, hand-painted Chinese wallpapers showing gardens with flowering trees and shrubs and with brightly plumaged birds in the foliage, and they hung upon their walls Chinese pictures painted on silk or glass. It was the lightness and gaiety of these decorations, in contrast to the dark and heavy furnishings they superseded, that made this fashion so successful.

'Chinese Chippendale' furniture was popular at this time; this had great beauty of design, although it resembled Oriental types only remotely. Even Chinese wallpapers were imitated

The Royal Pavilion, Brighton

THE MUSIC ROOM, ROYAL PAVILION, BRIGHTON
Designed with chinoiserie decoration for the Prince
Regent in 1815

by European craftsmen, as well as furniture of lacquer and imitation bamboo, porcelain ornaments of Chinese figures and groups, and porcelain table-ware with Chinese designs such as the willow-pattern.

The Chinese taste in decoration and furnishing reached its highest pitch of magnificence in the Royal Pavilion at Brighton, the seaside pleasure palace of the Prince Regent, later George IV. The Pavilion was decorated with Chinese wallpapers, and furnished with lacquer cabinets and bamboo chairs, sofas, and stools, made in China for the European market about 1800. In 1815 the Pavilion was enlarged and transformed, and the interior was adorned with immense wall paintings of Chinese scenes in red, yellow, and gold; there were gilded domes, carved dragons, and chandeliers in the form of lotus flowers. Except for lacquer and porcelain, little of this was genuine Chinese workmanship, almost everything being the chinoiserie work of English craftsmen. The Brighton Pavilion was one of the last great schemes of decoration in

the Chinese taste, although traditional Chinese patterns are still popular in, for example, porcelain.

See also CHINESE ART.

CHORALE, *see* HYMNS.

CHRONICLES, *see* HISTORIES.

CHURCH ARCHITECTURE, ENGLISH. 1.
The plan of Christian churches was early evolved to suit the ritual of the services. In spite of changes in the decorative style, this plan has remained essentially the same throughout the centuries. English churches have at all periods followed Continental European styles, but these have been modified to suit the conditions and character of the English (*see* BRITISH ART).

The main body of the church running east and west consists of nave in the centre and aisles at the sides; at right angles to the nave are the north and south transepts; farther east is the chancel, where the ALTAR (q.v.) is placed (Fig. 1). The nave is divided from each aisle by an arcade which supports the wall above it. This wall itself is divided horizontally into the triforium, an arcade of small arches, and the clerestory, a row of windows above it (Fig. 2). The stone VAULT (q.v.) or wooden roof is not so much supported by these arcades and walls as by buttresses built against the outside walls of the church. The height and weight of the vaults built in the 13th century and later needed massive buttresses and flying buttresses to support them. Only large churches and cathedrals have all these features, smaller ones being usually simpler in design.

The majority of medieval English churches were built over long periods, either by being enlarged as the community they served grew richer, or being rebuilt in part or wholly. Before the 12th century many churches were wooden and only one, at Greenstead in Essex, has escaped destruction. A few stone buildings of early dates exist, often incorporated in later churches, such as the 7th-century crypt at Hexham. Not only were the churches enlarged at various periods so that parts are in different styles, but donors added CHANTRY Chapels, elaborate TOMBS, or ROOD SCREENS (qq.v.) in the style of their time. Sometimes a church was modernized: the Norman abbey church at Sherborne, for example, was given a facing in

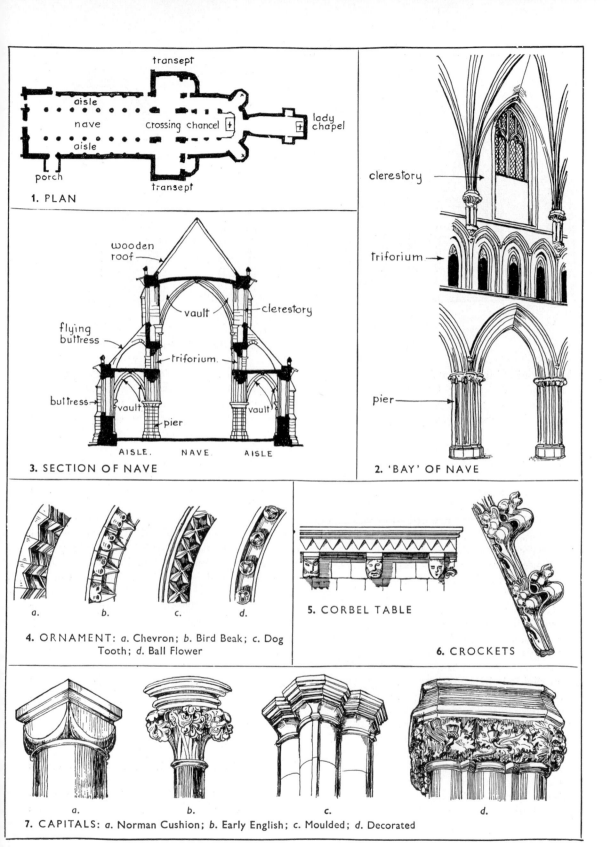

1. PLAN

transept

aisle

nave crossing chancel

aisle

porch

transept

lady chapel

3. SECTION OF NAVE

wooden roof

vault

clerestory

flying buttress

triforium

buttress

vault

pier

vault

AISLE. NAVE. AISLE

2. 'BAY' OF NAVE

clerestory

triforium

pier

4. ORNAMENT: *a.* Chevron; *b.* Bird Beak; *c.* Dog Tooth; *d.* Ball Flower

a.   *b.*   *c.*   *d.*

5. CORBEL TABLE

6. CROCKETS

7. CAPITALS: *a.* Norman Cushion; *b.* Early English; *c.* Moulded; *d.* Decorated

a.   *b.*   *c.*   *d.*

FIGS. 1—7. DETAILS OF ENGLISH MEDIEVAL ARCHITECTURE

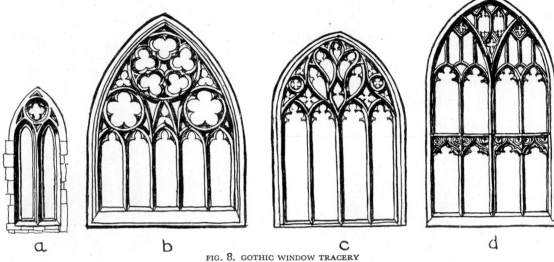

FIG. 8. GOTHIC WINDOW TRACERY
a. Early English; *b.* Geometric; *c.* Decorated; *d.* Perpendicular

the Perpendicular style in the late 14th century, as also was Gloucester Cathedral. Salisbury Cathedral is one of the few examples of a large church built all in one style, most of it between 1220 and 1266 (*see* Plate 2); at Durham a grand central tower was added in the 15th century to the Norman body, and at Westminster Abbey the nave is 100 years later than the 13th-century chancel. Many parish churches, especially in East Anglia and Somerset, were entirely rebuilt in the 15th century when the wool trade was flourishing, but in some cases only the nave, which belonged to the people, was rebuilt and the chancel, the concern of the rector of the parish, was left as it was.

2. SAXON. Saxon builders, who were not very skilful, built small churches with thick walls, narrow, rounded arches, and tiny windows. Sometimes, instead of an arch, two stones were leant together to form a triangular head of a window or door (*see* ARCH). Often fat round pillars divided the windows, and little arcades of arches decorated the walls. These were built of rough-hewn stones with dressed stone at the corners, arranged alternately vertically and horizontally in 'long-and-short' work. The churches usually consist of a rectangular nave, divided from a smaller rectangular chancel by an arch, as at Bradford-on-Avon, Wiltshire. Sometimes, at Earl's Barton in Northamptonshire, for instance, there is a tower at the West End.

3. NORMAN. The Normans built large churches in the Continental style of ROMANESQUE ART (q.v.) with nave and aisles, central tower, and semi-circular apse at the east end. They used the round arch, which was often large and elaborately carved. The Normans themselves were not great sculptors, and the decoration of their churches shows the traditional English love of ornament in the 'chevron' and other geometric forms, and stylized animal forms such as the 'bird beak', which were used in the 12th century (Fig. 4). The capitals are a simple 'cushion' shape or carved with foliage and figures, as in Canterbury Cathedral (Fig. 7 *a, b*). The round pillars are often immensely fat, as at Durham and Tewkesbury Abbey. On the outside flat pilaster buttresses give extra strength, and along the top of the walls there is a band or 'corbel table' of grotesquely carved stones (Fig. 5). Windows are small and walls thick.

4. EARLY ENGLISH. The English architecture of the first phase of GOTHIC ART (q.v.), dating from the end of the 12th century to the second half of the 13th century, is called Early English. Arches are pointed, and windows are tall, narrow 'lancets', either single or grouped in twos, with a circular or quatrefoil window pierced in the wall above each pair (Fig. 8 *a*). From this time the windows were filled with STAINED GLASS (q.v.).

Early English churches are lighter in appearance than the Norman. In the larger churches flying buttresses carry the weight of the vault

STAINED GLASS PANEL IN THE EAST WINDOW OF YORK MINSTER

The window, which has the largest area of stained glass in the world, has 81 panels illustrating the Revelation of St. John the Divine. In this one the Angel forbids St. John to worship him. The window was made in 1405–1408 by John Thornton of Coventry

over the aisle roofs to the buttresses, which stand out from the walls and are crowned with pinnacles (Fig. 3). The pillars of the nave arcades are made to look slender by the thin shafts, often made of grey Purbeck marble, which are attached to them, and which carry the eye upwards to the high vault. The capitals are carved with formal leaves curling over at the top, or simple, deeply cut mouldings (Fig. 7 b); the vaults are divided into a series of compartments by diagonal and transverse ribs.

5. GEOMETRIC AND DECORATED. From about the middle of the 13th century the decoration of churches became more elaborate. The tracery in the head of the windows is arranged in geometric patterns, the curves filled with smaller curves called 'cusps' (Fig. 8 b). Stiff carved leaves ('crockets'), or 'ball-flowers', run up the sides of pinnacles and windows, especially in churches in the west of England, as, for example, at Worcester (Figs. 4 d, 6). The carving becomes more naturalistic (Fig. 7 d), and carving spreads to 'spandrels', the triangular spaces between the arches of arcades, and other parts of the building. Ribs are added to the vaults, carved bosses covering the joints where they cross (see p. 441).

The geometric shapes of the window tracery soon became more flowing as corners were smoothed out (Fig. 8 c). Decorated windows were sometimes astonishingly intricate, as in the west window of Carlisle Cathedral. Everywhere in the church the same lavish ornamentation is evident and the same love of curving, flowing lines, as, for instance, in the ogee or S-shaped arches. Towers are often surmounted by tapering spires.

6. PERPENDICULAR. By the middle of the 14th century a new style had developed in England which was much simpler than the Decorated. By this time the windows had become so large that they practically filled the walls between the buttresses. To make them still bigger the arches were flattened. The glass was supported by vertical 'mullions' and horizontal 'transoms', the mullions being carried right to the top of the window (Fig. 8 d). This emphasis on vertical and horizontal lines is the basis of Perpendicular ornament. The walls are panelled with tracery like that of the windows; the vertical mouldings on the pillars of nave arcades are increased in number and run straight up into the head of the arch, uninterrupted by capitals. The 'fan' vault allows a much flatter roof, in keeping with the flat heads of the windows.

J. R. H. Weaver

SAXON TOWER OF EARL'S BARTON CHURCH, NORTHANTS

A. F. Kersting

ST. WOOLLOS CATHEDRAL CHURCH, NEWPORT, MON.

This Norman Church has rounded arches. The door is decorated with chevron and billet ornament

SHOTTESBROKE CHURCH, BERKSHIRE, BUILT IN 1337

EVERCREECH CHURCH, SOMERSET, LATE 15TH CENTURY

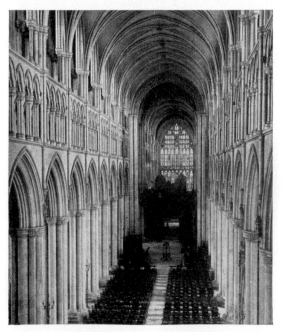

THE NAVE OF BEVERLEY MINSTER

A Gothic church of the 14th century

ST. MARY-LE-STRAND, LONDON

Built by James Gibbs (1682–1754)

7. RENAISSANCE. Few churches were built in England for some while after the Reformation in the 16th century; and by the time church-building was resumed, the Renaissance style of architecture had fully established itself. The form of worship had also changed: less emphasis was placed on the mysteries of religious ritual and more on the word of the preacher; in fact, by the end of the 17th century, when Sir Christopher Wren rebuilt the parish churches of London to replace those destroyed in the Great Fire, the church had become simply a meeting-hall for listening to sermons. The plan of the church was a simple rectangular hall with a shallow chancel opening off it, the hall being generally divided into nave and aisles by rows of pillars. There was usually a gallery with seating for more of the congregation at the west end, and sometimes galleries over the aisles as well, with seats facing inwards. Externally these Renaissance churches were plain rectangular structures, usually with round-headed windows and restrained classical doorways and cornices, and sometimes with porticoes. Many had square towers crowned with cupolas, or with miniature classical temples such as Wren introduced when he designed the spires of his City churches (*see* Vol. V, p. 492).

The same type of classical church persisted until in the mid-19th century the increase in population and a revival of religious activity led to the building of many new churches in the GOTHIC REVIVAL style (q.v.). Since then most English churches have been based on Gothic models.

See also BRITISH ART; MEDIEVAL ART, EARLY; ROMANESQUE ART; GOTHIC ART; GOTHIC REVIVAL; ST. PAUL'S CATHEDRAL.

CHURCH MUSIC, *see* SACRED MUSIC; PLAINSONG.

CLASSICAL ART. This is a term which can be used in two ways, in a narrower or a wider sense, though in order to understand the wider meaning it is necessary to know something of the narrower. In its narrower sense it means the art of ancient Greece or ancient Rome; in its wider sense it means the art of any later age in which the ideas and ideals of antiquity were the main inspiration of the artist. It can, indeed, further be applied to types and phases of art in which the artist has been inspired by similar

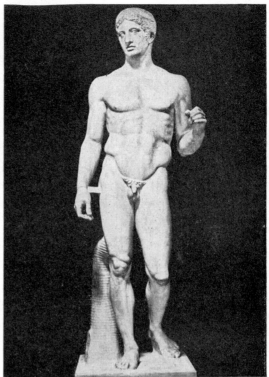

Anderson

THE 'DORYPHORUS'

Marble copy of a bronze by Polycletus (5th century B.C.)

ideals to those of antiquity, even though he knew little or nothing of antique art.

Only a certain kind of antique art can properly be called classical—broadly speaking, that produced in Greece in the hundred years after the middle of the 5th century B.C. (*see* GREEK ART). By then the problems facing earlier artists had been overcome: sculptors could represent the human form naturalistically, in action or at rest, with complete ease. Most sculpture represented gods, but naturalism was not out of place since the Greeks thought of their gods as men, though grander and more perfect than ordinary men. Since they were more perfect, they were also more beautiful than any individual man; consequently the artists sought for an ideal beauty not only in features and limbs but above all in the proportions of the human body. The sculptor Polycletus worked out from the study of the nude figures of Greek athletes a rule or canon of proportions, which he embodied in his athlete statue known as the 'Doryphorus', and which was accepted as the standard of perfection. Features, also, were generalized rather than particularized; if the figure was in action, or showing emotion, the artist sought for the mean which was common to all men, rather than the extreme which might be felt by one man at one moment. In female figures, too, the same combination of the most perfect features, taken from a number of different models, may be seen.

Classical art, therefore, is ideal, rather than individual and personal. It is a balanced and an intellectual rather than an emotional art. It is calm rather than violent, for violence is transitory, and it seeks always for eternal values rather than for changing moods.

The calm, ordered beauty seen in classical sculpture was also sought by architects. They, too, found it through a system of proportions, in which the size of every part of the building, even of the smallest moulding, was calculated and fixed in relation to other parts, and all to the whole (*see* ORDERS OF ARCHITECTURE).

Archives Photographiques

'LA BELLE JARDINIÈRE' BY RAPHAEL (1483–1520)
This is classical in the clear, geometric composition with the figures arranged in the shape of a pyramid, and in their static poses and restrained expressions. (*Louvre*)

Moreover, just as sculptors avoided violent emotions, architects avoided strong dramatic emphasis on any single part of the building. They used instead a quiet repetition of simple forms—columns with mouldings above them—making the main motive of their design a balance between uprights and horizontals, and thus achieving the harmony they desired.

Classical Greek art has had a long influence in Europe. It appealed greatly to the Romans when they conquered Greece. They borrowed Greek architectural forms, brought some Greek statues to Rome, and copied many more. Indeed, many Greek originals are known to us only through such copies. Unfortunately many of these copies were weak and even a little vulgar, and consequently later ages, to whom the Greek originals were almost unknown since Greece was under Turkish domination, held these poor copies to be representative of the classical ideal. Much Roman art, however, is also truly classical in its search for ideal beauty. This is specially true of the work produced under the Emperors Augustus (27 B.C.–A.D. 14) and Hadrian (A.D. 117–138), who were both high-minded men who wished to establish a good and serious standard of values among their subjects. So here, as always, art reflects the outlook of the society for which it is produced.

We know relatively little about classical painting in the antique world, since hardly anything except minor works, such as painting on vases, has survived. But descriptions exist in, for instance, the writings of Pausanias and Pliny, which show that the same attempt to find rules leading to the creation of ideal beauty was normal to painters as well as sculptors.

Such descriptions are part of the heritage of classical literature which has played so great a part in the civilization of western Europe (*see* GREEK LITERATURE). Writers, also, sought to achieve perfection of form and to express noble ideas in beautiful language. The same discipline of rules can be found, though here the rules are concerned with the order of a sentence or the structure and scansion of a poem. This literature, and the visible remains of sculpture and architecture, gave rise to the view that antiquity was a Golden Age in which the achievements of man were more noble than in any subsequent age. Artists and their patrons turned to antiquity for inspiration; sometimes they had a true perception of the underlying

Earl of Derby

'THE WOMAN OF MEGARA GATHERING THE ASHES OF PHOCION' BY NICOLAS POUSSIN (1594–1665)
Phocion was an Athenian general, so the subject is classical as well as the treatment, with the balanced groups of trees and classical buildings

and eternal value of the search for ideal beauty, for which they felt the need in their own lives, while at other times they imitated the outward forms only, because it was fashionable to do so.

It is perhaps at the time of the RENAISSANCE (q.v. Vol. I) that the impact of classical art can be most clearly seen, though indeed earlier masters, including GIOTTO himself (q.v. Vol. V), had been influenced by its humane and dignified conceptions. In the 15th century some Italian artists show in their figures the same search for essentials, the same feeling for the heroic grandeur of the human body, that appears in classical antiquity. Their conscious imitation of classical models led them to use antique dress and to represent antique subjects, but they did not render completely the concept of ideal beauty. In the early years of the 16th century in Rome, however, at the time known as the High Renaissance, a truly classical art appeared. The study of classical writers, above all of PLATO (q.v. Vol. V), resulted in an attempt to combine the noblest classical thought with Christianity, and for this combination the classical concept of

ideal beauty was the perfect form of expression. It can be seen most strongly in the work of RAPHAEL and in the early works of MICHEL-ANGELO (qq.v. Vol. V), but almost all contemporary Italian artists were touched by it. Raphael's art is perhaps the most perfect example of the classical spirit since antiquity. It is not simply a revival or a copying of classical forms, for the artist discovered for himself that the eternal values that he and his contemporaries were seeking could best be expressed in art by the calm purity of ideal beauty.

The same approach can be seen in the mature works of the great 17th-century French artist, Nicolas POUSSIN (q.v. Vol. V). The ordered reasoning of the classical ideal has always had a special appeal to the French, and never more than in the middle of the 17th century, the age of CORNEILLE, of the foundation of the French Academy, and of the great mathematician and philosopher, René DESCARTES (qq.v. Vol. V). Just as French writers, for instance, sought to impose order and logic of thought and action on the DRAMA (q.v.), so Poussin in his paintings,

Duke of Sutherland

THE LEVESON-GOWER CHILDREN BY GEORGE ROMNEY (1734–1802)
Though the faces are carefully studied portraits, the poses, drapery, and composition suggest classical models

whether they were of Christian or antique subjects, pursued relentlessly his search for an ordered ideal beauty (*see* FRENCH ART). He found much in classical antiquity and in the work of Raphael to help him; he drew on the developing science of mathematics to reinforce his conviction that simple forms—the pyramid, the cube, and the cylinder—have in themselves an abstract ideal beauty. He used these as the basis of his figure compositions and his landscape paintings, thus introducing a new aspect of ideal beauty which was to influence modern painters such as CÉZANNE (q.v. Vol. V). His figures are ideal types rather than individuals, displaying in their actions feelings which are known to all men, but which are shown on the highest plane. Both Poussin and Corneille express the thought of their own time in an heroic art which seeks for a perfect balance between form and content, and both have their place among the great classical artists of Europe. In England this balance was sought especially by writers in the late 17th and early 18th centuries, that is, in the AUGUSTAN AGE (q.v.).

Classical architecture, too, has had a continuous influence. From the early years of the Renaissance classical buildings were studied, and the design of buildings was based on antique forms. The classical orders have ever since formed the basis of much architectural design, as for instance in the GEORGIAN ARCHITECTURE (q.v.) of England.

In the middle of the 18th century renewed interest in classical art led to the Neo-classical Revival throughout Europe. Some of those who have sought for the classical ideal have failed to achieve great art because they thought that an imitation of antique art was enough— in other words that the form was all that mattered, and not the ideas that were being expressed. This was the weakness of much Neo-classical art. It was primarily the result of a fashion for antiquity, fostered partly by the development of the Grand Tour, which made a journey to Rome an indispensable part of the education of every young gentleman, and partly by the excitement caused by the rediscovery of the buried Roman cities of Herculaneum and Pompeii (q.v.) and then by a growing awareness of ancient Greece. Little Greek temples were set up as summer-houses in English gardens, and ladies in classical costumes mourn their dead husbands on innumerable tombs, cut with the smooth and rather empty technique of poor copies of Greek statues. Robert Adam (q.v. Vol. V) used Greek patterns in the decoration of his houses, but often on architectural forms which have not the proportions of true classical art. The fashion extended to pottery, and Josiah Wedgwood (q.v. Vol. V) reproduced on his wares the motifs from Greek vases. Some Neo-classical works have a fragile charm of their own, but it is on the whole a graceful, senti-mentalized, and rather empty imitation appro-priate to an age which regarded 'enthusiasm' as bad taste. It is not surprising that the Romantic Movement (q.v.) of the 19th century, which ultimately destroyed Neo-classicism, be-lieved in the unclassical ideals of the expression of violent and personal emotions.

Though much of 18th-century art shows the danger of imitating outward form, the classical ideal of a disciplined, ordered beauty can be seen in most 18th-century music. In the works of Bach, as in those of Nicolas Poussin, there is a mathematical precision of form, but neither Bach nor Mozart (qq.v. Vol. V), the two greatest classical composers, seem to have had any difficulty in combining the lovely content of melody with the discipline of form. If one com-pares the music of Mozart with that of Wagner (q.v. Vol. V), it is easy to understand how the term classical can be applied to music. Mozart, like a classical poet, accepts certain rules govern-ing the structure of a piece of music, and pro-duces form and content perfectly combined. Wagner, a Romantic composer, makes his own personal form, ignoring the older rules, and creates a tempestuous music emphasizing the changing passions of the characters of the drama, which is impossible to understand unless one knows the plot. This lies at the other extreme from all true classical art, which aims at a disciplined clarity of statement and at a perfec-tion both of form and content. These charac-teristics have been sought and achieved by many European artists and writers at different periods, sometimes without conscious reference to an-tiquity.

See also Art; Greek Art; Italian Art.

See also Vol. I: Greek Civilization; Roman Civiliza-tion.

CLEOPATRA'S NEEDLE, see Monuments.

CLERIHEW, see Comic Verse, Section 3.

CLOISTER. This is a courtyard, attached to a cathedral or abbey, and also to be found in old university buildings. It is surrounded by a covered walk, which looks into the central space (called the 'garth') through an arcade. The cloister (or rather its surrounding paved walk, called the ambulatory) provided a covered pas-sage from the cathedral or abbey-church to its subsidiary buildings; it served as a meeting-place and as a place where the clergy or monks could take air and exercise in private and where, in warm weather, they could perform tasks such as copying the scriptures and doing the abbey's accounts. Sometimes there were wall-fountains where the monks could wash before going to meals. The cloister was generally in the most sheltered position, south of the nave and west of the transept. It was customary to set aside at certain times of the day one side of the ambulatory for clergy of high rank. The garth is sometimes planted as a garden; some-times it is simply an area of grass.

Many cathedrals and monastic buildings in England and on the Continent have beautiful cloisters, though they are rare in French cathe-drals, because these were not connected with monasteries. Several Spanish cathedrals, notably Avila and Barcelona, have exceptionally fine cloisters which provide shelter from the hot sun. Among the oldest as well as the most beautiful are the Romanesque cloisters at the churches of St. Trophime at Arles, in France, and Monreale

Archives Photographiques

13TH-CENTURY CLOISTER OF ST. HILAIRE, AUDE, FRANCE

in Sicily. Among English cathedrals the best cloisters are to be found at Canterbury, Durham, Norwich, Salisbury, Wells, and Gloucester, the last being notable for its intricate fan vaulting. On the Continent there are a number of cloisters with two-storey ambulatories (for example, Verona and Assisi) and at least one (at Monte Oliveto Maggiore, in Tuscany) with three stories.

See also MONASTIC ARCHITECTURE.

COINS, *see* Vol. VII: COINS.

COLOSSEUM. This huge amphitheatre in Rome was so named in the Middle Ages because it stood near a colossal statue of the old pagan sun-god. It had been built by Vespasian on the site of an artificial lake belonging to Nero's Golden House, and replaced an earlier building destroyed in the fire of Rome under Nero (A.D. 64). It was enlarged and completed under the Emperor Titus and dedicated in A.D. 80. The oval plan measures 576 yards in circumference, 206 yards long, and 170 yards across. The outside wall, originally about 162 feet high, is built in four storeys. The first three consist of open arches, each storey decorated with a different ORDER OF ARCHITECTURE (q.v.): Tuscan in the lowest, Ionic in the second, and Corinthian in the third. Under the arches stood marble statues. Titus added a fourth and top storey, decorated with pilasters and windows. The windows are alternately large and small, and above the small ones, which are set level with the pilaster-bases, the Emperor Domitian (A.D. 51–96) added bronze shields. A row of stone corbels projecting from the top of the outside wall held wooden poles to which an awning was attached. The eighty arches of the lowest storey gave access to a corridor from which sixteen staircases led up to the auditorium. The seats, which held 45,000 spectators and were originally marble-covered, rested on barrel-vaults lying transversely across seven concentric rings of pillars encircling the arena and increasing in height towards the outside. Above the highest row of seats the top gallery was treated as a colonnaded portico with standing space. The arena was fitted for gladiatorial combats and wild beast fights and could be flooded for mock sea-battles. It was also the scene of many Christian martyrdoms.

See also ROMAN ART.

THE COLOSSEUM, ROME

COLOSSUS OF RHODES, *see* WONDERS OF THE WORLD.

COLOUR, *see* PAINTING METHODS. *See also* Vol. III: COLOUR.

COMEDY. 1. Comedy probably evolved from rough country revels held in ancient Greece (*see* GREEK DRAMA). The aim of comedy has always been to amuse or delight audiences, but, as there are many ways of causing mirth, so there are many different kinds of comedy. It ranges from the romantic other-worldliness of Shakespeare's *A Midsummer Night's Dream* to the fashionable social comedies of RESTORATION DRAMA (q.v.). Its humour, which depends sometimes on situation, sometimes on the wit of the dialogue, can be delicate or cruel. Comedy deals always with the relations between man and his fellows, and the dramatic interest is therefore dispersed among a group of characters; not, as in tragedy, concentrated on one figure and his conflicts. The main characters of comedy can be persons of any social class, while tragedy prefers the great and princely. And comedies always have a happy ending.

The greatest comedies of the world were written in Athens in the 5th century B.C., in Elizabethan and Restoration England, and in 17th-century France. The greatest comic writers of those periods were respectively ARISTOPHANES, SHAKESPEARE, Congreve, and MOLIÈRE (qq.v. Vol. V).

Three of the many types of comedy are easily distinguishable: satiric comedy (*see* SATIRE), which springs from the true satirist's wish to improve society by mocking its vices; the comedy of manners, in which the author, while accepting the code of his society, is urbanely and wittily amused and amusing about its manners and its modes of behaviour; and the comedy of romance, with a love interest at the heart of its plot, usually with a country setting, moving laughter by humour rather than by wit, and giving delight by its harmonious poetry. Other types merge into burlesque, farce, and light entertainment.

2. *Classical Comedy.* The comedy of ancient Greece and Rome, and the Renaissance comedies which are based on classical models, usually contain elements from all three types. The witty, satiric plays of the Athenian poet Aristophanes ridiculed literary and political ideas and

Phot. Larousse

A FARCE ACTED BY STROLLING PLAYERS IN THE 16TH CENTURY

the personalities of his day. They made fun of what was going on in the city or the nation, and they often introduced real characters—a topical note which was seldom found in tragedy. It was said that during a performance of the *Clouds* of Aristophanes which introduced SOC-RATES (q.v. Vol. V) the philosopher himself got up to let the audience see how much the character on the stage resembled him. This kind of Attic comedy has had no successful imitators, though the satire it initiated has been a main theme of comedy. After Aristophanes, the Athenian dramatist Menander (342–291 B.C.) developed what came to be known as Greek 'New' comedy. These plays were less satiric, humorous rather than witty, and mirrored contemporary life. The plots usually turned on a love entanglement, which ended happily, but only after various obstacles to the lovers' union had been overcome. Often the identity of a child, established through some trinket, led to the reconciliation of its estranged parents. Me-

nander was closely imitated by the Latin writers, Plautus (*c.* 254–184 B.C.) and Terence (*c.* 190–159 B.C.), who in turn served as models for Renaissance writers. Terence's six urbane plays strongly influenced Molière and the Restoration writers, while Plautus's robust comedies, which had greater variety, had a correspondingly wider influence. They included romantic, domestic, and sentimental comedies, burlesque, and farcical comedies such as *Miles Gloriosus*.

All types of modern comedy derive from these plays. For example, the first English comedy, *Ralph Roister Doister* (*c.* 1553), has as its chief character a boastful soldier closely modelled on *Miles Gloriosus*. But the native comic genius of each country, while taking over all that it needed from the classical models, had its own vigorous growth. Comic characters and situations of a truly English type can be found in the medieval MIRACLE PLAYS (q.v.). The second English comedy, *Gammer Gurton's Needle* (1566), adopted the construction and division into acts of classical plays, but its farcical plot, its village characters, and its broad humour are entirely English.

3. *Satiric Comedy.* In England satiric comedy is best represented by Ben JONSON (q.v. Vol. V). In Jonson's plays the characters are so dominated by their 'humour', or ruling tendency, that it is difficult to find anyone who is normal. This 'comedy of humours', as it is called, harshly exposes vices which cause unhappiness: in *The Alchemist*, the avarice of the confidence trickster, and the credulity of those who long for sudden riches; and in *Bartholomew Fair*, the hypocrisy of the Puritan. Among Restoration dramatists, William Wycherley (*c.* 1640–1716) alone has the 'savage indignation' of the satirist. The plays of Molière, France's greatest comic dramatist, have something of satiric comedy as well as the comedy of manners in them. Molière's satire is searching, but, unlike Ben Jonson's, genial; the humour springs both from dialogue and situation, and farce and burlesque contribute to it. Molière's aim, as he himself stated, was primarily to teach lessons of morality and conduct. In the present century, Bernard SHAW's problem-plays (q.v. Vol. V) have a strong vein of satiric comedy. These are mainly conversation-pieces, almost comedies of debate, in which, like Molière, Shaw tried to make people think as well as laugh.

4. *Comedy of Manners.* The intention of this type of comedy is simply to entertain, by wit rather than humour, and it demands a highly cultivated and worldly audience. Such an audience was provided in the 17th century by fashionable London society for the plays of Congreve and others (*see* RESTORATION DRAMA); by the brilliant Court of Louis XIV for Molière; and by 18th-century Venetian society for the social comedies of Goldoni (1707–93). With the rise of the middle classes in the 18th and 19th centuries, the comedy of manners became sentimental, moral, and less comic. Indeed, the spirit of comedy is more evident in Gay's *Beggar's Opera* than in any English drama of that period. Only GOLDSMITH and SHERIDAN (qq.v. Vol. V), who unfolded amusing and complicated plots with a fresh, sparkling wit, protested against the sentimental drama and outlived it. Sheridan's *The Critic* is a clever burlesque of the absurd tragic dramas of his day. At the end of the 19th century the comedy of manners reappeared in the elegant, artificial plays of Oscar Wilde (1854–1900). In the 20th century

Somerset Maugham and Noel Coward have written plays in the same tradition.

5. *Comedy of Romance.* This type of comedy was raised by Shakespeare to a degree of perfection never before or since attained (*see* SHAKESPEARIAN DRAMA). Shakespeare owed to his predecessors the structure of his dramas, and the plots of ten of his comedies. For his first, *The Comedy of Errors*, for example, he borrowed and blended the plots of two of Plautus's plays. His settings owe much to the PASTORAL convention (q.v.), and the blank verse which he mainly used was already wrought for him. But the poetry, the characters, and the quality of his comedies are his own. His great understanding and his dramatic genius created characters who live and move within the borrowed plots so convincingly that his comedies have been called comedies of nature. Nature in all her moods plays an important part. The sunlight would not be so radiant without the contrasting shadow of natural disaster, of death, shipwreck, and storm. Even though the disasters and deaths prove to have no substance, but to be shadows indeed, they contribute to the effect. Shakespeare blended all that he inherited with all that he conceived to produce his thirteen enchanting and varied comedies, each with its own unity of feeling, ranging from the light fantastic revelry of *A Midsummer Night's Dream* to the deep serenity of *The Tempest*.

Romantic comedy was treated in many different ways by Shakespeare's contemporaries and successors. Chapman added melodrama; Dekker, in such plays as *The Shoemaker's Holiday*, grafted lively, realistic pictures of city life on to conventional romantic plots; Beaumont and Fletcher produced mock-heroic burlesques such as *The Knight of the Burning Pestle*; and Fletcher's plays included tragi-comedy, such as *The Faithful Shepherdess*, or combined a romantic plot with a 'comedy of humours', as in *Monsieur Thomas*.

Thereafter the conventional plots of romantic comedy deserted the drama for OPERA (q.v.) and light opera. Of the plays of the last hundred years, those of CHEKHOV (q.v. Vol. V) can be described as comedies, because of their ironic humour; but the laughter they induce is near to tears. Synge's *Playboy of the Western World* with its poetry, its Irish landscape, and its swaggering hero is a new version of the old romantic comedy of error.

See also DRAMA; GREEK DRAMA; SHAKESPEARIAN DRAMA; RESTORATION DRAMA.

COMIC VERSE. Some poetry can be funny in the way that a circus clown is funny: the clown shocks his audience into laughter by means of antics that are ludicrous, incongruous, or fantastic, and comic verse also produces its humorous effects by these means. Its humour is more boisterous than intellectual; it is akin to wit and SATIRE (q.v.), but lacks the subtlety of the one and the pointed purpose of the other.

Comic verse falls roughly into three categories, which sometimes overlap: (1) funny stories told in verse, (2) verse in which the language itself produces the humorous effect, and (3) nonsense verse.

1. *Funny stories.* Many great English poets, for example, CHAUCER (q.v. Vol. V) and Skelton, have written amusing stories in verse. Matthew Prior, in the early 18th century, was a master in this vein, and in the 19th century this type of verse became very popular. Poets in the 19th century often obtained a comic effect by means of an incongruity between their gruesome or solemn subject-matter and the light way in which they treated it. Thomas Hood (1799–1845), an extremely accomplished poet in both serious and comic styles, excelled at comic-gruesome verses and at producing an amusing effect by contrasts:

> Play on, play on,
> My elfin John,
> Toss the light ball—bestride the stick—
> (I knew so many cakes would make him sick!)
> ('A Parental Ode to My Son')

R. H. Barham in *The Ingoldsby Legends* (1840) treated medieval stories in a grotesque way. These poems were favourites for drawing-room recitations in Victorian days, although some of their humour seems a little too gruesome for modern taste:

> Oh! tis shocking to view
> The sight which the corpse reveals!
> Sir Thomas's body, it looks so odd—he
> Was half eaten up by the eels!

W. S. Gilbert also knew the comic effect produced by the mock-shudder, and frequently used it in his *Bab Ballads* (1869):

> . . . When I ups with his heels, and smothers his squeals
> In the scum of the boiling broth.
> ('The Yarn of the *Nancy Bell*')

Many modern writers shock their readers into laughter in a similar way, notably Hilaire Belloc in his *Cautionary Verses* and Harry Graham in *Ruthless Rhymes*:

> The Aged Patriot groaned and died:
> And gracious! how Lord Lundy cried!
> (Hilaire Belloc)
> Making toast at the fireside,
> Nurse fell in the grate and died;
> And what makes it ten times worse,
> All the toast was burnt with nurse.
> (Harry Graham)

2. *Comic effects produced by the language itself.* Incongruous similes have caused amusement through the ages, for example, Shakespeare's 'His eyes were green as leeks', Samuel Butler's 'And like a lobster boiled, the morn From black to red began to turn', and John Gay's song beginning 'My passion is as mustard strong'. Many poets have also been fond of using puns, in particular Thomas Hood:

> Ben Battle was a soldier bold,
>   And used to war's alarms;
> But a cannon-ball took off his legs,
>   So he laid down his arms.
>
> Now as they bore him off the field,
>   Said he, 'Let others shoot,
> For here I leave my second leg,
>   And the Forty-Second Foot!'
> ('Faithless Nellie Gray').

Hood also wrote poems which amuse by virtue of their ingenious rhymes or metres, as does his 'Nocturnal Sketch' with its triple rhymes at the end of each line. W. S. Gilbert also displayed extreme ingenuity and gusto in rhyming and metre:

> For your brain is on fire—the bedclothes conspire
>   of usual slumber to plunder you:
> First your counterpane goes, and uncovers your
>   toes, and your sheet slips demurely from under
>   you;
> Then the blanketing tickles—you feel like mixed
>   pickles—so terribly sharp is the pricking,
> And you're hot and you're cross, and you tumble
>   and toss till there's nothing 'twixt you and the
>   ticking . . .
> ('Nightmare')

Poets of the 19th century were also fond of PARODY (q.v.), but the humour of this is usually more witty than comic. Modern writers sometimes use comically distorted words to produce a humorous effect:

In spite of her sniffle
Isabel's chiffle.
Some girls with a sniffle
Would be weepy and tiffle . . .
But when Isabel's snivelly
She's snivelly civilly,
And when she's snuffly
She's perfectly luffly.

(Ogden Nash)

3. *Nonsense poetry.* The best nonsense poetry was written in the mid-19th century by Edward Lear and Lewis CARROLL (q.v. Vol. V). Their poetry, unlike other forms of comic verse, was written for children, and some of it is clearly derived from nursery rhymes.

The difference between Lear and Carroll has been said to be that the latter wrote nonsense by exaggerating sense, and made up his nonsense words in an intellectual way, but Lear wrote nonsense that is an excess of poetic imagination and coined words for the sake of their colour and sound alone. Lear is the better poet of these two men of genius, but Carroll's *Hunting of the Snark* is the longest and most successfully sustained nonsense poem in the language, and his 'Jabberwocky' and 'White Knight's Song' perhaps the most famous shorter poems of this kind:

'Twas brillig, and the slithy toves
　Did gyre and gimble in the wabe;
All mimsy were the borogoves,
　And the mome raths outgrabe.

('Jabberwocky')

He said 'I hunt for haddocks' eyes
　Among the heather bright,
And work them into waistcoat-buttons
　In the silent night'.

('White Knight's Song')

Edward Lear had an exquisite sense of rhythm, and his nonsense verses often have a romantic melancholy so that the reader finds himself carried along with sympathetic emotions as he reads about the fortunes of the Dong with the luminous Nose who dwelt on 'the great Gromboolian plain, Through the long, long wintry nights'; of the Jumblies whose 'heads are green, and their hands are blue'; of the Pobble with his Aunt Jobiska; and of the Courtship of the Yonghy-Bonghy-Bo:

On the coast of Coromandel,
Where the early pumpkins blow,
In the middle of the woods,
Lived the Yonghy-Bonghy-Bo.

The well-known 5-line verse known as the limerick (after its supposed place of origin) was

ILLUSTRATION BY EDWARD LEAR TO HIS LIMERICK 'THERE WAS AN OLD MAN OF AOSTA'

not actually invented by Lear, but he first made
it popular. The first collection of his limericks,
with his own illustrations, was published in
1846. These verses are always pure nonsense,
and nearly always the last line ends with the
same words as the first:

> There was an Old Man of Aosta,
> Who possessed a large cow, but he lost her;
>   But they said: 'Don't you see
>   She has rushed up a tree?
> You invidious Old Man of Aosta!'

Nowadays the limerick has grown more
sophisticated: its humour is more pointed and
less nonsensical, and the fifth line does not
usually repeat the first:

> There was a young belle of old Natchez
> Whose garments were always in patchez.
>   When comments arose,
>   On the state of her clothes
> She drawled 'When Ah itches, Ah scratchez'.
>
> (Ogden Nash)

Some later variations of the limerick consist
of a verse with rhymes which are similar to the
eye but not to the ear, such as *dough* and *cough*,
or a verse where the ear supplies the missing
rhyme:

> There was an old man from Dunoon,
> Who always ate soup with a fork,
>   For he said 'As I eat
>   Neither fish, fowl nor flesh,
> I should finish my dinner too quick.'

Another form of nonsense jingle that is very
popular nowadays is the 'clerihew', originated
by Edmund Clerihew Bentley in 1905. Modern
comic verse usually avoids elaborate metres
and rhymes, and the clerihew is no exception
to this. It is a 4-line verse, loosely constructed,
and usually makes its comic effect by absurdly
incongruous statements about famous people:

> Edward the Confessor
> Slept under the dresser
> When that began to pall,
> He slept in the hall.

or

> What I like about Clive
> Is that he is not longer alive.
> There is a great deal to be said
> For being dead.

CONCERTO. The modern concerto with
soloist and full orchestra is the outcome of a
very long development in the organization of
music. It comes from an instinct as old as
music itself—an instinct for obtaining variety
and unity by contrasting and combining a solo
effort and a mass effort. This principle can be
seen in many children's games, in folk-dances
where one dancer or a pair of dancers take the
lead and others follow, and even in the versicles
and responses which have always formed a part
of religious liturgies.

The actual word concerto was formerly applied to various types of composition in which
more than one group of performers was engaged;
in the 18th century it came to be allotted specially to the works of certain Italian masters, in
which a soloist or a group of soloists was combined with an orchestra. The soloists were the
concertino; the main body of players was the
ripieno. Among the most famous of these 18th-
century *Concerti Grossi*, as they were called, were
the 'Brandenburg' Concertos of J. S. BACH and
the Twelve Grand Concertos of HANDEL (qq.v.
Vol. V).

The form of these concertos varied to some
extent, but was generally based on that of the
contemporary SONATA (q.v.). Generally there
were three or four movements; sometimes, as in
the first 'Brandenburg' Concerto, some dance
movements were included, which made the
concerto not unlike a suite (*see* DANCE MUSIC).

The fifth 'Brandenburg' Concerto shows that
the part allotted to the soloist in an 18th-century
concerto could be a very brilliant and prominent
one; and as the technical ability of players increased, the tendency to write music which displayed their skill also increased. Side by side
with this development went the growth of skill
in the composition of the SYMPHONY and the art
of ORCHESTRATION (qq.v.). In the latter half of
the 18th century, moreover, people were beginning to want music of an emotional, dramatic,
and personal kind, and the concerto with its
emphasis on the individuality of a soloist was
able to supply this want. MOZART (q.v. Vol. V),
gifted equally as performer and composer, and
possessed of a fine dramatic instinct, was specially
qualified to write as well as to produce concertos.
He wrote over forty, for various instruments,
and solved in doing so most of the problems that
arise in the composition of a work in symphonic
style for soloist and orchestra.

During the 19th century the pianoforte developed from the comparatively light-toned

Walker Art Gallery, Liverpool

THE FAMILY OF SIR WILLIAM YOUNG
Conversation Piece by Zoffany (1733–1810)

instrument that BEETHOVEN (q.v. Vol. V) knew into the concert-grand of the modern platform (*see* KEYBOARD INSTRUMENTS, Section 4, Vol. IX). The power and brilliance of players increased too, and technical skill became so great as to be sometimes oppressive. The old idea of a concerto as a shared performance between one or more soloists and an orchestra, with responsibilities of equal importance, partly gave way to a conception of the concerto as a solo performance with accompaniment provided by an orchestra; this tended to rob concerto form of some of its former balance and perfection. In recent years there has been something of a swing back, and many modern composers have tried to restore the old relationship between soloist and orchestra.

The form of the concerto has changed but little since it was established by Mozart. It is usually in three movements. The first movement is like that of a sonata or symphony, except that in most cases the principal subjects are stated twice at the opening, first by the orchestra and then by the soloist. In detail, however, there are considerable differences, due to the material of particular concertos: each work must be examined separately and treated as an individual. The second movement is generally a slow one. The finale can be either in sonata form, or in rondo form, or even a set of variations (*see* MUSICAL FORM).

At the climax of the first movement and sometimes again in the last it was usual to introduce a cadenza: that is, a passage of solo-work leading up to the final cadence, often improvised by the soloist. In recent times this opportunity for brilliant execution has sometimes been misused, and cadenzas have earned rather a bad name in modern concert halls. But a well planned cadenza can add much to the effect of a movement, and even (as in the Brahms Violin Concerto) provide some of the finest movements of the work. A concerto movement, moreover, which has no cadenza can sound curiously incomplete. It is safe to say that in classical concertos where opportunity is provided for a cadenza the composers designed their movements in such a way that they sound unbalanced if the cadenza is omitted. Sometimes the cadenza is written by the composer, but sometimes later composers have provided cadenzas which are now performed.

See also MUSIC; SONATA; SYMPHONY.

CONCERTS, see Vol. IX: CONCERTS.

CONDUCTING, see Vol. IX: CONDUCTING.

CONVERSATION PIECE. This term is applied to a kind of portrait painting which flourished in England in the mid-18th century. Conversation pieces are usually of only moderate size and show members of well-to-do families naturally grouped as if in conversation. The background is always part of the property of the sitters—their private park or a room in their house—and for that reason the conversation piece is one of the most personal kinds of painting. It is a portrait not only of the people but also of their property.

Pictures which look at first sight like the English conversation piece were painted in Holland in the 17th century by such artists as Ter Borch or Metsu. But these pictures of Dutch ladies and gentlemen, often grouped round a spinet, represent the life and activities of a class rather than portraits of individuals (see GENRE PAINTING), and their names are never given. The English conversation piece is essentially of particular individual people—'The Family of Sir William Young' (see p. 95), for example. The families concerned seem to have desired that some hint of their prosperity, though not too ostentatious to exceed the bounds of good taste, should be given in the picture. Two of the most famous and successful painters of English conversation pieces are Copley, an American, and Zoffany, a German. Perhaps, being foreigners, they could see the English character more truly than native artists.

The few conversation pieces painted by Thomas GAINSBOROUGH (q.v. Vol. V) are among the best of all. Though some artists still occasionally paint them, on the whole conversation pieces were the product of the elegance and refinement of English 18th-century society and virtually ended with it.

See also BRITISH ART; PORTRAITS.

CORINTHIAN ORDER, see ORDERS OF ARCHITECTURE.

COUNTERPOINT, see HARMONY.

CROSSES, STONE. The finest early standing stone crosses in the Christian world are in Britain. Several of these date from the 7th and 8th centuries, and for the skill and beauty of their carving they have no equal. They are something of a mystery, for no other stone carving of that date exists in western Europe, and it is improbable that the native inhabitants of Britain should suddenly have achieved, unaided, such an extremely high standard of stone carving. Some of the types of ornament used, such as the vine scroll, originated in the Mediterranean and Near Eastern countries, and so it is presumed that these crosses were carved at first by workmen from eastern Italy or Byzantium who accompanied the churchmen who brought Christianity from Rome in the 7th century.

All the crosses are damaged, but considerable portions of many remain, the finest and most ambitious of them being the crosses at Ruthwell in Dumfriesshire, Bewcastle in Cumberland, and the more damaged cross at Reculver in Kent. These three have more elaborate and accomplished figure carving than any of the others, some of which are decorated almost entirely with designs of birds and beasts, interlacing, and vine scrolls. Most of these crosses are in the north, possibly an accident of survival. A few of them were put up as memorials, but the erection of high crosses, probably of timber, had probably been introduced earlier by Irish missionaries. Some very elaborate stone crosses sculptured with interlacing patterns have survived in Ireland from the 9th and 10th centuries, notably those at Clonmacnoise and Monasterboice (see p. 253).

Though the skill of carving declined for a time, crosses continued to be erected on holy sites, in churchyards, and in places where people gathered together such as in markets, where they were used as centres for preaching. Late in the Middle Ages the market crosses in the big towns became buildings of considerable importance and were used for other purposes besides preaching. Crosses continued to be erected in churchyards and used as centres for preaching; there was a famous one in London outside St. Paul's Cathedral.

Rather different are the Eleanor Crosses built by Edward I in memory of his queen. She died at Hardby in Lincolnshire in 1290, and from

THE MELBOURNE AND MILBANKE FAMILIES. PAINTING BY GEORGE STUBBS (1724–1806)

ROBERT ANDREWS AND HIS WIFE. PAINTING BY THOMAS GAINSBOROUGH (1727–88)

PLATE 6 CROSSES, STONE

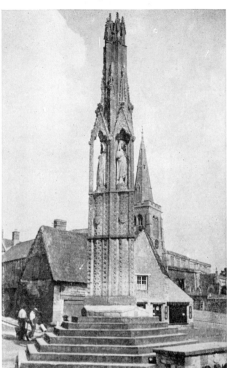

LEFT: THE RUTHWELL CROSS
7TH CENTURY
The sculptures represent St. John the Baptist, Christ, two Saints, and the Flight into Egypt

RIGHT: THE ELEANOR CROSS, GEDDINGTON, NORTHANTS.
It was set up in 1294 to mark one of the resting places of Queen Eleanor's funeral cortège

BELOW: THE POULTRY CROSS, SALISBURY
A 14th-century market cross

there to Westminster, where she was buried, Edward I erected a cross at every place where the funeral procession rested. There were probably eleven altogether, including those at Lincoln and Charing Cross. Three nearly complete ones survive at Geddington and Hardingstone, both in Northamptonshire, and at Waltham Cross; all three are complicated in design but very beautiful. They have all lost the actual crosses which were on the top of the monuments.

See also SCULPTURE.

CRYSTAL PALACE. This is the popular name of the iron and glass building put up in Hyde Park, London, to house the Great Exhibition of 1851 and afterwards re-erected on Sydenham Hill, South London, where it remained until it was burnt down in 1936.

It was designed by Joseph Paxton (1801–65), head gardener to the sixth Duke of Devonshire. Paxton had had much experience of building in iron and glass while constructing plant-houses and conservatories at the Duke's Derbyshire estate, Chatsworth. The promoters of the Great Exhibition, faced by strong public objections to the erection of a solid brick building in Hyde Park, were undecided what to do when Paxton presented a solution to the problem.

Apart from its intrinsic beauty (which eminent critics of the time, such as RUSKIN (q.v. Vol. V), were unable to discern) and its simple appropriateness for its purpose, the significant thing about the Crystal Palace was that it was wholly made of prefabricated parts, and was thus a forerunner of a type of building construction much used today. Its columns and walls and its ridge-and-furrow roofs were made of standard lengths of iron and covered with standard-sized sheets of glass, all delivered from the factory ready for use; consequently the building was put up in the very short time of 7 months.

It consisted of a flat-roofed hall with aisles, 1,851 feet long, 72 feet wide, and 64 feet high, crossed by a transept with an arched roof 104 feet high (*see* Vol. VII, p. 183). When the building was re-erected on Sydenham Hill it was given three transepts instead of one, and the whole building, instead of only the transept, was covered with an arched roof.

See also Vol. VII: EXHIBITIONS.

CUBISM, *see* MODERN ART, Section 3.

D

DANCE MUSIC. The earliest known dance music was that used to accompany FOLK DANCING (q.v. Vol. IX) on village greens. These tunes were made up by the village musician in the first place, and were handed down from father to son by memory, since no one except those in the service of the Church could understand MUSICAL NOTATION (q.v.) in early days. In time the lively rhythms and short symmetrical phrases of these folk-dances and songs began to attract the attention of the 'learned' composers, who had previously only written sacred masses and motets for trained choirs to sing. When KEYBOARD INSTRUMENTS (q.v. Vol. IX) came into fashion in the 16th century, composers such as Byrd and Farnaby wrote sets of variations on existing dance tunes for the virginal and spinet, or else original dance tunes based on the rhythms of popular dances. These were not intended to be used as an accompaniment for dancing, but were written purely for the pleasure of the player or listener. The pavan, a stately dance in duple time, and the galliard, a lively dance in triple time, made a very strong appeal to Elizabethan composers (*see* BALLROOM DANCING, Vol. IX). Recently Vaughan Williams resuscitated both these old dance-forms in his ballet *Job*.

In the 17th century, composers became dissatisfied with writing isolated dances, and began to produce 'suites' containing three, four, five, or more contrasting dances. BACH's dance suites (q.v. Vol. V) are still outstandingly popular. They nearly all contain an allemande, of moderate speed and in quadruple time, and a courante, a rather livelier running dance in triple time. For a slow dance Bach was particularly attracted to the sarabande, the characteristic rhythm of which is easily recognized because

of the emphasis often given to the second of the three beats in each bar, and he would frequently end his suites with a lively jig, which invariably has three little running notes to each big beat in the bar. Sometimes he included a minuet, at that time a stately dance in triple time, sometimes a gavotte with lively phrases always beginning on the third of the four beats in the bar, and sometimes the slightly quicker bourrée with the phrases beginning on the last of the four beats of the bar. Rather less common were the passepied, the musette, the rigaudon, and the hornpipe. All these were of folk origin from various countries throughout Europe and the British Isles. They all fall into two sections, each of which is repeated. The minuet is frequently followed by a contrasting interlude (again in two sections) known as the trio, after which the opening minuet is repeated without its own repeats.

The minuet was the only one of these old dance-forms to attract the attention of 18th-century composers. HAYDN and MOZART, and even BEETHOVEN (qq.v. Vol. V) when young, often used it for the third movement of their sonatas, quartets, symphonies, and divertimentos, though in their hands it became rather quicker than in Bach's day. Mozart, in order to make money, often wrote independent minuets in a simple, popular style that could be used to accompany the dancing at Court balls and in public dance halls.

There was a big revival of interest in dance-forms in the mid-19th century, when composers in the smaller countries of Europe were attempting to break away from the dominating German and Italian traditions and to write their own national music. CHOPIN (q.v. Vol. V), an ardently patriotic Pole, wrote many of his piano pieces in the form of the mazurka, a lively Polish peasant dance in triple time with a jumpy rhythm, and the polonaise, a more dignified and aristocratic Polish dance in triple time. Both Smetana and DVOŘÁK (q.v. Vol. V) introduced a breath of fresh Czechoslovakian air into their operas, orchestral works, chamber and piano music by means of the national polka and furiant rhythms, the former a lively duple time dance, and the latter a still more lively tug-of-war between duple and triple rhythm within a three-four time-signature. Other very popular dance forms borrowed by nationalist composers include the Hungarian czardas, in which a slow section, known as the lassu, alternates with the rapid friss; the Russian gopak, a lively dance in duple time; and the Spanish seguidilla in quick triple time, the bolero in slightly slower triple time, and the habanera in moderate duple time. Spain is outstandingly rich in folk dances of pronounced rhythmic character, and in consequence composers from all over Europe (and particularly France) have been drawn to writing new music in the Spanish dance style—Ravel's orchestral *Bolero* is but one of many instances.

There is one dance-form which has enjoyed a longer life and a more universal appeal than any—that is the waltz in simple triple time. It derived in the first place from the old German dances called Ländler, but far from only attracting the attention of German and Austrian composers (such as BEETHOVEN, SCHUBERT, and BRAHMS) it was taken up in the course of time by CHOPIN, TCHAIKOVSKY, GRIEG, DEBUSSY, SIBELIUS (qq.v. Vol. V), and many others of different nationalities. It reached the peak of its popularity in 19th-century Vienna, when Strauss (father and son) and Lanner composed

hundreds for their own famous dance bands to play at Court balls and in the fashionable pleasure gardens of the city.

Serious composers nowadays seem less interested in dance forms than their predecessors. BARTÓK (q.v. Vol. V) has written some Bulgarian and Roumanian dances, and certain sophisticated modern composers, such as Milhaud, Stravinsky, and Walton, have now and again flirted with the JAZZ idiom (q.v.) which reached Europe from America early this century. But for the most part, dance music is now left to the care of commercial musicians, and is written almost entirely for use in the dance-hall instead of as an art-form for the delight of the cultured listener.

See also JAZZ; SONATA; BALLET MUSIC.
See also Vol. IX: DANCING, HISTORY OF; BALLROOM DANCING; FOLK DANCING.

DECAMERON, *see* Vol. V: BOCCACCIO.

DECORATION, *see* ORNAMENT.

DELLA ROBBIA, *see* TERRACOTTAS.

DESIGN. Design means the conscious, or planned, control of the shape, structure, materials, and appearance of any man-made thing, whether it is simple like a cup or complicated like a ship. Whatever it is, the designer must first consider what purpose is to be served, what size and shape will be most suitable, what kind of structure and materials will best make the shape desired, and how it should look in form and colour, and possibly in pattern and texture as well, when finished. All these considerations must be kept continually in mind, so that they are reasonably balanced in the final result.

A design is not really successful unless it succeeds in all these particulars. For instance, a

Griffith Institute   *Wallace Collection*

THE INFLUENCE OF MATERIAL ON DESIGN

Left: Egyptian figure, 12th Dynasty, carved in hard granite. The forms are simple and details are reduced to a minimum
Right: Musical clock made in France in 1763. The case is ormolu (gilt bronze), a material which allows intricate detail

Heal and Son

THE INFLUENCE OF PURPOSE ON DESIGN

Left: 17th century state bed at Knole, Kent. Rich material and gorgeous decoration have been lavished on this bed
Right: Modern cherrywood bed. The simple design is suited to a small bedroom

cup may be a good size and shape to drink from, made of china that will hold hot liquid without cracking, and it may be charmingly decorated; but if the handle is too small or too awkward to hold, the design is unsuccessful. Similarly a ring may fit the finger easily, be made of a suitable kind of metal, and set with beautifully cut jewels, but if the gems are so large that they look clumsy, or the colours clash when put together, then it is not a good design. The design of the cup fails in its fitness for purpose, and that of the ring in its appearance.

The good designer must know as much as possible about the conditions relating to the purpose in mind, what are the best and most suitable materials available, and of what good workmanship, whether by hand or machine, should consist.

The design of a building or a ship raises more complicated problems than that of a cup; yet the principles of design are the same. In designing a building, the architect must consider climatic and geographical conditions, how the building should be placed on its site in relation to its surroundings, how people are to get in and out, what the building is to be used for: whether, for example, one large enclosed space will serve (as for some railway stations) or whether a

number of spaces, perhaps of differing shapes and sizes, are needed (as for a monastery or a palace); whether the spaces should be on the same or at different levels (as the stalls and galleries of a theatre); how access from one space to another should be arranged (by corridors or open arcades, by lifts or stairs). The height of the building compared with its other dimensions is also important; the building may vary from narrow and high (like a Gothic cathedral or a skyscraper) to wide and low (like some modern factories). A sense of proportion guides the actual form in which the building finally takes its shape and character, arising from the necessities of the plan. At various times, appearance rather than practical reasons has decided the shape of the plan, as in some Renaissance palaces and baroque churches; sometimes the decision is guided by tradition, as in most churches, where the purpose remains the same even though different materials or styles are being used.

The architect, bearing in mind the purpose of the building, must decide what materials and type of structure will be most suitable; the latter depends a great deal on the former: for example, frame building (timber, cast iron, steel), wall load-bearing (stone, marble, brick), post and lintel (timber, stone), dome, arch, vault (stone, brick), shell, cantilever (reinforced concrete). Then he must consider whether the building needs decoration, whether it is to be lit by windows or artificial lighting, and how it is to be heated and ventilated. Finally the details, such as what door handles shall be used, are all the concern of the architect, the designer of the building.

Whatever the design may be for, whether the highly complicated design for a building or the relatively simple one for a cup, the significant factor governing design is purpose. The purpose is usually mainly practical in character, but there are other kinds of purpose as well, such as magic, ritual and ceremony, symbolism, ornament, display, or social convention. The Christian crucifix, bishop's crozier, and chalice all have a ritual purpose, and all three are likely to be richly formed and decorated; the last, however, also has a utilitarian purpose (as a drinking vessel). The purpose of personal jewellery is ornament, and it sometimes also indicates social status. Purposes of ostentation and display are served by many objects ranging from the table ornaments in decorative porcelain of the 18th century to the triumphal arch of classic Rome. The medieval standing salt (the large ceremonial salt-cellar used by the nobility), the Islamic window screens of pierced carved woodwork, which admitted light and air to buildings while preventing people from seeing in (see p. 212), the state beds used for the formal levées of the aristocracy in the late 17th century in France

and England were all made partly for use and partly to conform to a current social convention.

Design, as we have already said, is influenced by the physical properties of the material, or combination of materials, in which the object is made. Almost any material has some limitations peculiar to it, either from its own nature, or from the way in which it is used; though these technical limitations tend to vary or lessen as discoveries have been made in the use of tools and machinery. Some materials are inflexible, such as stone, slate, or marble, and can be used only in certain limited ways after being quarried, by cutting, carving, or dressing the surface. Other materials, such as clay, metals, and glass, can be produced or treated in diverse ways to take on almost any shape, though the size may be limited. Wood can be used in a straightforward manner by cutting and jointing to make fairly simple shapes which can then be carved, inlaid, or veneered; or it can be produced in a more complicated way in the form of plywood, flat, curved, or moulded to more complex shapes. There are natural plastic materials such as clay, used for pottery, or synthetic materials such as bakelite, used for many purposes including parts of furniture. The question of whether the object has to bear any weight other than its own, or endure some stress or strain, also affects its size and shape, as, for example, in most furniture.

Within all the limitations of material and purpose, aesthetic reasons have always contributed

British Museum　　　　　　　　　　　*Victoria & Albert Museum*

THE INFLUENCE OF PERIOD ON DESIGN

Left: Greek cup, wide and shallow in shape with design painted in black on white. 5th century B.C.
Right: 18th-century chocolate cup made at Worcester, painted with flowers in colour on a white ground

to design: that is to say, design has depended on what people at different periods have thought beautiful and suitable. Though the purpose and even the material of objects may be the same, their shape and decoration at different periods may vary fundamentally. The wine-cup of classic Greece was often of the two-handled saucer shape, called the *kylix*. This, made in pottery, consisted of a very simple, shallow bowl, with two ear-shaped handles, on a small plain foot. It was unglazed and was painted with mythical scenes in black, white, or brown on the inside or round the outside of the bowl. This may be contrasted with the cups for hot chocolate, fashionable in 18th-century Europe. These were in very fine porcelain, elegant and charming in design, and included not only the deep, two-handled cup itself but a matching lid and saucer. All were painted with designs such as bouquets of flowers in natural colours on a white ground. In each case the object, while serving its purpose, has been designed with great regard for beauty of appearance, and both express the character of the society which produced it and which in turn it served.

Thus the finished product, whether it comes from a single hand or is the result of a team working together, is the solution of a problem involving practical requirements and aesthetic considerations; herein lies the essence of design, the physical expression of a mental intention.

See also ART; INDUSTRIAL ART.

DETECTIVE STORIES.

Detective stories combine the appeal of the thriller—excitement, suspense, and dangerous adventure—with that of the intellectual puzzle—a carefully reasoned conclusion from all the evidence fairly presented. Though several earlier works have something in common with modern detective stories, the American Edgar Allan Poe (1809–49) was really the first detective story writer. His stories are usually short and marked by grotesque imagination—for instance, in one of his stories the criminal is a monkey: but his solutions are very closely reasoned—in this way combining the qualities of both thriller and intellectual puzzle.

The Moonstone (1868) by Wilkie Collins has been called the best of all detective stories. Collins constructed his plots skilfully, giving the illusion of truth by means of a series of narratives

Meade Collection

SHERLOCK HOLMES

Poster advertising the *Strand Magazine* in which most of Conan Doyle's stories of Sherlock Holmes appeared

by different characters. But he preserved a romantic mystery by making *The Moonstone* a story of oriental fanaticism, as well as of sober English detection. For part of the solution he used certain little-known scientific facts, a device followed by many others, such as R. Austen Freeman in our own day. One of the best-known detective story writers is Sir Arthur Conan DOYLE (q.v. Vol. V). His detective, the famous Sherlock Holmes, proceeds by minute observation of details, deep scientific knowledge, and bold and astonishing deductions. He comes nearer than any other detective to solving his problems by pure thought. Though the majority of Conan Doyle's stories are of the intellectual puzzle type, a few, such as *The Hound of the Baskervilles* and *The Speckled Band*, are also thrillers.

G. K. Chesterton (1874–1936) used the detective story as a means of propaganda, and his detective, Father Brown, is also a philosopher. He was the first to rely mainly on psychological solutions. The detective asks what sort of person would have committed this crime, and so arrives at the solution without direct proof. Chesterton's contemporary E. C. Bentley wrote *Trent's Last Case* (1912), perhaps the cleverest of all detective stories, in which three separate, consistent, and seemingly convincing solutions are presented in turn.

Well-known recent writers include Dorothy Sayers, whose mysteries are solved by the charming Lord Peter Wimsey, and Agatha Christie, author of more than fifty stories, most of which end in the success of her detective Hercule Poirot by hard thinking with 'the little grey cells' and inspired guesswork. Ronald Knox works in Poe's tradition of strictly rational deduction from evidence; and so, to a large extent, did A. E. W. Mason.

Nearly all detective stories have one character who is a master detective. He may be a policeman, like A. E. W. Mason's Inspector Hanaud or Ngaio Marsh's Inspector Allen; but more often he is an amateur who conducts a battle of wits with the police, often making fun of the slow-witted superintendent. The detective is often something of a character with certain distinguishing traits: Sherlock Holmes has his pipe; Hercule Poirot his moustaches and his pernickety passion for order and neatness; Peter Wimsey his facetiousness. He is often accompanied by a companion who acts as a foil, who helps to lead the reader astray, and who is able to follow the detective's reasoning only with the greatest difficulty. The reader is intended to identify himself with this character—Conan Doyle's Dr. Watson or Agatha Christie's Hastings—and to share his surprise at the detective's brilliance.

Detective stories usually reverse the normal time sequence of the novel; they start with what happened last, the crime, and work backwards. The main part of the story contains an account of the detective's investigations with many false trails and much suspicion of innocent characters; and the climax is the discovery of the criminal.

A detective story may be regarded as a battle of wits between author and reader, in which the author must play fair. The reader is not interested if he can find the solution too easily; but if, when he comes to the solution, he realizes that he could not have discovered it because something essential was withheld from him, he feels cheated. The search for improbable solutions has gone so far as to make the detective, or in one case the narrator of the story, the culprit. But tricks of this kind are no longer effective once the reader becomes acquainted with them.

Since 1918 the number of detective stories written each year has vastly increased: indeed, they are probably the most widely read of all books of fiction. Like the cinema, they appeal to all classes and nearly all levels of intelligence.

See also NOVEL.

DIARIES. A diary is a record written day by day of a person's thoughts and experiences; and as such it is a formless and intimate kind of literature. Diaries are often inconsistent or repetitive, for the diarist may change his opinions or forget what he has previously written; but though they may be scrappy, they are at their best excellent records of the past. They reflect events, great and small, with the vividness of an eye-witness: an historian may explain why Charles I was executed, but the diarist Sir William Dugdale (1605–86) was able to describe how the execution looked, what it felt like to be watching, and how the soldiers dipped their swords in the King's blood. Samuel Pepys, who lived at the time of the Great Fire of London, writes in his diary an account which could only have been written by someone who had watched it all happening:

Everybody endeavouring to remove their goods, and flinging them into the river or bringing them into lighters that lay off; poor people staying in their houses as long as till the very fire touched them, and then running into boats, or clambering from one pair of stairs by the waterside to another. And among other things, the poor pigeons, I perceive, were loth to leave their houses, but hovered about the windows and balconies till they burned their wings, and fell down.

Diarists, of course, rarely have great events like these to record; their diaries are mainly records of ordinary, trivial matters of daily life, little experiences which, except in a diary, would not have seemed worth noting down. They may describe food and clothes, the weather, the crops, prosperity and poverty, the price of things in the shops, and what people thought of the Government, of wars, and

Miss S. Awdry

NUTTING PARTY IN SEAGRY WOODS

Drawing by Kilvert of an incident described in his diary on 4 September 1875. 'We had a grand scramble ... clambering over the high gates gathering nuts ...'

foreign countries. John Evelyn (1620–1706) in his famous diary made a picture of his times covering more than 60 years, and including accounts of several European countries in which he travelled.

Diaries often have an amusing mixture of great public events and private concerns. James Woodforde (1740–1803), who records in his diaries all the details of the life of a country parson in the 18th century, mentions the first news of the French Revolution in one sentence between the purchase of a crab and a visit from his brother. His personal record gives interesting information about the normal recreations of a Norfolk parson in 1782: 'About 12', he writes, 'went out coursing, ran two good courses and killed one of the hares which Jack found sitting and for which I gave him as usual 1s. 0d. My young greyhound Hector performed incomparably.' Some diaries catch great men in their leisure hours unaware that any record would be left for posterity. In her diary Fanny Burney (1752–1840) gives an account of George III and the American War of Independence, but also describes how the King ran wildly in pursuit of her in Kew Gardens. Pepys writes unflattering details of Charles II's condition when he landed in England at the Restoration: 'a sad, poor condition for clothes and money ... and how overjoyed the King was when Sir J. Greenville brought him some money'.

Diaries often give detailed and true records of people's feelings. They describe petty quarrels and amusements, depressions and excitements, the pleasures and discomforts of family life, love, hate, fear, and hope. Pepys, for example, gives a very intimate picture of the personal life of himself and his young wife, Elizabeth. He describes his pleasure in her appearance:

My wife seemed very pretty today, it being the first time I had given her leave to weare a black patch—

and his satisfaction with her behaviour:

Talking with my wife, in whom I never had greater content, blessed be God! than now—she continuing with the same care and thrift and innocence, so long as I keep her from occasions of being otherwise, as ever she was in her life, and keeps the house as well.

A man will sometimes write in his diary what he would not tell his closest friend, and because he is usually writing spontaneously what he thinks and feels at the moment, his diary may give a truer picture than any autobiography can, for the autobiographer is conscious of his audience and he is writing about things which may be by then some time past. The Rev. Francis Kilvert, one of the best Victorian diarists, whose diary is intimate and personal and little concerned with public events, writes:

Left Clyro for ever. A chapter of life closed and a leaf in the book of Life turned over. The day I came to Clyro I remember fixing my eyes on a particular bough of an apple tree in the orchard opposite to the school and the Vicarage and saying to myself that on the day I left Clyro I would look at that same branch. I did look for it this morning but I could not recognize it.

Such passages often bring to the reader's mind similar trivial things which have at some time been of importance to him also.

The keeping of diaries of some sort is probably very old indeed, but the vast majority of diaries are never published. Of those that have been made public and widely read, except for one famous French diary of the 15th century, known as the *Journal d'un bourjeois de Paris*, the great majority have been written since 1600. A wide variety of people have kept diaries which have come down to us. They include religious leaders such as WESLEY and George Fox, the founder of the Quakers, monarchs such as Queen VICTORIA, civil servants such as PEPYS (qq.v. Vol. V), the most famous of all diarists, scholars such as Edward Gibbon the historian, politicians, clergymen, landowners, and many others. Some wrote because they were lonely or bored, using their diary as a substitute for a friend; some, perhaps, to satisfy an urge to write. Most never intended their works to be read—Pepys even wrote in a code invented by himself. Boswell, who wrote from 1760 onwards and is only now being published, is the most outspoken of all diarists. Boswell and Pepys record all their feelings and thoughts with unashamed honesty, and each provides a very complete picture of a man as well as a period in history.

Many diaries like these were not made public until long after their author's death, sometimes to spare the feelings of living people, or because surviving relations feel that such candour may damage the dead author's reputation. Often, however, they have been simply lost and forgotten, and are eventually discovered by accident. Diaries have been found in extraordinary circumstances: that of SCOTT (q.v. Vol. V), the polar explorer, which contains records of the greatest interest and importance, was found by his body after he and his party had perished of cold and hunger.

Some few diaries, especially of recent years, have been written from the first for publication. These are usually the work of professional writers such as the French author, André Gide (1869–1951); and though they may be cleverer and better constructed, they are liable to lack the spontaneous intimacy of genuine diaries written without an audience in mind. Of recent diaries not intended for publication those of the Italian Ciano and the German Goebbels give intimate portraits of MUSSOLINI and HITLER (qq.v. Vol. V) respectively, and of the conduct of the Second World War from the Axis side. Their authors were so confident that their writings were secret that they said things about their countries' policy which they would never have admitted in public. Had they not belonged to defeated nations, their confidence would probably have been justified. The paradox of diaries is that what is least intended for publication is often the most interesting when published.

See also LETTERS.

DIVINE COMEDY, THE. DANTE (q.v. Vol. V) wrote this great EPIC (q.v.) during his exile from Florence between 1302 and 1325. It

Earl of Leicester

DANTE AND VIRGIL IN HELL
Devils attack Virgil, and Dante hides beside the mouth of Hell. From a 14th-century manuscript of *The Divine Comedy*

consists of three parts (or *canticas*)—*Hell*, *Purgatory*, and *Paradise*, and comprises in all some 14,000 eleven-syllabled lines of verse, arranged in groups of three, rhyming ABA, BCB, CDC, and so on (called *terza rima*). The *canticas* themselves are divided respectively into 34, 33, and 33 parts (or *cantos*), making 100 in all.

The *Divine Comedy* describes the poet's visionary journey in the year 1300 through Hell, Purgatory, and Paradise, with Virgil, the ancient Roman poet, and Beatrice, the love of Dante's youth, as his guides. At the outset Dante is lost in a dark wood, which symbolizes his own lack of spiritual direction, and there he meets Virgil. Virgil conducts him down the pit of Hell, which is imagined like a wide funnel converging on the earth's centre. As they go, they meet the shades of the eternally damned, many of whom are friends or figures of Dante's time. Their conversations, sometimes tender, sometimes angry, take place against a terrifying background of crags, demons, and cruel punishment. In the deepest part they find the tall figure of Lucifer, fixed in ice; they climb up his hairy body to emerge at the other side of the earth on the island of Purgatory. Its form is the opposite of Hell, for it is a mountain rising to heaven, divided into seven terraces, where repentant sinners are finally cleansed. Here the people and conversations are calm, the atmosphere full of hope for eventual salvation. At the summit, in the Earthly Paradise, Virgil turns back, and Beatrice, appearing in a symbolic procession, takes Dante up to Paradise. This is imagined as a series of ten heavens circling the Earth. Here, in the company of saints and other famous Christians, the ultimate truths of science and theology are explained to Dante as he passes through the heavens into the Divine Presence in the Empyrean.

In this visionary representation of a spiritual crisis in his own life, Dante has portrayed the progress of the sinner from dejection to salvation. He did so with all the varied passions of his own experience, and through the complex knowledge and beliefs of his times. The very vastness of its physical structure and of its all-embracing view of Man, the Universe, and the Creator, makes *The Divine Comedy* one of the greatest poems in the literature of the world.

See also ITALIAN LITERATURE; EPIC POETRY; Colour Plate, opp. p. 288.
See also Vol. V: DANTE.

DOME. This is a form of roof, shaped like an inverted bowl, covering a large part of any building. A small dome, such as that rising from the ridge of a sloping roof, or surmounting a large dome, is called a cupola. The Romans were the first people to build large domes successfully, the most famous surviving Roman example being that of the Pantheon (*see* ROMAN ART). The dome reached its peak of development during the BYZANTINE CIVILIZATION (q.v. Vol. I) which followed the Roman. Since the Pantheon is a circular building, it was not difficult to build a circular dome supported on its walls; it was a far more difficult problem to

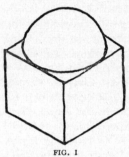

FIG. 1

roof a square building with a dome, for it could only rest on the walls at four points and some method had to be found for supporting it at the corners of the walls (Fig. 1). Various methods of building out from the corners were tried before the problem was solved by the Byzantine builders. One way was to build an arch (called a squinch) across the corners from one wall to the other, thus making an octagonal shape on which the circular base of the dome could be fitted (Fig. 2 *a*); another was to build the courses of stone at the corners so that one projected in-

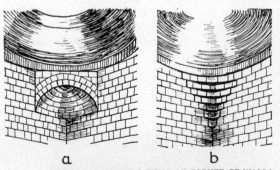

a   b

FIG. 2. *a.* SQUINCH SUPPORTING DOME AT CORNER OF WALL;
b. PROJECTING COURSES OF STONE

wards above the others, until a circular shape was obtained (Fig. 2 *b*). But neither of these methods was strong.

The perfect solution of the problem was to build sections of a larger dome (called pendentives) at each corner, which carried the walls

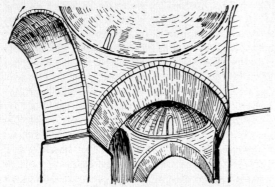

FIG. 3. DOMES SUPPORTED ON PENDENTIVES

upwards until they became circular and formed an adequate support for the dome (Fig. 3).

Domes were particularly suited to Byzantine churches, which were often built in the form of a Greek cross with a central dome over the middle, and smaller or half-domes covering subsidiary parts of the building, all visible externally (*see* BYZANTINE ART). The largest dome in existence is that of ST. SOPHIA (q.v.) in Istanbul.

The Byzantine style of domed church spread to southern France, as far west as Périgueux, where the cathedral (A.D. 1120) somewhat resembles St. Mark's, Venice. Eastwards the style spread throughout the Arab world. The Dome of the Rock (Mosque of Omar) was built in Jerusalem at the end of the 7th century (*see* Vol. V, p. 313), and as the Islamic religion conquered Egypt, Persia, and parts of India and North Africa, as well as the Arab lands, the use of the dome for mosques and shrines went with it. During the succeeding centuries it took different forms, such as the slightly pointed dome of Egypt and the bulbous dome of India and Persia (*see* p. 449). Often it was covered with coloured tiles or geometrical ornament.

In Europe the dome went out of use during the periods of Romanesque and Gothic architecture, but returned during the Renaissance after the architect BRUNELLESCHI (q.v. Vol. V), in the early 15th century, had roofed the cathedral of Florence with a dome. Other great Renaissance domes are those of ST. PETER'S CATHEDRAL, Rome, the Invalides, Paris (1706), and ST. PAUL'S CATHEDRAL, London (qq.v.). An impressive 19th-century dome is that of the Capitol at Washington (completed 1865) (*see* Vol. III, p. 472). Dome-like forms have lately been reintroduced as a result of the invention of shell-concrete, an economical method of roofing large spaces by the use of a thin, curved, membrane-like structure of reinforced CON-CRETE (q.v. Vol. VIII).

See also BYZANTINE ART.

DON QUIXOTE, by Cervantes, *see* SATIRE. *See also* Vol. V: CERVANTES.

DORIC ORDER, *see* ORDERS OF ARCHITEC-TURE.

DRAMA. Drama (from a Greek word meaning 'a thing done' or 'performed') originated in religious festivals, when ancient myths were re-enacted by dancers and singers (*see* RITUAL, Vol. I). Many ancient peoples produced primitive religious ceremonies of a dramatic kind, but the Greeks alone raised such songs and movements into an art-form. The idea of presenting a story by acting its chief incidents in a theatre, with actors to speak the words of its characters, is now so familiar that it is difficult to recognize the greatness and originality of the Greek achievement (*see* GREEK DRAMA). Since that day, the theatre has moved audiences to pity and terror in TRAGEDY or amused and delighted them in COMEDY (qq.v.). Greek plays and their Latin successors have influenced the themes, plots, characters, structure, and presentation of the drama as we have come to know it.

The chief dramatists of Rome were Plautus (*c.* 254–184 B.C.) and Terence (*c.* 195–159 B.C.) —both comic writers, who borrowed their plots and characters freely from the Greeks. Seneca (*c.* 5 B.C.–A.D. 65), the only Latin tragic dramatist whose work survives, had a considerable influence on Elizabethan drama over 1,500 years later. With the fall of Rome, drama vanished from Europe until in the Middle Ages it again began to grow out of religious ritual, this time the ritual of the Christian Church (*see* MIRACLE and MORALITY PLAYS). With the rediscovery of the culture of Rome in the 15th and 16th centuries, the playwrights and critics of the RENAISSANCE (q.v. Vol. I) became aware of the dramatic form which the Greeks had invented and which the Romans had imitated, and they adopted, modified, and eventually mastered it. As the native genius of each country expressed itself in these inherited forms, Europe's second age of great drama dawned.

Medieval plays had varied between day-long performances and short interludes at banquets or during elaborate Court entertainments. The Greek philosopher ARISTOTLE (q.v. Vol. V), however, had said that a play should be of 'a length to be taken in by the memory' and 'which allows of the hero passing by a series of probable or necessary stages from misfortune to happiness, or from happiness to misfortune'. Renaissance dramatists, accepting the classical theory and practice, wrote their plays at a length which took from 2 to 3 hours to perform. The Greek dramatists had used a chorus to sing choral odes which commented on the action of the drama and divided the performance into parts. From this evolved the division of modern dramas into acts—usually five, though sometimes less. In Renaissance Italy the chorus also suggested that combination of music and drama which the Italians developed as OPERA (q.v.), and which has always been the main dramatic mode of Italy.

The first THEATRES (q.v. Vol. IX) since Roman times were built in Italy, where the first dramas of the Renaissance were produced, and where also the classical literary convention of the PASTORALS (q.v.) was adapted to create a new dramatic form. The best plays of this period were the flowing comedies of Ariosto (1474–1533) and the pastoral plays of Tasso (1544–95): these were called the *commedia erudita* in contrast with the popular folk-form of drama known as *commedia dell' arte*. In the latter there was no written dialogue, the actors simply knew in a general way what they had to do and improvised their own dialogue (*see* HARLEQUI-NADE AND PANTOMIME, Vol. IX). From Italy the impulse towards drama passed in particular to Spain, England, and France.

The founder of Spanish drama, Lope de Vega (1562–1635), was the most prolific of dramatists, claiming to have written over 1,500 plays, more than 450 of which survive. His dramas, based on themes from his country's history and romances, present a lively picture of Spanish life. His great successor, Calderón (1600–81), was more interested in religious mysteries than in the passions of mankind, and his one-act religious plays, called *autos*, though now neglected, are supreme of their kind. His tragedies, which usually hinged on a point of honour, excelled in brilliant dialogue, picturesque situation, and surprise.

English drama in the 66 years from the open-ing of the first theatre in 1576 until the closing of all theatres by Parliament in 1642 is of un-rivalled splendour and variety, perhaps the greatest glory of English literature. Dramatists equalled the superb achievement of the great Elizabethan adventurers in their patriotism and daring. The earliest comedy is Udall's *Ralph Roister Doister* (1553); *Gorboduc* (1561–2) by Thomas Norton and Thomas Sackville, modelled on Seneca, and the chronicle play *The Famous Victories of Henry V* are the earliest tragedy and historical drama. Companies of players were formed under the patronage of great noblemen (*see* ACTING, HISTORY OF, Vol. IX); and new public theatres, with huge, rush-strewn plat-form-stages open to the sky, arose in London. Man was the centre of an exciting new world, and his passions and actions were presented with brave fervour. Written for rapid presenta-tion on the great platforms, without scenery, and with much left to the imagination of a quick-witted audience, the plays would chronicle an entire reign, tell of the clash of armies, or show the majesty of some great ruler over-thrown by towering ambition or other cause. Vigorous, excited audiences heard plays full of rich, brilliant poetry such as Marlowe's heroic conqueror spoke to his love in his play *Tambur-laine the Great*:

> Now, bright Zenocrate, the world's fair eye,
> Whose beams illuminate the lamps of heaven,
> Whose cheerful looks do clear the cloudy air,
> And clothe it in a crystal livery,
> Now rest thee here on fair Larissa plains,
> Where Egypt and the Turkish empire parts
> Between thy sons, that shall be emperors,
> And every one commander of a world.

The greatest dramatist of the period—and of all time—was William Shakespeare (*see* SHAKE-SPEARIAN DRAMA), of whom Dryden later said: 'he was the man who of all modern, and perhaps ancient poets, had the largest and most compre-hensive soul'.

In the 17th century Jacobean drama tended more and more to recreate the appearances and situations of daily life; but in spite of this exter-nal realism, it moved away from that true reality which Shakespeare defined as holding the mirror up to nature. Elizabethan tragedy had always been closely interwoven with romance and with the violence and horror of the Italian revenge-plays (*see* TRAGEDY); but in the greatest Elizabethan tragedies all other interests were

Garrick Club

A SCENE FROM SHERIDAN'S 'THE SCHOOL FOR SCANDAL' WITH THE ORIGINAL CAST
Painting by James Roberts, 1777

made subservient to the tragedy itself. In the later plays the romantic or the macabre tended to compete with the tragic motif—the romantic in the plays of Beaumont and Fletcher, for example, the macabre in those of WEBSTER (q.v. Vol. V). In comedy, the characters and situations become exaggerated and eccentric —for example, Ben JONSON's *Silent Woman* is about a man who cannot bear the slightest noise. The historical play, which reached its highest peak with SHAKESPEARE and MARLOWE (qq.v. Vol. V), died out altogether. Blank verse, the metre of the greatest Elizabethan plays, became flat and frequently gave way to prose. But at their greatest the Elizabethans created a native drama splendid in quality and variety, in characterization and stage-craft, upon which later dramatists freely drew.

In France, the theatre produced great writers of an entirely different kind. French tragedies were strictly constructed according to rules which were built up from the dictates of Aristotle. Aristotle declared that a play should have three unities—unity of action (that is, a single plot with no side-issues), unity of place (there could be no change of scene), and unity of time (the whole action should take place within 12 or 24 hours). The best tragedies in this strict, severe style were written in the 17th century by CORNEILLE and RACINE. The third great dramatist of this remarkable age was MOLIÈRE (qq.v. Vol. V), who has been called the supreme genius of comedy.

In 1660, with the restoration of Charles II to the throne of England and the overthrow of the Puritan rule, the playhouses were re-opened, and playwrights were again active (*see* RESTORATION DRAMA). Heroic plays replaced tragedy, and John DRYDEN (q.v. Vol. V) was their most distinguished author. Many of these plays, written in rhymed couplets, were extravagant and unreal. Comedy was artificial, too, though the best of the comedies, Congreve's *The Way of the World*, for example, reflect the times in their wit and sparkle, their elegance and licentiousness. During the 18th century a taste for the sentimental and the moral prevailed, and to suit this taste Shakespeare's dramas were often rewritten and sentimentalized; even *King Lear* was rewritten with a happy ending. The witty comedies of two Irishmen, GOLDSMITH and SHERIDAN (qq.v. Vol. V), in the 1770's, such as *She Stoops to Conquer* and *The School for Scandal*, form the only oasis in the dramatic desert of two centuries. Perhaps the creative skill of the teller of tales and the maker of characters went into the new literary form, the NOVEL (q.v.).

The ROMANTIC MOVEMENT (q.v.) brought no revival to drama in England, where, almost throughout the 19th century, the theatre was dominated by grotesque melodramas, farces, and fantastic 'spectacles'. But in Germany the crowded poetic tragedies of GOETHE and SCHILLER (qq.v. Vol. V), full of violent action and high speeches, gave a fresh impulse to a new national drama, which had begun with Lessing's *Nathan the Wise* (1779). In France *Hernani*, by Victor HUGO (q.v. Vol. V), presented in 1830, defied the dramatic conventions to which French drama had long subscribed, and the play's success revolutionized French drama. In his exciting historical plays Alexandre DUMAS (q.v. Vol. V), though no rival in literary merit, surpassed Hugo in his sense of theatre.

In England, at the end of the 19th century, the traditional comedy of manners was reintroduced by Oscar Wilde (1854–1900). At the same time the Norwegian Henrik IBSEN, and later the Irishman George Bernard SHAW (qq.v. Vol. V), who was himself greatly influenced by Ibsen, produced a more realistic form of drama which was largely concerned with social problems. The problem plays of Ibsen, especially, were usually concerned not only with a specific social problem but with the conflict it set up in the characters; and in this respect plays such as *Hedda Gabler* are psychological as well as social dramas. A less direct approach to social problems is seen in Russian 19th-century drama, especially in the plays of CHEKHOV (q.v. Vol. V).

In *The Cherry Orchard*, for example, Chekhov does not try to enlist sympathy for any social doctrine, nor to indicate a solution for a social problem, but shows a bewildered and ineffectual family in the grip of great social change—the breaking up of the old estates. Post-revolutionary Russian drama, however, broke away from this method of suggesting social conflict by atmosphere and mood, and became frankly propagandist.

At the beginning of the 20th century an Irish group of writers revived the poetic drama which, in England, had suffered an eclipse for centuries —the few attempts such as Milton's *Samson Agonistes* and Shelley's *The Cenci*, though great poetry, have not been successful on the stage. The best known of the Irish dramatists is J. M. SYNGE (q.v. Vol. V), whose plays, whether in prose such as *The Playboy of the Western World* or in verse such as *Deirdre of the Sorrows*, are charged with poetry. But despite the lead given by Synge and other Irishmen, such as W. B. Yeats and, later, Sean O'Casey, it was not until the 1930's, with the experimental verse-dramas of T. S. Eliot, W. H. Auden, Stephen Spender, and others, that any successful poetic drama was produced in England. T. S. Eliot's *Murder in the Cathedral* (1935) has for its theme the martyrdom of St. Thomas à Becket, while *The Family Reunion* (1939) is a modern version in terms of everyday life of the Greek myth of Orestes pursued by the Furies. Others, notably French dramatists and the American Eugene O'Neill, have gone to Greek mythology for plots, feeling that the deep and universal significance of Greek myths can be restated in terms of modern life.

Today dramatists are little bound by convention and can say very much what they like in any way they like. They can write in the accepted formal manner, as in the comedies of W. Somerset Maugham or Noel Coward, or they can use remarkable effects of staging and lighting to show what a man is thinking or dreaming (*see* THEATRE, Section 7, Vol. IX). Plays can now be presented, not only on the stage, but in films, on radio, and on television, and these mediums have immeasurably increased the audience for drama.

See also TRAGEDY; COMEDY; GREEK DRAMA; MIRACLE PLAYS; MORALITY PLAYS; SHAKESPEARIAN DRAMA; RESTORATION DRAMA.
See also Vol. IX: ACTING, HISTORY OF; THEATRE, HISTORY OF.

DRAWING. To a great extent drawings are the preparatory designs and experiments in composition used by an artist before his work is completed. Painters, sculptors, and architects have nearly all used such preliminary workings, and many are now prized not only as works of art, but also for the insight they give into the artist's mind and method. A highly finished drawing, done as a complete work of art in itself, is a far rarer thing.

Artists usually make their drawings on paper, but parchment and vellum have sometimes been used. They draw with pen, brush, metal-point, charcoal, black and red chalks, and pencil, or with a combination of any of these. Much of the black ink used by earlier artists has faded to a predominantly yellow colour in the course of time. A brown wash, made from wood soot, called bistre, was also used, mainly in the 15th century in Italy, but not as universally as the INK (q.v. Vol. IV) used for ordinary writing. In the 18th century, sepia, made from the dye of the cuttle-fish, was discovered.

Some artists draw with the point of the brush; DÜRER (q.v. Vol. V) and other artists frequently used Chinese white on blue paper in this way. In Italy, in the 16th century, many artists, especially those from Florence and Umbria, used a metal-point, made of silver, lead, or some other metal, with which they made preliminary soft indentations on prepared paper; these markings can often be seen under drawings finished in ink or chalk. This method was particularly popular for drawing in sketch-books, as ink was difficult to carry on journeys, and pencil or chalk easily rubbed. Sheets of drawings in metal-point from several of Raphael's sketch-books still exist. Raphael often worked up the slight sketches he had made of his assistants in the studio into figures or groups of figures in his paintings.

Charcoal, being a cheap substance, was much used for large-scale cartoons, or working drawings, which an artist often prepared before painting frescoes on walls. The artist prepared these cartoons from his original drawings, on the same scale as the finished work. He then cut them into manageable strips and held them over the wet plaster, while he pricked the outlines of the drawing on to the surface; he then painted over the little holes in the plaster and filled in the detail (*see* PAINTING METHODS). For paintings on panel or canvas the pricking

Ashmolean Museum

A KNEELING SAINT. SILVERPOINT DRAWING BY RAPHAEL
(1483–1520)
Raphael may have used this study of a boy for the figure of Mary Magdalene in the 'Crucifixion' in the National Gallery. The drapery is lightly suggested

method was sometimes used, but more often a smaller original drawing was enlarged by the square method. By this method the drawing was covered with a network of small squares, and the panel by an equal number of squares on a larger scale. By drawing in each of the larger squares lines corresponding with those in the smaller squares on the drawing, an enlarged copy was produced. Charcoal cartoons were easily rubbed and damaged, and not many have survived; an important one by HOLBEIN (q.v. Vol. V), for a fresco in Whitehall Palace is still preserved, however (*see* Vol. V, p. 219).

Black and red chalk, being more adhesive, spoils less easily by rubbing. Black or Italian chalk, which has a greyer tone than present-day black chalk, was mainly used in the 16th and 17th centuries. Red chalk alone was used by MICHELANGELO, Andrea del Sarto, and other great draughtsmen; and in the 18th century WATTEAU (qq.v. Vol. V) produced exquisite

ABOVE: LANDSCAPE WITH DISTANT CASTLE. PEN AND WASH
DRAWING BY CLAUDE (1600–82)

LEFT: BLACK CHALK DRAWING BY TINTORETTO (1518–94),
SQUARED FOR TRANSFER TO A PAINTING

THE HOLY FAMILY. PEN AND WASH DRAWING BY THE ITALIAN PAINTER TIEPOLO (1696–1770)

drawings by using black and red chalk together, heightening his effects with white. The pencil, made of graphite, did not enjoy much popularity before the 19th century, but it is universally used today.

Drawings are valuable, apart from their beauty, because they help us to understand how a picture was created. Landscape paintings are often done in the studio from recollection aided by sketch-book drawings done on the spot. CLAUDE (q.v. Vol. V) is known to have gone out into the Roman country-side to draw from nature, but his paintings were ideal classical compositions built up in the studio from the fusion of these direct observations recorded in drawings. Constable used his nature studies more faithfully. Figure drawings, done for practice, may be useful at any time for a composition. When a painting is first commissioned or imagined, the artist probably first roughs out a hasty sketch of the whole composition, which he then copies and alters in increasing detail. Then he works out individual figures, either from the life or from his sketch books, perhaps producing many variants of the same idea until he is satisfied. When the composition is finally planned, he can make a larger and much clearer drawing to submit for approval, if necessary. Then he sets up the panel or canvas, and begins the painting. This method of building up a work of art shows the close and intimate relationship between a painting and a drawing, the life-line between the mind and the hand. It is drawing which gives the feel of line and solidity, the bones under the flesh, as it were, in a painting. For this reason drawing is an important part of the training of art students.

Nearly all the main European painters have left drawings, some in greater quantity than others; these have been scattered around the world, and are eagerly sought after by collectors—English collectors in particular. In England the three main collections of European drawings accessible to students are at Windsor Castle and in the British and Ashmolean Museums. Windsor houses the great collection of drawings by LEONARDO DA VINCI, representative of all the mediums that had been invented in his day. He mainly used pen and ink, but also chalks, particularly for drapery studies, and metal-point for meticulous work (*see* Vol. V, p. 272).

Raphael and Michelangelo, who are magnificently represented in the British and Ashmolean

British Museum
RED AND BLACK CHALK DRAWING BY WATTEAU (1684–1721)

Viscount Hinchingbrooke
THE MONTAGU SISTERS. PENCIL DRAWING BY INGRES
(1780–1867)

Museums, also varied their medium. Raphael used mainly metal-point in his earliest drawings, pen and ink for the studies done when he was in Florence, and in his later Roman days red and black chalk. Frenchmen and Englishmen during the 17th and 18th centuries used other coloured chalks, besides red and black. Landscape artists preferred ink washes; Claude mastered the art so completely that he could capture the depth, light, and atmosphere of a place with an amazing economy of effort. REMBRANDT (q.v. Vol. V) used the same technique not only for landscape but also in his plentifully-peopled historical scenes, which spring to life whether brushed in broadly or sketched more carefully with the pen.

WATER-COLOUR painting (q.v.) is a technique closely akin to drawing. It was used particularly by the English landscape painters of the 18th and 19th centuries. In TURNER's water-colours the pencil foundation is often visible beneath the washes of atmospheric colour. Ingres made pencil drawings which have a great solidity in contrast to the nervous and dazzling wash drawings of his contemporary DELACROIX, which are drawn with a brush in a monochrome ink or water-colour (qq.v. Vol. V).

The temperament of an artist has much to do with his choice of working materials, and his preference will be obvious in any study of his drawings. A truly great artist experiments with everything which may possibly serve his purpose in the creation of a great work.

See also PAINTING METHODS; WATER-COLOUR.

DRYPOINT, *see* ETCHING AND ENGRAVING, Section 4.

DUTCH ART. Until the 16th century Holland was part of the Netherlands, which also included what is now Belgium and part of northern France. The few artists who belonged to the northern territory worked in the style of the southern painters (*see* FLEMISH ART). In the 16th century, the northern provinces of the Netherlands, which were Protestant, broke away, under the inspired leadership of WILLIAM THE SILENT (q.v. Vol. V), and formed the independent kingdom of Holland; while the southern States remained Catholic and under Spanish domination. Holland soon blossomed out into a century of extraordinary commercial prosperity, and at the same time produced, in the short space of a hundred years, a more dazzling array of great painters than any other country has done, with the exception of Renaissance Italy. When we think of Dutch art it is usually this school of painters that we mean; and it is astonishing that it can stand comparison with the arts of other countries which cover many centuries and include great architecture and sculpture as well as painting.

The 17th century was a period of artistic brilliance all over Europe, though in fact the Dutch painters had relatively little contact with those of other countries. Early in the century a few Dutch painters visited Italy and brought back ideas, particularly from the followers of Caravaggio, who painted figures with strong contrasts of light and shade (*see* CHIAROSCURO). But the greatest Dutch painters—REMBRANDT, VERMEER (qq.v. Vol. V), Hals, and Ruisdael—seem to have known Italian art only through engravings and such pictures as happened to be in Dutch collections.

There was, indeed, a lack of sympathy between Holland and the rest of Europe: Holland was Protestant and its wealth was in the hands of the merchants, whereas the other countries to the west and south were Catholic and the patrons of art were the Church and the royal Courts. So, while Catholic Italy and Flanders produced grandiose decoration which could be applied equally well to a florid church or to a splendid palace (*see* BAROQUE ART), the taste of the Dutch merchants, who wanted small pictures to decorate their modest houses, and the ban on church decoration in Protestant churches, resulted in an art consisting chiefly of portraits, interiors, and landscapes. Rembrandt was the only Dutch painter to produce many religious paintings.

A type of portrait which is scarcely found outside Holland is the life-size group of members of a society or guild. These portrait groups express the republican spirit of the Dutch, with their stiff and formal poses, their clothes of sober cut (with occasional splashes of bright colour), and the equal emphasis on each figure. But it required great ingenuity to compose such a group into an interesting picture and to avoid making it look like a school photograph. The Dutch painters got over the difficulty by varying the attitude of the figures as much as possible. In the groups by Rembrandt and Hals almost all the figures are turning or looking in slightly

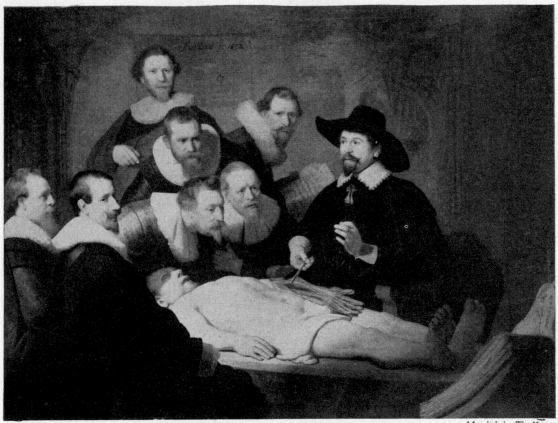

Mauritshuis, *The Hague*

'THE ANATOMY LESSON'. PAINTING BY REMBRANDT, 1632

different directions, and most of them appear unaware of each other's existence. This makes a satisfactory composition but not a very lively picture; in Rembrandt's 'Anatomy Lesson' few of the students appear to be paying any attention to the subject.

The portraits express the solid worth of their subjects in the realistic treatment of the head and details of dress. Hals excelled as a portrait painter by his uncanny ability to seize the fleeting expression on a person's face. Rembrandt became more and more interested in the character of his sitter and the expression of deep emotion (*see* Plate 11).

The painters of interiors and daily life are particularly characteristic of the Dutch School. Some of these, such as Steen or Maes, were chiefly interested in the people in the rooms and their occupations (*see* Vol. X: Colour Plate, opp. p. 448); others, such as Vermeer and de Hooch, in the light effects. Ter Borch and Metsu seemed to be more interested in the

textures of costumes than in daily life or light effects. Of all these Vermeer is perhaps the most remarkable. To him a jug or a table-cloth is as significant as a human face, and he paints each with equal care. He is particularly interested in the relation of one part of the picture to another. The position of the smallest object and the smallest spot of light is worked out with geometrical exactness and painted in a way which tolerated no false steps. It was perhaps the most subtle and sophisticated type of painting there has ever been, but it represented an extreme of refinement in a very limited sphere beyond which no progress could be made (*see* Vol. IX: Colour Plate, opp. p. 304).

Another original contribution of Dutch art was in LANDSCAPE PAINTING (q.v.). Painters for the first time painted landscapes naturalistically and for their own sake, not as a background to other subjects. Holland had become a great sea power, holding its own against the English navy; popular subjects, therefore, were seascapes and

LANDSCAPE. PAINTING BY
JACOB VAN RUISDAEL
(1628/9–82)
National Gallery

BELOW: LANDSCAPE WITH
CATTLE. PAINTING BY
ALBERT CUYP (1620–91)
National Gallery

river and canal scenes, which not only depicted magnificent warships and small fishing fleets but showed a great feeling for the changing light and moods of nature. Van Goyen painted calm river scenes, the van de Veldes scenes of the Dutch fleet (*see* Vol. X, p. 397), and van de Cappelle calm seascapes under blue skies.

Jacob Ruisdael and Albert Cuyp were two of the greatest landscape painters who depicted in their different ways the effects of sun and shadows with great feeling. Koninck expressed the calm flat character of the wide Dutch landscape, and Hobbema recorded the details of country life (*see* p. 236). Others, such as van der Heyden, show us the clean streets of Dutch towns and cool spaciousness of their churches.

The buildings for which the pictures were painted also reflect the stolid character of the Dutch burghers. Built in brick with high-pitched, stepped gables and small, panelled rooms, they were, to a great extent, the fore-runners of our own GEORGIAN ARCHITECTURE (q.v.), while the many-storeyed belfries of the Protestant churches influenced the great English architect, Sir Christopher WREN (q.v. Vol. V). The hub of Dutch life of the time, the great city of AMSTERDAM (q.v. Vol. III), was replanned early in the 17th century on a geometrical basis. The rings of streets, with canals down the centre of each, were arranged round the old town, and others radiated symmetrically from it.

The Dutch pottery of the 17th century was prized not only in Holland but particularly in England, where it was called 'delft' from the town where it was chiefly made (*see* EARTHEN-

National Gallery

INTERIOR OF A DUTCH HOUSE. PAINTING BY PIETER DE HOOCH
(1629–*c.* 1683)

WARE, Vol. VII). The pots and tiles (used to panel walls and fireplaces) were decorated in blue or purple on a white ground in imitation of the 'blue and white' porcelain which was imported at the time from China.

When the power of Holland waned in the 18th century its art also sank into insignificance. The most notable modern Dutch artist, Van Gogh, spent most of his life in France (*see* POST-IMPRESSIONIST PAINTING).

See also FLEMISH ART.

E

EARLY CHRISTIAN ART. Christianity grew up in the Roman Empire, and at first the early Christians employed artists and builders who were used to building and decorating ordinary Roman houses, temples, law-courts, and market-places. These artists knew how to represent the gods and goddesses, and how to commemorate great generals by painting or carving the incidents of their campaigns (*see* ROMAN ART). The first Christian buildings, therefore, look much like Roman buildings of the same time, and Christ and the saints look like pagan gods and famous Romans.

For the first three centuries Christians lived in danger and uncertainty; while some emperors tolerated them, others persecuted them. During these unsettled years, they seldom built churches but held services in rooms in large private houses; in times of great danger they probably worshipped in underground burying-places excavated in the rock, called catacombs. The most famous of these catacombs are just outside Rome, but there are others near Naples, Syracuse, and Alexandria. They consist of long galleries with little rooms opening out of them and connected by passages and steep stairways. The bodies were placed on shelves cut out of the walls and were then sealed in with slabs of marble or tiles, which were sometimes carved or decorated. As many of the most venerated of the Christian teachers and many heroic martyrs were buried here, the catacombs came to be regarded as places of great sanctity.

Probably at quite an early period the Christians began to decorate the walls of the catacombs with paintings. Many of the subjects are symbolic, that is to say, a quite ordinary object is represented but, to those who understand, it stands for some sacred person or idea. Thus the fish is a symbol of Jesus Christ because the five letters of the Greek word for fish *IXΘYΣ* (*ichthus*) are the first letters of the five Greek words which mean 'Jesus Christ, the Son of God, Saviour'; a ship means the Church in which the faithful are carried safely over the sea of life; an anchor means hope; a peacock stands for immortality; and the harvest for the Last Judgement. Other favourite subjects are Jonah and Daniel who, besides being themselves witnesses to God's mercy, symbolize the Resurrection. Occasionally Christ Himself is represented. He is not seen as He must have appeared during His earthly life but, according to His own description, as the Good Shepherd. He is young, handsome, and beardless. In representing Him the artists wished to show His divinity by giving Him the features commonly associated with a Roman god such as Apollo. The pictures are thought to be derived from representations of Orpheus, a legendary Greek poet, who charmed the wild animals by playing to them on his lyre. In the same way the portraits of the apostles are founded on those of pre-Christian philosophers and poets.

In these paintings the figures are graceful and full of life; they are generally seen in the open air surrounded by hills, trees, flowers, and animals, whose beauty recalls the lovely descriptions of nature in Roman poetry. The landscape is rendered naturalistically, and seems to recede into the background, for the artists had a considerable understanding of perspective. The figures seem to be solid and their limbs to move naturally under their drapery. After about the 5th century artists became less interested in trying to reproduce the actual appearance of things, and their work takes on a spiritual and unrealistic character. It is, however, brilliantly successful as decoration.

Books were a necessity to the Christian community; some of these Christian books are illustrated, and the pictures are carried out in much the same style as the catacomb paintings. Silk weaving is another technique at which the early Christians, especially those of Egypt, excelled. They often wove biblical figures and angels into their designs.

A good deal of early Christian sculpture has also survived. There are very few statues—that is, figures in the round—but there are a great many stone tomb-chests or sarcophagi, which are decorated with elaborate carving in which

THE CATACOMB OF ST. PRISCILLA.
ROME

BELOW:

JACOB AND RACHEL AT THE WELL
Illumination from the Vienna
Genesis, a Bible picture book of
c. A.D. 500. The parchment is
painted purple and the text
written in gold

The late Rev. F. R. P. Sumner

ST. APOLLINARE IN CLASSE, RAVENNA, BUILT BY THE EMPEROR JUSTINIAN *c.* A.D. 530

The church is modelled on a classical basilica. In the mosaic in the apse the cross represents Christ, and the sheep the faithful being presented to Him

figures are shown in relief (*see* TOMBS). Sometimes the Christians, like the Romans, carved portraits of the dead person on the front of the chest, but they generally included some Christian symbol in the design. Many of these sarcophagi still survive in Roman provinces in southern France and Spain, where they were copied by the Visigoths who overthrew the Roman rulers. Often scenes from the Old or New Testament were represented. The designers of the reliefs seem to have been more original than the painters, for they often illustrated the Bible stories in a straightforward way without using symbolism. These carvings were used later on as models for painters and illuminators.

Great changes took place when, in 313, the Emperor CONSTANTINE (q.v. Vol. V) gave the Christians permission to worship freely. All through his life he bestowed wealth and privileges on them, and finally was himself baptized. The Christians began to build great churches. For these they adapted the plan of Roman basilicas, buildings which had a wide central space in which markets were held and justice sometimes administered, and lower and narrower side aisles separated from the central space by columns. The central space (the nave of the Christian church) was lighted by windows above the roof of the aisles. The apse, a curved projection at one end of the basilica where the judge used to sit, was, in the church, placed at the east end and used for the altar and for seats for the priests. A forecourt at the west end was used by the catechumens (newly converted Christians who had not yet been baptized). The outside of these first churches was very plain, but inside they were decorated with marble panels and mosaics. The columns which separated the nave and the aisles were often brought from pagan temples, many of which were by this time disused and falling into ruins. Sometimes the wall above the columns was flat (*see* Vol. I, p. 117); sometimes there were arches between the columns. The type of building with the arched colonnade has become the most usual plan for Christian churches ever since. There are many fine early churches in Rome, some

Alinari

CHRIST AS THE GOOD SHEPHERD
Mosaic in the Mausoleum of Galla Placidia, Ravenna, 5th century A.D.

very large indeed, showing how numerous and wealthy the Christians had become just before the barbarian invasions of the 5th century.

Many of the churches are decorated with Mosaics (q.v.), which give a richer effect than painting and are very durable. The tiny cubes of coloured glass reflect the light and make the colours glow. At first the mosaic workers chose old Roman subjects. Thus at Santa Constanza in Rome there are little harvest scenes carried out in soft colours against a white ground, while, in the tomb of Galla Placidia, which was built in the 5th century and is the earliest surviving building in Ravenna, there is a fine mosaic representing the Good Shepherd. In this the Christ, young and beardless, is dressed magnificently in gold; the fleece of the sheep is most skilfully suggested by grey shading, and there is a charming landscape background and a blue sky.

Gradually a new style began to be used. The figures are placed almost motionless against a plain gold or blue background. Symbols, especially great crosses, sometimes appear above the head of Christ and sometimes take the place of

His figure altogether. Christ Himself is shown as a rather tragic black-bearded figure. This new style was Christian from the beginning and had lost most of its connexion with classical art (*see* Byzantine Art).

See also Medieval Art, Early.
See also Vol. I: Christianity.

EASTERN MUSIC, *see* Oriental Music.

ECLOGUE, *see* Pastorals.

EFFIGY, *see* Tombs.

EGYPTIAN ART. Art in Egypt appears to have developed from the earliest times in the service of the divine king who, like the Church in medieval Europe, was the chief patron of artistic enterprises. Even in historic times most of the reliefs, statues, and architecture which have survived were created to sustain the divinity of the Pharaoh, particularly after his death. Ancient Egyptian art is, therefore, inseparable from Egyptian ideas about the functions of kingship and the immortality of the Pharaoh

Lehnert and Landrock

THE PALETTE OF NARMER. IST DYNASTY, *c.* 3200 B.C.

The King, wearing the crown of Upper Egypt, slays his
adversary the Chief of the Delta. Below, defeated foes are
in flight (*Cairo Museum*)

(*see* EGYPTIAN CIVILIZATION, Vol. I). A characteristic art-form and expression were first worked
out by the master-craftsmen of the Court, and
the fashions thus created were carefully followed
by lesser craftsmen who catered for the needs of
humbler folk.

During the 1st Dynasty, about 3300 B.C. (*see*
chart, Vol. I, p. 157), the earliest work of art
which we can place definitely is a ceremonial
slate palette dedicated by King Narmer in the
temple of Hieraconpolis. It is carved with reliefs
commemorating the King's victories, the available space being organized so as to tell a story
with force and precision. This palette shows in
essence all the characteristic features of subsequent Egyptian art. At this time, Egyptian
drawing had not discovered perspective, and
throughout the rest of its history it was so bound
by the authority of the conventions used by the
earliest artists that there was little attempt to
represent depth and space. During the 3rd

Dynasty, about 2800 B.C., permanent mortuary
buildings in stone, such as the Step Pyramid of
Djeser, began to replace perishable mud-brick
tombs. From this time Egyptian art took on its
monumental character, a development which
reached full expression in the 4th Dynasty, when
the vast PYRAMID buildings (q.v.) absorbed most
of the energies of a vigorous school of master-
craftsmen. The architecture, statues, and
painted reliefs which they made inspired for a
long time succeeding generations of artists.
During this period the privilege of a 'goodly
burial' ceased to be confined to the king and his
family, and was extended to the Court as well.
The craftsmen, who had been trained on the
enormous tomb erections of the kings of the 4th
Dynasty, produced works of art for the numerous
tombs of the ruling classes, though the quality
of the work is very uneven. The naturalism of
the surviving sculptures in copper as well as
wood and hard and soft stones from this period
generally reflect the religious belief of the time.
The artist's intention was to produce literally
'a speaking likeness' of the deceased—a statue
in which a spiritual essence of the dead man
could reside for evermore. The reliefs that
decorated the walls of tomb-chapels show scenes
of an ideal life which it was devoutly hoped the

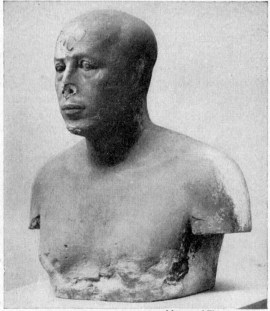

Museum of Fine Arts, Boston

PRINCE ANKH-HAF. OLD KINGDOM, *c.* 2600 B.C.

Bust in painted limestone in the restrained realistic style

Lehnert and Landrock   *Cairo Museum*

LEFT: MYCERINUS AND TWO GODDESSES. OLD KINGDOM, *c.* 2600 B.C.
Statue in dark slate in the classic style of Egyptian art to which later sculptors often revert (*Cairo Museum*)

RIGHT: STATUE OF AMENEMHET III FROM THE RUINS OF THE KING'S MORTUARY TEMPLE. MIDDLE KINGDOM, *c.* 1780 B.C.
Though in the traditional style, the weary melancholy of the features is characteristic of a more realistic school

deceased would enjoy in eternity, as though by mere representation all the needs of such an existence could be magically provided for. The ancient Egyptians never wholly discarded such beliefs in a material after-life, not even later when, it appears, they began to have some doubt about the persistence of a successful earthly life. Relief sculptures may have been replaced later by less expensive wall-paintings, but the subjects remain substantially the same, though their representation underwent considerable changes in style and emphasis.

The culture of the Old Kingdom was swept away by the anarchy that followed the collapse of the 6th Dynasty about 2300 B.C. The character of Middle Kingdom culture that began to succeed it about 2000 B.C. was very different. Disillusion and resignation superseded the old optimism, and the Pharaoh as the type of the ideal divine ruler was largely replaced by a heavenly king, the god Osiris. The art of this period betrays a different emphasis and mood, while still using the traditional forms. The life-like statuary in painted limestone gave way to a

Lehnert and Landrock

TRIUMPHAL STATUE OF TUTHMOSIS III. NEW KINGDOM,
c. 1460 B.C.
The King, holding sceptres, strides forth upon the symbols
of the traditional foes of Egypt (*Cairo Museum*)

more monumental sculpture in sombre hard-stones, and the portraits of the rulers of this period were concerned more with showing the king as a care-worn 'shepherd of his people' than as an aloof deity. Although monuments from this period are not numerous, there have survived a fair number of 'stelae' (inscribed tomb-stones) and statues, especially from Abydos, the great centre of the worship of Osiris. These show that the ordinary citizen had improved his position and was now able to claim many of the privileges of royalty. Consequently there was a good deal of cheap, crude art which can easily give a false impression of an age which at its best had a rare unity of form and expression.

The Middle Kingdom came to an end about 1675 B.C., and there followed a period of foreign domination, with the migrations of new peoples into Egypt, bringing new ideas. Then in 1580 B.C. strong leaders drove out the conquerors, and the New Kingdom was established, with power over the neighbouring states.

The art of the first phase of the 18th Dynasty depicts the Pharaoh as the all-conquering champion of an imperial age. The great wealth and resources that poured into Egypt from her foreign dependencies not only stimulated a taste for luxury and brought new techniques and materials but encouraged a more widespread patronage of the arts. The later rulers of the 18th Dynasty attempted to discard the traditional idea of the Pharaoh as a god, and to build up instead a conception of him as the mere earthly representative of the supreme god. AKHNATEN (q.v. Vol. V), who was particularly attracted by these new ideas, necessarily abandoned the traditional forms of art which were intimately associated with the old conceptions of monarchy. In attempting to find fresh artistic expression for new ideas the conservative Egyptian artists did not go very far outside the old conventions, though the later monuments display a strong naturalism that already had been evident in the popular (as distinct from the regal) art of the time. The early work of Akhnaten's reign, perhaps through the influence of the King himself, is more revolutionary, but after Akhnaten's death there was a violent reaction in favour of the old values both in monarchy and art. The old conventions were worked over and refined rather than worked up into something new. In the 19th and 20th

HEAD OF A MAN IN GREEN SCHIST. *c.* 100 B.C.

The realistic emphasis on lined features shows the influence of Greek Hellenistic ideas upon traditional Egyptian practice (*Berlin Museum*)

LEFT: HEAD OF A QUEEN FROM AMARNA. NEW KINGDOM, *c.* 1360 B.C.

Part of an unfinished statue with body and crown of different materials. The sad, spiritualized expression reflects the religious fervour of the age (*Cairo Museum*)

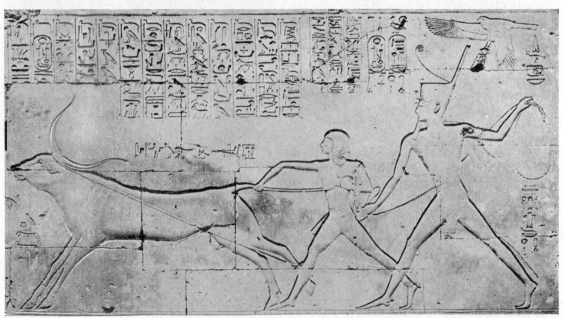

RAMESES II WITH A SON LASSOOING A SACRIFICIAL BULL

Sunk relief from the 'Bull Corridor' in the temple of Sethos I at Abydos. New Kingdom, *c.* 1300 B.C. The style shows a refinement of traditional forms

Gardiner Ph.

PECTORAL OF SENUSRET II. MIDDLE KINGDOM, *c.* 1850 B.C.

The design of this breast ornament in chased and engraved gold is made up of some of the names and titles of the king. The other side is inlaid with semi-precious stones
(*Cairo Museum*)

dynasties, though the art often showed un-expected invention and technical resource, it steadily degenerated into an empty form from which the life had fled. In this it reflected the decay of monarchical government which oc-curred at this period.

When, in 1085 B.C., at the end of the 20th Dynasty, the prestige of the Pharaoh was de-stroyed, the keystone of Egyptian culture col-lapsed. In the twilight of this Late Period, attempts were made in times of political stability to revive the old traditions in kingship and art, but for the most part only the form could be resurrected, since the spirit was no longer felt. The artists copied whatever of the art-forms of the Old, Middle, or New Kingdoms they wished, and often such work was highly accomplished technically, but little more. The Egyptians, far more than any other nation of antiquity, had always been interested in portraiture; and to-wards the end of this period there came an emphasis upon realistic portrait sculpture. This interest in the exact drawing of the human face may have been the result of new ideas from outside, and perhaps of a more searching study of Middle Kingdom statuary. It may indeed have influenced ROMAN ART (q.v.).

Impressive as the achievements of the Ancient Egyptians are in the field of painting, sculpture, and architecture, perhaps the most characteris-tic expression of the Egyptian genius is to be found in the applied arts. Egyptian jewellery of the Middle Kingdom in the form of crowns,

pendants, clasps, and mirrors in exquisitely worked gold and silver, inlaid with semi-precious stones, has never been surpassed in taste and execution (*see* Vol. I, p. 158). Even in pre-historic times great skill was shown in the making of vessels from hard stones (*see* Vol. I, p. 379), and this craft survived till classical times. Egyptian joinery and woodwork at its best was not equalled until the Italian Renais-sance, and the many toilet accoutrements of the New Kingdom in wood, ivory, and glass, such as were found in TUTANKHAMEN'S TOMB (q.v.), are among the most charming products of the ancient world. From antiquity, in fact, the tradition of fine work in Egypt in metals, wood, ivory, glass, pottery, and textiles, sur-vived into modern times and contributed much to the glories of BYZANTINE and ISLAMIC ART (qq.v.).

See also PYRAMIDS; SPHINX; TUTANKHAMEN'S TOMB.
See also Vol. I: EGYPTIAN CIVILIZATION.

EIFFEL TOWER. The French engineer, Gus-tave Eiffel (1832–1923), designed this steel tower

Fox Photos

THE EIFFEL TOWER

as the central feature of the Paris Exhibition of 1889. It stands on the left bank of the Seine in line with the Pont d'Iéna and the Palais de Chaillot (formerly the Trocadero) on the right bank, forming together one of the axial layouts for which Paris is famous.

During the second half of the 19th century French engineers were leading the world in the use of iron and steel for building. The series of exhibitions held in Paris, of which that of 1889 was the most spectacular, gave them their opportunity to experiment in these new materials. The Eiffel Tower was the object of angry protests when it was first built, but it is now regarded as one of the structures which reveal most clearly a new type of beauty made possible by the use of new materials.

A television transmitter to be added in 1957 will make the tower 1,033 feet high. It is an open-work structure supported on four spreading legs. The bases of the legs are linked by arches which are ornamental rather than functional. There are three viewing platforms; one immediately over the arches, one higher up, and one at the top, all reached by lifts.

See also Vol. VII: EXHIBITIONS.

ELEGY. In Greek and Latin literature 'elegy' had not the restricted sense it tends to have in England—that is, a poem of lamentation. In classical literature an elegy is a poem written in elegiac metre; the characteristic of this metre is the elegiac couplet, the first line of which is a dactylic 6-foot line called a hexameter and the second a roughly dactylic 5-foot line or pentameter.

$$— \cup \cup \ | — \cup \cup \ | — \cup \cup \ | — \cup \cup \ | — \cup \cup \ | — \cup$$
$$— \cup \cup \ | — \cup \cup \ | — \ || — \cup \cup \ | — \cup \cup \ | \cup$$

Because Greek and Latin metres were based on the varying length of syllables, it is difficult to reproduce them in modern languages. Coleridge described this metre and rendered it approximately in English thus:

—	∪ ∪	—	∪∪	— ∪ ∪	—	∪	— ∪∪
In the hex	ameter	rises the	fountain's	silvery

— ∪
column

— ∪ ∪	— ∪∪	— || — ∪ ∪	— ∪∪	—
In the pen	tameter	aye || falling in	melody	back

The earliest elegiac poems date from the end of the 8th century B.C. Greek elegiac poems were of one of the following types: banquet-poems, addresses to armies, historical pieces, inscribed dedications, laments, or epitaphs. Of all these, the most famous is Simonides' inscription for the 300 SPARTANS (q.v. Vol. I) killed at Thermopylae, a couplet in which the poet makes the dead speak—

Go tell the Spartans, thou who passest by,
That here obedient to their laws we lie.
(Translation by William Lisle Bowles)

Two Greek elegiac poems are of especial interest to English readers: the *Lament for Daphnis*, one of the earliest pastoral poems by Theocritus in the 3rd century B.C., which served as model for Milton's *Lycidas*; and Bion's *Lament for Adonis* (c. 100 B.C.) on which Shelley partly modelled his *Adonais*.

The most important Latin elegists all lived in the time of the Emperor Augustus: Gallus, Propertius, Tibullus, and OVID (q.v. Vol. V). All of them wrote principally—though not exclusively—love-elegies. Gallus, all of whose works are lost, naturalized the elegiac metre and first devoted it to themes of love. Propertius addressed many of his four books of elegies to his mistress, Cynthia, and in them he traces the course of his love for her from ecstasy through disillusion to aversion. As well as these he wrote elegies with historical or mythological themes, and also his famous epitaph for a noble Roman lady. Tibullus's melodious elegies have two main themes, love and the longing for a quiet country life. Ovid made the elegy more rhetorical and invented new types, such as his letters from exile.

Poems which were classified strictly by their form in classical times have come to be grouped rather by their subject-matter. Thus elegy from the Renaissance onwards falls into two main classes—laments, based on Greek models, and love-elegies, on Latin models. In the 17th-century volume entitled *Poems by Donne . . . with Elegies on the Author's Death*, we find that most of Donne's own elegies are passionate love-poems. Again, the *Roman Elegies* (1795) of the German poet Goethe have love as their main theme, a love that has revealed the whole classical world to the poet.

But the most notable modern elegies are either laments or meditations on death. Pre-eminent among the former are Milton's *Lycidas* (1637), where by pastoral convention the dead friend, Edward King, figures as a shepherd; *Adonais*

(1821), in which Shelley weeps for the death of Keats, but affirms his immortality, 'He is made one with Nature'; and Matthew Arnold's *Thyrsis* (1867) on the death of his friend and fellow poet Clough (*see* PASTORALS).

The 18th century produced many meditations on death, among them Thomas Gray's *Elegy Written in a Country Churchyard*, perhaps the best-known of all English elegies. It is the prototype of the elegy *On Tombs* by the Venetian poet, Ugo Foscolo (1778–1827). This noble poem, prompted by a government order for the burial of all bodies in public cemeteries under similar tombstones with standardized inscriptions, meditates on the human values that this order outrages; asserts that the past, by inspiring the present, lives on; and warns that the present dies if it abandons the past.

See also VERSIFICATION.

ELGIN MARBLES. These are sculptures and architectural fragments from the Parthenon and other Athenian buildings, acquired in Athens by Lord Elgin and now in the British Museum. Lord Elgin, appointed Ambassador to Turkey in 1799 when Greece was part of the Turkish Empire, went to Athens with an expedition to draw and take casts of the ancient sculptures there. The Parthenon had been blown up in 1687 during the war between the Turks and the Venetians; when Lord Elgin saw how badly the sculptures belonging to it and to neighbouring buildings were faring from neglect and from deliberate destruction, he obtained permission to remove them altogether, so that they should be saved for future generations. They were brought to London between 1802 and 1812; in 1816 they were bought for the nation.

The Parthenon, from which most of the sculptures come, was a temple of Athena Parthenos (the virgin goddess) built in 447–432 B.C. (*see* ACROPOLIS, ATHENS). The sculptor Phidias was responsible for the decoration. This, perhaps the most beautiful of all Greek temples, belonged to the Doric ORDER OF ARCHITECTURE (q.v.). The pediments were filled with figures, and round the outside were also stone slabs, called metopes, with carvings in relief (*see* p. 316). In addition, running round the inner side of the colonnade, was a continuous sculptured frieze. These sculptures are some of the finest ancient sculptures which have survived.

British Museum

DETAIL FROM THE WEST WALL OF THE PARTHENON FRIEZE
The frieze depicts a procession of the Athenian people in honour of the goddess Athena

The east pediment portrayed the birth of Athena (goddess of wisdom); the west, the contest of Athena and Poseidon (the god of the ocean) for the land of Attica. The frieze depicted the four-yearly sacred procession in honour of the goddess. The metopes were all scenes of battle: gods and giants, Greeks and Amazons, Greeks and Trojans, and Greeks and Centaurs.

See also ACROPOLIS, ATHENS; GREEK ART.

ELIZABETHAN DRAMA, *see* DRAMA; SHAKESPEARIAN DRAMA.

EMBROIDERY, *see* Vol. XI: EMBROIDERY.

ENAMEL, *see* Vol. VII: ENAMEL.

ENCAUSTIC PAINTING, *see* PAINTING METHODS, Section 2.

ENCYCLOPAEDIAS. The word 'encyclopaedia', which means instruction in the whole circle of knowledge, is used for a work containing information on all branches of knowledge, arranged systematically, usually in alphabetical order. 'Encyclopaedia' is also used for a comprehensive survey of one field of human knowledge, usually arranged alphabetically; though such a work is sometimes called a Dictionary. The *Oxford Junior Encyclopaedia* is a compromise between these two kinds of work. It resembles the first kind in that all the volumes together present a survey of human knowledge. Each volume resembles the second kind in that it deals with one branch of knowledge.

The earliest comprehensive encyclopaedia we know of was compiled in China in the Ming period (*see* CHINESE CIVILIZATION, Vol. I). The *Great Standard* of the Emperor Yung Lo, begun in 1408, was an immense work of over a million pages; but no complete copy of it has survived fires, wars, and other disasters, only a few volumes being extant. Another vast encyclopaedia in 5,020 volumes was printed at Peking in 1726. The British Museum has a copy of this, received in 1878.

Although in Europe the idea of a comprehensive encyclopaedia was unknown before modern times, classical authors and authors of the Middle Ages produced works of so wide a range that they might be considered as the forerunners of encyclopaedias. One of these is the *Natural*

Warburg Institute

THE MANDRAKE. FROM ISIDORE OF SEVILLE'S 'ORIGINS OR ETYMOLOGIES'

From a 9th-century copy by Hrabanus Maurus. The mandrake was supposed to scream when pulled out of the ground

History of Pliny the Elder in the 1st century A.D. Some of the subjects on which it discourses are physics, geography, physiology, animal life, plants, medicine, minerals, and the arts. Pliny's intellectual curiosity cost him his life: he attempted to observe too closely the eruption of the volcano Vesuvius, and was asphyxiated.

Men of the Middle Ages liked informative books: they cherished the old ones, and wrote new ones. Isidore of Seville's *Origins or Etymologies* (7th century), the 13th-century Frenchman Vincent de Beauvais's *Mirror of History* (*Speculum Historiale*) and *Mirror of Nature* (*Speculum Naturale*), and the late 13th-century Italian Brunetto Latini's *Treasure* were all popular encyclopaedic works. Of the several encyclopaedic works of the 17th century the most famous, Bayle's *Dictionnaire historique et critique* (1697–1702), was translated into English, four English editions being published. It was a pioneer work in scientific biography and in the critical presentation of religion and legend.

Ephraim Chambers published the first English encyclopaedia in 1728, under the title *Cyclopaedia* or *An Universal Dictionary of Art and*

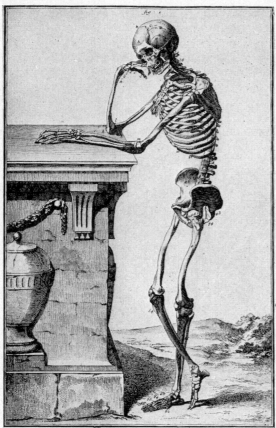

ILLUSTRATION TO 'ANATOMY' IN THE FRENCH ENCYCLOPÉDIE

Sciences. Later editions with supplements appeared, and a French translation was made. It was used as the basis of the French *Encyclopédie*, one of the most famous books of the 18th century, under the editorship of DIDEROT (q.v. Vol. V) and D'Alembert. It took 20 years to complete, and appeared between 1751 and 1780 in thirty-five volumes. Its contributors included all the most eminent writers and thinkers of 18th-century France, among them Voltaire, Rousseau, Montesquieu, and Buffon. It was attacked both by the State authorities and by the Church because it criticized existing institutions—which were so bad that to describe them was inevitably to censure them—and because it attempted to give a rational rather than a religious explanation of the Universe. It had enormous influence in developing radical and revolutionary opinion in France.

The most ambitious encyclopaedia in English, the *Encyclopædia Britannica*, first appeared in three volumes between 1768 and 1771 in Edinburgh. In subsequent editions it was enlarged, and different publishers have at various times undertaken it. It is now in American ownership, and published under the auspices of the University of Chicago. The 14th edition in 1929, published both in New York and in London, consisted of twenty-four volumes. The German *Brockhaus's Encyclopaedia*, started in 1796, the French *La Grande Encyclopédie* (1886–1903), and the Italian *Enciclopedia Italiana* (1929–37) are all important national works. *Chambers's Encyclopaedia* (in no way connected with Ephraim's), completed in 1868, was published by the Edinburgh firm, W. R. Chambers. It has had many editions since, and it is now published by George Newnes. These are the most important of the many encyclopaedias produced in Europe during the last two centuries.

See also Vol. IV: REFERENCE BOOKS.

ENGLISH LITERATURE. The first familiar name in the history of English literature is CHAUCER (q.v. Vol. V) for, although much had been written and recorded before his day, it can only be understood by those who have learned Early English or Anglo-Saxon (*see* ENGLISH LANGUAGE, Vol. IV).

Anglo-Saxon literature is haunted by a quality of tragedy: darkness and storm, winter journeys and long exile, death and disaster are the ever recurrent themes. Poems such as *The Wanderer* and *The Seafarer* are early examples of great English sea poetry; and *The Battle of Maldon* (A.D. 991) is one of the finest battle poems. In the desperate struggle against an overwhelming Viking army the heroic words of the warrior Byrhtwold inspire his companions to 'battle-death and glory':

> The will shall be the harder, the courage shall be
> keener,
> Spirit shall grow great, as our strength fades away.

The greatest existing single work is BEOWULF (q.v.), an epic poem full of heroic deeds which tells the story of great fights against fearful monsters. The excitement of the story is heightened by the strong rhythm and the use of alliteration—that is, two or more accented words in the line beginning with the same letter. The poetic quality is strengthened by the free use of poetic synonyms, such as 'battle-gleam' (spear), 'swan-road', or 'whale-path' (sea), and the heroic conventional phrases which, repeated again and again, made it easy for people to remember the story as they listened to it being told. Most Anglo-Saxon poetry is anonymous and the earliest mention of a poet by name is in Bede's great *Ecclesiastical History* (*see* HISTORIES), in which he tells how Caedmon, a cowherd at Bede's own monastery in Yorkshire, was inspired by a vision to 'sing the beginning of created things'. Only a fragment of this 'Song of Creation' survives; but a long poem called *Genesis* is also often attributed to Caedmon. *The Dream of the Rood* (Cross), one of the finest religious poems existing, is most likely by Cynewulf, a Northumbrian.

Anglo-Saxon prose is at its best in the great Chronicles—the first real historical records in Europe—begun at the command of King ALFRED. They record important events in the history of Wessex, and give magnificent accounts of battles against the Danes.

After 1066 the language and literature of the Court was Norman-French; the language for official and learned use was Latin. English was used only in popular literature, that is, in the BALLADS, tales, and FABLES (qq.v.) told by storytellers. The wandering MINSTRELS (q.v. Vol. IX), who sang in the halls of castles and manors in the 12th and 13th centuries, brought lovesongs and romances from France—tales of chivalry in which every knight had his lady, and in which very strict conventions were observed (*see* ROMANCE LITERATURE). The literature of the people included, as well as songs and stories, the earliest attempts at English drama—the MIRACLE PLAYS (q.v.). These were at first part of the church services—dramatizations of the Christmas and Easter stories; but gradually they moved away from the Church and became more secular and more elaborate. The medieval trade guilds became responsible for the performance of the plays which, besides their religious teaching, included comic characters and scenes. The MORALITY PLAYS (q.v.), which followed the miracle plays, had only a slight connexion with the Church. The greatest of all the medieval plays is *Everyman*, a story, like Bunyan's *Pilgrim's Progress*, of man's pilgrimage from birth to death, most movingly and poetically told. The last great English medieval allegorical poem was William Langland's *Piers Plowman* in which the poet, himself a countryman, gives a vivid and terrible picture of 14th-century English life (*see* ALLEGORY).

CHAUCER, also writing towards the end of the 14th century, is called the first modern poet because he re-established native English as a great literary language. Although the language of the CANTERBURY TALES (q.v.) is rather different from modern English, especially in spelling and in stress, it is easier for us to read than are the miracle plays or even *Piers Plowman*. Chaucer used the language with a new mastery; colloquial and easy, he could be charming, witty, romantic, serious, satirical, and coarse. *The Canterbury Tales*, one of the first books printed by Caxton, might be called the forerunner of the NOVEL and the SHORT STORY (qq.v.), as well as laying the foundations of English poetry. From this time onward, as printing became more common, people grew less dependent on hearing poems and stories from professional minstrels, and more accustomed to reading the works of great writers for themselves.

Though most of the longer medieval allegorical poems were somewhat dull, there were many delightful songs, carols, and short lyrics, and it is from these that Elizabethan poetry sprang. The RENAISSANCE, with its revival of interest in classical literature, and the REFORMATION (qq.v. Vol. I) had profound results for literature. The rhythm and vocabulary of CRANMER's Book of Common Prayer, together with existing translations of the Bible, became the basis for the magnificent prose of the 17th and 18th centuries (*see* TRANSLATIONS). The closing of the monasteries had weakened the Church's authority over learning, and the Elizabethan age opened in an irrepressible mood of daring and experiment—though it was still by no means safe to question accepted beliefs too openly, and most of the writers of the time got into trouble for the freedom of their ideas. It was an age of incredible richness. The outstanding names, SPENSER for pure poetry, MARLOWE for melodrama, RALEIGH for history and travel, SIDNEY for romance, SHAKESPEARE for the whole range of poetry and drama, history and romance, are backed by innumerable lesser names, all crowded into this wonderful period at the end of the 16th and beginning of the 17th centuries. It was the first great age of ANTHOLOGIES (q.v.)—the most famous of them being *Tottel's Miscellany*, printed as early as 1557. Ballads, stories, and traditional plays by strolling players continued to be popular among the illiterate and the country people. Although the reading public was growing, it was not necessary to read to be able to enjoy the blank verse of Marlowe, Shakespeare, Ben JONSON, and others (*see* DRAMA).

Though born an Elizabethan, the poet John DONNE belongs in spirit to the age of scientific inquiry, the 17th century: with a truly original mind, though owing something to the poetry of Raleigh, he broke the conventions of Elizabethan love poetry and founded the school of METAPHYSICAL POETRY (q.v.), in which intellectual intensity counted for as much as passion of the heart.

On the 17th-century stage the demand was for tragi-comedies such as Dekker's, for the violent tragedies of WEBSTER and Tourneur, and for MASQUES (q.v. Vol. IX), with their charming songs and their emphasis on spectacle. But in 1642 the Puritans closed the theatres, and when they reopened with the Restoration both playwrights and audiences had changed. Congreve, Vanbrugh, and others wrote for a sophisticated audience, many of whom, having been in exile in France during Cromwell's rule, were familiar with French models, especially with MOLIÈRE (*see* RESTORATION DRAMA). The emphasis was on brilliant dialogue and complicated, highly artificial plots, an emphasis which remained until the end of the 19th century when SHAW and the Norwegian IBSEN revolutionized the drama.

The 17th century, dominated by the lonely, magnificent figure of MILTON, is as much an age of prose as of poetry. The English language is for the first time widely used in works of scholarship, such as HOBBES's *Leviathan*, Clarendon's *History of the Rebellion*, Burton's *Anatomy of Melancholy*, BACON's *Essays*, and the scientific writings of the first members of the Royal Society. Yet NEWTON wrote his great *Principia* in Latin, and most of Milton's prose works are in Latin. Indeed, it was only after long deliberation that Milton decided to write his greatest poem, PARADISE LOST (q.v.), in English.

The outstanding literary figure of the late 17th century, the beginning of the AUGUSTAN AGE (q.v.), is DRYDEN—satirist, playwright, critic and, with Pope, the greatest master of the heroic couplet (*see* VERSIFICATION). The work of Dryden was brought to its climax in the 18th century by JOHNSON with his magnificent common sense, by SWIFT with his bitter determination to make people listen to the truth, and by POPE, the supreme poet of English SATIRE (q.v.).

But alongside this serious literature of the late 17th and early 18th century a more popular kind of literature was evolving. Newspapers were becoming popular; DIARIES and LETTERS (qq.v.) were written and preserved; the new coffeehouses provided the ideal background for all sorts of minor literary activity—sketches, dialogues, and gossip-writing were the raw material of the *Tatler* and *Spectator* (*see* PERIODICALS); even news-reporting became creative in the hands of DEFOE in such books as *Robinson Crusoe* and *Moll Flanders*.

After a strict censorship of plays was imposed in 1737, the genius and invention which had gone into drama was directed into the NOVEL (q.v.), and the novel-reading public, first catered for by Defoe, was soon able to weep over Richardson's new novels of sentiment.

FIELDING's parody of Richardson's *Pamela* led to a new realistic, humorous novel; and STERNE, Smollett, Fanny Burney, and others all made their contribution to a form of writing which reached its peak in the 19th century when Jane AUSTEN, SCOTT, DICKENS, THACKERAY, George ELIOT, and HARDY were the giants.

At the end of the 18th century there was an inevitable reaction from existing standards of art. The young artists and poets of the ROMANTIC MOVEMENT (q.v.) revolted against the formal perfection of the Augustan age. The tradition of popular poetry—the poetry of ordinary people as opposed to consciously literary people—had never been broken; in Scotland, for instance, the tradition was flourishing in the songs and poems of BURNS. In addition there are, in any age, original writers who remain outside fashionable convention—such poets as BLAKE who, in his *Songs of Innocence and Experience*, wrote lyrics in the simplest everyday language. But the conscious adoption of a new style, the deliberate attempt to change the way of poetry to make it capable of expressing man's simplest and noblest thoughts and feelings in language which was direct and truthful, was left to WORDSWORTH, who, with his friend COLERIDGE, published the revolutionary *Lyrical Ballads* in 1798. Like all innovations it was greeted with mockery, but it changed the course of poetry, and made possible the work of the younger romantics, SHELLEY, KEATS, and BYRON, each profoundly original.

For those to whom poetry did not appeal there were the new novels of horror, such as Walpole's *Castle of Otranto* and the novels of Mrs. Radcliffe; eccentric fantasies such as

Peacock's stories and DE QUINCEY's *Confessions of an English Opium-Eater*; and entertainment for the casual reader, such as the essays of LAMB and of HAZLITT. Serious readers had the historical work of Gibbon and HUME and, later, that of MACAULAY and CARLYLE. Though the 19th century is dominated by great men such as TENNYSON, BROWNING, DICKENS, THACKERAY, ARNOLD, and RUSKIN, there was a tremendous output of every sort of literature. In the mid-19th century the PRE-RAPHAELITES turned to medieval heroic literature, reviving ARTHURIAN LITERATURE and the old SAGAS (qq.v.); CHILDREN's BOOKS (q.v.) were taken seriously, and by the end of the century such classics as *Alice in Wonderland* and the *Jungle Books* had been written. R. L. STEVENSON, Wilkie Collins, and Conan DOYLE popularized stories of adventure and DETECTIVE STORIES (q.v.). The first circulating libraries had encouraged popular novels, and had done much to divide the reading public into highbrow and lowbrow.

In the 1890's the original writers of the day revolted against and often deliberately flouted Victorian public opinion, which seemed to them dull and stifling. Although much of this writing was extravagant and second-rate, poets such as Dowson and Lionel Johnson had something serious to offer; Oscar Wilde was the first original and brilliant playwright since the Restoration; and W. B. YEATS, one of the most influential poets of our own time, as a young man was associated with the writers of the 90's.

The early 20th century was dominated by the novels of WELLS and Arnold Bennett, and the plays of SHAW. In our own time, perhaps the greatest achievements have been the perfecting of the SHORT STORY (q.v.), the revival of the drama, and the development of *vers libre*, that is, poetry which depends on rhythm and sound, not on rhyme and set form (*see* MODERN POETRY). The greatest single experiment in literature, James JOYCE's *Ulysses*, was an attempt to use language in a new way, to renew words and phrases that have grown stale with use. In the 20's, the outstanding names were T. S. Eliot for poetry, Virginia Woolf for prose; and in the 30's young writers, such as Auden, were especially concerned with political and social problems. Since the Second World War, literature has tended to become more personal, more lyrical, and more romantic, as in the poems of Dylan Thomas.

The great writers whose names are in capital letters in this article have separate biographies in Volume V.

See also POETRY; DRAMA; NOVEL.

ENGRAVING, *see* ETCHING AND ENGRAVING. *See also* Vol. VII: ENGRAVING.

EPHESUS, TEMPLE OF ARTEMIS, *see* WONDERS OF THE WORLD.

EPIC POETRY. An epic is a noble poem which, in continuous narrative, celebrates the great achievements of one or more heroes of history or tradition. The first known epics are Homer's *Iliad* and *Odyssey* (*see* HOMERIC LITERATURE), composed probably about 700 B.C. The epic and the choral ODE (q.v.) are the earliest known forms of Greek poetry. Epics in the direct line of succession from Homer are found in Latin, French, Portuguese, Italian, and English.

There are other epics which seem to have arisen quite independently of the classical, notably the Anglo-Saxon *Beowulf*, and also the Sanskrit *Mahābhārata* and *Rāmāyana*. These two epics of the Hindus are thought to have been composed about 500 B.C., and written down 200 to 300 years later. The *Rāmāyana* tells of Rama's war against the Giant, Ravan, who carries off Rama's wife, Sita, and whom Rama slays. Rama is one of the many incarnations of Vishnu, a Hindu god, of whom Buddha is another incarnation (*see* HINDUISM, Vol. I).

BEOWULF (q.v.), the most important poem of Old English literature, over 3,000 lines in length, survives in only one manuscript of the late 10th century, a manuscript which in 1731 was damaged by fire. Its author was an unknown Christian (possibly 8th century, and possibly recomposing an earlier pagan version). Such historical events as it relates belong to the 6th century. In alliterative verse it tells how the hero, Beowulf, comes across the seas from Sweden to Denmark to fight and finally slay the monster, Grendel, and his more terrible mother. Beowulf returns home, and later joins battle with a ravaging dragon, from which, though victorious, he receives his death-wound. In the famous elegiac passage which closes the poem, his people mourn his death and their loss. The unity of *Beowulf* depends on its telling the story of one man, and not of one action. It does not follow Aristotle's rule that 'the construction of the stories should clearly be like that of a drama; they should be based on a single action, one that is a complete whole in itself, with a beginning, middle, and end. . . '. *Beowulf* has, nevertheless, epic simplicity and grandeur, strength in language, freshness in imagery; it recreates a world more primitive than that of Homer, a twilight world where heroic man battles against the forces of nature and monsters.

We know from ancient writers that there was a considerable body of Greek epic literature after the *Iliad* and the *Odyssey*; but it is a Roman poet, VIRGIL (q.v. Vol. V), who wrote the next great epic. His work owes much to the Greeks, and something to Quintus Ennius (239–169 B.C.), the originator of Roman epic poetry, who in his *Annales* took the Greek hexameter (6-foot line) as his metrical model. Virgil's great poem, the *Aeneid*, is a national epic designed to celebrate Rome and Rome's origins. It recounts the wanderings of the Trojan Aeneas from his arrival in Sicily, 7 years after the Trojan war, to his final settlement in Italy, where he founds a Trojan settlement in Latium, whence the Roman race sprang. Virgil skilfully extends this bounded time into the past and the future by dialogue and by prophecy; for example, in Book II, Aeneas relates to Dido the fall of Troy and subsequent events (*see* TROJANS, Vol. I); again, in Book VIII, a shield presented to Aeneas bears prophetic pictures of the future history of Rome down to the battle of Actium. Thus into the comparatively short story of Aeneas's wanderings the poet interweaves the whole history of Rome from its inception to its fullest expansion (*see* ROMAN CIVILIZATION, Vol. I). This noble poem has had a very great influence on European poets, especially on DANTE (q.v. Vol. V) in the early 14th century.

In Book VI of the *Aeneid*, Virgil describes how Aeneas, with the Cumaean Sibyl, descends into the underworld, where they see many of the dead, and visit, among other places, the entrance to Tartarus where criminals suffer torments, and the fields of Elysium where the blessed enjoy happiness. Dante, the greatest poet of the Middle Ages, so much admired Virgil's poem that in his DIVINE COMEDY (q.v.) he has Virgil for his guide through Hell and Purgatory; In Heaven, Dante's first love Beatrice, now an angel, guides him. This great religious epic—

which Dante called a comedy because, unlike a tragedy, it has a happy ending—not only describes realistically the regions of the next world, but in its story of one soul's pilgrimage through the universe, it interprets the life of the spirit.

France in the Middle Ages was the wellspring of literature, and this literature begins with the CHANSON DE ROLAND (The Song of Roland) (q.v.), written probably in the late 11th century. This long poem, telling of the wars of Charlemagne against the Saracens and of Roland's part in them, has little historical accuracy, and is little influenced by classical epics. It is the earliest of a great series of heroic poems of adventure and war, which from their diffuseness, their short-line couplets, and their episodic form, are not true epics, and are more akin to romances (*see* ROMANCE LITERATURE).

The interest in classical forms which the RENAISSANCE (q.v. Vol. I) called forth made for a revival of interest in the epic. Among the many epics of this period one of the most interesting is the Portuguese poet Luis de Camoens' *The Lusiads* (*Os Lusiadas*, 1572). In this classical epic the poet celebrates the descendants of Lusus, mythical ancestor of the Portuguese; and in particular Vasco DA GAMA (q.v. Vol. V) and his explorations of East Africa and the East Indies. Although Camoens died in misery, this greatest of Portuguese poets is now fittingly entombed next to his hero, Vasco da Gama.

In Italy, especially in the 16th century, a modified type of epic, owing much to the romances of chivalry, appeared. Among these are Torquato Tasso's *Gerusalemme Liberata* (Jerusalem Delivered), which tells the story of the First Crusade in romantic terms; Boiardo's *Orlando Innamorato* (Roland in Love); and its sequel by Ariosto, *Orlando Furioso* (The Madness of Roland), which tell of Roland's adventures in love and war (*see* CHANSON DE ROLAND).

MILTON (q.v. Vol. V) published in 1667 in England his noble epic, PARADISE LOST (q.v.), in twelve books of magnificent blank verse, whose opening lines state its theme—

Of Man's First Disobedience, and the Fruit
Of that Forbidden Tree, whose mortal taste
Brought Death into the World, and all our woe
With loss of Eden, till one greater Man
Restore us, . . .

Milton tells the story of the fall of the angels from Heaven, the temptation and the fall of man. Like Virgil, Milton devotes part of his epic (the last two books) to prophecy, but he uses this device less skilfully than Virgil, and these two books might be said to mar the structure of the poem. *Paradise Lost* shows clearly the interweaving of the Hebrew and Greek influence in Milton's mind. Its greatness of theme, thought, characterization, and language have won for Milton a place second only to Shakespeare among English poets. Its sequel *Paradise Regained* (1671), which recounts Christ's temptation in the wilderness, is far less successful. No really great epic has been written since *Paradise Lost*.

See also HOMERIC LITERATURE; BEOWULF; DIVINE COMEDY; CHANSON DE ROLAND; PARADISE LOST.

EPIGRAM. This was originally an inscription, usually in verse; later, an epigram came to mean a short poem ending in a witty turn of thought; and by the end of the 18th century the term was used for any pointed or satirical saying.

The first Greek verse epigrams appeared in the 7th century B.C., usually as epitaphs on tombstones, sometimes on signposts. They consisted of one or more lines of graceful information. Simonides was the first great poet to write such epigrams. Below is a translation of one to his hound:

> Although beneath this grave-mound thy white bones now are lying,
> Surely, my huntress Lycas, the wild things dread thee still.
> The memory of thy worth tall Pelion keeps undying,
> And the looming peak of Ossa, and Cithaeron's lonely hill.

(Translation by F. L. Lucas)

In Simonides' hands epigrams kept their brevity and their purpose, but became as well beautiful and moving.

Gradually the themes of Greek epigrams became more varied, and they were no longer used only for inscriptions. Some treated of pastoral scenes and village life; others of love and wine and books. The themes and the tone of later Greek epigrams are rather similar to those of the sonnet nearly 2,000 years later. The length of the epigram varied, but its metre was almost always that of the elegiac couplet (*see* ELEGY). The following is an epigram by Callimachus (310–240 B.C.), translated by William Cory:

> They told me, Heraclitus, they told me you were dead;
> They brought me bitter news to hear and bitter tears to shed.
> I wept, as I remember'd, how often you and I
> Had tired the sun with talking and sent him down the sky.
>
> And now that thou art lying, my dear old Carian guest,
> A handful of grey ashes, long, long ago at rest,
> Still are thy pleasant voices, thy nightingales, awake,
> For Death, he taketh all away, but them he cannot take.

Alcaeus of Messene in the 3rd century B.C. was the first to write epigrams with a bitter twist to them—invective epigrams—and it was this kind which the Romans preferred when they adopted the form. The greatest of all the many Roman epigrammists was Martial (A.D. 40–104).

Martial published twelve books of epigrams. He was a keen observer of his contemporaries, high and low, good and bad, and he wrote of them with extraordinary detachment. He was many-sided: tender, satiric, flattering, and obscene in turn. His satiric epigrams, which greatly influenced Renaissance and post-Renaissance writers, were short poems ending in a witty turn of thought, about a real person usually under an invented name. Here is one of the more playful of them:

> The golden hair that Gulla wears
> Is hers; who would have thought it?
> She swears 'tis hers, and true she swears
> For I know where she bought it.

The epigram was a favourite literary mode of the European Renaissance, and by the 17th century in England it had the kind of popularity it had had in Augustan Rome. Ben Jonson, Campion, Harington (who translated the Martial epigram above), Donne, and, later, Herrick and Crashaw all wrote epigrams—usually satires on society, but sometimes epitaphs. Campion, in the Preface to his *Book of Airs*, summarizes the attitude of his age to epigrams, thus: 'What Epigrams are in Poetry, the same are Airs in Music, then in their chief perfection when they are short and well seasoned.'

Voltaire in France and nearly all English writers of the AUGUSTAN AGE (q.v.) wrote epigrams—sharp, pointed, and satirical. Besides their epigrams, much of what they wrote was epigrammatic. In particular this is true of Pope, who wrote neat couplet epigrams like this:

> You beat your pate, and fancy wit will come;
> Knock as you please, there's nobody at home.

The 18th-century poets, notably Goethe and Schiller in Germany and Blake, Burns, Shelley, and others in England, continued to produce epigrams. Coleridge wrote a much-quoted epigram on the epigram—

> What is an Epigram? a dwarfish whole,
> Its body brevity, and wit its soul.

As a verse-form, epigram has lived on in the work of Landor, W. B. Yeats, and many others; and in its modern meaning of a pointed saying, it is, as at all times, ubiquitous. Two English writers who used it most effectively are the historian Edward Gibbon, and the dramatist Oscar Wilde.

See also SATIRE.

EPITAPH, *see* EPIGRAM; ELEGY.

ESKIMO ART, *see* AMERICAN-INDIAN ART.

ESSAYS. The name essay was first used by MONTAIGNE (q.v. Vol. V) in 1580 for some writings of his own; but the essay form itself goes back at least to the ancient Greeks. It is a word impossible to define, though its original meaning of 'an attempt' gives a clue to its use. One might call it the rag-bag of literature, a classification for writings that do not fit into the categories of novels, plays, biographies, and so on. An essay can be about any subject, and the author often allows his mind to wander from one subject or mood to another. An essay is usually short and in prose; but POPE wrote two essays in verse, and in the 18th century the word was used to include full-length treatises such as LOCKE's *Essay on Human Understanding* (qq.v. Vol. V).

Few well-known writers have written essays and nothing else, but most have at least occasionally written essays. The examination system and the vogue of the weekly essay by undergraduates at universities have meant that most professional writers start with considerable experience of essay-writing. Most essays nowadays are first published in newspapers and periodicals, and then, if the author is successful, his essays may be collected and published as a book.

As essays often deal with well-worn subjects, whether momentous like Bacon's or trivial like Lamb's, the greatest interest lies in the style. Essays do not generally attempt an exhaustive treatment of their subject, and often suggest much more than they actually state. Indeed, sometimes a short essay, read in two minutes, may provide food for hours of meditation. The essay is a very personal literary form, in which we are given the author's own individual response to the subject. In an essay about railways, for instance, we may gain little or no information about engines or the track or the work of railwaymen, but may read instead about the author's feelings and experiences when waiting for 2 hours in the rain on a small country station platform, with the waiting-room locked because the station-master has gone home for the day. The essay is generally unexpected and often humorous. By an unfamiliar approach the author may make us realize the familiar in a new way. 'It is a thousand to one', said Chesterton, 'that the reader is looking at something he has never seen; that is, never realized.' His own essay on 'A Piece of Chalk' is a good example of this. He describes a sketching expedition on the chalk downs of Sussex. In his box of chalks he had every colour but white. When he needed white chalk he was about to stop work until he realized: 'I was sitting on an immense warehouse of white chalk. The landscape was made entirely out of white chalk. White chalk was piled mere miles until it met the sky.'

We can group essays into four main types: (1) the essay of personal reflection, where the subject seems to be chosen at random, and is merely the vehicle of the author's wit; (2) the brief impressionistic analysis of an idea or a character; (3) the persuasive essay on a public question; and (4) the learned essay on a specialized scholarly subject.

The first kind has flourished ever since Montaigne's time, and intermittently before him. Today, some papers, such as the *Observer*, set apart a special place in the paper each week for such an essay. Perhaps the most celebrated contemporary writer of this kind is Max Beerbohm. Fantasy and absurdity often abound in such essays. DE QUINCEY invites us to read about 'Murder Considered as One of the Fine Arts'; LAMB traces the origin of roast pork to a mythical fire in which pigs were accidentally burnt; SWIFT makes a detailed comparison of a man to a broomstick.

'Surely man is a broomstick. But a broomstick, perhaps you'll say, is an emblem of a tree standing on its head; and pray what is man but a topsy-turvy creature, his animal faculties perpetually a-cock-horse on his rational, his head where his heels should be.'

In the 18th century ADDISON, Steele, and later Samuel JOHNSON (qq.v. Vol. V), used this method in a more restrained style. They undertook the great labour of producing alone complete journals which appeared daily or at frequent intervals. Steele and Addison collaborated in the *Spectator* and the *Tatler*; Johnson produced the *Idler* and the *Rambler* (*see* PERIODICALS). The names of these collections of journalistic essays exactly indicate their manner and purpose. They are the work of learned men on holiday, and convey in polished prose the illusion of casual conversation.

The second type, though not common today, has a long history. The ancient Greek Theophrastus wrote a series of very short 'character essays' which are witty and penetrating analyses of flatterers, superstitious men, boors, and many other types. He was imitated by a number of 17th-century writers, who skilfully created a recognizable character in about 200 words, written in a concise and memorable style. Consider this description of 'A mere formal man': 'His life is like one that runs to the Churchwalk, to take a turn or two, and so passes. He hath stayed in the world to fill a number, and when he is gone, there wants one, and there's an end.'

When ideas not characters are the subject, one thinks first of Francis BACON (q.v. Vol. V). His essays, published between 1597 and 1625, are very short meditations on fundamental subjects—truth, love, envy, death, and the like. Brilliant as they are, they aim not so much at originality as at putting into words what everyone has obscurely felt. For example, 'Certainly it is heaven upon earth to have a man's mind move in charity, rest in Providence, and turn upon the poles of truth', and again: 'Men fear death as children fear to go in the dark; and as that natural fear in children is increased with tales, so is the other.' Bacon's *Essays* are packed with passages which have been so much quoted that we know them without realizing with whom they originated. Essays of Bacon's type flourished for about 200 years after his time.

The third type, the persuasive essay, has been most common from 1800 to the present day, and reached its climax in the later 19th century. This is the most serious and impressive form of essay and usually the longest. Matthew ARNOLD (q.v. Vol. V) used it to attack all that he hated about his own time, *laissez-faire* liberalism, neglect of culture, ignorant distrust of foreign countries. His contemporary, RUSKIN (q.v. Vol. V), preached a moral and aesthetic revolution: 'The most beautiful things in the world are the most useless; peacocks and lilies for instance', and again: 'The purest and most thoughtful minds are those which love colour most' (*The Stones of Venice*). In his book of essays, *Unto This Last*, and other writings he preached a conception of social justice that savoured both of socialism and of feudalism: 'Whereas it has long been known and declared that the poor have no right to the property of the rich, I wish it also to be known and declared that the rich have no right to the property of the poor.' A little earlier MACAULAY (q.v. Vol. V) had brought his formidable apparatus of argument to bear on the idea that the state of England had not improved between 1680 and 1830. In his reviews he annihilated certain forgotten writers in phrases like this, 'But Mr. Robert Montgomery's readers must take what grammar they can get and be thankful,' or, 'We take this to be, on the whole, the worst similitude in the world'. The Victorian essayists in general, if they held an opinion at all, held it very strongly indeed.

The fourth type, the learned essay, is more restricted in its appeal. It usually appears in one of the learned journals, each of which is devoted to one subject of study—medicine, law, archaeology, and so on. These papers have a limited circulation and are bought mainly by libraries; but they are essential to academic progress, for in some subjects, and especially in science, not to know what others are doing in the same field is like working in the dark. Journals of this kind are usually published quarterly, occasionally more frequently. A few such journals began in the 18th century and they have increased in numbers in the 19th and 20th centuries.

In general, one may say that as the essay is the freest of all literary forms, it is nearest to the speaking voice. As long as there are famous writers whom thousands would like to meet, if they could, the popularity of essays is unlikely to decline.

See also LETTERS; DIARIES; PERIODICALS.

ETCHING AND ENGRAVING. 1. Etching and engraving on metal, together with the closely related techniques of drypoint, mezzotint, and aquatint, come under the general heading of intaglio printing (*see* PRINTING, Section 1, Vol. VII). In all these processes the ink which will form the printed picture is contained in small lines or dots sunk in a metal plate, and is transferred to dampened paper by means of heavy pressure.

Each process of making the lines or dots in the plate lends itself to different kinds of effect. Etching is appropriate for a free and rapid method of drawing, though it can also be handled very deliberately. Engraving, sometimes called 'line engraving', is more suitable for disciplined, formal design and draughtsmanship. Aquatint produces areas of tone which resemble washes of water-colour. Mezzotint produces rich gradated tones, and has been much used in the reproduction of oil paintings.

The processes are sometimes employed together on the same plate—engraving to give precision to etchings, drypoint to add richness, and aquatint to render flat tones. Etching, drypoint, and aquatint are usually drawn direct on the plate by the artist, but engravings and mezzotints are more often made by a craftsman from artists' drawings or paintings.

2. ENGRAVING. The lines of an engraving are cut into the metal—usually copper or steel—with a pointed tool, called a graver or burin, which removes a thin shaving of metal. The tone of the line to be printed is determined by the depth to which the graver is thrust into the plate; a narrow, shallow line produces a fine line on the print; a wide, deep incision produces a darker, broader printed impression. When fine lines are cut close together the effect is a grey tone; by varying the strength of the lines and their closeness to each other gradations of tone are produced. Lines may be cut across each other, or 'cross-hatched' (*see* Vol. V, p. 149).

3. ETCHING. This word comes from an old German word meaning 'to eat', because the lines of the picture are eaten into the copper (or sometimes zinc) plate by means of dilute nitric acid. The polished copper plate is coated with a thin film of wax which resists acid. The design is drawn by scratching through the wax with a metal point, thus leaving the plate exposed in a series of lines or ticks. The plate is then placed in a shallow dish of acid which attacks the parts of the plate exposed by the scratched lines. After a time which may vary from a few seconds to many minutes the plate is taken out of the acid, and the lines which the artist wishes to print very lightly are covered with an acid-resistant varnish. The plate is immersed once more in the acid, which continues to eat into the remaining exposed lines, thus making them deeper and wider so that they will print heavier lines. This process of 'stopping out' is repeated as often as the artist thinks necessary to give him the range of tones he desires.

4. DRYPOINT. This technique is similar in some ways to engraving, for the lines are incised with a tool and not bitten with acid. In appearance, however, drypoints are more like etchings. The incision or furrow in the plate is made with a steel or diamond point held and handled in much the same way as in writing with a pencil. The stroke of the point rarely completely removes the shaving of metal; it leaves a burred edge along the line, which holds ink and gives to drypoint its characteristic soft quality. Only a small number of prints, perhaps no more than thirty, can be taken from such a plate, as the burr is lost by the repeated pressure of printing.

5. AQUATINT. Like etching, this is made by eating away the plate with acid. The surface is prepared by covering the plate with a layer of resin dust which, when heated, sticks to the plate and acts as an acid 'resist' in much the same manner as the wax in etching, except that the resin leaves tiny spots of exposed copper, into which the acid bites, giving the final print its grained effect. As in etching, variation of tone is obtained by 'stopping out' the parts to be printed light, and etching more deeply the darker areas (*see* Vol. VII, opp. p. 128).

6. MEZZOTINT. The whole surface of the copper plate is first covered with a multitude of minute pits that are dug into the plate with an instrument possessing hundreds of sharp points (*see* Fig. 1). This instrument is rocked across the plate in many directions until the whole surface is rough. Each little hollow will retain ink, which will be transferred to the sheet of paper when the plate is printed. The artist, using a steel scraper, scrapes away more or less of the surface where he wishes more or less light tones to be printed. Where he does not scrape at all, the roughened surface will hold a good deal of ink and print almost black; where he partly scrapes down, but does not entirely destroy the pitting, some ink will still be retained in the pits and the area will print a light tone. For high lights he scrapes the pits right away and burnishes the flat surface so that no ink will cling to it.

7. PRINTING. All these processes are printed in practically the same way. The plate is warmed, and stiff ink is dabbed all over so that every line is filled. Superfluous ink is then wiped off the surface of the plate (which corresponds to the white parts of the print), leaving ink in the hollows only. Damp paper is placed on the plate and covered with a blanket; the whole is then passed under a heavy roller which transfers the ink to the paper. Artists often proof their plates during the 'stopping out' process to see how the work is progressing. Many of Rembrandt's etchings, for example, exist in different 'states', the first light in tone and later ones growing gradually richer. The number of prints which can be taken from plates, especially copper, is limited, as the metal is worn down and later impressions become pale and blurred. Only about fifty impressions can be taken from copper, but several hundred can be printed from a steel plate. For this reason copper etchings are sometimes electrically faced with steel.

Because all these processes, as well as WOOD-ENGRAVING AND WOODCUTS and LITHOGRAPHY (qq.v.), are printed, the impressions are often called 'prints'. Prints from plates or blocks made

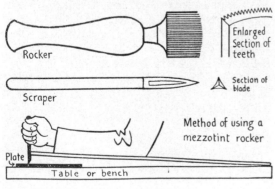

FIG. I. MEZZOTINT TOOLS

Rocker

Enlarged Section of teeth

Scraper

Section of blade

Plate

Table or bench

Method of using a mezzotint rocker

British Museum

ST. JEROME IN HIS STUDY. ENGRAVING BY DÜRER

by the artist himself are original works of art in the same sense as a painting is an original, for they reproduce directly the artist's work.

8. HISTORY. Engraving on metal is a very ancient craft, but it was not until the 15th century that metal plates were engraved with the sole intention of taking prints from them. The first dated line engraving is one of a series of scenes from the Passion, bearing the date 1446. The earliest engravers were German, but their names are rarely known. The greatest of the early engravers, whose technique is unsurpassed, is Albert DÜRER (q.v. Vol. V). He also made a few etchings and drypoints. His subjects range from nudes and classical themes to the Passion of Christ. Dürer and his contemporaries often produced series of prints, usually with religious or moral themes, in which a story is told in pictures. The earliest dated etching (1513), by the German Urs Graf, shows a girl bathing her feet. Another German, Altdorfer (1480–1538), was a prolific and charming etcher, particularly of landscapes. The art of etching reached its greatest height in the work of REM-BRANDT (q.v. Vol. V). Nobody before or since has used etching in a greater variety of ways or

British Museum

SIX'S BRIDGE. ETCHING BY REMBRANDT

with such grandeur of design, ease of execution, and mastery of drawing. Whether his subject is a freely drawn landscape, a painstaking portrait, or a deeply meditated religious subject, there is the same sure touch of the great master. He frequently mixed drypoint with the normal etching technique.

Engraving was used from the 16th century onwards for reproducing paintings and, until the invention of PROCESS REPRODUCTION (q.v. Vol. VII), many of the famous works of the great Masters were known to the majority of people only from engravings.

The 17th century was an age of great portrait engravers and etchers, among whom possibly the finest after Rembrandt was Anthony VAN DYCK (q.v. Vol. V). Van Dyck produced a series of portraits of famous men, a number of which he etched himself, the others being engraved from his drawings. Jacques Callot (1592–1635) made many etchings of gypsies, beggars, and prisoners, and recorded the horrors of the Thirty Years War in his series 'The Miseries of War' (see Vol. X, pp. 376 and 486). Much of our knowledge of what London looked like in the 17th century comes from the etchings of the German, Wenceslas Hollar (1607–77).

British Museum

LE PETIT PONT. ETCHING BY CHARLES MERYON

In his landscape etchings CLAUDE (q.v. Vol. V) shows how expressive the medium can be.

About 1642 von Siegen invented the mezzotint process, which was at first used for original pictures, but was soon to be used for the reproduction of paintings.

In the 18th century HOGARTH (q.v. Vol. V) made engravings and etchings showing the sordid side of the life of his times. He painted many of his pictures especially for engraving, and he did his own engraving. The Italian Piranesi (1720–78) produced large romantic engravings of Roman antiquities, which were popular with the young nobles who travelled to Rome. Later came the invention of aquatint and its masterly use in the hands of such men as Thomas Rowlandson (1756–1827), the English caricaturist, and, greater still, the Spaniard GOYA (q.v. Vol. V), whose eighty-two plates of the 'Disasters of War' expressed the horrors of the Peninsular War with great intensity.

William BLAKE (q.v. Vol. V) recorded his mystic visions in many remarkable etchings and engravings (see Vol. IV, p. 197). The delightful pastoral etchings of Samuel Palmer (1805–81) have had considerable influence on 20th-century artists.

Etching, engraving, and aquatint were used in the late 18th and early 19th centuries for book illustration, especially for books of architecture and picturesque views. Many flower books were also produced, Thornton's *Temple of Flora* being an example in which mezzotint was used. Many of these prints were coloured by hand. Later, etching was used to illustrate novels as well as topographical books,

British Museum

OPENING THE FOLD. ETCHING BY SAMUEL PALMER

as, for example, the famous illustrations of George Cruikshank (1792–1878) for Dickens's *Oliver Twist*. Charles Meryon (1821–68), a colour-blind etcher, captured magnificently the beauty of Paris.

Towards the end of the century artists began to use etching once again for pictures which were not merely illustrations to books but independent works of art, and in the early 20th century etchings and aquatints of landscape and portrait subjects were popular. WHISTLER (q.v.

British Museum

BLACK LION WHARF. ETCHING BY J. MCNEILL WHISTLER

Vol. V), one of the greatest masters of etching, gave a fine feeling for atmosphere in his series of the Thames and Venice. Today the mediums are again being used for book illustration, but only for limited editions. The French artist Rouault has produced a series of prints called *Miserere* which, like the 16th-century series, are related by a common theme.

See also Wood-engraving and Woodcuts; Lithography.

See also Vol. IV: Books, History of; Illustration.

See also Vol. VII: Printing; Process Reproduction.

ETRUSCAN ART.

It is not known for certain who the Etruscans were. It appears that, some time between 900 and 800 B.C., small bands came by sea from Asia Minor to central Italy, where they subdued the local inhabitants and settled down. The part where they lived was called Etruria and is now known, from an alternative form of their name, as Tuscany. The fertility of the soil and the rich mines of iron and copper gained them great wealth, and they were soon trading freely with their neighbours, especially those from western Asia and Greece.

Etruscan art may be divided into three periods. During the first, 750–600 B.C., the Etruscans looked chiefly for their models to western Asia, for Greece had not as yet much to offer them. During the second, 600–450 B.C., they fell under the influence of Greek art. During the third, 450–100 B.C., their art gradually declined until finally it was swallowed up in Roman art.

The chief products of the first period were bronze pails, jugs, and jars, engraved and often decorated with figures of men and animals which were made separately and then fastened on; gold jewellery in the form of ear-rings, clasps, and necklaces, decorated with granulation (minute dots of gold); and a characteristic grey-black pottery called 'bucchero'.

Vast numbers of Greek vases from Corinth, Athens, and elsewhere have been discovered in tombs of the second period, and it seems likely that Greek artists actually came to Etruria to work. In addition to the products of the previous period, the Etruscans now made statues and statuettes of bronze and also of clay (*see* Terracottas). At this time no good stone was known to them, and in general they used bronze and clay where the Greeks used marble. They carried out a certain amount of sculpture, however, in coarse stone. Their temples were much like the Greek temples, but instead of having a surrounding colonnade, they had only a deep porch in front and plain walls at the sides and back. They were made of wood and faced with clay. They also used clay for making ornamental sarcophagi (coffins). They continued to make bucchero vases and at the same time also imitations of Corinthian and Athenian pottery.

Important families frequently had elaborate tombs, the usual form being a communal burial-chamber covered by a large mound. The walls were decorated with paintings, which also showed the influence of Greek art. Also a vast number of engraved seal-stones were made at this time.

In the third period, although jewellery, bronzes, terracottas, and pottery were still made, the quality was not so high. Sarcophagi of clay and of stone were made, and were often decorated with portraits of the deceased.

See also Greek Art; Roman Art.

See also Vol. I: Roman Civilization.

Anderson

APOLLO OF VEII
Large terracotta statue, late 6th century B.C.

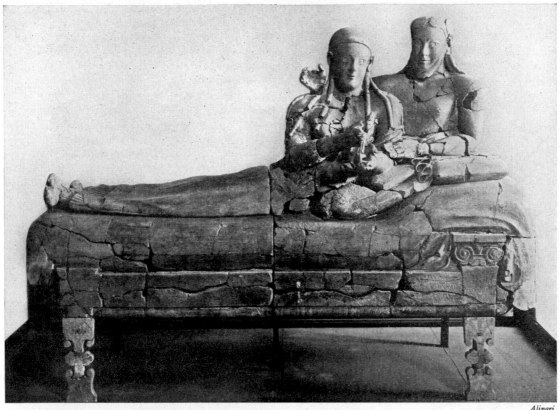

Alinari

ETRUSCAN CLAY SARCOPHAGUS, *c.* 520 B.C.

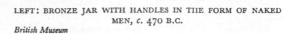

LEFT: BRONZE JAR WITH HANDLES IN THE FORM OF NAKED
MEN, *c.* 470 B.C.

British Museum

EVERYMAN, *see* MORALITY PLAYS.

EXPRESSIONIST ART. The term 'Expressionism' is applied to a movement in modern continental Europe in which artists, and also writers and dramatists, seek by new techniques to express their inmost feelings rather than to describe the real outside world in the traditional methods of their craft. The word was coined by artists who wished to show their opposition to IMPRESSIONIST PAINTING (q.v.), the style in which the aim of the painter was to represent the outside world simply as it appeared to the eye, without attempting to express his own emotion or to exercise his imagination in any way. The Expressionists believed that the artist should find inspiration not in the appearance of the outside world, but in his own imagination and his emotional reaction to what he saw. They were inspired chiefly by the works of two

National Museum, Oslo

THE CRY. PAINTING BY EDVARD MUNCH

northern painters, the Dutchman Van Gogh (1853–1890) and the Norwegian Edvard Munch (1863–1944). In the work of both of these artists, the expression of emotion was more important than naturalism. With violently twisting lines and brilliant colour Van Gogh distorted landscapes into expressions of his own violent temperament, while Munch chose subjects themselves full of emotion and planned his paintings so that each line and touch of colour heightened the impact of the subject on the spectator (*see* POST-IMPRES-SIONIST PAINTING).

The first Expressionist group, called *Die Brücke* (The Bridge), was founded in Germany about 1905. Its members painted in strong patterns of line and colour, but were inclined to use bright colours and startling simplifications of form for their emotional effect, rather than for their decorative value. For this reason the Expressionists began very early to explore PRIMI-TIVE and AFRICAN ART (qq.v.). Satire and a deliberately frightening quality began to appear in their paintings. Emil Nolde, who joined the group, used elements taken from primitive art to express religious emotion. The sculptor Ernst Barlach tried to recapture the direct and moving qualities of medieval art in his wooden carved figures by means of a medieval simplicity of technique. Oscar Kokoschka followed Van Gogh in using a feverishly twisting brush-stroke to convey emotion, investing landscapes and portraits with a strange violence.

A second Expressionist group, called *Der Blaue Reiter* (The Blue Rider), was formed in 1911, and its chief members were Franz Marc (killed in the First World War), the Russian Wassily Kandinsky, and Paul Klee. They attempted to express emotion not so much by distortion of natural forms, as by using line and colour to convey emotion by themselves, apart from the things represented. Kandinsky went so far as to develop what is called 'Abstract Expressionism', where there is no imitation of nature, but a pattern of coloured lines and patches which still are intended to evoke particular emotions in the spectator. Klee was interested less in the expression of emotion than in a sort of abstract fantasy. Starting from an abstract play of lines and colours, he would allow a subject gradually to suggest itself; the result is usually whimsically fantastic rather than emotionally striking.

The term Expressionism is sometimes used for all forms of art in which the artist distorts nature in order to achieve a powerful emotional effect, whether or not he belonged to the German movements. It is applied, for example, to the French religious artist Georges Rouault, who, like the Germans, used a similar technique for its emotional rather than its decorative effect. He, too, turned to medieval and primi-tive art for inspiration, recalling in his later work the religious images of the Middle Ages.

See also MODERN ART; MODERN POETRY.

THE TOWER OF BLUE HORSES. OIL PAINTING BY FRANZ MARC, 1913–14

F

FABLE. This is a short story, either in prose or verse, which attempts to convey a lesson in or observation on manners, behaviour, or morals. The characters in the story are often animals that think and talk like men. The fable is a very ancient form of long-continued and widespread popularity.

Greek fables are ascribed to Aesop, who is said to have been a slave in Samos in the 6th century B.C. The earliest of several Greek collections of fables now extant was made by Babrius in the 2nd century A.D.; this was used by a 14th-century monk, Maximus Planudes, who made the collection familiar to us under the title *Fables of Aesop*. These fables have become so well known in many countries that many of their phrases have enriched the language: for instance, 'sour grapes', 'to cry "wolf"', 'a wolf in sheep's clothing', 'a dog in the manger'. Below is the fable from which we have adopted the last phrase:

A dog lay in a manger, and by his growling and snapping prevented the oxen from eating the hay which had been placed for them. 'What a selfish Dog!' said one of them to his companions; 'he cannot eat the hay himself, and yet refuses to allow those to eat who can'.

Nearly all the fable-writers of Europe, such as the Frenchman La Fontaine (1621–95), admit their debt to Aesop, many of their fables being merely new versions of his. Jean de la Fontaine is incomparably the greatest fabulist of modern Europe, and one of the most brilliant writers of the reign of LOUIS XIV (q.v. Vol. V). His fables are written in elegant, witty verse. The animal characters are most convincing as animals, but at the same time clearly mirror recognizable types of men to be found in the life of Louis XIV's Court and times—king,

THE ASS WHO IMITATED THE LAPDOG
Woodcut from the first printed edition of Aesop's *Fables*,
Naples, 1485

courtiers, nobles, merchants, peasants, clergy, lawyers, and children. Although La Fontaine writes as an observer of life rather than as a moralist, each of his fables points a moral. In some the moral is stated, usually at the end of the fable; in some it is implicit. All the fables present the view that men's folly and wickedness have made a world where virtue is little rewarded. La Fontaine took some of his themes from oriental sources—from the fables of an Arabian fabulist, Lokman, and from an ancient collection of Hindu stories, *Bidpai*, both translated in the 13th century.

Many other writers have produced memorable fables—for example, the Latin poet HORACE (q.v. Vol. V), who wove into his epistles and satires fables such as the *Town and Country Mouse*. The French divine Fénelon (1651–1715) wrote a book of fables to teach a royal pupil his duties; and Jonathan SWIFT (q.v. Vol. V), in his *A Tale of a Tub*, designed the brilliant fable of the *Spider and the Bee*. The spider represents the anti-classical writers who maintained that creative writing should, like the spider's web, be designed and spun out from within. The bee represents the writers who argued that they should not rely wholly on their own genius, but should find inspiration in the classics. These, like bees, fill their 'hives with honey and wax; thus furnishing mankind with the two noblest of things, which are sweetness and light'.

See also Vol. I: FABULOUS CREATURES.

FAERIE QUEENE, THE, by Edmund Spenser, *see* ALLEGORY. *See also* Vol. V: SPENSER.

FAIRY-TALES, *see* CHILDREN'S BOOKS. *See also* Vol. I: FAIRY-TALES AND TRADITIONAL TALES.

FAUST. Faust in literature stands as a symbol of modern man striving for higher knowledge along forbidden paths. That he has become such a figure is largely the work of the German poet, GOETHE (q.v. Vol. V), whose dramatic poem of 12,000 lines was the first complete attempt to present the salvation of Faust.

Georg (or Johann) Faust (*c.* 1480–1540) was born in Knittlingen (Württemberg). According to contemporary sources he studied magic in Cracow and travelled widely in Germany practising his art. He had no great reputation, however, and was frequently attacked as a mountebank and charlatan. After his death tales of his enterprises in magic were collected, the first so-called *Faustbook* appearing in 1587. This was translated into Dutch and French, and in England, where the legend had been known since 1588, the *Historie of the damnable life and deserved death of Doctor John Faustus translated into English by P. F. Gent* appeared in 1592. This was the source of the *Tragical History of Dr. Faustus* by MARLOWE (q.v. Vol. V). The drama was taken to Germany by a company of strolling players who travelled on the Continent in the 17th century. There it eventually became a puppet play, and in this debased form was known to the young Goethe.

In 1759 the German writer Lessing, in a scene of a projected drama which he never completed, restored the Faust tradition to serious literature. He was the first to attempt the salvation of Faust. Marlowe and the authors of the *Faustbooks* had no hesitation about Faust's fate; he was a sinner, and Marlowe portrayed his 'damnable life and deserved death' with matchless poetic power. However, in the 18th century,

the Age of Enlightenment, when striving for knowledge was ranked among man's highest aspirations, writers such as Lessing thought that Faust deserved to be saved; and it fell to Goethe to work out his salvation. Goethe began his *Faust* in 1772, and only ended it in the year of his death (1832). After a *Prologue in Heaven* in which the Lord gives Mephistopheles permission to tempt Faust by any means he may devise, we first meet Faust, the discontented seeker after knowledge, and also Gretchen, whom Faust seduces and deserts. Gretchen is imprisoned and executed for killing her child by him. The first part of the tragedy, the most poignant that Goethe ever wrote, ends with Faust's vain attempt to rescue Gretchen from prison. The second part describes how Faust, having recovered from his sense of guilt, visits the Emperor's Court, is associated with the resuscitated Helen of Troy, and carries out warlike and colonizing enterprises. He dies at the age of 100, and in heaven Gretchen intercedes with the Virgin to obtain his salvation. Although many critics still hold that the first part is a far greater work than the second, the true meaning of the drama as a whole has become more widely recognized. Faust's salvation cannot be divorced from his life and character as presented in the earlier part of the poem.

Since Goethe, many writers, especially in Germany, have used the Faust theme, mainly in dramatic form. Many of these have dealt with the damnation rather than the salvation of the hero. The most notable are Lenau's tragedy (1836), Heine's 'dance-poem' (1851), Thomas Mann's prose work *Doctor Faustus* (1947), and also the French poet Paul Valéry's unfinished comedy, *Mon Faust* (1946).

See also GERMAN LITERATURE.

FIGURES OF SPEECH. These are established modes of expression which, by differing from the normal and expected, make what is said more vivid. They occur not only in literature, but also in everyday speech, and even in SLANG (q.v. Vol. IV).

Some figures of speech point out likenesses in unlike things; some express contrasts or seeming contradictions; some make statements opposite to their real meanings; some use a name other than its own to signify an object; some depend on twisting a statement into another shape; and so on. But all figures of speech have a common purpose—to make what is said more vivid, more startling, more memorable; and all of them employ the same means to this end—they spur the reader's imagination, making it leap from one idea to another. And the enlivened imagination is capable of comprehending and holding the ideas offered.

1. COMPARISONS. 'Simile' and 'metaphor' contrast two objects, persons, or events in order to emphasize what they have in common. Simile does this by an explicit comparison, metaphor by an implied comparison. The simple statement, 'He fought bravely and well', could, by using a simile, become, 'He was like a lion in the fight'. But if the comparative word is omitted, we are left with an implied comparison, that is, a metaphor—'He was a lion in the fight'. In both, the comparison emphasizes what the man and lion have in common, namely, courage and strength, without using the words 'courage' and 'strength'.

In *The Rime of the Ancient Mariner* Coleridge wrote brief prose summaries beside every few stanzas of the events that they relate; and often we find that a main difference between the prose rendering and the poetic lies in the use of metaphor, as here—

The ship driven by a storm toward the south pole.

And now the STORM-BLAST came, and he
Was tyrannous and strong:
He struck with his o'ertaking wings
And chased us south along.

With sloping masts and dipping prow,
As who pursued with yell and blow
Still treads the shadow of his foe,
And forward bends his head,
The ship drove fast, loud roared the blast,
And southward aye we fled.

In this second stanza, the double comparison of the ship with a pursued man, and of the storm with a pursuing enemy, is developed in detail. Because Homer often developed his similes at length, such a simile is often called a 'homeric simile'. In the same way, the comparison in a metaphor is often extended to show a series of likenesses; and we call it an 'extended metaphor'. The famous passage in which Brutus persuades Cassius of the wisdom of fighting at Philippi is an example of this:

There is a tide in the affairs of men
Which taken at the flood leads on to fortune;
Omitted, all the voyage of their life
Is bound in shallows and in miseries.
On such a full sea are we now afloat,
And we must take the current when it serves,
Or lose our ventures.

     (*Julius Caesar*, Shakespeare)

No one has formulated the importance of metaphor better than Aristotle, who, in discussing diction in *The Art of Poetry*, said: 'But the greatest thing by far is to be a master of metaphor. It is the one thing that cannot be learnt from others; and it is also a sign of genius, since a good metaphor implies an intuitive perception of the similarity in dissimilars.'

Metaphor is quicker and more arresting than simile, and its images can add beauty, movement, and power. But it must be used with care. In many words and phrases a metaphor lies sleeping. Such metaphors, if thrown together, often become muddled, as in 'Bottlenecks will be ironed out'. They are then called 'mixed metaphors'. There is an example of this in Hamlet's famous soliloquy:

. . . Or to take arms against a sea of troubles
And by opposing end them?

Very near to metaphor is 'personification'; that is, representing as a person something that is not a person—a ship, perhaps, a country, or an idea. We are using personification in the song, 'Rule, Britannia!', or when we say of a ship, 'She can do 14 knots'. Collins personified honour as a pilgrim and freedom as a hermit in his 'Ode written in the year 1746':

There Honour comes, a pilgrim grey,
To bless the turf that wraps their clay;
And Freedom shall awhile repair,
To dwell, a weeping hermit, there!

A special case of personification, when nature is credited with human emotions, is known as the 'pathetic fallacy':

Thee Shepherd, thee the Woods and desert Caves,
With wild Thyme and the gadding Vine o'ergrown,
And all their echoes mourn. (*Lycidas*, Milton)

2. NAME CHANGE. Some figures of speech use other than their real names to identify the subjects they are describing. For example, instead of naming the thing meant, the writer names one of its attributes or symbols. This is called 'metonymy'. James Shirley in 'A Dirge' writes:

> Sceptre and Crown
> Must tumble down,
> And in the dust be equal made
> With the poor crookèd scythe and spade.

If, like Coleridge, Shirley had prose marginal notes, he might well have cast this stanza as 'Both kings and peasants must die'. By using the symbols of their callings, and so emphasizing the contrast in their lives, and the levelling quality of death, he makes his statement more rich and powerful.

3. CONTRASTS AND CONTRADICTIONS. 'Antithesis' startles the reader's attention by using contrasting or seemingly contradictory expressions. 'A wise son maketh a glad father; but a foolish son is the heaviness of his mother' (*Proverbs*) makes its effect by using words of opposite meaning in parallel phrases; while 'O strong and long-lived death, how cam'st thou in?' ('Elegy on Mrs. Boulstred', Donne) uses the seemingly contradictory words 'long-lived' and 'death' in juxtaposition to each other to add power to the phrase. 'Syllepsis', the unexpected coupling together of words which convey unrelated ideas, such as 'Love and murder will out' (*The Double Dealer*, Congreve), has the same effect. The statement 'John is no fool' makes the hearer at once think of the exact opposite of 'fool', and is therefore a more effective way of saying 'John is intelligent'.

4. APPARENT MIS-STATEMENTS. Another figure of speech, often used by orators, depends upon an ironical mis-statement which the reader or hearer has to interpret. Mark Antony used irony when he said, 'And Brutus is an honourable man' (*Julius Caesar*, Shakespeare), since he meant the opposite, and intended his audience to understand that he meant the opposite.

Sometimes a deliberate understatement is used to gain effect. Swift, when he wrote, 'Last week I saw a woman flayed, and you will hardly believe how much it altered her person for the worse' (*A Tale of a Tub*), evokes more horror in his reader by this understatement than he would by the most impassioned description. The opposite, an over-statement or 'hyperbole', is commonly used in slang; for example, 'I'm dead', 'I'm cooked', 'I'm frozen', for 'I'm tired', 'I'm hot', 'I'm cold'. Hyperbole can also be used with great poetic effect: 'They were swifter than eagles, they were stronger than lions' (2 Samuel xxiii) wrote David of Saul and Jonathan. Another rarer kind of mis-statement is when an adjective referring to a future event is used as though the event were already past:

> So the two brothers and their murder'd man
> Rode past fair Florence. (*Isabella*, Keats)

We understand that the man is not yet murdered, but about to be; and the effort of imagination demanded by this—as by all the other 'mis-statement' figures—ensures its effect.

5. APOSTROPHE AND RHETORICAL QUESTION. To apostrophize someone, generally a dead or absent person, in a public speech or poem is to call upon them in an exclamatory way. Wordsworth, for instance, in his Sonnet to Milton begins:

> Milton! thou shouldst be living at this hour:
> England hath need of thee:

Another device often used by orators is the rhetorical question, that is, a statement made for effect in the form of a question. It has the effect of persuading the hearer to endorse the statement. At the time of Wat TYLER's rebellion (q.v. Vol. V), John Ball in his revolutionary sermon (1381) put the doctrine of social equality in this powerful and memorable form:

> When Adam delved and Eve span
> Who was then the gentleman?

6. INTERRUPTION, INVERSION, AND REPETITION. An effective rhetorical device is to break off the question or statement in the middle, thus giving the unspoken words greater force:

> If we should fail— (*Macbeth*, Shakespeare)

An inversion of the natural order of words: 'Home they brought her warrior dead' (*The Princess*, Tennyson), or a repetition of significant words: 'Break, break, break, On thy cold grey stones, O Sea!' (Tennyson), are other devices for gaining emphasis, as is the interruption of a statement by an address to an absent person:

> The very deep did rot: O Christ!
> That ever this should be!
> Yea, slimy things did crawl with legs
> Upon the slimy sea.
> (*The Ancient Mariner*, Coleridge)

7. PLAY ON SOUND. The choice of words as well as their arrangement plays an important part in gaining effect. When the words chosen suggest their sense by their sound (a device called 'onomatopoeia') their effect is enhanced. Pope both explains and uses the device in this passage:

True ease in writing comes from art, not chance,
As those move easiest who have learned to dance.
'Tis not enough no harshness gives offence,
The sound must seem an echo to the sense.
Soft is the strain when zephyr gently blows,
And the smooth stream in smoother numbers flows;
But when loud surges lash the sounding shore,
The hoarse, rough verse should like the torrent roar.   (*Essay on Criticism*)

A pun is a play on sounds which have more than one meaning. Often this is used for fun:

They went and told the sexton
And the sexton toll'd the bell.

But it is also often used quite seriously, especially by Shakespeare, who in a sonnet punned thus on his name, Will:

Whoever hath her wish, thou hast thy *Will*,
And *Will* to boot, and *Will* in overplus.

8. DRAMATIC ARRANGEMENT. A writer sometimes makes his ideas or statements succeed each other in a series, each more forceful than the last, until he reaches a climax. For example, John of Gaunt, when describing his feeling for his country, says:

This blessed plot, this earth, this realm, this England.   (*Richard II*, Shakespeare)

On the other hand, the writer may seek his effect by a sudden anti-climax or bathos from an impressive to a trivial statement—a device dear to satirists and humorists:

Poetic Justice, with her lifted scale,
Where, in nice balance, truth with gold she weighs,
And solid pudding against empty praise.
          (*The Dunciad*, Pope).

FLAMBOYANT ARCHITECTURE, *see* GOTHIC ART, Section 3.

FLEMISH ART. A foreigner who looks at the art of the Netherlands—that is, Flanders (roughly the modern Belgium) and Holland—can hardly fail to be struck by the fact that the two countries have always shown a natural aptitude both for trade and for painting, and at times in their history when they have had successful mer-

THE TOWN HALL, LOUVAIN, BELGIUM
It was built in the 15th century

chants they have also had brilliant painters (*see* DUTCH ART). In addition, the Flemings have had a strong tradition of excellence in the minor arts—particularly weaving of materials, tapestry, and lace-making—and they have preserved these traditions (which still flourish) in spite of constant wars and religious disturbances.

The most notable Flemish works of art which date from the Middle Ages are the vast town halls, which reflected the growing prosperity of their cities. The largest of these was the 13th-century Cloth Hall at Ypres, destroyed in the First World War but rebuilt to the old pattern. Perhaps the finest is the town hall at Louvain. This building is an example of how the Flemings, who did not show any great originality in either architecture or sculpture, decorated their buildings with sculptured figures in order to give them the same rich effect that their paintings have. The Louvain town hall is more like a gigantic

Alinari

THE PORTINARI ALTAR-PIECE BY HUGO VAN DER GOES (*c.* 1435–82)
In the centre panel of the triptych is the Nativity and in the wings are donors and Saints

casket than a building; but for richness of pictorial effect few buildings can rival it.

From the 12th to the 14th century Flanders was dominated by France, and Flemish artists worked at the Courts of the dukes of Burgundy. The chief characteristic of their art was a realism

Foto Mas

PIETÀ BY ROGIER VAN DER WEYDEN (*c.* 1400–64)
In the Prado Museum, Madrid

which is pre-eminent in the sculpture of Claus Sluter, who worked for the Duke of Burgundy till his death in 1406. He carved a grand series of large figures of Hebrew prophets for a fountain in the monastery of Champmol near Dijon, and also portraits of the duke and duchess which are the first realistic portraits of medieval art. A similar realism is seen in the illumination in the *Très Riches Heures* painted for the Duke of Berri by the Limbourg brothers in 1416. In the calendar of this manuscript the months are illustrated by scenes of Court and peasant life and accurate views of castles (*see* Vol. VI, p. 6; Vol. X, p. 152).

In the 15th century the Flemish merchants became so prosperous that the power passed from the great lords to the cities, and in these cities the great Flemish school of painters worked. The first and most famous of these painters, Jan van EYCK (q.v. Vol. V), appeared in the 1420's working in a style and technique which had no precedent. His paintings showed a command of light and perspective which the Italians themselves were only just mastering and, though he did not invent the technique of oil painting, he was the first great master to use it. Tempera and fresco fade in the damp northern climate (*see* PAINTING METHODS), and oil is more permanent and more suited to the brilliant and meticulous rendering of detail at which the Flemish painters excelled.

Jan van Eyck and his brother Hubert were followed in the 15th century by a large number of brilliant painters, of whom the most important were Rogier van der Weyden, Hugo van der Goes, Memlinc, and Dirk Bouts. Although Rogier van der Weyden, at least, is known to have painted a series of important historical scenes for the town hall at Brussels, these no longer exist, and the surviving work of this brilliant group consists of religious pictures, usually altar-pieces, and portraits. In these the taste of the wealthy merchants who commissioned the artists plays an important part. The sacred scenes are realistically treated; the Holy Family are ordinary people seen in a natural landscape or room, and the donor of the picture is often portrayed as though he was taking part in the scene. The pictures of Rogier van der Weyden, in addition, show a depth of human feeling which perhaps only the great Dutch painter Rembrandt has equalled.

Flemish and Italian art grew up at about the same time without being fundamentally influenced by each other. But the two arts interacted in several interesting instances. Rogier van der Weyden, for instance, visited Italy in 1450, and then introduced Italian features into some of his paintings. Again, soon after 1475,

when the gigantic 'Portinari' altar-piece commissioned from Hugo van der Goes by the Medici agent in Flanders arrived in Florence, it created a sensation, for it was the largest oil-painting the Italians had ever seen.

During the 16th century the Netherlands came under Spanish rule, and after a bitter struggle the Protestant northern States broke away to form what is now Holland. In Flemish art these political developments were reflected in the sharp cleavage which now set in between the Court style and the popular style. In the 16th century the Court artists for the most part tried to imitate Italian models without properly understanding them, because this was the fashion. The result was an uninspired mixture of Flemish realism and Italian subjects. The art of the people, however, is represented by the very moving and beautiful pictures of Pieter BRUEGHEL the Elder (q.v. Vol. V). His art is old-fashioned—in many ways more medieval than the art of the van Eycks and their school more than 100 years earlier. Brueghel, for instance, seems to show in many of his paintings the old medieval dislike of empty spaces, and he fills up

Musées Royaux, Brussels

'THE FALL OF ICARUS' BY PIETER BRUEGHEL THE ELDER (1525–69)
Icarus is falling into the sea below the ship on the right

'THE JUDGEMENT OF PARIS' BY RUBENS (1577–1640)

the horizon with mountains which do not exist in the Flemish landscape he painted. He was antagonistic to classical mythology: in his picture of the Fall of Icarus, for example, he shows the main incident only in the background, and the principal figure, the ploughman, is turning his back on it. In the warmth and beauty of his paint, in the freshness of his landscape backgrounds, and in his deep sympathy for the folly and suffering of the ordinary man, Pieter Brueghel is one of the greatest Flemish painters.

In the 17th century, however, the magnificent art of Flanders' greatest painter, Peter Paul RUBENS, sprang from the Court tradition, as did that of his pupil, VAN DYCK (qq.v. Vol. V). Pictures of low-life and tavern scenes continued to be painted by such artists as Teniers and Brouwer, somewhat in the vein of Brueghel but without his genius (*see* GENRE PAINTING).

The outward career and activities of Rubens were opposed to all that Brueghel stood for, yet in reality the two have much in common and are equally representative of the Flemish genius. Rubens visited Italy at an early age and stayed there 8 years, absorbing everything that that country had to offer an artist. Italy was at that time just about to evolve BAROQUE ART (q.v.), and Rubens, on his return to Antwerp in 1608, formed independently a northern baroque style of painted decoration, peculiarly Flemish. Both in Italy and in Flanders baroque art is religious and bombastic, calculated to appeal by its magnificence to the emotions of the spectator. Rubens painted for princes and wealthy churches; he himself lived like a prince, and part, at least, of his life was spent as a diplomat. In addition to the immense decorations and religious subjects which were his chief delight, he painted a number of portraits and, at the end of his life and purely for his own amusement, a series of landscapes. Finally, in his great 'Kermesse' (Fair) now in the Louvre, he showed that he had as much understanding of the common people as Brueghel.

The most talented of Rubens' immense studio of pupils, Anthony Van Dyck, had not the tremendous vigour of his master But his sensitive spirit made him excel in portraiture, in which he based himself to a great extent on Italian painters, and his influence on painting in England, where he lived for some years, was very great (*see* Vol. V, p. 83).

Flemish architecture was a peculiar mixture of medieval and Renaissance elements which became the model for Elizabethan architecture in England. Flemish tomb-sculptors fled to England in large numbers towards the end of the 16th century to escape religious persecution, and it was a member of one of these families who carved the bust of Shakespeare above his tomb at Stratford on Avon (*see* Vol. V, p. 411).

In the 17th century the Flemings built a series of churches in a particular Flemish baroque style largely inspired by the decorations of Rubens. Rubens himself, however, is only known to have designed one building (his own house at Antwerp). But it is impossible to look at a characteristic example, the façade of the Jesuit church at Louvain, with its wealth of rich, sculptured ornament, without being reminded of another Flemish building of 200 years earlier—the town hall in the same town of Louvain. These qualities of vigour and pictorial richness characterized Flemish art during more than 200 years of its greatness. It is not surprising, therefore, that the weaving of tapestries—the richest and most luscious form of interior decoration—has also flourished in Flanders. So renowned were the tapestry weavers that the name Arras, one of the chief centres of manufacture, became used as another name for tapestry. Most of the palaces of Europe were decorated with Flemish tapestries.

Since the 17th century Flemish painting has hardly achieved international status, and Flemish artists have usually worked outside their own country.

FLORENTINE PAINTING.

In Florence, where the Renaissance in Italy started, painting was only one among very many kinds of artistic activity (*see* ITALIAN ART, Section 3). The great Florentine painters were in many cases equally distinguished as sculptors or as architects, and consequently they tended to look at the world not so much from the point of view of the painter as from that of the all-round artist who was also a painter.

The first great Florentine painter, GIOTTO (q.v. Vol. V), was not so notably versatile as many later artists, although in addition to his main work as a painter he was responsible for the design of at least part of the belfry in Florence which bears his name (*see* Vol. III, p. 167). Giotto is admired now for the qualities of grand simplicity and of drama in his paintings, but to his contemporaries his great distinction seemed to rest in the fact that he copied nature more closely than any painter had done before him. To us it is clear that he stopped short of a completely faithful imitation of nature and used certain mannerisms—a set type of somewhat rigid drapery, a set type of face with slit eyes and cotton-wool beards—which he invented himself and which are satisfying in his hands. His followers copied these tricks without also making Giotto's close observation of nature, and so for about 100 years after Giotto's death Florentine painting declined in quality.

About 1420 a young genius of the highest order, MASACCIO, started painting in a new way. He had made some study of antique Roman art

Anderson

'THE TRINITY' BY MASACCIO (1401–28)
Fresco in the church of S. Maria Novella, Florence. The perspective of the architecture, which is based on classical forms, suggests space and reality

National Gallery

'THE ROUT OF SAN ROMANO' BY PAOLO UCCELLO (1397–1475)

National Gallery

'THE MARTYRDOM OF ST. SEBASTIAN' BY ANTONIO POLLAIUOLO
(*c.* 1432–98)

and was a friend of the great Florentine architect BRUNELLESCHI, who had made a more prolonged study of the subject, and of the sculptor DONATELLO (qq.v. Vol. V). No Roman paintings were then known, and so Masaccio was compelled to base his pictures almost entirely on the study of nature, though infusing into them the spirit of classical sculpture. He was only about 27 when he died, and his achievement is without parallel in the history of art. Instead of the type of picture which his contemporaries were painting, in which the figures lack depth and are often shown against a gold background, Masaccio painted scenes in which the figures are arranged naturally in space and appear to have solid bodies. Furthermore he arranged that the light in his pictures (most of which were wall-paintings) should all come from the same direction—namely, from the direction of the window of the chapel in which the pictures were painted. It seems impossible that one man—and he so young—could have invented unaided so many important things, and it was perhaps because of the very suddenness of Masaccio's achievement that his followers could not quite live up to his high example. An understanding of PERSPECTIVE (q.v.) and anatomy seemed to come naturally to Masaccio, but his followers, many of them men of great ability, developed the new discoveries and reduced them to a rule.

These scientific studies, indeed, became something of an obsession with Florentine painters in the first half of the 15th century. Some, such as Uccello, made a special study of perspective; the Pollaiuolo brothers and Signorelli were more interested in anatomy and movement. The older Fra ANGELICO used the new knowledge to bring reality into religious painting, and BOTTICELLI (qq.v. Vol. V) gave religious and mythological subjects a lyrical quality which makes his figures at the same time fairy-like and very human (Plate 1). Fra Filippo Lippi's Madonnas are still more human. But the charm and humanity of these painters lack the vitality and technical accomplishment of Masaccio's painting.

At the end of the 15th and beginning of the 16th century Florentine painting flowered for the third time in the hands of two of the greatest geniuses that art has ever produced—LEONARDO DA VINCI and MICHELANGELO (qq.v. Vol. V). Leonardo's nature was perhaps basically that of an artist, but he devoted much of his energies to scientific study. He was thus a true Florentine, though an extreme one. He used in his pictures the results of his scientific observations (of plants, birds, or water) and developed the art of light and shade to an extent even beyond Masaccio. Michelangelo was a typical Florentine in another way. His paintings on the ceiling of the

Archives Photographiques

'THE VIRGIN AND CHILD AND ST. ANNE' BY LEONARDO DA VINCI (1452–1519)

Sistine Chapel (*see* VATICAN), which are among the greatest works of art in the world, show a knowledge of anatomy and a power of draughtsmanship which have never been surpassed (*see* Vol. I, p. 221).

That so many talented artists were active in Florence in the 15th century was made possible by the patronage of the MEDICI FAMILY (q.v. Vol. V), at whose Court artists and writers were welcomed and encouraged, and whose fame was commemorated by such works as the wall-paintings by Benozzo Gozzoli in the Medici Palace (*see* Colour Plate, Vol. V, opp. p. 336) and the tombs in the Medici Chapel by Michelangelo (*see* p. 454). But in the early 16th century political upheavals and wars reduced their power. Leonardo and Michelangelo, for example, who began their careers in Florence, later worked mostly in other cities, and Florence ceased to have either patrons or artists of quality.

See also ITALIAN ART.
See also Vol. III: FLORENCE.

FOLK-SONG. This is essentially music of the people. A man ploughing a field, perhaps, or

Anderson

THE HOLY FAMILY (THE 'DONI' TONDO) BY MICHELANGELO (1475–1564)

felling a tree, may think of a tune and whistle it to himself as he works. He thinks of some words to go with it; or perhaps the words come first. In the evening he sings it to his friends, and they all sing it after him, making alterations here and there. Later, they all sing it to their friends. It is not written down, and as it passes from singer to singer it gets changed still further. This is why there are often many versions of one folk-song, and why one cannot speak of any one composer of a folk-song. Folk-song is evolved by the people and continues to exist because it stays in people's memories, and because living people continue to sing it. If a written song is not sung for a hundred years it still exists in its musical score; but if a folk-song is not sung it may be lost in a generation or two because the people who knew it have died.

All peoples all over the world and at all times have evolved folk-songs of some sort; and since the everyday joys and sorrows, and everyday emotions, and to some extent even the every-day tasks of people have been very similar, the same themes are treated over and over again— love-songs, cradle-songs, and mourning-songs, patriotic or war-songs, working- and drinking-songs, narrative-songs, dancing- and sporting-songs, and so on. Some nations have more songs of some special kinds than other nations. In England, for example, generations of mariners have evolved fine sea shanties which they sang as they weighed anchor or reefed in sail; and songs about the open air, hunting, and poaching have always been popular. France is rich in lullabies, while Hungarian folk-song tends to be romantic and reminiscent.

Most folk-songs have purely entertainment value, but many working-songs were intended to help people to do their jobs more effectively. Many sea shanties are of this type: if the work was not going well the mate would call for a

shanty, not only to encourage the spirits of the men but also because the strong rhythm of the shanty helps to achieve a concerted pull on the ropes at the right moment. In the chorus of the well-known sea shanty 'What shall we do with the drunken sailor?', for example, there is a very strong beat at the beginning of each bar which stimulates the sailors to pull at the right moment when hauling in the anchor (see Fig. 1).

The work-songs of the Negro slaves in America served the same purpose, as some of their titles show—'Nine Foot Shovel', ''Dis Timber Got to Roll', 'Chain Gang Boun'. The strong beat of many of them was marked by a 'huh' as the hammer blow was made, or as the pick went into the ground or the axe into the tree. Many folk-songs accompanied dancing (see FOLK DANCING, Vol. IX); others helped people to remember stories and fables, which were told and sung in verse form (see BALLADS). The old street-songs, with which merchants used to advertise their wares, also were a simple kind of practical folk-song.

Though the subjects of folk-songs are similar, the musical style differs from one nation to another; the distinguishing features of its folk-tunes always express unmistakably the salient characteristics of any race. Sir Hubert Parry, in *The Evolution of the Art of Music*, wrote: 'The natural music of a demonstrative people is rhythmic and lively; of a saturnine people, gloomy; of a melancholy and poetical people, pathetic; of a matter-of-fact people, simple, direct, and unelaborated; of a savage people, wild and fierce; of a lively people, merry and light; of an earnest people, dignified and noble.' It is because folk-song is the expression of the national temper that 'nationalist' composers (such as Borodin, Balakirev, and Mussorgsky in Russia; Bartók and Kodály in Hungary; and Falla in Spain) have turned to it as a major source of inspiration. Folk-song quickly becomes one of the most potent symbols of nationality when a nation is threatened by absorption or extinction.

The differences in musical character from one nation to another may lie in the SCALES (q.v.) employed, in melodic patterns, in rhythmic figures, or in the form. A Scots tune, for example, may betray itself by the 'Scotch Snap' (♪♩); a Russian tune by its downward move-ment and repeated phrases; while many French

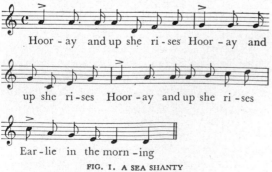

Hoor - ay and up she ri - ses Hoor - ay and

up she ri - ses Hoor - ay and up she ri - ses

Ear - lie in the morn - ing

FIG. I. A SEA SHANTY

HUNGARIAN

RUSSIAN

DANISH

FRENCH

Refrain:-

SCOTS

ENGLISH

FIG. 2

folk-songs are characterized by their form—a couplet together with a refrain made up of nonsense syllables, 'tra-la-la', 'ton reloton', for example (*see* Fig. 2).

In spite of the revival of interest taken in folk-song during the 19th century, and the many societies founded to foster its growth and to undertake research, folk-song is a dying art; the growth of large cities and, more recently, wireless, films, and television have hastened its decay. Great quantities of folk-music, however, often dictated by very old country singers, have been preserved in printed collections or on gramophone records. It is impossible to generalize about the age of the songs which have survived; some, particularly those from remote districts, are undoubtedly of great antiquity, while others, obviously influenced by modern 'composed' music, are probably not old at all.

See also SONG, HISTORY OF; NEGRO SPIRITUALS.
See also Vol. I: FOLK-LORE.
See also Vol. IX: FOLK DANCING.

FOLLY (Building), *see* LANDSCAPE ART.

FONT. This is the basin, usually of stone, used to hold the water during the ceremony of baptism in a church. It is generally placed at the west end of the church. In early Christian times (before the 9th century) baptism took place in a separate room leading off the church, or even

National Buildings Record

FONT IN WINCHESTER CATHEDRAL, 11TH CENTURY
It is made of black marble from Tournai, Belgium, and carved with scenes from the life of St. Nicholas

National Buildings Record

FONT IN SAXMUNDHAM CHURCH, SUFFOLK, 15TH CENTURY
In the panels are angels and the symbols of the Evangelists

a separate building, called the 'baptistery'. In Italy baptisteries were built throughout the Middle Ages. The same name is now sometimes used for the part of the church itself where the font stands, such as a transept or the area beneath the tower.

The commonest shape of a font was square or round before the 13th century and octagonal afterwards, the bowl being raised on a pedestal and often on steps as well. Sometimes the pedestal takes the form of a group of columns. In Gothic churches the style in which fonts are designed closely follows the changes that took place in GOTHIC ART (q.v.) generally. Fonts were often richly carved and sometimes had a tapering wooden cover, carved and painted or gilded.

See also CHURCH ARCHITECTURE, ENGLISH.
See also Vol. I: SACRAMENT, Section 2.

FORBIDDEN CITY, PEKING, *see* PEKING, FORBIDDEN CITY.

FORGERIES (Art). A 'fake' or forged work of art is an imitation of the work of an artist, generally done long after his death, and passed off as his work. When a master's paintings are scarce, and collectors are willing to pay large sums for them, the forger sees his chance.

In the 15th century, at the time of the RENAISSANCE (q.v. Vol. I), when classical sculpture was particularly prized, a number of pieces imitating the antique are known to have been forged. But on the whole the craze for 'antique' pictures, furniture, and china only developed in the last century, largely on account of the decay of those arts at the time. That was the great period of forgery, though forging still continues.

Specimens of the minor arts—furniture, porcelain, or metalwork—are easier to forge than paintings or sculpture, for, in general, every picture or statue is unique. Very few painters or sculptors have made copies of their own work, and where two versions of a work of art appear it is usually possible to tell which one is the forgery. The Spanish painter, El GRECO (q.v. Vol. V), however, who painted in a way not difficult to imitate, kept on repeating his own compositions; consequently many spurious El Grecos exist, and it is said more are made every year. In most cases the forger can make only slight variations on known paintings, which he will pass off as 'try-outs' by the original artist.

In the 1930's and 1940's the Dutchman, Hans van Meegeren, successfully forged paintings which were sold as the work of VERMEER (q.v. Vol. V). Van Meegeren had a genius for imitation without directly copying, and he took endless pains to ensure that his materials—canvas, pigment, and oil—were correct in every detail. The quality of his painting was so high that his pictures were thought to be important works. In most cases forgers imitate the minor work of a master; sketches supposed to be by TURNER and CONSTABLE (qq.v. Vol. V) are very common, as are small pictures which are claimed to be Italian primitives. These very early works are scarce and, being primitive, they are easier to imitate. Detection of such works cannot be undertaken without plenty of knowledge of genuine work. The paint and wood or canvas may be examined under the microscope to make sure that they do not contain substances unknown to the early painters; such scientific aids to detection, however, are usually less helpful than the eye of an expert.

The forging of furniture, porcelain, or metal-work can be very difficult to detect, since no piece is unique. For instance, a set of twelve identical Chippendale chairs might have been made originally by the firm of Chippendale, and if six more turn up in the 20th century no one can say that they must be forgeries merely because they are exactly like the others. The forger of the minor arts has merely to copy his model, and, assuming that the material is of the right kind, detection rests on quality of craftsmanship alone. Here again the practised eye can usually tell the difference; if a genuine and a spurious work of the same kind can be placed side by side (though this is seldom possible), the difference in quality is often apparent.

One remarkable class of forgery is almost impossible to detect. This is the French furniture and Sèvres porcelain of the Louis XVI period (1774–93). Soon after the Revolution broke out in 1789 the old style of furniture was superseded in France by another. But foreign buyers (particularly English) continued to demand the older style, and the demand has not ceased to this day among the very rich. As a result the French cabinet-makers soon started deliberately to copy their own earlier style, which was sold abroad as the genuine article. As in some cases the maker may actually have been the same man, there was virtually no difference, although the aim was dishonest and the work technically a forgery, since the date of manufacture was falsely given. During the same period the Sèvres porcelain works went bankrupt, and a quantity of china, which had been left unpainted in the store-rooms of the factory for some years owing to minor faults, was sold off and painted in the style of 20 and 30 years earlier. There was a great demand abroad for this china, as for the Louis XVI furniture. It is sometimes impossible even for the expert to be sure whether a piece of Sèvres was painted at the time supposed or a generation later.

FOUNTAINS. Italy is the great country of fountains, those in Germany, Spain, and elsewhere deriving originally from Italian types. Well-heads were traditionally rather elaborately decorated in Italy. Some very early examples of fountains are found in the cloisters of the great monasteries, such as the fine late 12th-century fountain in the cloisters of Monreale in Sicily. Among the simplest types are the wall fountains which are particularly popular round about Florence. They consist of a semicircular basin into which water spouts from some such device as a nozzle in a lion's mouth, the whole thing being framed in an arch like a doorway. These are sometimes found in public places, but are more usually placed in the courtyard of a house.

In the Middle Ages big public fountains were erected in towns to give a general water supply. This type usually had a circular or polygonal basin, in the middle of which stood a pier with a pinnacle top; water flooded into the basin from nozzles in the pinnacle. During the Renaissance the fountain became more elaborate, with a series of basins one above the other, usually diminishing in size and crowned with elaborate figure sculptures. Water flowed from the sculpture, trickling down from basin to basin. Such fountains gave great scope in the 15th and 16th centuries for free-standing figure sculpture. DONATELLO (q.v. Vol. V) modelled a bronze group of Judith and Holofernes for a fountain in Florence; the water spouted out of the corners of the bronze wineskin on which Holofernes is

Alinari

FOUNTAIN OF THE LABYRINTH IN THE GARDENS OF THE
ROYAL VILLA, PETRAIA

Designed in the 16th century by Tribolo. The bronze
figure is by Giovanni da Bologna

sitting. In the next century, a great series of varied and elaborate fountains was erected in the Boboli Gardens in Florence. Such fountains were used particularly in Florence and northern Italy, where the supply of water was adequate but not too abundant.

In the 16th century the popes repaired the classical Roman aqueducts, and so produced an immense water supply in Rome. This made possible a different kind of fountain in which sculpture was combined with large quantities of water in motion, the flashing light and movement of which appealed to the taste of the 17th century (*see* BAROQUE ART). In these fountains the design of the movement and flashing of the water is almost more important than the actual sculpture. The cascade was a feature of the great gardens of the late 16th and early 17th centuries in Italy, wherever there was enough water. In most cities in Italy, however, water is not so plentiful, and so the fountains were designed with the sculpture as the main feature— the water merely dribbling and tinkling as it falls from small jets or from basin to basin.

Fountains in the Italian style were erected all over Europe; the most notable English example is the cascade at Chatsworth in Derbyshire. The great fountains at VERSAILLES (q.v.) follow the Roman type. There was no natural abundance of water on the site, but the grandiose taste of the age of Louis XIV would not be denied, and water was made available regardless of cost.

FREE VERSE, *see* MODERN POETRY.

FRENCH ART. The art of France, although it was never at any one time quite so brilliant as that of the Italian Renaissance, has nevertheless maintained a higher standard over a longer period than that of any other country. From the 11th century to the present day there have been few periods when the French have not been in the forefront in either painting, sculpture, or architecture, as well as in the minor arts, such as tapestry, porcelain, and furniture making.

Two qualities have been invariably present in French art, sometimes the one, sometimes the other being predominant. These are realism— the desire to portray in art a scene or figure as it really is as opposed to a fancy version of it; and classicism—the love of the qualities of grandeur, austerity, and cool repose which is characteristic of CLASSICAL ART (q.v.). The second of these

qualities appears at a very early stage in some of the details of Romanesque churches in the south of France where the presence of a great many Roman ruins exercised a strong influence on medieval French artists. ROMANESQUE ART (q.v.) probably started in France, and before the end of the 11th century magnificent churches were being built, of which perhaps the most striking examples are the two great abbeys built by William the Conqueror at Caen (*see* Plate 14).

In the 12th century the French began to build cathedrals in the northern cities, transforming the massive Romanesque style into the tall, pointed Gothic. They were the innovators of the new style, and within 150 years, from the mid-12th century to the end of the 13th, they produced the supreme achievements of GOTHIC ART (q.v.). Refinements and modifications came later, but nothing in the whole history of Gothic art can really compare in splendour (in architecture, sculpture, and stained glass alike) with the five greatest French 12th- and 13th-century cathedrals—CHARTRES (q.v.), Paris, Amiens, Rheims, and Beauvais. At the end of the 13th century their architectural inventiveness seems to have been largely exhausted, and the ravages of the Hundred Years War during the 14th and 15th centuries made the production of such great works impossible. Indeed, so many great cathedrals had been built in the 13th century that there was hardly need for new ones. The finest French Gothic buildings in the 14th, 15th, and 16th centuries are either smaller churches or additions to existing cathedrals. At this period the patrons of art were no longer the cities but individual people, and the most notable centres of art were the Courts of the dukes, particularly the dukes of Burgundy, who were almost as powerful and wealthy as kings. Here were painted exquisite ILLUMINATED MANUSCRIPTS (q.v.), realistic portraits, and fairy-like pictures of religious scenes. TAPESTRIES (q.v. Vol. VII) and IVORY CARVINGS (q.v.) also reflect the charm and grace of life at these Courts. Sculpture was used less to decorate buildings and more for individual monuments.

By the beginning of the 16th century the power of the monarchy had increased and that of the great nobles diminished. King Francis I was anxious to make his Court as magnificent as it was strong, and he set out to entice as many as possible of the great Italian artists of the High Renaissance to his Court at Fontainebleau. One

CHÂTEAU DE MAISONS AT ST. GERMAIN-EN-LAYE. DESIGNED BY FRANÇOIS MANSART (1598–1666)

L'INSPIRATION DU POÈTE. PAINTING BY NICOLAS POUSSIN (1594–1665)

PLATE 8   FRENCH ART

ABOVE:
THE ENCHANTED CASTLE
PAINTING BY CLAUDE (1600–82)

THE SWING
PAINTING BY J.-H. FRAGONARD
(1732–1806)

of the first of these was the great LEONARDO DA VINCI. A large number of other Italians followed Leonardo, including the famous goldsmith and sculptor, Benvenuto CELLINI (qq.v. Vol. V). Their works in France and those of the Frenchmen working with them, with their high-flown subject-matter and Italian style, represent the classical side of French taste. At the same time there were realistic portrait-painters, such as Clouet and Corneille de Lyon.

The religious upheavals which took place in France in the late 16th and early 17th centuries interrupted the artistic tradition, and it was not until well into the 17th century that art was able to flourish again. Two painters of this period, Nicolas POUSSIN and CLAUDE Lorraine (qq.v. Vol. V), were so imbued with classical ideals that they both passed their entire adult lives in Rome, though working largely for French patrons. Poussin's religious and mythological paintings are austere because of the geometric precision of the composition and the idealized figures. In the few landscapes which he painted he arranged the elements—trees, water, and buildings—as carefully on geometric lines as he did in his figure subjects (*see* p. 85). Claude was a landscape painter who sought to paint the moods of nature and above all the effect of light, but his landscapes were carefully composed on classical lines. Contemporary with them was the great architect François Mansart, whose buildings, particularly the Château de Maisons, set an example of classical elegance and good taste which the French have seldom, if ever, lost.

In the meantime political developments were taking place in France which profoundly affected the arts. The famous statesman, Cardinal RICHELIEU (q.v. Vol. V), had spent his whole political career in humbling the great nobles and building up the authority of the Crown. His work, continued by Cardinal Mazarin, reached its culmination under LOUIS XIV (q.v. Vol. V) and his minister, Colbert. The latter realized that the Academy of Arts, which had been founded in 1648 (*see* ACADEMIES), was an institution which, by ensuring that artists were kept under control, could be made to help build up the prestige and splendour of the Crown. In the latter half of the 17th century the main artistic talent of France was absorbed in building and decorating the Palace of VERSAILLES (q.v.). This great palace was built to impress the world with the personal glory of Louis XIV, and the style

in which the artists worked was nearer to the BAROQUE ART (q.v.) of Italy than the classicism of Poussin and Mansart.

At the beginning of the 18th century this baroque style gave way to ROCOCO ART (q.v.), a style principally of exquisite interior decoration in which the walls, furniture, and tapestries abound with free and graceful ornament. The great painter of the period is Antoine WATTEAU (q.v. Vol. V), whose small-scale pictures of picnics (*Fêtes Champêtres*), with lovers dressed in exquisitely painted silks and satins, have a fairy-like quality. The light-hearted and decorative paintings of Boucher and Fragonard suited the gay Court of Louis XV.

Furniture, tapestry, and porcelain reflected the same tastes as the paintings of the 17th and 18th centuries. Under Louis XIV the furniture was elaborate and richly decorated; the craftsman Boulle gave his name to a style of inlay of metal (*see* Vol. VII, p. 244), and tortoise-shell and rare woods were used for marquetry (*see* INLAY AND MARQUETRY, Vol. VII). The tapestry works at Gobelins, founded by the State in 1662, continued to produce tapestries from designs of the leading painters throughout the 18th century. The Sèvres PORCELAIN works (q.v. Vol. VII), also a royal factory, was started in the mid-18th century.

While the Court art of the 17th and 18th centuries was predominantly classical in subject, there were realistic painters who were working for middle-class patrons. In the 17th century the brothers Le Nain painted homely scenes akin to those of the contemporary Dutch painters. In the 18th century Chardin painted STILL LIFE (q.v.), subjects which were in complete contrast to the frivolous gods and goddesses of Boucher.

At the end of the 18th century Jacques Louis David introduced a style which was strongly opposed to the rococo and was even more severely classical than that of Poussin. His style suited the spirit of the French Revolution and of Napoleon's Empire which followed; and David, who had himself been a whole-hearted supporter of the Revolution, became the chief painter of the new Court. The architecture, furniture, and costume of the Empire all reflect the spirit of classical art.

The history of French painting from that time to the present day has been very varied. During the first 50 years of the 19th century the scene

'THE OATH OF THE HORATII' BY J. L. DAVID (1748–1825)

is dominated by two painters—Ingres, who followed David in the classical style, and DELACROIX (q.v. Vol. V), the leader of the ROMANTIC MOVEMENT (q.v.). These two were bitterly opposed to each other, but each, in his different way, painted scenes equally removed from ordinary life. Ingres painted subjects from classical antiquity, or modern people in as classical a style as possible; Delacroix painted anything which was removed in space or time from 19th-century France, such as scenes from Oriental life or from history (*see* p. 388). LANDSCAPE PAINTING (q.v.) of this period was much influenced by English painting, especially that of Constable.

In the 40's and 50's of the 19th century Gustave COURBET (q.v. Vol. V), in reaction against both Ingres and Delacroix, painted the most ordinary scenes in as truthful a way as possible. His example gradually led French artists to pay attention not so much to what they painted as to the way in which they painted. They began to realize that what one sees is not necessarily the same thing as what one knows is there, and they deliberately aimed at rendering in their pictures only the first impressions of a scene as recorded by the eye. This movement became known as IMPRESSIONIST PAINTING (q.v.). In order to render the lightness and brilliance of colour in sunlight, Georges Seurat and his followers used a 'pointillist' technique—that is, instead of mixing the paint to obtain the actual colours of their subject, they applied tiny dots or points of unblended colours and left it to the eye of the spectator to make the fusion (*see* p. 205).

Edgar Degas, though ranking as an Impressionist, had original aims and was profoundly interested not only in the way he painted but also in his subjects—frequently theatrical scenes, particularly ballet dancers (*see* p. 333). Degas's work shows the influence of

Archives Photographiques

'THE STUDIO OF THE PAINTER' BY GUSTAVE COURBET, 1855

RIGHT: 'THE PIPER' BY EDOUARD MANET, 1866

the great 19th-century invention, photography. People with a camera in their hands are often tempted to press the trigger indiscriminately and to produce pictures in which the arrangement appears haphazard. Degas in his paintings did this deliberately, choosing unexpected points of view—from an odd angle or from high up (*see* Vol. VII, p. 281). Another painter, Toulouse-Lautrec, specialized in similar subjects, but treated them more satirically.

POST-IMPRESSIONIST PAINTING (q.v.) was a reaction against Impressionism. Its first and greatest painter, Paul CÉZANNE (q.v. Vol. V), was interested in depicting the solidity of objects rather than their appearance under different lighting conditions (*see* Plate 12). The sculptor Rodin combined an interest in realistic form with the expression of emotion (*see* p. 52).

Cézanne was such a great and profound painter that since his death in 1906 many painters have worked on his principles—sometimes, like the Cubists, carrying them to extremes. In the 20th century France is still the most important art centre, and painters from all countries study there; some, like the Spaniard Picasso, remain there to work and to lead the French school of painters (*see* MODERN ART).

Archives Photographiques

FRENCH LITERATURE, The FRENCH LAN-
GUAGE (q.v. Vol. IV) developed gradually from
Latin during the early Middle Ages, but it is not
until the 11th century that Old French can be
said to have become established as a language
distinct from Latin (*see* ROMANCE LANGUAGES,
Vol. IV).

There are two principal strains in Old French
literature, one idealistic and ennobling, the
other realistic and often satirical. In the first
category are the epic *Chansons de Geste*, of which
the most famous is the magnificent 12th-century
CHANSON DE ROLAND (q.v.), and the later poems
of chivalry and courtly love, the themes of which
were often based on stories from the ARTHURIAN
LEGEND (q.v. Vol. I). In the second category are
the 13th-century *Fabliaux* and the greater part
of the allegorical poem the *Roman de la Rose*
(*see* ROMANCE LITERATURE). During the Middle
Ages, too, other forms of literature, such as
lyric poetry and drama, had their beginnings.
The great 15th-century lyric poet VILLON (q.v.
Vol. V) still used medieval themes and styles,
although his work also has a startling air of
modernity.

The early 16th-century Renaissance in France
coincided with the emergence of France as a
modern State, and with the beginnings of the
REFORMATION (q.v. Vol. I). The Renaissance,
with its rediscovery of Greek and renewed
interest in Latin literature, brought with it a
sudden stimulating of intellectual curiosity concerning all the fields of human knowledge and
endeavour, a tremendous appetite for learning,
and an air of optimistic belief in human progress. The effect on literature was to replace
the medieval forms in poetry and in drama
with those of antiquity—the ODE and ELEGY,
TRAGEDY and COMEDY (qq.v.). Of the host of
great writers during this century three may perhaps be singled out. There was RONSARD (q.v.
Vol. V), leader of a group of poets who called
themselves *La Pléiade*, who was responsible in
large measure for the splendid flowering of LYRIC
POETRY (q.v.) at this time. Then there were
two great prose-writers: RABELAIS, the earliest
French novelist, and MONTAIGNE (qq.v. Vol. V),
the essayist. Rabelais reflected in his lively style
his remarkable scholarship, his wit and imagination, and all the qualities of the early Renaissance optimism; Montaigne, on the other hand,
was a representative of a sadder generation—that
of the fierce Wars of Religion (1562–98)—for

whom the earlier optimism was being replaced
by scepticism.

The 17th century is the age of Classicism,
when writers strove after clarity and perfection
by applying logical principles of order and simplicity both to their language and to the structure of their works (*see* CLASSICAL ART). In
France the Wars of Religion had induced a
general desire for peace and order, for the tacit
acceptance of the established order in Church and
State; and this affected the manners and tastes
of polite society and, consequently, the literary
fashions of the day. In 1635 Cardinal Richelieu
founded the Académie Française, an event which
contributed greatly to the stabilizing of the language and to the forming of standards of literary
criticism (*see* ACADEMIES). During the early part
of the century also, the literary *salons*, social
gatherings of people of literary importance, became fashionable in Paris. During the second
part of the century the enlightened patronage of
LOUIS XIV (q.v. Vol. V) and the Court of Versailles helped to bring French literature to its
maturity. Almost all forms of literature except
lyric and epic poetry had great exponents in the
17th century. Above all, writers were interested
in human nature, in human passions, and in the
problems of man in society; consequently most
of the literature of the time is in part didactic,
and there are many moralists, such as La
Bruyère (1645–96). Best remembered of all are
the dramatists, for both tragedy and comedy
reached their greatest heights in the works of
CORNEILLE, MOLIÈRE, and RACINE (qq.v. Vol.
V). Writers were interested in philosophical and
religious problems, and the influence of the ideas
of DESCARTES (q.v. Vol. V), which exalted the
power of reason, was enormous.

By 1680 a new spirit of inquiry was beginning
to weaken the tacit acceptance of the established
order. Descartes, while believing in the omni-
potence of reason, had for the most part
deliberately avoided examination of religious
and political problems; but now these problems,
too, came under the examination of reason. The
18th century is often called the Age of Reason,
and this is an apt title for an age which produced
political theorists such as Montesquieu (1689–
1755), and inquiring thinkers such as DIDEROT
and VOLTAIRE (qq.v. Vol. V). But the 18th
century also produced a totally opposed strain
of nervous sentimentality, to be found in the
writings of the great dramatists Marivaux

(1688–1763) and Beaumarchais (1732–99), in the famous novel *Manon Lescaut* by Prévost (1697–1763), and even in the works of Voltaire and Diderot in certain moods. Undoubtedly the most influential 18th-century writer was ROUSSEAU (q.v. Vol. V), in whose writing both reason and sentiment were mingled. Rousseau's works had a tremendous effect upon the thought of western Europe. A penetrating political theorist, a fervent lover of nature, Rousseau helped to prepare for both the FRENCH REVOLUTION (q.v. Vol. X) and the ROMANTIC MOVEMENT (q.v.).

The Romantic Movement was a reaction against 18th-century rationalism; but it was also, even more clearly, a continuation of 18th-century sentimentality. This European movement was beginning in France in the first years of the 19th century and was in its decline by 1850. The political upheaval of the Revolution, the glories and final defeat of Napoleon, and the changes in the social structure of the country consequent upon growing industrial development, all had a profound effect upon writers of this half-century, producing in some acute dissatisfaction with their environment and a hatred of contemporary society, and in others excitement at the high task of leadership awaiting the artists in the modern world.

The most significant literary developments were the revival of lyric poetry and the establishment of the NOVEL (q.v.) as a live and important literary form. The greatest of the many 19th-century Romantic poets was undoubtedly HUGO (q.v. Vol. V), whose technical mastery, inexhaustible imagination, and poetic eloquence gained him universal recognition. The great novelist BALZAC (q.v. Vol. V) gave a remarkable and realistic picture of the society of his time and showed a profound understanding of humanity in the many novels grouped together under the title of *La Comédie Humaine*; and STENDHAL (q.v. Vol. V) in his analytical novels observed with penetration and gave a vivid impression of the political ideas of the time.

During the second half of the 19th century there was a movement towards the perfection of form in poetry. Many would say that from BAUDELAIRE and RIMBAUD (qq.v. Vol. V) comes the finest poetry ever written in French: both contributed a new intensity to poetic expression and opened up new realms of experience for poetic treatment. Their work gave rise to the school of poets known as Symbolists, of whom Mallarmé was a leader. These poets aimed at representing ideas and emotions by indirect suggestion rather than by direct statement, and they came to attach symbolic meanings to particular objects, words, or sounds. Their poetry was often obscure; they delighted in word-music, used ALLEGORY (q.v.), and experimented with new *vers libre* forms (*see* MODERN POETRY).

In the novel, the realistic technique of Balzac was developed further by novelists such as Zola (1840–1902), who, by working out certain ideas about heredity in his novels, added a scientific strain to the realism of Balzac. Zola in his later work propagated a kind of Utopian Socialism in the manner of a Romantic artist rather than a realist. The great novelist FLAUBERT (q.v. Vol. V) was a realistic writer in so far as he observed and documented the world around him, but he was primarily interested in style, and evolved a prose style that has much of the power of suggestion found in poetry.

We are too close to the literature of the 20th century to be able to make a fair estimate of it. But certain names are established firmly; as those of the poet Valéry (a pupil of Mallarmé), the novelist PROUST (q.v. Vol. V), and the novelist, dramatist, critic, and moralist Gide. It is true to say that activity in French literature is now as intense as at any time during its long history, as is shown, for instance, by the work of the philosopher Sartre, the novelist Camus, and the dramatist Anouilh.

See also Vol. I: FRENCH.
See also Vol. IV: FRENCH LANGUAGE.

FRESCO, *see* PAINTING METHODS, Section 4.

FUGUE, *see* MUSICAL FORM, Section 7.

FURNITURE, *see* Vol. XI: FURNITURE.

FUTURISM, *see* MODERN ART, Section 4.

G

GENRE PAINTING. The French word 'genre' means 'category' or 'type'; it has long been applied to pictures which portray scenes from everyday life, although it is not used of present-day painting. The most satisfactory results of this kind of painting have been homely scenes—peasants eating, drinking, or dancing, or a mother supervising the affairs of the household—in which the artist felt himself completely at home. Genre painting is distinct from the CONVERSATION PIECE (q.v.). In the latter the figures are portraits of specific people, but in

genre they are essentially anonymous and typify Everyman at home (*see* Vol. IX, p. 189).

In the purest examples of genre painting—by the 17th-century Flemings Brouwer and Teniers, or the Dutchmen Steen and the brothers Ostade—there is no attempt to tell a story or point a moral; the characters are shown going about their daily occupations (*see* Vol. VII, p. 45). A great many of these pictures show scenes of eating and drinking, which are important items in a peasant's life.

In one type of genre painting the painter's motive has been mixed. For example the great Flemish painter, Pieter BRUEGHEL the Elder (q.v. Vol. V), painted a number of pictures representing Biblical scenes—such as the 'Massacre of the Innocents' or the 'Procession to Calvary'—which in fact are contemporary scenes of life in Flanders. The main characters of the story are usually inconspicuous, or in the background.

Another type of disguised genre painting which flourished particularly in England in the 18th century was the satirical picture (*see* CARICATURE). HOGARTH (q.v. Vol. V) and Rowlandson painted scenes of everyday life of the most realistic kind but with a moral purpose. The characters are usually shown drinking themselves to death as a result of debt, or gambling, or stark mad in an asylum. The painter's object, therefore, was not purely artistic; he thought of himself as a social reformer—as the novelist Charles Dickens did—and tried by his pictures to warn people of the evil consequences of their actions (*see* p. 405).

It was but a step from this kind of picture to another form of genre painting—the sentimental family picture of the Victorian era. Pictures with titles such as 'The Last Day in the Old Home' also tell a story, but their purpose, in this case, is to please the spectator by permitting him to say 'How like ourselves!'

Another form of genre, popular 50 years ago, was the so-called 'problem picture' which showed a genre scene, the meaning of which the spectator was invited to unravel for himself from the clue supplied by the title. A famous example by Orchardson shows an elderly man in the foreground listening with rapt attention to a girl singing in the background. As the picture is called 'Her Mother's Voice', one deduces that the man is a widower and the girl his daughter.

In the 20th century much of the former de-

National Gallery

'THE IDLE SERVANT' BY THE DUTCH PAINTER NICOLAS MAES
(1632–93)

Sir Hickman Bacon

'TAVERN SCENE' BY THE FLEMISH PAINTER ADRIAEN BROUWER (*c.* 1605–38)

mand for genre painting has been met by photographs in newspapers and magazines: photographs bearing such titles as 'Chelsea Pensioners going to Church' or 'Ploughing on the South Downs' are essentially the same in subject and appeal as were the older painted versions.

GEORGIAN ARCHITECTURE. This is the name given to the type of Renaissance architecture evolved in England (and in the English colonies, especially the eastern States of what is now the U.S.A.) during the 18th century. It lasted roughly from the beginning of George I's reign in 1714 until the end of the century, when changing fashions led to the development of REGENCY ARCHITECTURE (q.v.).

The Georgian age is specially notable for its houses, large and small, town and country; and even the buildings other than houses (the churches, market-halls, and public buildings) had a largely domestic character; for England at that time was a country ruled by its citizens, merchants, and landowners, who preferred buildings of a prosperous but discreet solidity to the splendour and showmanship found in con-

temporary buildings in countries dominated by kings and prelates. Moreover, for the Protestant religion, with its emphasis on the word of the preacher rather than on the colourful celebration of ritual, churches designed as simple meeting-halls were appropriate (*see* p. 82).

Georgian architects inherited from their predecessors a style of house which, though Renaissance in its details and decoration, and developed from ideas brought from Italy in the 17th century, was essentially English. To architects such as Sir Christopher WREN (q.v. Vol. V) and his contemporaries England owes her tradition of fine craftsmanship in brick and simplicity of outline. As the Georgian age progressed, a greater delicacy of detail became fashionable, seen in the change from the robust, deeply undercut ornament of the William and Mary house to the thin surface ornament of the late Georgian, and the increasing slenderness of window-bars. Houses remained relatively plain, symmetrical, rectangular structures, mostly in brick but often with stone trimmings. At first their sloping roofs projected over classical cornices of stone or painted wood; later they were

A. F. Kersting

THE CIRCUS, BATH, DESIGNED BY JOHN WOOD THE ELDER AND COMPLETED IN 1754

partly concealed behind parapets. Stress was laid on the correct and agreeable proportioning of a comparatively small number of almost standardized parts, ornament being confined to a few places, such as the door, which often had a pillared porch, and, in larger houses, to the stone surrounds of some of the windows. Town houses, especially, had ornamental iron balconies and railings. Churches, too, were plainly rectangular, usually with a pillared portico and a square tower at the west end (*see* CHURCH ARCHITECTURE, ENGLISH, Section 7).

Early in the 18th century an especially formal style became fashionable, known as the Palladian style because it was modelled on the work of the Italian architect Andrea PALLADIO (q.v. Vol. V), who was greatly admired by those young aristocrats who completed their education with the Grand Tour of Europe. The principal advocate of the Palladian style was Lord Burlington, himself an amateur architect; he sent a succession of promising young men to study in Italy, and these became the most sought-after architects in England (*see* AUGUSTAN AGE).

One result of the rise of the middle classes in the Georgian age and the cultivation of the civic and domestic, rather than the aristocratic, virtues was that groups of domestic buildings were for the first time considered as one architectural unit; consequently there emerged the squares, the terraces, and the crescents which, designed

in the discreet but elegant Georgian taste, constitute the chief architectural riches of so many English towns. Grand, landscaped compositions were built at Bath, and later, fancifully ornamented, tree-planted terraces at Cheltenham; in the Bloomsbury area of London there was a more formal sequence of squares; elegant streets were built in outlying villages such as Chelsea and Hampstead, and neatly laid-out residential areas in numerous provincial towns. Whatever the form, the individual house was subordinated to the architectural conception of the whole. This depended on the rhythm of repeated windows and doorways, sometimes with the centre houses, otherwise identical, marked by pediments and pilasters. Ornament, too, was considered as a unit in a repeating pattern, and the Georgian street demonstrated the effective use of standardized, prefabricated elements, such as were to assume such importance two centuries later (*see* MODERN ARCHITECTURE).

This Georgian town architecture, coinciding as it did with the building up of new residential areas by the great landlords, represents the first conscious attempt in England to develop town-planning into an art with its own principles and ideals (*see* TOWNS, HISTORY OF, Vol. XI).

Under the Burlington régime, the qualities of a design were judged by its adherence to a strict set of rules, and it was in part the cold rigidity of the Palladians which produced, towards the end of the century, a reaction in the direction of the fanciful and the romantic, heralding the eventual disintegration of the formal Georgian style. The fanciful was encouraged by the study of antique buildings at POMPEII (q.v.) and Athens, on which new styles of decoration were based. The romantic element revived interest in the Middle Ages, and consequently, a Gothic flavour was given to Georgian architecture which led to the GOTHIC REVIVAL (q.v.). This process of disintegration was hastened by the growth of industrialism, which upset the whole social structure of the 18th century, of which Georgian architecture was an expression.

See also CLASSICAL ART.
See also Vol. XI: HOUSES, HISTORY OF.

GERMAN ART. In the Middle Ages there was no single German nation and very little contact between the people of the various parts of what is now Germany. This situation produced distinctive styles of art. There are, however, some characteristics which are common to all and which we recognize as German.

In the 9th century, while Saxony and the East were still barbarian, the Frankish ruler CHARLEMAGNE (q.v. Vol. V), who was crowned Holy Roman Emperor in 800, drew artists and scholars from Rome, Byzantium, and Northumbria to his Court at Aachen in western Germany. Most of his buildings have perished, but the most important of them, the cathedral at Aachen (Aix-la-Chapelle), still stands. It is an octagonal building, based on the Byzantine church of S. Vitale at Ravenna; but some of the details, particularly the main doors, show how closely the artists copied Roman models. Small objects are more easy to preserve than buildings, and a number of manuscripts of Charlemagne's time and IVORY CARVINGS (q.v.) remain; these also show a dependence on Roman and Byzantine styles (*see* MEDIEVAL ART, EARLY).

After the death of Charlemagne interest in the arts declined, though during the 11th century rich ILLUMINATED MANUSCRIPTS (q.v.) were made, and a style of church architecture was introduced, with an apse and altar at both ends, which became characteristic of German medieval churches. In the 11th and 12th centuries a school of metal workers in Hildesheim produced notable works, including a pair of large bronze doors for the church decorated with scenes in relief which were technically very competent

Foto Marburg

ECKHART AND HIS WIFE UTA
Figures in Naumburg Cathedral, 1260–80

and of high artistic merit (*see* BRONZE SCULPTURE).

In Germany ROMANESQUE and GOTHIC ART (qq.v.) started much later than in Italy, France, or England, and was largely derived from French models. However, the Germans did develop one form of Gothic building which was important in itself and extremely characteristic of their feeling for architecture in all ages. This was the 'hall church' in which the side aisles and nave are all the same height, instead of having a high central nave and lower side aisles. A church of this kind gives a greater sensation of space than an ordinary Gothic church gives. In the latter the eye is drawn upwards and forwards to the High Altar, but in a hall church all the parts are equally important. Not all architecture has this feeling of space, but it has always been an important element in German architecture.

Though German sculpture of the Gothic period, like the architecture, derived a good deal from the French, it has an individual character. German artists have always been interested in

Wallraf-Richartz Mus., Cologne

'THE MADONNA WITH THE VIOLET' BY STEFAN LOCHNER
(c. 1410–51)

Bibl. de Colmar

THE RESURRECTION: PANEL OF THE ISENHEIM ALTAR-PIECE
BY MATTHIAS GRÜNEWALD, 1509–11

portraying the human form, not the ideal form of classical art but the variety and idiosyncrasy of individual character. At the same time there is a mystical element in German art, and these two characteristics have been used over and over again to intensify each other. In the 12th-century sculpture at Bamberg in Bavaria the human element is uppermost, for instance, in the figures of Adam and Eve on the portal—the earliest example of the nude figure in medieval art; and the series of 13th-century portrait figures at Naumburg in central Germany express intense human emotions.

The altar-piece, which in Italy and Flanders is nearly always painted, in Germany is often carved in wood. The panels, which were painted and gilded, are more like pictures than sculpture but the figures stand out in full relief.

The first notable German schools of painting (as distinct from illumination) were those which flourished in the 15th century at Cologne and in Westphalia. Of these the Cologne school was perhaps the more important, and its chief painter, Stefan Lochner, one of the greatest German artists. There is a gentle grace in his work which is unlike the usual emotional quality of German art, and its other-worldly feeling makes it very different from the extremely realistic type of painting which was being produced close by in Flanders at the same time (*see*

FLEMISH ART). The Westphalian artists, on the other hand, are sometimes brutally realistic.

In the 15th century there occurred in Germany an event of the utmost importance—the invention of printing. Its most obvious effect on art was the growth of the craft of ENGRAVING (q.v. Vol. VII) to illustrate printed books. The earliest German artist to devote much of his time to engraving was Martin Schongauer. He ushered in a period which produced the greatest German painters and engravers—DÜRER, HOLBEIN (qq.v. Vol. V), Cranach, Grien, Altdorfer, and Grünewald (*see* ETCHING AND ENGRAVING). These all lived in the 100 years from the mid-15th to the mid-16th centuries, and all, though in different degrees, were inspired by the same motives. Their works, in the first place, are usually very emotional. German artists have always been obsessed, in particular, by the idea of death. Dürer could rarely draw a young couple making love without also showing a skeleton brandishing an hour-glass in the background to indicate that such delights will not last for ever (*see* Vol. V, p. 149). In the works of Grünewald this emotional and unrealistic tendency reached its height: Christ's flesh in the Crucifixion is dark green and His face, in the Resurrection, light lemon colour. This sounds, and is, extravagant. But it was produced by a religious feeling which was more intense than anything we can see in the art of other countries at this period.

These artists gave in their pictures an impression of infinite space which is akin to the feeling of space to be found in the architecture. In Altdorfer's battle picture, for instance, the extreme distance is shown under lurid and unnatural lighting conditions which make it positively disquieting. The artist was not interested in those qualities of repose to be found in Roman or Italian or French art. He sought to communicate to the public his own terrifying, even nightmare, visions, and the strong sensations to which German art often gives rise is a measure of the artist's success.

This remarkable group of artists shared another most incongruous characteristic: they became infatuated, particularly Dürer, with contemporary ITALIAN ART (q.v.), in spite of the fact that its essential qualities were the

RIGHT: THE APOSTLES JOHN AND PETER
Painting by Albrecht Dürer (1471–1528)
Ältere Pinakothek, Munich

opposite of their own art. Indeed, the outstanding feature in Dürer's career is that his whole conscious effort was spent in trying to assimilate the art of the Italian Renaissance, while his own deepest instincts were firmly rooted in the Middle Ages.

During most of the 17th century Germany was so disrupted by war that hardly any art was produced. One notable painter, however, Adam Elsheimer, who worked chiefly in Rome, painted small pictures, often on copper, which, though of religious subjects, are chiefly interesting for their dramatic landscape backgrounds. But the 18th century was more stable and saw the rise of the Prince Bishops, who built enormous and magnificent palaces and churches in southern Germany which had remained Roman Catholic. The style they used was BAROQUE (q.v.), a style which combined the qualities of religious fervour of an emotional kind with princely splendour. The Germans, though they developed the baroque style three-quarters of a century later than the Italians who first evolved it, pushed it to far greater lengths. Here again the German sense of space found its fullest scope. German baroque architects, particularly Balthasar Neumann, treated the interiors of their churches so daringly that the walls may be said to be moulded as if by a sculptor rather than built by an architect. Walls and ceilings curve in every direction, and the effect of complex space is overwhelming.

In the 19th century artists with the age-old qualities of German art—emotional, romantic, and unprogressive—produced pictures and architecture of every kind but of little importance. German 18th-century writers on the art of Greece and Rome, particularly Winckelmann and Lessing, were largely responsible for the revived interest in Greek art which swept Europe in the early 19th century. But the artists who represented it, at least in Germany, were not of great consequence.

During the First World War a style known as EXPRESSIONIST ART (q.v.) arose. This was characteristically German in that its main object was not to record the painter's reactions to the things he saw around him so much as to reveal his personal emotional life. Most artists have done this to a certain extent, but the Expressionists went so far that they did not hesitate to transform the things they saw in order to express their own feelings—horses, for instance,

might be painted bright blue or red (*see* Colour Plate opp. p. 144). After the war German architects and artists were inspired by developments in France and England but tended to develop these ideas much further. A group of artists at Dessau started a school, the Bauhaus, which sought to integrate architecture and all the arts of decoration. When Hitler came to power in 1933 progressive art was prohibited, and the expressionist painters and artists of the Bauhaus sought refuge in America and Britain.

GERMAN LITERATURE. German literature as a whole may be described as essentially romantic, if we take this term in its widest sense. That is to say, from its beginnings in the 9th century to the present day the authors have shown a marked trend to present complex rather than simple thoughts and feelings, to examine life from an individual rather than a social point of view, and to reach out for things that lie behind and beyond ordinary experience. The greatest works of German literature in poetry and drama all show this quality even when they conform to the standards accepted in the European tradition. This does not mean, however, that the best works are produced where the romantic spirit appears in its most concentrated form. The German character has always tended to drive things to extremes, and this failing makes itself felt in the literary work of the Romantic School which flourished during the first quarter of the 19th century, as well as in the dramas of great writers such as Heinrich von Kleist, who lived in the Romantic era without belonging to the Romantic School (*see* ROMANTIC MOVEMENT).

The romantic trend already appears in the Middle Ages. Here, the most characteristic work is Wolfram von Eschenbach's *Parzival*, a long verse EPIC (q.v.) describing a spiritual quest. The greatest lyric poet of that time, Walther von der Vogelweide, breaks away from tradition by writing highly personal, as well as topical poetry. *Parzival* has much in common with Goethe's FAUST (q.v.) and also with his novel *Wilhelm Meister*. But GOETHE (q.v. Vol. V) had a profound admiration for the ancient Greeks and, without slavishly imitating them, was influenced by them in his own writings. Goethe stands at the head of an influential group of German classicists which includes Lessing, SCHILLER (q.v. Vol. V), and Hölderlin, as well as a host of minor writers. Their objective standards of

THE BATTLE BETWEEN ALEXANDER AND DARIUS III. PAINTING BY ALBRECHT ALTDORFER, 1529

Though the subject is classical, the figures are dressed in contemporary costume and set in a romantic landscape

judgement and taste kept under control the German tendency to exaggerate and create formless works, with the result that they produced what are generally regarded as the greatest works in German literature.

The influence of the Greeks is only one among many in German literature. English, French, and Oriental influences are also strong at different times, and occasionally at one and the same time. In fact, there is no other literature in western Europe in which foreign models play such an important part. Yet German writers use foreign models not in order to become like them, but to develop an individual style from them. This is particularly true of the writers belonging to the revolutionary movement called 'Storm and Stress', which flourished from about 1770 to 1785. The name comes from the title of a play by Klinger which has all the characteristics of the style—emotional intensity, love of the weird and the mystical, wildness of style and subject. Among these writers the younger Goethe and Schiller were pre-eminent, before they turned towards classicism.

German literature is particularly rich in LYRIC POETRY (q.v.) of a personal kind. From the great German minnesinger (love poet), Walther von der Vogelweide (1160–1230), the stream runs unhampered in the work of 17th-century poets such as Gryphius, 18th-century poets such as Klopstock, Hölderlin, and Goethe, 19th-century poets such as Heine and Mörike, and 20th-century poets such as George and Rilke. There are some notable examples of tragedy in German literature, particularly in the work of Schiller, Kleist, and Hebbel. Germany has produced very little comedy, which needs an objective outlook which the majority of German writers do not possess. It is not true to say that German literature is poor in great comedies because the Germans lack a sense of humour (there are great humorists from Jean Paul to Morgenstern), but a sense of the comic only will not produce good comedy. German writers have excelled in the *Novelle*, a special form of the short story popular in the 19th century. Its flowering in that century has something to do with the rise of the middle classes, as one may see from the work of its greatest exponents, E. T. A. Hoffmann, Theodor Storm, and others.

No other literature of western Europe shows so many regional variations. The reason is not far to seek. From about the 15th century, and especially after the coming of Protestantism, Germany was divided into many small States, principalities, duchies, and even towns, which all had political independence. This made for great divergence and variety in the literary life of the country, particularly since there were also great differences in the speech in different parts of Germany, based on the dialects of the different tribes that originally had settled in the country. Germany never possessed a single centre of culture such as Paris or London, and this accounts for the individualism of German writers throughout the history of its literature. One must, moreover, distinguish between German literature and literature written in the German language. The latter would include the literatures of Austria and the German-speaking parts of Switzerland, which have not been dealt with in this article.

See also Vol. IV: GERMANIC LANGUAGES.

GLASS, see STAINED GLASS. *See also* Vol. XI: GLASSWARE; Vol. VII: GLASS-MAKING.

GLEE, see SONGS, Section 3.

GOLD AND SILVER WORK, see Vol. VII: GOLD AND SILVER WORK.

GOLDEN BOUGH, THE, by Sir James G. Frazer, *see* HISTORIES.

GOTHIC ART. 1. The art of the northern countries of Europe in the 13th, 14th, and 15th centuries is called Gothic. The name was given to the buildings of the Middle Ages by the architects of the Renaissance who thought them barbarous, like the GOTHS (q.v. Vol. I) who had helped to overthrow the Roman Empire. Since at this time architecture was the most important of the arts, and the use of the pointed arch the most characteristic feature of the buildings, Gothic art is sometimes described as 'the art of the pointed arch'.

The use of the pointed arch made it possible to build very lofty churches and to roof them with a stone VAULT (q.v.). From inside the building these vaults look as if they were supported only on the very slender shafts and pillars of the nave, but actually their weight and thrust is mainly counterbalanced from the outside by flying buttresses. In a Gothic building pressure in one direction is always met and

Herbert Felton

CHOIR AND SANCTUARY OF WESTMINSTER ABBEY, REBUILT
BY HENRY III

The work was begun at the east end in 1245. The plan
and proportions were influenced by those of Rheims
Cathedral, which was also used for coronations

cathedrals, for people had come to want great
cathedrals to glorify and enrich their towns.
Although a good deal of the money for the
building of cathedrals was given by kings,
bishops, and nobles, much was also subscribed
by ordinary citizens. Sometimes people made
their contribution by giving manual labour: at
CHARTRES (q.v.), for instance, when the cathedral was burnt down, the chroniclers say that
rich and poor harnessed themselves to the carts
which carried the stone up the hill.

No doubt rivalry between different towns
prompted the masons to choose ever more daring
plans. Sometimes this led to disaster, and we
hear of towers falling and vaults collapsing.
Most of the great buildings, however, are still
in excellent condition, which shows the skill of
the masons who designed them. The builders
had no scientific training to help them calculate
the weight of material and the thrusts of arches,
but had to rely on tradition and their own experience and observation.

Foto Marburg

THE PRESENTATION IN THE TEMPLE. FIGURES FROM THE WEST
PORTAL OF RHEIMS CATHEDRAL, 13TH CENTURY

The figures stand in front of columns. SS. Joseph and
Anne on either side have a swaying movement produced
by resting the weight on one leg

counterbalanced by an exactly equal pressure
from another. Gothic art, therefore, can be said
to depend on the understanding of the laws of
balance. This Gothic love of balance and
counterpoise is seen in the sculpture and painting as well as in the architecture. Architecture
is the most important art in the Gothic period,
but sculpture in stone, wood, and ivory, wall-
painting and illumination, metal-work, weaving, and embroidery were also brought to
perfection.

2. EARLY GOTHIC. The Gothic style was first
perfected in France, and spread from there
throughout Europe. In England the style of the
first half of the 13th century is called Early
English. This develops into the Geometric and
Decorated styles at the end of the century (*see*
CHURCH ARCHITECTURE, ENGLISH).

In the Gothic period, especially on the
Continent, the finest buildings were no longer
monasteries, as in ROMANESQUE ART (q.v.), but

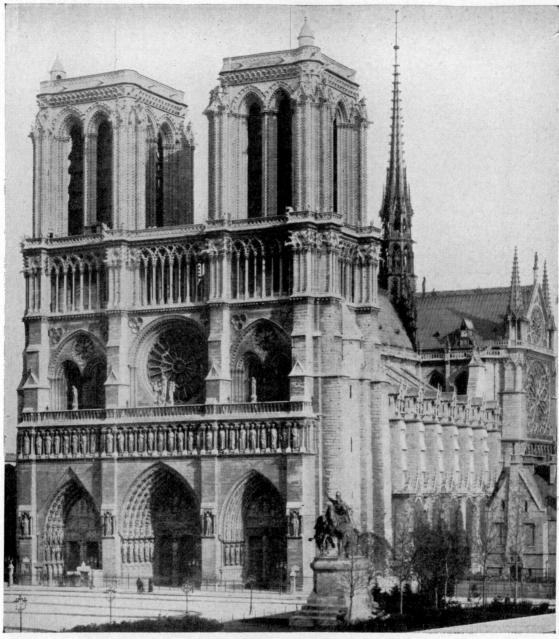

NOTRE DAME, PARIS

The west front was begun in 1208. The design reflects the structure of the interior with its three aisles, clerestory, and triforium

Since the main beauty of a Gothic church is its soaring arches, the masons seem to have felt that elaborate carving would have been out of place inside the buildings. The capitals, for instance, are either plain or decorated with a few crisply curling leaves. The shape of the windows is very simple; some of them are slender, pointed openings (lancets), but others are wider with the lower part divided into two traceried arches and the heads filled with a circle. They were often filled with STAINED GLASS (q.v.) with figures and scenes enclosed in geometrically shaped medallions, the spaces in between being filled with leaf designs.

While the interior of early Gothic churches was rather plain, the exterior, especially the west end, was most elaborately designed to form one great composition. In French cathedrals there are usually four storeys. At the bottom are three deeply recessed porches, with successive rings of arches from which sculptured angels look down towards the life-sized figures standing on each side of the door. Above these deeply shadowed porches comes a line of figures in niches, which makes a strong horizontal division between the porches and the great rose window above. This window is the central feature of the whole composition. The rose, which serves to light the west end of the nave, is flanked on either side by tall windows which light the aisles. Above the windows is an arcade which links the two great towers at the corners and screens the gable of the roof. The towers usually contain narrow, soaring arches. The composition is divided vertically by the four buttresses which support the towers.

The same love of balance and contrast can be seen in the sculpture as in the architecture. The figures nearly always rest their weight on one foot, with a slight tilting of the line of the shoulders and hips; this is counterbalanced by a turning of the head. The movements of the body are interpreted by the drapery. At this period there is little attempt at portraiture, the sculptors merely suggesting some differences of age and character. These differences are only lightly and subtly suggested in France but are much further stressed in the more emotional art of Germany. Important carvings in relief were also carried out, especially in the head of the arches above the great doorways and below the standing figures at the side. The subjects above the doors are often Christ and the Evangelists or the Last Judgement, or scenes from the Life of Christ and the Virgin. The most attractive reliefs are those on a small scale. The Church taught that man could begin to work towards his own redemption by both manual work and serious study, so both are illustrated in the sculpture. Many animals, plants, and birds are also represented in the doorways and other parts of the cathedrals to show that God created the natural world as well as Man. Some of these, especially the gargoyles, which decorate the waterspouts carrying rainwater off the roof, are fantastic grotesques.

Inside the cathedrals and larger churches there were great opportunities for WOODCARVING (q.v.) on the magnificent screens, stalls, bishops' thrones, and bench-ends. Here again some of the scenes are fantastic and satirical (*see* ROOD SCREENS; MISERICORDS).

Towards the end of the 13th century, as individual wealth increased and life became more settled, beautiful works of art were made not only for religious purposes but also to enrich the lives and houses of the wealthy. Secular subjects, also, such as scenes drawn from ROMANCE LITERATURE, were used as subjects for paintings and IVORY CARVINGS (qq.v.) (*see* Vol. IX, p. 126).

Gothic art reached its peak at the end of the 13th century. At this time domestic architecture as well as the building of churches was brought to perfection. Crusaders returning from the Holy Land brought back new ideas of castle-building, and the castles, which were often surrounded by moats, were both very beautiful and practically impregnable to besiegers without artillery (*see* CASTLES, Vol. XI).

3. DECORATED AND FLAMBOYANT. In the 14th century buildings, sculpture, and painting tended to become over-elaborate, especially in France. In Germany and England new ideas were introduced. The whole weight of the vault was carried by buttresses set at right angles to the walls, and the latter, freed from the need to be strong, were often largely replaced by huge windows filled with elaborate tracery. In England this style is called 'Decorated'; in France 'Flamboyant', meaning flame-like. Sculpture was used much more freely inside buildings than before, and often important parts of the buildings were entirely covered with a pattern of tiny carved leaves which give great richness to the surface and produce fascinating effects of light and shade. Richly carved TOMBS and CHANTRY chapels (qq.v.) were included in the buildings.

4. PERPENDICULAR. The Decorated style did not last long in England and, before the end of the 14th century, was replaced by the Perpendicular style, which is plain and austere. In this style the stress is placed on the upright or perpendicular mullions of the windows and the very slender shafts which run up the walls to support the vault, sometimes without even being interrupted by capitals. In order to give uniformity to the building, the walls are usually divided into tall, narrow panels by means of very shallow tracery applied to their surface—

ELY LADY CHAPEL, 1321–49

The windows have elaborate decorated tracery, the vault is of the lierne type. The arcading and the niches for figures
of saints in the window splays are richly carved and have ogee arches

the shape of the panels again stressing the perpendicular. This style, which is only found in England, originated in the west country, the first and one of the finest examples being in Gloucester Cathedral. There, the Romanesque choir is completely covered with a screenwork of perpendicular shafts and panels, entirely hiding the original 12th-century work; and the east apse was taken down and replaced by an enormous window in which the new simple tracery is seen to perfection. This remodelling of a Romanesque building, which was begun in 1337, shows how conscious people in the Middle Ages were of fashion in architecture.

Among the finest Perpendicular buildings are the series of royal chapels built at Windsor, Eton, King's College, Cambridge, and Westminister All these are simple oblong buildings, beautifully proportioned and decorated with skilful craftsmanship, and roofed with magnificent fan vaults. A great many English parish churches, especially in the wool-growing districts of East Anglia, the Cotswolds, Yorkshire, and the west country, were either rebuilt or drastically altered in the 15th century. These very large churches would have seemed less bare and cold than they do now when the walls were decorated with mural paintings, the windows filled with stained glass in which saints, scenes from the Bible, and all kinds of heraldic devices were portrayed in glowing colours, and the churches enriched with magnificently carved rood screens, benches and pulpits, often richly painted and gilded. In the eastern counties the double hammer-beam roofs, ornamented with angels with outspread wings, were almost as elaborate in construction and craftsmanship as the fan vaults of the royal chapels.

The sculpture and painting in these churches was not always of the highest quality, but the subjects represented are interesting, as they reflect the religious life of the people of the time—a time when the saints were much reverenced. The saints were made recognizable by their emblems, and sometimes long and fantastic episodes from their legends were represented. The stories of the Gospels were also often illustrated. In the Christmas scenes especially, there is a great stress on homely details, the figures usually wearing the clothes of the late Middle Ages. The artists possibly took their ideas from scenes in the MIRACLE PLAYS (q.v.) which were acted in the churches or the churchyards during the great church festivals. In the Passion scenes Christ is represented more as a suffering Man than as the triumphant Saviour. German artists especially made the crucifixion scenes almost unbearably painful to look at. One much-repeated subject was that of the Virgin holding the dead Christ on her knees.

Domestic building underwent great changes in the late 14th and 15th centuries (*see* HOUSES, HISTORY OF, Vol. XI). Castles were gradually transformed into pleasant dwelling houses. In England these were comparatively modest; but abroad, especially in France, the kings and nobles built enormous and fantastic châteaux, such as those in the Loire valley. With their high-pitched roofs, round towers surmounted by pointed spires, great gateways, and carved open staircases, all reflected in the still waters of moats and lakes, these châteaux look like fairy palaces. In the cities guild halls and town halls were sometimes even more elaborate than the châteaux of the nobility (*see* PUBLIC BUILDINGS). The finest are in the cities of the Low Countries (Holland and Belgium), which were the most important commercial centres of the Middle Ages (*see* p. 149).

The late Middle Ages was a period of great interest in learning, and many of the colleges of Oxford and Cambridge, with their beautiful

Archives Photographiques

'PIETÀ' AT VILLENEUVE-LES-AVIGNON. BY AN UNKNOWN SOUTH FRENCH PAINTER
The painting was probably inspired by one of the many carved representations of the Virgin of Pity

F. H. Crossley

ANGEL ROOF, WOOLPIT, SUFFOLK, 15TH CENTURY

The hammer-beam construction made it possible to span a wide roof with short timbers. The ends of the hammer-beams are carved with angels

chapels, great halls, libraries, quadrangles, and gateways, were built and endowed at this time. As in the domestic buildings of the period, the builders used many architectural devices which were derived from traditional church design.

Although scholars in northern Europe had many contacts with their fellows in Italy, northern artists and architects remained almost completely untouched by the Renaissance in ITALIAN ART (q.v.). Apart from minor details, the Gothic tradition remained fundamentally unchanged down to the mid-16th century.

See also CHURCH ARCHITECTURE, ENGLISH.

GOTHIC REVIVAL. Gothic architecture was considered barbaric by the scholars and artists of the 17th and 18th centuries, whose interests were centred almost entirely on the ideals and forms of CLASSICAL ART (q.v.). But in the middle of the 18th century, though GEORGIAN ARCHITECTURE (q.v.) remained typical of the period, an interest in the Middle Ages became fashionable, and with it a revival of Gothic architecture. It was regarded as romantic, and its revival coincided with a liking for the romantic in literature (*see* ROMANTIC MOVEMENT). At first only a Gothic appearance was given by the use of pointed windows, castellations, and other features in buildings that remained fundamentally Georgian. A few houses were built in a more completely Gothic style, such as Horace Walpole's 'little Gothic castle' at Strawberry Hill, Twickenham (begun 1753), and Fonthill, Wiltshire, begun in 1796 for the romantic novelist, William Beckford.

It was not until well into the 19th century that a more thorough-going Gothic revival began, inspired by new feelings about religion, and by a notion that these were best expressed by buildings reminiscent of the more spiritually minded Middle Ages. The Gothic style was declared to be the only possible style for churches: it was truly devotional, its advocates argued, while Renaissance buildings were pagan. And soon a movement was afoot for recognizing Gothic as the only proper style for all kinds of buildings. Its leader was the architect A. W. N. Pugin, a deeply religious man, a great student of medieval art and architecture, and a skilful designer, especially of Gothic ornament. He published a book called *Contrasts*, which had a profound influence, in which he depicted medieval architecture as the setting for an ideal civilization, and identified Renaissance architecture with all the evils he saw in the England of his day. Among other things Pugin was responsible for the ornamentation and furnishings of the Houses of Parliament, built between 1840 and 1852 to the designs of Sir Charles Barry (*see* Vol. X, p. 197).

The Gothic Revival was largely confined to England, and expressed itself especially in churches. The particular phase of medieval Gothic chosen as a model was that of the 14th century, known then as 'middle pointed'. At first the details of this period were carefully copied, but later architects designed with more originality, choosing their models from all times and all countries. In this they were stimulated by RUSKIN's (q.v. Vol. V) eloquent descriptions of Venetian Gothic and by others who made a study of medieval buildings.

The 19th century produced a number of great church architects, among whom the most original was William Butterfield, the most prolific Sir Gilbert Scott, and probably the most generally talented George Edmund Street. By the middle of the century choice of style had become the most important question in architecture, and a great controversy raged, called the

National Museum, Athens

ATTIC GEOMETRIC VASE, MID-8TH
CENTURY, B.C.

It was set over a grave. A funeral
scene is depicted in the centre, with
mourners beside the corpse

RIGHT: MAN CARRYING A CALF

Archaic figure of about 570 B.C.
found on the Acropolis, Athens

insisted that the solution should harmonize with rules of decoration and proportion already worked out. The artist, starting from the achievements of his predecessors, constantly directed his interest to something new. In some periods interest in pattern was predominant, in others composition or emotion; but development was constant.

1. EARLY PERIOD. From the 12th to 8th centuries B.C. potters decorated vases in brown paint with lines and circles combining in complicated patterns until most of the vase was covered with a design. In this 'Geometric style' animals, and human figures in funeral processions, in chariots, or dancing, were drawn, but these also fitted into geometrical patterns. The bodies were triangular, the limbs stick-like, the heads were knobs; the artists drew head and legs in profile and body full-face, and showed depth by placing figures one above another. Childlike as was the drawing, the effect is lively, fresh, and decorative. Solid bronze statuettes of men, and particularly horses, in the same style are the earliest sculpture.

In the 8th century B.C., Greek travellers in Egypt and Asia Minor were impressed by the sight of large-scale sculpture with narrative scenes and rows of decorative monsters (see ASSYRIAN and EGYPTIAN ART). Greek artists became interested in rendering life realistically and in story-telling.

The first nearly life-sized statues were made about 650 B.C., in stone. These statues are stiff and board-like. In the beginning of this, the 'Archaic Period', the sculptor, to avoid cutting the stone deeply, rendered features and muscles as markings on the surface. The head on its massive neck is large, often flat-topped, with heavy wig-like hair, enormous eyes, and ears unnaturally set; the limbs are close together as though still imprisoned in the original block.

'Battle of the Styles', between the advocates of Gothic and the advocates of classical as the best kind of period dress to use. At first Gothic had the better of it, but for non-religious buildings it was eventually defeated by Renaissance and Neo-classical styles, largely because of the obvious unsuitability of Gothic for the many new types of building—railway-stations, hospitals, stores, factories, and so on—which the new industrial age required. But the Gothic Revival in its various forms continued to dominate church architecture well into the 20th century, though with increasing competition from rival styles (see MODERN ARCHITECTURE).

See also GOTHIC ART; CHURCH ARCHITECTURE, ENGLISH.

GREEK ART. Greece is a land of brilliant outlines and hard contrasts of light and shade. It is natural to the Greeks, therefore, to dislike haziness and in art to insist on proportion and the importance of line and pattern. Ancient Greek artists, in studying problems such as the natural representation of the human body or the rendering of three dimensions on a flat surface,

The statues usually have dignity, often grace, and harmony and pattern bind together the whole. The poet AESCHYLUS (q.v. Vol. V) said in the early 5th century B.C. that though the new statues were wonderful works, the old had something divine in them.

Sculptors of the 6th and early 5th centuries studied the forms of the body, gradually working out its proportions. Muscles acquired volume, arms were free of the body, weight might be thrown on to one leg. The head might turn or bend, and hair was shown in different ways. Male statues were usually nude, but the drapery of female statues began to develop substance of its own, while allowing the body its own shape. Folds made a beautiful system of patterns, delightful in themselves and an essential part of the lines of the whole statue. It also became possible to have an interesting view of a statue from any angle, instead of only a plain front or side view.

These statues were painted, as was usual throughout the Greek period. Many, buried in the debris after the Persians had sacked the Athenian ACROPOLIS (q.v.) in 480 B.C., were excavated with their colour still preserved. The hair was yellow, reddish-brown, or black, the flesh pink for women, ruddier for men, the eyes dark (sometimes inlaid in another material), the clothes variously coloured, often with elaborate borders. Our idea of white statuary comes from the loss of colour through weathering.

2. GREEK ARCHITECTURE. Greek architects also used colour to pick out details of their buildings, or as a wash to cover poor materials. Early Greek temples were small hut-like buildings of rubble or mud-brick, sometimes thatched. Colonnaded temples of stone are rare before the 6th century. The design was simple—a rectangular building on a foundation of usually three steps, with columns at the porch, at either end, or all round (see Vol. I, p. 203). The Greeks did not use the arch, their buildings depending for effect on the strong contrast of light and shade on horizontals and verticals. Figure sculpture in the round filled the triangular gable (pediment) at the ends, and reliefs were carved on the horizontal beams supported by the columns. The sculpture usually told a story, often that of the god or hero of the place. The difficulty of filling the triangular shape of the pediment was overcome by having kneeling and lying figures at the corners. Pediment figures with elaborate

scenes of movement have been preserved from temples at Aegina (early 5th century), Olympia, and the Parthenon. In the reliefs (see Vol. I, p. 207), the artists had to solve the problems of showing in a depth of a few inches figures overlapping and receding in space. This was brilliantly achieved on the Parthenon frieze, where horsemen are shown effectively grouped (see ELGIN MARBLES).

3. VASE PAINTING. Little is left of large-scale Greek painting, but we can follow its influence in vase painting, an art practised by painters of great skill. In the late Geometric period the match-stick figures filled out, the heads developed features, and the limbs shape. Scenes began to tell stories. In the 7th century influences from the East made popular friezes of lions, bulls, and winged monsters. The brown paint was enlivened with gay touches of red, white, and yellow. Human beings, hereafter the centre of Greek interest, are painted more often fighting, hunting, or taking a lion for a walk on a lead. The vases were strongly and finely made, with shapes beautiful and suitable for their purpose. The pottery of Corinth was supreme in

Alinari

ATTIC BLACK FIGURE VASE, *c.* 540 B.C., SIGNED BY THE PAINTER EXEKIAS

Castor says good-bye to his parents before leaving for a journey. To the left Pollux is greeted by a dog

Giraudon

ATTIC RED FIGURE CUP, *c.* 500 B.C., SIGNED BY THE POTTER
EUPHRONIOS
Young Theseus, escorted by Athene, visits the goddess
Amphitrite at the bottom of the sea

Greece in the 7th century, but in the 6th century Athens took the lead.

A more sober style known as Black Figure then became popular. The figures, mostly human or divine, were shown in black silhouette against the reddish clay of the vase (*see* Vol. I, p. 205). White paint might be added for women's flesh, and for details. Markings on the figures are shown by incision—a scratching away of the paint to show the ground beneath. The beauty of Black Figure largely depends on the firmness and delicacy of the incision. The greatest Black Figure painter was Exekias, an Athenian of the middle 6th century. His figures are full of energy and well-bred dignity, his compositions well designed, and the whole vase perfectly finished in every detail.

About 525 B.C. Black Figure began to be superseded by Red Figure (*see* Vol. I, p. 208), in which the background was painted black, and the figures left in the natural colour of the clay. The inner markings were shown by lines of lustrous black paint, which could be thinned to brown. The paint brush was easier to manipulate than the incision tool, and allowed greater variety of line, and, later, the addition of shading to show roundness. Red Figure vase painting was at its greatest at the end of the 6th and in the early 5th centuries. The problems of three-quarter views, foreshortening, and the rendering of action were being solved, while the feeling for pattern remained strong.

Later, vase painting degenerated as fewer

first-rank artists applied themselves to it. Vase painters tended to imitate wall painters, such as Polygnotus, who were painting on a scale and with complications, such as the rendering of perspective, beyond the scope of a vase painter. Consequently the vase designs lost their unity, and with it life; and, though some delicate and pretty work was done in the late 5th and early 4th centuries B.C. (*see* Vol. I, p. 209), much was ornate and even vulgar, and by the end of the 4th century the art was dead.

4. CLASSICAL SCULPTURE. The victories over the Persians in the early 5th century were followed by a graver, grander style, which found characteristic expression in sculpture, as at OLYMPIA (q.v.). It was a period of increasing naturalism, and the sculptor, certain of his mastery of body forms, turned to representing all forms of action. Myron's Discobolos, an athlete hurling the discus, made about 450 B.C., is interesting from all points of view. The curved body is tensed for violent action, but the moment shown is that before the actual cast, with the

THE DISCOBOLOS (DISCUS THROWER). COPY OF A BRONZE
FIGURE BY MYRON, *c.* 450 B.C.

British Museum

DEMETER, FOUND IN HER SANCTUARY AT CNIDUS
Probably by the Athenian sculptor Leochares, *c.* 330 B.C.

discus at rest at the top of its swing—the most fitting moment for sculpture. It was in bronze—indeed most sculptors of this period were bronze workers; hollow bronze casting (*see* BRONZE SCULPTURE) was invented in the 6th century, but no works remain earlier than the 5th. Few life-size bronzes survive, except in copies, but we have one, by an unknown sculptor, which must be among the greatest—the bronze statue of Zeus hurling a thunderbolt, found in the sea off Cape Artemisium (*see* Vol. I, p. 197), and dated about 470–460 B.C. The god's spread arms and legs form an interesting cross-shaped design. He is a mature man of fine development, full of divine majesty.

Phidias, between 450 and 430 B.C., made the two most famous statues, the Athene of the Parthenon, and the Zeus of Olympia (*see* WONDERS OF THE WORLD). Both are known only by late copies and descriptions. They were colossal, with ivory flesh and golden garments. It was said that the sight of the Zeus could make a man forget his sorrows. The sculptures of the Parthenon show Phidias' largeness of style and design, splendid strength, delicacy, and subtlety. His contemporary, Polycletus, about 440 B.C. made a statue of a youth holding a spear, embodying what he considered the ideal proportions of the human figure (*see* p. 83).

In the 5th century emotion was shown in the whole figure rather than in the face, which was generally calm, though not uninterested or unintelligent. Fourth-century sculptors such as Scopas, who made popular the fashion of deepset

Anderson

MOSAIC OF THE BATTLE OF THE ISSUS FROM POMPEII, BASED ON A LATE 4TH-CENTURY B.C. GREEK WALL PAINTING
On the left Alexander, bareheaded, charges the Persian king Darius, who flees in his chariot

GREEK COINS

1. Syracuse, *c.* 500 B.C. Head of Arethusa surrounded by dolphins
2. Elis, *c.* 421–365 B.C. Head of Zeus's eagle
3. Heraclea Lucaniae, *c.* 380–281 B.C. Heracles wrestling with the Nemean lion
4. Tarentum, *c.* 430–380 B.C. Taras, the city's hero, riding a dolphin
5. Macedon, 336–323 B.C. Alexander the Great wearing the lion skin of Heracles
6. Acrapas, 5th century B.C. The crab is the city badge
7. Bactria, *c.* 160–150 B.C. King Eucratides

Ashmolean Museum

eyes under shadowing brows, concentrated on representing intellectual feeling and emotion through the face, and this led to a development of portraiture. Earlier portraits had idealized the subject, producing a type rather than an individual. Drapery became dramatic, with swirling folds, creating complications of light and shade, and indicating different textures. The human body was soft and graceful but lacked the earlier strength and dignity. This change is seen in the works of PRAXITELES (q.v. Vol. V) whose gods are beautiful, but without the fire of divinity.

5. HELLENISTIC PERIOD. In the Hellenistic period (3rd to 2nd centuries B.C.), when Greek civilization spread over the Mediterranean and Near East, some works such as the VENUS DE MILO (q.v.) continued earlier traditions. The VICTORY OF SAMOTHRACE (q.v.) is full of life and grand in conception. But in statues like the Laocoon, who with his sons was strangled by serpents, the technically skilful attempt to render the horror of the subject leaves a feeling of emptiness, and statues with dramatic subjects such as dying barbarians lose their effect by overstressing the emotions.

The painting of the Hellenistic period is well known from copies found at POMPEII (q.v.) and Herculaneum. Interest in perspective and elaborate colour schemes continued, and a new interest developed in still life and landscape, not yet as a scene, but as a setting for figures. Pictures were also executed in lively and decorative MOSAIC (q.v.).

Portraiture was the most living branch of this late Greek art. The features of rulers appeared on COINS (q.v. Vol. VII). These, with gems, and small works in ivory and precious metals, are in design and execution among the finest Greek works of art.

Greek art does not end with the Roman conquest of Greece, or even with the transition from the ancient to the medieval world; it develops as BYZANTINE ART (q.v.), and has been at the foundation of the art of western Europe. Its lasting influence is due to its sense of reason and balance, its concentration on humanity, and its sheer beauty.

See also CLASSICAL ART; ORDERS OF ARCHITECTURE.
See also Vol. I: GREEK CIVILIZATION.

GREEK DRAMA. The Greeks were the first European people to lift primitive religious RITUAL (q.v. Vol. I) into that branch of art and literature which we know as DRAMA (q.v.). The first Greek drama was produced in Attica, one of the states of ancient Greece, in the 6th century B.C., and from it has descended all modern European drama. Only a few later plays, however, imitate the form of a Greek play at all closely (the most famous example in English is MILTON's *Samson Agonistes* (q.v. Vol. V), and even there the choruses are very unlike their Greek models). Few Greek plays have survived, and we know little about the conditions in which they were originally produced. Most of the Greek theatres which can be studied from their ruins were built after the great age of Greek drama was over, and the evidence about costumes, scenery, music, dancing, and the diction and gestures of the actors is scanty (*see* ACTING, HISTORY OF, Vol. IX).

The Greeks recognized two main types of drama: TRAGEDY (from a Greek word meaning 'goat-song', so called either because a goat was the prize or because a goat was sacrificed as part of the ritual) and COMEDY (qq.v.) (from a word meaning 'revel', or perhaps 'village-song'). Both these types reached their highest development in Athens.

The first tragedy is said to have been composed by an Athenian, Thespis of Icaria, and seems to have been performed by a single male actor and a chorus. Dialogue was exchanged between the actor and the chorus-leader, and when the actor retired into the dressing-room (called *skēnē*, 'tent'), the chorus danced and sang in the open space (called *orchēstra*, 'dance-floor') round the altar of the god. We cannot be certain how this performance originated: the Greek philosopher ARISTOTLE (q.v. Vol. V) claimed that it had developed from the dithyramb, a choral hymn in honour of Dionysus, the god of wine; but it is probable that the ritual origins of Greek tragedy were older and more complex than Aristotle realized.

Tragedy first received official recognition as an art in 534 B.C., when Pisistratus, tyrant of Athens, established a competition at the great spring festival of Dionysus. We do not know the original rules for this competition; but early in the 5th century it was established that each competitor must submit to the city authorities a set of four plays (called a tetralogy), of which three must be tragedies and the fourth a 'satyric' play (so called because the chorus had to appear as satyrs, the half-animal companions of Dionysus). The four plays could be either on different subjects (as in the earliest known tetralogy with which AESCHYLUS (q.v. Vol. V) won the first prize in 472 B.C.), or all on the same theme, in which case the three tragedies formed successive acts of a single drama (as in the *Oresteia* of Aeschylus, the only 'trilogy' to survive), with the satyric play burlesquing some episode in the story. Another condition was that the plays had to be performed by a chorus of twelve (later fifteen) members and two (later three) actors, all male; the only limit to the number of parts assigned to each actor was the necessity of getting the actor off the stage to change his costume and the mask which all actors then wore. In the 5th century B.C., it seems to have been expected that the subjects should be based on what we know as GREEK MYTHS (q.v. Vol. I), which

the Greeks regarded as ancient and almost sacred history; that a tetralogy should not much exceed 5,000 lines in length; and that violent action (particularly bloodshed) should never take place on the stage, but be reported by a messenger. From the tetralogies submitted the authorities chose three for production at the festival, allotted the actors, and made arrangements for training the casts. After the performance, a carefully selected jury awarded prizes to the three chosen dramatists, and the winner of the first prize went off to celebrate with his friends—as the tragic poet Agathon does in Plato's dialogue the *Symposium* (or 'Banquet').

There was little change in the form of 5th-century tragedies—no doubt because of the ritual purpose of the plays and the rules of the competition. The dialogue is very stylized, often with symmetrical speeches or a rapid interchange of single-line remarks, and the dialogue sections are marked off from one another by elaborate choral songs, which were accompanied by dancing. The effect must have been much more like a combination of opera and ballet, with suggestions of oratorio, than anything which we are accustomed to call a play.

Of the enormous number of tragedies which must have been performed at Athens (for the competitions lasted for many centuries), only thirty-two have survived, and all except one (the *Rhesus*, by an unknown author) must have been produced in the 5th century. Of these, seven are by Aeschylus, seven by SOPHOCLES, and seventeen by EURIPIDES (qq.v. Vol. V). Fragments of other plays survive, and some can be partly reconstructed; but only the *Rhesus*, perhaps written in the 4th century, gives us any real idea of the work of any other tragic poet. Of the satyric plays, only Euripides' *Cyclops* is complete, though a considerable part of Sophocles' *Huntsmen* and some tantalizing fragments by Aeschylus, whom the ancients regarded as the greatest writer of satyric plays, still survive.

Greek comedy developed later than tragedy (the first competition was instituted at Athens about 487 B.C.), and Aristotle thought that it originated in the rough revelry of country rituals held to ensure the success of the vintage. From that source it derived a strong element of crude humour, which had been eliminated from tragedy, though still appearing in satyric plays. As a literary form, comedy may have originated in Sicily (the first famous comic poet was

Epicharmus of Syracuse), but from the middle of the 5th century all the great writers were either Athenians or foreigners living at Athens. From that time, the history of comedy falls into three periods. 'Old' comedy is represented by nine of the eleven plays of ARISTOPHANES (q.v. Vol. V), and by a number of fragments from other poets who were active in the second half of the 5th century; the plays have an even more elaborate choral structure than tragedy, and are highly satirical and topical, full of knockabout fun and high spirits. 'Middle' comedy, which covers the first two-thirds of the 4th century, and which we know from Aristophanes' last two plays and from other sources, is quieter than 'Old' comedy and derives much of its fun from bringing tragic myths into line with modern ways of acting and thinking. 'New' comedy lived on into the 3rd century; it can be judged by extensive fragments of plays by Menander (342–c. 291 B.C.), the most famous comic poet of his time, which have been discovered in Egypt, and by many adaptations by the Roman dramatists Plautus and Terence. The subjects of 'New' comedy are usually taken from middle-class life; penniless youths, angry old men, faithful servants, and unfortunate maidens are involved in complex plots with a happy ending. It was this type of romantic comedy (see COMEDY, Section 5) which so much influenced the comic dramatists of the Renaissance and which has created stock characters in the comic drama of most countries.

See also DRAMA; TRAGEDY; COMEDY; GREEK LITERATURE.

See also Vol. I: GREEK CIVILIZATION.

See also Vol. IX: THEATRE, HISTORY OF, Section 1.

GREEK LITERATURE.

The history of ancient Greek literature begins with Homer, who lived perhaps about 700 B.C., and the epic works which go under his name are described in the article HOMERIC LITERATURE (q.v.).

EPIC POETRY (q.v.) continued to be composed after Homer's time; but even in the 7th century B.C. epic poetry was becoming of less importance than LYRIC POETRY (q.v.). There were two main kinds of lyric poetry: choral, which was originally chiefly religious in purpose and was performed by choirs which sang and danced to lyre or flute accompaniment; and personal, sung by a single person and claiming to express his or her experiences and opinions. Sparta is the earliest known centre of choral lyric, the most important poets being Terpander of Lesbos and Alcman. Towards the end of the 7th century B.C., Corinth and Sicily developed the narrative and dramatic elements in choral lyric to the almost complete exclusion of the religious elements. In the meantime, personal lyrics were being composed in many parts of Greece. Archilochus of Paros was a great innovator in technical (especially metrical) matters; Tyrtaeus of Sparta and Callinus of Ephesus preached the citizen's duty to fight and die for his country; Mimnermus of Colophon wrote of the individual's duty to enjoy life while he could. Towards the end of the century the two great lyric poets of Lesbos, Alcaeus and SAPPHO, both emulated Archilochus in the passionate expression of their own feelings and in their fondness for technical innovations.

In the 6th century personal lyric poetry is represented by the political poems of the Athenian SOLON, by the satires of Hipponax of Ephesus and Xenophanes of Colophon, and by the love-songs and drinking-songs of Anacreon of Teos. Choral lyric lived on only in the west of the Greek world, but was revived in old Greece towards the end of the century. About this time Athens began her rise to the intellectual leadership of the Greek world. Great literary competitions, especially the yearly competition for tragedy instituted in 534 B.C., were established in Athens, and these stimulated interest in literature. Towards the end of this century prose was becoming recognized as a literary medium, especially for philosophy, medicine, chronicles, and geography.

By the beginning of the 5th century, lyric poetry was no longer popular, though some choral lyric was still being written, especially by Simonides and his younger contemporary, the Theban Pindar. At Athens the greatest interest was in drama, and in 487 B.C. a competition for comedy was added to that for tragedy. Among the many playwrights the tragedians AESCHYLUS and SOPHOCLES, and the comedian Cratinus, were the greatest. By the second half of the century drama had become by far the most popular form of poetry in Greece, and in Athens EURIPIDES in tragedy and ARISTOPHANES in comedy were of the first rank (see GREEK DRAMA).

During this great period in Greek literature, important works were being written in science and philosophy, especially by members of the medical school at Cos, of whom the greatest was traditionally HIPPOCRATES. Even more significant, however, for the later history of literature was the study of the proper use of the spoken word—*rhētorikē*, that is, the art of the public speaker (*see* RHETORIC). This study, originated by Protagoras, was carried on mainly in Sicily, especially by Gorgias of Leontini. The growing interest in prose style can be traced both in oratory, which first became important as literature towards the end of the century, and in the histories of Herodotus of Halicarnassus, and THUCYDIDES (*see* HISTORIES).

The 4th century B.C. was an age famous for its great prose, especially for the philosophy of PLATO and ARISTOTLE and for the oratory of DEMOSTHENES and many others. The historical works of this century are mostly lost, except for those of Xenophon, who also wrote memoirs, essays, and a romance.

After the death of Alexander the Great (323 B.C.), though Athens still remained an important centre for the study of philosophy, literature and science soon found a new home in the *Mouseion* (shrine of the MUSES (q.v. Vol. I)) founded at Alexandria in Egypt by Ptolemy I about 300 B.C. So began what is called the Hellenistic age, in which Greek became a world language and Greek culture spread widely among non-Greek peoples. Poets tended to look back to their predecessors as models, and technical skill and complicated displays of learning excused the lack of originality in the writer's thought. The period, therefore, could boast few genuine poets; even in the early 3rd century B.C. only Theocritus, Callimachus, and Apollonius of Rhodes deserve the title. On the other hand, Hellenistic prose literature is outstanding, both in technical subjects (especially botany, medicine, mathematics, astronomy, and geography) and in more literary fields such as philosophy (where Philo and Plotinus are perhaps the most important), history (including the work of the Jewish historian Josephus), and biography and essays (in which PLUTARCH is unchallenged). In the 2nd century A.D., at a time when the old beliefs and literary traditions were decaying, the philosopher Lucian wrote brilliant satirical essays and humorous dialogues in a sparkling, vivid style. Almost every aspect of life and thought in the ancient world was written about; this universality of Hellenistic literature may perhaps help us to understand why Greek so quickly became the first language of Christianity, and why it is still a living language today, with an important medieval and modern literature.

Those writers whose names are printed in capital letters have separate biographies in Vol. V.

See also Vol. I: GREEK CIVILIZATION.
See also Vol. IV: GREEK LANGUAGE.

GREGORIAN CHANT, *see* PLAINSONG.

GULLIVER'S TRAVELS, by Jonathan Swift, *see* SATIRE. *See also* Vol. V: SWIFT.

H

HARMONY. 1. When two or more musical sounds of different pitch are sung or played at the same time, and are chosen so that the result is euphonious or sounds well, it is called harmony.

If a single voice sings a song, the sound may be thought of as a thread of sound running along more or less horizontally. Thus the tune of the hymn 'On Jordan's Bank' may be written as in Fig. 1.

If four different voices, treble, alto, tenor, and bass, sing different sounds together the result may be shown as four lines of melody (Fig. 2). In this case one does not only hear the four lines of melody independently. At each point four sounds are heard together one below the other; they are therefore related to each other not only horizontally as the melody passes from one note to the next, but there is also a relationship

FIG. 1

Soprano
Alto

Tenor
Bass

etc.

FIG. 2

etc.

FIG. 3

between each of the four sounds sung at the same time. This may be represented by vertical lines (Fig. 3).

The vertical groups of notes are called chords. These chords are built up of notes at definite intervals from each other based on the notes of the scale of the key in which the music is written. There is a chord based on every note of the scale, consisting of that note and the third and fifth above it (Fig. 4). These three notes are the basis of chords; they can appear in any order and can be repeated at octaves higher or lower. Chords can be built up from them by the addition of sevenths and other intervals, but however elaborately these chords are arranged or decorated (as in piano music) they underlie all Western music.

C major

G major

FIG. 4. THE CHORDS OF C MAJOR AND G MAJOR

1. Tonic; 2. Supertonic; 3. Mediant; 4. Subdominant; 5. Dominant; 6. Submediant; 7. Leading tone. The chords with stars are common to both keys

The most significant chords are the tonic, subdominant, and dominant, that is, those based on the first, fourth, and fifth notes of the scale. These, therefore, are especially used to emphasize the pause at the end of the phrases of melody (*see* MELODY AND RHYTHM). A composition is built up of a series of phrases; in order to round off the end of the composition and give it a sense of finality the final phrase ends with the tonic chord, preceded usually by either the subdominant or the dominant.

Too long a stretch of harmonies based on one scale would become uninteresting; variety, therefore, is given by changing from one key to another. This is called 'modulation'. Some keys are closely related to each other because their scales have a large number of notes in common (Fig. 4). Modulations are most common between keys which are closely related in this way. The closest relationship occurs between keys in which the tonic of one is the dominant of the other. Fig. 1, for example, starts in C major, but ends in the key of its dominant, **G major.**

J. S. Bach

FIG. 5

2. Counterpoint. Contrapuntal music or 'counterpoint' is built up of a number of independent melodies which, nevertheless, combine to give the harmonic interest. Fugue and canon (*see* Musical Form, Sections 7 and 8) are examples of counterpoint. In Fig. 2 some of the parts (particularly the tenor) have very little melodic interest, so that the music cannot be said to be contrapuntal. In Fig. 5, on the other hand, each of the three parts has an individual character and independence. This, then, is good counterpoint, as well as being good harmony.

3. History. The Plainsong (q.v.) sung in the medieval church consisted of melody only. If boys and men sang together, the melody would be duplicated at an interval of an octave, the men's voices being lower in pitch. Soon the melody was sung by some voices at intervals of a fourth and fifth (Fig. 6 *a*). This was known as 'strict organum'. In free organum, the added part did not confine itself all the time to moving at a distance of a fourth or fifth from the original melody, but moved in 'oblique motion' (one part repeating a note while the other moved up or down) or, later, in 'contrary movement' (the parts going in opposite directions) (Fig. 6 *b* and *c*). Before there was any standard and accurate Musical Notation (q.v.) it was possible to give melodic variety to the different parts, but rhythmic variety was impossible until a way of writing down note values had been invented. Even when this had been achieved, and the strands became more independent in rhythm as well as melody, composers at first still paid more attention to the melodies themselves than to the harmonies they produced by being combined.

The perfecting of counterpoint which had

been built up slowly for a period of over 600 years came about during the 16th century. Music was still based upon horizontal strands of rhythmic melody, but they were combined in such a way that the intervals between simultaneous notes produced satisfactory harmonies. Perhaps the most crucial time in the development of the technique of musical composition was the latter part of the 16th century and the beginning of the 17th. In the Middle Ages composers thought entirely of the horizontal aspect of the music. Gradually they began to pay more attention to the harmonies which resulted from the combination of melodies. Finally the harmonic aspect became the most important factor, though contrapuntal writing has always played a large part in much fine music.

When composers began to give more consideration to the vertical aspect of their com-

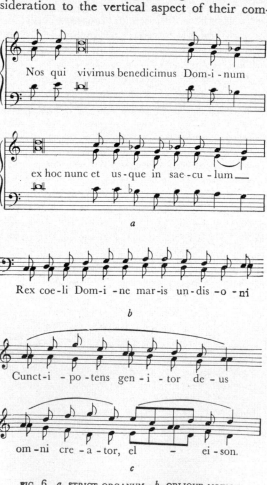

Nos qui vivimus benedicimus Dom-i-num

ex hoc nunc et us-que in sae-cu-lum

a

Rex coe-li Dom-i-ne mar-is un-dis-o-ni

b

Cunct-i-po-tens gen-i-tor de-us

om-ni cre-a-tor, el — ei-son.

c

FIG. 6. *a.* STRICT ORGANUM. *b.* OBLIQUE MOTION. *c.* CONTRARY MOVEMENT

positions, they found that there were only a limited number of harmonies which could be built on the modes on which plainsong melodies were based, and that modulation was impossible. Greater freedom was possible only with the development of the major and minor SCALES (q.v.).

The 'New Music' of the 17th century was a violent reaction against the counterpoint of the preceding age, and musicians turned to the possibilities of harmony rather than counterpoint as a means of expression. Yet the instinct for counterpoint still remained and saw a new flowering in the works of J. S. BACH and, to a lesser degree, of HANDEL (qq.v. Vol. V) and his contemporaries. In Bach's counterpoint the two factors, vertical and horizontal, are more or less equal partners. Bach's harmonic structure is strong and well organized, but is generally brought about by the combination of the parts, which, while retaining their horizontal character, are designed to combine together to produce harmonic results.

In the period of HAYDN and MOZART (qq.v. Vol. V) and the so-called 'classical' period in general, the vertical triumphed over the horizontal. Harmony was no longer the product of interwoven strands, but was the essential basis of the music. However much the 'parts' might move about, they were almost completely dependent upon the harmonic progression of the chords. To make richer and more interesting effects, notes, called 'chromatic notes', were introduced which did not belong to the key in which the music was composed. Chromatic notes were used from the time of Bach and Handel but became progressively more common until, in the 19th century, there was a great increase in the use of chromatic sounds, and the use of discords was developed. In the latter part of the century this trend increased to such an extent that the music was not felt to be in any particular key. The inevitable result was that either a reaction or a complete break with the past had to come. Composers made various experiments to try and find a satisfactory way out of the disorganization of harmonies produced by the excessive use of chromaticism. Some tried a return to a much more classical use of keys, and even to the old modes and contrapuntal style, though using discords in a modern way. Others made experiments with new scales, and therefore with a new system of harmony, and began to write twelve-note music, based on the equality of every note of the chromatic scale (*see* MODERN MUSIC).

See also MUSIC; MUSIC, HISTORY OF; SCALES; MELODY AND RHYTHM.

HERALDRY, *see* Vol. IV: HERALDRY.

HEROIC COUPLET, *see* VERSIFICATION, Section 4.

HISTORIES. 'History', from a Greek word, means 'an investigation'. Herodotus, a Greek of the 5th-century B.C. was the first known historian, 'the father of history'. He was the first to use the word 'history' (in the title of his work), and the first to envisage such writing, not as a transcription of legend, myth, and traditional story, but as an investigation into what men have done and why. And this he undertook so that men's deeds might not be forgotten. He read and travelled widely to collect information; he says, again and again, 'I wanted to know, so I went to see.' In the nine books of his *History*, Herodotus traced the enmity between Europe and Asia, culminating in the struggle between Greece and Persia. He wrote vividly, simply, and with zest.

The other great Greek historian is THUCYDIDES (q.v. Vol. V), who was a younger contemporary of Herodotus. His (incomplete) history, in eight books, recounts the war between Athens and Sparta (the Peloponnesian War) as far as the year 411 B.C. But he prefaces this by a survey of events leading up to the war. Thucydides made a great contribution to historical method by clearly formulating the principle that historical investigation must rest on evidence. His own work shows that he reported faithfully what he judged to be true; and because he wrote of the immediate past and present, he could accumulate evidence and check it. He took part in the war of which he wrote, and his first-hand knowledge of military affairs was a great asset to him as a war-historian. He understood political affairs, too, and was able to trace political events to their causes. What chiefly interested him was not so much the events as the laws by which they happen.

The first important Roman historian was LIVY (q.v. Vol. V) who wrote in a work of 142 books—of which 35 survive—the complete history of Rome from her beginnings till 9 B.C. To a Roman, Rome was the world; and Livy's great conception was, for a Roman, the equivalent of a world history. It was the first time anything of the sort had been done. By contrast Livy's compatriot, Tacitus, confined himself to a short period. His *Annals* and *Histories* tell the story of Rome under the Emperors for some 80 years, A.D. 14–96. They present a dark but not unjust picture of the corruption and demoralization of life in Rome; and they show Tacitus' special interest in the characters of men and their effects on history. Two other works of his are the *Germania*, which describes the Germanic peoples and their institutions; and the *Agricola*, a biography of his father-in-law, Agricola, in which he describes the Roman conquest of Britain. Tacitus originated a concise, meaningful, subtle style, so characteristic that we now describe such a style as Tacitean.

The Christian influence on historical ideas in the 4th and 5th centuries was revolutionary. St. AUGUSTINE (q.v. Vol. V) in the 5th century A.D., in his *City of God*, expounded the doctrine that the past, present, and future of mankind are due, not to the will of man, but to the will of God. From this comes the now familiar idea that historical processes do not depend on man's actions only, but have an independent power of their own. Thus, although Brutus and Cassius could assassinate Caesar, they could not prevent the triumph of Caesarism and the downfall of the Republic (*see* AUGUSTUS CAESAR, Vol. V). But, though historical thought gained from this, historical method lost. To the medieval historian, intent on discovering and revealing God's plan for mankind, men's actions were relatively unimportant, and so he neglected the historian's first duty—to find out what happened.

Another contribution of Christian thought to history was the idea that no one race or community was more important than another; therefore the Christian demanded, not a Roman or Jewish history, but a universal one. As a consequence, a single chronological framework was adopted—a chronology which dated everything backward and forwards from the birth of Christ. This was worked out by Isidore of Seville in the 7th century, and popularized by the Venerable BEDE (q.v. Vol. V) in the 8th. Bede's greatest work, the *Ecclesiastical History of the English Nation*, though written in Latin, is the first great English history. It describes England from 55 B.C. (Caesar's invasion) to A.D. 731, and contains information unobtainable elsewhere.

The chronicles and annals of the Middle Ages, compiled in most of the great monasteries of Europe, are more often valuable as sources for history than as histories in their own right. Monks of Winchester, Canterbury, and Peterborough—probably in the first place at the command of Alfred the Great—wrote the *Anglo-Saxon Chronicle*, which relates events in England down to the middle of the 12th century. Later, Froissart and Holinshed were famous chroniclers. Froissart dealt with Flanders, France, Spain, Portugal, and England in the period 1325–1400; he was a great traveller, and painted a vivid picture of the period, the literary merit of his work excusing his historical untrustworthiness. The Holinshed *Chronicles*, written by Holinshed and several other writers, describe England, Ireland, and Scotland. They were first produced in 1577, and were much used by Shakespeare and other Elizabethan dramatists to provide material for their historical plays.

The last of the histories in the medieval tradition (though much later) was the *Discourse on Universal History* (1681) by the French divine, Bossuet, who traces divine intervention at every stage of man's history. With the coming of the Renaissance, interest once more was centred on man. Much of the valuable work in history at this time consisted in clearing away accepted legends and resuming critical standards.

The great religious and political controversies of the 16th and 17th centuries prompted men to examine and publish documents which would

Larousse

FROISSART WRITING HIS CHRONICLE
Illumination from a 15th-century manuscript

National Gallery of Canada

'THE DEATH OF WOLFE' BY BENJAMIN WEST (1738–1820)

In art as in literature at the end of the 18th century there was an interest in the realistic portrayal of historical events

uphold argument and counter-argument, and the recently invented printing-presses made this possible. The Reformation conflict produced in England John Foxe's *Book of Martyrs* (1563), which quotes freely from documents, and Thomas Fuller's *Church History of Britain* (1655) and *Worthies of England* (1662). More and more collections of documents appeared, and the new histories were based on such records. Stow produced his *Survey of London* (1598) which laid the foundations for the history of municipal affairs. William Dugdale collected many documents and used them with great skill for his *Antiquities of Warwickshire* (1656). The most important English collection was Thomas Rymer's *Foedera* (1704–35): twenty volumes of State papers, legal documents, charters and rolls, which provided for the first time a scientific basis for the writing of English history.

Clarendon's *True Historical Narrative of the Rebellion and Civil Wars in England* was published in 1702–4, nearly 30 years after its author's death. It is half history, half memoir, and is the most important single work on the 20 years it covers. Towards the end of this century, Edward Gibbon produced the greatest of historical works in English literature, *The Decline and Fall of the Roman Empire* (1776–88). This deals with a period of 13 centuries, from the age of Marcus Aurelius to the fall of Constantinople in 1453, and thus links the ancient world with the modern. Gibbon's highly latinized style is eloquent, dignified, quotable. Many of its epigrams are familiar, such as this: 'All that is human must retrograde if it does not advance.' As an historian he was learned, truthful, and as well-informed as it was then possible to be. But his description of the growth of Christianity as a purely human phenomenon provoked criticism.

Since Gibbon's day, a whole new field of evidence has been literally unearthed by historians and archaeologists. Excavations have revealed cities, monuments, tombs, works of art, coins, papyri, inscriptions (*see* ARCHAEOLOGY, Vol. I).

Philologists have been able to read many lost languages, though some scripts, such as Etruscan, still remain unsolved. Historians have been able to show that Greece and Rome were the heirs of many brilliant earlier civilizations—EGYPTIAN, SUMERIAN, BABYLONIAN, MINOAN (qq.v. Vol. I). Schliemann, the great German amateur archaeologist, made discoveries which revolutionized our view of early Greek history.

The 19th century was a time of intensive research, particularly in Germany, where Niebuhr applied rigorously the principles which determine the reliability of evidence, and also showed how by inference something can be known which the evidence did not disclose. His great contemporary and compatriot, Mommsen, author of *Roman History* (1854–6), said: 'All historians are Niebuhr's pupils.'

The most outstanding English 19th-century histories are: Grote's *History of Greece* (1846–56), the first important modern work on Greek history; a *History of England* (1849–61) by MACAULAY, a vast and detailed study of the period from James II to William III; and the *French Revolution* (1837) by CARLYLE (qq.v. Vol. V), in which he brings to life the drama of the revolution.

A work which rivals Carlyle's for vivid re-creation is the *History of France* (1833–67) by the Frenchman, Michelet. In this century of developing nationalism, Michelet is the greatest of many historians whose preoccupation with their own countries led them to produce work of markedly national, sometimes patriotic, bias.

Now that the range of history has become so vast, historians have as a rule to confine themselves to a single topic or period. Nevertheless, within these confines we get great works such as Stubbs's *Constitutional History of England* (1874–8), and Frazer's monumental work in eleven volumes, *The Golden Bough* (1890–1915), provides us with much of our knowledge of primitive life, customs, and superstitions (see FOLK-LORE, Vol. I).

Besides work by a single author, important co-operative works have been compiled, such as the various *Cambridge Histories*, and the *Oxford History of England*. In these, specialists contribute articles or volumes on single aspects or periods.

Lord Acton's precept, 'Study problems, not periods', summarizes the attitude of many modern historians. Some of the most influential trends of thought in modern history spring from the 18th-century Italian, Vico, whose theory of historical cycles reappears in Spengler's *Decline of the West* (1918); from the German philosophers, HEGEL and KANT, who conceived of history as a gradual realization of man's freedom; from Karl MARX (qq.v. Vol. V), who saw mankind's story in terms of a class-struggle resulting from inequality of possessions; from the Italian, Croce, for whom history was the reliving in one's own mind of past experience. A contemporary work on a vast scale, Arnold Toynbee's *A Study of History*, is a comparative study of civilizations.

See also BIOGRAPHY.

HOMERIC LITERATURE. The earliest literature of Greece (and therefore of Europe) passes under the name of HOMER (q.v. Vol. V). To him the early Greeks ascribed a great number of narrative poems called EPIC (q.v.) from the fact that they were composed in the metre which the Greeks call *epos*, but which we call the heroic hexameter (see VERSIFICATION, Section 3). Except for two long poems these epics have been lost, and are known to us only from short summaries in prose, or from occasional quotations and references in later writings. There are also a number of shorter poems in honour of various gods, known as the Homeric Hymns, and a poem called *The Battle of the Frogs and the Mice*, which parodies the style of serious epic.

Since the end of the 5th century B.C., however, the two long poems already referred to have been generally regarded as the only true Homeric literature. The earlier and longer of these (nearly 16,000 lines) is known as the *Iliad* ('about Ilion'—*hē Ilias*); the second and shorter (just over 12,000 lines) as the *Odyssey* ('about Odysseus'—*hē Odysseia*).

Strictly speaking, the *Iliad* is only indirectly about Ilion (or Troy): it refers only in passing to the famous events in Troy's history—the abduction of Helen, wife of King Menelaus of Sparta, by the Trojan Prince Alexandros (also called Paris); the gathering by Agamemnon, King of Mycenae and Menelaus' brother, of an avenging army of Achaeans (Greeks); and the 10 years' siege and sack of Troy (see TROJANS, Vol. I). All these serve only as a background to the main theme of the poem, which is, as the author himself tells us in the first line, 'the wrath of Peleus' son, Achilles'. In the 10th year of the siege, Achilles, the bravest and most terrible

ACHILLES KILLS A TROJAN AT THE TOMB OF PATROCLUS TO AVENGE HIS FRIEND'S DEATH
Painting from a Greek vase

of the Achaean heroes, quarrels bitterly with Agamemnon over a captive woman, part of Achilles' share in the booty. Feeling that Agamemnon has dishonoured him, Achilles withdraws from the fighting until Agamemnon shall offer full amends for the insult. The disasters which then befall the Achaeans finally induce Achilles to send his dearest friend, Patroclus, to resist the Trojans. When Patroclus is killed by Hector, the Trojan leader, Achilles himself in grief and rage returns to the battle, kills Hector, and drags his body away to the Achaean camp. Achilles, reconciled to Agamemnon, gives Patroclus a stately burial; and is then induced to give up his impious plan of mutilating Hector's body, which instead he restores to Hector's father for burial. The poem, therefore, ends with the symbolic reconciliation of Achilles with the gods and with his deadliest enemy.

The main theme of the *Iliad* deals only with the events of about 40 days in the last year of the siege; but the poem as a whole extends much more widely in time and space. This effect is produced mainly by the free use of reminiscence, by which the author describes not only the previous course of the expedition but also events which occurred far away and long ago (such as the wars of Lapiths and Centaurs in Book I, the adventures of Bellerophon in Book VI, or the history of the Trojan royal house in Book XX). Prophecy is also used occasionally (mainly by the gods) to describe events which are destined to happen later. The narrative is given balance by the skill with which the characters of the main actors are contrasted with one another, and by the care with which the author relieves his tale of violence and slaughter. He does this by inserting scenes from ordinary life, glimpses, for example, of domestic life in Troy or in the Achaean camp, or by the use of elaborate similes, or even by descriptions of works of art, such as the scenes from the peaceful city on Achilles' shield in Book XVIII. The *Iliad* is a tragic story: the young and passionate Achilles is doomed to die far from home in a quarrel in which he is not directly concerned, and the more mature Hector, home-loving and god-fearing, loses all that he holds dear in a vain struggle for a cause which he knows to be unrighteous.

Compared with the *Iliad*, the *Odyssey* has a simpler structure and tells a less tragic, though perhaps more exciting, story. The character-drawing is less elaborate; but there is much greater variety of scene and action, and suspense is more freely and dramatically used to overcome the difficulty that everyone knew the story pretty well already. The main theme is the return of Odysseus, King of Ithaca, to his home after 20 years' absence (10 years at the siege of Troy and 10 of wandering). Almost everyone except his wife, Penelope, supposes him to be dead; and the young noblemen of the district are trying to compel Penelope to marry one of themselves. When it seems that even Penelope can hold out no longer, Odysseus arrives in disguise and, helped by his son Telemachus and a few faithful servants, kills the suitors and regains his home and kingdom.

The author begins the story in the 10th year after the taking of Troy, with Odysseus marooned on a remote island belonging to the sea-nymph, Calypso. He describes Odysseus' adventures from that point until, about 40 days later, he is reconciled with the kinsfolk of the dead suitors. Odysseus' earlier adventures are introduced into this simple scheme by allowing Odysseus himself to tell them (in Books IX–XII) to his benefactor, King Alcinous of Phaeacia. A further theme is added by the account of how the young Telemachus went to Pylos and Sparta to seek news of his father, and how he learned from Nestor and Menelaus what had befallen the Achaeans on their way home from Troy. Here, as in Odysseus' account of his visit to the world of the dead (Book XI), and in other suitable places, the *Odyssey* describes past events. Some connexion with the future is given by the ghost of the seer Tiresias, who reveals something of Odysseus' life after his homecoming and foretells how he is to die.

The poems give almost no clue as to their date of composition, their author (or authors), or the public for which they were intended. This 'Homeric problem' has worried students of Greek literature for centuries. It has become specially important since in 1788 the French scholar Villoisin first published the ancient commentaries (known as *scholia*) from the margins of two Homer manuscripts in Venice. The intensive study of Homer's text which this made possible, combined with the recent astonishing results of archaeology, have drawn attention to inconsistencies in details of Homer's narratives and to surprising differences of period both in language and in the description of customs, weapons, clothes, and such like. These have led some scholars to think that both poems are the products of a long evolution through the minds and mouths of nameless bards. Other scholars believe that there was once (perhaps about 850 B.C.) a great poet who composed an *Iliad* and an *Odyssey*, and that less competent bards later inserted passages of their own, thus damaging the original poems irretrievably. The most recent, and perhaps the most probable, view emphasizes the essential unity of plan, which was apparent to Aristotle as it is to the modern reader. It explains the archaisms of language or customs as fossils which have become embedded in the epic language, and points out that such inconsistencies can easily be found in works of comparatively modern times whose single authorship is undoubted. On this theory, the *Iliad* in substantially its present form was composed by an Ionian Greek, who perhaps called himself Homer, in about 700 B.C., for recitation at some great festival. The *Odyssey* was composed some years later, in much the same way and for the same purpose, and perhaps (but not certainly) by the same author.

See also GREEK LITERATURE.
See also Vol. I: GREEK CIVILIZATION.

HOUSES, *see* Vol. XI: HOUSES, HISTORY OF.

HYMNS. In the early Christian Church the hymn was a song of praise mainly for congregational singing. At first, when the congregation was Jewish, psalms were sung to a Hebrew melody; but later, when the Church consisted mainly of Greeks and Romans, other passages from the Bible were sung in Latin to Greek melodies resembling PLAINSONG (q.v.). Some of these hymns, such as the *Te Deum* (We praise Thee, O God), are still sung in church services. In the 4th century St. Ambrose, Bishop of Milan, introduced hymns of regular metre (known as 'Long Measure' in modern hymn-books) into the services of the Church. These were sung in unison, without any accompaniment, to plainsong melodies, each hymn usually having its own tune, which might be an elaborate one with several notes to each syllable, or a simple one with one note to each syllable, as they are sung in our churches today. When a second melody was combined with a plainsong melody, this was known as a 'descant'. (In the modern sense a descant is a tune which is sometimes sung above a hymn tune by the soprano voices.) After the invention of descant, many of these tunes were used as themes for Masses and motets (*see* ANTHEM). They were invariably set in the tenor or baritone part, probably because plainsong was associated with the voice of the priest.

In medieval times, simple plainsong hymns were often sung between the scenes of the MIRACLE PLAYS (q.v.), which were popular throughout Europe. In 1585 the Italian composer Palestrina made a collection of hymns for every festival of the Christian Year, written for three or more voices. The German Protestant reformer LUTHER (q.v. Vol. V) made many collections of hymns, realizing their value both for instructing the people in the Christian religion and for gaining new converts. Some of these tunes were simplified forms of the old plainsong, others were folk-tunes, while others were composed by Luther himself, the most notable being *Ein' feste Burg* (A safe stronghold). These hymns, which came to be known as 'chorales', were sung in German for the first time, instead of in Latin as was the custom in the Roman Catholic churches. J. S. BACH (q.v. Vol. V) used them as the basis of many of his CANTATAS (q.v.).

In the early days of the Reformation many of the psalms were set to verse (known as 'metrical versions') so that the common people, few of whom could read, could more easily memorize them. Many of these 'versions' came to England and Scotland from Geneva, the headquarters of Calvinism, and are still popular, especially in the Scottish Presbyterian churches. During the reign of Elizabeth I two Englishmen, Sternhold and Hopkins, published a new collection of 'versions' of psalms which replaced the earlier ones. In these the melody was still set in the tenor part, the congregation apparently filling in the other parts as best they could. Sternhold and Hopkins's collection was supplanted in 1696 by that of Tate and Brady, a good example from which is the well-known metrical version of Psalm 34, 'Through all the changing scenes of life'. Many of the tunes were set for the treble part, though some were still allotted to tenor voices.

For many centuries churchmen had hesitated to use any hymn verses in Divine Service which were not directly inspired by the words of the Bible; but in the 18th-century hymns composed by George Herbert, Isaac Watts, and John and Charles Wesley were being sung in church services. The Wesley brothers, whose preaching induced a revival of religion in England at a time when it was at its lowest ebb, relied greatly on the use of hymns not only to instruct the people but also to introduce a warmth and tenderness into public worship which was sadly lacking. The 18th century was remarkable for its many noble hymn tunes inspired by the poetry of the finest minds of the age. These were graceful and melodious, yet always dignified, and it is no wonder that so many of them have lived.

In 1861 *Hymns Ancient and Modern* first appeared; in this an attempt was made to collect together the best of the past, with some contemporary work as well. The latter, however, was typical of the somewhat sentimental poetry and music of the period, and gave place, about the turn of the century, to more virile and forthright examples, such as are to be found in the *English Hymnal*, *Songs of Praise*, or the revised edition of *Hymns Ancient and Modern*. Though the form and nature of hymns have varied considerably through the ages, the purpose of the hymn—a congregational act of choral worship —has remained unchanged.

See also MUSIC, HISTORY OF; SACRED MUSIC.

I

ICONS. These are religious pictures painted upon panels for the devotional use of members of the ORTHODOX EASTERN CHURCH (q.v. Vol. I). They vary in size from quite small panels intended for either personal or ritualistic use, to the large, often double-sided icons designed for processional purposes or for setting on the 'iconostasis', or screen, dividing the nave of the church from the chancel. The method of painting originally came from the tomb portraits of Graeco-Roman Egypt; it was soon adopted in

Museum of Fine Arts, Moscow

ST. GEORGE

14th-century Byzantine icon, painted in Constantinople

the Christian world, and by the 12th century icons had become universal in the Orthodox East.

The earlier icons generally show either a single figure, the Virgin and Child, two closely associated saints, or Christ standing between the Virgin and St. John the Baptist. In the 13th century New Testament scenes became customary, and gradually the panels tended to become crowded, being covered, for example, with a series of small scenes illustrating the life of a particular saint. The figures were generally placed against a gold ground, the scenes against a mountainous or architectural setting and a gold sky. Sharp, clear colours were used, the highlights being brightly picked out and shadows omitted. There was no striving for realism, no concern with anatomy, perspective, or truth of colour. The purpose of the icon was not to charm, but to inspire and uplift. Furthermore, the personages and scenes were invariably depicted in the exact manner laid down as correct by the Fathers of the Church, no deviations from rule being permitted. Although the figures had to appear

Tretiakov Gallery

THE VIRGIN OF VLADIMIR

Detail of a 12th-century Byzantine icon which set the style for hundreds of years human and easily recognizable, they were not to seem as though they belonged to the everyday world. The artist and the people believed that the merit lay, not in realism and innovation, which were forbidden, but in the intensity of feeling invested in the painting, in the perfection of line, and in the quality of the colour.

The earliest Christian panel paintings were made by Byzantine artists in the 6th century; but they are extremely rare, the majority probably having been destroyed during the 8th century when such paintings were forbidden (*see* BYZANTINE ART). Most of the few surviving icons of the 9th to 12th centuries are now in Russia, the finest being the magnificent panel of the Virgin and Child known as 'Our Lady of Vladimir'. In the 13th and 14th centuries examples are known from all countries belonging to the Orthodox Eastern Church, which differ according to the national style of each country. Most of the finest work came from Constantinople, but beautiful icons also came

THE ANNUNCIATION
14th-century Byzantine miniature mosaic icon

from the Greek mainland and from Russia. By the 16th century, by which time many schools had been established, especially in Russia, Italian influence began to blend with the Byzantine (*see* Colour Plate opp. p. 400).

In addition to the paintings on wood, which constitute the most traditional type of icon, other materials were also used; the small MOSAIC icons (q.v.) formed of minute glass squares set in wax, which date from the 10th to the 14th centuries, are the most precious. Such icons were always rare and now very few exist.

Metal icons, generally either of silver or copper, were quite common. These usually had a repoussé design hammered out from the reverse side, and a scroll design in filigree was sometimes added. From the 16th century onwards moulded copper 'diptychs' and 'triptychs' (sets of two or three hinged panels) were in general use in Russia, Greece, and the Balkans, the more elaborate Russian examples often having enamel as well. It was also the custom to screen the most venerated of the painted icons with a silver repoussé cover, often studded with precious or semi-precious jewels, which left the original face of the icon exposed.

See also BYZANTINE ART; RUSSIAN ART.

IDYLL, *see* PASTORALS.

ILIAD, THE, *see* HOMERIC LITERATURE.

ILLUMINATED MANUSCRIPTS. An illuminated manuscript is a text written by hand (Latin *manus*) on vellum or parchment—thin skins, specially prepared (*see* PAPER, Vol. IV)— and adorned with coloured designs or illustrated with pictures. The decoration is called illumination because it often includes gold which lights up or illumines the page. The first illuminated manuscripts date from the late Roman period, and the art was practised all through the Middle Ages until the invention of printing in the mid-15th century. Illumination is important in tracing the history of medieval art, for illuminated manuscripts have survived in great numbers and are often as fresh and bright as on the day on which they were finished. Most of the wall-paintings, on the other hand, which decorated churches and other buildings, have perished, and those which remain are often faded and have lost much of their detail.

The writings of the Greeks and Romans were

Trinity College, Dublin

DETAIL OF THE BEGINNING OF ST. JOHN'S GOSPEL IN THE
BOOK OF KELLS, AN 8TH-CENTURY IRISH GOSPEL

The huge letters are filled with trumpet design and interlaced decoration, and the figure is unrealistic, the hair and
drapery being transformed into interlaced designs

more often recorded on papyrus rolls than in books (*see* BOOKS, HISTORY OF, Vol. IV) and were only occasionally illustrated. The Early Christians preferred books, partly because they were more durable and partly because a whole Bible would have occupied many rolls. Under Constantine, the first Christian Roman Emperor, many religious books were written; some of those from Constantinople, the new capital, are very rich and are written in gold or silver letters on purple vellum. Those with pictures illustrating the Bible were copied and re-copied throughout the Middle Ages. Later Byzantine manuscripts are even finer; those which were for the use of the Emperor and his courtiers have illustrations in which the figures look solid and natural and are placed in landscapes; others, mainly those used in monasteries, have tiny pictures round the margins of the pages; both types were copied later in western Europe (*see* p. 54).

Another important school of illumination in the early Middle Ages grew up in Ireland. The Irish had been converted to Christianity by St. Patrick in the 5th century and Irish missionaries began to go to other parts of Europe. The Irish loved books, especially the Gospels, and a number of fine illuminated Gospel books have survived from the late 7th and the 8th centuries. These are enriched by pages entirely covered with patterns, which are placed before the beginning of each Gospel; the first word of the text begins with a huge initial letter, elaborately shaped and filled with tiny scrolls, interlaces, and fantastic animals. Many of these patterns are like those used for centuries to decorate metalwork. Sometimes pictures of the Evangelists and scenes illustrating the Life of Christ are also included, but the artists were not interested in making the figures look lifelike, and they wove their hair and the folds of their garments into interlacing patterns.

Irish books of this kind were taken to Europe by the missionaries and were copied in the monasteries until a new style was introduced by CHARLEMAGNE (q.v. Vol. V), who became Emperor in A.D. 800 and who ruled over France, western Germany, and north Italy. With the help of the Pope he reformed the monasteries within his dominions and tried to make them centres of learning. He encouraged the monks to copy books and probably brought back new models for them from Italy, where Byzantine works were obtainable. The illuminations coming from different monasteries vary very much in style, and this probably reflects the different styles of the models given to the illuminators. Some of the figures are placed out-of-doors and are carefully shaded in order to look solid, while others, which have a look of majesty and spirituality, are placed within an elaborate frame of architecture and are outlined in thick, black lines and painted in flat, brilliant colours. In one very interesting manuscript, known as the Utrecht Psalter, each separate phrase used by the Psalmist is illustrated by groups of tiny darting figures outlined in wildly zig-zagging pen strokes and scattered about in a landscape of hills and trees.

In the late 9th and 10th centuries King Alfred in England and the Emperors in Germany encouraged religion and learning, and great schools of illumination grew up in both countries. The pictures in English manuscripts are usually surrounded by elaborate frames of richly curling acanthus leaves. The figures are drawn with broken outlines, and the drapery looks as if it was being stirred by a strong wind. Both figures and leaves are painted with thick colour, and the highlights are suggested by jagged patches of white. Other English manuscripts of this period are illustrated by delightful outline drawings, often in bright coloured inks.

ABOVE: ST. MATTHEW, FROM AN EARLY 9TH-CENTURY GOSPEL
RIGHT: ST. MARK, FROM A GOSPEL OF *c.* 800
These show two types of Carolingian illumination; on the
left the realistic human figure, and on the right the stiffer
figure with its symbol above

DAVID AND THE LION. INITIAL AT THE BEGINNING OF THE
BOOK OF MICAH IN THE WINCHESTER BIBLE, *c.* 1165

LEFT: THE THREE MARY'S AT THE TOMB. FROM THE BENE-
DICTIONAL OF ST. ÆTHELWOLD, MADE AT WINCHESTER *c.* 980
FROM THE DEVONSHIRE COLLECTION

PAGE FROM THE METZ PONTIFICAL, 1302–16

A Pontifical contains those services at which only a Bishop
may officiate. The illumination shows a Bishop dedicating
a church by sprinkling it with Holy Water

In the illustrations of German manuscripts the
meaning of the scenes is interpreted in an emotional and spiritual way, the figures being set
against an empty background painted purple
or gold, which accentuates their exaggerated
gestures.

Towards the end of the 11th century, as
ROMANESQUE ART (q.v.) gradually developed,
these lively compositions were replaced by severe
designs with flat, rigid figures enclosed in simple
frames. Romanesque illuminations express the
dignity and mystery of the Christian doctrine;
the favourite subjects are Christ in Majesty and
the Last Judgement. An attempt was made to
interpret the Bible in a new way by placing
scenes from the Old Testament next to those
from the New, which they were held to fore-
shadow. Many great Bibles for ceremonial use
in church services were illuminated at this time;
in these, each book begins with a very large

initial letter, which forms a frame either for
scenes with little figures or beautiful leafwork
ornament. These initials are skilfully combined
with the large clear script to form most impressive pages.

From the middle of the 12th century GOTHIC
ART (q.v.) spread throughout Europe, but the
Gothic style in illumination was not fully developed until nearly 100 years later. Many
psalters were illuminated for educated and
wealthy laymen to use in their private devotions,
as well as other religious books and books on
plants, and also bestiaries—moralizing treatises
on animals—as in earlier times. Romances, with
subjects which were sometimes contemporary
and sometimes founded on stories from Ovid
(*see* ROMANCE LITERATURE), were often illustrated, the illumination being sometimes carried
out by lay painters instead of being produced in
the *scriptoria* of the monasteries. The names of
some of these craftsmen, including that of one
woman, have been preserved.

The workmanship is extremely skilful; the
figures are drawn in very fine pen lines, and their
simple, graceful outlines are thrown into relief
by backgrounds of highly burnished gold or of
tiny chequer patterns in gold, red, and blue.
Over the figures there are often minutely
traceried arcades. There is no feeling of space,
and everything is lighted by a clear, equal
brilliance.

At the beginning of many psalters is a calendar
with pictures illustrating an occupation characteristic of each month, and this is sometimes
followed by a series of scenes showing the main
events in the Life of Christ. The text is ornamented with initials which are combined with a
very delicate arrangement of leafy stems running

LOWER BORDER OF A PAGE FROM THE ORMSBY PSALTER,
MADE IN EAST ANGLIA *c.* 1295

Decorated with grotesques and accurately drawn and
coloured birds and butterflies

down the left side of the page and turning at right angles at the bottom—thus stressing the way in which the eye travels down the page and from left to right in reading. Charming little figures of people, animals, and grotesques (fantastic interweaving of human and animal forms with foliage) are sometimes placed on the bottom stem. The French psalters are small and very finely executed, but in England the work is bolder. In a series of very large psalters made in East Anglia at the beginning of the 14th century, many of the more important pages are completely surrounded by rich frames of leaves and flowers, among which are scattered birds, animals, grotesques, and scenes from contemporary life (*see* Vol. I, p. 481). Both the drawing and the colouring are naturalistic and very fine.

In the 14th century, Books of Hours became more popular than psalters for private use (*see* Colour Plate, Vol. IV, opp. p. 48). The spirit of tenderness which St. FRANCIS (q.v. Vol. V) had infused into religion led artists to try to express the more human feelings of love, joy, or sadness expressed by the people in the Gospel stories. Italian artists, especially those in the school of SIENESE PAINTING (q.v.), took the lead in this movement, but they were soon imitated in France and other European countries. The artists abandoned the flat, decorative style of the Gothic period and tried to make the figures look lifelike by introducing more shading and placing them in front of landscape backgrounds. At first these consisted of a series of flat-topped, arid hills seen one behind another, with the gold and chequer work still used for the sky. Soon, however, both the hills and the foreground came to be spangled with grass and flowers, like the grounds of contemporary tapestries, while the skies were either shaded from dark to light blue or painted dark and lit by stars.

At the beginning of the 15th century a magnificent Book of Hours, known as *Les Très Riches Heures du Duc de Berry*, was painted by Pol de Limbourg and his brothers. The artist who painted the calendar pictures at the beginning of the book chose scenes to illustrate the occupations of the months from his own observation— a hunting party riding through the woods outside one of the duke's many châteaux, for example. He seems to have had a real understanding of figure drawing, landscape, natural lighting, and perspective (*see* Vol. VI, p. 6).

British Museum

THE ADORATION OF THE MAGI. FROM THE BREVIARY OF ISABELLA THE CATHOLIC, QUEEN OF SPAIN, 1497

Written in Spain with Flemish illuminations, the scene resembles paintings of the period

Flemish illuminators developed this realistic style and painted scenes from the everyday life of the towns and country-side. In their wide borders they built up patterns using very accurately drawn flowers, such as carnations, roses, and thistles, combined with snails, butterflies, and other insects. Although these illuminations are often very beautiful in themselves, they are less appropriate for adorning books than those of the earlier period, which are more closely related to the script. The representation of solid-looking figures and landscapes which recede into space breaks up the unity of the flat page, especially when the scenes are forced into the conventional shapes inside initial letters. The full-page illustrations are now pictures in miniature rather than illuminations.

A good deal is known about the technique of illumination at this time. An Italian illuminator in the 14th century wrote a book in which he describes the way in which he worked. First the manuscript was ruled and written by the scribe, who left blank spaces for the pictures and decorated initials. The illuminator drew in the figures in ink with a quill pen; then he treated the parts to be gilded, first with fish or stag's horn glue, well moistened in the mouth, then with size, and finally with prepared white of egg. Then he applied thin gold leaf, and when this had stuck, he laid the page on a polished board and burnished the gold by rubbing, preferably with a wolf's tooth. The colours were ground on a stone slab and filtered, and then mixed with white of egg or size, with a spot of honey to stop them cracking. They were applied either with a pen or brush. White was added to the highlights, and the shadows were shaded with dull pink or grey. A greyish-green layer of paint was usually applied under the whites and pinks of the faces and hands to give extra brilliance. Most of the colours, such as the beautiful blue (lapis lazuli or ultramarine) and the bright green (malachite), occur in nature, as do the soft browns, yellows, and reds. The more brilliant red (vermilion) is red lead, and some colours, such as saffron, are prepared from plants. The writer of the book made it very clear that his craft was different from both that of the scribe and the painter, although some of the processes which he used were also used by painters.

ILLUSTRATION, *see* Vol. IV: ILLUSTRATION.

IMPRESSIONIST PAINTING. An artist of any period who seeks to convey a rapid impression of the thing he sees may be described as an impressionist. In the art of the past, the paintings of RUBENS are more impressionistic than those of the methodical, detail-loving van EYCK (qq.v. Vol. V). Today, however, the term refers to the school of French painters who, working during the second half of the 19th century, made 'impressionism' their deliberate aim.

The 16th-century Flemish painter BRUEGHEL (q.v. Vol. V) was one of the first to note the varying atmospheric effects peculiar to the different seasons of the year and times of the day, and this became more and more the preoccupation of the landscape painters of the 17th, 18th, and 19th centuries, at first in Holland and then in France and England. TURNER and CONSTABLE (qq.v. Vol. V), for example, both forestalled some of the achievements of the French Impressionists, Constable's impressionism being most marked in the oil sketches he did in the open air, which he later worked up into finished pictures for exhibition.

Working in the open air became the cornerstone of the French Impressionists' creed. More than Turner or even Constable, landscape painting for them became a hand-to-hand conflict with nature herself, and not a composition reflecting the mood that the scene had aroused in the artist, and which he slowly evolved in the studio from brief sketches. To say that the Impressionists ignored the mood and sought only the effect would be an exaggeration, since art cannot be separated from the thoughts and feelings of the artist; but undoubtedly a part of the Impressionists' aim was the attempt to share the almost impersonal vision of the recently invented camera, while at the same time deliberately trying to paint effects too subtle or too bold for the camera to record.

The name 'Impressionist' was given to these young French painters by a critic reviewing their first collective exhibition in 1874. Claude Monet, the pioneer of the group, had sent for exhibition a harbour scene entitled *Impression:*

National Gallery

VETHEUIL: SUNSHINE AND SNOW. PAINTING BY CLAUDE MONET, 1881

Rising Sun. This artist had already been painting in the open air for 10 years or so, using the lighter range of colours he had derived from Edouard MANET's example (q.v. Vol. V). Monet's ideas spread to Sisley, Pissaro, Renoir (who painted figures rather than landscapes), and to the other members of the group. Since these men believed that the landscape should be begun and finished in the open air, face to face with nature, they began to question the traditional methods of landscape painting and the nature of light and shadow. Light, even the brightest sunlight, became the Impressionists' main quest, and shadow they saw as composed of a variety of tones and colours from which light itself was seldom absent. They perceived that the same thing looked quite different under varying conditions of light. This led Monet to paint the same scene again and again under different atmospheric conditions.

In order to render the infinite atmospheric subtleties apparent to the eye, the Impressionist artists developed a new theory of colour, and with it a new method of laying their paint on canvas. This theory is known as 'pointillism'. Instead of mixing the primary colours on his palette, the artist applied pure colours to the canvas with quick, short brush-strokes, placing them side by side so that when seen at a distance they blended together. This gave a more truthful impression of the glittering complex of colours in nature.

The Impressionists were at first despised and ridiculed, except by a few far-sighted dealers and connoisseurs; but their style was later imitated so widely throughout the world that it became accepted as the normal academic style of painting. Many of the imitators took no account of the revolutionary developments which were made soon afterwards in POST-IMPRESSIONIST PAINTING (q.v.), from which today's various styles of painting have emerged, and the original Impressionist style soon ceased to be a pioneer movement.

See also FRENCH ART.

Tate Gallery

MEADOWS IN SPRING. PAINTING BY ALFRED SISLEY (1839–99)

Art Institute of Chicago

SUNDAY ON THE GRANDE JATTE. PAINTING BY GEORGES SEURAT (1859–91)

INDIAN ART

INDIAN ART. India and Pakistan, for a period united under British rule, were originally made up of a number of separate States, in each of which the people and the way of life differed, as they do in the nations of Europe. The art of the different regions is equally distinctive, though there are common features due to the various religions, HINDUISM, JAINISM, BUDDHISM, and ISLAM (qq.v. Vol. I), which spread through India at different times. Indian art has a long, continuous history covering over 2,000 years, and its traditions are still alive today. The art, too, not only of most of the neighbouring countries, such as Burma, Ceylon, and Afghanistan, but also of Tibet, Siam, Indonesia, and Indo-China is based on, or is influenced by, Indian art.

India has, perhaps, the greatest number of monuments in the world. There are countless ruins of temples, *stūpas* (memorial monuments), and palaces, and over a thousand temples and monasteries hewn out of the living rock, which are no longer used. Many of the ancient temples and palaces are still in use. The art is essentially religious. As in the medieval art of the West, the names of individual artists are seldom recorded.

The most important art in India is sculpture. The temples were profusely decorated with carvings inside and out, and their design was more that of monuments than of buildings. The rock and cave temples, for example, were carved into the rock or cut out of it just as sculpture is carved out of a piece of stone. The rich decoration of the buildings sometimes seems too ornate for Western eyes; but its purpose is more than mere decoration: a temple represented, so to speak, a fervent prayer to the deity, and the richer it was, the more effective the prayer would be. It was therefore considered wrong to leave any part of a wall bare.

In Indian sculpture, as in that of Greece and Rome, the nude human figure is very important; but, whereas in the latter case man was glorified for the beauty of his form, the Indian aim was different. The human figure was used to express passionate emotion or to show some quality of the god such as power or wisdom. To achieve this, the figures might be given several heads, arms, or legs, or animal heads (*see* Vol. I, p. 225). They are often reminiscent of figures in fairy-tales.

Painting also has always been important in India. The sculptures were coloured, and the

Birmingham Museum
BUDDHA FROM SULTANGANJ
Bronze figure, 5th century A.D.

walls of temples, palaces, and halls were decorated with paintings. Some of these wall-paintings date back to the 1st century B.C. Also miniatures were painted in water-colours, either as illustrations to manuscripts or as pictures which were bound together in albums. There were no easel paintings in oils comparable to Western pictures.

Until recently our knowledge of Indian art did not go back much further than the 3rd century B.C. But earlier ruins of big towns have been discovered in the valley of the river Indus and elsewhere, the inhabitants of which obviously enjoyed a considerable degree of civilization (*see* INDIAN CIVILIZATIONS, Vol. I). Sculptures were found and clay cylinders with figures and inscriptions on them dating from 2000 or 3000 years B.C. These show some connexion with ancient Mesopotamian civilization.

Little is known about the period between the civilization of the Indus Valley and the historical period which begins in the 3rd century B.C.

Early literature mentions palaces, painting, and crafts; but as buildings and works of art were mainly in wood, ivory, and other perishable materials, hardly anything of them remains. In earlier times the majority of Indian buildings were wooden, and the style of the stone buildings and caves (mostly temples) is clearly developed from architecture in wood.

Indian art from the 3rd century B.C. to modern times is divided into three main periods: the Early Period, lasting to the 3rd century A.D., the Golden Age or Classic Period, from the 4th to the 7th or 8th centuries, and finally the Late Period. The Early Period starts with the Mauryan Emperors, who brought much of India under one strong rule. The great ruler ASOKA (q.v. Vol. V) devoted much of his time to Buddhism. Many Buddhist temples were built, but most of these, being wooden, have been destroyed. A number of tall stone columns surmounted by carved animals date from Asoka's reign (see Vol. I, p. 240).

The most important monuments of the Early Period are the *stūpas* of Bhārhut, Sānchī, and Amarāvatī, and works at Mathurā. Originally the *stūpas* were simple earthen or brick mounds erected on tombs, but later they were domes built over relics and decorated with sculpture (*see* PAGODA). They were surrounded with sculptured railings enclosing a space for processions. The sculptures on the gates of the railings and on the railings and domes chiefly depict scenes from the life and the previous lives of the Buddha. The sculpture is fresh and natural, but there is little attempt to suggest an effect of space. The vivid scenes are full of detail, showing how people lived at the time. Most of the sculptures of Mathurā in the first three or four centuries A.D. were carved in mottled red sandstone.

In the Classic Age the art is monumental and spiritual. Instead of lively scenes which might have been taken from daily life, there are grand figures of gods which, by their expression and

PART OF A ROCK TEMPLE AT ELLORA, 8TH CENTURY A.D.
The whole temple, including the free-standing sculpture, is carved out of the rock

majesty, are remote from human life. The composition, often round a central figure, helps to stress the religious idea behind. The great technical skill of the sculptors adds to the impressiveness of the figures. The rock temples of Ajantā (*see* Vol. I, p. 241) and Ellora in Hyderabad and the caves of Elephanta belong to this period.

Buddhist, Hindu, and Jain rock temples were made in the Classic Age. Some were monasteries with cells for the monks, others halls in which the worshippers congregated. At Ajantā there are twenty-nine Buddhist caves of both sorts, and most of them are profusely decorated with sculpture and paintings, which cover the walls, columns, and ceilings. The paintings show scenes from the life of the Buddha and people connected with his story. There are many figures of the Buddha himself because it was thought that the more often he was represented the greater the piety. He is shown with various gestures which all have a religious significance.

At Ellora there are Hindu caves and a temple cut out of the rock. In many ways the sculpture which adorns it has the same quality as at Ajantā, but the Hindu figures and scenes are more vivid and dramatic. The huge temple, 96 feet high and 164 feet long, with a courtyard 276 feet by 154 feet, with several separate buildings and free-standing sculptures, is all cut out of the rock. Every part is covered with sculpture in relief or in the round, representational or ornamental, and everywhere the workmanship is unsurpassed.

Most buildings and sculptures which now exist belong to the Late Period. In the various areas different architectural styles developed in which an elaboration of detail is characteristic. The temples become a complicated mass of halls, towers, and roofs, richly decorated all over with sculpture. Charm and grace predominate in the sculpture, and the figures are full of excited movement and dancing poses (*see* Vol. I, p. 226). The development of the temples can be traced from small shrines built in the 6th century to the gigantic temples, such as those in Konārak and Madura, which date from the 13th and 17th centuries respectively. At Madura there is a central shrine with a colossal pyramid-shaped tower which is covered with sculpture arranged in horizontal bands. Surrounding the central tower are five others, as well as courts and halls and elaborate gateways.

The general characteristics of Indian art can be seen in all parts of India, yet the different regions had their own distinguishing features. One might compare this with the art of Europe where, for instance, in the Middle Ages GOTHIC ART (q.v.), whether in an English or a French church, was recognizably Gothic, and yet was equally clearly either English or French.

The chief regional styles are those of southern India, northern India, the Deccan, and Gandhāra. There are also areas where the styles are mixed. Typical of the southern style are the pyramidal towers such as at Madura, which are often very high and richly sculptured. The temples of the northern style have towers with curved outlines as, for instance, in the province of Orissa. In the Deccan the ground plans of temples are star-shaped. They are rather low and are built on plinths, the bases richly decorated with several bands of sculpture.

The art of Gandhāra in Pakistan and in Afghanistan differs from that of other parts of India because, as a result of the invasion of Alexander the Great in 326 B.C., a considerable contact existed between the Mediterranean countries and north-west India. The existing sculpture dates from the 1st to the 6th or 7th centuries A.D., a long time after Alexander's invasion; but still thousands of sculptures belonging to this period show a mixture of Buddhist-Indian and Greek or Roman styles. In other parts of India the art shows little Western influence.

From the 11th century the religion of Islam, brought by foreign invaders, spread over India. ISLAMIC ART (q.v.) differed in many ways from the native Indian art. Sculpture, so important in other Indian art, was not used, and painting was confined chiefly to miniatures and book illustrations (*see* Colour Plate, Vol. V, opp. p. 64). It was an art of the Court, and its greatest period was under the emperors of the Mogul dynasty (1526–1857). Typical of Islamic architecture are the mosques and elaborate tombs, such as the TAJ MAHAL (q.v.) near Agra.

Little is known of Indian crafts in ancient times, though we can see from sculpture and painting that jewellery was always very important. India is especially rich in precious stones. Metalwork, above all vessels and arms, and textiles have been preserved from the last 500 years. Transparent silk fabrics from India are famous.

See also Vol. I: INDIAN CIVILIZATIONS; INDIAN PEOPLES.

THE NORTH GATEWAY OF THE STŪPA AT SĀNCHI, 1ST CENTURY A.D.
The gateway is carved with figures and reliefs representing Buddhist subjects

PLATE 10   INDIAN ART

THREE TYPES OF HINDU TEMPLE

ABOVE LEFT: KHAJURAHO TEMPLE, 950–1050

This is the northern Indian style

ABOVE RIGHT: PART OF THE WALLS OF THE TEMPLE OF HALEBID IN THE DECCAN, 12TH–13TH CENTURY

BELOW: TEMPLE AT MADURA, 1623–59

The pool in the foreground is used for ritual bathing

INDIAN LITERATURE. Ancient Indian literature may be broadly divided into two groups: that written in the Aryan languages of the land lying to the north of the Vindhya hills, and that written in the Dravidian languages of the land lying to the south (*see* INDIAN LANGUAGES, Vol. IV). Aryan literature, the older and the more important of the two, began as early as the 15th century B.C., and the bulk of it was written in Sanskrit. The relationship of Sanskrit literature to the modern Indian literatures can in many ways be compared with that of Greek and Latin literatures to the modern European literatures; but the reign of Sanskrit, both before and after it became a dead language, was longer. It had a predominantly religious character which it communicated to the modern Indian literatures. Of the numerous religious works written in Sanskrit the Vedas, the Upanishads, and the *Bhāgavad-gitā* are the greatest (*see* SACRED BOOKS, Vol. I). The *Rāmāyana* and the *Mahābhārata* are the greatest of the many EPICS (q.v.). The literature also includes dramas, long romances, and short tales and fables. Sanskrit drama has no tragedy, as it was considered unaesthetic to represent suffering on the stage. The long romances use the device of enclosing narrative within narrative, so that there are several subsidiary stories besides the main story. Of the countless tales and fables in Sanskrit, the animal FABLES (q.v.), primarily intended for children, have enjoyed the widest popularity. La Fontaine retold some of them in his *Contes*. The greatest period of Sanskrit prose and poetry began about A.D. 300. The most pleasing quality of the poetry of this period is its verbal and rhythmic music, and Kālidāsa (*c.* A.D. 400) is the greatest Sanskrit poet. In his best-known lyric, the 'Cloud Messenger', an exiled husband asks a rain cloud to carry a message of love to his wife. The poem describes the mountains, rivers, and cities over which the cloud will pass. Kālidāsa also wrote several poetic plays.

Besides Sanskrit, the literary language, there were several dialects in the Aryan half of ancient India. Many of the sacred books of Buddhism, as well as the delightful *Jātaka* tales are in these dialects. The *Jātaka* tales are about the Buddha in his previous births as animals.

Tamil, the classical Dravidian literature, flourished between A.D. 100 and 900. The *Kurāl* of Tiru-Vulluvar, sometimes called the Tamil Veda, is the oldest and the most venerated devotional work. There are also many devotional poems and hymns.

In the 13th century Moslem rule was established in northern India (*see* INDIAN CIVILIZATIONS, Section 4, Vol. I). This period saw the rise of modern literature, such as Gujarathi, Marathi, Hindi, and Bengali in the north, and Telegu and Malayalam in the south. Persian was the official language of Moslem India, and a new language and literature, Urdu, grew out of a mixture of Persian and Hindi. With the exception of Urdu and some early pieces in Hindi, the whole of medieval Indian literature consists of devotional poems and songs. There were folk-tales and fairy-tales and fairy-stories in all the languages, but they remained in people's memories and were not written down until much later.

When British rule was established in the 19th century and English education was introduced, Indian writers became familiar with English literature and imitated Western literary forms, such as the essay, the short story, the novel, and the drama (as distinct from the ancient Sanskrit drama). Bengali, the leading literature of this period, produced Rabindranath TAGORE (q.v. Vol. V), the greatest writer of modern India. Many of Tagore's poems have appeared in English translation, such as his poems of childhood in *The Crescent Moon*:

> 'Where have I come from, where did you pick me up?' the baby asked its mother.
> She answered, half crying, half laughing, and clasping the baby to her breast,—
> 'You were hidden in my heart as its desire, my darling'.

See also Vol. I: INDIAN CIVILIZATIONS.
See also Vol. IV: INDIAN LANGUAGES.
See also Vol. V: TAGORE; IQBAL.

INDIAN MUSIC, *see* ORIENTAL MUSIC, Section 2.

INDUSTRIAL ART. This term is usually applied to the making of useful objects with a pleasing appearance. The industrial arts, therefore, may include pottery, glassware, furniture, silverware, textiles, and jewellery (a craft almost entirely ornamental in aim). In the past such things were mainly made by hand with the aid of simple tools. Factories for the mass production of pottery by hand existed in ancient Egypt, Greece, and Rome, and for centuries in

DESIGN FOR A CAST-IRON GRATE

The fussy shape, further elaborated by decoration, is typical of the period

From *The Illustrated Exhibitor*, the catalogue of the Great Exhibition, 1851

China. In Europe, communities of monks revived the crafts after the Dark Ages; later, the CRAFT GUILDS (q.v. Vol. VII) upheld good standards of workmanship and design until their disappearance in the 16th century. Whether an article was made from start to finish under one roof, or whether the work of various specialists was co-ordinated as a cottage industry, little distinction was then made between designer and craftsman.

Fashions in design spread slowly through Europe. Sometimes the artists moved from country to country, as, for example, the monks of the Middle Ages or the political refugees of the later Huguenot persecutions. Sometimes the works of art themselves were transported, as with the Byzantine illuminated manuscripts and carved ivories in early Christian times, or objects of all kinds brought home by travellers of Renaissance days. Pattern-books, too, were in circulation, such as the Flemish ones on woodwork in the 18th century.

As manufacturing enterprise grew, the work of craftsmen often came to be directed by a master designer; for the most part the names of both craftsmen and designers remained unknown, though occasionally a well-known artist, for instance HOLBEIN (q.v. Vol. V), might design for crafts such as jewellery and plate. Names of factories, such as the Sèvres porcelain factory, were often well known, as were a few individual craftsmen who published books of designs, such as the furniture makers, Chippendale, Sheraton, and Heppelwhite.

But, with the Industrial Revolution, and inventions such as the steam-engine, the spinning-jenny, and the weaving machine there came a great change. The machines led to mass-production, and Britain became the leading industrial country. The demand for more and more goods for world-wide markets resulted in little concern with design, and although well-designed hand-made objects might be copied, the results were often spoilt because defects in workmanship were covered up with poor decoration. Although the Royal Society of Arts (established 1754) held small exhibitions and awarded prizes to encourage good design, confusion of thought arose, and the word 'design' began to be considered as meaning only ornament applied, often quite unsuitably, to an object.

In order to improve the standards of design the British Government established a National Gallery of Art and schools of design, and in 1852 founded a Museum of Ornamental Art, now the Victoria and Albert Museum (*see* ART GALLERIES). Private persons, notably William MORRIS (q.v. Vol. V), attacked the design and quality of machine-made things. Morris established a company for handicrafts, particularly metalwork, stained glass, wallpaper, chintzes, and furniture. The Art-Workers' Guild and the Arts and Crafts Society were formed in the 1880's. But neither the artist-craftsman nor the art-school student was in close touch with industry, while the manufacturer, on his side, thought of art as an extra to be bought and

Murphy Radio

RADIO SET DESIGNED BY R. D. RUSSELL, R.D.I.

added, rather than as an integral part of the design and production of his goods.

As the 20th century advanced, conscious interest in design became more general. The British Institute of Art and the Design and Industries Association were formed, and international Exhibitions of Industrial and Decorative Arts took place in Munich and Paris. The pottery and glass industries in Sweden (where the influence of Morris had been felt) began to employ artist-designers in their works, and in London the Worshipful Company of Goldsmiths held competitions and offered travelling scholarships. The Royal Society of Arts continued its encouragement, and finally, in 1944, the Government set up the Council of Industrial Design. Yet the artist-designer, in Britain at any

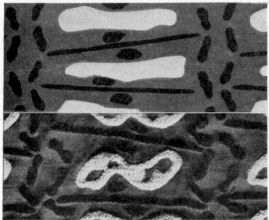

The Ambassador

DESIGN FOR A TEXTILE BY W. A. BROOK, AND THE FINISHED TEXTILE

rate, still has not an important enough place in industry. The reason is partly economic; many manufacturers feel that they cannot afford to employ a full-time designer closely connected with a product at every stage of its manufacture, but prefer, as for instance in printed textiles, to buy designs from a 'free-lance' designer or from an organized design studio, and to alter them if need be.

The profession of industrial designer has recently come into existence chiefly in connexion with new industries, such as those which manufacture in large numbers such articles as radio sets, motor-cars, or electric irons. It is the designer's duty, working with experts in PRODUCTION ENGINEERING (q.v. Vol. VIII), to

devise an article which will look attractive, which will prove convenient in daily use, and which can be manufactured as economically as possible.

See also DESIGN.
See also Vol. VII: INDUSTRIAL REVOLUTION.

INTERLUDES, *see* MORALITY PLAYS.

IONIC ORDER, *see* ORDERS OF ARCHITECTURE.

IRONY, *see* FIGURES OF SPEECH, Section 4.

ISLAMIC ART. This is the art of those countries where the Moslem religion prevails (*see* ISLAM, Vol. I), and covers a wide area and a long period of time. The Islamic world has included peoples differing in race and artistic traditions but united by a common religious outlook. For this reason the artistic products of widely separated regions of the Islamic world, however they vary in detail, all possess a certain quality which stamps them as Islamic.

Moslem doctrine forbids the representation in art of any living creature, either human or animal. Islamic art, therefore, is largely confined to decorative effect, and Moslem artists have concerned themselves particularly with architecture, book production, and the decorative arts such as pottery, weaving, and metalwork. Figures and animals are sometimes represented in spite of the religious prohibition, but they are rarely realistic. Large-scale painting and sculpture are hardly known. While the Christian Church took narrative art into its service in order to illustrate and glorify the truths of its faith, Islam has refused to do so.

Moslem architects devoted themselves to the building of MOSQUES (q.v.), palaces, houses, and tombs. Potters manufactured the coloured tiles which so often adorn the walls of Moslem buildings, and also supplied ornaments and vessels for eating and drinking. Their pottery is particularly noted for its colour and design. Glassmakers, besides making vessels of everyday use, produced for the mosques beautiful lamps decorated with gilding and enamels. Metalworkers produced works of bronze or brass inlaid with gold and silver. Perhaps the finest form of decoration was achieved by the weavers, whose richly coloured carpets were intended for wall coverings as well as floors. Moslems consider the copying of the Koran (*see* SACRED BOOKS,

Creswell

PIERCED STUCCO WINDOW GRILLE WITH GEOMETRIC DESIGN
From the Mosque of Ahmed ibu Tulun, Cairo, A.D. 876–9

Section 8, Vol. I) and the decoration of its pages as a meritorious religious act; thus handwriting is to them an important art. Reverence for the Koran text was shown in the inscribing of isolated verses or phrases on the walls of buildings and even on objects of everyday use.

Islamic ornament tends to be abstract rather than naturalistic. One of its most typical elements is the 'arabesque', an often very intricate pattern formed by the curling stem of a plant which is punctuated by leaves, buds, and flowers. Its origin has little to do with the Arabs but rather belongs to the Moslem artists of Egypt in about the 10th or 11th century. The arabesque is an admirable form for decorating a plain surface,

Victoria & Albert Museum

MARBLE FOUNTAIN BASIN DECORATED WITH ARABESQUE
ORNAMENT. SYRIAN, A.D. 1278

for it is lively but at the same time restful. Sometimes the plant form becomes far removed from nature, and is made to form an intricate geometric pattern. The arabesque is only one of many decorative ideas used by the Moslem artists; and some of these, such as the many-pointed star, depend on considerable geometric skill. Such was the Moslem love of ornament that even when portraying an animal artists often tended to develop it into an ornamental abstraction. Animal heads, for example, may sprout from the stem of an arabesque, and a fabulous monster like the bronze winged griffin at Pisa has its whole surface covered with abstract patterns and Arabic writing.

Islamic art was developed at the end of the 7th century when the Islamic world was united under one single ruler, the Caliph. The Arabs, having no artistic traditions themselves, employed the artists and craftsmen of the conquered peoples to build mosques and palaces worthy of their dignity as rulers of a mighty Empire (*see* ARABS, Vol. I). Each of these peoples contributed to Islamic art, particularly the Egyptians, Syrians, and Persians. At first the Caliph ruled from Syria, and the finest surviving monument of this period is the Omaiyid Mosque at DAMASCUS (q.v. Vol. III) which shows the typical plan of a mosque. When in the 8th century the Caliphs moved to what is now Iraq, Persian methods of building were adopted, but were so transformed to suit the ideas of the new religion that this art can be truly called Islamic.

During the 9th century the political unity of Islam began to break up. Spain established a Caliphate of its own and evolved a style which later spread to North Africa and is known as MOORISH ART (q.v.). A distinctive art flourished in Egypt from the 10th century, the finest surviving monument of which is the al-Azhar Mosque and University, founded about 970 (*see* UNIVERSITIES, HISTORY OF, Vol. X). Succeeding generations have left behind them a wonderful series of mosques and public buildings in CAIRO (q.v. Vol. III).

By the 10th century the wandering Turkish tribes of central Asia were securing power in Persia, and giving a great impetus to the arts. Between the 13th and 15th centuries, in spite of devastating raids by the Mongols, some magnificent illustrated manuscripts were produced in Persia. Then, in 1501, foreign rule came to an end in Persia, and a purely native dynasty secured the throne and inaugurated a great artistic period (*see* PERSIAN ART).

The OTTOMAN TURKS (q.v. Vol. I) began to acquire their vast Empire in the 14th century. Their best artistic achievements were in Asia Minor during the 15th and 16th centuries, when splendid mosques partly inspired by Byzantine churches were built, and Turkish pottery and textiles were famous throughout Europe.

Lastly, the Moslem art of India has a character all its own (*see* INDIAN ART). The Turks had established themselves in northern India in the 11th century, and in the 16th century the Moguls, also of Turkish race, founded their Empire. The greatest of the Moguls was the Emperor AKBAR (q.v. Vol. V), who united his Hindu and Moslem subjects under a wise and beneficent rule. Hindu and Moslem co-operated in the building of mosques and palaces, and a distinctive style known as Mogul art evolved. In the paintings of the period the style shows a fusion of Persian and Hindu elements (*see* Colour Plate, Vol. V, opp. p. 64). The splendour of Akbar's civilization was carried on by his successors, Jahangir and Shah Jahan, who built the TAJ MAHAL (q.v.).

See also MOORISH ART; PERSIAN ART; MOSQUE.
See also Vol. I: ISLAM; ARABS.

Anderson

BRONZE GRIFFIN, 11TH CENTURY
In the Camposanto, Pisa

ISLAMIC LITERATURE, *see* ARABIC LITERATURE.

ISLAMIC MUSIC, *see* ORIENTAL MUSIC, Section 4.

ITALIAN ART. The art of Italy—in painting, sculpture, and architecture, and also in literature and music—represents the most remarkable all-round artistic achievement that any one country has made since the time of Christ. The reason for this wonderful flowering in Italy is as much a mystery as any other manifestation of the human genius. But the fact that in Italy there were more traces of the lost greatness of the art of Imperial Rome than in any other country un-doubtedly gave the strongest stimulus to Italian artists at different times.

1. THE MIDDLE AGES. Though the grandest buildings of Imperial Rome, such as the COLOSSEUM (q.v.), the Pantheon, and the amphi-theatres at Verona and Pola, existed and could be seen during the Middle Ages, it was some time before the conditions of life in Italy were sufficiently settled to permit artists to profit by their example. Moreover, most of the best

British Museum

GLASS LAMP MADE FOR A MOSQUE, 14TH CENTURY
The bowl was filled with oil in which a wick burnt

Roman sculpture lay buried and unknown throughout the Middle Ages. There had been a brilliant artistic movement at Ravenna as early as the 6th century, but this drew more on Eastern than on Roman examples for its inspiration (*see* BYZANTINE ART). The continual warfare and insecurity of life which followed in the 7th and 8th centuries were most unfavourable to artistic production (*see* DARK AGES, Vol. I). It was not until the late 9th century that a truly Italian form of art began to develop, and then its energies were turned more to architecture than to sculpture or painting.

ROMANESQUE ART (q.v.) was based on that of Imperial Rome to the extent that the builders used the stone VAULT and the ARCH (qq.v.) as the Romans had, but they made little use of the ornaments of Roman architecture. Romanesque art flourished simultaneously in several districts of Italy, particularly in Lombardy in the north and Apulia in the south, and it reached its highest development in the 12th century. Many large churches were built, such as St. Ambrose at Milan and the cathedral at Parma, which are even now among the most impressive in Europe.

The Romanesque style spread from Italy to the northern countries of Europe; but GOTHIC ART (q.v.), which followed it, developed first in northern Europe and spread to Italy. Although there are some fine Gothic churches, such as the cathedral at Florence, Gothic architecture never really suited either the tastes or the needs of the Italians.

In the meantime in the 13th century the Italians began to take a much more definite interest in Roman art. The Emperor Frederick II employed sculptors at Capua who must have studied examples of Roman art so thoroughly that their works were later sometimes mistaken for late Roman ones. In the late 13th and early 14th centuries the sculptors Niccolo and his son Giovanni Pisano did important work which showed that they had studied Roman as well as Gothic models. A new spirit was developing in art which is expressed perfectly by a contemporary Florentine painter—the first painter we have yet had cause to mention—GIOTTO (q.v. Vol. V).

2. GIOTTO. It is difficult to exaggerate the importance of Giotto in the history of both Italian and European painting. Although his paintings do not look very lifelike to us, they immediately became famous because they were so much more lifelike than any which had been painted before. But the important development which Giotto's paintings reveal is not so much an increase in artistic ability as a radical change in people's outlooks. Artists in the Middle Ages who painted unlifelike figures did so not because they were unable to do better but because it was not their aim to make them lifelike. The beauties of the material world meant little to them compared with spiritual beauties. But by the end of the 13th century, when Giotto lived, people were beginning to take more interest in their surroundings; and so it was that he, earlier than any other great artist, modelled his painting on nature.

His example was so great that for a century painters in his home town of Florence were content to copy his style slavishly, without attempting to progress along the lines which he had indicated. During this time painters in Siena, a town

Alinari

'THE ADORATION OF THE MAGI' BY NICCOLO PISANO
Relief on the marble pulpit in the Baptistery, Pisa, 1260

Mansell

ST. JOHN THE EVANGELIST ASCENDING TO HEAVEN. FRESCO BY GIOTTO (*c.* 1266–1337) IN THE BARDI CHAPEL, FLORENCE
The figures appear to be solid and there is an effect of space around them, although Giotto had little knowledge of
anatomy or perspective

near Florence, were working in a different style (*see* SIENESE PAINTING), but although many of their paintings were exquisite, they were medieval in spirit rather than forerunners of the Renaissance, as Giotto's paintings had been.

3. THE EARLY RENAISSANCE. The real Renaissance in painting, sculpture, and architecture began in the early 15th century, and went much farther than either of the earlier two movements (*see* RENAISSANCE, Vol. I). The first fully fledged Renaissance artists came from Florence (*see* FLORENTINE PAINTING). It was to Rome, however, that the Florentine architect BRUNELLESCHI (q.v. Vol. V) went to study the ruins and to learn to make a new style of architecture. He measured the Roman buildings and examined their joints, and so rediscovered the principles of proportion and the methods of construction on which they had been built. His dome over the cathedral in Florence, which dominates the city, and the chapels and churches which he built there are the first great architectural monuments of the Renaissance. Brunelleschi is said to have dug for ancient sculptures and coins among the ruins in Rome; and he was a friend of DONATELLO

(q.v. Vol. V), the Florentine sculptor who was to adorn the new buildings with many beautiful works. Donatello brought back into marble and bronze figures the true anatomy which the Greeks had used in their sculpture, and which the Romans had copied. In his life-size bronze statue in Padua of the soldier Gattamelata on horseback he deliberately made the rider look like another Caesar, dressed in half Roman costume, and his charger a horse from a Roman chariot team (*see* Vol. I, p. 400). In his relief-sculptures Donatello made use of PERSPECTIVE (q.v.), thus revealing to painters new possibilities of design and expression which had been unknown to antiquity.

The first painter to use these ideas was the Florentine, MASACCIO (q.v. Vol. V). Masaccio set his figures among buildings designed in the Renaissance style, and, partly by the perspective of these and partly by painting real landscape, he gave a depth to his scenes which was something new. He made the figures themselves seem men and women of flesh and blood, solid and grandly proportioned as they had not been in the works of the Gothic painters. So few

Anderson

THE TRIUMPH OF THE DUKE AND DUCHESS OF MONTEFELTRO. PAINTING BY PIERO DELLA FRANCESCA (*c.* 1416–92)
On the back of the panels are portraits of the Duke and Duchess

antique paintings of high quality have survived that Masaccio can hardly have been influenced by them, but he used types and gestures in some of his pictures which he probably saw in Graeco-Roman sculptures.

At this point men's imagination took wings, and art was used in ways which had been unknown for more than a thousand years. In the Middle Ages art had been turned almost exclusively to religious uses; now princes and wealthy citizens demanded to have their portraits painted and their houses decorated. For the latter purpose the myths and legends of Greece and Rome were found to provide delightful material for the artist's imagination. Streets were ornamented with statues and sculptured fountains, and churches were built in shapes based on pagan temples. The new interest in science and nature led artists to study anatomy and perspective in order to make figures and landscapes more lifelike. Artists were often expected to be expert in more than one field, and so arose those miracles of versatility, ALBERTI and LEONARDO DA VINCI, who excelled in almost every field of the arts and sciences, and MICHEL-ANGELO (qq.v. Vol. V) whose works in sculpture, painting, and architecture were equally epoch-making.

For 100 years, from about 1420 to about 1530, works of art of all kinds were poured out with unparalleled splendour. Numerous centres—Florence, Umbria, Ferrara, Padua, Vicenza, Milan, and Venice—all produced SCHOOLS OF

ART (q.v.), each markedly individual. The Florentine sculptor Ghiberti modelled reliefs which are more like pictures than sculpture, for the figures have life and movement and space around them (*see* p. 51). The Umbrian painter, PIERO DELLA FRANCESCA, used light to give reality and solidity to his figures and a dramatic effect to his compositions. MANTEGNA (qq.v. Vol. V), who began his career in Padua, was the most enthusiastic classicist of all. His paintings seem intended to resemble Roman reliefs, and he chose classical subjects such as the Triumph of Caesar, and dressed his figures in Roman costumes.

4. HIGH RENAISSANCE. In the first quarter of the 16th century, the greatest Italian architect, BRAMANTE, and the two greatest painters of the day, RAPHAEL (qq.v. Vol. V) and Michelangelo, were all working in Rome at the same time in the VATICAN and on the new ST. PETER'S CATHEDRAL (qq.v.). The works of the last two, the decoration of the ceiling of the Sistine Chapel and of the State apartments (the 'Stanzi'), represent perhaps the highest peak of European painting, and approach nearer than at any other time the ideals of CLASSICAL ART (q.v.) (*see* Vol. I, pp. 221, 402).

Correggio, who belonged to the School of Parma in north Italy, was one of the few great artists (apart from the Venetians) who were working outside Rome at this time. His figures of the Madonna and Child and of antique goddesses seem years ahead of their time and many

By gracious permission of H.M. the Queen

DETAIL FROM THE TRIUMPH OF CAESAR. PAINTING BY ANDREA MANTEGNA (*c.* 1430–1506)

of his compositions have something of the movement and dramatic quality of the baroque style,
which developed a century later.

This period, called the High Renaissance, was
so intensely brilliant that it could hardly last.
It was external circumstances of an unexpected
kind which killed it. In 1517 Martin Luther
nailed his attack on Catholicism to the door of

the church at Wittenberg, and so started the
final stage of the REFORMATION (q.v. Vol. I).
Ten years later, in 1527, the army of the
Emperor Charles V sacked Rome. To anyone
living in Italy at the time it must have been
apparent that an epoch was over. As long as the
authority of the Roman Catholic Church was
undisputed it could afford to be tolerant and

DANAE. PAINTING BY CORREGGIO (1494–1534)

Anderson

permit artists to follow their natural bents unchecked; but under this threat to its existence it had to impose a very severe control. The Church laid down general rules to control intellectual and artistic activity—in fact, it assumed the kind of despotism which was completely alien to the almost unrestricted intellectual freedom of the Renaissance.

During this period VENETIAN PAINTING (q.v.) alone maintained a high standard of art. Venice had always stood rather apart from the rest of Italy, and her Renaissance started later than it did elsewhere. Now her greatest painter, TITIAN, although constantly modifying his style, nevertheless continued painting magnificently until well into the second half of the 16th century, at a time when other schools of Italy were in turmoil. At Vicenza, near Venice, the architect PALLADIO (qq.v. Vol. V) built villas in a style closely modelled on Roman examples.

5. MANNERISM AND BAROQUE. The wars and the opposition of the Church shook men's faith in the Renaissance ideals, and self-confidence was replaced by fear and uncertainty. The art which is called 'Mannerism' reflects this uncertainty. Artists, following the example of Michelangelo and Raphael, painted pictures which lack the reality of their masters. The figures are elongated and contorted, and instead

of a clearly defined space within the picture, figures and architecture seem to float in a dream world. The Carracci brothers, on the other hand, tried to revive the spirit of the Renaissance by painting classical subjects in which they kept as closely as possible to classical models.

The despotic character of the Church's control of art helped to produce in the 17th century a remarkable result which could not have developed in any other way. By the 17th century the Roman Catholic Church was more secure and no longer in mortal danger. Believing that men's faith is controlled not so much by reason as by the emotions, it encouraged BAROQUE ART (q.v.), which appealed directly to the emotions.

Lorenzo BERNINI (q.v. Vol. V), the greatest of the baroque artists, was, like other great Italians, sculptor, architect, and painter. Caravaggio's paintings are dramatic and forceful because of their arresting composition and strong contrasts of light and shade (*see* CHIAROSCURO). The end of the long period of Italian art came, appropriately, in Venice, where it had started later. In Tiepolo she produced one of the greatest of all decorative painters and one who carried her art up to the middle of the 18th century.

It is interesting to note that the unification of Italy (*see* ITALIANS, Vol. I), so long desired and only achieved in the 19th century, although associated with notable movements in literature and in music, especially in the operas of VERDI (q.v. Vol. V), produced no great painting, sculpture, or architecture.

See also FLORENTINE PAINTING; SIENESE PAINTING; VENETIAN PAINTING.
See also Vol. I: RENAISSANCE.

ITALIAN LITERATURE. Italy has not only given to the world some of the greatest writers of all times, including DANTE, PETRARCH, and BOCCACCIO (qq.v. Vol. V), but she has also exerted more continuous influence on the literature of western Europe than any other country. Especially during the RENAISSANCE (q.v. Vol. I), all Europe looked to Italy for leadership in the arts. With an unbroken tradition, dating from the early 13th century, Italy has produced at all periods, with the notable exception of the 17th and early 18th centuries, writers of the first order, whose works were translated and spread throughout Europe.

The beginnings of Italian literature, by comparison with other languages such as French, came late, for Latin remained the language of literature and learning in Italy until the early 13th century. Then poets at the Court of Frederick of Sicily began to imitate in Italian the love-poetry of Provence (see ROMANCE LITERATURE). Artificial and conventional as it was, this poetry began a literary tradition in Italian which flourished so rapidly, especially in Florence, that within less than 100 years Dante wrote in this medium his famous DIVINE COMEDY (q.v.), and during the succeeding 50 years there followed the exquisite love-sonnets of Petrarch and the fine humorous tales of Boccaccio. This trio of Tuscan writers of the 14th century determined by their example the language and forms of Italian literature for many centuries.

For some 70 years after Boccaccio's death in 1375 no work of comparable greatness was written in Italian, partly because, in the early part of the Renaissance, writers applied themselves with new vigour to Latin, and for a time neglected Italian. Cultured men devoted themselves to scholarship and moral philosophy rather than to poetry, until, under the MEDICIS in Florence (q.v. Vol. V), a revival of Italian literature took place, aided by the patronage and example of Lorenzo the Magnificent. The poets drew fresh inspiration from classical literature, striving to create in Italian the perfection of style they admired in the ancients. As the Courts of the Italian city-states of Ferrara, Urbino, and Mantua increased in social brilliance, they fostered the development of literature. From the courteous, refined social background of Ferrara came at the close of the 15th and in the early 16th century two poems of chivalry, based on the legends of Charlemagne and Arthur—the *Orlando Innamorato* of Boiardo and the *Orlando Furioso* of Ariosto (see CHANSON DE ROLAND). Ariosto's poem, which attained great fame in Europe, is the most representative work of the age, for in its entirely fantastic subject-matter, and intricate web of chivalrous adventure, treated with all the polished seriousness of a great artist, it exemplifies the Renaissance poet's search for purity of form and harmony of expression, untroubled by the coarser reality of life.

Italy's background at that time was turbulent —the scene of intrigue and warfare, with little

Anderson

THE FLIGHT INTO EGYPT. PAINTING BY ANNIBALE CARRACCI (1560?–1609)

security; yet there is no obvious reflection of these events in the contemporary literature. They do not appear to disturb the perfection of Castiglione's *Courtier*, which, written in Urbino (1528), and translated into several languages (including English in 1561), had a great effect on the manners and accomplishments of the European courtier. In the writings, however, of MACHIAVELLI (q.v. Vol. V), especially his *Prince*, which marks the beginnings of modern historical and political thought, and in the histories of Guicciardini, the history of the times is reflected; for both men were preoccupied by the political decay and division of Italy.

The more literary writers of 16th-century Italy gave themselves wholeheartedly to the imitation of the classics and of the great models of Italian literature, principally Petrarch and Boccaccio. Social conditions much favoured the gallant SONNET (q.v.) in the Petrarchan manner, and it was through these imitations that Petrarch came to have so great an influence on the poetry of France and England. In prose, Boccaccio's tradition of story-telling was imitated, among others, by Bandello, from whose tales Shakespeare drew the stories of some of his plays. Writers also attempted, though not very successfully, to create from classical models types of literature hitherto unknown in Italian, tragic and comic dramas, for instance. Tasso (1544–95), who proposed to write a religious epic with his *Gerusalemme Liberata*, succeeded in creating a heroic romance of great beauty in the tradition of Ariosto. Yet the spirit of Tasso's poetry was very different from Ariosto's, a difference partly attributable to the change which had come over Italy, due to the Church's campaign against the ideas of the Reformation and the restraints which she put on the advancement of knowledge.

In the 17th century, though Europe still looked to Italy for the arts, she, in fact, produced no great poets, though the name of GALILEO (q.v. Vol. V) stands high in the history of science. During this period, however, there flourished the 'Commedia dell'Arte', a kind of popular improvised comedy, with conventional characters and plots. This spread throughout Europe, and traces remain in the HARLEQUINADE (q.v. Vol. IX).

Italian literature revived in the 18th century under the impulse of new ideas from France and England, both of which countries had surpassed her in philosophy and the sciences. The influence of these new ways of thinking brought about a reaction against artificiality and a move to bring literature closer to real life. Consequently there was a great quantity of new writing in Italy, though much of it was merely destructive. In drama, Goldoni (1707–93), inspired by Molière's example, attempted to substitute a more human social comedy for the fantasy of the 'Commedia dell'Arte'; while Alfieri (1749–1803) aimed at giving Italy the classical tragedy of great emotions she had hitherto lacked. Parini (1729–99), partly inspired by Alexander Pope, wrote delightful poetic satire about the contemporary society in north Italy. The climax of this revival of Italian literature was reached in the poetry of Foscolo (1778–1827), with its powerful personal and patriotic emotions and pure classical form in the best Italian tradition (*see* CLASSICAL ART). After Foscolo, the classical tradition began to give place to Romantic influences which came mostly from France and Germany.

The ROMANTIC MOVEMENT (q.v.) in Italy never produced the great poetry which characterizes French or English Romanticism. Its greatest poet is Leopardi (1798–1837), who wrote lyrics of deep sentiment and pure form. The novel became very popular, and in this form Manzoni (1785–1873), in his *I Promessi Sposi*, wrote the finest prose since Boccaccio. The historical novel, however, became too quickly a vehicle for patriotic sentiment or for sentimentality, and there were no other great novels until late in the 19th century, when there came a reaction against Romantic idealization in literature. This reaction is represented by the virile classicism of Carducci's verse (1835–1907), and in the novels and short stories of Verga (1840–1922), based on the miseries of Sicilian life. Other novelists and short-story writers occupied themselves with the social and spiritual problems which had arisen with the scientific and industrial developments of the late 19th century. D'Annunzio (1863–1938) wrote novels, and also poetry, of refined and exotic sensations which earned him a European reputation. The modern writer best known in Europe is the novelist and dramatist Pirandello (1867–1936), who took as his themes social and domestic situations which demonstrate his own philosophy of life. In Pirandello's work sentimental romanticism and scientific realism have given place to a scepticism symptomatic of a modern civilization groping for a new sense of human values. Another famous contemporary writer, Croce (1866–1952), found these values in philosophy and art, and his literary criticism and aesthetic theories have exerted a great influence on modern Italian thought.

In general, it is true to say that Italy has produced much great poetry and little great prose. This must be attributed partly to national temperament and partly to the early foundation and unbroken continuity of the poetic tradition, which is perhaps the most striking feature of Italian literary development.

IVORY CARVING. Ivory is a very dense substance; it is hard enough to be durable and to allow the carver to work with great precision, but it is more easily worked than stone. The pores contain a waxy solution which helps to polish the surface. Ivory varies from almost pure white to a deep cream; it has characteristic markings, and when cut thinly is semi-transparent. It cannot always be distinguished from stag's horn and the teeth of the walrus and the sperm whale, and objects made from all these materials are usually classed together.

Victoria & Albert Museum

A LION DEVOURING A GAZELLE. ASSYRIAN KNIFE HANDLE, 7TH CENTURY B.C.

In prehistoric times ivory was easily obtainable, for mammoths and mastodons ranged in large numbers over the whole of Europe, as well as Asia and Africa. The cave dwellings of the late Stone Age in France and Spain have yielded many ivory objects, some carved in the round and others simply incised with pictures of animals drawn in a clear outline (*see* PREHISTORIC ART). These drawings are surprisingly naturalistic and show that primitive man had great powers of observation. In the New Stone Age, as the climate changed and the great animals retreated southwards, ivory objects

became scarcer in Europe; but ivory was carved from the earliest times in Egypt and Assyria. The Egyptians obtained large quantities of ivory by trading with the peoples of the upper Nile. They used it, among other things, for decorating furniture. In Assyria the surface of the carving was often heavily ornamented with inlay of semi-precious stones set in grooves or cells. But in some small objects, such as knife handles carved into the shapes of animals, the craftsman showed a full appreciation of his material.

Ivory was extensively used in the decoration of the great palaces of KNOSSOS (q.v.) in Crete, and ivory statuettes have been found there, especially of women, wearing tiaras and robes trimmed with gold, which are lifelike and full of character. Little ivory carving has survived from Greece, but it is recorded that the heads and hands of some of the large statues were made of ivory and then painted; how they obtained blocks of ivory large enough for this purpose is not known.

Most of the Roman ivory carvings which survive belong to the 4th century, that is, to the period after the capital had been moved to Constantinople. The most characteristic carvings are those known as 'Consular diptychs'. Diptychs, originally used either as notebooks or for sending letters, were usually made of two small wooden panels hinged together; the inner faces were slightly hollowed and coated with wax on which it was possible to write with a pointed instrument called a stylus. On especially important occasions ivory was used instead of wood. The insides were hollowed but not waxed and were written on in ink, and the outsides were elaborately carved. At a later date these same diptychs were used to record the names of benefactors to churches or as book covers, and were preserved in monastic libraries. One of the finest, now in the Victoria and Albert Museum, was probably used originally to announce a marriage. On it is carved the figure of a woman pouring libations on an altar which stands under a tree. Most of the diptychs, however, were sent by Roman consuls to other important personages of the Empire to announce their appointment. These diptychs were often carved with portraits of the consuls themselves, and sometimes little scenes showing chariot races or fights with wild beasts were placed below.

Ivory carving is especially important in BYZANTINE and early MEDIEVAL ART (qq.v.)

because very little full-scale sculpture survives from these times. In the 6th century ivories made for churches, especially those from great cities such as Alexandria, are very lifelike, and the figures have some resemblance to classical statues; in others the figures are stiff and motionless and are designed mainly to inspire people with a sense of reverence. They are similar in style to early Byzantine MOSAICS and ILLUMINATED MANUSCRIPTS (qq.v.). At a slightly later date, when making pictures or statues of sacred personages was forbidden in the Byzantine Empire, ivory carvers turned for their subjects to very natural representations of battle scenes, horse races, animals, and birds. The figures are often dressed in Greek costume; some of them are nude. In the 9th century, when the prohibition was removed, many beautiful ivory carvings of religious scenes were made in Constantinople and other cities of the Eastern Empire (*see* p. 54).

As ivory was probably difficult to obtain in western Europe in the early Middle Ages, bone carvings were made instead. When Charlemagne established his Empire in western Europe he encouraged artists of all kinds to copy works of art from Italy and the Byzantine Empire. Many beautiful ivories were carved, in some of which the figures are very stiff and are sitting under arches, but in others they move about freely with lively and expressive gestures.

In the Romanesque period ivory was used to decorate objects used in church ritual, such as bishops' crosiers, crosses, reliquaries in which the bones of saints were preserved, and combs

Victoria & Albert Museum

LEAF OF THE CONSULAR DIPTYCH OF THE CONSUL AT CONSTANTINOPLE IN A.D. 517
Below the consul are servants leading horses and boys plaguing an old man by attaching a crab to his nose

used when the celebrating priests changed their vestments during Mass. These are usually decorated with designs composed of scrolls and dragons, which are most skilfully adapted to the shape of the object. Elaborate reliquaries in the form of miniature churches were made of enamelled metal, with little ivory figures in niches set in the sides. Some of the finest book-covers and other reliefs were produced in Spain and show a blend of Arabic with various Christian styles. The surfaces are so deeply pierced that the tall and emaciated figures set off by dark shadows have an intense and often tragic appearance. The figures are surrounded with leaf-work frames. Chessmen were made in ivory and walrus tooth, particularly in Scandinavia.

In the 13th and 14th centuries the craft of ivory carving was centred in Paris, although a few important English carvings survive. The French work varies very much in design and quality. A few quite large free-standing figures were made, but the most characteristic objects are little ALTARS (q.v.) in two or three leaves for use at private devotion. The leaves are divided horizontally into several tiers so that a large number of little scenes, usually representing the Nativity scenes and those of the Passion, can be represented. The figures, which are placed under pointed arcades, are most minutely carved and often stand almost free from the background. Colour decoration and gilding is often used still further to enhance the richness of the carving.

In the Gothic period ivory was used more and more for non-religious objects such as marriage caskets, mirror cases, and combs, decorated with delicately carved representations of scenes from romances, or people hunting or playing chess (*see* Vol. IX, p. 126). In Italy a few great artists of the Gothic period, such as Giovanni Pisano, carved statuettes, but ivory was more often used for inlay, where it is combined with ebony and semi-precious stones. After the 16th century little ivory carving of importance was produced in Europe.

Ivory carving in India and the Far East has always been important. The extreme fineness to which it can be cut especially suits the intricate patterns loved by Indian craftsmen (*see* INDIAN ART).

See also SCULPTURE.

Victoria & Albert Museum

HEAD OF A PASTORAL STAFF, ENGLISH, 11TH CENTURY
The ivory is carved with scenes from the Nativity and Passion

Victoria & Albert Museum   *Archives Ph.*

LEFT: IVORY TRIPTYCH, FRENCH, LATE 13TH CENTURY
In the lowest tier are Nativity scenes; in the centre, the Crucifixion; and above, the Last Judgement with the righteous entering Heaven and the wicked being pushed into the jaws of Hell

RIGHT: VIRGIN AND CHILD FROM VILLENEUVE-LES-AVIGNON, FRANCE. 13TH CENTURY

A free-standing figure carved from a large piece of ivory

J

JAPANESE ART. Much of Japanese art was inspired by China. In China all branches of art were already highly developed when, in the 7th century A.D., the first temples were built in Japan, the first pictures painted, and the first sculptures made. These were mostly the work of Chinese and Korean artists who went to Japan from the 6th century onwards, when BUDDHISM (q.v. Vol. I) was introduced into the country. The art of Japan until about the 9th century was therefore predominantly Chinese or Korean in character, and a study of CHINESE ART (q.v.) is necessary to understand Japanese art.

Since the Japanese never had to submit to successful invasions of foreign peoples, and also because they treated their art treasures with exceptional care, many works have been preserved from the early periods which add much to our knowledge of Chinese and Korean art. A number of Japanese Buddhist temples and other buildings in wood, still preserved today, are amongst the oldest monuments of their kind in the world. Painting too, and sculpture in wood and bronze, as well as works of the applied arts from the 7th and 8th centuries, are often preserved in the places for which they were originally made. To this date belongs the Hōryūji temple near Nara with its frescoes which were only recently damaged by fire, and a large part of its sculpture. The Imperial depository Shōsōin in Nara can be regarded as the oldest museum in the world, although it was not originally intended as such. A Japanese empress in the year A.D. 756 dedicated to the Buddha her household goods—mainly LACQUER (q.v.), pottery, wood, glass, and metal objects, and textiles—all magnificent examples of mostly Chinese craftsmanship; and these objects still fill the wooden depository that was erected for them. The contents of the Shōsōin are of immeasurable value for our knowledge of East Asiatic art and culture as a whole.

When in the 10th century the once mighty Chinese Empire of the T'ang dynasty was in a state of disintegration, Japanese art began to acquire a character of its own. Japanese Buddhist painting and sculpture revealed an unusual gracefulness, and a school of painting arose, the Yamato school, which for the first time showed unmistakable Japanese features. Literary, religious, and historic works were illustrated vividly, often with great dramatic power, mostly in shining colours on horizontal rolls (*Makimono*). The entire life of the people is reflected in these rolls.

In the 13th century there was a new wave of Chinese influence. The sculpture at this time, in its closer relationship to nature, echoes Chinese sculpture of the Sung period (A.D. 960–1279). Before long, Chinese painting in black Indian ink was adopted and, as in China, landscape and plant and animal life became the favourite subjects. Various schools appeared, often named after the masters who founded them. The pupils were usually members of the master's family or were adopted by him, so that the style of a particular school was often carried on for many genera-

SHŌSŌIN, AN IMPERIAL TREASURE HOUSE AT NARA, JAPAN
The wooden building and its contents date from the 8th century

CHINESE POTTERY AND PORCELAIN

From left to right: Blue and white wine ewer, Period Chia Ching (1522–1566). Tomb figure of a Court Lady, T'ang dynasty (618–909). Wine pot, Sung dynasty (960–1279). Peach bloom vase, Period K'ang Hsi (1662–1722). Celadon plate with fish, Sung dynasty. Famille verte vase, Period K'ang Hsi

Museum of Fine Art, Boston

ILLUSTRATION TO A JAPANESE NOVEL 'HEIJI MONOGATARI'
Detail of a long hand-scroll, Yamato School, 13th century

tions by one family. This is a Japanese habit which occurs in other branches of art as well as in painting. The greatest master of ink-painting was Sesshū (1420–1506).

In the Tokugawa period (1603–1868) the art became more truly Japanese than, except for the Yamato School, it had ever been before. Admiration for Chinese art continued and schools of painting influenced by China existed in Japan, but in much of the art a new style was developed, based on the fusion of Chinese elements and those of the Yamato School. Characteristics of this style are elegance, the spirited and brilliant transformation of nature into decorative designs, unrivalled technical skill, and endless patience in execution. New subjects appeared, new colour combinations were used, and gold backgrounds played an important part. The Kano School, which began as purely Chinese, soon showed these new characteristics. From the middle of the 16th century its most important achievements were brilliant folding screens (*Byobu*) and paintings on movable walls (*Fusuma*) in palaces and temples. Most strikingly Japanese were the works of the Kōetsu School, whose leading masters were Kōetsu (1557–1637) and Kōrin (1658–1716). To the West, however, the Ukiyoye School (School of Life), the first to make coloured wood-

cuts, is the best known. These woodcuts were produced for sale to the poorer classes as a cheap substitute for paintings. The favourite subjects of the Ukiyoye painters were the activities and pleasures of the ordinary people of the big towns, such as actors and tea-house beauties. When Japan started to trade with the West in the middle of the 19th century, her works of art were seen in the West for the first time, and artists such as MANET, WHISTLER (qq.v. Vol. V), and many others were deeply influenced by the Japanese colour woodcuts, which were more easily exported than paintings.

The same spirit as in painting is also apparent in the crafts of the Tokugawa period. Lacquer, in particular gold lacquer, has always been used more in Japan than in China. The writing box (*Suzuribako*) in which the Japanese keep their writing utensils—brush, Indian ink, ink-stone—and the *Inrō*, a dainty little box for perfumes or pills worn attached to the girdle by a decorative button (*Netsuke*), are mainly of lacquer. The *Netsukes*, frequently made of wood or ivory, are miniature sculptures of astonishing variety and fineness of execution. In metalwork the sword is the most important. Every Japanese of the upper classes used to carry two swords, which he cherished almost religiously. Never has so much inventiveness and labour been expended on an

Private Coll. Japan

Japanese Coll.

LEFT: LANDSCAPE IN STORM. PAINTING IN INK BY SESSON (1504–89)

COCK, HEN, AND CHICKENS. PAINTING IN COLOURS ON SILK BY ŌKYŌ (1733–95)

BELOW: NETSUKE. IVORY CARVED BUTTON, 18th CENTURY

TSUBA. INLAID IRON SWORD-GUARD, 18th CENTURY

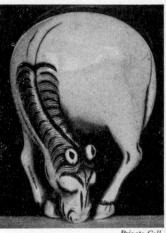

Private Coll.

individual article as was lavished by the Japanese on the guard and on other decorated parts of their swords. Japanese pottery is also a very important craft. Their most exquisite productions are for the tea ceremony, a gathering where tea is drunk in a very ceremonial manner and most costly vessels are used. The high quality and style of Japanese tea pottery is in no small measure due to the Japanese invasion of Korea at the end of the 16th century. Korean potters came as prisoners to Japan, and under their influence pottery was produced in which sometimes elegant, sometimes consciously peasant forms with simple lead glazes, predominated. It was, in the main, STONEWARE, but pure decorated PORCELAIN (qq.v. Vol. VII) was also made in great quantities more or less after Chinese models. Much of the pottery which reached the European markets, in particular that from Satsuma and Imari, is a type of inferior ware of poor taste made mostly for export.

See also CHINESE ART; LACQUER.
See also Vol. I: JAPANESE.

JAPANESE LITERATURE.

The oldest Japanese book still preserved (though most of it is in Chinese) is the history called *Kojiki* (A.D. 712). But it was not until the Tokugawa period (1603–1868) that more than a small proportion of the population could read. By the 18th century, a flourishing printing trade had grown up in the main cities, and a great deal of popular literature was produced. This increase in book-production has continued, until today more books are published in Japan than in almost any other country.

The Japanese have a strong military tradition, and thus we naturally find in their old literature much about battles. The 'war-tales' of medieval times describe civil wars, especially those between the Taira and Minamoto clans, and tell of the exploits of famous warriors such as Minamoto Yoshitsune and his faithful retainer Benkei. There are, too, many works describing vendettas and bloody revenge. Yet the Japanese have another, less harsh, side to their character; they are strongly emotional, fond of beauty, and possess a great love of nature, and it is this aspect which we see in their poetry. Japanese poems are LYRICS (q.v.), suggesting in a few brief lines the writer's feelings—his unhappiness, for instance, at losing his lady's love, or his sadness at seeing the cherry-blossoms fall (a common symbol for the briefness and uncertainty of human life). Much Japanese poetry and many prose works have a note of pessimism or melancholy, partly due to the influence of BUDDHISM (q.v. Vol. I).

The first great flourishing of Japanese literature took place at the Imperial Court in the 9th, 10th, and 11th centuries. It consisted mainly of love lyrics and romances, written by the nobility, and in particular the Court ladies, for their own restricted circle, and was typical of the elegant, luxurious, and rather effeminate society which produced it. One outstanding work of the time is *The Tale of Genji*, by Lady Murasaki Shikibu, the most famous novel in Japan, which tells of the career of an imaginary prince, and gives us a very good picture of life at the Imperial Court.

By the 13th century the actual government of Japan was no longer in the hands of the Emperor and his ministers, but of the military caste, and until the mid-19th century Japan was under a feudal system (*see* JAPANESE, Vol. I). The earlier part of this period produced, besides the 'war-tales', the *No* plays, the classical drama of Japan, while the latter part, the Tokugawa period, is important for the growth of popular literature

Museum of Eastern Art, Oxford

GIRL WASHING CLOTH. COLOURED WOODCUT BY HARUNOBU (1725–70). UKIYOYE SCHOOL

such as novels, ghost stories, and humorous tales, and the PUPPET plays (q.v. Vol. IX) and *kabuki* plays. The *No* and the *kabuki* plays (and to some extent the puppet plays) are still performed today, but the *No*, having little action and no scenery, are not widely popular as are the *kabuki*, which are full of action and movement. A typical *kabuki* is *The Loyal League*, the story of the forty-seven *samurai* (retainers) of a feudal lord who vowed to avenge his death, and who carried out their intention knowing that they themselves would be condemned to death for carrying on a vendetta. This play gives us a good idea of the atmosphere of feudal Japan, where custom and law laid great stress on the individual's duty of loyalty to his feudal lord, his duty to his parents, and so on. In much of the popular literature of the Tokugawa period, however, it is by no means true that the call of duty is always obeyed.

Since the introduction of modern Western civilization into Japan after the restoration of imperial power in 1868, Japanese literature has tended more and more to follow Western models.

See also Vol. I: JAPANESE.
See also Vol. IV: JAPANESE LANGUAGE.

JAPANESE MUSIC, see ORIENTAL MUSIC, Section 1.

JAZZ. The early history of jazz is bound up with that of the West African Negroes who were exported as slaves to the West Indies, to New England, and to the delta of the Mississippi (see AMERICAN NEGROES, Vol. I). Their degradation under the American Slave Code was so complete that, apart from work songs (see FOLK-SONGS), until some time after the emancipation of the slaves in 1865, all their primitive musical instincts seem to have been stifled. At first their music was purely vocal, but gradually they began to use instruments—sometimes secondhand, sometimes home-made. Uneducated and ignorant of Western musical technique, their music was all improvised. The work songs evolved into the 'Blues'—songs deeply expressive of sadness, fear, even satire upon the lot of the black man at the expense of the white, but never of vindictiveness or hatred. Most of these traditional blues were in a twelve-bar form with four beats to the bar, and the placing of the chords varied very little. Within these simple structural limits countless thousands of blues were extemporized.

When they began to use instruments the Negroes attempted to reproduce on them all the effects which had characterized their singing of the blues, such as the *vibrato* (a trembling of the voice) and a way of sliding from one note to another. These instrumental techniques played an important part in forming jazz, for jazz is essentially an instrumental style. The negroes loved BRASS BANDS (q.v. Vol. IX), and about 1890 they began a process of 'jazzing' (as they called it) their brass band marches by improvising, singly or collectively, elaborate decorations, and by shifting the accent from the strong to the weak beat (see SYNCOPATION). The strong beat, which was a necessity in binding together these syncopated elaborations, was derived partly from the marches and partly from the excited clapping and stamping characteristic of Negro religious services (see NEGRO SPIRITUALS) rather than from the original West African drum rhythms, which were much more complicated. Later, the string bass and piano took over the function of providing a clear and regular beat, allowing the other instruments even more latitude in the way of syncopation, or even slight variations in the actual tempo.

The terms 'Jazz' and 'Ragtime' have become confused, although they were originally distinct. Ragtime, or 'rag', originated in the imitations which Negro pianists gave of banjo techniques, combined with the tricks of syncopation they had learnt from the jazzing of brass band music. Rag was essentially a rhythmic style, while jazz referred more to the instrumental and harmonic character of the extemporized variations on well-known marches and dances. Jazz was played by a band, at first without a piano, while ragtime was originally performed on a piano alone. Ragtime had a highly syncopated tune with a regularly accented beat in the bass, usually at a moderate speed and with two beats to the bar. Jazz grew up in New Orleans; rag in St. Louis.

At the beginning of the 20th century white men began to play in the jazz style (their renderings being sometimes known as 'Dixie-land' to distinguish them from the Negro originals of New Orleans). Round about 1920 jazz spread throughout the United States, and from thence all over the world.

'Boogie-woogie', which like rag is played on a piano, is an elaborated version of the old blues songs. The term 'swing' came into use about 1935 to describe a later phase of jazz, and one much influenced by the pianists' rag. It usually has a simple harmonic basis in strict time provided by guitars, piano, percussion, and other instruments, with a solo melody, often improvised and in a very free time and syncopated style, played by a trumpet or saxophone.

To the Negroes music was always closely associated with movement, and rhythm is certainly the outstanding characteristic of jazz. Movement was indeed the origin of the old Negro work songs and, through the march, movement was the inspiration of jazz. Jazz has always been closely connected with dancing, although it is by no means only performed as an accompaniment to dancing. In the early days European dances, such as the waltz and the polka, were frequently 'jazzed' by Negro musicians; and jazz has subsequently evolved countless dances, and ways of dancing of its own, such as the Fox-trot, Charleston, Conga, and Jive.

See also DANCE MUSIC.
See also Vol. IX: BALLROOM DANCING; DANCE BANDS.

JEWELLERY, see Vol. XI: JEWELLERY.

JOURNALS, see PERIODICALS.

K

KEY, MUSICAL, *see* SCALES.

KNOSSOS. From very early times, perhaps as early as 3000 B.C., the capital of Crete was Knossos (or Cnossus), the centre of the MINOAN CIVILIZATION (q.v. Vol. I), so named from Minos, the legendary King of Crete. About 2000 B.C., Crete, the seat of the first empire in history to be based on naval power, became very wealthy. Large towns grew up with splendid palaces, of

Ashmolean Museum

VASE WITH COLOURED DESIGN FROM THE EARLY PALACE AT KNOSSOS

Maraghiannis

BLACK STEATITE (SOAPSTONE) FILLER IN THE FORM OF A BULL'S HEAD

This was used for filling large vessels with wine. The liquid was poured in at the back of the neck and out of a small hole in the lower lip. From the Little Palace, Knossos

which the most magnificent was the so-called Palace of Minos at Knossos.

Sir Arthur Evans began to excavate the ruins of this palace in 1900, and he suggested that this was the labyrinth of the Minotaur legend, the word being derived from *labrys*, the double axe which was the sacred symbol of the great mother-goddess of Crete. The King was evidently thought of as a divine figure, and so his palace was also a centre of public worship. For this reason the building and the works of art which have been found amongst the ruins represent the finest products of Minoan art of all periods except the very early. There had, perhaps, been a palace on the site in the early period, but most of the early work had been cut away when the site was levelled to build the Palace of Minos.

The Palace of Minos consisted of buildings round a great central courtyard. To the west was an official block containing the Throne Room, the Palace Shrine, stores for wine and oil, and some great columned reception halls on the first floor. On the eastern side of the courtyard was the domestic quarter with a grand staircase serving some five storeys or more of the personal living-rooms of the royal family and their attendants. In addition there were crypts with sacred pillars in the centre and repositories for religious objects.

The walls of the rooms were covered with brilliant paintings in which men, animals, birds, and plants were rendered with great freedom

Ashmolean Museum

PRIEST KING. RELIEF PAINTING FROM THE PALACE OF MINOS
AT KNOSSOS

and naturalism. The artists, however, followed certain conventions which distinguish Minoan art from that of any other people. In the palace ruins handsome vases of gold, silver, and bronze have been found, and very fine pottery, sometimes of little more than egg-shell thickness, adorned with formal but highly effective floral designs in colour on a black ground. The craftsmen of Knossos excelled in miniature work, in engraved gems, jewellery, small figures of ivory and pottery, 'fillers' in the form of ox-heads used for filling the wine jars, and vases made of a local stone and carved in low relief.

In the middle of the 16th century B.C. much of Knossos was destroyed by a violent earthquake followed by a fire. The Palace of Minos, however, was soon rebuilt on a grander scale; new pictures were painted on the walls, some of them modelled in relief, and the palace was filled with new works of art. The exquisite freshness of the earlier painting was succeeded by a more pompous grandiose style; the brightly coloured

pottery and delicate egg-shell cups were replaced by great wine jars and vases with designs in dark brown or red varnish on a light ground, with naturalistic floral or marine designs or running spirals. Instead of paintings of gardens with birds, cats, and apes, there were processions of persons bringing offerings to the king in the Egyptian manner, or representations of the dangerous sport of catching a bull by the horns and vaulting over it, which was doubtless a part of the religious ceremonial (*see* Vol. I, p. 318).

About 1400 B.C. disaster again overtook Knossos, probably as the immediate result of an earthquake followed by fire, and the palace was destroyed. Invaders from Greece brought an end to the Minoan Empire, and the palace was never reoccupied, except by poor Minoan refugees who squatted in the ruins and erected a small shrine to the goddess whose symbol was a double axe.

See also Vol. I: MINOAN CIVILIZATION.

KREMLIN. In medieval times all Russian towns of importance contained a fortified area called a kremlin. It was enclosed by wooden walls and served as a citadel, much as an ACROPOLIS (q.v.) did in a Greek city. During the 15th century, however, when Moscow became the centre of the Muscovite kingdom, the capital's Kremlin acquired a symbolic meaning; and now the term is normally taken to mean Moscow's citadel.

The original Moscow Kremlin dated from the 12th century, and, like all the others, was built of wood. In 1485 Moscow's increased power and prosperity decided the Tsar, John III, to adorn and tidy his capital. He sent to Italy for architects, and three of these were entrusted with the task of replacing the Kremlin's crumbling oak walls with pink brick, retaining the original isosceles shape of the enclosure. Within 7 years the work was completed. The regular outline of the high, battlemented walls was broken at various points by towers of Italian outline, alternating with pyramid-shaped ones of Russian design. Until the Second World War some 7,000 feet of these walls survived. There were five great gates concealing drawbridges, of which the main gate, Spasskiye Vorota (the Salvation Gate), still gives access to the Red Square. In its tower, the Redeemer Tower, still hangs the peal of bells erected in 1626 by the

S.C.R.

THE KREMLIN, MOSCOW
View of the outer wall and one of the Kremlin's cathedrals

English architect, Christopher Galloway. These are rung on State occasions and are heard today when the people of Moscow gather before Lenin's tomb in the Red Square for an official celebration. Russia's largest church bell is still preserved in the Kremlin.

Until 1703, when St. Petersburg replaced Moscow as Russia's capital, the Tsar and the Patriarch of the Church, together with the more important officials, resided in the Kremlin. Of recent years various government departments and an important museum have been installed within the walls. The Tsar's ancient palace and council chamber, as well as several churches, are still there, and today the head of the State and his main advisers once again live within the Kremlin enclosure.

See also RUSSIAN ART.
See also Vol. III: MOSCOW.

JAPANESE GOLD LACQUER COVER OF A WRITING BOX, 18th CENTURY

L

LACE, *see* Vol. VII: LACE-MAKING.

LACQUER. China is the native country of the art of lacquer, though different forms of lacquer have also been made in Japan, India, and Europe. In Europe in the 17th and 18th centuries, when objects of Chinese and Japanese lacquer-work were introduced for the first time in quantity, they were often wrongly called Indian. In fact, they were not made in India but had been shipped from there. A certain kind of lacquered Chinese screen was known as a 'Coromandel screen' because it was shipped to Europe from the Coromandel coast of India. The term 'japanning', although derived from the word Japan, is used for both Chinese and Japanese lacquer-work.

Lacquer is a liquid which is applied as a

Museum, Peking

CHINESE RED AND YELLOW LACQUER PLATE CARVED WITH DRAGON AND PHOENIX DESIGN, MING PERIOD, 16TH CENTURY

shining coating to objects of wood, metal, porcelain, papier-mâché, and other materials, and which afterwards hardens. Chinese lacquer is the sap of a tree which grows in central and southern China, and is obtained, much as rubber is, by tapping the tree. The raw material goes through a long process before it is ready for use. The surface on which it is to be applied has also to be carefully prepared. From three to twenty or even more coats of lacquer may be needed to cover the object, each being dried, smoothed, and polished. After that the object is generally painted or carved. The lacquer itself is usually black or red, and into it are sometimes inlaid mother-of-pearl, ivory, gold, silver, amber, and turquoise. The decoration follows the patterns used in other forms of CHINESE ART (q.v.).

Lacquer has been used in China from earliest times to protect or decorate all sorts of objects such as boxes, bowls, furniture, and sculpture. By the Han dynasty (206 B.C.–A.D. 220) the technique was fully developed; in the T'ang dynasty (A.D. 618–906) lacquered objects, which were often inlaid, were particularly splendid. Most surviving Chinese lacquer is red and carved, and dates from later periods; in the Ming period (1368–1644) the quality is particularly fine, the lacquers being frequently decorated with landscape scenes, animals, and flowers.

Chinese lacquer was introduced into Japan in the 6th or 7th century A.D. and soon became a branch of JAPANESE ART (q.v.). The Japanese, however, used gold lacquer for their finest work. Though it is not so grand, Japanese lacquer of the last centuries often surpasses the Chinese in faultlessness of execution.

Indian lacquer (usually called 'lac' in England), which was also used in Burma, is an incrustation deposited on certain Indian trees by an insect (see SHELLAC, Vol. VII). It is less stable and lustrous than Chinese lacquer, and its decoration seldom reached such a high artistic level. European lacquer is a mixture of resins, oils, and pigments which was used to imitate Chinese and Japanese lacquer (see GUMS AND RESINS, Vol. VII). European cabinet makers sometimes used panels from Chinese screens for furniture, such as cabinets and table tops.

See also CHINESE ART; JAPANESE ART.

LANDSCAPE ART. The art of landscape design (as distinct from that of garden design) began in England in the 18th century. Previously, both in England and abroad, the immediate surroundings of a house consisted of a garden formally laid out with walks, hedges, flower-beds, and small trees, generally enclosed by low walls or forming a series of terraces, together with the necessary kitchen gardens and outbuildings. No account was taken of the more distant surroundings; the gardens stopped abruptly where the fields began, except that sometimes an avenue of trees would be extended beyond the close neighbourhood of the house (see GARDENING, HISTORY OF, Vol. VI).

During the 18th century landowners began to take an interest in the view from their houses and to alter and improve the arrangement of the landscape far beyond their garden walls. This interest in designing landscapes was stimulated by a new style of LANDSCAPE PAINTING (q.v.) that had grown up on the Continent (exemplified in the work of CLAUDE (q.v. Vol. V) and other artists) and by the habit of foreign travel, which not only brought Englishmen into contact with the work of these artists but made them acquainted with the more dramatic scenery of Italy and Switzerland. When they returned to their own estates they tried to reproduce there the beauties they had admired abroad. This was a time when the landowners were the most powerful people in England, and consequently they wanted to contrive settings for their country mansions as magnificent in their own way as the town palaces of other nations and periods. So they began to devise landscapes covering huge tracts of country, of which their own mansions were the focus. So sure were they of the permanence of their way of life that they often planned as much for their descendants as for themselves, their designs depending for perfection on trees which would not have grown up until long after they were dead. The landscape they created was of the kind that we think of as most typically English, though it is not generally realized that English scenery is so much a man-made affair: clumps of trees were planted in distant fields where they improved the composition of the landscape, rivers were diverted, and lakes and water-courses formed. Monuments or imitation classical temples were often built on hill-tops or far places in a nobleman's park so that they formed part of the view from the house.

Landscape gardeners of the 18th and early 19th centuries, a time when everything Romantic and Gothic was admired (see GOTHIC REVIVAL), often built Gothic arbours, battlemented look-out towers, or artificial ruins as part of the ornament in the grounds of a great place. Such buildings came later to be called 'follies'. They were sometimes extravagantly fantastic—rock-strewn hermitages, grottoes lined with shells, and equipped with furniture made from the skulls of horses—anything which was considered to be romantic and picturesque.

Landscape design developed in course of time into an elaborate and specialized art of its own, based on carefully worked out principles. Its practitioners called it 'the art of the Picturesque', this word being used in its literal sense of forming a picture. Each view was a carefully considered composition, irregular in character (in contrast with the formality and symmetry that prevailed on the Continent), and taking its inspiration from the natural characteristics of the site. As time went on, more emphasis came to be laid on the inspiration of nature and less on artificially picturesque composition.

Among the principal landscape artists working in England in the 18th century were two architects, Kent (1684–1748) and Chambers (1726–96), and also the famous Capability BROWN (q.v. Vol. V) who was succeeded by Humphry Repton (1752–1818), the fashionable

BLENHEIM PARK, OXFORDSHIRE
The palace was designed by Vanbrugh, and the park later laid out by Capability Brown. He dammed up a small stream to make the lake

artist whom Mr. Rushworth in Jane Austen's *Mansfield Park* called in to improve his estate, Sotherton Court. The literary character of the romantic picturesque movement is shown by the fact that several famous poets were among its leaders, notably Pope and Shenstone, and also Horace Walpole. Shenstone's own garden, 'The Leasowes', was one of the first examples of the English landscape style, and many other amateurs made important contributions both to the theory and practice of the art, and wrote elaborate treatises on the subject.

The art of picturesque landscape, a purely English art, has been one of England's great contributions to European art. But it could hardly survive long into the age of industrialism, though the fashion it set for irregular planning has influenced design in the suburbs up to our

THE CHESTNUT AVENUE AT LANGLEY PARK, KENT, BEFORE AND AFTER IMPROVEMENT
From Humphry Repton, *Sketches and Hints on Landscape Gardening*, 1794

own day. Not until the mid-20th century did opportunities again occur for landscape design on the scale practised in the 18th century. Today the judicious planning of new electrified industries in open country, the sweep of new arterial roads across the landscape, and the wide powers of control over the use of land that have been put into the hands of TOWN AND COUNTRY PLANNING authorities (q.v. Vol. X) all make it possible once again to fashion the landscape deliberately and imaginatively. The landscape designer is again in demand.

Other countries where attention has been given to the design of landscape on a large scale are Persia, China, and Japan; but the type of man-made scenery found there belongs more to the category of garden design, as do the landscaped gardens of the Italian Renaissance. Oriental gardens, however, have this in common with the English landscaped park, that they observe rules of design based on a philosophical theory as well as on mere architectural effect.

See also Vol. VI: GARDENING, HISTORY OF.

LANDSCAPE PAINTING. During the 19th century the art of landscape painting was practised in England more than any other branch of painting; in fact, England led the world at this period in landscape painting. Amateurs, in particular, nearly always paint landscapes. Yet it is a much newer branch of art than, for example, figure painting, and in some countries it has never been popular.

Painters have looked at landscape in many different ways. Some, when painting a tree, have been interested chiefly in the shape and structure of the leaves and how they join on to the branches; others have been fascinated by the complexity of the branches and have preferred trees in winter, without their leaves. Some painters have favoured placid landscapes with meadows and streams; others have preferred dramatic rocks and mountains or stormy seas. Others again have been much more interested in the play of light on objects than in the objects themselves. They have studied the different appearance of landscapes in the varying moods of nature or at different seasons. Certain painters, having selected the type of landscape they wished to paint, have then tried to reproduce faithfully what interested them in it. Others have rearranged the objects they have seen in accordance with their own design for the picture.

In the Middle Ages painters showed little inclination to record nature, and the little that appears in pictures is purely decorative and formal. But in the Renaissance people recognized the endless variety and beauty of the landscape just as they were becoming interested in the achievements of mankind, especially the achievements of the ancient Romans. The 15th-century landscapes, whether in Italy in, for example, the work of Giovanni BELLINI, or in the north in that of the van EYCKS (qq.v. Vol. V) or Dierk Bouts, show that the artist was studying the landscape with the same care and interest as he studied the appearance of the men and women whom he portrayed. The landscapes were painted in a straightforward manner and often with striking realism. But they were not the main subject of the picture, being only the background against which the main element in the picture, the figures, were seen. Early in the 16th century the Flemish artist, Patenier, painted a number of pictures in which the landscape was so much more important than the figures that it would be natural to classify them as landscapes rather than as figure-pieces with landscape backgrounds. But it was not until the 17th century that landscape as an independent form of art really came into its own, and it is in this century, together with the 19th, that the greatest landscape paintings have been produced.

In the 17th century there were two main schools of landscape painting—the French and the Dutch. The French artists—of whom the most famous were Nicolas POUSSIN and CLAUDE (qq.v. Vol. V)—lived and worked not in France but in Rome, for they and their colleagues were as fascinated by the splendour of ancient Rome as the Italians of the Renaissance had been. Consequently their landscape painting is not a straightforward rendering of the scenery around Rome, but an attempt to idealize what they saw and to make it conform with the spirit of Roman art. Although those two great masters differed in many ways from each other—Poussin was chiefly interested in the structure of the trees and rocks which he painted, Claude in the circulation of light and air round them—they were at one in this important respect, and the work of both is known as 'classical' landscape (see CLASSICAL ART). It was a noble and educated form of painting and, although it never portrayed any specific landscape quite as it really

National Gallery

THE AVENUE, MIDDELHARNIS. PAINTING BY MEINDERT HOBBEMA, 1638–1709

was, it showed a kind of ideal form of it, which was what a great many people would have liked the real landscape to be (*see* p. 85 and Plate 8).

A number of 18th-century painters followed the example of Claude, including the Englishman, Richard Wilson, who introduced important variations of his own (*see* Plate 4). Many painters, misunderstanding Claude's aim, concentrated on the picturesque features, such as temples and ruins, which in his pictures were only incidental. Thus there arose in the 18th century a whole school of not very distinguished 'ruin painters' whose work influenced landscape painting, particularly in England. Wealthy British tourists were among the chief patrons of such art, especially of Venetian 18th-century landscape painting, which in the hands of the painter Canaletto was often little more than accurate topographical rendering of the fantastic beauty of Venice (*see* Colour Plate, Vol. IX, opp. p. 208). Canaletto's Venetian contemporary, Guardi, preferred a more romantic and

fairy-like type of landscape painting, and something comparable with this was being practised independently by French landscape painters such as Fragonard and Hubert Robert.

As the art of Poussin and more particularly of Claude was misunderstood and perverted during the 18th century, so was that of the other great 17th-century school of landscape painters —the Dutch. The Dutch painters approached nature in as straightforward a way as had the 15th-century Flemish painters. They had little or none of Claude's desire to improve on what they saw in nature, but different artists were interested in different aspects of it. Albert Cuyp painted placid landscape (usually with cattle) bathed in glowing light. Jacob Ruisdael's pictures and those of Meindert Hobbema and Philip Koninck are usually of the flat expanses of Holland in cloudy weather. The van de Veldes, van de Cappelle, and others painted shipping—Holland at that time was a major naval power (*see* Vol. X, p. 397); while others painted street scenes in their native towns (*see* Dutch Art). Almost the only attempt to improve on nature in any of these works was the occasional introduction of mountains or waterfalls, which do not exist in Holland but which the painters had probably seen, or heard of, in Norway or Italy.

During the 18th century many English collectors bought 17th-century Dutch landscape paintings of this realistic type, and this may account in part for the spectacular outburst of landscape painting in England early in the 19th century. Most painters, such as John Constable (q.v. Vol. V), were content, like the Dutch, to record the scenery as it really was. Constable succeeded in portraying the very essence of the English landscape—the smiling meadows, the sparkle of the sun on rain or dew, or the stormy and uncertain clouds (*see* Colour Plate opp. p. 448). The Norwich school of painters, of whom John Crome was the best known, had comparable aims, as had the Water-Colour painters (q.v.) such as Girtin or de Wint. The important exception to this type of landscape painter was J. M. W. Turner (q.v. Vol. V). He was prob-

ably the greatest landscape painter who has ever lived, and he stands outside any category because at one time or another he practised in each of them. Early in life he absorbed the manner both of Claude and the Dutch, and made striking essays in both, with original variations. Late in life he visited Venice and painted it with a magic of light such as the native Venetian painters had never achieved. Finally he dissolved the forms of his landscapes altogether in the play of light and shade, thereby anticipating (as Constable had done to a much lesser extent) the work of French Impressionist Painting (q.v.).

In 19th-century France the example of Constable greatly assisted French landscape painters such as Corot and Theodore Rousseau, who chose similarly undramatic subjects. Later in the 19th century the progress of landscape painting in France followed the chequered and exciting course of French Art (q.v.) in general at this period. Nearly all the greatest painters of this revolutionary period—the realistic Courbet, the Impressionist painters Monet, Pissarro, and Sisley, and the Post-Impressionist painters

Tate Gallery

A FROSTY MORNING; SUNRISE. PAINTING BY J. M. W. TURNER, 1775–1851

Though an early painting, exhibited in 1813, its shows Turner's interest in natural effects of light and atmosphere

THE PALACE OF THE POPES, AVIGNON. PAINTING BY COROT, 1796–1875

LANDSCAPE WITH VIADUCT. PAINTING BY PAUL CÉZANNE, 1839–1906

(q.v.) Van Gogh and Cézanne achieved some of their finest results in landscape painting and devoted much of their time to it. Of these, Courbet chose the most solid and the most ordinary types of landscape for his subject—woods, the coast of northern France, or streams flowing near massive cliffs. Monet, the most extreme of the Impressionists, seems to have been content to paint any sort of landscape as long as the light was interesting. He would even paint the same object several times in the same day under different lighting conditions. Van Gogh and Cézanne painted chiefly in the sunny Mediterranean landscape of the south of France, Van Gogh delighting in the vibrating effect, which with him seems almost alive, of strong sunlight or strong wind on corn. Cézanne, alone of 19th-century landscape painters, tried, like Poussin and Claude, to rearrange the landscape to emphasize its repose and harmony.

In the 20th century landscape painting is still the main field of activity for many painters, whose work follows the general trends of MODERN ART (q.v.).

See also WATER-COLOURS.

LATIN LITERATURE.

Latin was a literary language from the middle of the 3rd century B.C. to the end of the 17th century A.D.; and though we conventionally classify Latin authors as classical, medieval, or Renaissance, no hard and fast lines can be drawn to separate one period from the next. This article deals only with the classical period, taken as ending with the death in A.D. 524 of Boethius, author of *The Consolations of Philosophy*, which was first translated into English by Alfred the Great.

Within the classical age of Latin literature, definite periods are quite easily recognizable. First comes the age of the wars with Carthage (264–146 B.C.), in which Latin authors were learning to translate from GREEK LITERATURE (q.v.) and adapt Greek models to Roman subjects and conditions. Of the many authors working in the period only the epic poet Ennius, the comic poets Plautus and Terence, and the satirist Lucilius are now recognized as of first-class importance.

In the second period, that of the late Republic (c. 80–43 B.C.), the most important development is the perfection of Latin prose as a vehicle for philosophy, history, oratory, and letter-writing (both private and official). CICERO (q.v. Vol. V),

famous as an orator and letter-writer and for his works on the technique of oratory (*see* RHETORIC) and on philosophy, has had an incalculably great influence on the development of prose literature in every European language. In the field of history JULIUS CAESAR's war memoirs (q.v. Vol. V) and Sallust's historical essays have been nearly as influential. In poetry this age is marked by the lyric and short epic poems of Catullus (c. 84–c. 54 B.C.) and his circle, and by the philosophical epic *On Nature*, by Lucretius (c. 94–55 B.C.), all of which decisively influenced the great poetry of the next period. The poems of Catullus and Lucretius still exist and directly influence modern writers.

With the third, or 'Augustan', period, called after the Emperor AUGUSTUS (q.v. Vol. V), Latin poetry culminates in the work of VIRGIL, HORACE, and OVID (qq.v. Vol. V), and the less often read, but still influential, Propertius. In prose, the Augustan period produced the great historian, LIVY (q.v. Vol. V) and the first Roman writer to devote himself entirely to the study and teaching of rhetoric, the elder Seneca (55 B.C.–c. A.D. 37), who is important because rhetoric was regarded by the Romans as the basis of all sound education, although after the fall of the Republic it was no longer so important as a political weapon.

In the so-called 'Silver' (or Post-Augustan) age of Latin literature, the most important period lasted from about A.D. 50 to 117, the date of the death of the Emperor Trajan. In the early part of this period the philosopher Seneca the younger (c. 5 B.C.–A.D. 65) wrote tragedies which had a deep influence on Renaissance drama. His nephew Lucan (A.D. 39–65) wrote an epic poem on the civil war between Caesar and Pompey, which strongly affected Roundhead, Whig, and Liberal thought about tyranny. Petronius wrote a novel, the *Satyricon*, which is the ancestor of such works as the *Decameron* and the CANTERBURY TALES (q.v.); and the *Natural History* of the elder Pliny (A.D. 23–79) was the chief ENCYCLOPAEDIA (q.v.) of the Middle Ages.

In the later part of this period, the most original, and perhaps the greatest, writer was the historian Tacitus (*see* HISTORIES). Quintilian wrote a famous treatise, *On Educating the Orator*, which has had a decisive effect on later educational thought. From the epigrams of Martial, the satires of Juvenal, and the letters of the younger Pliny we get a vivid picture of the

Roman world of the late 1st century A.D., in which Christianity was beginning to make its way.

Between the deaths of Trajan (A.D. 117) and Constantine (A.D. 337) most of the important Latin literature was Christian, with writers such as Tertullian and Lactantius, who was sometimes called 'the Christian Cicero'. The most important pagan writer was the novelist, Apuleius, whose *Golden Ass* is still a classic. The 4th and early 5th century produced much poetry (both secular and religious), history, and philosophy. The writers included the professor-poet, Ausonius of Bordeaux, the philosopher-bishop, St. Augustine of Hippo (q.v. Vol. V), and the Court poet, Claudian. Boethius' work, with its fascinating combination of poetry and philosophy, reminds us that the classical spirit lived on for at least a century after Augustine, and that the last of the Romans is himself the first great author of the Middle Ages.

Apart from the individual contributions of the greatest Latin authors, such as Cicero, Virgil, and Tacitus, the fact that Latin so long remained the common language of educated men throughout the western world might be considered the most remarkable achievement of classical Latin literature, by means of which the language was developed as a uniquely flexible instrument for the formulation and communication of thought.

See also Epic Poetry; Lyric Poetry; Histories; Ode; Pastorals.
See also Vol. I: Roman Civilization.
See also Vol. IV: Latin Language.

LETTERING. The design of fine lettering ranks high among the crafts. The materials and tools with which letters have been made have at all times played their part in creating the forms of letters. The Egyptians wrote with reed-brushes on papyrus, producing a flowing line with even strokes; the Assyrians used soft clay to write upon, incising the letters with wedge-

ABCDEFGILM NOPQRSTVX

FIG. 1. THE ROMAN ALPHABET FROM THE INSCRIPTION ON TRAJAN'S COLUMN

shaped sticks, hence the wedge-shaped form of Cuneiform Writing (q.v. Vol. IV). The Romans wrote on papyrus as well as on wax tablets, but their most important contribution to the art of lettering was made in the inscriptions which were incised with chisels in stone. In these the shapes and proportions of the letters were worked out to such a degree of refinement that they have remained the model for all subsequent letters, and craftsmen have at all times returned for inspiration to the original Roman letters (*see* Handwriting, Vol. IV).

Roman capitals have thick down strokes and thin up or horizontal strokes, the curved strokes swelling where they approach the vertical. The strokes terminate in a little flourish, called the 'serif'. The letters O, C, G, D, and Q are almost circular, and the proportions of B, P, R, S, E, and F are based on two small circles placed one above the other (Fig. 1).

Not only is the proportion of each letter important but also the space between them. As a rule the area round the letters is equal, and not the distance between them; round letters, therefore, are placed closer than ones with vertical lines.

In the Middle Ages the lettering used in books was at first copied from Roman originals, but gradually its character changed. Capitals became very ornamental, and their shapes were altered to allow pictures to be fitted into them. For instance, in medieval psalters the B beginning the first Psalm *Beatus Vir* was often enlarged to fill the whole page, and a drawing of the Tree of Jesse (showing the ancestors of Christ) filled

Crown Copyright

PART OF THE INSCRIPTION ON HENRY VII'S TOMB IN WESTMINSTER ABBEY, DESIGNED BY TORRIGIANO the spaces in and around the letter. The tail of the letter was sometimes prolonged and elaborated to make a pattern down the side of the page (*see* ILLUMINATED MANUSCRIPTS).

In Italy in the 15th-century the Renaissance fostered an interest in antiquity which led to the copying of many books by Latin authors. The copyists used the early medieval style of lettering in which many of the books they found had been written. From this style developed the design of modern letters and PRINTING-TYPE (q.v. Vol. VII), both the upright (roman) and sloping (italic) forms. Artists became interested in the shapes of the letters they found on Roman inscriptions; DÜRER (q.v. Vol. V) worked out the proportions with minute care, showing how the parts, even the serifs, are related to the whole and each letter to the others; but his letters have not the flowing beauty of the Roman originals.

From the 16th century to the end of the 18th century CLASSICAL ART (q.v.) was the basis of all the arts, and lettering followed the Roman forms, though changes in fashion are reflected in the proportions; the sturdy 17th-century letters, for instance, give way to finer, more elegant shapes in the 18th century. At the end of the 18th and beginning of the 19th century the romantic interest in exotic arts was reflected in lettering. In the so-called Egyptian letter all the strokes are of equal thickness, including the serifs. Alphabets were designed without any serifs and, though based on Roman letters, were often distorted and ugly. The proportions of the Roman letters were not appreciated and the forms were twisted and tortured, making them difficult to read and unsuitable for

L.T.E.
SANS SERIF LETTERING BY EDWARD JOHNSTON

the purpose which they had to serve. Sometimes all the letters were made the same size, so that narrow ones had to be made unduly wide and wide ones too thin; sometimes they were ornamented to look like twigs or twisted plants; often different styles were mixed.

In the late 19th and early 20th centuries artists turned again to the Roman inscriptions and medieval manuscripts, and designed alphabets based on traditional lettering. Edward Johnston (1872–1944), one of the greatest of these masters of the art of lettering, was anxious to see good lettering everywhere—on foundation stones, street-name plates, advertisements, and every kind of notice. He designed an alphabet without serifs ('sans serif') which was used in the London Underground railways; and from this sans serif printing types were developed in the 1930's.

Modern craftsmen know, as the Romans did, that not only are the proportions of the letters important but that the materials used should determine the style of letter: painted letters should be large enough to allow the full use of the brush; very small letters are difficult to cut in stone; a close-grained material, such as metal, is best for fine and subtle lettering; raised letters take longer to cut out of any material than incised ones, but they are usually more legible. It is realized, too, that the refined lettering of Trajan's Column is not suitable for all purposes of modern display, and that variety of style gives interest. But good lettering, whatever the style, has always followed the proportions of Roman letters.

See also Vol. IV: HANDWRITING.

LETTERS. Personal letters, which unite description with individual feeling, so that the personality of the writer is revealed, are an interesting literary form. Very few such letters have survived from the Middle Ages in England. People wrote only when they had something important to say, and letters were usually brief and

LETTERING OF 1850
From the title-page of the first edition of Dickens's
David Copperfield

awkwardly stiff in style. One of the earliest surviving, written about 1400 when English was only just becoming the language of all classes, shows what difficulty people had in writing personal notes. Dame Mountford wrote to her cousin in haste:

Tres chere cousin, je vous prie bring a writ of trespass envers Richard Ford of Solihull . . . the which trespass they did to the walley (value) of twenty marks . . . inscrit en haste en la manere de Cod-barrow.

In the 15th century several families of land-owners wrote series of business letters in English which have been preserved. The most famous of these collections is the *Paston Letters*, which give us many interesting glimpses of the times. Although there are some hundreds of such letters, very few have such a delightful personal note as the one in the *Stonor Letters* from the merchant Thomas Betson to the lady who was soon to marry him and who was then 12 years old:

Be a good eater of your meat alway, that ye may wax and grow fast to be a woman . . . and to greet well my horse and pray him to give you four of his years to help you withal. . . . Written at Calais the first of June, when every man was gone to his dinner, and the clock smote noon and all our household cried after me and bad me come down. 'Come down to dinner at once!'

More letters have survived from the 16th and 17th centuries, but although they are less awkward, they are mostly written in an elaborate, dignified style without personal warmth. The letters of Dorothy Osborne (1627–95), however, written to her future husband, Sir William Temple, are an exception. She described her own moods, her pleasures, such as wandering in the garden at night to smell the jasmine, and the books she read. She teased Sir William and gave humorous descriptions of her neighbours, including Sir Justinian Isham, the pompous widower with four daughters, who wished to marry her:

Would you think it, I have an ambassador from the Emperor Justinian that comes to renew the treaty [i.e. of marriage]? In earnest, 'tis true, and I want your counsel extremely, what to do in it. You told me once that of all my servants [i.e. those who wished to marry her] you liked him the best. If I could do so too, there were no dispute in't. Well, I'll think on't, and if it succeed I'll be as good as my word; you shall take your choice of my four daughters.

She went to the heart of the matter when she wrote:

All letters methinks should be free and easy as one's discourse; not studied as an oration, nor made up of hard words like a charm.

The 18th century saw many great letter-writers. Jonathan SWIFT (q.v. Vol. V) wrote a series of letters, 1710–13, called *The Journal to Stella*, in which the formidable Dean told the inner story of his daily doings, his hopes and fears, pleasures and irritations. He often wrote in bed before or after sleep, in a scribble:

methinks when I write plain, I do not know how, but we are not alone, all the world can see us. A bad scrawl is so snug. . . .

He sometimes used a 'little language' of words known only to him and Stella. His letters were not meant for publication. His great friend POPE (q.v. Vol. V), on the other hand, caused his own letters (altered to show himself in a better light) to be published as if against his will; but they have lost their power to convince. The letters of Samuel JOHNSON (q.v. Vol. V) are an example of the more formal style of letter-writing. His most famous letter is the one to Lord Chesterfield (himself the author of a series of formal letters to his son on how to be a gentleman). Chesterfield offered Johnson help and patronage, but only when it was too late. Johnson wrote:

Is not a patron, my Lord, one who looks with un-concern on a man struggling for life in the water, and, when he has reached ground, encumbers him with help? The notice which you have been pleased to take of my labours, had it been early, had been kind; but it has been delayed till I am indifferent and cannot enjoy it, till I am solitary and cannot impart it, till I am known and do not want it.

Johnson did not always reply promptly to his friends:

Do not fancy that an intermission of writing is a decay of kindness. No man is always in a position to write; nor has any man at all times something to say.

Johnson's massive style lends itself to solemnity, but he could also be playful, and was sym-pathetic with his friends. The letters of William Cowper, mostly to his cousin Harriet Hesketh, are an example of informal letter-writing. He wrote in an easy, crystal-clear style with gaiety and gentle wit about all the tiny happenings

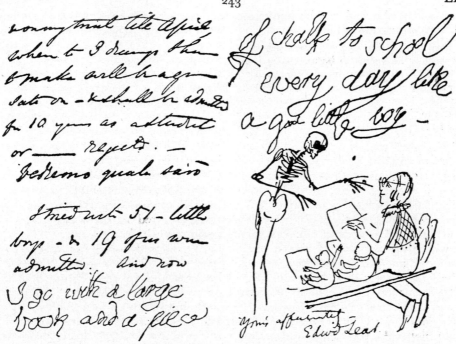

PART OF A LETTER FROM EDWARD LEAR
It describes how he joined the Royal Academy Schools in 1851. From *Letters of Edward Lear*, T. Fisher Unwin, 1907

of his quiet life at Olney. His interest makes the commonest things seem fresh:

The very stones in the garden walls are my intimate acquaintance. Everything I see in the fields is to me an object, and I can look at the same rivulet, or at a handsome tree, every day of my life with new pleasure.

When nothing happened he wrote a delightful letter on 'Nothing'. Rarely the underlying horror of his life—he thought he was damned—appeared:

My days are spent in Vanity. . . . Nature revives again; but a soul once slain lives no more.

From the end of the 18th century the formal style disappeared (except in the brief, crisp letters of the Duke of Wellington). Letters tended to become more and more like written talk, with a wide variety of subjects. All great letter-writers give us the feeling of meeting an exceptionally interesting person and of knowing him better than we know most people in life. No English letters do this more successfully than those of Charles LAMB (q.v. Vol. V). This 'most lovable of men' wrote to many people in many different moods, but his humour is everywhere present. An example of his easy lively manner comes from an early letter to COLERIDGE (q.v. Vol. V):

Godwin has called upon us. He spent one evening here. Was very friendly. Kept us up till midnight. Drank punch and talked about you. He seems above all men mortified at your going away. Suppose you were to write to the good-natured heathen. . . . I have scribbled over a queer letter, as I find by perusal; but it means no mischief.

I am, and ever will be, yours ever, in sober sadness,
C. L.

Write your German as plain as sunshine, for that must correct itself. You know I am homo unius linguae: in English illiterate, a dunce, a ninny.

It was once said of Lamb when old that 'in a jest or few light phrases, he would lay open his heart'. Jokes and puns did not prevent depth of feeling nor delicate sympathy. His letters also contain much pleasant and valuable literary criticism, as well as ideas and descriptions which he later treated more elaborately in his *Essays of Elia*.

In the letters of John KEATS (q.v. Vol. V) the drama of his short life unfolds. He wrote to Fanny Brawne, whom he loved, painfully moving letters. He wrote to his brother George and his other friends, describing his activities, his ambitions, the books he read, and his passionate thoughts about the nature of life:

You perhaps at one time thought there was such a thing as worldly happiness to be arrived at. . . . I scarcely remember counting on any happiness—I look not for it if it be not in the present hour—nothing startles me beyond the moment. The setting sun will always set me to rights—or if a sparrow come before my window I take part in its existence and pick about the gravel.

The letters of any historical character help to reveal his personality as nothing else does; but of the many interesting collections of letters in the 19th century there are few which stand really well on their own. Among the most interesting are those of Thomas CARLYLE (q.v. Vol. V) and his wife, with their wit and brilliance, their satirical humour, and their uneasy love for each other. The famous story of Robert and Elizabeth Barrett BROWNING (q.v. Vol. V) is best read in their many letters to each other. Towards the end of the century the letters of Gertrude Bell (1868–1926) not only reveal an outstanding personality—poet, scholar, fashionable woman, explorer—but also give us interesting information about the Arabs and tell a wonderful story of adventure, with all the zest and vivid detail which are among the marks of a good letter.

See also DIARIES; ESSAYS.

LIBERAL ARTS, see ART.

LIEDER, see SONG, HISTORY OF, Section 6.

LIMERICK, see COMIC VERSE, Section 3.

LITERARY CRITICISM. The word critic is derived from a Greek word meaning 'judge', and the literary critic's job is to interpret, weigh, and value literary works. Some critics aim at assessing the effects of literature on society and its influence on readers' minds; others are concerned with the techniques of writing—form, vocabulary, and style. Biographical critics inquire into a writer's life and try to assess how far the experiences of his life have influenced his writing. Some critics are most interested in the aesthetic and emotional impression a work makes on the mind of an intelligent reader. Criticism deals with both past and present literature; but not all countries or periods have produced much literary criticism. At some periods criticism has not been considered a

serious occupation for an intelligent man, while at others some of the greatest writers have turned their genius to this purpose. Primitive peoples accept all literature which satisfies the universal desire to listen to a story and to celebrate the brave deeds of their ancestors; they apply no critical judgement. Again, as criticism proceeds by comparison, the critic must know many works before he can properly criticize any. He must have books accessible, and these were rare before the invention of printing. An age in which there is a spirit of inquiry and analysis and a sceptical attitude to earlier authorities is likely to produce good literary criticism. Such conditions occurred in classical Greece but rarely again until the last 300 years.

The ancient Greek philosopher ARISTOTLE (q.v. Vol. V) laid the foundations of criticism in his brief and masterly *Poetics*, which has been discussed, attacked, and defended by critics ever since, but has never been refuted or superseded. His criticism dealt with such questions as why it is that events which in life would be painful and shocking can cause the highest pleasure when imitated in the theatre; he analysed devices of surprise and suspense, and laid down that a work should contain nothing irrelevant to its main subject.

There was no systematic criticism in English till the Restoration, and Johnson calls DRYDEN (q.v. Vol. V) the 'father of English criticism'. Dryden's *Essay of Dramatic Poesy* (1668) is a wide-ranging discussion in dialogue form of the merits of classical drama compared with the drama of his own time. At this time there were long discussions, both in England and France, about the so-called 'rules of composition' or 'unities' (*see* DRAMA), rules which, taking their authority from Aristotle, had become more rigid than Aristotle had ever advocated. French theory was more rigid than English. Dryden preached moderation in the application of rules.

In the 18th century critics laid great stress on smoothness and regularity in verse, and in their concern for order and propriety often took the side of the French against Dryden. Samuel JOHNSON (q.v. Vol. V), however, the finest critic of the period, approached literature through his extensive knowledge of life and character, and his *Lives of the Poets* (1779) has been called a 'masterpiece of the judicial bench'.

In the early 19th century the most important criticism was written by great poets who were impatient at what they thought the unreasonable restrictions imposed on 18th-century writers. WORDSWORTH (q.v. Vol. V), for instance, demanded that poetry should be written in the kind of language men actually speak. Criticism at this time was inclined to be intolerant, especially of 18th-century literature, just as, in a different way, the 18th-century critics had been intolerant of what did not agree with their ideas, especially of the METAPHYSICAL POETRY (q.v.) of the 17th century. Literary criticism at this time was represented by HAZLITT, whose essays range from criticism of Elizabethan drama to contemporary poets, and by COLERIDGE (qq.v. Vol. V).

With a few exceptions Victorian criticism is less successful. Matthew ARNOLD (q.v. Vol. V), in *Essays in Criticism* (1865) and other works, thought that literature should deal with moral ideas. Profoundly interested in problems of education and culture, he saw literature as a remedy for the distressing state of the world. His almost religious seriousness in dealing with literature has been imitated by some recent critics. Walter Pater (1839–94) was an aesthetic critic who ranged over a wide field of ancient and modern literature and art, and was himself an artist in words. It is noteworthy that though there have been many critics who were not themselves creative writers, most of the best and most celebrated ones have been.

Today the more serious newspapers and periodicals and the wireless have carried literary criticism to a wider public, but reviews in the remainder of the press frequently consist of no more than a description of a book in a very few lines with little serious judgement. Much of the best criticism published today is later reprinted in book form.

See also ESSAYS.

LITHOGRAPHY. This was originally a method of producing prints from a drawing made on stone, and some artists still use stone, although metal plates are now used commercially. The word is derived from the Greek words *lithos* (stone) and *graphein* (to draw).

Lithography is known as planographic or surface printing because the print is obtained from a flat surface, not, as in WOOD-ENGRAVING and ETCHING AND ENGRAVING (qq.v.), from a raised or hollowed surface. The process is based on the fact that grease and water do not mix. The artist makes his drawing with a greasy crayon or greasy ink upon the lithographic stone, which is a kind of limestone. The stone is then treated with gum and acid, and a damp cloth is wiped over it. The greasy strokes of the drawing repel the moisture, whereas the rest of the surface of the stone retains it. While the stone is still damp, greasy printing-ink is spread over it. The damp parts of the stone reject the ink, but it sticks to the greasy lines of the drawing. To obtain a print, paper is laid over the inked drawing, and pressure applied to transfer the ink from the stone to the paper.

As an artistic medium the advantage of lithography is its ability to give the most delicate as well as the richest tones on the same drawing. Carefully graded tones can be combined with free, dashing brushwork; textures can be obtained by spattering lithographic ink, and fine white lines made by scratching with a pointed instrument. Most important European painters since 1800 have produced lithographs; but although the artist himself draws on the stone or plate, it is usual for a printing craftsman to prepare and print it.

The process was discovered by a German named Senefelder about 1798. It became the chief medium for topographical prints, among the finest being those by Richard Parkes Bonington (1802–28). At first lithographs were made in black and white, colour being added by hand, as in some of the magnificent flower-books of that day. Later it became common to print all over the drawing a grey or buff tint from a second stone. By scraping through this tint, high-lights were obtained. Then came the practice of using several stones, each printing a different colour, to obtain richer effects. While delicate, transparent inks were used, the effect was delightful; but when printers used thick, opaque inks in an attempt to imitate oil paintings, the result was the unpleasant, though popular, oleograph of Victorian times.

Among the greatest lithographers are the Spanish painter GOYA (q.v. Vol. V), who made a magnificent series of bull-fighting scenes in 1825, and the French painter Honoré Daumier (1808–79), whose satirical cartoons are among the finest lithographs ever made (*see* CARICATURE). Other French artists used lithography, at first in black and white and later in colour, notably the Frenchman Toulouse-Lautrec (1864–1901), who lithographed many POSTERS (q.v.).

British Museum

THE FAMOUS AMERICAN BULLFIGHTER, MARIANO CEBALLOS. LITHOGRAPH BY GOYA (1746–1828)

It was not until after 1900 that artists in Britain began to use lithography to any extent, though since that time it has been used with great understanding. Since 1930 lithographic printing direct from the artist's plate has been a popular medium for book illustration, particularly of children's books.

For more than a century lithography has been used commercially as a purely reproductive process for the multiplication of maps, music, posters, labels, folders, and booklets. As a commercial process, photography has been applied to lithography so that it is no longer necessary for a draughtsman to draw on to the stone. Moreover, stone has been replaced by metal plates that can be treated so that they 'take' ink and water in much the same way as stone (*see* PROCESS REPRODUCTION, Section 5, Vol. VII).

See also WOOD-ENGRAVING AND WOODCUTS; ETCHING AND ENGRAVING.

See also Vol. IV: BOOKS, HISTORY OF; ILLUSTRATION.

LOUVRE. This palace of the French kings in Paris is probably the largest in the world. It was used as a royal palace until the abdication of Napoleon III in 1870, and is now used to house, among other things, two museums and a number of government offices. The building assumed its present shape by the joining of two distinct palaces several hundred yards apart. The first was the Louvre proper, originally a medieval castle, situated near the Seine; the second was the palace of the Tuileries which ran inland at right angles to the Seine. These two were united in the opening years of the 17th century by an immensely long building known as the Grande Galerie, which runs along the bank of the Seine. During the 17th century the east end of the building (where the old castle had been) was largely remodelled under Louis XIV. He summoned the great artist BERNINI (q.v. Vol. V) from Italy for the purpose; but the French statesmen and artists were so jealous that Louis had to dismiss Bernini and entrust the job instead to a brilliant French amateur, Claude Perrault. Perrault was responsible for the present east front, one of the greatest masterpieces of French architecture. At this period the Louvre and the Tuileries were still only joined on the river side to the south; the area between the north end of the Tuileries and Perrault's block was a maze of narrow streets and houses. There were repeated projects throughout the 17th and 18th centuries to demolish these and to build a long northern wing corresponding with the Grande Galerie on the south; but it was not till the mid-19th century that this was achieved. In 1871, during riots in Paris at the end of the Franco-Prussian War, the palace of the Tuileries was burnt down by the mob and it was never rebuilt. The two vast wings thus stretch westwards today from the site of the old castle and are not directly connected with each other.

The Louvre museum contains paintings, sculpture, and furniture from the former French royal collection, including two of the most famous works of art in the world—the so-called VENUS DE MILO (q.v.) and the portrait of Mona Lisa by LEONARDO DA VINCI (q.v. Vol. V). It is both the largest and the finest single museum in the world, combining most of the functions of three separate museums in London—the British Museum, the National Gallery, and the Victoria and Albert Museum (see ART GALLERIES). The less important objects of decorative art are housed in a separate museum (Musée des Arts Decoratifs) in part of the wing of the palace opposite to that occupied by the Louvre museum.

See also Vol. III: PARIS.

LYRIC POETRY. There were three kinds of poetry in Greece: EPIC (q.v.), Lyric, and Dramatic. Lyric was poetry accompanied by music, and its most splendid form was the choral ode. We use the term 'lyric poetry' in a very general way to signify poetry that is not narrative or dramatic: ODE, ELEGY, SONNET (qq.v.), all

Donald McLeish

THE EAST FRONT OF THE LOUVRE, PARIS, DESIGNED BY CLAUDE PERRAULT (1613–88)

belong to this class. But when we speak of 'a lyric' we mean a short poem conveying some thought or sentiment of the poet's own; and such a poem is usually divided into stanzas or 'strophes'.

Some lyrics are as familiar to us sung as spoken, and these lyrics are usually called songs. Such are Ben Jonson's 'Drink to me only with thine eyes'; the madrigals and lute-songs of the Elizabethans; the songs of Shakespeare's plays, like 'O Mistress Mine, Where are you roaming?'; and the German *Lieder* (songs) of the 18th and 19th centuries, of which Heine's are particularly well known (*see* SONGS). But the lyric that is no longer sung nor accompanied has not lost its music; the music is wrought into the poem in rhythm and rhyme and melodious sound-pattern.

There are lyrics in all languages, in all ages; and not only in Europe, but in China, India, Persia, everywhere. Here, for example, is a beautiful Red Indian love-song:

Early I rose
In the blue morning;
My love was up before me,
It came running up to me from the doorways of the
   Dawn.

On Papago Mountain
The dying quarry
Looked at me with my love's eyes.
                    (Translation by Mary Austin.)

Lyrics have a multitude of forms, an infinity of themes. They express whatever the heart can feel, the senses apprehend, or dream suggest; they sing of human love, of nature, and of God. And so, in an approximate way, they are love-songs, nature poems, or religious lyrics.

Although lyrics are universal, they are not always and among all peoples of equal excellence. Some ages and some cultures have been more fertile soil for the lyric than others; and most notably Greece in the 7th century B.C., Rome in the 1st century B.C., Provence in the 11th century, Renaissance Italy and France, England in the 16th and 17th centuries, and all Europe during the ROMANTIC MOVEMENT (q.v.) of the 19th century.

Little Greek lyric poetry has survived, and most of what has survived is contained in the *Greek Anthology* (*see* ANTHOLOGIES). Only fragments survive of the lyric poets whom the Greeks held in the highest esteem—Anacreon of the 6th century B.C., Alcaeus of the 7th century B.C., and his contemporary SAPPHO, the greatest of all women poets. The few of their poems that we know have some of the highest lyric qualities, simple spontaneity, passionate feeling, a moment of time with a suggestion of timelessness, a sequence that is imaginative, not logical; all these are present in such a lyric as this of Sappho's:

The moon has set,
And the Pleiades.
Time is passing, passing,
And still I lie alone.

Of Latin lyrists, the greatest are Catullus and HORACE; Catullus is best known for his passionate love-lyrics, such as the one beginning *Odi et amo* (I hate and I love), and for the poems in which he dwells on his brother's death—

Atque in perpetuum, frater, ave atque vale.
(So, brother, for all time, hail and farewell.)

Horace's lyrics, by contrast, are urbane, discreet, measured, with rhythms adapted from the Greek. He used in Latin the metres of the great Greek lyric poets, much as our own Elizabethan poets used the Italian sonnet form.

About A.D. 1100 rhyme first established itself throughout Europe, adding a new beauty and music to poetry and quickening the poetic impulse, first in Provence, then in northern France, Germany, Italy, England, Scandinavia. New forms were invented in great variety, the Provençal poets, for example, aimed at never using the same stanza twice. The basic measure of their lyrics was the 10-syllabled line; this became one of the most important metrical lines, for it later appears in the sonnet, and it is the 'heroic' line, the metre of England's greatest poetry (*see* VERSIFICATION).

By the 14th century many lyrical forms, mainly French and Italian, had established themselves, among them the 14-line sonnet, the 'rondeau', in which the opening words are twice repeated, and only two rhymes are used throughout the 10 lines; and the 'ballade', a longer form of two or three 8-line stanzas in which a refrain is interwoven. In Villon's 'Ballade of Dead Ladies', for example, each of the three stanzas describes women famous for their beauty in bygone days, and each ends with the refrain, 'But where are the snows of other years?' The ballade usually ends with an 'envoy', that is, a short stanza addressing a princely personage.

In England, lyric poetry has been, since the 14th century, one of the main glories of the literature. In the 14th and 15th centuries, four out of every five lyrics were religious. One of the most beautiful of these religious lyrics, found in a 15th-century manuscript, has for its theme the Virgin Mary:

> I sing of a maiden
> that is makeles,
> King of all kings
> to her son she ches.
>
> He came also stylle
> ther his mother was
> As dew in Aprylle
> that falleth on the gras.
>
> He came also stylle
> to his mother's bower
> As dew in Aprylle
> that falleth on the flower.
>
> He came also stylle
> ther his mother lay,
> As dew in Aprylle
> that falleth on the spray.
>
> Mother and maiden
> was never none but she.
> Well may such a lady
> Godes mother be.

(The spelling is partly modernized.)

CHAUCER, by introducing French and Italian forms and metres, made the 14th-century lyric more supple and various; but two lesser poets of the 16th century, Wyatt and Surrey, were greater in their influence. With them begins the English Renaissance in poetry. They introduced into England a knowledge and love of the French and Italian lyric poetry, with the dignity, restraint, and simplicity it had derived from classical models. They are precursors of the great Elizabethan lyrists, SPENSER, SIDNEY, SHAKESPEARE, Ben JONSON, DONNE; and of their successors, HERRICK, who sang 'Of brooks, of blossoms, birds and bowers', the METAPHYSICAL poets (q.v.), and MILTON and Marvell. This was the great age of song and lyric in England; and many collections and anthologies of this period have anonymous poems as beautiful as those by famous poets. The subtlety and richness of classical and Renaissance diction, the elaborate rhyming of Provence forms, the alliteration of Old English, and the refrain which was characteristic of such folk-songs as ballad and carol, all lend something to the perfection of such a lyric as this from *The Tempest*:

> Full fathom five thy father lies;
>   Of his bones are coral made;
> Those are pearls that were his eyes;
>   Nothing of him that doth fade
> But doth suffer a sea-change
>   Into something rich and strange.
> Sea-nymphs hourly ring his knell
>   Ding-dong.
> Hark! now I hear them,—ding-dong-bell.

The main stream of 18th-century poetry is not lyrical. But BLAKE and BURNS, at the end of the 18th century, were great English lyric poets. The true singing tone of Robert Burns's poems derives from the old Scottish airs for which he made them. His love-poetry, celebrating his many loves, is strong, ardent, warm:

> Oh, my love's like a red, red rose,
>   That's newly sprung in June;
> Oh, my love's like the melody
>   That's sweetly played in tune.
>
> As fair art thou, my bonny lass,
>   So deep in love am I;
> And I will love thee still, my dear,
>   Till a' the seas gang dry.
>
> Till a' the seas gang dry, my dear,
>   And the rocks melt wi' the sun:
> I will love thee still, my dear,
>   While the sands o' life shall run.
>
> And fare thee well, my only love!
>   And fare thee well a while!
> And I will come again, my love,
>   Though it were ten thousand mile.

William Blake is above all a poet of the imagination. He gave most of his life to composing long prophetic works, which are obscure and difficult. His lyrics, published in *Poetical Sketches* (1783), *Songs of Innocence* (1789), and *Songs of Experience* (1794), seemingly simple and clear, sing themselves more easily into the memory than the understanding. Blake himself described his songs as 'showing the two contrary states of the human soul'; that is, innocence and experience. To present spiritual states and events, he uses symbols; he does this in a striking way when he symbolizes the two contrary states of the human soul, in *Songs of Innocence* as the lamb:

> Little Lamb, who made thee?
> Dost thou know who made thee?

and in *Songs of Experience* as the tiger:

> Tyger! Tyger! burning bright
> In the forests of the night,
> What immortal hand or eye
> Could frame thy fearful symmetry?

The 19th century brought, in all the arts, a revolt against the formalized decorum of the 18th century, and this revolt we call the ROMANTIC MOVEMENT (q.v.). Lyric, the poetry of emotion and passion and imagination, burst into new flame. GOETHE in Germany, Leopardi in Italy, Victor HUGO in France, Lermontov in Russia, and in England a galaxy of poets— WORDSWORTH, COLERIDGE, KEATS, SHELLEY, BYRON, SCOTT—were among the many creators of the new lyric poetry. What these poets had in common was the belief that imagination is the most powerful faculty of man; that the world created by the imagination can illumine the familiar world; and that this world of the imagination is best revealed by particular instances of the familiar world. They believed that you are able, in Blake's words:

> To see a World in a Grain of Sand
> And a Heaven in a Wild Flower,
> Hold Infinity in the palm of your hand
> And Eternity in an hour.

The poets who set more store by imagination than reason were not content with the poetic forms of the 18th century; they revived the old forms of BALLAD and FOLK-SONG (qq.v.), the intricate rhyming forms of the Renaissance, especially the sonnet, and adapted the classical forms of ode and elegy to suit their themes. They wrote of nature, love, beauty, freedom, and death. They wrote few poems which could by orthodox measure be termed religious; but some of their nature poems record the spiritual experience of communion with nature, and are very near to religious lyrics in their awe, their fervour, their love. This great flame of poetry died as quickly as it flared. Some of its poets died young, some suffered death of the imagination. But its glow lived on in the lyrics of the Victorian age. And none of the many and great lyrists since their day is without debt to the Romantic poets, however indirectly—a thought that echoes back from the first stanza of this lyric of Shelley's:

> Music, when soft voices die,
> Vibrates in the memory;
> Odours, when sweet violets sicken,
> Live within the sense they quicken.

> Rose leaves, when the rose is dead,
> Are heap'd for the belovèd's bed;
> And so thy thoughts, when thou art gone,
> Love itself shall slumber on.

The poets whose names are printed in capital letters have biographies in Volume V.

See also POETRY; ENGLISH LITERATURE

M

MADRIGAL, *see* SONGS, Section 2.

MAGAZINES, *see* PERIODICALS. *See also* Vol. IV: MAGAZINES AND PERIODICALS.

MANUSCRIPTS, *see* ILLUMINATED MANUSCRIPTS.

MASQUE, *see* Vol. IX: MASQUE.

MASS, MUSIC FOR, *see* SACRED MUSIC.

MAUSOLEUM, *see* TOMBS; WONDERS OF THE WORLD.

MEDALS. The first medals, which date from Roman times, developed from COINS (q.v. Vol. VII), which they resembled, having profile portraits with a laurel wreath on the front (obverse), and allegorical designs, often taken from the major works of art of the time, on the back (reverse). Medals were used as gifts or rewards to commemorate or record great events in public or private life and to express and gratify pride in achievement. The vast number of medals made throughout the world provides an indelible record of history. They are awarded by learned societies, institutions, sports associations, and so on, and in greater numbers by the Crown or head of the State for services rendered to the country. State or official medals are worn as a decoration, and each medal has its own coloured ribbon from which to suspend it (*see* MEDALS AND DECORATIONS, Vol. X).

Medals can be made in limited numbers by making a model the actual size of the medal and moulding and casting from it; this permits bold relief in the modelling. The more usual method is to strike or stamp the device on a blank disk of a softer metal, such as gold, silver, or copper, from a hard metal die that has been engraved by hand. In this method the relief is usually low. This delicate art of engraving is called die-sinking, and is derived from the very ancient art of gem engraving. It was practised as early as the 7th and 6th centuries B.C. in Greece, when coins were first introduced. Dies are engraved on special steel with chisels and punches. The design is drawn in reverse with a sharp steel point on the flat, smooth surface of the die, and hollowed out with chisels to form a mould. Repeated patterns are impressed into the steel with punches. The delicate details of the engraving are finished with minute chiselling aided by small files and tiny points of oil-stone. The steel die is hardened and tempered before the medals are struck.

The moulding and casting method was much favoured by artists during the Renaissance in Italy and was used by the great medallist and painter Antonio Pisano, called Pisanello (*c.* 1395–*c.* 1455), and his followers. The work of this artist and his successors reached an unsurpassed degree of perfection.

For the obverse the artist would model in wax a portrait, invariably in profile; for the symbolic and allegorical designs on the reverse Pisanello sometimes included reliefs of animals and birds with extraordinarily fine detail, or scenes which, though only an inch or so wide, suggest space and atmosphere. Though none of the medallists

Victoria & Albert Museum

BRONZE MEDAL CAST BY PISANELLO
Malatesta Novello, whose portrait is on the other side, kneels at the foot of the Cross

British Museum

BRONZE MEDAL OF OLIVER CROMWELL STRUCK FROM A
HAND-ENGRAVED DIE BY THOMAS SIMON, 1653

when the transition from manual or hammer striking of coins and medals to mechanical or press methods was taking place. Die-sinking was still done by hand, and Simon was skilled in this technique, as well as in modelling medals in wax to be cast into metal and chased. The designs on the reverses of some of his medals are most minute in detail, and include scenes with many figures, such as the sitting House of Commons on the medal commemorating the battle of Dunbar (1650), or the naval engagement on the reverse of the Naval Reward Medal of 1653, commemorating victories over the Dutch. Simon's medals are remarkable for their vivid portraiture, particularly of Cromwell and Charles II.

In the 19th century die-engraving by hand was superseded by the pantograph die-engraving machine, with which an artist's design can be reduced and cut mechanically on the die. All important medals or coins are now struck from machine-engraved dies, and the hand die-engraver's place has been taken by the sculptor or modeller. The invention of the engraving machine has widened the scope of the art, bringing new possibilities of beauty or extravagance to the medal. The artist makes his wax relief model about four or six times larger than the ultimate medal, and casts it in plaster of paris.

of the Renaissance approached this master's grandeur of style, imagination, or sensitive modelling, it was a time when many fine medals were made.

The finest English die-engraver was Thomas Simon (c. 1623–65), who was working at a time

CORONATION MEDAL OF H.M. QUEEN ELIZABETH II STRUCK
FROM A MACHINE-ENGRAVED DIE BY CECIL THOMAS, F.R.B.S.,
1953

LEFT: THE FUNERAL OF PRESIDENT CARNOT, 1894. MEDAL
STRUCK FROM A MACHINE-ENGRAVED DIE BY OSCAR ROTY

From this a copper electrotype or a metal casting is made, which is placed at one end of the panto-graph arm of the engraving machine. At the other end of the arm, the cutting or reducing end, is a blank steel die. The model and the die revolve in unison, and as they turn a feeler, like a gramophone needle, passes over the model. A corresponding cutter at the other end of the machine reproduces in miniature in the steel die the forms of the model. When the dies are hardened they can be used in presses capable of exerting a pressure up to 100 tons for the striking of the medal.

Now that medals can be easily produced in great numbers, they are used, especially in France, to commemorate even domestic events, or are produced solely for collectors. This has resulted in the development of the plaque or one-sided medal which is often not circular in shape.

See also Bronze Sculpture.
See also Vol. VII: Coins.
See also Vol. X: Medals and Decorations.

MEDIEVAL ART, EARLY.

After the Roman Empire had been overwhelmed by successive waves of barbarian invasion in the 5th century, a great contrast developed between the art of the Mediterranean regions and that of northern Europe. While both Italian and Byzantine Art (qq.v.) retained links with the art of Greece and Rome, the peoples north of the Alps reverted to an art which was similar to that of the Celtic people of the Iron Age (see Prehistoric Art, Section 4). They used art mainly to decorate small portable objects such as arms, horse trappings, and household utensils. Much of their work is very fine, for the craftsmanship is precise, and the abstract patterns which they employed are related to the shapes of the objects which they wished to decorate. The metalwork is enriched with coloured enamels and with inlays of garnet and coral.

Beautiful work was produced in England both by the British and by their Saxon conquerors. The people who especially excelled in these arts, however, were the Irish, for their native culture had developed undisturbed by either Roman or barbarian invasions. Irish art had been stimulated by the introduction of Christianity. St. Patrick, who began his mission in 432, probably taught the people the art of writing and inspired them to produce the ornaments

Courtauld Institute

CROSS AT MONASTERBOICE, IRELAND, ERECTED BY MUIDACH, ABBOT OF MONASTERBOICE, WHO DIED IN 923

and vessels needed for the church services. Irish Christianity depended almost entirely on the monasteries and, in order to build permanent dwellings for the monks on the remote and rocky headlands which were their favourite abodes, huts shaped like bee-hives were erected, which, unlike the dwellings of the peasantry, were built of stone (see Dwellings, Primitive, Vol. XI). These monasteries also had a small oratory and a high ceremonial pillar. At first the pillars were decorated with a simple incised cross, but gradually they took the form of crosses themselves and, by the 8th century, they were often decorated with interlace, strap-work, fantastic animals, and even human figures (see Crosses, Stone). These crosses are among the first examples of monumental carving in Europe. The Irish were great missionaries. From a monastery on the Scottish island of Iona, Irish missionaries converted Northumbria, bringing

THE ANNUNCIATION TO THE SHEPHERDS. ILLUMINATION
FROM THE GOSPELS OF THE EMPEROR HENRY II, 1002–14

The wings, drapery, and large hands, set against an empty
gold ground, give great emotional force to the scene

their art as well as their religion. Two of the
finest of the high crosses are found in northern
England (*see* Plate 6).

At about the same time the monks began to
decorate their manuscripts. The earliest of
these, which is called the Book of Durrow, contains some pages which are completely covered
with decoration of the same kind as that used in
metalwork, curious representations of the Evangelists' symbols and great decorated initial
letters. This art, like that of the crosses, was
transplanted to Northumbria, and one of the
most magnificent of these ILLUMINATED MANU-
SCRIPTS (q.v.) is the Lindisfarne Gospels.

Christian missionaries came to Northumbria
from Rome as well as from Ireland, and probably brought with them works of art. Consequently the style of the Northumbrian crosses
and manuscripts is a mixture of the Irish with
its love of decoration and of Byzantine art with
its tradition of naturalistic figures. The art
which resulted was carried by Irish and Northumbrian monks to continental Europe.

When in 771 CHARLEMAGNE (q.v. Vol. V)
became ruler of the Franks, he sought the help
of the Church at Rome in reforming the
monasteries, setting up schools, and converting
the heathen Saxons by the sword. Owing to his
personal initiative great changes were brought
about in architecture and art. His most impressive building is his cathedral at Aachen
(Aix-la-Chapelle), his capital city, in which an
attempt is made to copy the 6th-century
octagonal church of San Vitale at Ravenna.
More important for the future development of
architecture are the great abbey churches, such
as those of St. Gall and St. Riquier, which are
built on the basilican plan with a nave and two
aisles, but have transepts both at the crossing
and the west end, and a western apse.

It is known that many of the churches of
Charlemagne and his successors were decorated
with wall-paintings and stucco reliefs, but
nothing remains to indicate their appearance.
Sometimes, as in the cathedral of Aachen,
mosaics, columns, and marble facings were
brought back from Italy to add to the effect of
magnificence. It is practically certain that
Charlemagne brought manuscripts, ivory carvings, and other small objects from Italy also,
and he may have introduced southern craftsmen. The models which the scribes of his own
palace and of the different monasteries copied
must have been of varying schools and periods,
for only in this way is it possible to explain the

HEADSTONE OF A GRAVE OF A VIKING BURIED ON THE SITE OF
ST. PAUL'S CATHEDRAL, *c.* 1035

The carving represents a fight between a lion and a serpent.
The body of the serpent and the tail of the lion develop
into leaves and stems

A. Gardner

THE ROMSEY ROOD. LATE 11TH-CENTURY CRUCIFIXION ON
THE WALL OF ROMSEY ABBEY, HANTS

The body is naturalistically treated and very sensitively
modelled

astonishing variety of styles to be found in the illumination and ivory carving of the Carolingian period.

The second half of the 9th century was a very unsettled period. Charlemagne's empire broke up after his death, and the coasts of England, Ireland, and the Continent were raided by the heathen VIKINGS (q.v. Vol. I) from Scandinavia, who burnt both monasteries and cities. The Vikings themselves brought with them a highly developed and very beautiful form of animal ornament.

In the late 9th century King Alfred re-established order in England, and the Vikings, who had conquered about half the country, were absorbed and converted. In Germany, which had formed the eastern part of Charlemagne's empire, the dukes of Saxony set up a strong rule. Finally, 200 years after Charlemagne the Emperor Otto I established a close alliance with the Church and also became a great patron of

architecture and art. A number of magnificent churches and cathedrals were built during the 10th and 11th centuries in Germany, and illumination, IVORY CARVING, and BRONZE SCULPTURE (qq.v.) were all brought to great perfection at this time (*see* GERMAN ART).

In England in Saxon times many churches were built, but very little of the original work remains to show us what they were like. The smaller parish churches were often embellished by little arcades with round pillars, and the outside walls were decorated with arcades (*see* CHURCH ARCHITECTURE, ENGLISH). Large-scale sculpture as well as small ivories were produced, in which the figures are firmly modelled and rounded in a way which recalls the work of Greece and Rome. The artists seem to have drawn their inspiration mainly from late Carolingian art. The Anglo-Saxon manuscript illuminations have a richness and a sense of unity between figures and decoration which seems to be a heritage from Irish art.

By the end of the 11th century new tendencies can be seen in the art of almost all countries, and the way was prepared for the monumental ROMANESQUE ART (q.v.) which spread through Europe in the 12th century.

MEDIEVAL ROMANCE, *see* ROMANCE LITERATURE; ARTHURIAN LITERATURE.

MELODY AND RHYTHM. Music consists of sounds arranged in patterns, and these patterns are usually dependent on the pitch of the sounds, that is, whether they are high or low, and their duration in time—whether they are long or short. The arrangement according to the duration and accentuation of the sounds is called 'rhythm', and 'melody' when there are also variations in pitch. The two are very closely connected; it is possible to have rhythm without melody—a clock ticking or a drum beating produce a rhythm but no melody—but melody without rhythm is impossible.

Rhythm in music must not be confused with the 'time-value' or length of the notes; it is concerned with the grouping of the notes by accenting certain of them. Normally the accents occur at regular intervals, nowadays indicated by dividing the music into bars containing an equal number of beats. The number of beats in each bar is shown by the 'time signature' (*see* MUSICAL NOTATION, Section 6). In the example given in

Fig. 1 *a* the relative length of the notes is clear. But if the tune is sung to the words 'Down the

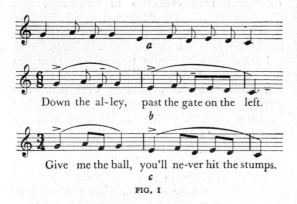

Down the al-ley,   past the gate on the   left.

b

Give   me the ball,   you'll ne-ver hit the stumps.

c

FIG. 1

alley, past the gate on the left' (Fig. 1 *b*), its rhythm is quite different from what it would be if it were sung to 'Give me the ball, you'll never hit the stumps' (Fig. 1 *c*). In Fig. 1 *b* there are two main beats (each subdivided into three) in a bar ($\frac{6}{8}$ time), and in 1 *c* there are three main beats (subdivided into two) in a bar ($\frac{3}{4}$ time). The first beat in each bar has the strongest accent.

Sometimes the regular rhythm is disturbed by accenting beats which are normally weak. This is called SYNCOPATION (q.v.).

Notes of any pitch may be used to make a melody but a random choice of notes does not produce a melody which sounds well to our ears. Musicians have always selected a group of sounds on which to build their melodies. Their selection has been governed by different ideas at different times and in different places; the result has been a great variety in the sound of melodies. To people who are used to the type of melodies found in Western music of the last 300 years, ORIENTAL MUSIC (q.v.) sounds strange and discordant, just as Western music must sound incomprehensible to the Chinese.

The selections of sounds on which melodies are based are called SCALES (q.v.). Most Western music since the early 17th century is based on the major and minor scales, though some composers now use others (*see* MODERN MUSIC). Melodies based on the major and minor scales do not always use only the notes of the scale (or key) in which they are written; they may introduce other notes or they may change to a different key. In the latter case the melody will usually return to the original key.

An analysis of the folk tune 'All Through

the Night' shows how the melody is constructed (Fig. 2). The 'sections' are the smallest units which form patterns; they are grouped together to form 'phrases'. The broad rhythmic pattern is achieved by an accent on the first note and the middle note of each section (the first note of each bar); the third note of each bar has a slighter accent. Repetition plays an important part in the pattern. Both the rhythm and melody of sections A and B are repeated no less than three times. The rhythm of section C^1 is repeated in C^2, but the melody is given interest by variety; it consists of two descending groups of four notes, similar in shape to the second half of C^1 but on different notes, so that each group starts on a fresh note. Similarly the rhythm of each half of section A is similar, but the pitch of the notes varies.

PHRASE 1ᵃ

Section A1   Section B1

PHRASE 1ᵇ

Section A2   Section B2

PHRASE 2

Section C1   Section C2

PHRASE 1ᶜ

Section A3   Section B3

FIG. 2

The most important notes in the scale are the first, called the 'tonic' or 'keynote', and the third and fifth, which together form the tonic chord on which a piece of music nearly always concludes (*see* HARMONY). To achieve an effect of finality the melody has to end on one of the notes of the tonic chord. In 'All Through the Night' the melody, which is in the key of G major, ends on G, the keynote, and this gives the feeling of a satisfactory finish. The other appearances of Phrase 1 also end on the keynote, but, because the rhythmic pattern is not felt to be complete until the end, the music is kept going. Phrase 2, on the other hand, ends on the

LA PREMIÈRE SORTIE. OIL PAINTING BY PIERRE AUGUSTE RENOIR, 1841–1919

semitone below the keynote, and this carries the music on into Phrase 1 c.

The pattern of phrases in 'All Through the Night' is only one of many patterns which are used in building up melodies (see MUSICAL FORM). They are all based on the principle of the balance of repeated and contrasted phrases. In the repetitions the rhythm is often the same, but the pitch of the notes may vary. The rhythm of the first two lines of 'God Save the Queen' is the same, but the notes of the melody change. If the rhythm changed it would give the same effect of lameness that a couplet of poetry would give if it had too many syllables in the second line or accents in the wrong places (see VERSIFICATION).

At the end of every phrase in a melody there is a feeling of pause, sometimes only slight (as at the end of Phrase 2, Fig. 2), sometimes more definite (as at the end of Phrase 1). These pauses, or 'cadences', have exactly the same function as punctuation in literature; they divide the musical sentence into smaller sections, making it more intelligible because they make its structure clearer.

Most melodies will be found to depend on these principles, which are capable of great subtlety, variety, and elaboration. Composers, however, often rely not upon fully organized and complete melodies, but upon fragments of themes, sometimes part of a melody which is not heard in its complete form until in a late stage of the work.

Different types of melodies and rhythms are associated with definite ideas and subjects. Dances have particular rhythms; the rhythm of the waltz, for instance, is made up of groups of three notes, and marches are always in a steady rhythm with the chief accent on the first of each four beats. A lilting melody flowing gently from one note to another may suggest a lullaby, and one with strong contrasts of pitch, such as 'The British Grenadiers', is stirring and gives a sense of activity.

This association of melody and rhythm with definite ideas is a powerful help to composers, who can suggest the solemn tread of the funeral march or the gay movement of a polka. Rhythm can impart to music the sense of repose as well as the sense of movement, and it is to a large extent his imaginative use of the opportunities offered by these powers of rhythm and melody that determines a composer's musical character.

See also MUSIC; HARMONY; MUSICAL NOTATION; SCALES.

METAPHOR, see FIGURES OF SPEECH, Section 1.

METAPHYSICAL POETRY. 1. Poets often express their meaning indirectly by comparison or by implied comparison, that is, metaphor. In the 17th century some poets used unexpected metaphors, in order, by associating things fantastically unlike in themselves, to command the startled reader's attention. To this group of writers Dryden, and later Dr. Johnson, attached the odd label 'metaphysical' as a term of reproach for the speculative and learned quality of their poetry.

The name has stuck. But to us now 'metaphysical' implies not only the characteristic usage of learned and witty expressions and the far-fetched imagery which Dr. Johnson deplored, but the bold, questioning spirit of the 17th century—a century of revolution in philosophy, politics, economics, and social affairs. In philosophy, ideas which had been accepted for hundreds of years were challenged, and a new movement to discover the secrets of nature by experiment gained ground. In politics the violent reaction to the doctrine of the divine right of kings led to the CIVIL WAR (q.v. Vol. X), the execution of Charles I, and the establishment of the Protectorate in 1649. The middle classes—mainly Puritan and Parliamentarian—vastly increased their power at the expense of the King's party. Although the metaphysical poets were nearly all of the King's party, they were all, as products of that revolutionary period, affected in some way by the new spirit of revolt against authority.

John DONNE (q.v. Vol. V) is the first of the metaphysical school both in time and fame, and his work includes the two major themes of the metaphysical poets, love and religion. His love-poetry, passionate, mature, and harsh, treats of the relation between himself and woman; his religious poetry of the relation between God the eternal and himself a mortal. His successors in love-poetry—Carew, Suckling, and Lovelace—and in religious poetry—Herbert, Vaughan, Crashaw, and Traherne—while sharing his themes and using many of the techniques he used, were very different from him and from one another in their approach and attitude.

2. *Metaphysical Love Poets.* Thomas Carew (1598–1639), who spent most of his life in embassies and at the Court, wrote a fine elegy to

Donne, many love-poems and songs, and a masque. His writing is elegant, urbane, sophisticated in matter and manner. Let us compare a couplet from his contemporary HERRICK (q.v. Vol. V):

> Sweet, be not proud of those two eyes,
> Which starlike sparkle in their skies;

with a stanza from Carew which also compares a woman's eyes with stars:

> Ask me no more where those stars 'light
> That downwards fall in dead of night;
> For in your eyes they sit and there
> Fixèd become, as in their sphere.

How much more striking Carew's version is, interweaving the felt strangeness of stars falling with the intellectual strangeness of astronomy, giving the metaphor such force as overcomes our resistance to it.

Carew's friend, Sir John Suckling (1609–42), the first of Pope's 'Mob of Gentlemen who wrote with Ease', is remembered chiefly for his 'Ballad Upon a Wedding' and for his graceful, gay, witty love-poems:

> Why so pale and wan, fond lover?
>   Prithee, why so pale?
> Will, when looking well can't move her,
>   Looking ill prevail?
>   Prithee, why so pale?

Richard Lovelace (1618–58), handsome, cultivated, idealistic, and loyal, who suffered imprisonment and impoverishment in the King's cause, wrote courtly and miscellaneous songs, celebrating honour, beauty, and love. Two of them, 'To Althea, from Prison' and 'To Lucasta, Going to the Wars', are among the best-known poems of this period:

> Stone walls do not a prison make,
>   Nor iron bars a cage;
> Minds innocent and quiet take
>   That for an hermitage;
> If I have freedom in my love,
>   And in my soul am free;
> Angels alone that soar above
>   Enjoy such liberty.

Abraham Cowley and Andrew Marvell both wrote some metaphysical poetry. Some of Marvell's best poetry combines the wit and subtlety of the metaphysical poet with the grace of the cavalier, the seriousness of the Puritan, and the elegance of one who has taken Greek poetry as a model.

3. *Metaphysical Religious Poets.* This period produced four of the greatest of English religious poets. George Herbert (1593–1633), a priest of the Church of England, published most of his poems in one volume, *The Temple.* Of his poetry he says it presents 'a picture of the many spiritual conflicts that have passed betwixt God and my soul, before I could subject mine to the will of Jesus, my Master'. This drama is presented with quiet intensity of tone, in simple terse language, with—in spite of his great learning—homely similes, and with form and rhythm matched to the ebb and flow of his mood. A famous example of this is 'The Collar', which begins:

> I struck the board, and cried, No more!
>   I will abroad.

and ends,

> But as I raved and grew more fierce and wild
>   At every word,
> Methought I heard one calling, *Child!*
>   And I replied, *My Lord.*

Richard Crashaw (1612–49), much influenced by the Spanish mystics, joined the Church of Rome in 1645. To him religion is the soul's pursuit of the knowledge and love of God, which he expresses in the ardent images of physical love. Sensuous, musical, ecstatic at its best, at its worst it succumbs to a jungle-growth of extravagant 'conceit'. Here is a stanza from 'The Weeper', celebrating the tears of Mary Magdalene, interesting to compare with the stanza quoted from Carew above:

> Heavens thy fair eyes be;
> Heavens of ever-falling stars;
> 'Tis seed-time still with thee
> And stars thou sowest, whose harvest dares
> Promise the earth to countershine
> Whatever makes Heaven's forehead fine.

Henry Vaughan (1621–95), known as 'the Silurist' because of his love of his native Brecknockshire, a county once inhabited by an ancient British tribe, the Silures, sees the soul of man in darkness longing to return to the unwavering light of God and eternity:

> I saw eternity the other night
> Like a great ring of pure and endless light,
> All calm, as it was bright:

His religious poems were published in a volume called *Silex Scintillans,* and comprise many evangelical and devotional pieces from amongst which the great contemplative poems stand out.

Thomas Traherne's (1637–74) poems, not published during his lifetime, first appeared in a volume printed in 1903 from a manuscript discovered in a London bookstall. Traherne, a devout Anglican, celebrates the joy of childhood and the wonder of the revelation of God in earth and sky and sea, flowers and grains of sand and 'especially Ones Self'. His are songs of innocence, not songs of experience.

The metaphysical poets have never enjoyed such appreciation as in our time. The active intellect confronting new ideas, the passionate sensuality which produces equally love-poetry or religious poetry, the muscular subtlety of language and wit which results from rebellion against convention and cliché, all these are sympathetic to the 20th century.

METRE, *see* VERSIFICATION.

MEZZOTINT, *see* ETCHING AND ENGRAVING, Section 6.

MINIATURES. These are small paintings; although the term can be applied to paintings in medieval ILLUMINATED MANUSCRIPTS (q.v.), it is commonly used for small separate paintings, generally portraits. The vogue for miniature portraits lasted over 300 years, from about 1520 to 1850. Early miniatures were usually painted in WATER-COLOURS (q.v.) on vellum mounted on a piece of card (often cut from a playing-card); after 1700, miniaturists began to paint on polished ivory with more transparent colours, and attained great brilliance.

The miniature arose out of the merging of two traditions, that of the illuminated manuscripts and that of the metallic portrait MEDALS (q.v.), which are the earliest kind of miniature portrait; these were round—and so were the first miniatures, such as those by Holbein. But miniature portraits are the most intimate form of painting, made for relatives or for lovers, to be worn as jewels on the dress or carried about as a love token, often worn over the heart. Their shape, therefore, was soon modified from round to oval to suit the conventional locket form. Their frames were often of gold and set with precious stones of great value.

Although the British have always excelled in miniature painting, the first miniature artist of

Victoria & Albert Museum
A YOUNG MAN WITH A BACKGROUND OF FLAMES. MINIATURE BY NICHOLAS HILLIARD (*c.* 1547–1619)

importance was the German-Swiss, Hans HOLBEIN (q.v. Vol. V), who painted some of the finest miniatures in the world. The greatest 16th-century British artist, Nicholas Hilliard (*c.* 1547–1619), was a miniaturist. Son of an Exeter goldsmith and trained as a goldsmith, Hilliard was producing excellent miniatures by the time he was 13, and until Queen Elizabeth's death in 1603 he was the leading miniature painter. His style combines the old-fashioned quaintness of medieval painting with the liveliness of contemporary French work and the solid sense of human individuality of the great Flemish portrait painters. He was a master craftsman and a genius at design, incorporating mottoes and symbolic illusions (such as a background of flames behind a passionate lover) into his portraits, which are as richly worked and concentrated as a Shakespearian sonnet, and just as alive. Many of the great Elizabethans sat to him, and Elizabeth herself was painted often by him. At the end of his life he lost favour to a former pupil of his, Isaac Oliver, and died in poverty. Oliver, who was scarcely less gifted than Hilliard, painted with more marked light and shade in the realistic and fashionable Flemish manner (*see* Vol. V, pp. 143, 416).

The great British 17th-century miniaturist, Samuel Cooper (1609–72), was influenced by

Fitzwilliam Museum

LADY MARGARET LEY. MINIATURE BY SAMUEL COOPER
(1609–72)

Victoria & Albert Museum

PORTRAIT OF A GENTLEMAN. MINIATURE BY
RICHARD COSWAY (1742–1821)

VAN DYCK (q.v. Vol. V), but his style was strong enough to remain individual, and his portraits, which include most of the distinguished men and women of Cromwell's and Charles II's time, are real people. Indeed, they make the work of the fashionable large-scale portrait painters of the day, such as Lely, look like dolls. In the 18th century more and more miniatures were painted on ivory, a practice popularized by the Italian woman painter, Rosalba Carriera (1675–1757). The technique was brought almost to perfection by the superb English miniaturists of the second half of the 18th century, especially by John Smart (1741–1811), George Engleheart (1750–1829), and Richard Cosway (1742–1821). Cosway was perhaps the best; although his portraits are rather affected, with eyes larger and necks longer than they were, they are unsurpassed in their light and brilliant elegance. Cosway often used a rather larger oval than had been normal till his day, up to 3 inches high instead of between 1 and 2 inches. The French school, including such painters as J. B. Isabey (1767–1855), practised a more highly polished but very elegant type of miniature painting.

In the 19th century a rectangular shape came into fashion, and miniatures tended to get bigger and bigger until they began to look like small oil paintings. The last of the great miniaturists was Sir William Ross (1794–1860); but even before his death, the development of photography was already killing miniature painting as a living form of art. The photograph fulfilled the demand for small, accurate, intimate likenesses more efficiently and far more cheaply than the painted miniature, and the art survives now largely as a curiosity.

From the 17th century onwards, enamel miniatures, painted on china or metal and then fired, were also popular; the best-known practitioners were the Frenchman J. Petitot (1607–91) and the German C. F. Zincke (1683–1767), both of whom worked for some time in England.

See also PORTRAITS; SILHOUETTES.

MINOAN ART, see KNOSSOS. *See also* Vol. I: MINOAN CIVILIZATION.

MINUET, see DANCE MUSIC; SONATA.

MIRACLE PLAYS. This early form of English DRAMA (q.v.), based on stories from the Old and New Testaments, was popular between the 13th and 16th centuries. The plays, sometimes called Mystery plays, were first performed in a very simple way as part of the church services. About the 10th century, for example, the Gospel story of the meeting of the Angel and the three Marys before Our Lord's empty tomb was presented, in Latin dialogue, by monks as part of the Easter service:

'Quem quaeritis in sepulchro, o Christicolae?'
'Iesum Nazarenum crucifixum, o Caelicola.'

('Whom do you seek in the tomb, O Christians?'
'Jesus of Nazareth, the crucified, O heavenly One.')

Later, other scenes from the life of Christ were portrayed and were developed into more elaborate episodes, English gradually taking the place of Latin.

By the 14th century these scenes had been expanded into plays that were performed outside the church. Though probably still written by monks, they were usually paid for and acted by laymen, members of the CRAFT GUILDS (q.v. Vol. VII) of important towns, each town having its own series of plays. There were about forty short plays in a 'play-cycle', telling the whole Biblical story from the Creation and Fall to the Redemption and Day of Judgement. Each guild was usually responsible for one play, which was performed on a special two-decker waggon called a PAGEANT (q.v. Vol. IX), with suggestive scenery such as a huge dragon's mouth to represent the entrance to Hell. The plays were usually given in procession on the great religious festival of Corpus Christi (which falls in late May or June), and were acted in turn at various 'stations', or stopping-places. They started as early as 4.30 a.m. and went on till dusk; sometimes they lasted for 2 or 3 days. Each guild usually played a scene appropriate to its trade; the carpenters, for example, played Noah building the Ark.

The plays were intended to instruct simple people. They told the Bible stories in terms of contemporary life; the actors mostly wore their usual working clothes; and the shepherds in the story of the Nativity, for example, grumbled about working conditions as they were in the 15th century. In this way the Christian story was made more real and vivid to the audience. Scenes were sometimes played with a rough humour, even with coarseness. Noah's wife, for instance, was usually shown as an obstinate quarrelsome old woman who had to be carried

National Buildings Record

A 14TH-CENTURY EASTER SEPULCHRE IN THE CHURCH AT HAWTON, NOTTS, AT WHICH THE EASTER RITUAL WAS ENACTED

In the central niche is the risen Christ, with the sleeping soldiers below and the Ascension above

struggling into the Ark; Herod was a blusterer; the Devil sometimes a clown.

Of the Miracle plays which have survived, the twenty-five Chester plays are the earliest, the most devotional, and the least comic. There is real pathos in the *Sacrifice of Isaac*, which was acted by the Guilds of Barbers and Wax Chandlers. Some of the forty-eight York plays present vigorous character-sketches, of which Pilate in the *Passion* is perhaps the best. The second *Shepherds' Play*, one of the thirty-two plays which made up the Wakefield (sometimes called the Towneley) cycle, is perhaps the best of all Miracles. Its first half is a comedy about sheep-stealing, where the stolen sheep is hidden in a cradle; the second half tells the story of the Nativity. The Shepherds are down-to-earth, grumbling characters, but the sight of the Christ-child draws from them a sweet and tender devotion, which is as typical of the Miracles as the

crude knockabout humour. The verses spoken
by the Third Shepherd are characteristic:

> Hail, darling dear,
> Full of Godhead!
> I pray thee be near
> When that I have need.
>
> Hail, sweet is thy cheer (appearance).
> My heart would bleed
> To see thee sit here
> In so poor weed (clothing)
>   With no pennies.
>
> Hail! put forth thy dall, (hand).
> I bring thee but a ball;
> Have, and play thee withal,
>   And go to the tennis.

While there are no character studies, no suspense, and no great poetry in Miracle plays,
there is fun and devotion, energy and simplicity.
They were written in several verse-forms with
much alliteration. Unfortunately the surviving
texts are a patchwork by many writers, and have
many mistakes, so that they are sometimes difficult to read in the original.

Though the REFORMATION (q.v. Vol. I)
checked the popularity of the Miracles, which
gradually gave way to the more elaborate
MORALITY PLAYS (q.v.) and comic Interludes,
they continued to be acted from time to time
until the end of the 16th century.

See also DRAMA; MORALITY PLAYS.

MISERICORD.

MISERICORD. The word comes from the
Latin *miserēri* and *cor* (pity and heart). In architecture it is used to describe the little projecting
brackets which are often constructed on the
underside of the folding seats or stalls in the
chancel of cathedrals, abbey churches, and some

Picture Post

MISERICORD IN EXETER CATHEDRAL, 1255–79
The first elephant ever seen in England was presented to
Henry III in 1255

Mrs. T. Cox

MISERICORD IN NORWICH CATHEDRAL, 14TH CENTURY
The carving of an owl mobbed by birds is composed to
make a support for the little shelf

large parish churches. In the Middle Ages long
parts of the service, including the Psalms, had
to be said or sung standing, which must have
been very tiring, especially for monks who had
to say nine services in the course of 24 hours.
To give a little support, the partitions between
the stalls were shaped to form comfortable arms
with projecting knobs, often carved, on which
the hands could rest, and, when the seats were
tipped up, the misericord brackets could be
leant against.

Usually the seat and the bracket were made
out of one thick piece of oak. Round the edge
were mouldings which curved down and ended
in circular designs of leaves or figures carved in
low relief. The central part supporting the
bracket was carved in much bolder relief, and
sometimes the background was entirely cut away
so that the design appeared to stand completely
free.

The earliest misericords in England, dating
from the 13th century, were usually decorated
with leaves, scrolling stems, and dragons. In the
14th century the carvings became more elaborate; the subjects included figures from
legends and romances, fantastic animals, scenes
intended to be humorous, such as animals
playing musical instruments or satirical scenes
making fun of the clergy or of henpecked husbands, as well as leaves, flowers, animals, and
birds. Two of the most interesting series of
14th-century misericords are those at Wells
and Norwich Cathedrals. At Wells there are
carvings of animals, such as bats, hares, and
rabbits, which show great accuracy of observation. In this series exquisitely carved leaves of
oak, ivy, and other common plants fill the circular designs at the sides. Misericords are found

in churches in most Continental countries. There is a fine 14th-century series in the cathedral at Cologne. A very large number survive in England, France, and Germany which date from the 15th and early 16th centuries.

Biblical subjects are seldom carved on misericords; the carver, perhaps, felt himself free to indulge his own fancy in work of so humble a nature, which would not be seen unless the seats were tipped up. In spirit the carvings on the misericords are often similar to the little figures of birds, animals, and fantastic people found in the foliage borders of ILLUMINATED MANUSCRIPTS (q.v.), where they form a contrast to the serious pictures which are the main part of the decoration of the page. It is possible that the carvings

MISERICORD IN HENRY VII'S CHAPEL, WESTMINSTER, EARLY 16TH CENTURY
An avaricious clerk upsets a bag of ill-gotten gold as the devil seizes him

were intended to form a similar contrast to the great representations of Christ and the saints painted on the walls of the choir and displayed in the stained glass windows. The clergy seem to have raised no objection either to the broadness of some of the humour or to the rather pungent satire on clerical life, and especially on the avariciousness of the clergy, which is conveyed by some of the carvings.

MODERN ARCHITECTURE. This term can mean either buildings put up at the present time, or the style of design that has been evolved to suit the present time and that could belong to no other. Modern architecture in the second sense began as a rebellion against the practice of imitating the styles of the past, a practice which had dominated architecture since early in the 19th century. The pioneer modern architects at the beginning of the 20th century felt that it was unreasonable for buildings thus to appear in the style of an earlier period, and that the present should have the self-confidence to speak, as it

were, in its own language. They also thought that period design placed unnecessary restrictions on a building's usefulness. There are numerous technical advances, such as steel and reinforced concrete construction (*see* BUILDING CONSTRUCTION, Vol. VIII), of which full advantage cannot be taken if buildings are restricted to forms and proportions dating from centuries before these were invented; and the efficient planning of complex structures such as hospitals, factories, and railway-stations is impossible if their appearance has to imitate that of the buildings of an age when such things hardly existed.

The first architects who tried to design without imitating the past felt the need to make something of a display of the freedom they had gained; consequently the 'modern' architecture of the 1920's and 1930's was deliberately reduced to its bare bones to display its structure, and was absolutely without ornament. Ornament was something specially identified with period architecture and was, in addition, usually the work of a craftsman's own hand. There was no place for this kind of ornament in the new architecture because the detailed parts of a building which used to be decorated were now often made by machinery. Modern architects, therefore, sought beauty not in elaboration of ornament but in perfection of finish and elegance of proportion. They were determined to make the most of the new building techniques which science had lately made possible, and to emphasize that structure was the true basis of architecture. They therefore made a point of using steel, concrete, and plate-glass whenever possible and in their most dramatic and easily recognizable shapes, that is, in shapes that arose naturally from the form of the construction used (these were called 'functional' shapes). Architecture became more and more a kind of refined engineering.

From these conditions arose the type of building we associate with this early phase of modern architecture—buildings geometrical in outline, simple in detail, with plain white walls and large windows. But soon the modern architects began to understand that their somewhat puritanical outlook did not allow them to produce buildings with a sufficient range of effects to stand as symbols of their civilization, as good architecture should. They realized that richness of form and texture has a permanent place in architecture, and so have the traditional materials—brick,

FLATS AT MARSEILLES DESIGNED BY LE CORBUSIER AND
COMPLETED IN 1952

stone, and timber; in fact, they reminded themselves that it was part of their own creed to avoid having preconceived ideas of any sort. The modern idea is to keep an open mind, fitting design and technique to the needs of each particular building. Consequently, since the Second World War, modern architecture has lost much of the bleakness of its conscientiously revolutionary phase; it is more human, and the uniformity of appearance in every part of the world is beginning to give way to differences of style deriving from the climate, materials, and social customs of different regions.

These developments in style do not, however, alter the fact that profound and permanent changes have come over architecture; the design of a building is now the outcome of a close study of the purpose it has to serve, the ideals it ought to express, and the most appropriate structure and materials for achieving these. Buildings are thus designed from within outwards, a great change from the days when a picture of the finished exterior was first conceived and the internal arrangements forced to conform to it.

The architect has become more of a planner, and this has widened his scope enormously. It has brought him into collaboration with the industrialist. Factories were previously put up by engineers, generally without much planning or thought for their appearance. Architects have now shown how, by studying production processes and planning the layout and the buildings accordingly, they can increase a factory's efficiency. They have proved that well-designed buildings assist output by providing better working conditions. The modern architect's emphasis on planning has likewise induced him to study TOWN AND COUNTRY PLANNING (q.v. Vol. X) and landscaping, that is, the planning not of isolated buildings but of groups in relation to each other.

Modern architecture evolved gradually as the ideas of a number of original thinkers were accepted and adopted one by one during the late 19th and early 20th centuries. One of the first of these was William MORRIS (q.v. Vol. V), who conducted a crusade to restore honest craftsmanship as the basis of good design. He helped to rid architecture of shams and pretensions, but his influence was limited by the fact that his remedy for the widespread ugliness that had accompanied industrialization was to return to the Middle Ages, not to move forward into an age when machinery would be accepted and treated as a new source of beauty.

The ground had already been prepared for such a step forward by the great engineers who, early in the 19th century, helped to transform England from an agricultural into an urban industrial country, building splendid and vigorous bridges, docks, and warehouses that owed little to the period styles then fashionable among the architects. The last of these engineers was Joseph Paxton, whose CRYSTAL PALACE (q.v.) of 1851 was the first large building to be made of standardized prefabricated parts. A similar role was played a generation later by French engineers who built a series of daringly original iron and glass structures at the Paris exhibitions, of which the EIFFEL TOWER (q.v.) remains. The focus of new architectural developments had moved away from Britain to the continent of Europe and to America. In the Middle West of America Louis Sullivan and others were building office-blocks and department-stores with a design which grew naturally from their steel-frame construction (see SKYSCRAPER), and Frank Lloyd Wright was designing informally planned houses with long horizontal lines and wide window openings, the importance of which, however, was not recognized till many years

ANTI-TUBERCULAR CLINIC, ALESSANDRIA, ITALY
Designed by the Italian architect Ignazio Gardella, and built in 1937–8

afterwards. In Holland, before the end of the century, several buildings of simple nobility had been built in brick and iron with their structural parts frankly revealed. In Germany a period of straightforward industrial building led to the linking of design and industry and eventually to the founding of the influential *Bauhaus* school of design, where architecture and all the arts of design dependent on it were studied. In Austria, Sweden, Finland, and France there were pioneers in creating an appropriate and effective style of architecture out of the newly invented technique of reinforced concrete; and later the Swiss pioneer, Le Corbusier, made known in his writings his ideas of the house as a 'machine for living in' and exemplified them in the most poetical and imaginative way.

See also ARCHITECTURE.

MODERN ART. 1. Before the end of the 19th century certain painters—Gauguin and Van Gogh among them—were growing to believe that the artist's task was less to produce good imitations of nature than to use lines, colours, and shapes to express his ideas and feelings (*see* POST-IMPRESSIONIST PAINTING). In the 20th century this revolt against naturalism has increased in strength. Many artists believe that rather than copying the real world they should be creators of new objects, and that it is more important for a picture or a carving to be beautiful or striking as a coloured pattern or a shaped piece of stone than faithful as an exact image of some place or person.

Sculptors claimed that the artist should not sacrifice the qualities possessed by his material (stone, wood, or metal) in order to achieve realism. Before the First World War, sculptors such as the Frenchman Aristide Maillol, though they still believed that the recognizable human form was the sculptor's proper subject, tried at the same time to preserve the feeling of the stone's weightiness, and to retain the spirit of the original block from which the figure was carved. In the work of younger sculptors today, the stone or piece of clay is sometimes altered only enough to suggest the growing of a living form out of the block.

Artists, no longer wishing to be true to nature in a merely 'photographic' sense, have had to

Tate Gallery
FAUVISM: 'THE POOL OF LONDON'. PAINTING BY ANDRÉ DERAIN
The shapes are rendered as a flat pattern of brilliant colours

Archives Photographiques
FAUVISM: 'THE ARTIST AND HIS MODEL' BY HENRI MATISSE, 1917
Strong black lines emphasize the pattern of coloured shapes
and create an illusion of solid form in the figures

find another purpose. Their search has led to endless experiments, to a long series of different 'movements', and also to a new appreciation of non-naturalistic types of art—the art of the Middle Ages, of primitive pre-classical Greece, of Africa and some parts of Asia, and of the art of children.

2. THE FAUVES. One group of artists, including Henri Matisse (born 1869), Maurice Vlaminck, and Albert Marquet, felt that the main task of the painter was simply to please and excite the eye of the spectator. They used nature, the places and things they saw, as a starting-point, but were interested less in truth to nature than in striking, brilliantly coloured patterns. Matisse and his friends thought it artistically dishonest to pretend that a picture was anything but a flat canvas covered with lines and patches of colour. Therefore, like medieval or Eastern painters, they did not try to represent space or volume. The violent distortions of nature and the brilliant colours used by this group in France so shocked one critic that he named them *Les Fauves* ('the wild beasts').

3. THE CUBISTS. Before long, painters such as the Spaniard, Pablo Picasso (born 1881), and the Frenchman, Georges Braque (born 1881), began to feel that it was not sufficient for a painting to be merely a pleasing decoration of flat patterns, and began to seek a stronger and more serious form of art. In such diverse sources as the work of the Post-Impressionist painter, CÉZANNE (q.v. Vol. V), and the native sculptures of West Africa (*see* AFRICAN ART), they found a tendency to reduce things to simple geometrical shapes, which led them to formulate a new attitude to nature.

Many artists, when they look at a figure, see its basic form as a series of simple shapes; in a head, for instance, the neck is a cylinder, the skull a sphere, while the whole head fits into a cube. Picasso and Braque believed that, instead of using these shapes merely as a foundation on which to build the subtle natural forms, the artist should actually depict these geometrical

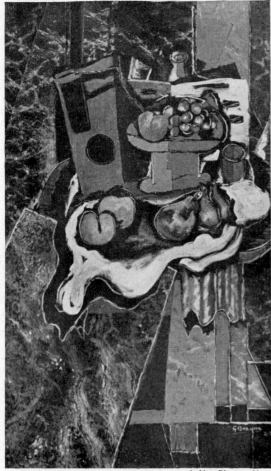

CUBISM: 'STILL LIFE WITH A MARBLE TABLE'. PAINTING BY
GEORGES BRAQUE, 1925

Cubism has become decorative rather than geometric

CUBISM: 'SEATED WOMAN'. PAINTING BY PABLO PICASSO

The figure is split up into geometric fragments, representing
different points of view, which are spread over the canvas
so that only a few parts remain easily recognizable

forms alone—should paint not the outer 'skin' but the structure beneath it. About 1908 they began to paint in that way.

Before long the 'Cubists', as they were rather inaccurately called, began to think that it was not enough to paint things as they appear from one point of view only. They wanted to show the essential structure of things—not only, for example, the nose as it appears in profile but also the nose from the front. So in painting a head, they might put in two separate noses, from two points of view.

The results of this attempt to analyse the structure of objects were strange and difficult to understand. There followed a simplification, even more difficult to understand, in which part

of an object would be used as a sign for the whole, these fragments being arranged in a flat geometrical pattern. Thus Cubism, which began to lose ground to SURREALISM (q.v.) in the middle 1920's, has three main phases—the 'geometrization' of shapes, followed by the use of several viewpoints at once, and, finally, the arrangement of fragments of things in a flat pattern.

Cubist sculpture was governed by similar principles. Picasso himself made early cubist heads which are chiselled into geometrical shapes. Later he built up 'constructions' of flat pieces of metal or wood and wire, which bore only a distant relationship to real things. The Roumanian sculptor, Constantin Brancusi, starting from a study of African art, invented a style close to Cubism in its use of simplified shapes.

4. THE FUTURISTS. During this century Paris has been the world's artistic centre, and artists elsewhere were deeply influenced by the French experiments. Many, like Picasso, went to Paris to work; others started similar movements at home. In Italy a group of young artists, inspired by Cubism, invented a style of their

FUTURISM: 'SINGLE FORM OF CONTINUITY IN SPACE'.
SCULPTURE BY UMBERTO BOCCIONE, 1913

Movement is represented by curling extensions to the figure. The 'scientific' title and machine-like form of the head reflect the interests of the futurists

ABSTRACT: 'COMPOSITION IN YELLOW AND WHITE'. PAINTING
BY PIET MONDRIAN, 1933

The artist attempts to imitate no part of reality and to arouse no emotion beyond the pleasure derived from the arrangement of geometrical shapes

own just before the First World War, and called it 'Futurism'. They were worshippers of everything modern—machinery, speed, and science. It was probably a garbled version of Einstein's Theory of RELATIVITY (q.v. Vol. III) that led them to attempt to represent the 'fourth dimension'—time—in painting and sculpture. This they did by painting things 'in motion'. They would, for instance, suggest a moving arm by painting in all the successive positions occupied by the arm while it moved.

5. ABSTRACT ART. Both painters and sculptors also turned to abstraction. The Fauves had sought decorative patterns in nature, and the Cubists had translated real things into geometrical shapes; but some painters argued that these shapes were sufficient in themselves and that artists had no need to start from nature at all. So they painted pictures which were simply arrangements of coloured rectangular or circular shapes. One of the Russian abstract artists, Malevitch, painted a picture which consisted of one white square placed in another.

Many abstract sculptors made constructions of metal, stone, or concrete which were simply three-dimensional patterns of a geometrical sort. Others allowed the shape of the original block of material to suggest the form into which it was to be carved or modelled; they let a form 'grow' from the block, and often this form would take on the appearance of something living, although not usually that of any particular creature. The sculpture of Hans Arp followed this 'organic' principle, and many younger artists, such as the Englishman Henry Moore, have been influenced by it. The cold 'cleanness' and absence of fuss in the works of abstract painters and sculptors have much appealed to modern architects and industrial designers.

6. OTHER MOVEMENTS. The various trends in modern art are not always clear cut, but to some extent merge with one another and produce variations. Two developments, EXPRESSIONISM, the expression of the inmost emotions of the artist rather than the realistic world, and SURREALISM (qq.v.), the expression of his subconscious feelings, have parallel developments, especially in poetry and drama.

Many individual artists do not fit into any category, while most of those who began as Fauves, Cubists, or Surrealists developed other styles after the decay of those movements. Picasso's painting, for instance, has changed

Tate Gallery

RECUMBENT FIGURE. SCULPTURE BY HENRY MOORE, 1938

The artistic effect of the weightiness and texture of stone is considered more important than a naturalistic rendering

several times since he abandoned pure Cubism in the early 1920's. In 1937 he painted a picture, 'Guernica', as a protest against the bombing of the town of that name during the Spanish Civil War. In it, distortions of a cubist type are used, not to explore the structure of the physical world, but to express the artist's horror of war and destruction. Similarly, other artists have learnt from cubist and abstract art how to give a firm geometrical foundation to more or less naturalistic paintings.

See also EXPRESSIONIST ART; SURREALISM.

MODERN MUSIC.

At all times there have been composers who were called modern because their inquiring minds led them beyond the accepted styles of their day, as when BEETHOVEN went far beyond the confines of classical form in his later quartets and sonatas, or when WAGNER (qq.v. Vol. V) wrote continuous 'music-drama' instead of conventional OPERA (q.v.) in set numbers. Nevertheless the changes that have been taking place in the language of music since the beginning of the 20th century are more drastic than any that have been known since the old modes gave way to the key system about 300 years ago (*see* SCALES). Soon after 1900 there was a reaction from the romantic composers who had tried to make music tell stories and paint pictures (*see* PROGRAMME MUSIC), and musicians began to return to the attitude of the older classical composers, who were far more interested in creating beautiful patterns in sound than in trying to make their compositions describe life. To rid music of all its romantic associations composers found that they needed to discard many of the accepted ways of using the notes of the scale, both in melodies and in chords, and to assemble these notes afresh in patterns that the human ear had never heard before. As it was a time of general unrest and disillusionment, there was much dissonance in this new music of the 20th century.

DEBUSSY (q.v. Vol. V) was the first important revolutionary. Although he continued to use descriptive titles for many of his piano-pieces, his music is completely impersonal, and only concerned with the relation of sounds to each other. After making up new chords that often shocked his teachers, he ignored all the rules in the harmony-books prescribing how chords ought to be approached and followed. After his death in 1918, another group of French composers known as *Les Six* went still farther towards making music unemotional and abstract; to ensure that their music was neither romantic nor expressive, they sometimes wrote pieces in which each instrument played in a different key. Milhaud, one of the most prominent of the group, wrote symphonies for a mere handful of instruments lasting only a few minutes, as a protest against the enormous orchestras and excessive long-windedness of the 19th-century composers. He even set agricultural and horticultural catalogues to music, instead of evocative poetry. All the group often imitated the rag-time and JAZZ (q.v.) that had just reached Europe from America as a way of mocking those who took music seriously.

Paris was the centre of this artistic revolution, and composers from all countries worked there, including the Russian Stravinsky. Before the First World War Stravinsky shocked everyone with his audacities in his opulently scored

BALLET MUSIC (q.v.) written for Diaghileff's famous company; in *The Rite of Spring*, for example, he not only wrote in different keys at once, but sometimes in different rhythms at once as well. After the war he turned against big orchestras and made austerity his ideal. For a while he would write only for wind instruments because he considered their tone more impersonal than strings; for his opera *Oedipus Rex* he chose the 'dead' Latin language, and in some of his songs he used no words at all.

Another important revolutionary was the Viennese Schönberg. He started as an out-and-out romantic; then, realizing that there was no farther to go in that direction, he began at the beginning again and invented a new way of composing called the 'twelve-tone technique'. In this the composer arranges the twelve semitones (all the notes between octaves) in any order he likes, but having once formed his 'row', he has to go on using these same notes in the same order throughout the piece. His only liberties are using the 'row' upside down, back to front, or at a higher or lower pitch. With so many rules to worry him, he has little or no time to think about emotion. Some of Schönberg's followers, notably Alban Berg and the little-known Norwegian, Fartein Valen, have managed to write fine music in this system, but they are the exception rather than the rule. Another notable experiment was made by Alois Haba, a Moravian, who, instead of using the twelve semitones such as are found on the piano keyboard, began to compose with notes smaller than semitones, known as microtones. BARTÓK (q.v. Vol. V) in Hungary allowed his tunes to be influenced by some of the old scales and irregular rhythms of his country's authentic folk music.

Not all composers today are as revolutionary in their methods as those mentioned above. Shortly before the Second World War the extreme passion for merely manipulating sound in novel ways began to subside, and composers once again found room for sentiment and emotion in their music. This can be readily appreciated if some of William Walton's and Benjamin Britten's earliest works are compared with their more recent achievements. All the same, the new techniques developed during the earlier part of the century are still making their influence felt.

As a result of Stravinsky's experiments, rhythm today is often a matter of irregularly instead of regularly recurring accent, expressed in unsymmetrical rather than symmetrical phrase lengths, or musical sentences. Since Schönberg tried to give the twelve semitones equal status in his twelve-tone technique, the 'doh' and 'soh' around which each scale is built (*see* TONIC SOL-FA) no longer stand out as important notes; and this, together with the novel experiments in chord-building started by Debussy, has seriously weakened (though not entirely destroyed) the system of keys on which music had been organized for the last 300 years. The move towards economy started by *Les Six* has resulted in shorter, terser, and less extravagantly scored symphonies, concertos, and choral works. In short, the contemporary idiom is very much like a new language which has to be learnt before the age-old sentiments which it contains, such as joy and sorrow, can be recognized and enjoyed.

See also MUSIC; MUSIC, HISTORY OF; MELODY AND RHYTHM; HARMONY; SCALES.

MODERN POETRY. People's ideas of poetry, as of painting and other art forms, tend to change violently, each age rebelling against its predecessor, and seeking fresh ways of expressing itself. The poets of any one period, though different as individuals, generally also have much in common; and so we group their work under some common title—such as METAPHYSICAL POETRY or poetry of the ROMANTIC MOVEMENT (qq.v.). The poetry of the 20th century, especially that since the First World War, we call, for the purposes of this article, 'modern poetry'.

About 1910 a new kind of poetry began to appear, in reaction to the inferior imitators of such great Victorian poets as Tennyson, Browning, Swinburne, and Rossetti. These early 20th-century poets experimented in metres, often substituting for traditional metres variable rhythms, or mingling traditional metres freely, not in accordance with the accepted rules of poetry. Such experimental verses were called *Vers Libres*, or free verse. In its vocabulary and use of words the new poetry was even more revolutionary. The forerunner of this revolution was the Roman Catholic poet, Gerard Manley Hopkins (1844–89), whose poetry, though written in the 19th century, was little known until its general publication in 1918. Hopkins, for whom the world was a revelation of God's grandeur, tried to express his conception of nature's radiance and man's pain in new powerful rhythms and in words 'counter, original, spare, strange'—to use the words by which he himself describes God's created world in his poem 'Pied Beauty':

Glory be to God for dappled things—
  For skies of couple-colour as a brinded cow;
    For rose-moles all in stipple upon trout that
      swim;
Fresh-firecoal chestnut-falls; finches' wings;
    Landscape plotted and pieced—fold, fallow, and
      plough;
    And all trades, their gear and tackle and trim.

All things counter, original, spare, strange;
  Whatever is fickle, freckled (who knows how?)
    With swift, slow; sweet, sour; adazzle, dim;
He fathers-forth whose beauty is past change:
    Praise him.

From BROWNING and Thomas HARDY (qq.v. Vol. V), the new poets acquired realism, so that they treated in prosaic or colloquial terms themes that the romantics and Victorians would have treated in abstract terms. And they wrote about subjects which the 19th-century poets would have thought unsuitable for poetry. The modern poets were greatly influenced by the French 'Symbolists' of the late 19th century, to whom the mystery of a poem was more important than its meaning, and who used a great variety of symbols and images to express their ideas. Sometimes a symbol has more than one significance, as in Edith Sitwell's poem 'The Raids of 1940', where the symbol 'rain' at first represents bombs falling, but later in the poem signifies Christ's blood:

Still falls the Rain—
Dark as the world of man, black as our loss—
Blind as the nineteen hundred and forty nails
Upon the Cross.

In W. B. Yeats's poems the tower recurs as a varying symbol; in T. S. Eliot's *The Waste Land* water is the symbol of life. Modern poets have extended the variety of symbols and images, drawing inspiration from anthropological works such as Frazer's *The Golden Bough*, from psychological studies such as those of Freud, from various religions, and from not only the classical myths and legends but also those of Ireland, India, and Byzantium.

YEATS (q.v. Vol. V) exemplified during his long life a general change in the attitude of poets. He grew up strongly under the influence of the doctrine brilliantly summarized by Oscar Wilde in 1891 as 'Art never expresses anything but itself'. By 1916 Yeats had veered so far from this doctrine as to say 'What moves natural men in the arts is what moves them in life'. 'Easter Rising 1916', the poem in which he celebrates a tragedy of contemporary Irish nationalism, could never have been written by the Yeats of 20 years before, the Yeats who wrote of Celtic romance and mystery. As his subject-matter became more realistic, his style hardened and sentimentality gave place to sincerity. His verse retained its perfection of form, its emotional construction, and its poetic passion, but acquired the sharp unexpected wit which was characteristic of the 17th-century metaphysical poets whom modern poets admire and emulate. Yeats's poem 'A Prayer for Old Age' has this characteristic, especially in its fourth line:

God guard me from those thoughts men think
In the mind alone;
He that sings a lasting song
Thinks in a marrow-bone;

From all that makes a wise old man
That can be praised of all;
O what am I that I should not seem
For the song's sake a fool?

I pray—for fashion's word is out
And prayer comes round again—
That I may seem, though I die old,
A foolish, passionate man.

T. S. Eliot's poetry is completely different from Yeats's, and yet their professed aims are not dissimilar. When Eliot says that the poet's business is to find 'the emotional equivalent of thought', he is saying something very near to what Yeats was saying in the first stanza of the poem quoted above. And when Eliot says that the concern of Dante or Shakespeare was 'to express the greatest emotional intensity of his time, based on whatever his time happened to think', we can understand what he tries to do in his own work. He does it by presenting, without comment, a situation or chain of events adequate to reveal or evoke a particular emotion; the reader must do the rest—must interpret the symbols, perceive the suggestions of the images, understand the thought, hear the music, and at the same time receive the poem as a whole. This is perhaps a little like listening to a symphony, where we keep in mind the themes, their developments and recurrences; we hear both the harmonies and the different instruments that produce them; we experience the emotion the music evokes—and all this simultaneously, not separately. In poetry, as in music, the better we know the work the more possible we find it to do this.

Eliot's use of images, which was immediately affected by Ezra Pound (like himself an American who had settled in Europe), is precise, powerful, compressed, and original. Such a line as

I have measured out my life in coffee spoons

conveys in an instant a character, his way of life, his ironical despair of himself, his sense of the futility of the world he lives in. The sudden transitions of Eliot's poetry, which present difficulty to an unaccustomed reader, give it great range and impact. Thus in the second movement of *The Waste Land* a sudden shift of scene and characters, accompanied by an abrupt change of diction and metre, is made with no explanation; the reader must transfer himself (as in Shakespeare's plays) from high life to low, and must interpret the clues. For example, the refrain 'Hurry up please its time' places the scene as a pub:

'What shall we ever do?'
                    The hot water at ten.
And if it rains, a closed car at four.
And we shall play a game of chess,
Pressing lidless eyes and waiting for a knock upon
    the door.

When Lil's husband got demobbed, I said—
I didn't mince my words, I said to her myself,
HURRY UP PLEASE ITS TIME
Now Albert's coming back, make yourself a bit
    smart.
He'll want to know what you done with that money
    he gave you
To get yourself some teeth. He did, I was there.
You have them all out, Lil, and get a nice set,
He said, I swear, I can't bear to look at you.

Books have been written analysing the poetry and technique of T. S. Eliot. It is not only poetry of great quality, but it has had enormous influence on modern poets. It is not easy to understand; even Eliot recognized some of the difficulties, and in notes to *The Waste Land* referred his readers to the sources of the symbols. The mysticism and morality that inform his poetry make its deeper meanings hard to reach; he makes his own poetical structure, metres, transitions. The movements of his poems re-

semble the movements of music rather than those of any known poetical forms. The title of his recent work, *Four Quartets*, confirms this.

Eliot's early works were not easy because of the symbols and the sudden transitions; the difficulty of his later works lies rather in their philosophic and mystic content. They have themes such as memory, consciousness, time. He no longer uses dramatic technique and experimental metres; the lines of his later works are nearer to those of Old English poems such as Langland's *Piers Plowman* than to any metres used since Chaucer (*see* VERSIFICATION, Section 2). But, just as music can be an experience on many levels, the deepest disclosing itself only as a synthesis of all the others, so this poetry can convey much even to unfamiliar readers who cannot pierce the heart of its mystery.

We might wonder why modern art, including poetry, should be so different from its predecessors. Certainly our age is in violent contrast to the Victorian, and the great issues and events of our fast-changing world have moved artists to violent reactions. Poets of the First World War—Robert Graves, Siegfried Sassoon, and Wilfred Owen—expressed their horror of slaughter, their pity for the slain, their hatred of a complacent society, as in this stanza from 'Anthem for Doomed Youth' by Wilfred Owen:

What passing-bells for these who die as cattle?
    Only the monstrous anger of the guns.
    Only the stuttering rifles' rapid rattle
Can patter out their hasty orisons.
No mockeries for them from prayers or bells,
    Nor any voice of mourning save the choirs,—
The shrill, demented choirs of wailing shells;
    And bugles calling for them from sad shires.

Between the wars a group of poets—among them Cecil Day Lewis, W. H. Auden, and Louis MacNeice—felt the urgency of social and political problems and wrote poems of social passion, such as MacNeice's 'Among these Turf-Stacks', of which this is the second stanza:

But those who lack the peasant's conspirators,
The tawny mountain, the unregarded buttress,
Will feel the need of a fortress against ideas and
    against the
Shuddering insidious shock of the theory-vendors,
The little sardine men crammed in a monster toy
Who tilt their aggregate beast against our crum-
    bling Troy.

One of the attitudes shared by many diverse poets is a hatred and fear of the modern industrial mechanized world, which they often hold responsible for 'man's inhumanity to man'. They turn against the wasteland, destruction, death; not the death of the individual, for they contemplate this with stoicism, but the death of the soul of mankind. 'Images of stone' is one of the most recurrent phrases in modern poetry. They universalize each sharp particular experience, as Edith Sitwell did the experience of the air raids of 1940 in the poem already quoted.

Yeats reacted by exaggerated praise of the big house and the peasant; Eliot and Edith Sitwell feel and express a despair; D. H. Lawrence sets against the artificiality of modern civilization his doctrine of warm, natural life; Walter de la Mare, W. H. Davies, and Dylan Thomas turn from it to magic, to nature, to youth. The poets turn towards the quickening, living, compassionate impulse, whether they define it in terms of Christ, or an unknown god, or, as Dylan Thomas did, as 'The force that through the green fuse drives the flower'.

See also ENGLISH LITERATURE.

MODES, MUSICAL, *see* SCALES.

MONASTIC ARCHITECTURE. The collection of buildings in which a community of monks lives, worships, and works is called a monastery or abbey (*see* MONK, Vol. I). In the Middle Ages the various Christian Orders held so dominating a position that the monasteries grew to a great size, not only as religious communities but as the principal centres of learning and education, of the care of the sick, and even of political power. The form of monastic buildings became more or less standardized in the 11th century, a period when many monasteries were built. The most powerful monastery of the Benedictine Order was at Cluny, in France, which had an enormous range of buildings. Branches, or 'daughter houses', were founded all over Europe, including England, by Cluniac monks who modelled their buildings on those of Cluny. The largest and most important monasteries in England, however, were built in the 12th century by the Cistercians. Their order was founded in the late 11th century as a protest against the extravagance and worldliness of the Cluniac Benedictines and, though the plan of their monasteries is similar to the Cluniac, the style of building and decoration is much more austere. Most of the monasteries in England were

disbanded and destroyed during the Reformation in the 16th century. Their plans can often be traced from the ruins that remain, and some idea of how grand these buildings must once have been is conveyed by the beautiful ruins of the Benedictine abbey of Glastonbury and of the Cistercian abbeys of Rievaulx, Fountains (*see* Vol. I, p. 325), and Tintern.

PLAN OF ROCHE ABBEY, YORKS, A CISTERCIAN MONASTERY

The most important building in the monastery was the church. On the south side of the nave was the CLOISTER (q.v.), round which the domestic buildings were grouped. Off the east side of the cloister were the parlour and CHAPTER HOUSE (q.v.), with the dormitory over them reached by the day-stair. A night-stair for the use of monks attending services in the night led from the north end of the dormitory straight into the south transept of the church. At the other end of the dormitory were the privies. Off the south side of the cloister was the refectory, where the monks had their meals. At the western end of this was the kitchen. On the west side of the cloister were offices and storehouses, which in later times had a library over them. East of this central group of buildings was the infirmary, and nearby a guest-house and the abbot's private lodging. The whole, together with the orchards, gardens, and fishponds, and any subsidiary buildings such as workshops, was

Archives Photographiques

REFECTORY OF THE ABBAYE DE ROYAUMONT, OISE, FRANCE,
c. 1250

p. 348) and below Mount Sinai) exist to this day. Other religions besides Christianity have monastic orders—especially Buddhism, the monasteries of which, composed of cells, refectories, libraries, and other buildings grouped round a central shrine, and sometimes cut out of the living rock, are common all over India, China, and Japan (*see* p. 207). In Tibet the Lamaistic monasteries (Lamaseries) built on the tops of hills are the most prominent buildings in the country (*see* Vol. I, p. 473).

See also CHURCH ARCHITECTURE, ENGLISH.
See also Vol. I: MONK.

MONUMENTS. To build something in stone has always been a favourite way of keeping alive

THE MONUMENT OF LYSICRATES, ATHENS

enclosed in a series of courtyards and surrounded by a wall, through which a great gateway led. The monastery, therefore, could be defended against an enemy, if necessary.

The plan described above was varied to suit the special needs of certain monastic orders; for example, the Cistercians, who had large numbers of lay brothers, provided a lay brothers' dormitory west of the cloister, and the refectory, instead of being parallel to the south side of the cloister, was often at right angles to it. The Carthusians had individual cells instead of a dormitory. Yet the general plan remained the same, except that it became more elaborate as the monasteries grew in size and in the range of their activities, and as they adopted a more luxurious standard of life. The infirmary often was an almost self-contained establishment with its own chapel and refectory; the abbot's lodging often had a private chapel, and sometimes, as at Glastonbury, a separate kitchen; and travellers' rest-houses, further libraries, and other buildings were added.

The Greek Orthodox church developed its own type of monastery, and many of these (like the famous ones on Mount Athos (*see* Vol. I,

the memory of a person or event. Sometimes the building serves a practical purpose as well—the PYRAMIDS of Egypt (q.v.), for example, were both monuments to the kings who built them and coverings to their tombs. Sometimes a monument has no purpose beyond the embellishment of a public place.

Apart from the pyramids, Egyptian monuments took the form of sculpture or of obelisks, which were tall, square pillars of stone, tapering to a pointed summit and inscribed on their sides with hieroglyphics. They stood in pairs by the entrance to temples. They usually consisted of a single huge piece of stone, so their transport and erection was a remarkable engineering feat. Many Egyptian obelisks were removed by Roman emperors and set up in Rome. The tallest obelisk known, 105 feet high, which came from the Temple of the Sun at Heliopolis, now stands in the Piazza of St. John Lateran, Rome. The 68-foot obelisk known as Cleopatra's Needle, which now stands on the Thames Embankment in London, also came from Heliopolis; while that in the Place de la Concorde, Paris, came from Luxor.

Crown Copyright

THE MONUMENT, LONDON. BUILT BY SIR CHRISTOPHER WREN TO COMMEMORATE THE GREAT FIRE, 1666

and fountains, their monuments usually took three forms: tombs, triumphal arches, and pillars of victory. The tombs, containing either a sarcophagus (stone coffin) or an urn filled with ashes, were generally square or circular in shape and richly sculptured; sometimes, after the Roman conquest of Egypt, they were pyramidal, and sometimes they had the shape of a temple.

Triumphal arches were put up to victorious emperors and generals at the end of a military campaign. They were often very large and bore carvings in relief depicting the events they commemorated and an inscription cut in the stone across the top (*see* ROMAN ART). The Roman type of triumphal arch was much copied in Renaissance and later times, the most impressive example being the Arc de Triomphe in Paris, erected in 1806. The Marble Arch, London, which originally stood at the entrance to Buckingham Palace, is an adaptation of the Roman triple-arch type.

TRAJAN'S COLUMN (q.v.) in Rome is, perhaps, the finest pillar of victory; the column of Marcus Aurelius (A.D. 174), also in Rome, is another. A smaller type of Roman commemorative column was the 'rostral column', erected to celebrate naval victories and adorned with representations, projecting from the face of the column, of the prows of ships.

In the Middle Ages there was no comparable public display of monuments, though sculptured tombs inside churches became very elaborate as the Gothic period progressed, sometimes to the extent of being miniature buildings in their own right (*see* CHANTRY). Richly decorated crosses were set up at central points in medieval towns to commemorate some person or event. These sometimes had the practical function of providing shelter for a small market or a fountain (*see* CROSSES, STONE).

Greek monuments most commonly took the form of statues; but there were also sculptured TOMBS (q.v.), as well as small monuments commemorating the winners of athletic or musical contests. One of these in Athens, consisting of a circular group of columns on a square base, is known as the Monument of Lysicrates (335 B.C.). It is in a good state of preservation, and its unusual delicate carving was much studied by architects and scholars in the 18th century.

The Romans, especially of all ancient peoples, commemorated their great men and their military victories by erecting monuments, and with these they adorned their own cities and the cities their soldiers occupied. Apart from statues

Donald McLeish

THE ARC DE TRIOMPHE, PARIS

Begun by Napoleon to commemorate his victories of 1805–6. The sculptures represent battles and figures symbolizing France. Beneath the arch is the tomb of France's unknown soldier, commemorating the First World War

During the Renaissance the public monument, with many of its Roman forms, was revived. Great men were commemorated by stone or bronze statues, sometimes on horseback and in Roman dress—for instance, Donatello's statue of Gattemelata in Padua (*see* Vol. I, p. 400). Notable events were also commemorated: 'the Monument', a 202-foot fluted column designed by Wren, marks the starting-point at Billingsgate of the Great Fire of London in 1666. The 18th-century enthusiasm for LANDSCAPE ART (q.v.) led to the erection of monuments to people, battles, and other events in the parks of great houses or crowning hills. For this purpose all the traditional shapes were adapted: columns, obelisks, pyramids, and temples; and new ones were also devised.

Classical forms continued to be used throughout the 19th century for architectural monuments. Among these are Napoleon's column in the Place Vendôme, Paris, which has spiral bands of relief in imitation of Trajan's column; the column in Trafalgar Square, London, surmounted by the statue of Lord Nelson; and the

George Washington obelisk, 555 feet high, in Washington.

The most common modern monuments have been war-memorials, which have often taken the form of Gothic or Celtic crosses as well as Roman columns and triumphal arches. The most famous British war-memorial is the cenotaph (literally 'an empty tomb') in Whitehall, designed by Sir Edwin Lutyens to commemorate those who fell in the First World War.

See also SCULPTURE.

MOORISH ART. In the 8th century the Moslem Arabs from North Africa overran the whole of southern Spain and established a kingdom there. The capital of this Moorish kingdom was Cordova, and this became one of the great centres of Arab civilization in the early Middle Ages (*see* MOORS, Vol. I). The art of the Moors, which was a branch of ISLAMIC ART (q.v.), spread from Spain to North Africa, and also to some extent influenced the Christian kingdoms of medieval Spain (*see* SPANISH ART). Magnificent specimens of the work of Moorish artists are still to be seen in Andalusia, especially at Cordova, Seville, and GRANADA (q.v. Vol. III).

The Great Mosque of Cordova, built in the 9th century, is perhaps the finest monument of the western Islamic world. Since the 13th century it has been used as a Christian cathedral. Basically its layout is similar to that of the Great Mosque of Damascus (*see* MOSQUE). The roof of the sanctuary is supported on a forest of pillars which form no less than nineteen naves. Two stages of arches are used to give added height to the sanctuary. These include the 'horse-shoe' and cusped arch, which are typical of Moorish architecture (*see* p. 21). In front of the *mihrab* (that is, the niche in the wall marking the direction to Mecca) is a dome, and the *mihrab* itself is decorated with mosaics and carved panels of floral and arabesque patterns that were to become the stock-in-trade of Moslem artists in Spain and North Africa.

Many features of the Great Mosque of Cordova appear in the mosques of the North African cities. A distinctive feature of these mosques is a beautiful type of minaret, a square tower surmounted by a square lantern. The faces of the minaret, either of stone or brick, are decorated at different levels with windows, 'blind' arches or arcades, carved panels, or painted decoration (*see* p. 278).

At the beginning of the 13th century Moslem rule in Spain was confined to the kingdom of Granada. The rulers of Granada built the palace of the Alhambra on the hill above the city, probably the best-known example of Moorish art, with its cool marble courts and fountains, delicate columns and arches, and wall decoration of carved and painted stucco (*see* Vol. I, p. 327). About the same time, the Christian king, Peter the Cruel, enlarged the Alcazar of Seville which is similar in style to the Alhambra.

The Moslems of Spain also contributed to the minor arts. They made fine bronze vessels, jewellery, silks, brocades, and carpets. They excelled in the carving of ivory and in making pottery. Particularly fine are the earthenware dishes and vases decorated in gold lustre, a technique which came from the Near East, was introduced to Europe by the Moors in the 12th century, and was later transmitted to Italy.

See also ISLAMIC ART; SPANISH ART.
See also Vol. I: MOORS.

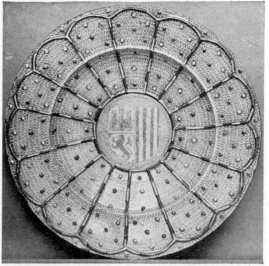

British Museum

LUSTRE DISH, *c.* 1480

In the centre are the arms of Ferdinand of Aragon and Isabella of Castile

Ph. Mas

NAVES IN THE GREAT MOSQUE AT CORDOVA, SPAIN, A.D. 848

Monuments Historiques, Rabat

THE KOUTUBIYAH MINARET, MARRAKESH, MOROCCO,
12TH CENTURY

MORALITY PLAYS. These plays, which probably developed from the MIRACLE PLAYS (q.v.), flourished in England in the 15th century. Miracle plays presented Biblical scenes from the Creation to the Last Judgement, whereas the Moralities were concerned with man's behaviour in this life. In these plays a man's impulses, duties, and interests, and his virtues and vices were personified as actors on the stage, and each tried to influence the hero (*see* ALLEGORY). A favourite scene was a lively battle between the Virtues and Vices for possession of man's soul, and the summons of Death was often shown because it made man examine his life seriously to see whether he himself was likely to go to Heaven or Hell.

From simple beginnings Moralities became very elaborate: one of the best of them, *The Castle of Perseverance*, has as many as thirty-four characters. In this play, Mankind, who is on friendly terms with all the Seven Deadly Sins, is shown following World. Penitence rescues him and places him in the castle of Perseverance, which is then attacked by his former friends. Mankind gives in to them, but is summoned by Death and eventually finds Mercy. The last words are spoken by God:

> King, kaiser, knight and champion,
> Pope, patriarch, priest, and prelate in peace,
> Duke doughtiest in deed, by dale and by down,
> Little and mickle, the more and the less,
> All the states of the world, is at my renown (power).
> To me shall they give account at my digne dais
>   (great judgement seat).
> When Michael his horn bloweth at my dread doom
>   (judgement),
> The account of their conscience shall put them in
>   press (difficulty)
>   And yield a reckoning
>   Of their time how they have spent,
>   And of their true talent,
>   At my great Judgement
>   An answer shall me bring.

One of the last and best Moralities, and one of the simplest, is *Everyman* (*c.* 1495), which is either the translation or the original of a Dutch play called *Elkerlijk*. God sends Death to summon Everyman to a pilgrimage, bringing a 'sure reckoning'. Death confronts Everyman:

> Everyman, stand still; whither art thou going
> Thus gaily? Hast thou thy Maker forgot?

Everyman searches for companions to accompany him on his dread journey, but Fellowship, Kindred, and Goods refuse to go with him. Everyman's Good Deeds wishes to come, but she is too weak to stand. Everyman visits Confession, which strengthens Good Deeds, and eventually she and Knowledge, Beauty, Strength, Discretion, and Five Wits all agree to accompany him. But only Knowledge and Good Deeds stand by him to the last, and even Knowledge leaves Everyman on the brink of the grave. When he is gone Knowledge says:

> Now hath he suffered that we all shall endure;
> The Good Deeds shall make all sure.
> Now hath he made ending;
> Methinketh that I hear angels sing
> And make great joy and melody,
> Where Everyman's soul received shall be.

In both these plays, although the characters are abstractions, their speech is varied, alive, and occasionally beautiful. The verse is rough but vigorous. The plots and situations are interesting, and there is some rough humour and satire. There have been successful modern revivals of both these plays. A German version of *Everyman* is performed in the cathedral square as part of the Salzburg Festival every year.

The growing demand for entertainment and the rise of small groups of professional actors brought about a new kind of play, developed from the Moralities but with no religious purpose, called an Interlude. Interludes in the 16th century were short, comic, often satirical pieces in simple verse, played by four or five actors in banqueting halls, the courtyards of inns, and so on (*see* THEATRE, HISTORY OF, Vol. IX). They were called 'Interludes' because they evolved from the short pieces of entertainment interposed between the acts of a morality play to add to the entertainment value. A typical Interlude is John Heyward's *Playe called the Four Ps*, in which a Palmer (professional pilgrim), a Pardoner, a Pedlar, and a Poticary (apothecary) each claim to be able to tell the biggest lie. The Palmer eventually wins the prize by saying that 'he never saw or never knew any woman out of patience'.

Plays of this kind, with the emphasis on entertainment rather than instruction and with entirely secular themes, show how independent drama had grown of the authority of the Church, and are the forerunners of the great dramas of the Elizabethan age.

See also DRAMA; MIRACLE PLAYS.

MORTE D'ARTHUR, by Sir Thomas Malory; *see* ARTHURIAN LITERATURE.

MOSAICS. In ancient Mesopotamia and Egypt precious and delicate objects were sometimes decorated with a glazed brick or mother-of-pearl inlay (*see* SUMERIAN ART). Mosaic work, which consists in forming patterns or pictures from pieces of coloured marble, stone, metal, or glass, is probably an elaboration of this old technique.

Mosaic floor decorations first appeared in the late Greek and Roman worlds. In the technique called *opus Alexandrinum*, porphyry and other precious marbles were cut into slabs, circles, and bands and arranged in geometric patterns. In

OPUS ALEXANDRINUM. DETAIL FROM THE FLOOR IN ST. JOHN STUDION, CONSTANTINOPLE, 12TH CENTURY

the finer *opus sectile* technique, the patterns were made of uniform stone or marble cubes, varying in size in different mosaics from $\frac{1}{4}$ inch to roughly 2 inches across. In the earlier floors as few as five or six colours sufficed to produce extremely intricate geometric patterns, or representations of single figures of birds, animals, flowers, or fruits, set against a white ground and enclosed in a clearly outlined frame. Often the entire

OPUS SECTILE. DETAIL FROM THE PAVEMENT IN THE IMPERIAL PALACE, CONSTANTINOPLE, 5TH CENTURY

ROMANO-BRITISH MOSAIC PAVEMENT WITH A SEA GOD, FROM
A VILLA AT VERULAMIUM, ST. ALBANS

composition was carried out in black and white.
Early in the Christian era the colour range and
decorative schemes became more elaborate, and
human figures were introduced into the more important decorations. There are some extremely
fine examples of the earliest Byzantine floor
mosaics at Antioch and at the Imperial Palace
at Constantinople (Istanbul). The mosaics represent agricultural, hunting, and fishing scenes
set in enchanting landscapes, as well as animals
in repose. The backgrounds are in white, and
cubes of deep blue and green glass are used to
suggest solidity in the figures.

The earliest glass mosaics so far recorded,
found at POMPEII (q.v.) and dating from the 1st
and 2nd centuries A.D., are unambitious and
small in size. The Byzantines elaborated this
type of work for the decoration of walls and
ceilings, using small cubes of coloured glass,
gold, or some semi-precious substance such as
mother-of-pearl, set in plaster. Miniature
mosaics were used for ICONS (q.v.). The technique required the highest skill, for the mosaicist
had to work very fast, sketching his designs upon
the damp plaster foundation and firmly fixing
his cubes before the plaster had time to set.
These mosaics, so exciting in the effect produced
by the light reflected from the coloured 'tesserae'
or cubes, made a splendid form of decoration.

By the 4th century it was not unusual for the
interior walls and ceilings of the richer churches
to be covered with mosaic decorations. The
scenes, which were always religious, were often
separated from each other by decorative bands of
vividly coloured geometric patterns or enchanting floral or animal motifs. At first the pattern
was set against a dark blue ground, and then a
gold one. It became the rule with church
mosaics for Christ to appear in the dome, the
four evangelists beneath Him, the Virgin in
the main apse, and scenes from the scriptures
along the upper levels of the walls, with portraits of saints below. Secular wall mosaics, now
destroyed, decorated the Imperial Palace at Constantinople; the only surviving secular Byzantine
mosaics date from the 12th century and are in
the Palazzo Reale in Palermo.

The earliest Christian mosaics are to be found
in Italy, at Rome and Ravenna, with less important examples at Milan, Naples, and Capua.
There are others at Parenzo, now in Yugoslavia,
at Salonica in Greece, and in the monastery of
Mount Sinai. In the mosaics of the 4th and 5th
centuries in Rome the figures are foreshortened,
rigid, and somewhat Roman in appearance, and
early Christian symbols, such as the Cross or
sheep, frequently appear. At Ravenna the
Byzantine element predominates, most of the
mosaics having been inspired, first by Galla
Placidia, the daughter of the Byzantine Emperor
Theodosius the Great, then by the Emperors
Theodoric and Justinian (see pp. 120 and 121).
The royal donors are shown on some of the
mosaics wearing their eastern court dresses (see
Vol. I, p. 89). The elongated religious figures,
although restrained in pose, are forceful and full
of the deep devotional spirit that characterizes
BYZANTINE ART (q.v.).

During the 8th century, when pictorial representations of the human figure were for a
period of some 100 years forbidden throughout
Byzantium, some outstanding compositions were
produced elsewhere. The Mosque of the Dome
of the Rock at Jerusalem contains splendid
mosaics, and there are even finer ones in the
Great Mosque at Damascus. These, essentially
Byzantine in style, consist entirely of patterns
and nature scenes without figures. Their extraordinary vigour and liveliness is due partly to
the astonishing variety and subtlety of their
colours, partly to the imaginative blending of
formal yet realistic landscapes with fanciful build-

T. Talbot Rice

THE CRUCIFIXION. 11TH-CENTURY BYZANTINE MOSAIC FROM
THE CHURCH AT DAPHNI, GREECE

ings, and partly to the treatment which suggests details rather than defining them rigidly.

The 9th century was the great period for Byzantine wall mosaics. In the cathedral of ST. SOPHIA (q.v.) at Constantinople deeply sensitive religious scenes were executed in an astonishingly wide range of delicate, powerful colours, together with decorative panels of unparalleled ornateness. Many other churches within the Empire contained almost equally splendid mosaics. During the 9th and 10th centuries, although mosaics are a very costly form of decoration, religious centres as far removed as St. Germigny-les-Près, near Orléans in France, Kiev in Russia, the cathedral of St. Mark in Venice, as well as the Italian churches of Murano and Torcello, acquired their own mosaics. In the 12th century the Holy Roman Emperors erected some remarkably fine mosaics in Sicily at Cefalu, Palermo, and Monreale, and these in their turn were surpassed in the 14th century by the mosaics in the church of the Chora (Karieh Cami) in Constantinople. The exquisite workmanship of these mosaics, their

shimmering colours and profound sentiment, are unequalled anywhere.

During the 12th century an Italian family of marble-workers, called the Cosmati, decorated marble pulpits, columns, church candlesticks, and slabs with inlaid strips of marble and gold tesserae arranged in geometric or spiral patterns. This novel form of mosaic work, which became extremely popular, was called Cosmati work in honour of its inventors.

See also BYZANTINE ART.

MOSLEM ART, *see* ISLAMIC ART.

MOSQUE. This is the Moslem place of worship (*see* ISLAM, Vol. I). The Moslem can perform his prescribed acts of worship wherever he happens to be, provided he turns towards Mecca, but it is the duty of every Moslem to attend at the mosque on Friday for the public recitation of prayers and the sermon.

The earliest mosque was the courtyard of Mohammed's house in Medina where the faithful assembled for prayer and to hear the Prophet's words. Their religion being the main driving force of the Arab armies of the 7th and 8th centuries, they built mosques in all the lands they conquered. In these early days the mosque was simply a rectangular space surrounded by a wall where the faithful ranged themselves behind the prayer leader, facing the direction of Mecca. The side towards Mecca was called the *qibla*, and along it was built a roof of palm leaves supported on palm branches to protect the congregation against the heat of the sun.

Their conquests soon brought the Arabs in contact with the long-established civilizations of Persia and Byzantium. The inhabitants of these countries possessed imposing churches and temples, but the Arabs had no artistic or architectural tradition. Sometimes the Moslems took over the whole or part of a church and converted it into a mosque. But soon they wanted to build their own places of worship which might stand comparison with those of the Christians and Zoroastrians. With the aid of foreign craftsmen and architects they began to build more elaborate mosques. One of the earliest is the Omaiyid Mosque of DAMASCUS (q.v. Vol. III) built by the Caliph al-Walid in A.D. 708. This consists of a paved rectangular court surrounded on three sides by a covered portico. On the fourth,

Donald McLeish

THE OMAIYID MOSQUE, DAMASCUS, 8TH CENTURY
Beyond the arcade is the Bride's Minaret and to the left
the Treasury of the mosque

a long side, is the prayer sanctuary, the roof of which is supported by columns arranged in three aisles running from side to side. A broad nave surmounted by a cupola passes through the centre of these aisles and leads to the *mihrab* or niche, set in the centre of the *qibla*. To the right of the *mihrab* is the *mimbar*, or pulpit consisting of a steep flight of steps leading to a raised platform. In the middle of the other side of the court is a minaret from which the crier or *muezzin* calls the faithful to prayer. This plan was repeated, though with modifications and variations, in many of the great mosques.

Another type is the 'cruciform' plan, which first appeared in Persia in the 12th century, an example being the Royal Mosque of Isfahan. In this, instead of the covered porticoes and aisled sanctuary, each side contains a vast niche. Yet another type was developed by the Ottoman Turks, probably under Byzantine influence, an example being the Suleiman Mosque in Constantinople. This is a large square or rectangular structure surmounted by a vast dome.

The mosque, therefore, developed out of foreign architectural forms adapted to the needs of Moslem ways of worship. For example, the aisled sanctuary of the Omaiyid Mosque can be traced back to the aisled basilicas of Greek and

THE NORTHERN AND EASTERN NICHES OF THE ROYAL MOSQUE, ISFAHAN, 1625-30

Roman times, the minaret to the bell towers of the churches of Syria, and the niches of the 'cruciform' plan to those of the houses of ancient Persia.

See also ISLAMIC ART; MOORISH ART; PERSIAN ART. See also Vol. I: ISLAM.

MOTET, see ANTHEM.

MUSEUMS, see ART GALLERIES. *See also* Vol. X: MUSEUMS.

MUSIC. The raw material of music is SOUND (q.v. Vol. III): music is sound selected, arranged, and organized into patterns. There are three aspects of this organization: MELODY AND RHYTHM are the patterns made by the changing pitch and speed of the sounds, and HARMONY (qq.v.) is the combination of sounds of different pitch. Melody, rhythm, and harmony are all fused together in our modern Western music, but this is not so in all music. PLAINSONG (q.v.), for example, is pure melody: it was untrammelled by our modern regular rhythms, and was never meant to be harmonized. In some ORIENTAL MUSIC (q.v.), on the other hand, native drummers have developed rhythm into an extraordinarily subtle art uncomplicated by melody and harmony.

The elaborate harmonized music of the West is a rare phenomenon in the whole history of the world's music. While it has produced vast new resources of expression, it has weakened some of the old ones. Melody is less freely expressive when it is determined by harmony; and rhythm, chained to harmony and shackled to vocal and instrumental melody, is a poor, feeble thing when compared with native drum rhythms.

The rhythmical part of music has, perhaps, the greatest influence on men. Some people are 'tone-deaf' (or, to use a more accurate expression, 'pitch-deaf'), but people are never entirely 'rhythm-deaf'. Rhythm lies too near the centre of our being for us to be able to do without it: our very heart-beats produce a rhythm, our steps when walking. Because of its rhythm music has always been associated with physical movement, especially with DANCING (q.v. Vol. IX), not only recreational dancing but also war dancing, ritual dancing, and so on (*see* FOLK DANCING, Vol. IX). From very early times, also, men have used rhythmical songs to help them to do ordinary, everyday jobs.

Eastern people sing as they fetch water from the well; farmers sing as they reap; woodmen sing as they fell trees; sailors sing as they haul on the ropes (*see* FOLK-SONG). Rhythm, whether that of a large military band or of a solitary drummer or piper, helps troops on the march. Indeed, if no music is provided, soldiers will spontaneously provide it for themselves by singing or whistling.

Music also appeals to man's sense of wonder, his sense of mystery. The sound of tom-toms in the jungle can be terrifying, the solemnity of a funeral is enhanced by the playing of a dead march. Even among pagan people, music has played a part in the mysteries of religion. It has formed part of religious RITUAL (q.v. Vol. I), especially in the Christian Church, which has always known how music can raise men's minds from worldly matters to a contemplation of divine things in a way which is quite beyond the power of words.

All music, not only ritual and religious music, is a form of expression: it can express emotions of sadness, happiness, courage, pity, and so on. Great music communicates feelings which are beyond the power of words to express; and since there is no barrier of language, music has been truly called an 'international language'. A symphony by a Russian composer, for example, does not have to be translated before a Frenchman or an Englishman can understand it. But music, though it may tell us what words cannot, can express only abstract ideas and emotions, not concrete facts. Even PROGRAMME MUSIC (q.v.), which sets out to describe things, can do so only in terms of music.

To express an abstract idea perfectly in terms of music is just as much a triumph of the mind as it is to express a concrete idea perfectly in terms of words. To express his feelings in sound, a composer needs to know how music is organized. The problem of MUSICAL FORM (q.v.) in a musical work is an intellectual one: it is only the brain which can see all the possibilities of a musical idea—what is its most appropriate musical form, what instrument can best play it (*see* ORCHESTRATION), how it can be harmonized, and so on. There are many other technical problems such as, for instance, how to represent sound on paper (*see* MUSICAL NOTATION).

A composer, therefore, has to learn a technique, just as a surgeon has to learn how to use a knife, or an aircraft designer how to use blue-prints, calculate stress, and so on. Because the technique of Western music has become so involved, composers need a long and thorough training to master it. Not all music has been so elaborate, however. Much the largest proportion of the world's music, taking into consideration the music of all lands and of all ages, has been folk music: anonymous music created and developed by ordinary people.

The enormous technical development of the West, however, has vastly increased the expressive powers of music. It has enabled the composer to write long works which, because of their balance and contrasts, are not repetitive or dull. The development of MUSICAL INSTRUMENTS (q.v. Vol. IX) has provided many new resources for creating sound: large orchestras, small combinations of instruments such as the string quartet, choirs, brass bands, organs, solo voices and instruments, and combinations of these. In place of the narrow musical limits of unaccompanied vocal song and native drum-beating of PRIMITIVE MUSIC (q.v.) there are all the varied resources of the SYMPHONY, CONCERTO, SONATA, OPERA, ORATORIO, BALLET MUSIC (qq.v.), and many other styles of musical composition.

See also MUSIC, HISTORY OF; MODERN MUSIC.

MUSICAL FORM.

1. A composition is built up by the repetition, contrast, and balance of musical ideas; this is its form. A piece of music consisting of a string of musical ideas without any relationship one to another could hardly give the listener any lasting satisfaction. Even less satisfying would be a piece consisting of one musical idea only, repeated over and over again in the same way; for an interesting musical idea, well able to bear repetition, would still need other ideas to provide contrast to it; moreover there would need to be balance between the various sections in order to satisfy the ear.

In the Middle Ages nearly all music was sung, and the PLAINSONG (q.v.) melodies were designed to follow the words of church services rather than to make purely musical patterns. Form was achieved by the repetition of verses and by antiphonal singing—that is, the verses were sung alternately by two voices or choirs. Modern musical forms have developed since the 16th century side by side with the development of instrumental music and modern rhythms. There are a limited number of ways in which

musical ideas can be arranged, but the basic patterns allow an infinite variety of treatment.

2. BINARY FORM. Many well-known traditional songs, such as 'Barbara Allen' or 'The Bailiff's Daughter of Islington', consist of two principal musical themes, the one balancing the other. This is known as binary form (*see* Fig. 1). Elizabethan instrumental music and also the 17th- and 18th-century suites of Purcell, Bach, Handel, and Scarlatti frequently used this form.

FIG. I. BINARY FORM

3. TERNARY FORM. This much more common, and in many ways more satisfying, form consists of a musical theme (often repeated), a contrasting theme, and finally a repetition of the first theme (*see* Fig. 2). Examples of simple ternary forms are the 'Skye Boat Song' and 'Charlie is my Darling'; it is also the stock form for all marches-and-trios, minuets-and-trios, as well as the earlier aria form (*see* SONG, HISTORY OF, Section 4). 'Where'er You Walk' is an admirable example, with its opening section, its contrasting section, and its restatement of the first section.

FIG. 2. TERNARY FORM

4. SONATA OR FIRST MOVEMENT FORM is a development of the ternary form, so called because it was frequently used in the first movement of the SONATA, as well as in orchestral compositions such as the SYMPHONY and CONCERTO (qq.v.). It differs from simple ternary form in presenting two main themes instead of one. The first is given out in the main key of the movement; this leads on through a short connecting passage to the second subject, which is not only in a different key but is also of a different character. This opening section is called the exposition. In the second or 'development' section the composer gives rein to his fancy in the expansion and treatment of his subject; in the third section or 'recapitulation' he brings back the opening section (this time rearranged so that it is all in the main key) to give a sense of proportion and balance. It is not always easy to follow the form when one is listening to a movement of any length, for the main themes appear in many different guises.

This is the usual pattern for the first movement of a sonata:

Exposition:
    (1) 1st main theme (in main key of the movement)
    (2) joined by a linking section to
    (3) 2nd main theme, contrasted in style to the first (in a related key).

Development:
    in which all the themes are used together freely (passing through many keys).

Recapitulation:
    (1) 1st main theme repeated again (in main key of the movement)
    (2) joined by a linking section to
    (3) 2nd main theme (this time in main key of the movement)
sometimes rounded off by a short, final passage colled a 'coda'.

5. RONDO FORM. This is another extension of ternary form, in which one or more further sections are added between the repetitions of the opening theme. Thus, if the opening theme is called A, the second B, and so on, the simple A B A of ternary form becomes in a rondo A B A C A or even A B A C A D A. An elementary example of this is the song 'Cherry Ripe', by Horn. The rondo may be used as a separate composition, or one of the movements in a larger composition may be in rondo form.

6. VARIATION FORM. The early keyboard composers often drew their material from the popular songs of the day, but they had to invent some method of giving to the repetition of the tunes the variety which the changing words of the verses provided in the songs. They achieved this by making each statement of the tune more elaborate than the one before it, while keeping more or less the same harmonies throughout. This was the earliest type of variation form, and is to be heard at its best in Handel's variations known as 'The Harmonious Blacksmith'. Haydn and Mozart frequently used this form in their pianoforte sonatas, and composers have written individual works in it, particularly for the pianoforte. Bach's 'Goldberg' Variations were written for one of his pupils named Goldberg. The musician Diabelli sent a theme to a number of composers, among them Beethoven, who, though at first unwilling to use it, later composed thirty-three variations on it. Brahms wrote one of the finest examples—Variations on the St. Anthony Chorale; and Elgar further developed the form in his 'Enigma' Variations.

7. FUGUE. This is a form in which the melody is interwoven by different voices or parts. It is often extremely complex, although it usually has only one theme, and that a short one, which is called the Fugue subject. It is divided into three sections, the exposition, the middle, and the final. Each voice or part introduces the subject in turn, but alternates from one key to another, for example, the first part may introduce the subject in the key of C, the second will follow with the subject in G, the third in C again, and so on. The entries of the second and fourth parts are called 'answers'; thus, the first part introduces the subject, the second then enters with the answer while the first takes up a short contrasting tune, called the 'counter-subject'. When the third part enters, the second takes over the counter-subject, and so on. This forms the exposition. In the middle section both subject and counter-subject, or even snatches of each, are treated in a variety of ways, and touch many different keys; between their appearances contrasting material is inserted, called 'episodes'. In the final section the composer often uses a 'stretto', or 'pedal', or both; in the stretto he creates an atmosphere of excitement as each part, announcing the subject for the last time, cuts in before the previous part has finished its subject. The pedal is almost as thrilling; a low bass or high treble note is held, while the other parts move rapidly towards the final chord.

Fugues may be written for voices or instruments. Bach developed this form to the highest perfection and his 'Forty-eight Preludes and Fugues', written for the clavichord, are among the world's great musical compositions.

8. CANON. This is not so much a form in itself as a device which may be used in forms such as sonata-form or fugue. It is particularly useful in fugue because it is a kind of counterpoint (*see* HARMONY) and the basis of fugue is the contrapuntal weaving of melodies. The principle of canon is that two or more statements of the same melody overlap each other, that is, one voice sings exactly the same tune as another, but a

BEETHOVEN SYMPHONY NO. 4.

a

BACH '48'. BOOK II. FUGUE IN C MINOR

BACH '48'. BOOK I. FUGUE IN D MINOR

c

FIG. 4. CANON

little later (Fig. 4 *a*). One particular kind of canon is the fugue stretto, which we have already mentioned. Sometimes whole songs for

several voices are constructed on this principle of one melody constantly overlapping; these are often called rounds (*see* SONGS, Section 4).

The different statements of the melody are not always exactly the same. Each one may be at a different pitch: in Fig. 4 *a* it is an octave lower than at its first appearance. One voice or instrument may play the melody twice as slowly or quickly as the other (Fig. 4 *b*); or the answering voice has the melody in contrary motion, that is, it moves down where the first voice has moved up, and vice versa (Fig. 4 *c*). A canon in which the answering voice sings the original melody backwards is called a crab canon, or *canon cancrizans*. Such ingenious devices usually look more effective on paper than they turn out to be in performance, and only the greatest composers, such as Bach, can give them real artistic life.

9. The term 'musical form' is sometimes used to mean the style of a composition as a whole rather than the arrangement of the elements within the composition. The various types of orchestral composition, such as the SYMPHONY, CONCERTO, and OVERTURE (qq.v.), all have their particular arrangement. Many types of composition, such as the minuet, gavotte, and waltz, had their origin in DANCE MUSIC (q.v.), and in these the form is dependent on the dance which inspired the music. The original purpose of other compositions, such as the march, has determined their style and rhythm.

See also MELODY AND RHYTHM; HARMONY.

MUSICAL INSTRUMENTS, *see* Vol. IX: MUSICAL INSTRUMENTS.

MUSICAL NOTATION. We have grown so accustomed to being able to write down music that it is difficult to realize how great were the problems which confronted the men of countless generations who tried to represent musical sounds on paper. Even when a fairly satisfactory system had been worked out people never stopped trying to improve on it or to find new methods. All the systems, however, which have appeared at different times and in different places could be roughly divided into the two groups represented by our modern system of signs printed on five lines and by our TONIC SOL-FA system (q.v.).

1. NEUMS. Our five-line system was evolved by the Church in the Middle Ages. The practice arose of marking the Scriptures with accents

ACCENT	EARLY NEUMS	NEUMS USED NOW	MODERN EQUIVALENT

FIG. I

which showed the inflexion of the reader's voice. The acute accent (´) showed that he would lift his voice, the grave (`) that he would let it fall, and the circumflex (ˆ) that he would raise and lower it on one syllable. These signs were probably first used in church services about A.D. 680. At this time rhetoric was a widely studied art, and the rise and fall of the voice were governed by many rules; to our ears the effect would probably seem exaggerated. As the rules governing inflexions increased, the use of the accent signs became more exact, and so began our modern system of notation.

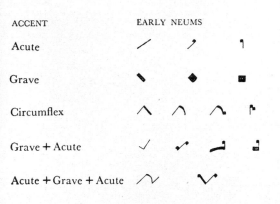

EARLY NEUMS
Antiphon for the Feast of Epiphany from a 10–11th-century manuscript

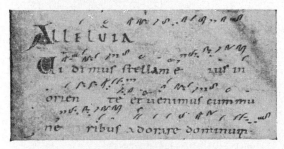

NEUMS WITH STAFF LINES
The darker line is red and the lighter one yellow. Detail from an antiphon from a 13th-century manuscript

In time, the three basic signs were modified, extended, and combined, until at last there was a whole series of markings running along the top of the words indicating whether the music rose or fell.

From at least the 9th to the 15th century the notation based on the accents was evolving into a series of musical symbols, called 'neums', to represent single notes or groups of notes (Fig. I). These, however, varied enormously at different times and in different places. A form of neum notation, based on 13th- to 15th-century methods, is commonly used today for PLAINSONG (q.v.).

2. STAFF. At first the neums did not show how much the notes rose or fell or which were the same. Then, at the beginning of the 11th century, a red line was drawn across the page indicating that all the notes which fell on this line were the same. Soon a second line appeared, this time a yellow one. Other horizontal lines were added, but gradually the system of using four was agreed upon for the chant sung in church, and this is still used for plainsong.

The set of lines is known as the staff. Staves have had up to fifteen lines, but the five-line staff has become generally accepted for modern music. For notes higher or lower than the staff, 'leger' lines (small parts of additional lines) are used (*see* Fig. 3).

3. CLEF. The notes indicated by the lines and spaces of the staff are the white notes of the piano. (The notes apply, of course, to all instruments; we are only taking the piano as an example.) The interval (or change of pitch) between the white notes is in some cases a tone and in others a semitone. In neum notation the sign 𝄢 or 𝄡 was placed at the beginning of the staff. The former showed that the line on which

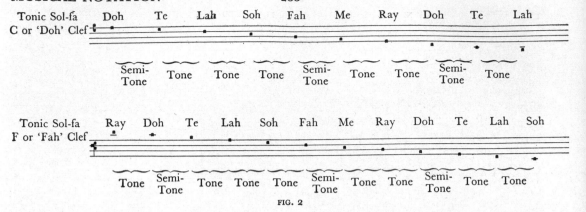

FIG. 2

it was placed was fah (*see* TONIC SOL-FA); the latter indicated doh. From these the relationship of the other notes could be calculated. This sign became known as the 'clef' (meaning key), for without it one could not tell whether the interval from one line to the next space was a whole tone (doh to ray in Tonic Sol-fa) or semitone (me to fah) (Fig. 2).

In modern music three clefs are used. The treble or G clef has the sign ⟨clef⟩ for G centred on the second line from the bottom to show that the note G above middle C falls on this line. The bass or F clef has the sign ⟨clef⟩ centred on the second line from the top, indicating that the

Treble or G Clef   Bass or F Clef   Tenor   Alto
C Clefs

FIG. 3

notes on that line are the F below middle C. The C clef may have the sign for middle C (⟨sign⟩) on the second or third line (Fig. 3). The treble clef includes nearly the full range of a soprano singer, the bass clef that of a bass singer, and the C clefs those of tenor and alto singers. Piano music uses the treble clef for the right hand and the bass clef for the left hand.

4. ACCIDENTALS. Since the lines and spaces only indicate the notes on the white keys of the piano, additional symbols are used to indicate the black notes—the 'flats' and 'sharps'. The flat sign (♭) shows that a note is to be lowered a semitone, and the sharp sign (♯) raises a note a semitone. Such 'accidentals', as they are called,

also affect the note if it is repeated within the same unit of rhythm—the 'bar'. To restore it to its normal pitch the 'natural' sign (♮) is used. When certain notes are to be flattened or sharpened throughout a composition, the signs are not used each time the notes occur, but are placed in their appropriate position at the beginning of the staff after the clef (Fig. 4 *b*) and also at

a b c

FIG. 4. *a*. Clef. *b*. Key signature. *c*. Time signature

the beginning of each line of staff down the page. If, for instance, the work is written in the key of E major, F, C, G, and D will always be sharpened. The signs at the start of the staff are called the 'key signature' because they indicate the key in which the music is written (*see* SCALES, Section 3).

5. VALUES OF NOTES. In plainsong music the lengths of the notes were not precisely related to each other but were controlled by the words to which the music was sung. The rhythm of modern music and use of a number of instruments or voices performing together has made

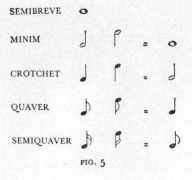

FIG. 5

THE INSCRIPTION OVER HELL GATE—'ALL HOPE ABANDON YE WHO
ENTER HERE'

Water-colour by William Blake (1757–1827) illustrating Dante's *Divine Comedy*

it necessary to show the exact length of each note. The longest note in present use is called the semibreve, the note half as long is the minim, and the crotchet, quaver, and semiquaver are each half as long as the one before it (Fig. 5).

Quavers and semiquavers are frequently joined together in groups:

The length of 'rests' or silences has to be indicated as precisely as that of notes, and corresponding signs are used: semibreve (−−), minim (−−), crotchet (𝄽) or (𝄾), quaver (𝄿), and semiquaver (𝅀). A dot placed after a note or rest indicates that it is to be held half as long again: ♩. = ♩ + ♪; −−· = −− + 𝄾. A dot over or under a note means that it is to be played 'staccato', that is, the sound is to be as short as possible without the time allotted to it being shortened. A 'tie' (⌢) between two notes of the same pitch shows that there is to be no break between them, that they are to be performed as one long note equal to the sum of both of them:

The tie is not the same as the phrase mark, which groups together two or more notes of different pitch to show that they are members of the same musical phrase or idea, or sometimes, in music for various instruments such as wind and string, that they are to be performed in one breath or in one movement of the bow:

6. Bars and Time Signatures. Vertical lines were originally drawn across the staff to show the end of a section of the music. About the end of the 17th century these vertical lines or 'bar lines' were used to divide off an equal number of beats into bars. The figures at the beginning of a piece of music show how many beats there are in a bar (or 'measure' in America). The lower figure shows what kind of beat is used; the minim, being half a semibreve, is indicated by the figure 2, the crotchet, being quarter of a semibreve, is shown by 4, the quaver ($\frac{1}{8}$) by 8. The top figure shows the number of beats in the bar; thus $\frac{3}{4}$ means that there are three crotchets in a bar, $\frac{6}{8}$ means six quavers, $\frac{2}{2}$ means two minims. The sign 𝄴 means $\frac{4}{4}$ (four crotchets)

and 𝄵 means $\frac{2}{2}$ (two minims); these are survivals from medieval theories of rhythm. The 'time signature' comes after the key signature at the beginning of the staff (Fig. 4c).

7. Ornaments. The harpsichord and similar Keyboard Instruments (q.v. Vol. IX) were incapable of sustaining notes. Various methods called 'ornaments' were devised to give the effect of a sustained note, and these are shown by signs. Chief amongst the ornaments still in use is the trill (*tr*〰) which indicates that the note shown is to be played in rapid alternation with the one above it (Fig. 6a). A 'mordent'

performed thus:

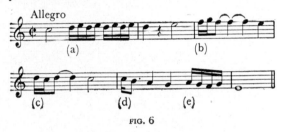

FIG. 6

(𝆛) shows that the principal note and the note above it are to be played very quickly before the principal note (Fig. 6b). An 'inverted mordent' (𝆙) uses the note below the principal note (Fig. 6c). The 'grace-note' or 'acciaccatura' is shown as 𝆕, and means that this note is to be played as quickly as possible. It has no time value itself, but robs the following note of a fraction (Fig. 6d). The 'turn' (∞) on a note is just what its name implies (Fig. 6e).

8. Expression Marks. Many signs are used to indicate the way music should be played. Expression marks, such as piano (soft), forte (loud), crescendo or $<$ (getting louder), diminuendo or $>$ (getting softer), seem to have become established first of all in lute music during the first half of the 17th century. Other words and signs have increased rapidly. The language most generally employed is Italian, and this has the advantage that the comparatively small vocabulary required is now

FIRST PAGE OF THE MANUSCRIPT SCORE OF ALAN RAWSTHORNE'S 'STREET CORNER' OVERTURE
The top group are woodwind, then brass, percussion, and strings

widely familiar amongst musicians of all nationalities. The practice of using other languages, however, seems to be steadily increasing. The rapid growth of the number of signs used by composers has naturally left less and less room for the personal decisions of performers. Great players pay scrupulous attention to a composer's markings; but there are, of course, many shades of tone, phrasing, and tempo which cannot be shown even by our modern abundance of signs, and which distinguish a live performance from a dead one.

See also MUSIC; SCALES.

MUSIC, HISTORY OF. 1. ANCIENT MUSIC.

No one knows exactly how music-making first began, because there is no record of it in primitive times. The earliest records we do possess come from the Assyrians, who discovered a way of writing down music by means of symbols used in writing (*see* MUSICAL NOTATION). Their instruments consisted of harps, lyres, pipes, and primitive trumpets, besides drums of various kinds which were used mainly to accompany the dance (*see* MUSICAL INSTRUMENTS, Vol. IX). They sang or played a simple melody in unison, without attempting to blend different sounds as in modern music. We have many sculptures and pictures of the instrumental music of the ancient Egyptians, who used the harp and lyre and also some wind and percussion instruments. Much more is known of Jewish music, for there are many allusions to it in the Bible. Everyone in Israel sang, we are told, and the lyre and timbrel (or tambourine) were played by the women. 'Professional' musicians are first heard of during the reigns of David and Solomon; many of them were attached to the Court and sang the Temple services.

So much was written about the music of ancient Greece by the Greeks themselves that its meaning and purpose is quite clear to us; and its influence on the music of western Europe has been great. The Greeks rated music very high in the order of subjects to be taught, even believing that good and evil, order and disorder, depended upon the music sung or played. About 550 B.C. Pythagoras, when experimenting with strings of various lengths, scientifically 'discovered' the various notes, ranging from high to low, of a SCALE (q.v.), or 'mode' as it was then called. The Greeks, like the Assyrians, wrote down their music by using symbols, the letters of the alphabet, to indicate the different sounds of the scale. Like that of most other ancient nations, Greek music consisted mainly of singing a simple melody, which their chief instruments, the lyre and pipe, accompanied by playing exactly the same tune as the singers.

The Romans added little to musical history, but depended on the Greeks to provide what music they wanted.

2. MEDIEVAL MUSIC. For many centuries after the coming of Christianity, the development of music centred round the Christian Church. At first the music was mainly Jewish; but as the Church expanded and spread to Greece and Italy, the music of these countries was adopted. The Church began to make much use of music in its services, not only as a help to worship but as a means of gaining new converts (much as the Salvation Army has done). The music, which was sung in unison, that is, all the singers singing the same melody, with little use of instruments, was based on the Greek modes and was necessarily simple in melody and rhythm, for the tunes had to be learnt by ear, there being no way of writing them down. The church services and the music, called PLAINSONG (q.v.), to which they were set were standardized in the 4th century by St. Ambrose, and remained unchanged until the end of the 6th century, when Pope GREGORY (q.v. Vol. V) introduced more variety into the music. The plainsong is still heard in the services of the Roman Catholic Church, and to some extent in the English Church.

Although in the 7th century efforts were made to preserve melodies by recording them in writing, it was not until the 14th century that a notation at all resembling modern notation began to be used. At this time there was a development from simple melody towards HARMONY (q.v.). In earlier centuries the different voices had sung the same melody together, though at the different pitches suited to the pitch of boys', women's, or men's voices. Gradually, however, the melodies sung by each voice became more independent—that is to say, the various singers sang different melodies at the same time, but in such a way that the complete effect sounded harmonious. The principles of harmony, however, were not fully developed until the 16th century.

Probably as early as the Norman Conquest priests began to present the stories from the Gospels and legends of the saints in dramatic form,

CHRIST SURROUNDED BY ANGELS. PAINTING BY FRA ANGELICO (1377–1455)
The angels are playing trumpets, portable organs, cymbals, drums, rebecks, gitterns, and harps

interspersed with much singing. These 'plays' developed into the MIRACLE PLAYS (q.v.) of the 14th and 15th centuries. The music used for them was similar to the plainsong of the church services.

While scholars were studying music and making rules for its performance, another kind of music was growing up, with no rules and no written notation. This was the FOLK-SONG (q.v.) of the country people, who sang about the things that mattered to them—their work, their holidays, their joys and sorrows. During the Middle Ages there were also MINSTRELS (q.v. Vol. IX), professional musicians who were either attached to a nobleman's house or who traversed the country singing songs in praise of noble deeds. These popular singers soon broke away from the traditional tunes of the Church, and were probably the first to adopt our modern scales: indeed, a 13th-century song, 'Sumer is Icumen In', is actually written in the modern major scale. The minstrels experimented with vocal music and, no doubt, when accompanying their songs on rebecks or gitterns, harps or lutes, often struck a chord sounding something like our modern chords. Ultimately it was the fusion of the church plainsong and the country-side folk-song which gave the great Elizabethan composers the material on which to work.

3. RENAISSANCE MUSIC. The spirit of inquiry stimulated by the RENAISSANCE (q.v. Vol. I) was as productive in music as in other arts. In some

ways music became simpler and more direct, in other ways more elaborate.

In church music simplicity was the new aim. In the Reformed Church of England, as the English language took the place of Latin in public worship, the more intricate types of plainsong were no longer heard. The music composed for the new services laid the foundations of the great tradition of English SACRED MUSIC (q.v.).

It was in Italy, the centre of Renaissance thought, that new types of secular music originated. The madrigal (*see* SONGS, Section 2), a composition for unaccompanied voices perfected by Palestrina (1525–94) and his school, soon came to England, inspiring English musicians also to compose madrigals. In the 16th century instrumental music independent of singing first began to be written. The instruments in common use were, for the well-to-do, VIOLS (q.v. Vol. IX) and virginals (*see* KEYBOARD INSTRUMENTS, Section 2, Vol. IX), and for minstrels and travelling musicians, RECORDERS and LUTES (qq.v. Vol. IX). There was no music as yet written for these instruments in combination, but instruments were sometimes used to replace voices, and many madrigals bore the heading 'apt for viols or voices'. The Italian Monteverdi was the first to realize that each group of instruments in the orchestra had its own character, and to use them by way of contrast (*see* ORCHESTRATION).

Composers for the virginals were more enterprising; they took a well-known song tune as their subject and elaborated it with runs and trills and passages up and down the keyboard, yet keeping the same little tune as a basis throughout the piece. Later these keyboard composers used dance tunes with good effect. In such pieces lies the germ of the suites of dances composed by Bach and Handel in the 18th century (*see* DANCE MUSIC).

The people of the Renaissance not only looked forward to new inventions and discoveries, but they also looked back to rediscover the past. The beginnings of OPERA (q.v.) can be seen in the attempts in 16th-century Florence to restore Greek drama; and a similar religious drama, called ORATORIO (q.v.), was developed. Songs accompanied by the lute became fashionable, and are notable for the excellence of both the music and the poetry. Especially beautiful madrigals, songs with lute accompaniment, and also music for MASQUES (q.v. Vol. IX), were written in England. This great activity culminated in the work of PURCELL (q.v. Vol. V), whose music led the way to new developments.

4. CLASSICAL MUSIC. In the 18th century the most important musicians were Germans and Italians, patronized as they were by the princes and nobles of these countries. Even religious music was composed for performance not only in churches but also at princely Courts, and it was there that orchestral music, such as the SYMPHONY (q.v.), was developed.

The 18th-century ORCHESTRA (q.v. Vol. IX) was not the same as we know it because some of the WOOD-WIND INSTRUMENTS (q.v. Vol. IX) were still crude, and violins were only just beginning to take the place of viols (*see* STRING INSTRUMENTS, Vol. IX). Moreover, the harpsichord (*see* KEYBOARD INSTRUMENTS, Vol. IX) still provided the background for string music. In his CANTATAS (q.v.), J. S. Bach set solo and chorus voices to an accompaniment of strings and harpsichord or organ, with occasional wind instruments added; and these he used with special consideration of the individual character of each instrument. His outstanding ability as an organist also led to a remarkable progress in the art of composition for ORGAN (q.v. Vol. IX) as well as in the standard of organ-playing.

The Italian Corelli (1653–1713), the first great violinist, was a highly skilled composer for the violin. Another Italian, Alessandro Scarlatti (1660–1725), introduced into his operas and cantatas harmonies which had never been used before.

In the 18th century the 17th-century developments in the use of instruments and in MUSICAL FORM (q.v.) and harmony were perfected. The music of this period is called 'classical' because the work of such composers as BACH, HANDEL, HAYDN, and MOZART (qq.v. Vol. V) has qualities of refinement and perfection of form and balance which are found also in CLASSICAL ART (q.v.). The classical composers paid great attention to the form of their compositions, showing their originality more by varied treatment within the accepted forms than by inventing new forms. There is clarity and order in their music, and the interest is centred more in purely musical qualities, such as beauty of melody and harmony, than in the expression of emotions through music.

5. ROMANTIC MUSIC. Just as the classical composers of the 18th century expressed the ideas which were to be found in all the arts of the time, so in the following period other aims were sought in music, art, and literature (*see* ROMANTIC MOVEMENT). The early music of BEETHOVEN (q.v. Vol. V) is classical in form, but later he

National Gallery

MUSICIANS AT THE COURT OF LOUIS XIV

Their instruments are flutes and a bass-viol.
Painting attributed to Robert Tournières (1667–1752)

introduced into his work an intensity of feeling which led the way to the 'Romantic' music of the 19th century. Music came to be considered not only for its own sake but as a means of expressing ideas which have not necessarily any direct connexion with it—feelings of joy, sorrow, love, or anger. PROGRAMME MUSIC (q.v.), as it is called, was built up round a story. Music, of course, had often been used to reflect ideas, but the romantic composers carried this much farther. To achieve their effects they did not follow the rules of classical composition rigidly but introduced new ideas to stimulate the imagination of the audience. With the development of the CONCERTO (q.v.), the solo performer became more important, and, as the mechanism of the wind instruments improved, the music written for these made increasing demands on the skill of the performers, not only in solo work but also in orchestral playing. CHOPIN and LISZT (qq.v. Vol. V) experimented with new forms of pianoforte composition.

During the first half of the 19th century the art of music developed speedily and widely, and rapidly became available not only to a small aristocracy but also to the rising middle classes. The public concerts started in the 18th century became increasingly popular, giving opportunity for the performance of large orchestral works, as well as of CHAMBER MUSIC (q.v.) and solo recitals. The performance of music by amateurs was helped by the introduction of the TONIC SOL-FA system (q.v.), and girls' education was considered incomplete unless they were proficient at the piano or could entertain their friends by singing.

Opera, the most obvious form of programme music, was to be found in almost every city in Europe, with the exception of England, and was the most popular type of music among the people. WAGNER (q.v. Vol. V) carried the romantic ideas even farther by conceiving the music and drama of his operas as one, each giving meaning to the other. To express his ideas he used every available resource both in the handling of instruments and in musical form.

6. MODERN MUSIC. Throughout most of the 19th century, German composers influenced every country in Europe; but at the end of the century there was a reaction against traditional harmony, led by DEBUSSY (q.v. Vol. V) and centred in France (*see* MODERN MUSIC). In every successive period of history music, like other arts, has reflected the spirit of the age, and the music of today, with its turbulence, and with harmony so dissonant to the ears of those accustomed to classical music, proves no exception to the general rule.

See also MUSIC; PRIMITIVE MUSIC; MODERN MUSIC; MUSICAL FORM.
See also Vol. IX: MUSICAL INSTRUMENTS.

MYCENAEAN ART, *see* Vol. I: MYCENAEAN CIVILIZATION.

MYSTERY PLAYS, *see* MIRACLE PLAYS.

N

NATIONAL SONGS, *see* FOLK-SONG; SONG, HISTORY OF, Section 5.

NATURE WRITING. There are literary works which owe their very existence to their creator's love of nature, and to his close observation of land and sky, of animals and plants. Among these is the *Georgics* of VIRGIL (q.v. Vol. V), a poem in four books about crops, seasons, and weather, the growing of trees, cattle-rearing, and bee-keeping. The *Georgics* is not merely an agricultural treatise; it is in form and spirit a work of great poetic beauty. It expresses the struggle between man and nature, the dignity of a farmer's work, and the virtue of the simple life.

Virgil could turn his genius both to this natural treatment of the country-side and to what is almost its opposite, the pastoral mode (*see* PASTORALS). But in later times his pastoral poetry was much more imitated than his *Georgics*—in English 16th- and 17th-century poetry, particularly, the pastoral was very popular. The poet was interested only in shepherds who sang and made love, and his scene was Arcadia, not the familiar English country-side. Herrick is one of the few poets of this period whose countrymen worked in the fields. What a contrast there is between a shepherd like William Browne's Thyrsis—

> On a hill that grac'd the plaine
> Thyrsis sate, a comely Swaine,
>   Comelier swaine ne'er grac'd a hill—

and the reapers in Herrick's poem, *The Hock-Cart or Harvest-Home*—

> Come Sons of Summer, by whose toile,
> We are the Lords of Wine and Oile:
> By whose tough labours, and rough hands
> We rip up first, then reap our lands.

Although English poetry from its beginnings is full of natural descriptions, and many of its most delightful lyrics, such as the 13th-century 'Sumer is Icumen in', sing of the pleasures of nature, it is not till the 18th century that a long poem was written about Nature in her varying aspects. *The Seasons* (1726–30), by the Scottish poet James Thomson, is the first of many such poems. It was succeeded by Collins's 'Ode to Evening' (1747); Gray's 'Elegy' (1750); Goldsmith's *Deserted Village* (1770); and Crabbe's painful and realistic picture of the misery of cottage-dwellers, *The Village* (1783).

The poets of the ROMANTIC MOVEMENT (q.v.), and notably Wordsworth, continued to write both rustic and nature poetry; but they went beyond the domestic landscape of villages and fields to the wild grandeur of mountain and cataract. Since Wordsworth's time we accept unthinkingly what was till then unthinkable: that Nature is one of the greatest themes of poetry.

Prose writers saw and recognized the English country-side before the poets did. Izaak Walton's book, *The Compleat Angler* (1653), has been one of the outstandingly popular books (there have been about 280 editions of it). It is at once a technical treatise on angling and a vision of rural England. Walton said that it was a picture of his own disposition, but he lavished as much care and love on the landscape as on the portrait. Rural England is the object of his contemplation and rejoicing, and angling a fit occupation for the calm contemplative:

. . . There I sat [he writes] viewing the silver streams glide silently towards their centre, the tempestuous sea; yet sometimes opposed by rugged roots and pebble stones, which broke their waves, and turned them into foam; and sometimes I beguiled time by viewing the harmless lambs; some leaping securely in the cool shade, whilst others sported themselves in the cheerful sun: and saw others craving comfort from the swollen udders of their bleating dams. As I thus sat, these and other sights had so fully possessed my soul with content, that I thought, as the Poet has happily expressed it:

> I was for that time lifted above earth;
> And possessed joys not promised in my birth.

The name of Gilbert White is inseparably linked with Selborne in Hampshire, where he was born, where he spent most of his life, and which he has lovingly and beautifully described

SELBORNE. FRONTISPIECE TO THE 1813 EDITION OF GILBERT WHITE'S 'NATURAL HISTORY OF SELBORNE'

in his *Natural History and Antiquities of Selborne* (1789) as well as in his *Naturalist's Calendar* and his *Journals*. He presents with the same interest and accuracy the majesty of the Downs or the feeding habits of the bat, the history of the red deer which had formerly inhabited Wolmer Forest or the evening manœuvres of rooks.

Richard Jefferies (1848–87) was as acute an observer as Gilbert White, but his work, notably *Wild Life in a Southern County* and *The Life of the Fields*, is the work of a poet and philosopher as well as of a naturalist. This extract from *Field and Hedgerow* is an example:

If you will look at a grain of wheat you will see that it seems folded up: it has crossed its arms and rolled itself up in a cloak, a fold of which forms a groove, and so gone to sleep. If you look at it some time, as people in the old enchanted days used to look into a mirror, or the magic ink, until they saw living figures therein, you can almost trace a miniature human being in the oval of the grain. . . . And I do not know really whether I might not say that these little grains of English corn do not hold within them the actual flesh and blood of man. Transubstantiation is a fact there.

Sometimes the grains are dry and shrivelled and hard as shot, sometimes they are large and full and have a juiciness about them, sometimes they are a little bit red, others are golden, many white.

W. H. Hudson is better known for a South American romance, *Green Mansions* (whose heroine, Rima, is the subject of the memorial to him in Hyde Park by Epstein), than for his numerous and moving nature-writings. Hudson, born in South America in 1841 of American parents, came to England when he was 28, and later became a British subject. Many of his writings are about birds—*Birds in London* (1898), *Birds and Man* (1901), *Adventures among Birds* (1913). Others treat of more general aspects of Nature; among them *Afoot in England* (1909), *A Traveller in Little Things* (1921), and his delightful record of the life of the Wiltshire Downs, its people, and their dogs and sheep—*A Shepherd's Life* (1910).

The American, Henry David Thoreau (1817–62), described many of America's varied landscapes. During the years 1845–7, he lived like a hermit at Walden Pond (Massachusetts) in a hut which he built himself, and there wrote his best-known work, *Walden, or Life in the Woods*. In this series of eighteen essays, he describes the natural life of the pond and its influence on his thought and belief. Several brief trips he made supplied him with material for *Excursions*, *The Maine Woods*, *Cape Cod*, and *A Yankee in Canada*, all published after his death. Thoreau, a stubborn individualist, was as unsentimental about nature as he was ardent. He said that he liked 'better the surliness with which the woodchopper speaks of his woods, handling them as indifferently as his axe, than the mealy-mouthed enthusiasm of the lover of nature'.

See also PASTORALS.

NEGRO ART, *see* AFRICAN ART.

NEGRO SPIRITUALS. Nearly all the missionary work to the Negro slaves in America was undertaken by Nonconformist ministers, and their emotional HYMNS (q.v.) were enthusiastically accepted. At about the beginning of the 19th century Presbyterian missionaries started the great 'Camp Meeting' revival, holding meetings in country districts in chapels improvised out of tents and covered wagons. The Methodists who followed the Presbyterians had even more emotional hymns; these made a

Verse 1. De gos-pel train am a-com-in', I
Verse 2. I hear de train a-com-in', She's

hear it jus' at han', I hear de car-wheels
comin' roun' de curve, She's loosened all her

rum - blin', An' roll - in' thoo' de
steam an' brakes An' strain-in' ev - 'ry

Chorus
lan', Den git on bo'd lit'-l' chil'-en, Git on
nerve.

bo'd lit'-l' chil-dren, Git on bo'd lit'-l'

children, There's room for ma-ny a mo'.

FIG. I

When Is - rael was in E-gypt's lan'

Let my people go. Oppressed so hard they

could not stand, Let my people go. Go down,

Mo - ses, Way down in E - gypt's lan',—

Tell ole 'Pharaoh to let my people go

FIG. 2

tremendous appeal to the Negroes who, during generations of slavery, had been denied all religious consolation and had received little human sympathy. But even the evangelical hymns did not satisfy the tumultuous emotional demands of the Negroes, and spontaneous song became characteristic of the camp meetings. Someone would sing a roughly improvised verse —usually very irregular from a poetical point of view—made up of odd jumbles of phrases from the scriptures and everyday speech. Everybody would join in with the chorus, or with periodical shouts of 'Hallelujah' or 'Amen'. When the singing became frenzied the people would mark time by clapping and stamping. One can easily imagine with what excitement the chorus to the song in Fig. I, for example, would be sung.

The imagery of the train, after its advent about 1830, appeared frequently in Negro spirituals. Many Negroes worked on the building of railways, which became to them a symbol of escape. Not all the spirituals were as exuberant as the one in Fig. I, however. Often they were filled with the deepest melancholy, a heartrending longing such as one can imagine filling the hearts of the Jews in captivity in Egypt, whose lot, as the Negroes realized, resembled their own in America (Fig. 2). To the Negroes the Bible was intensely real: the Old Testament stories were wonderful but literal events to be told, retold, and pondered upon (Fig. 3).

The most important musical characteristic is the intense rhythmic verve with which the

(Dorian Mode)

If there's an - y - bo - dy here like

weep - in'__ Ma - ry, Call up - on your

Jesus an' He'll draw nigh. O__ glo - ry,

glo - ry hal - le - lu - jah! Glo - ry be to

my God, who rules on high

FIG. 3

spirituals are performed. The feeling for rhythm may be an unconscious memory of African drum music, and it found an important outlet in Jazz (q.v.); the rhythms of the spirituals and the more intricate rhythms of jazz, however, show no direct connexion with African drum rhythms, which were far more complicated (*see* PRIMITIVE MUSIC). One frequent rhythmic feature is the Scotch Snap (♪♩.) (*see* Figs. 1 and 2). In the melodies the influence of the evangelical hymns can often be observed, though the spirituals avoided their banality. Some spirituals are based on modes and pentatonic scales (*see* SCALES), offering a refreshing contrast to the conventional major and minor scales of the missionaries' hymns. In this they betray their connexion with FOLK-SONG (q.v.) imported by European settlers.

See also Vol. I: AMERICAN NEGROES.

NORMAN ARCHITECTURE, *see* CHURCH ARCHITECTURE, ENGLISH; ROMANESQUE ART.

NOTATION, MUSICAL, *see* MUSICAL NOTATION.

NOVEL. 1. The novel is a prose story which describes some aspect of the lives of human beings. This story is usually complete in itself, whether it be concerned with a single episode or the whole lifetime of a character, or with the complicated interweaving of a dozen different lives; and its length is usually not less than about 50,000 words—often very much more.

In the present century prose fiction has become by far the most popular form of imaginative literature, much more widely read than poetry or drama; and as many as 2,000 novels are sometimes published in a year. Whether the author's theme be adventure or the unravelling of some social complication, he has to give an illusion of reality to his fictitious characters and incidents in order to hold the reader's attention. A modern novelist usually works out his plot in great detail before he starts to write, so that his carefully selected incidents will reveal his characters' personalities or help the action along. On the other hand, some of the great 19th-century novelists, such as Dickens, concentrated on the creation of living characters and let the plot develop in the haphazard way of life itself. This more haphazard development was partly conditioned by the fact that the novels were frequently first published in serial form in a magazine.

The novel can have other functions besides entertainment. The author may attempt to penetrate and expose the inner workings of the human mind, revealing and describing emotions not obvious from behaviour; or he may use the novel to propound some theory or to illustrate a moral precept. Such a 'novel of ideas' is successful only if the author is able to clothe his abstract theory with living characters, avoiding the temptation to distort or over-simplify life for his purpose.

2. EARLY HISTORY. The European novel was a product of the 18th century, the result of a profound change in taste which had been taking place, particularly in England, during the previous 100 years. Realism, insistence on fact, and unwillingness to take anything for granted characterized the mood of the 17th century, the century of great scientific discoveries. At the same time there arose a large new class of merchants and trades-people, who formed a literate public eager for entertainment and instruction.

There had been a few early works of prose fiction in England, for example Nashe's *Unfortunate Traveller* (1594), Bunyan's PILGRIM'S PROGRESS (q.v.), and the works of Daniel DEFOE at the beginning of the 18th century. In the 1740's, however, works of the three great originators of the novel, Richardson, FIELDING,

MR. B. FINDS PAMELA WRITING
Illustration by Joseph Highmore (1692–1780) to Richardson's first novel, *Pamela*

and Smollett, began to appear; these might be said to correspond roughly to the categories into which most novels can still be divided: novels of emotion or psychological analysis, 'novels of manners' (that is, the behaviour of people as social beings), and novels of action and adventure. In addition, the 18th century produced the first 'novels of ideas': SWIFT's *Gulliver's Travels*, Dr. JOHNSON's *Rasselas*, and, in France, VOLTAIRE's *Candide*.

The early novelists, with the exception of Richardson, were more concerned to give a general picture of the life of their time than to portray individual character. It is for this reason that Fielding and Smollett often take their heroes from place to place, from country houses to London inns, perhaps to places of amusement, to prison, or to sea. The hero's emotions and thoughts are never given in 'close-up': he is simply a central figure who passes through a succession of scenes and meets a variety of characters, so enabling the author to build up a complete picture of society.

This emphasis on a panoramic view frequently makes the 18th-century novelist appear indifferent to the feelings of his hero. Smollett's *Roderick Random*, for example, suffers agonies at school and again when he studies medicine, is hustled through a series of adventures and encounters in London, and then joins the navy where his tribulations begin afresh. No single man could have endured all that Roderick suffered; but Smollett was less concerned with Roderick than with his object of introducing as many scenes and characters as possible, and thus painting a broad picture of society in general.

Fielding's *Tom Jones* has the same object, but Fielding's greater artistry and deeper interest in human nature enabled him to make the hero convincing as a person as well as a device for changing the scene. These novels and their descendants (called 'picaresque' from the Spanish word for 'rogue') trace their ancestry back to CERVANTES' *Don Quixote*.

The novel took a great step forward when writers began to examine their characters' thoughts and emotions, making these as interesting to the reader as the life of action. In 1678 a Frenchwoman, Madame de La Fayette, wrote a story, *La Princesse de Clèves*, which concentrated on a simple and realistic analysis of feeling. The 'novel of emotion' was thus born in France (where it has found a congenial home ever since). The 18th-century English writer, Richardson, penetrated more deeply into the subtle processes of the heart than any previous prose writer had done, and his *Pamela, or Virtue Rewarded* (1740) was the first English prose story to combine the element of action and character-analysis within the framework of a controlled plot, and so is usually called the first modern novel.

3. THE NOVEL OF ACTION. The novel of action and adventure is still very much alive today. At the beginning of the 19th century it was enriched with a sense of history by Sir Walter SCOTT, who used the heroic past of his country as the setting for his tales of adventure, and made the dry bones of dead ages live in a way that was unique at the time. The adventure story for boys can be traced back to Captain Marryat, whose first books are contemporary with Scott's last ones, and who wrote exciting tales of the sea. Towards the end of the 19th century the genius of R. L. STEVENSON and KIPLING raised the adventure story to the level of great literature. This form of novel, in the hands of a writer experienced both in life and in literary technique, not only provides first-class entertainment but also enlarges the reader's knowledge of the world by describing unfamiliar places and unusual occupations. Kipling's stories of India, notably *Kim*, are an instance of this.

DETECTIVE STORIES (q.v.), originated in the mid-19th century by Wilkie Collins and later developed by Conan DOYLE, are primarily concerned with the manipulation of a plot, so that the reader is kept in suspense until the mystery is revealed, and convincing characterization is of secondary importance. Lack of interest in character is also a feature of modern 'horror' novels, many of which come from America, and which are descended from the 'Gothic' style of romantic fiction fashionable at the end of the 18th century. Ivied ruins, owls, skeletons, 'all delicious threatening horrors' were the subjects of these wildly fantastic novels, inaugurated by Horace Walpole's *Castle of Otranto* in 1764. Mary Shelley's *Frankenstein* (1818) is the prototype of the semi-human monster which readers meet again in the works of H. G. WELLS and the modern strip cartoon.

4. THE NOVEL OF MANNERS. This is the largest and most important category of novel, and the one to which England has made the greatest contribution. Fielding declared that the whole of human life was to be his subject, and he consciously tried to make his new literary form, the 'comic epic in prose' as he called it, both a realistic mirror and a critical consideration of the life of the time. Jane AUSTEN was not concerned with this panoramic view of society; she turned her extraordinary power of observation and keenly critical moral sense on to the complexities of personal relationships. It is this intense interest in life and marked concern with its moral problems which characterizes the great tradition of the 19th-century English novel and distinguishes it from the French. George ELIOT raised the novel to new heights by her own high moral seriousness, her lofty conception of life and its values, and her psychological insight.

The 19th century was rich in novels in England, France, and Russia. DICKENS and TROLLOPE were superb entertainers; Henry James, an American living in Europe, evolved new ways of using language to reveal shades and subtleties of meaning in highly-complicated personal relationships. The Russian novelists, Gogol, DOSTOEVSKY, and TOLSTOY paralleled the English writers in their serious view of life and art. France had novelists of unsurpassed technical brilliance such as FLAUBERT, but in general they seem to lack the human sympathy and sense of human values which make George Eliot's *Middlemarch* or Tolstoy's *War and Peace* completely satisfying as comments upon life as well as pictures of it.

5. THE NOVEL OF EMOTION. The novel of psychological analysis was not greatly developed in 19th-century England, possibly owing to the

Victorians' dislike and distrust of passion, in particular sexual passion. THACKERAY, for example, complained that he could not portray every side of a young man's life as the 18th-century writers had done, and Emily BRONTË's stormy and passionate masterpiece, *Wuthering Heights*, caused a good deal of shocked comment. The psychological novel developed, therefore, more freely in other countries—in France by STENDHAL and Flaubert; in Russia by Dostoevsky, who plunged below the surface of conscious thought as no previous novelist had done. Dostoevsky's novels in translation reached England and France shortly before the First World War, at about the same time that the psychologist Sigmund FREUD published his startling revelations of the hidden springs of human behaviour. This new knowledge of the workings of the subconscious mind provided important new material for the novelist, of which many writers, notably D. H. LAWRENCE, have since made direct use.

One of the most interesting and influential experiments in the portrayal of emotion was made in France by Marcel PROUST, who in his immensely long work, *Remembrance of Things Past*, explores the feelings of his various characters by means of a highly subtle and complicated interweaving of themes, changes of viewpoint, shifts of time and place, and the slow uncovering of layer beneath layer of personality. But, as with Flaubert, the reader feels that the vision of life that this tremendous literary achievement seeks to express is one of disgust and disdain for human nature, far removed from the profound humanity of the world's greatest novelists.

Towards our own day James JOYCE and Virginia Woolf have carried the expression of shades of emotion a step further still by means of the 'stream of consciousness' technique: their novels, that is to say, do not describe behaviour or even states of mind but rather the shifting interplay of impressions that crowd into the mind when it is in the very act of thinking. In Joyce's *Ulysses* and *Finnegans Wake* this technique becomes so involved that, like a scrambled jigsaw puzzle of thoughts, it is almost impossible for the reader to follow. It is difficult to imagine that the novel could be developed further along these lines. The novel which describes and comments upon man as a social being rather than as an individual consciousness is perhaps the most capable of development in the future.

The novelists whose names are printed in capital letters have biographies in Volume V.

See also SHORT STORIES; DETECTIVE STORIES; CHILDREN'S BOOKS.

NURSERY RHYMES. The rhymes we first hear in the nursery remain with us throughout our lives. Our mother or nurse learnt them when she was a child, and they are almost certainly the first to come to our minds when we ourselves look after children. It is possible to prove that many of them have been passed on from one generation to another for centuries.

Opie Collection

HEY DIDDLE, DIDDLE
Woodcut from Catnach's *Nursery Rhymes, c.* 1830

Almost everyone, from Elizabethan times onwards, has been familiar with the story of the 'Frog who would a-wooing go'; and, when wanting to know how many days there are in a month, has consulted the rhyme which begins, 'Thirty days hath September'.

At the beginning of the 19th century, when scholars were becoming interested in studying the origins of everyday habits and superstitions, several curious facts about nursery rhymes came to light. It was then noticed that almost identical rhymes were repeated by the children of other countries. It was realized that many of the words contained in the rhymes did not belong to our modern language.

In 1842 a young man, James Orchard Halliwell, who had been asked by a learned society to make a collection of the rhymes, published a book called *The Nursery Rhymes of England*. Nearly all the rhymes we know today are included in his collection, showing that 'Hey diddle, diddle' and 'Solomon Grundy', for example, were known to the early Victorian nursemaids. Halliwell's collection was not only far larger than any there had been before; it was also annotated, and he gave some indication

Opie Collection
MOTHER GOOSE
Woodcut, *c.* 1850

of the age of the rhymes. People began to become interested in discovering exactly when the rhymes did first appear. Little toy books were discovered. One, called *Tommy Thumb's Little Song Book*, and including such well-known pieces as 'Baa, baa, black sheep' and 'Little Tommy Tucker', had been published in 1744. Another, perhaps the most famous nursery-rhyme book, *Mother Goose's Melody*, may have been compiled about 1765 and contained over fifty rhymes, nearly all of them, such as 'Ding, dong, bell' and 'Ride a cock horse to Banbury Cross', favourites of today. Further research among old writings revealed that certain of the rhymes had been referred to at even earlier dates: 'London Bridge

Opie Collection
SIMPLE SIMON
Woodcut, *c.* 1820

is broken down' was cited in 1725, 'A was an Apple-Pie' in 1671, and the rhyme

Jack will eat no fat, and
Jill doth love no leane.
Yet betwixt them both
They lick the dishes cleane

appeared, exactly like this, in a book dated 1639. And a search through the works of Elizabethan dramatists shows that they knew songs such as 'There were three jovial Welshmen' and 'Tommy O'Linn and his wife and wife's mother'.

It now becomes pertinent to ask whether any of the characters in the rhymes were real people. A great many suggestions have been made. The original Jack Horner is said to have been steward to the last Abbot of Glastonbury. He was instructed to take a pie to King Henry VIII as a Christmas gift. Inside the pie were the deeds of the Manor of Mells, which Jack extracted while on the way. Thus goes the legend. What is certain is that a man named Horner did move into the Manor in 1543, shortly after the dissolution of Glastonbury Abbey. His descendants live there to this day, though they say that their ancestor bought the property. The rhyme, nevertheless, may well date from this period. Other

Opie Collection
LITTLE JACK HORNER
Woodcut from *Cradle Melodies, c.* 1850

nursery characters, also, were probably real people: for example, 'the brave old Duke of York' may have been Frederick, son of George III, and

Bessy Bell and Mary Gray,
They were two bonny lasses

were, according to tradition, two 17th-century beauties of Perthshire who built themselves a bower at a place called Burn-braes outside Perth to escape the plague, but who nevertheless

Opie Collection
DING, DONG, BELL
PUSSY'S IN THE WELL
Woodcut from Catnach's *Nursery Rhymes, c.* 1830

caught the plague and both died. The Elsie
Marley of the rhyme

> Elsie Marley is grown so fine,
> She won't get up to feed the swine,
> But lies in bed till eight or nine.
>   Lazy Elsie Marley

is identified as an alewife of Picktree in Co.
Durham who died in 1768.

In a few cases we know the exact origin of a
rhyme and who made it up. The man who did
not like Dr. Fell was the satirist Tom Brown.
His jingle perpetuates the memory of Dr. John
Fell (1625–86), one of the promoters of the
Oxford University Press, the publishers of this
Encyclopaedia. 'Twinkle, twinkle, little star'
was written by a young girl, Jane Taylor, and
published in *Rhymes for the Nursery* in 1806.
'Mary had a little lamb' was written by the
American authoress, Sarah Josepha Hale, and
published in 1830.

The rhymes which are believed to be oldest
are those which have equivalents in foreign languages. The invocation to the ladybird to fly
away home has parallels in France, Germany,
Switzerland, Denmark, and Sweden. The riddle
rhyme about Humpty-Dumpty is a favourite
throughout Europe. The similarity of some
Continental versions to ours may be judged by
the following from Germany:

> Hümpelken-Pümpelken sat op de Bank,
> Hümpelken-Pümpelken fēl von de Bank;
> Do is kên Dokter in Engelland
> De Hümpelken-Pümpelken kuräre kann.

The European versions of these rhymes appear
to be the original, and folklorists who have studied the problem are puzzled as to how the
rhymes came to us from across the sea. The most
plausible explanation they can give is yet the
most extraordinary, that the rhymes date from
an age before that usually covered in history
books. This may not seem so strange, however,
if we think again of the persistence with which
the jingles remain in our minds, even those which
are composed of unmeaning words. 'Onery,
twoery, Ziccary, zan' and 'Ena, meena, mina,
mo' are rhymes frequently used for counting
out at the beginning of a game. Yet it is fairly
certain that these words are relics of numerals
which were used by the Ancient Britons before
the Romans came to this country.

See also Vol. I: FAIRY-TALES; FOLK-LORE.

Opie Collection
THE HOUSE THAT JACK BUILT, *c.* 1820

O

OBELISK, *see* MONUMENTS.

OCEANIC ART. 1. Oceania consists of a large number of scattered islands and archipelagos in the Pacific Ocean, from New Guinea in the west to Easter Island in the east, and from Hawaii in the north to New Zealand in the south. The inhabitants fall into two main groups, the MELANESIANS, including the Papuans, in the west, and the POLYNESIANS (qq.v. Vol. I) in the region east of Fiji. Before the discovery of the islands, the Polynesians had reached a higher level of culture than the others. They worshipped a number of gods personifying

British Museum

PAINTED BARK-CLOTH MASK OF THE ELEMA TRIBES, PAPUAN GULF, NEW GUINEA

the sky, the sea, war, and so on, while the more primitive Melanesians believed in the power of ghosts and demons, and particularly the spirits of their ancestors (*see* ANCESTOR WORSHIP, Vol. I). These differences in culture and religion are reflected in their art, much of which is closely connected with supernatural beliefs and ceremonies. The Polynesians carved wooden and occasionally stone images of their gods in human form, and set them up in their holy places, while the Melanesians made masks for use by the members of secret societies, who impersonated spirits at funerals and other religious rites. Apart from art inspired by religion, useful objects were decorated simply for the love of pattern and colour, especially by the Papuans and Melanesians. Among the Polynesians the best decorative art was produced by the MAORIS of New Zealand (q.v. Vol. I) and the Marquesas islanders. Their arts, however, tended to degenerate soon after their contact with European explorers in the late 18th century, and comparatively little of the best old work, which was carved entirely with tools of stone, shell, or bone, has been preserved to the present day.

2. PAPUA AND MELANESIA. The richest development of art is found in the large island of New Guinea or Papua. The country is so much split up by high mountains and dense forests that each tribal area evolved its own distinctive style.

In northern New Guinea wooden figures carved in the round often depict ancestors quite realistically. Even more lifelike are the portrait heads in which the face is modelled in clay over the actual skull of the dead man. On the other hand, wooden masks and statuettes are generally carved in a conventional style with a long bird's beak in place of a nose, to represent a 'soul bird'. Some animals are rendered with great realism— for instance, crocodiles on canoe prows and hornbills on drums. Pigs' heads are modelled on large pots at some villages; at others the pots are covered with spiral patterns, deeply incised and painted in several colours. Generally speaking, the geometric patterns are derived from human or animal forms throughout Oceania.

On the south coast, in the region of the Papuan Gulf, masks are usually made of bark cloth on wicker frames, the features being outlined with strips of cane and painted white, black, and red. In these faces all pretence of realism is sacrificed to fanciful design. The eyes

British Museum

LEFT ABOVE: HUMAN SKULL WITH FACE MODELLED IN CLAY AND PAINTED, FROM NEW GUINEA
BELOW: PAINTED WOODEN MASK WITH FIBRE HEAD-DRESS, FROM NEW IRELAND
CENTRE: WOODEN DRUM ORNAMENTED WITH CARVED SCROLLS, A HORNBILL, AND A GROTESQUE FACE, FROM NEW GUINEA
RIGHT: CARVED AND PAINTED ANCESTOR FIGURE, FROM NEW IRELAND

and mouth are much distorted and often surrounded by sharply indented lines, producing a ghostly effect as befits their purpose. There is no sculpture in the round, but grotesque figure designs are carved in flat relief and painted on 'spirit boards' and shields, which are hung up in the men's club houses (*see* Vol. I, p. 20). Elaborate patterns are carved on the broad bark belts and painted on the loin cloths worn by men; and geometric designs are incised or 'pokerworked' on bamboo pipes, gourd vessels, and other useful objects.

At the eastern end of New Guinea there are no masks or statues, but almost all implements, utensils, and ritual objects are profusely decorated with patterns of curved lines, such as spirals, which are derived from birds' heads and snakes. The varying rhythm and balance of

these delicately flowing curves is best seen on the flat surfaces of canoe-prows, house boards, and dance paddles (*see* p. 363). A high degree of skill is shown in New Ireland in the figures of clan ancestors, which are carved by specialists for exhibition at great funeral feasts and INITIATION CEREMONIES (q.v. Vol. I). These figures are often enveloped in an intricate mesh of birds and fishes, representing good and evil spirits, carved in openwork and painted in vivid colours. In the same island simpler figures, commemorating important chiefs, are carved in wood and chalk.

In the Solomon Islands various styles of woodcarving are practised, both in flat relief and in the round; some of the figures show marked realism. The individual character of their art is displayed in wooden food bowls and troughs, which have boldly projecting figures of birds and

British Museum

LEFT: CARVED WOODEN IDOL FROM RAROTONGA, COOK ISLANDS
CENTRE: CARVED WOODEN IDOL FROM HAWAII
RIGHT: WAR GOD OF RED FEATHER-WORK WITH SHELL EYES, FROM HAWAII

fish at the ends. The surface is blackened and enriched by inlaying small triangular pieces of shell in bands. Shell inlay is a favourite form of decoration here and is applied to many objects, including the large head-hunting canoes. A stylized form of the FRIGATE BIRD (q.v. Vol. II) appears in many of their patterns, especially in finely fretted turtle shell ornaments and incised patterns on bamboo lime boxes.

3. POLYNESIA. Polynesian art is at its richest in New Zealand, where the characteristic curvilinear patterns resemble those of New Guinea or Indonesia. The Maoris carved figures in the round and in relief on houseposts and panels in a formal style; often a grotesque expression was produced by tilting the eyes and enlarging the mouth. They excelled in the sumptuous decoration of wooden surfaces, which were covered all

British Museum

WOODEN DOOR LINTEL FROM NEW ZEALAND WITH FIGURES AND SCROLLS CARVED IN OPENWORK over with patterns usually composed of human and demon grotesques intertwined with scrolls and spirals. These were carved in high relief or in openwork on house boards, lintels, and the prows of canoes, as well as on implements, wooden boxes, flutes, and other small articles. Jade pendants, called 'tikis',which were treasured as heirlooms, were carved in the form of little grotesque figures with shell eyes.

In central Polynesia (Samoa, Tonga) there was little figure or decorative carving except on clubs. In the eastern archipelagos (Society, Cook, Marquesas, Sandwich Islands) wooden idols were carved in various conventional styles, which never approach individual portraiture. In Hawaii the idols are given a highly grotesque expression with enormous mouths (*see* Vol. I, p. 371). Similar features are seen in war gods made of red feathers and furnished with shell eyes and dogs' teeth, as well as in carved figure supports for food bowls. In the Marquesas the face is modelled in a more refined style in low relief with large round eyes and flattened nose, and the same motifs appear in the patterns carved on bowls, paddle clubs, and other objects.

The colossal stone statues of Easter Island, where there was no timber for large-scale carving, are up to 36 ft. in height. The hollow eyes and thin lips and the simple but massive treatment of the body give the statues an air of serene and unearthly dignity. Ritual figures of birds and 'birdmen' were cut in bold relief on rock surfaces, and small wooden statuettes of ancestors with emaciated features were carved in a more lifelike style.

Throughout Polynesia decorative designs were painted or printed on sheets of bark cloth, and elaborate patterns were tattooed on the face or body in most islands.

See also PRIMITIVE ART.

ODE. This is a poem with a noble theme. In different ages and in different countries, poets have produced odes which vary greatly both in form and quality, the greatest being among the finest poems of the world. 'Ode' comes from a Greek word meaning 'song'. The form was invented by the Greeks, and was written to be sung by a full choir on great public occasions. The earliest known ode, Alcman's 'Maiden-Song' (7th century B.C.), displays the distinguishing features of the Greek ode: it was written for a festival of the gods, and celebrated both the gods

British Museum

COLOSSAL STONE STATUE FROM ORONGO, EASTER ISLAND, ORIGINALLY COLOURED RED AND WHITE, ABOUT 8 FT. HIGH

and those who took part in their festival; it told a story of gods or heroes; and it described the relations between men and gods. Pindar (518–438 B.C.), whose odes have never been surpassed, composed his choral songs and their music to celebrate the victories of athletes at the great Games festivals, such as the OLYMPIC GAMES (q.v. Vol. IX). In these songs, of which four books are known to us, he celebrates victory as a godlike attribute to which men may momentarily attain, and as an inspiration to the poet to recall the heroic legends of the victor's family. His poems, which were sung and danced by a large choir, have very intricate rhythms, and vary greatly in length (from 24 to 300 lines).

HORACE, who lived in the 1st century B.C., is the greatest Roman writer of odes. Horace's odes are very different from Pindar's; they were intended to be read, not sung and danced to a great audience. They owe much to the Greek lyric writers Alcaeus and SAPPHO, and so they partake of the nature both of ode and LYRIC POETRY (q.v.). Elegant, meditative, and restrained, they vary greatly in metre and tone, and their themes range from the pleasures of wine to the greatness of Rome.

European poets from the Renaissance onwards owe much to Pindar and Horace. The Renaissance lyricists first applied the word 'ode' to Pindar's torrential choral songs, to the calm melodies of Horace, and to those of their own lyrics which attempted great and noble themes in the classical manner. The French 16th-century poet Pierre RONSARD wrote, to rival Pindar, four *Books of the Odes*, which, however, neither eclipsed Pindar's star nor are among the best of Ronsard's own poetry.

Certain of Shakespeare's contemporaries attempted to write odes, but the first great Pindaric ode in English is MILTON's *On the Morning of Christ's Nativity*. The ode proper, following an invocation to the Muse, sings the coming triumph of Christianity and its victory over the dying gods of old. The great theme is presented in powerful language and flowing rhythm. While Milton was writing his Nativity ode, Ben JONSON was finishing his *Ode on the Death of Sir H. Morison*, which owes more to Horace than to Pindar, particularly in its epigrammatic quality:

> In small proportions we just beauties see;
> And in short measures, life may perfect be.

Andrew Marvell's *Horatian Ode upon Cromwell's return from Ireland* (1650), a conscious and successful imitation of Horace's heroic odes, celebrates Cromwell's greatness and the tragic events of the Civil War. Its description of the execution of King Charles is justly famous:

> He nothing common did or mean
> Upon that memorable scene,
> But with his keener eye
> The axe's edge did try;

Towards the end of the 17th century odes with music for singers and orchestra were written and performed in great numbers, the most successful being DRYDEN's well known *Alexander's Feast*, which he thought his best poem, and which HANDEL later set to music.

Neither of the two great 18th-century ode-writers, Thomas Gray (1716–71) and William Collins (1721–59), wrote their odes for musical performance, but the former's *Progress of Poesy* and *The Bard* and the latter's *Ode to Evening* have an innate musical quality:

> Like thy own solemn springs,
> Thy springs, and dying gales;

The poets of the ROMANTIC MOVEMENT (q.v.) —GOETHE in Germany, Victor HUGO in France, in England WORDSWORTH, COLERIDGE, KEATS, and SHELLEY—gave the ode fresh vigour and beauty. They widened its range of themes and deepened its emotional power by using it to express private experiences. Wordsworth, for example, in his great ode on *Intimations of Immortality*, tells of a spiritual loss—'that there hath passed away a glory from the earth'; he contemplates the nature of this lost radiance, and resolves his suffering and discord into a harmony:

> To me the meanest flower that blows can give
> Thoughts that do often lie too deep for tears.

Again, Keats in *Ode on a Grecian Urn* and *Ode to a Nightingale* mourns the despair and sorrow of life and time which only the eternity and deathlessness of art and music can lighten. In these three, as in the other 'romantic' odes, much of the character of the Greek odes has vanished with the audience, the music, and the dance. But much remains. Many formal characteristics persist; for example, the ode is almost always addressed to someone or something:

> O wild West Wind, thou breath of Autumn's being
> (Shelley).

Its rhythms are free and varied, not now with the freedom of dance movement but in accord with the free-moving imagination; its language is noble—even Wordsworth abandons in the ode his theory of everyday language for poetry—its images sharp and evocative, its detail clear and bright. The tone, too, is noble, symphonic. The victories it celebrates are victories of men's spirit; the relation between men and gods is no longer its theme, but instead the relation between men and their noblest conceptions: time, beauty, truth.

The poets whose names are printed in capital letters have biographies in Volume V.

See also POETRY; LYRIC POETRY.

ODYSSEY, *see* HOMERIC LITERATURE.

OIL PAINTING, *see* PAINTING METHODS, Section 5.

OLYMPIA. This was the chief sanctuary of Zeus (*see* GOD, Vol. I) in Greece, and was sacred to all Greeks. It was famous for the OLYMPIC GAMES (q.v. Vol. IX), held every 4th year in honour of Zeus.

The sanctuary consisted of a sacred enclosure containing two temples (one of Hera and one of Zeus), eleven State treasuries, and countless statues dedicated by victors in the Games. The athletic buildings were outside the walls of the enclosure.

The Temple of Hera, begun in the 7th century B.C., was originally of wood, but was later rebuilt in stone. Nothing remains of the sculpture except a stone head, perhaps of the statue of the goddess, which was made about 600 B.C. The Temple of Zeus, completed in 457 B.C., was built in the Doric ORDER OF ARCHITECTURE (q.v.). The sculptures which decorated it are some of the grandest in ancient art. The west pediment (gable) shows a battle between Greeks and centaurs; in the centre stands the god Apollo. The east pediment shows the beginning of a legendary chariot-race. Over the porches at front and back there are reliefs of the twelve labours of Heracles (*see* Vol. I, pp. 201 and 207).

The author of these sculptures is not known. Phidias made the statue of Zeus which was placed within the temple (*see* WONDERS OF THE WORLD), but he cannot be the sculptor of the statues and reliefs on the building, since they differ so greatly from the sculptures of the Parthenon, for which we know he was responsible.

Amongst the works of art discovered at Olympia, the most famous is a statue of Hermes holding the infant god Dionysus, made by the Athenian sculptor PRAXITELES (q.v. Vol. V) about 350 B.C. The temples are now ruined, and most of the sculptures which survive are in a museum on the site.

See also GREEK ART.
See also Vol. I: TEMPLE; GODS OF GREECE AND ROME.

OPERA, HISTORY OF. OPERA (q.v. Vol. IX) is the only musical form which was invented rather than evolved like the SYMPHONY or SONATA (qq.v.), for example, out of other and less developed kinds of musical composition. The first operas were composed at the end of the 16th century by members of an aristocratic group of amateur musicians in Florence, who were trying to create a musical style in which to deliver the lines of a play as they thought the Greeks had done in ancient GREEK DRAMA (q.v.). Their solution to the problem, *recitativo secco* (*see* SONG, HISTORY OF, Section 4), which delivered the words quickly, reproducing as nearly as possible the speed, accentuation, pitch, and so on of ordinary speech, introduced a break with musical tradition and a new way of composing music. Its inventors were primarily interested in how the ancients had declaimed the lines of their dramas, and, in the earliest opera which has survived complete, Peri's *Euridice* (1600), the purely musical interest is negligible.

The Italian musician, Claudio Monteverdi, whose first opera, *Orfeo*, was produced in 1607, gave musical life and interest to this new style. Monteverdi sought to convey by his music the ideas and emotions expressed by the words. He did not hesitate to write tuneful airs if these served convincingly to express the feelings of the characters in the drama, or to use the *recitativo secco* of the Florentines, particularly at exciting points in the story when it was important to tell the story with the least delay. He imbued the opera with more musical feeling, even allowing traces of real melody to creep in. He introduced choruses and dances: in fact he made use of all musical forms and styles known to him. Monteverdi's success depended on his power of conceiving the whole drama, all its characters, all its incidents, in terms of music, and this made him the first great opera composer.

In the period after Monteverdi's death the demands of the music tended to outweigh the demands of the drama. The history of opera has always been something of a tug of war between the music and the drama, and a proper correlation of the two is one of the qualities of great opera. Songs in a set form (arias) were introduced, irrespective of whether the form fitted into the dramatic situation or not. Alessandro Scarlatti (*c.* 1660–1725), for example, established a highly conventional style of Italian opera in which recitative and aria were carefully distinguished and the arias extended. These became widely popular with fashionable audiences throughout Europe, and were introduced to London by HANDEL (q.v. Vol. V).

These operas were governed by rigid conventions: there were always three female and three male soloists, no singer having two songs in succession; and the opera was in three acts,

Roger Wood

SCENE FROM MOZART'S 'MARRIAGE OF FIGARO': CHERUBINO, SUSANNA, AND THE COUNTESS
From a performance of the opera at Glyndebourne

each scene ending with an aria. With such rules, dramatic truth and life were impossible, and this led Dr. Johnson to call the opera 'an exotic and irrational entertainment'. Subsidiary entertainments were given between the acts of the opera, and from these the Italians developed a new style of opera called *opera buffa* (comic opera). This, though still using the recitative and aria of serious opera, discarded its conventionality and pomposity, together with its themes from mythology and classical literature, introducing instead modern themes, unashamedly gay and vigorous in their simple sense of fun. One of the most famous *opera buffa* is Pergolesi's *La Serva Padrona* (1733), which tells of the attempts of a serving-maid to trick her master into marriage.

A somewhat similar process went on in France, where opera had been established in Paris by an Italian, Giovanni Battista Lully (1632–87), in the employ of Louis XIV. Its recitative evolved in a way more suited to the French language. French opera also developed two things which Italian opera had practically ignored—the chorus and the BALLET (q.v. Vol. IX); but it was

as artificial and as far removed from the reality of everyday life as the Italian opera, and the development of the *opéra comique* served the same purpose as the *opera buffa* did in Italy.

In England the starchy conventions of the Italian opera were attacked by the popular *Beggar's Opera* (1728)—a 'ballad opera' in which the main action was carried on in ordinary speech, interspersed with songs which were already old favourites—a form which became very popular in England (*see* Vol. IX, p. 350). Far from dealing with legendary heroes, it told of the adventures of a highwayman. English ballad opera, the French *opéra comique*, and also the German form of humorous opera known as *singspiel*, differed from the Italian comic opera in using spoken dialogue.

In the mid-18th century GLUCK (q.v. Vol. V) completely remodelled the form of serious opera, though he kept to classical themes. Attacking the conventional layout of the story itself, he aimed to tell his story as simply as possible, but sincerely, without standardized sentiments and characters. Like Monteverdi, he wanted to deal with genuine human passions and emotions; but to do this he had to change not only the treatment of the plot, but also the style and form of the music, which he had to adapt to the needs of the drama. Amongst his most significant operas were *Orfeo* (1762) and *Alceste* (1767).

MOZART (q.v. Vol. V) continued the Gluck style in his opera *Idomeneo*, but his most famous operas—*The Marriage of Figaro, Don Giovanni*, and *Così fan Tutte*—although they broke from it in many ways, are all in the tradition of Italian comic opera. *The Magic Flute*, written to German words, had a great influence on later German opera: originally it set out to be a comic play with songs (in the *singspiel* tradition), but it gradually developed into a much more serious affair, concerning itself with moral and ethical ideas. Though the plot is muddled, the opera as a whole, which never fails to be entertaining, is woven into an artistic unity by the brilliance of the music.

In Paris the *opéra comique*, though intended for popular audiences, was more and more patronized by the nobility. Though it always remained topical, its character in other ways began to change: adopting devices from serious opera, it gradually replaced its somewhat ribald good humour by a sentimental pastoralism—for shepherds and shepherdesses were at that time fashionable in all fields of art (*see* ROCOCO ART). After the French Revolution the original comic element had virtually disappeared. Beethoven's one opera, *Fidelio* (1805), makes use of the spoken dialogue of the French *opéra comique*, and it shows the influence of the French Revolution in its theme of heroism, freedom, and liberation.

Inspired by the French composers and Beethoven, as well as by works such as Mozart's *Magic Flute*, a new type of romantic opera, full of wonder and mystery, was developed in 19th-century Germany. Legend and superstition provided popular themes of magic, witchcraft, and horror. Weber's *Der Freischütz* (1821), the first masterpiece in this new style, tells of a young huntsman making use of bullets forged by magic to win a competition—the condition of his marriage to his love. In a terrible and exciting scene in the Wolf's Glen in the depth of the forest at midnight the bullets are forged, and finally the Demon Hunter himself appears. Like many other romantic opera composers, Weber cast his net far, both in time and space, for the settings of his operas. *Euryanthe* takes place in medieval

France, while *Oberon* combines the mysteries of Western fairies with those of the medieval Orient. *Der Freischütz* uses spoken dialogue, but in *Euryanthe* the music is made continuous by a system of melodious and expressive recitatives.

Richard WAGNER (q.v. Vol. V) began where Weber left off. In his earlier works (such as the legendary story of *The Flying Dutchman*, 1843) there are still set numbers, but Wagner came more and more to think, not in terms of isolated pieces, but of whole scenes, acts, and finally operas. In his later operas (such as the RING (q.v.) and *Parsifal*) Wagner achieved a vast, closely-knit score of uninterrupted music. As he wrote his own words or librettos, his works were conceived as unities from the beginning. The use of leitmotives (the association of particular musical themes with particular people or objects) not only helped to bind the whole opera together, but also enabled the orchestra to comment on the drama and to play an intrinsic part in it. So close, indeed, was the relationship between the orchestra, the characters of the opera, the plot, and the staging that Wagner invented the term 'music drama' to describe his works.

In the 19th century the distinction between the French *opéra comique* and serious opera was merely technical. Gounod's *Faust* and Bizet's *Carmen*, for example, technically belong to the *opéra comique* tradition because they use spoken dialogue. Offenbach (1819–80) wrote many brilliantly gay and witty operas, such as the *Tales of Hoffmann*, which were akin in spirit to the earlier farcical stages of *opéra comique*, and influenced the operas of Gilbert and Sullivan.

In Italy opera continued to be the most important national musical form, and Italian composers had a wide influence in other countries, especially France. In the operas of Rossini (1792–1868), the music again begins to swamp the drama, and the technical extravagance of the solo singer to swamp the music. Although he wrote serious operas, Rossini is now best remembered by his comic operas such as *The Barber of Seville* (1816). Other 19th-century Italian composers, such as Bellini and Donizetti, wrote serious operas which are filled with elaborately beautiful melodies designed to show off the vocal tricks of the singers, with very stylized orchestral accompaniments.

At first Giuseppe VERDI (q.v. Vol. V) composed in much the same style, though his operas were always characterized by sincerity and

Roger Wood

THE CRAP GAME: SCENE FROM 'PORGY AND BESS' BY
GEORGE GERSHWIN

directness. With *Rigoletto*, *Il Trovatore*, and *La Traviata*, however, he rose to greater heights. He could write finer melodies than his predecessors, but he was primarily concerned that they exactly expressed the moods of the drama. In Verdi's operas there is not the same collaboration between orchestra and singers that there is in Wagner's: the vocal parts are nearly always the means of expression, with the orchestra in the background. In his two greatest operas, however, founded on Shakespeare plays, *Otello* (1887) and *Falstaff* (1893), and written when he was an old man, the music runs on without any break, and the orchestra is handled with greater skill than before.

Puccini (1858–1924), the greatest Italian composer after Verdi, was preoccupied with stories of crime and low life, as in his operas *La Bohème* and *Tosca*. In this he was influenced by two earlier French composers, Bruneau and Charpentier, who first introduced a new and harsh realism into opera. Charpentier's *Louise* (1900), for example, is set in the slums of Paris.

FOLK-SONGS (q.v.) were often introduced into operas, especially in the 19th century, when they were sometimes used by composers as a means

of starting a native school of opera. In Russia, for example, Glinka's *A Life for the Czar* (1836), Moussorgsky's *Boris Godunof* (1874), Borodin's *Prince Igor* (1890), and, to a lesser extent, Tchaikovsky's *Eugen Onegin* (1879) are based on folk-song and music, as in Czechoslovakia is Smetana's *The Bartered Bride* (1866), and in England, Vaughan Williams's *Hugh the Drover*. All these works either used folk-song, or were inspired by it and by local traditions.

The greatest opera composer since Wagner is Richard STRAUSS (q.v. Vol. V). His *Der Rosen-kavalier* (1911), with its courtly intrigue set in the 18th century, recalls Mozart's *Marriage of Figaro*, but its grandiose orchestration and voluptuous musical style are quite original. Modern operas in general have been characterized by their composers' personal idioms and ideas rather than by any particular tradition. This is true of DEBUSSY's delicately beautiful *Pelléas et Mélisande* (q.v. Vol. V), and of Alban Berg's sordid story of *Wozzeck* (1925), a moving work written in the twelve-tone system (*see* SCALES). George Gershwin's *Porgy and Bess* (1935), set amongst American Negro people and making use of JAZZ material (q.v.), is again quite individual.

See also MUSIC, HISTORY OF; SONG, HISTORY OF; OVERTURE.

See also Vol. IX: OPERA.

ORATORIO. About 1556 St. Philip Neri, founder in Italy of the religious order called the Congregation of the Oratory (hence the term 'oratorio'), introduced the practice of interspersing the recitation of biblical stories with settings of hymns (*Laudi Spirituali*). Out of this practice, and also from the incidental music used in medieval MIRACLE PLAYS (q.v.), as well as the elaborate chanting of the story of Christ's Passion by priests and choir (*see* PASSION MUSIC), grew what we now call oratorio. At the time of the birth of OPERA (q.v. Vol. IX), about 1600, there was little except subject-matter to distinguish an opera, such as Peri's *Euridice*, from the first real oratorio (a lengthy musical setting of religious words for soloists, chorus, and orchestra), such as Cavalieri's *Rappresentazione di anima e di corpo*, written in the same year.

Oratorio, indeed, has been described as a religious opera without the acting—though even this distinction has not always held good. One of the reasons for its popularity in Italy, the land

HANDEL AT THE HARPSICHORD AT A REHEARSAL OF AN ORATORIO

of its birth, and elsewhere was that it was one of the few forms of public entertainment allowed during Lent. Whether it used Italian or Latin words it took over all the secular musical forms, such as the madrigal and cantata which were also being absorbed into opera.

The similarity between oratorio and opera remained: there is nothing to distinguish the overtures, recitatives, and arias of Handel's oratorios, for example, from those of his operas, though the chorus usually plays a larger part in the oratorios. HANDEL's *Saul* (q.v. Vol. V), though less familiar than his *Messiah*, is more

typical of his many oratorios. Based on the familiar story in the first book of Samuel, it begins when David, having just killed Goliath, is being presented to Saul. The first part describes Saul's mounting jealousy of David, and his charge to his son Jonathan (David's best friend) to kill him. The second part, after the chorus has sung a little homily on the hatefulness of envy, tells how Jonathan intercedes for David, and Saul cunningly appears to relent. But the King's jealousy is renewed upon David's victorious return from the wars. In the third part Saul makes his famous visit to the Witch of

Endor. News of the death of Saul and Jonathan is brought to David. He laments the death of his friend Jonathan, and is proclaimed leader of the people. The really important incidents of the plot are told in the recitatives, while the arias expand and develop the emotional possibilities of the situation described in the preceding recitatives. The chorus, representing the Israelites, every now and again interjects rather pious and trite commentaries. The musical style is limited by the conventions of Italian opera; from a dramatic point of view the work keeps stopping and starting—getting under way for a recitative and then holding fire for an aria or chorus (see SONG, HISTORY OF, Section 4).

For a long time oratorio did not spread beyond Italy, although it influenced its German equivalents, the church CANTATA and PASSION MUSIC (qq.v.). The so-called 'Christmas Oratorio' of BACH (q.v. Vol. V) is really a collection of six cantatas designed for separate performance on six separate days between Christmas and the Epiphany. Later, however, oratorio kept pace with all the changing styles of musical composition. HAYDN (in *The Creation* and *The Seasons*) and MENDELSSOHN (in *Elijah* and *St. Paul*) (qq.v. Vol. V), amongst many other composers, maintained the division of oratorio into recitative, aria, and chorus, though their style of composition differed widely from Handel's and from each other's. ELGAR's oratorios (for instance, *The Kingdom* and *The Apostles*) were written without these subdivisions, in the same way that WAGNER (qq.v. Vol. V) in his operas discarded the smaller units of set numbers in favour of a lengthy and well-knit musical structure. Modern composers, such as Honegger (*King David*), Michael Tippett (*A Child of Our Time*), and Lennox Berkeley (*Jonah*), have continued to write oratorios in their own individual styles.

Many other composers have written lengthy religious works which, however they may have classified them, seem to fall within the category of oratorio. Typical of these is Elgar's *Dream of Gerontius*, the length and large orchestral and choral demands of which make Elgar's own description of it as a cantata seem inadequate. Unlike earlier oratorios, though in accordance with many modern works, the *Dream of Gerontius* is not based on the Scriptures: it is a setting of parts of a lengthy dramatic poem by Cardinal Newman, describing the progress of the soul of an ordinary man—Gerontius—from the moment of his death to his judgement. The work is in two parts, and in each it is continuous. It is easy to imagine how lame and halting the old style of a succession of recitatives, arias, and choruses would have been if it had been adapted to such a visionary conception as the *Dream of Gerontius*, with its swift dramatic movement, its choruses of angels and demons, and its approach to the very throne of God.

See also MUSIC, HISTORY OF.

ORATORY, see RHETORIC.

ORCHESTRATION. This is the art of scoring, that is, of writing music for the instruments of the ORCHESTRA (q.v. Vol. IX) to play. With some composers it is synonymous with the art of composing: ideas come to their heads not just as tunes or rhythms, but straight away in terms of instrumental timbre. Each instrument has a different 'timbre', or tone-colour, determined both by its shape and the material of which it is made (see MUSICAL INSTRUMENTS, Vol. IX); instruments made of brass, for example, have a more strident tone than those made of wood. Other composers think out their music in terms of a black and white sketch first, and then afterwards colour it, as it were, by orchestrating it. ELGAR is a good example of the first kind of composer, and BRAHMS of the second (qq.v. Vol. V). Indeed, Brahms often had difficulty in deciding whether to give his new works to the piano, the orchestra, or to the CHAMBER MUSIC repertory (q.v.).

All music was at first for voices only, and then instruments also began to take part. But the fact that Byrd could write, 'Fit for voyces or viols', above his *Psalms, Songs, and Sonnets* of 1611 is but one of many instances of how little the intrinsic character of instruments was considered in early times. The haphazard collection of instruments found in Monteverdi's opera *Orfeo* (1607) shows that composers scored for whatever was available to them in the household of their patron, and did not select the instruments on the grounds of each one's particular character. By the time of BACH and HANDEL (qq.v. Vol. V) it was customary to find strings and harpsichord, with flutes, oboes, bassoons, trumpets, and drums according to choice, constituting the normal orchestra of the day, but even the scores of these two great composers suggest that they

B.B.C.

THE B.B.C. SYMPHONY ORCHESTRA CONDUCTED BY SIR MALCOLM SARGENT

were not wholly aware that certain instruments were better fitted for certain kinds of musical tasks than others. Bach's instrumental movements are nearly always derived from one recurrent main theme which is taken up in turn by the different instruments selected for that particular movement; in the second 'Brandenburg' Concerto, for example, the trumpet is asked to be just as agile as the flute and oboe. When writing instrumental accompaniments to arias Bach would frequently choose a solo instrument (or possibly more than one) to play an important counter-melody (or melodies) against that of the singer throughout the movement, a system of scoring known as the *obbligato* method. The ideal of the period was to have the interwoven melodies clearly defined by the different instruments, regardless of each one's specific 'personality', with the harpsichord supplying the harmonies in simple chords. This accompaniment was called the *continuo* or figured bass; it was often indicated in the score by single bass notes with figures above or below them. These figures showed the player which chords the composer intended, but the system allowed a certain freedom of interpretation.

By the time of HAYDN and MOZART (qq.v. Vol. V), and chiefly owing to the pioneering work carried out by Johann Stamitz (1717–57) with his Mannheim orchestra, new ideas were afoot. The newly invented clarinet established its position among the flutes, oboes, and bassoons of the wood-wind section, and horns joined the trumpets as regular members of the brass department. Strings and drums held their old positions, but the harpsichord *continuo* disappeared. Not only had the orchestra begun to assume the shape by which we recognize it today, but com-

posers were at last beginning to regard it as a corporate entity. No longer did they select certain instruments, in the *obbligato* tradition, to play the whole tune in this movement or that, but called upon each one to contribute a little touch of its own peculiar tone-colour and character at any given moment to every movement, with much give and take. BEETHOVEN (q.v. Vol. V) called for still more instruments in his powerful symphonies, sometimes four horns instead of two, and sometimes a piccolo, double-bassoon, and trombone, as well as the normal wood-wind and brass instruments. The dynamic quality of his thought is frequently emphasized by important drum parts and sharper contrasts of colour than Haydn and Mozart used; but his style of scoring is essentially in their classical tradition.

It was after Beethoven that the art of orchestration began to attract unprecedented attention. As composers of the ROMANTIC MOVEMENT (q.v. Section 3) became less interested in formal design and more in telling stories, painting pictures, and creating 'atmosphere' in sound, so instrument-makers set out to widen the range of tone-colour available to them. Each of the WOOD-WIND INSTRUMENTS (q.v. Vol. IX) grew a family, as it were. To the flute were added the piccolo and bass flute; to the oboe the deeper cor anglais and heckelphone; to the clarinet the shrill E flat clarinet and bass clarinet; and to the bassoon the double-bassoon. The range of BRASS INSTRUMENTS was deepened by various trombones and tubas (beloved by Wagner); PERCUSSION INSTRUMENTS (qq.v. Vol. IX) and the 'effects' department included side-drums and bass drums, as well as timpani and all manner of novelties from glockenspiels and tubular bells to wind-machines (Schönberg in his *Gurrelieder* even requests a large iron chain). The HARP (q.v. Vol. IX), moreover, became a frequent visitor, lending a touch of magic whenever it appeared.

Instrument-makers also turned their attention to the mechanism of wood-wind and brass instruments; Theobald Boehm, a famous Munich flautist, invented a system of metal rods and keys which made wood-wind instruments much more agile, and the addition of valves to horns and other brass instruments enabled these to play far more notes than was hitherto possible. Even STRING INSTRUMENTS (q.v. vol. IX), which could not be enlarged or improved, were made to yield new sounds by different kinds of bowing —*tremolo* (vibrating the bow), *col legno* (hitting the strings with the wooden back of the bow), *ponticello* (playing with the bow close to the bridge), *sul tasto* (with the bow near the finger-board), and so on. The orchestra, in fact, became an enormous paint-box containing an infinite variety of pastel shades as well as primary colours; in the hands of masters such as BERLIOZ (whose *Treatise on Instrumentation* still remains a standard work), WAGNER, TCHAIKOVSKY, STRAUSS (qq.v. Vol. V), Rimsky-Korsakov, Stravinsky, and others the art of orchestration touched the limits of both brilliance and subtlety. Berlioz loved to bring the roof down with his tremendous *tuttis*, in which all the instruments played together, but he also had a sufficiently keen ear for delicate effects to be able to discriminate between the differences of tone produced, for example, by drum-sticks with wooden, leather, and sponge heads—his scores always stipulate which he requires.

A move towards greater clarity of texture, in contrast to romantic lusciousness, was started by the French impressionist composers, DEBUSSY (q.v. Vol. V) and Ravel. Nowadays, contemporary composers seem to be turning their backs still more on 19th-century orchestration and aiming at a kind that is more economical in numbers, more clean-cut in style, and often more brittle in actual sound (*see* MODERN MUSIC).

See also MUSIC, HISTORY OF; CONCERTO; OVERTURE; SYMPHONY.

See also Vol. IX: ORCHESTRA; MUSICAL INSTRUMENTS.

ORDERS OF ARCHITECTURE.

The style of architecture used by the Greeks and taken over from them by the Romans was based on a

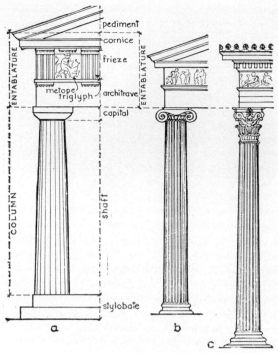

FIG. I. THE GREEK ORDERS
a. Doric. *b.* Ionic. *c.* Corinthian

system of construction consisting of vertical columns supporting horizontal beams as, for example, in Greek temples (*see* Vol. I, p. 470). Definite rules of proportion and the relationship which one part of a building should bear to another were laid down, and variety of design was strictly limited. Each variation in design was called an 'order'.

The Greeks used three different orders: the Doric, the sturdiest and simplest of the three; the Ionic, more slender and elegant, easily recognizable by the voluted (or spiral) capital of the column; and the Corinthian, which was developed later than the others and had a capital decorated with sculptured acanthus leaves. Each order consisted of a 'stylobate' (or stepped base), columns, and an entablature (Fig. 1). Each had its own type of ornamentation, which was never used on other orders. The column consisted of three parts, the base (the Greek Doric column, however, had no base), the shaft, which was grooved or 'fluted', and the capital or cushion on which the entablature rested. The entablature was likewise divided into three: the architrave, which was the beam running across the capitals of the columns; the frieze, a wide band above the architrave, sometimes ornamented with sculpture or other forms of decoration; and the cornice, the topmost projecting part corresponding to the eaves of the roof.

The Romans used five orders. They adopted and slightly altered the three Greek orders and added two more of their own (Fig. 2). Their favourite was the Corinthian, as being the most ornate, and they preserved the Doric as the simplest, though changing it considerably. The Roman Doric column, unlike the Greek, has a base. Their new orders were the Tuscan, an even simpler version of the Roman Doric with unfluted shaft, and the Composite, a very ornamental one with a capital combining the Ionic volute with the Corinthian acanthus-leaf motif. The Romans, unlike the Greeks, used the orders in conjunction with round arches, and superimposed one upon the other, as on the walls of the COLOSSEUM (q.v.) in Rome. They also applied them as decoration to walls which were not constructed on the column-and-beam system.

In the RENAISSANCE (q.v. Vol. I) architects drew their inspiration from Roman buildings and based their designs on the Roman orders; but the orders were used frequently in purely ornamental ways, in complete disregard of their original structural purpose. The outsides of buildings were ornamented by columns, half-columns, or flat columns (called pilasters) laid

FIG. 2. THE ROMAN ORDERS
a. Doric. *b.* Ionic capital. *c.* Corinthian capital.
d. Composite capital. *e.* Tuscan capital

against the wall, each column with its appropriate entablature. Sometimes huge columns embraced several storeys of a building while small columns and cornices decorated its doors and windows. Colonnades were a favourite motif, and round arches were used which rested directly on the capitals of columns. Plain walls were crowned with entablatures and even when the columns were absent the correct proportions of the chosen order were preserved. Later on, the parts of the various orders provided patterns for the sculpture-like ornament of the BAROQUE period (q.v.).

The later Renaissance architects took great pains to work out the exact proportions and relationship of parts used in the classical orders, and to set them down mathematically, using as a unit of measurement a 'module', which was one-half the diameter of a column at its base. At the end of the 18th century, the ancient Greek orders were even more meticulously measured and copied by scholars and architects.

See also GREEK ART; ROMAN ART.

ORGANUM, *see* HARMONY.

ORIENTAL MUSIC. This must not be confused with PRIMITIVE MUSIC (q.v.). According to legend the Chinese musical system, one of the oldest in existence, was established by the Yellow Emperor Huang-Ti before 2600 B.C. (*see* CHINESE CIVILIZATION, Vol. I). That Oriental music is so little known in the West is due partly to a lack of an adequate MUSICAL NOTATION (q.v.), and partly to the general decline of music in the East in recent years. Much of this music, however, shows a cultural development which is at least comparable to that of the Western world; but the two methods have developed along quite independent lines. The Oriental peoples directed all their efforts towards MELODY AND RHYTHM, while Western music has concerned itself far more with HARMONY and counterpoint (qq.v.). It is not surprising, therefore, that the East has developed subtleties of rhythm and nuances of pitch which make our SYNCOPATION and unvarying SCALES (qq.v.) seem almost amateurish. In spite of the many consistent features, traditions varied widely throughout the vast territories we vaguely describe as the Orient, and even from one local district to another. In this article we shall divide Oriental music into four geographical regions: (1) China and Japan;

(2) India; (3) Indo-China, Burma, Polynesia; (4) Persia, Arabia, and all the Moslem countries of the Eastern Mediterranean and North Africa.

1. CHINESE AND JAPANESE MUSIC. The chromatic scale of the ancient Chinese system was arrived at by a system of twelve *lüs* or pitch pipes

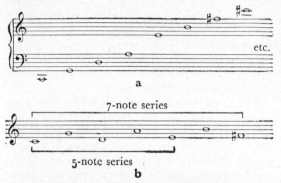

a

7-note series

5-note series

b

FIG. 1. THE NOTES OF THE CHINESE 'LÜS'

corresponding to a circle of perfect fifths (Fig. 1 *a*). These were telescoped within the range of a single octave (Fig. 1 *b*). The fundamental note was the note made by a standard tube, the 'yellow bell'. The *lüs* were used in many civic customs and religious rites. Melodies were based on a five-note or 'pentatonic' scale corresponding to our do, re, mi, sol, la or C, D, E, G, A. A seven-note scale which contained the next two notes of the series was also in use for a time. A melody could take any of the twelve *lüs* as its key-note in accordance with religious rites. Chromatic melodies or melodies making use of any notes outside the five-note scale did not exist.

The political and social importance of music was emphasized particularly by CONFUCIUS (q.v. Vol. V); and after his death music became so widely cultivated that in 246 B.C. the Emperor Shi Huang-Ti ordered all music books and instruments to be destroyed lest trade and agriculture should suffer. Music revived under the Han dynasty (206 B.C.–A.D. 220), and reached its classical period under the T'ang and Sung dynasties (618–1279). In this period huge orchestras numbering 300 or more instruments were used for ritual and courtly ceremonies. Music was divided into four categories: sacred, chamber, operatic, and folk music. Sacred music used vast collections of what we should classify as harps, lutes, mouth-organs, bells, oboes, chimes, and drums; but the chamber

music, performed on the traditional instruments (*ch'in*, a zither, and *p'ip'a*, a lute) was the most highly developed style. The traditional opera, which is of a serious nature, goes back to the 14th century. For the last three centuries Chinese music has been declining, the most vigorous form of the art being folk-song, still based on the ancient pentatonic scale.

Japanese classical music is derived from that of China. In addition to the pentatonic scale corresponding to C, D, E, G, A it also uses a scale corresponding to C, D, E♭, G, A♭, and a number of others. Much more use is made, particularly in the Japanese temple rituals, of minute melodic intervals which occur as grace notes, that is, infinitesimally short decorative notes occurring before the real melodic note. In the theatre the Japanese classical drama (the *Nō* plays) has developed a distinctive style of dramatic song in which recitatives alternate with arias (*see* JAPANESE LITERATURE).

2. INDIAN MUSIC. This also has very ancient traditions, which we can trace back some 3,000 years. The system of scales, however, seems first to have been stated clearly about A.D. 500. It divides the octave into twenty-two small intervals or *scruti* which, although they are not theoretically exactly equal, may be roughly thought of as quarter tones. These intervals are never used together in the same melody any more than the Chinese use all twelve of their *lüs*, but they are the basis of the scales or *ragas* of Indian music. The use of these is closely associated with the mood of the performer and varies with particular events or festivities, and even with the time of day. Solo singers are usually accompanied by a kind of lute (*tambura*), with or without hand drums. The *tambura* provides a drone accompaniment. In its rhythmic complexity and melodic subtlety this music frequently sounds extraordinarily complicated to Western ears.

3. INDO-CHINESE, BURMESE, AND POLYNESIAN MUSIC. In these countries there are various combinations of Indian, Chinese, Arabian, and other influences, though many districts have their own local traditions. The music of Annam, for example, is basically Chinese (particularly in its notation and instrumentation), but it is distinguished by a sincerity, intimacy, and love of simplicity. Burmese music shows Chinese influence as far as rhythm is concerned, though it is nearer Indian music in its use of scales.

नव्वर्धगप्रकृत्बनीउ । म्रर्ठ्छकीलीविलमउर्व   उम्वीष्वर्हरंवलवेउमीभ

British Museum

THE RAJAH BALWANT SINGH OF JAMMU AND MUSICIANS
Indian painting of the Kangra School, early 19th century

Chinese scales, on the other hand, influenced Cambodia, known for its royal ballet and court orchestras. Javanese music employs intervals which differ more widely from ours than those of Japan or even India. Its music was probably originally derived from China, and has become particularly noteworthy for a highly developed orchestral style.

4. ISLAMIC MUSIC. The last region is that over which ISLAM (q.v. Vol. I) has for centuries held sway: it stretches from the borders of India westwards to the Mediterranean and across North Africa. It has been the cradle of many civilizations—Babylonian, Assyrian, Egyptian, and Greek. Often their instruments have survived, but there seem to have been no musical treatises and no adequate musical notation by means of which we may reconstruct their music. Not until about the 9th century A.D. do we find the first Arabic musical treatises, and by this time far older Persian, Greek, and Arabic elements have already blended into a wider Moslem tradition. Arabic music is recognizable by its drawling, sliding style of singing and its extraordinarily complex elaboration of the vocal melody. The rhythm of its melodies is akin to that of Indian music, and it also has melodic

groupings (*maqāms*) similar to Indian *ragas*. Throughout the Moslem world melodies are accompanied by drums and sometimes stringed instruments. The drum rhythms are at their most intricate in Tunis, Algeria, and Morocco, though the metrical phrases are short. Phrases are much longer farther east (in Egypt, Syria, Persia), but there are fewer cross rhythms.

The music of the Near East has frequently influenced Western music. Gregorian chant (*see* PLAINSONG), it has been conjectured, was influenced by Greek and also by Jewish music, which in its turn has at many periods been coloured by Arabian music. Our kettle-drums are derived from Arabic models, and so were lutes. Arabic treatises on acoustics and instruments (*see* MUSICAL INSTRUMENTS, Vol. IX) date from before similar works by European writers. Many Moorish musical traditions have survived in Spanish DANCE MUSIC (q.v.).

ORNAMENT. In all ages and in all places ornament has been used in endless variety to decorate objects. Ornament may be added to an object, as in painted pottery, or it may be part of the material structure, as in patterns in woven materials. Its purpose may be simply to

GREEK WAVE

GREEK FRET

ROMAN GUILLOCHE

GREEK HONEYSUCKLE

ROMAN ACANTHUS

BEAD AND REEL

EGG AND DART

ROMAN FOLIAGE

CLASSIC PERIOD

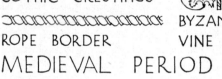

CELTIC INTERLACING

GOTHIC CRESTINGS

ROPE BORDER

MEDIEVAL PERIOD

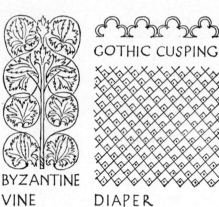

BYZANTINE VINE

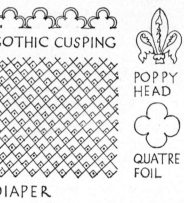

GOTHIC CUSPING

DIAPER

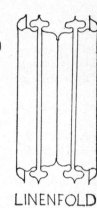

POPPY HEAD

QUATRE FOIL

LINENFOLD

FLUTING

GADROONING

GUILLOCHE & ROSETTE

LATTICE FRET

RENAISSANCE PERIOD

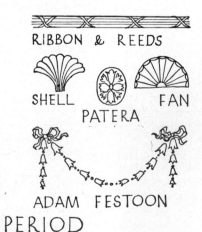

RIBBON & REEDS

SHELL   PATERA   FAN

ADAM FESTOON

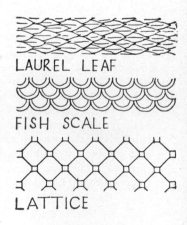

LAUREL LEAF

FISH SCALE

LATTICE

EXAMPLES OF ORNAMENT OF DIFFERENT PERIODS

make an object look more attractive—for instance, the patterns on curtains or carpets. It may be the traditional result of some bygone useful function: the lines stitched on the backs of gloves are descended from the metal guards of gauntlets in the days of armour. Ornament may have a symbolic meaning: the winged disk of ancient Egypt signified new life, the PHOENIX (q.v. Vol. I) and the peacock are Christian symbols for the resurrection and immortality. Some forms of decoration have a magical or religious meaning—the primitive Mediterranean sailor painted an eye on the bow of his boat to give it 'sight'; others, such as the paintings on Greek vases, may tell a story. Ornaments may signify ownership, as do coats of arms (see HERALDRY, Vol. IV), or rank, such as the coronet of nobility.

Ornament may be used to define the shape of an object, as do, for instance, the lines running round the lips of cups or edges of plates. It may stress the structural form, as, for example, the fluting of columns which emphasizes their vertical form, or it may fill a gap between two structural points, as do the carved spandrels between arches and piers in a Gothic church. It may excite the eye with colour and movement, as do the arabesque patterns of ISLAMIC ART (q.v.), or it may give a feeling of space—the effect given by ceilings patterned with stars or clouds.

The forms of ornament range from simple abstract patterns of lines or dots to complex designs including the naturalistic rendering of figures, animals, and plants. Pattern, that is, the formal arrangement of motifs, is an essential part of ornament. The arrangement may be symmetrical, one part of the design exactly reflecting another, or unsymmetrical; it may consist in the repetition of many units, or the careful placing of a simple shape so that it enhances the design of the object it decorates. The arrangement of patterns in relation to each other and to the object are an essential part of ornament.

Ornament has characteristic forms at different times and among different people and, like all art, expresses the ideas of the culture in which it flourishes. The refinement and precision of GREEK ART (q.v.) may be seen in the formalized leaf patterns and geometric ornament. The lavish splendour of Imperial Rome is reflected in the elaborate patterns of the capitals of their columns or their richly carved MONUMENTS

(q.v.). A more barbarian type of splendour can be seen in the flowing scrolls and enamel ornaments on Celtic metalwork or on Saxon jewellery. The changing cultures of the Middle Ages can be followed from the intricate patterns of interlacing animals in 7th- and 8th-century manuscripts (see p. 200) to the naturalistic rendering of plants and animals in GOTHIC ART (q.v.); from the crude but strong pattern with which the Normans decorated their arches (see p. 81) to the intricate carving of Perpendicular roofs.

From the time of the RENAISSANCE (q.v. Vol. I) much ornament has been based on classic forms, though always interpreted in a way which has accorded with the spirit of the times. The exuberant vitality of Elizabethan England is reflected in the lavish use of robust and bold ornament, while in the late 18th century Robert ADAM (q.v.) decorated rooms with the same motifs, but made them elegant and restrained to suit the polished society which used the rooms. There is a similar contrast between the grandeur and theatrical quality of the ornament in BAROQUE ART and the light-hearted, unsymmetrical decoration of ROCOCO ART (q.v.).

In the 20th century ornament takes many forms and is derived from many sources. A lack of ornament is also characteristic of the time; in MODERN ARCHITECTURE (q.v.), for example, many architects have thought that the structure of the building should not be hidden by ornament which has nothing to do with its function. The simplicity of the abstract patterns found in much PRIMITIVE ART (q.v.) has been related to the simple forms of modern processes of manufacture.

See also ART; DESIGN.

OVERTURE. In its most usual sense the word 'overture' means the piece of music which the orchestra plays before an OPERA, ORATORIO (qq.v.), or play. Its origins are to be found in the earliest operas, in which it was customary to begin the entertainment with a short orchestral introduction. These introductions (at this time often called symphonies or toccatas) were little more than short conventional flourishes designed to let the audience know that the play was about to start. Monteverdi's *Orfeo* (1607), for example, opens with a toccata of nine bars, which is directed to be played three times.

Composers soon began to elaborate these

movements, and in the early 18th century two distinct and elaborate kinds of overture had become popular. The French overture, associated with Lully (1632–87), began with a slow introduction, went on to a quicker movement, often in fugal style, and ended with a slowish dance tune such as the minuet. The Italian overture, associated with Alessandro Scarlatti (c. 1660–1725), had three sections, quick-slow-quick. As the principles of sonata form (*see* MUSICAL FORM, Section 4) emerged during the 18th century, the operatic overture was bound to be affected. Gluck's overture to *Iphigenia in Aulis* (1774), for instance, is a rather extended form of French overture; it begins with a short, slow movement, followed by ten bars of fanfare and then by a quick ('allegro maestoso') movement. The fanfare is repeated at the end, and leads straight into the opera. The 'allegro maestoso' section, however, is based on the sonata form.

Composers gradually began to think of overtures as something more than mere curtain-raisers. They tried to make the overture set the atmosphere for the work which was to follow and, indeed, to make it an important feature of the whole work from a dramatic point of view. Sometimes a composer would heighten the dramatic effect of his overture by using themes afterwards heard in the opera. This happens in Mozart's *Don Giovanni*, for instance, where the music used when the statue comes to life and appears at the feast is used in the Andante of the overture. In his *Magic Flute*, also, the trombone chords which summon the priests with great and solemn effect are heard in the overture. In this way, an overture such as Beethoven's *Leonora No. 3* (originally composed as an overture to his opera *Fidelio*) can give, in musical terms, a kind of summary of the whole plot of the opera. *Leonora No. 3* starts slowly with a long descending passage which gives an impression of passing from daylight down into the gloom of the dungeon where the hero, Florestan, lies chained. Then there follows a hint of his song in Act II ('In the springtime of life happiness has fled

from me') which makes a moving contrast with the vigour of the Allegro movement. Later we hear the trumpet calls which are used to denote the arrival of Florestan's liberators. When, in cases such as this, dramatic intensity became a first consideration, the conventions of the sonata form had often to be modified.

It became the custom to perform the overtures of operas and oratorios by themselves at orchestral concerts. In the case of overtures which ran straight into the first act (as, for instance, with Wagner's *Mastersingers*), a special ending was sometimes composed for concert performances. Gradually composers began to write overtures solely for concert performance, without any connexion with dramatic works; such are, for instance, Mendelssohn's *The Hebrides*, and John Ireland's *A London Overture*. Many works of this kind have been based on stories, or great characters, or places. William Walton based his overture *Portsmouth Point* on a picture by Rowlandson. Overtures that have some definite subject, as these have, are a kind of tone poem (*see* PROGRAMME MUSIC).

Even in many of these concert overtures such as *The Hebrides* or a modern work like Walton's *Scapino*, the connexion with sonata form is definite, because, in fact, it is hard to devise a form for an extended work of dramatic style without producing something that resembles sonata form. When the general character of the overture or the opera concerned is less ambitious, the composer may attempt nothing more elaborate than a medley of tunes exactly as they appear in the opera, strung together with a contrast of key and style but without development in the symphonic sense. If this kind of thing is well done, as in some of SULLIVAN's overtures (q.v. Vol. V), the result can be very effective.

Some composers, including J. S. Bach, have used the word overture in a rather different sense, to describe works usually for orchestra which are in effect suites (*see* DANCE MUSIC).

See also MUSICAL FORM; OPERA, HISTORY OF; ORATORIO; SYMPHONY; PROGRAMME MUSIC.

P

Mactavish

THE GREAT PAGODA AT SOOCHOW, KIANGSU PROVINCE
Ming period (1368–1644)

PAGODA. The origin and meaning of the word is uncertain. It is used for two quite different types of building: one is a monument found particularly in India, Ceylon, Burma, Siam, and Java; and the other belongs to China and Japan.

The Indian pagoda, there called a *stūpa*, is generally in stone and consists of a terrace, a dome, and a small pavilion crowned with umbrella-shaped roofs. It arose from a pre-Buddhist memorial mound erected for kings or over relics of saints. Gradually the *stūpa* became one of the most characteristic of Buddhist monuments built over relics of the Buddha, at places of religious importance, or in memory of religious events. Hundreds, even thousands, of *stūpas* were built in India, but only a small number have been preserved. One of the most famous is the great *stūpa* of Sānchī in Bhopal, begun in the 3rd century B.C., enlarged in the 2nd century B.C., and recently restored (*see* INDIAN ART). There are innumerable *stūpas* in Burma and Siam. In Java there is the Borobudur, the largest and most impressive pagoda in the world, built in the 9th century A.D.

The Chinese and Japanese pagoda is at first sight quite unlike the Indian and has greater variety of design. It is a tower divided into three to thirteen storeys by projecting cornices or roofs, or both, and crowned with different ornaments. It is built of brick or wood, and in Japan is always wooden. It is almost certain that it developed from an early type of Chinese tower of several storeys to which Indian elements were gradually added. The oldest Chinese pagoda to be preserved is built of brick and dates from the 6th century A.D. The oldest wooden one is Japanese and dates from the 7th century A.D. The Japanese adopted one particular type from the Chinese; its chief characteristic is the roof with **curved-up edges** covering every storey.

In China pagodas are not always connected with Buddhism, but in Japan they are invariably attached to Buddhist temples.

In the 18th century Western interest in Oriental culture led to the building of pagodas in Europe, such as the one in Kew Gardens built by Chambers in 1760–1 (*see* CHINOISERIE).

See also CHINESE ART; INDIAN ART; JAPANESE ART.
See also Vol. I: BUDDHISM.

PAINTING METHODS. 1. Various materials, animal, vegetable, and mineral alike, have been used, diluted with fluid, to produce the colours necessary for painting. For instance, blacks are made from carbon, yellows and greens usually from earths of different kinds ground into fine powder, carmine from the cochineal insect, madder from the root of a plant. Nowadays pigments are sold already made up and ready for use; but formerly each artist or an assistant had to grind and prepare the colours for himself.

Changes in the method of painting have gone hand in hand with changes in style, for as artists have found that the methods they were using would not give them the effects they were aiming at, so they have been compelled to seek for others. The different systems of painting are normally named according to the liquid—wax, **egg**, oil, or water—which has been used to make

National Gallery

ENCAUSTIC: DETAIL FROM A PORTRAIT OF A MAN
Greco-Roman, 2nd–3rd century A.D.

the colours fluid. These liquids are known as 'media'.

2. ENCAUSTIC. This was the method used by the Greeks and Romans. Wax was heated until it was liquid, then mixed with the powdered pigment and applied to the picture while it was still hot. From the few Greek or Roman paintings which exist we know that it was possible with this method to get rich colour effects. Although recent attempts have been made to revive the method, it chiefly remains a curiosity.

3. TEMPERA. This method was practised in the Middle Ages and was the standard one for easel pictures throughout the early part of the Renaissance in Italy. The medium used in tempera painting is egg, especially the yolk. The early Italian pictures were usually painted on wood, which in very early examples was covered with canvas; the canvas or wood was covered with a white coating known as a 'ground', usually made of a kind of plaster called gesso, on which colours showed up well. The method of applying the colours varied, though in all the early Italian pictures the final coat of paint rested on several coats of underpaint. In Byzantine and early Sienese tempera paintings the white gesso ground was completely covered with a green preparation made of an earth

which shows through in the outlines and shadows, producing an effect of modelling. The outlines of the pictures were traced on this 'ground', very often by punching small holes through the outlines of careful, full-sized drawings which were laid on top of the panel. The artists sometimes scratched the main lines of the picture on the 'ground' to guide them in their painting. After grinding the colours to a fine powder in water, they mixed them in equal quantities with yolk of egg. The background and details of the picture were often covered with gold which was burnished to make it shine. By the 15th century, or even earlier, the finished picture was covered with a protective hard varnish of oil.

The chief characteristic of tempera is lightness of tone. The original white gesso ground tends to give a luminous effect which the 15th-century Italians exploited with beautiful results. But this lightness had disadvantages. The darker parts, particularly of the flesh, could be indicated only by painting parallel lines, known as 'hatching', in darker paint on top of the colour used for the lighter parts. Effects of deep shadow were impossible. The method was difficult to handle; the colours could not be applied

National Gallery

TEMPERA: DETAIL FROM 'MARS AND VENUS' BY BOTTICELLI

Mansell

FRESCO: DETAIL FROM 'THE CREATION OF ADAM' BY MICHELANGELO

too wet, and it was necessary to work with a certain speed.

4. FRESCO. Most of the greatest paintings of the Renaissance in Italy are painted on walls. There are various methods of attaching paint to walls; both encaustic and oils, for example, can be used, and in Venice and elsewhere it was usual to paint pictures in oil on canvas which was then fixed to the walls or ceiling. But the most common method in Italy, at least in the earlier period, is the process known as 'fresco'. This technique consists of painting on to a coating of wet lime plaster on the wall. When the plaster dries, the painting becomes part of it and is permanent. In Italy there are, in fact, frescoes over 500 years old which are still excellently preserved. The method is difficult because the plaster must not be allowed to dry while the paint is being put on. Only as much plaster as can be painted over in a day is applied and it has to be kept continually wet. No corrections can be made once the paint is applied, and as the colours change when they dry great skill and experience is needed to judge the right colours to use.

In order to be able to work quickly at the actual painting the Italians made a full-sized DRAWING (q.v.), known as a cartoon, on paper or parchment, and transferred the design from this to the wall by punching holes or lines through the main outlines on to the plaster.

The painter could make his cartoon as slowly as he liked, working out the design of his picture on this; the only thing he had to do quickly was the actual painting. When the plaster was dry he could put on finishing touches in tempera; but great fresco painters always tried to do this as little as possible since tempera was not so permanent as true fresco.

The merits and defects of fresco painting are similar to those of the tempera method. It encourages a precise type of painting, light in tone, and deep effects of shadow are difficult to obtain. A school such as the Florentine, which excelled in tempera, was usually equally distinguished at fresco; whereas the Venetian school favoured neither tempera nor fresco but oil. Fresco was not often used in northern Europe as it is not permanent in a cold, wet climate.

Fresco and tempera reached their greatest perfection in the 15th and early 16th centuries in Italy, especially in FLORENTINE PAINTING (q.v.). The painting shows the limitation of the media—the precise outline and light tone—which emphasizes the drawing and gives a sculptural effect to the figures. Indeed, many of the painters were also sculptors.

5. OIL PAINTING. It was no doubt owing to its disadvantages that tempera painting was superseded by the oil medium. Exactly when oil painting started is not known, though it almost certainly came into use gradually. The early 15th-century oil paintings appear to be in a mixed technique of tempera underpainting with oil varnishes or glazes on top. This method was certainly known before the time of the van Eyck brothers (q.v. Vol. V), who used to be credited with the discovery of oil painting, because they were the first great artists to make extensive use of it.

Earlier oil paintings were on wood, but after the 16th century wood was largely replaced by canvas, which permitted broader effects more in keeping with the nature of oil painting. Rubens (q.v. Vol. V), however, in the 17th century, seems to have preferred working on wood, though he also painted a large number of pictures on canvas. The canvas used for oil paintings is fixed to a wooden frame known as a stretcher. Some painters, particularly modern ones, paint directly on to an untreated canvas; but this uses up a great deal of paint, which sinks into the fibres of the canvas, and the colours do not show up well. As with wood panels, therefore, canvases are usually treated with a 'ground' or 'priming', which hardens into a surface through which paint cannot penetrate. This can

National Gallery

OIL: DETAIL FROM 'A WOMAN BATHING' BY REMBRANDT

be of various materials, such as chalk or gesso, and also of various colours, such as white, green, or even red (Tintoretto and the Spanish painter, El Greco (qq.v. Vol. V), used red primings extensively).

The process of building up the oil painting and the amount of oil used with the colours has always varied from artist to artist. Velazquez and Gainsborough, for example, appear to have used oil-paints almost like water-colours, with the colours swimming in medium. Paint applied in this way is known as a glaze. Rembrandt (qq.v. Vol. V), on the other hand, seems frequently to have applied paint in parts of his pictures with little or no oil; when applied like this it is known as 'impasto'. Glazes are used on top of areas of more solid paint to make them look warmer and more luminous. Between the extremes of glaze and impasto there can be infinite variety in the proportion of pigment to oil used, depending on what effect the painter is aiming at. Types of oil used to mix with the colours vary greatly, among the most common being poppy oil, walnut oil, and linseed oil. Turpentine is also used to make the colours thinner.

Oil painting is able to achieve a greater richness of colour and tone than is possible with tempera. Even early oil paintings have a much more lifelike treatment of shadows than was possible with tempera, and later painters discovered that in oils they could suggest forms without giving them an exact outline, in a way which is far closer to nature than are the more precise shapes inevitable in tempera.

In this transformation the school of Venetian Painting (q.v.) played an important part. The Venetians made the change from tempera on wood to oil on canvas a natural and inevitable change. Their great artists, such as Titian (q.v. Vol. V), were all solely great painters, and not also sculptors and architects as were many of the great Florentine painters. Here in the early 16th century emerged the qualities of the painter as opposed to those of the draughtsman —tone, colour, and atmosphere.

6. Water-Colour. This was the last important method to be developed. The colours are mixed with water and painted usually on paper, but sometimes on fabrics such as silk, or on ivory or bone (*see* Miniatures). The water-colour method has long been used for putting finishing touches to drawings, and there exist

Ashmolean Museum
GOUACHE: DETAIL FROM 'THE BEAN STICKERS' BY CAMILLE PISSARRO

a number of drawings of this kind by such artists as LEONARDO DA VINCI and DÜRER (qq.v. Vol. V). But the method—apart from its use for miniatures—did not become really widespread as an independent form of art until the end of the 18th century, when a school of landscape painters sprang up in England. These are probably the greatest European exponents of the method. On account of its lightness and delicacy of tone, water-colour is particularly suitable for LANDSCAPE PAINTING (q.v.); but it is not easy to handle, and the colours, unlike oils, fade easily (see WATER-COLOURS).

7. GOUACHE AND POSTER-COLOUR. This is a branch of water-colour painting in which the colours, though also mixed with water, are much thicker in themselves and therefore opaque in effect. As they tend to dry evenly they are suited to POSTERS (q.v.), for these usually need bright splashes of colour rather than delicate variations of tone. Certain artists, such as Sir William Nicholson, who were distinguished in the older branches of painting, have also enjoyed reputations as poster artists.

See also PASTEL; WATER-COLOURS.

PAINTINGS, CARE OF. Although many famous pictures are centuries old, paintings are, by the nature of their material, very liable to decay. There are three parts of a painting, all of which may deteriorate by the action of time or ill treatment: the paint itself, the 'ground' or prepared surface on which the paint is laid, and the canvas or wood which supports the 'ground' and paint (see PAINTING METHODS). The commonest ailment to which old pictures are liable is blistering and flaking of the paint. This may be caused by too great heat—for instance, from being too close to a fire; but it more usually occurs when the 'ground' has rotted, so that in places the paint no longer adheres to it. When this happens it is necessary to insert new adhesive (preferably from the back) under the blistering paint, and then to iron down the blister with a heated blade.

Sometimes the canvas or wood decays. It is possible to reline pictures on canvas by sticking a new canvas on to the back of the old. When the wood on which a picture is painted is completely rotten (as when it is eaten away by worms) it is sometimes necessary to plane away all the remains of the wood and then to stick a new piece of wood or canvas to the back of the paint. This process is known as 'transferring' and is so delicate and difficult a task that it is resorted to only in extreme cases.

The commonest source of trouble from the visible parts of a painting is the varnish, which is put over the colours as a protection after they are dry. This is normally transparent when applied, but with the passage of time it tends to become yellow, or discoloured by dirt in the atmosphere, thus falsifying the colours. It may also contract and drag the paint with it. When this happens, as it does inevitably after 50 years or more, a process of cleaning becomes necessary —that is, the old varnish is removed and replaced by new. This is done by applying a solvent which dissolves the varnish but not the paint beneath it.

Paintings two and three centuries old will normally have been cleaned several times already, and restorers in the past usually took advantage of the cleaning process to touch up areas of the paint which had become damaged or worn with time. Old pictures may thus contain a certain quantity of later paint, known as 'repaint': indeed, some famous pictures, such as the 'Last Supper' by Leonardo da Vinci (see Vol. V, p.

National Gallery

'CHRIST BEARING THE CROSS' BY THE SPANISH PAINTER RIBALTA (1551–1628), BEFORE AND AFTER CLEANING

273), now consist almost entirely of repaint. If the varnish of a painting has become very yellow or opaque, it may be difficult or impossible to determine the extent of the repaint. Nevertheless the restorer should, if possible, have this knowledge before he begins work, since the repainted areas and the original paint will react differently to treatment. Also, if the areas of repaint are very great, it may not be worth while to attempt cleaning at all. It is at this point that modern science has come to the aid of the restorer. Ultra-violet light will usually show up the repainted parts which may be imperceptible to the naked eye, while infra-red rays and X-rays will penetrate the paint to

different levels and show up fundamental damage or changes made by the artist during the course of work, and covered up by him.

Most of the great modern art galleries are equipped with a scientific laboratory where such work is carried out. But it is better to prevent the ailments of pictures than to cure them. The best method of prevention is to control the atmosphere and temperature of the room so that it is neither too dry nor too damp, too hot nor too cold. The modern system of air-conditioning answers these requirements best, but it is expensive to install and to operate, and not many galleries are equipped with it.

See also PAINTING METHODS; FORGERIES (Art).

PALLADIAN ARCHITECTURE, *see* Augustan Age.

PARABLE. The word parable means placing side by side—that is, comparing. A parable tells 'an earthly story with a heavenly meaning'. We use the word almost exclusively of the stories told by Jesus Christ and reported in the New Testament by Matthew, Mark, and Luke. These stories resemble Allegory and Fable (qq.v.) in that they have a meaning and a significance other than their obvious meaning; and this we have to interpret. But they differ from allegory in that their first and exclusive object is to teach, in having always a simple theme, and in being always short. And they differ from fable in that they convey a spiritual truth or a moral instruction where the fable teaches a more worldly wisdom; and the fable's dearest device, the animal that talks, has no place in parable. Here is the parable of The Sower, and its interpretation:

A sower went out to sow his seed: and as he sowed, some fell by the way side; and it was trodden down, and the fowls of the air devoured it. And some fell upon a rock; and as soon as it was sprung up, it withered away, because it lacked moisture. And some fell among thorns; and the thorns sprang up with it, and choked it. And other fell on good ground, and sprang up, and bare fruit an hundredfold. And when he had said these things, he cried, He that hath ears to hear, let him hear.

And his disciples asked him, saying, What might this parable be? And he said, Unto you it is given to know the mysteries of the kingdom of God: But to others in parables; that seeing they might not see, and hearing they might not understand. Now the parable is this: The seed is the word of God. Those by the way side are they that hear; then cometh the devil, and taketh away the word out of their hearts, lest they should believe and be saved. They on the rock are they which, when they hear, receive the word with joy; and these have no root, which for a while believe, and in time of temptation fall away. And that which fell among thorns are they, which, when they have heard, go forth, and are choked with cares and riches and pleasures of this life, and bring no fruit to perfection. But that on the good ground are they, which in an honest and good heart, having heard the word, keep it, and bring forth fruit with patience. (Luke viii, Authorized Version.)

The themes of the parables are various: eight others have the same theme as The Sower, the spreading of the Gospel. Other recurrent themes

are life, judgement, duties, brotherly kindness. All are couched in the form of simple stories, whose terms are readily understood by simple people, by farmers, by fishermen. Christ explained why He used the form of parable. Had His audiences immediately understood His new teaching, they might have been repelled by it. But those who kept His words in their memory would arrive gradually, and more sympathetically, at their meaning.

See also Allegory; Fable.

PARADISE LOST. *Paradise Lost*, published in 1667, when John Milton (q.v. Vol. V) was nearly 60, is the greatest example of Epic Poetry (q.v.) in the English language, and among the greatest in the world. It is written in blank verse (*see* Versification) and is arranged in twelve books.

Milton took the story for his poem from the Bible—the story of how Adam and Eve disobeyed God and were forced to leave the innocent happiness of the Garden of Eden and to begin a new and harder life. In telling this story Milton attempts, as he says, to 'justify the ways of God to men'. He shows us a picture of Lucifer (Satan) and the rebel angels fighting against God for the soul of man, and he shows that, though the weakness of Adam and Eve causes them to lose Paradise, they are still in God's care, the Tempter's victory only providing God with larger opportunities for showing his love for mankind.

The theology of the poem is difficult; but the characters and scenery are clear and tremendously impressive. The first two books, which describe the fallen angels in Hell and their great leader, Lucifer, are as grand as anything in literature. Lucifer's words are heroic:

> What though the field be lost?
> All is not lost; th' unconquerable Will,
> And study of revenge, immortal hate,
> And courage never to submit or yield:
> And what is else not to be overcome?

The descriptions of the innocent life in Paradise are extraordinarily beautiful, and there is a noble feeling of tragedy in the account of how Eve is betrayed by her vanity and how Adam voluntarily commits the sin of eating the forbidden fruit rather than risk losing her.

The story is often interrupted by accounts of past or future events given by angels, a device for breaking up the narrative borrowed from Homer and from Virgil. For example, Adam is told the whole story of the creation and of the battle with Lucifer and his rebel angels. But though Milton makes great use of his wide knowledge of classical literature, *Paradise Lost* is entirely an original work. The style is individual and sublime, and the poet rightly claims that he is dealing with 'Things unattempted yet in Prose or Rime'.

See also Vol. V: MILTON.

PARODY. A poem or prose work which mimics the characteristics of an original so as to make the original appear ridiculous is a parody. A good parody immediately calls to mind the original that it mocks. The nearer it echoes the rhythms, the rhymes, the peculiar turns of speech, the vocabulary, and the structure of an original, the better the parody is.

One of the most effective kinds of parody is achieved by imitating the form of a poem, but using a ludicrously different theme. That is how G. F. Bradby parodied John Masefield's poem *Sea Fever*, which begins:

I must go down to the seas again, to the lonely sea
    and the sky,
And all I ask is a tall ship and a star to steer her by,

Here is the parody:

I must go back to a vest again, to a winter vest with
    sleeves,
And all I ask is an honest shop, where the shopmen
    are not thieves;
And a fair price, and a free choice, and a full stretch
    for dining,
And a smooth touch on the bare chest, and a smooth
    inner lining.

I must go back to a vest again, for that which worst
    I dread,
Is a bad cold, a head cold, and a day or more in
    bed;
And all I ask is a friend's advice, and a short time
    for thinking.
And a soft wool, and a man's size, and a good bit
    for shrinking.

Poets whose style is most easily recognizable because of unusual thoughts, images, or rhythms are most easily parodied. Swinburne's command of rhythms puts him in this class. But Sir Owen Seaman's parodies do more than echo Swinburne's rhythms; they use his themes too, and, by introducing ridiculous comparisons,

they deride the content as well as the form of Swinburne's verse. Here is a sample of Seaman's parody of Swinburne—

I sang of the faith that is fleeting
    As froth of the swallowing seas,
Time's curse that is fatal as Keating
    Is fatal to amorous fleas;

Swinburne himself was a subtle parodist. He parodied *The Higher Pantheism* of Tennyson, and its confused thought, in verses from which these lines are quoted—

Parallels all things are: yet many of these are askew:
You are certainly I: but certainly I am not you. . . .

Not only individual writers, but often a school of writers can be derided by a parody. A good example of this is Sir J. C. Squire's *Celtic School*, with its echoes from many Irish songs and lyrics:

There's a grey wind wails on the clover
    And grey hills, and mist around the hills,
And a far voice sighing a song that is over,
    And my grey heart that a strange longing fills.

A sheen of dead swords that shake upon the wind,
    And a harp that sleeps though the wind is
    blowing
Over the hills and the seas and the great hills be-
    hind,
    The great hills of Kerry, where my heart would
    be going.

For I would be in Kerry now where quiet is the
    grass,
    And the birds are crying in the low light,
And over the stone hedges the shadows pass,
    And a fiddle weeps at the shadow of the night.

With Pat Doogan
Father Murphy
Brown Maidens
King Cuchullain
The Kine
The Sheep
Some old women
Some old men
And Uncle white Sea-gull and all.
(Chorus) And Uncle white Sea-gull and all.

The first three stanzas are a smiling, tender parody of the mood and poetry of the *Celtic School*. But in the last burst of lines parody becomes burlesque, the smile changes to mocking laughter.

When a new kind of poetry, a new fashion, arises, it is often the occasion for parody: the members of the old school deride the new poets, and are themselves often derided in turn. For example, the French symbolist poets of the 19th century were parodied so well that poems intended as parodies are now considered as one aspect of symbolist poetry itself (*see* FRENCH LITERATURE). The poets of the ROMANTIC MOVEMENT (q.v.) in England were much parodied, particularly Wordsworth. Horace and James Smith's *Rejected Addresses* includes parodies of Wordsworth, Coleridge, Scott, Byron, and others. When Scott saw the parody of his *Marmion* in this, he said, 'I certainly must have written this myself, though I forget upon what occasion'. It is not altogether unflattering to be parodied.

Among the most widely known parodies in England are those that occur in Lewis Carroll's *Alice in Wonderland*, such as:

'Tis the voice of the lobster, I heard him declare,
You have baked me too brown, I must sugar my hair.

The original which this imitates is *The Sluggard*, one of Isaac Watts's *Moral Songs*, which goes:

'Tis the voice of the sluggard: I heard him complain
You have wak'd me too soon, I must slumber again.

Most parodies are written to be laughed over and forgotten; but some, especially those which ridicule a literary form rather than an author, have achieved immortality. The outstanding example is *Don Quixote*, a mock-heroic romance which CERVANTES (q.v. Vol. V) wrote to ridicule the medieval romances (*see* ROMANCE LITERATURE). All mock-heroic and mock-epic poems are, in the widest sense, parodies. They parody epic and heroic poetry generally, rather than any one poem in particular. Drama, too, has its parodies: George Villiers's comedy, *The Rehearsal* (1672), made fun of the heroic tragedies of Dryden and other Restoration dramatists, and Sheridan's comedy, *The Critic*, ridicules both the sentimental drama and dramatic criticism of his time.

Parody is as old as literature; Homer himself was parodied in the mock-heroic Greek poem, the *Battle of the Frogs and the Mice*. And Chaucer did not scorn to write a parody: *The Tale of Sir Thopas*, one of the CANTERBURY TALES (q.v.), in which he ridicules the romances of knight-errants.

There are other literary imitations which neither are nor mean to be true parodies. Forgeries, of course, belong to this class. But so do those verses, common in contemporary reviews, which appear to be parodies because they mimic an original very closely, but whose aim is to ridicule, not the original they imitate, but some politician or political event or doctrine. These are not true literary parodies. Again, when one poet imitates the well-known lines of another so that his own meaning shall gain by the evocation, he is not parodying, for he has no intention of ridiculing, but quite the contrary. Thus, when Mr. T. S. Eliot, in describing a beautiful woman and the luxury that surrounds her, says—

The Chair she sat in, like a burnished throne,
Glowed on the marble . . .

he knows that his words will remind the reader of Shakespeare's description of Cleopatra—

The barge she sat in, like a burnished throne,
Burned on the water . . .

But his purpose is a poetic purpose; he is adding to his words the evocation of Shakespeare's. Imitation, therefore, is not always parody, though parody is always imitation.

See also SATIRE.

PARTHENON, *see* ACROPOLIS, ATHENS; ELGIN MARBLES.

PART-SONGS, *see* SONGS, Section 4.

PASSION MUSIC. From very early times it has been customary to recite the Evangelists' accounts of the Passion of Our Lord as part of the Holy Week services. The Passion according to St. Matthew is read on Palm Sunday, according to St. Mark and St. Luke on the next Tuesday and Wednesday, and according to St. John on Good Friday. About the 12th century a certain amount of dramatic presentation was introduced to assist the congregation to follow the Latin more clearly. The Passion was sung by three priests: one (*Evangelista*) sang the main narrative at a normal speed and medium pitch; another (*Turba Judaeorum*) sang all the words attributed to the mob of Jews at a quicker pace and in a high voice; the third (*Vox Christi*) sang all the words uttered by Jesus in a slow, deep voice. Performances of the Passion in this style can still be heard in many Catholic churches during Holy Week: for the most part the story is sung in a simple, inflected monotone (*see* PLAINSONG), though the cry of Jesus '*Eli, Eli, lama sabacthani*' is set to a more expressive melody.

With the development of harmonized music, composers began to write settings of the words of the crowd (the *Turba*), which seemed to demand a collection of voices, to be sung by the choir. The earliest surviving settings date from about 1480, and there is an English setting, written about 1490 by Richard Davy. For the next 100 years or more a succession of great church composers produced these settings, the most famous being those of Lassus, Victoria, and Byrd. In the Lutheran Church it became customary to use German instead of Latin words, and to use a simpler musical style for the crowd choruses: the first St. Matthew Passion written in this manner by Johann Walther dates from 1530.

Almost parallel with this style of Passion developed another, in which the whole story, not merely the voices of the crowd, was sung by the choir. One of the earliest examples, by the Netherlander Jacob Obrecht, begins with a harmonized setting of the opening announcement, the *Introitus, Passio Domini nostri Jesu Christi secundum Matthaeum* (the Passion of our Lord Jesus Christ according to Matthew), which had formerly been sung by the *Evangelista* priest. Solo voices were not used, even for the words of Jesus. Many composers, both Roman Catholic and Lutheran, wrote these 'fully-composed' Passions (sometimes called 'motet passions'), but the most far-reaching developments were carried out by the Lutherans.

During the 17th century many changes took place in music, both in actual style and in instrumentation, and this spirit of musical adventure also influenced the fully-composed Lutheran Passion: solo voices were used; recitatives and airs in the new style were written (*see* SONG, HISTORY OF, Section 4); an orchestra was introduced; a more dramatic vein was considered permissible; and additions and alterations to the text of the Scriptures were allowed. Heinrich Schütz (1585–1672), the greatest composer of this period, was remarkable for the dramatic force of his passion music, his sincerity, his style of writing for choir, and for the naive realism with which he depicted the cock crowing, for example, or the rolling of the stone from the sepulchre. Schütz discarded the preliminary musical setting of the title ('The Passion of our Lord Jesus Christ', &c.), a survival from the time when the Passion was sung as part of the church service.

In the period between Schütz and BACH (q.v. Vol. V) the German Passion was strongly influenced by the Italian style of religious opera or ORATORIO (q.v.). Many experiments were made, such as discarding the biblical words in favour of rhymed paraphrases in the sentimental style of the day. The general atmosphere of the passion-oratorios was sentimental and cheap. Bach's Passions (the *St. John Passion*, 1723, and the *St. Matthew Passion*, 1729) returned to a severer and more dignified style. Both use the actual Bible words for the main story (set in recitative for the Evangelist or in short choruses for the crowd), while poetical texts are inserted for meditative arias and large choruses. Old Lutheran chorales (*see* HYMNS), wonderfully harmonized by Bach, are sung at suitable dramatic points throughout the Passion, summing up, as it were, the reflections of the listener on the sacred drama.

J. S. Bach was the last and greatest exponent of the German Passion tradition, few settings of the Passion in that manner having been made since. There have, however, been isolated works dealing with the crucifixion of Our Lord, such as Haydn's *Seven last Words from the Cross*. The medieval hymn *Stabat Mater*, telling of the sufferings of the Blessed Virgin at the Cross, has also been set to music by many composers, notably Palestrina, Pergolesi, Haydn, Rossini, and Dvořák.

See also MUSIC, HISTORY OF; ORATORIO.

PASTEL. This method of drawing or painting with coloured chalk derives its name from the Italian *pastello*, a 'little paste'. Pastel consists of ground-up colour mixed with some adhesive, such as gum-water or wax; this is rolled into the shape of a pencil or crayon and used like a pencil. The basis of most pastels is chalk; the pigments of the earliest known pictures in prehistoric caves were mainly chalk, and chalk has always been popular for drawing. The method has certain advantages over brush painting in water- or oil-colours; pastels do not fade as do water-colours, or, to a lesser extent, oil-colours, nor do they darken in time as all oil must do; and there are no difficulties about drying. On the other hand, pastel is light in colour and only suitable for small pictures; although chemical fixatives can now be sprayed on the pastel to bind it to its base, it smudges very easily; the picture must be sealed back and front against damp, and is almost impossible to clean if it gets dirty.

Pastel portraits, generally less than life-size and more like drawings than paintings, were in fashion in France and later in England in the 16th and 17th centuries. The most brilliant exponents at this time were the Clouet family, who worked in France in the late 16th century. The first pastel painter to achieve an international reputation on the same footing as the great oil-painters was Rosalba Carriera (1675–1757), an Italian woman portraitist. During the 18th century the French school was predominant; of those who worked mainly in pastel the greatest was Quentin de la Tour (1704–88), who produced portraits of the most subtle elegance and liveliness. Many of the great oil-painters also worked in pastel, including Nattier

RIGHT: MARY GUNNING, COUNTESS OF COVENTRY. PASTEL BY J. E. LIOTARD

Rijksmuseum, Amsterdam

Glasgow Art Gallery

DANCERS ON A BENCH. PASTEL BY EDGAR DEGAS

(1685–1766) and J. B. Perroneau (1715–83), while Chardin (1699–1779) produced, in his pastel self-portrait, one of the world's masterpieces. The Swiss J. E. Liotard (1702–89), who worked all over Europe and in the Middle East, made extremely skilful portraits which are almost photographically realistic. In England also there was a flourishing school, of whom the most notable artist was John Russell (1745–1806).

In the second half of the 19th century there was a great revival of the pastel, particularly in France. Edgar Degas (1834–1917), who always stressed the importance of drawing to the art of painting, was perhaps happiest in this medium, which is half-way between the two. He made many studies in pastel of ballet dancers and women washing in their tubs or ironing clothes.

See also PAINTING METHODS; DRAWING; PORTRAITS.

PASTORALS. When Marie Antoinette, the last Queen of France, played at being a shepherdess in the exquisite little palace at VERSAILLES (q.v.)—the Petit Trianon—she was playing in life a game that has been played in literature for centuries. She was enacting the pastoral convention. In pastoral literature the characters are shepherds and shepherdesses, who live a simple life in an idealized countryside, an Arcadia. There Nature is gentle and beautiful, peopled with nymphs and satyrs. It is a world of youth, and love, and song.

The pastoral mode has been popular at many periods. Poets, in particular, loved 'to tend the homely, slighted, shepherd's trade'; and we owe some of the finest elegies in the world, and many other beautiful poems, to the pastoral convention. Apart from two exquisite works more like novels than romances (*Daphnis and Chloë* by Longus, a Greek writer of the 3rd century A.D., and *Paul et Virginie*, its 18th-century successor, by the French writer Bernardin de Saint-Pierre) most pastoral prose works were Renaissance romances. Today the pastoral mode is quite out of favour, being regarded as too artificial and stiff.

The first great pastoral poet we know of is Theocritus, a Greek of the 3rd century B.C. At this period Alexandria was the literary centre of the Greek world, and the writers of the Alexandrian school of literature introduced a more personal, private kind of poetry—poetry to be read among friends, not, like the magnificent Athenian epics and odes, to be sung or declaimed on great public occasions. One of the most beautiful forms of this new poetry was the idyll, which Theocritus invented.

The *Idylls* of Theocritus present the old country life of Sicily. They usually tell some simple tale, often in the form of dialogue, and many of them have a refrain. The first Idyll contains the beautiful *Lament for Daphnis*, from which the stanza below, translated by Sir William Marris, is quoted:

So said he then—no more. And Aphrodite
Was fain to raise him; but the Destinies
Had spun his thread right out. So Daphnis went
Down stream: the whirlpool closed above his head,
The head of him whom all the Muses loved,
Of him from whom the Nymphs were not estranged.

Muses, forgo, forgo the pastoral song.

The influence of this lament can be seen and felt in many lovely laments and elegies: in the Greek poet Bion's *Lament for Adonis*, and in the poem this poet's death inspired, Moschus's *Lament for Bion*; in Virgil's Latin *Lament for Daphnis*; and in the three great English poems, *Lycidas*, where Milton mourns the death of Edward King, *Adonais*, Shelley's lament for Keats, and *Thyrsis*, which Matthew Arnold wrote after Clough's death (*see* ELEGY). In such poems the supernatural characters of pastoral—such as Echo, the loves, the muses, nymphs—mourn with the poet the death of a beloved poet-shepherd; as guardians and mourners they have life and purpose. Thus they avoid the role of mere picturesque onlookers which many nymphs of pastoral have had to play.

Theocritus's Roman successor was VIRGIL (q.v. Vol. V). His *Eclogues* describe country life, usually Sicilian life, in imitation of Theocritus. The descriptions lose in freshness, and the pastoral scene at second-hand is slightly artificial. But Virgil invented a device often imitated by later writers—the device of describing contemporary events in terms of a shepherd's life. For example, he refers in Eclogue I to the land confiscations in which he had himself lost his home. And it was Virgil who invented Arcadia, the earthly paradise to many a courtier and city-dweller since.

The writers of the Renaissance were enchanted with Arcadia and the shepherd's song. The Latin *Eclogues* of PETRARCH and the Italian

Eclogues of BOCCACCIO (qq.v. Vol. V) were the first imitations of Theocritus and Virgil. Boccaccio adapted the pastoral mode to romance in his *Admetus*; and many of the romance-writers followed his example, notably Sannazzaro in his *Arcadia* and the Portuguese poet Montemayer in *Diana*.

In England, too, the pastoral mode was adopted with enthusiasm. The first important work of SPENSER (q.v. Vol. V), *The Shepheard's Calendar*, consists of twelve eclogues—one for each month of the year—in the form of dialogues among shepherds. The *Arcadia* of Sir Philip SIDNEY (q.v. Vol. V) is a romance, with pastoral eclogues at the end of each book. The lyric poets used the pastoral device lightly and gracefully in their lyrics, songs, and madrigals. *The Passionate Shepherd to His Love* by MARLOWE (q.v. Vol. V) is one of the best known of these pastoral lyrics. Its first and last stanzas are:

> Come live with me and be my Love,
> And we will all the pleasures prove
> That hills and valleys, dales and fields,
> Or woods or steepy mountain yields.
>
> . . .
>
> The Shepherd swains shall dance and sing
> For thy delight each May morning:
> If these delights thy mind may move,
> Then live with me and be my Love.

Sir Walter RALEIGH (q.v. Vol. V) wrote *The Nymph's Reply to the Shepherd*, which charmingly mocks the pastoral poet for thinking that love and song and youth are all of life. Here are the stanzas parallel to those quoted from Marlowe:

> If all the world and love were young,
> And truth in every shepherd's tongue,
> These pretty pleasures might me move
> To live with thee and be thy Love.
>
> . . .
>
> But could youth last, and love still breed,
> Had joys no date, nor age no need,
> Then these delights my mind might move
> To live with thee and be thy Love.

Pastoral dramas were fashionable, too, and Lyly, Greene, Ben Jonson, and other Elizabethan dramatists wrote such plays. Shakespeare's *As You Like It* has made the pastoral element in drama familiar to generations.

MILTON (q.v. Vol. V) is the greatest of English pastoral poets. His MASQUE *Comus* (q.v. Vol. IX), his elegy *Lycidas*, and his two lovely idylls,

L'Allegro (The Cheerful Man) and *Il Penseroso* (The Contemplative Man), are all written in the pastoral mode. All, too, were written before Milton was 30; later he turned to epic forms. But Milton's poetry, even when he was young, was noble, harmonious, grave; his shepherd's pipe sounds like an organ.

By the second half of the 17th century pastoral poetry had become less popular, and, except for the elegies already discussed, few notable pastorals have been written since. In the 18th century the pastoral became as formalized as an 18th-century garden, as self-conscious as a Dresden shepherdess. Mallarmé, the 19th-century French Symbolist poet, used some of the familiar pastoral figures in his *L'Après-midi d'un faune* (The Afternoon of a Faun); but his interpretation is far removed from the traditional pastoral. His poem inspired DEBUSSY to translate it into music (with the same name), and NIJINSKY (qq.v. Vol. V) translated it into ballet.

See also NATURE WRITING.

PATTERN, *see* ORNAMENT.

PEKING, FORBIDDEN CITY. This palace of the Chinese Emperors is the innermost of four enclosures of the city of PEKING (q.v. Vol. III). It was called the Forbidden City or Purple Forbidden City, because the public were forbidden to enter the buildings and because purple mortar was used in building the walls. About 1,100 yards of wall, 22 feet high, ran from north to south. There are four magnificent gates.

The Forbidden City was built in the 15th century and repeatedly restored during the last Imperial dynasties of China (*see* CHINESE CIVILIZATION, Vol. I). When China became a republic in 1911 part of the palace was turned into a museum. The buildings, which are among the most impressive in the world, are typical of Chinese architecture. Mostly of only one storey, they are arranged on marble terraces round vast rectangular courts (*see* Vol. I, p. 108). The most important features are the enormous curved roofs covered with tiles, often doubled or even tripled, and resting on short wooden columns.

The Imperial Palace, like Chinese buildings in general, is constructed chiefly of wood; the space between the wooden pillars is filled in with stone, brick, or mud.

See also CHINESE ART.

PERIODICALS.

PERIODICALS. Before the 17th century there were no newspapers or periodicals. Then news sheets containing miscellaneous information began to be produced two or three times a week. The *Tatler* (1709–11) edited by Sir Richard Steele was the first of such periodical papers to have literary value. The *Tatler*'s aim was 'to expose the false arts of life, to pull off the disguises of cunning, vanity and affectation, and recommend a general simplicity in our dress, our discourse, and our behaviour'. It was intended to please 'persons of all conditions, and of each sex'—indeed, Steele was, perhaps, one of the first writers specially to consider women readers. After the first few numbers the news-items were dropped, and each number consisted usually of a short essay in which an imaginary character or an incident of town-life was amusingly described, and absurdities of fashion or habit thus shown up. Occasionally a more serious note was struck, as in the condemnation of duelling and gambling. Virtue was illustrated by descriptions of such characters as Aspasia (Lady Elizabeth Hastings), who was praised with the famous remark, 'To love her is a liberal education'.

Steele was helped by Joseph ADDISON (q.v. Vol. V), and in March 1711 Steele and Addison together started a successor to the *Tatler* called the *Spectator*. This ran till December 1712, and again for a few weeks in 1714, appearing daily. Its aim, like the *Tatler*'s, was 'to enliven morality with wit, and to temper wit with morality'. The papers were supposed to be written by a grave man, Mr. Spectator; various characters were invented, including the famous Sir Roger de Coverley, a country squire; but most of the descriptions were of London life. Neither the *Tatler* nor the *Spectator* was political. The *Spectator* included more essays on general literary subjects, such as, for instance, Addison's papers on Milton, and on the imagination. Both periodicals are valuable for the picture they give us of the age, but especially for the balanced, gentlemanly, entertaining way in which they are written. They set a high standard of behaviour in restrained manners and good taste, and made a smooth, agreeable style popular. They set a fashion for such periodicals, and Samuel JOHNSON (q.v. Vol. V) modelled his *Rambler* and *Idler* upon them. His writing is less light and cheerful, but his thought is more profound.

Johnson also contributed to a new kind of periodical founded by the publisher Edward Cave, called the *Gentleman's Magazine* (1731–1914), a miscellany of literary articles, parliamentary reports, music, maps, and so on, which was published monthly, and the success of which attracted several rivals.

The next development came (like so many other literary developments) at the beginning of the 19th century. Two great reviews were founded, to be published three or four times a year, the aim of which was to survey literature, art, science, politics, and public events, to criticize them intelligently, and so to improve understanding and taste. The first of these was the *Edinburgh Review*, founded in 1802, and edited, with the help of Sidney Smith, by Francis Jeffrey till 1829. It was advanced in politics, but very conservative in literary taste. It was so brilliantly written that its first number astonished and delighted the reading public, and it became extremely popular. A rival paper was founded in 1809, also in Edinburgh, called the *Quarterly Review*, supported by the Tory party and by Sir Walter SCOTT (q.v. Vol. V). It was edited by William Gifford till 1823, and then by John Gibson Lockhart, and soon became as famous as the *Edinburgh*. Both periodicals were notable for the violence of their criticism, particularly of modern poets (the *Edinburgh* hated the 'Lake School'—Wordsworth, Coleridge, and Southey; the *Quarterly* hated the 'Cockney School', especially Leigh Hunt, Shelley, and Keats). But Scott's contributions in the *Quarterly* were understanding and impartial, especially his notice of Jane Austen's *Emma* and the review of one of his own books, in which he condemns the insipidity of his heroes.

Two brilliant magazines, aiming more at entertainment than did the reviews, were founded about the same time. One was *Blackwood's Edinburgh Magazine* (1817), which soon had many notable contributors, among them DE QUINCEY (q.v. Vol. V). Like the *Quarterly*, it was Tory in politics and attacked Leigh Hunt, Lamb, Hazlitt, and Coleridge. *Blackwood's* still continues, featuring mainly tales from outposts of the Empire. The other magazine was the *London* (1820–9), which opposed *Blackwood's*, and published some of the most brilliant work of the writers whom *Blackwood's* condemned. The abusive enmity between the two magazines

BACCHUS AND ARIADNE. OIL PAINTING BY TITIAN, *c.* 1480–1576

resulted in the tragic death of John Scott, the first editor of the *London*, in a duel.

There were many other reviews and magazines in the 19th century on the same lines but less violent in style, and most of the great writers of the age contributed important essays to one or other. Among these were the *Athenaeum*, *Fraser's Magazine*, and the *Cornhill* (edited by Thackeray).

About 1880 a number of small weekly periodicals began to appear, often with pictures, which aimed at entertaining the masses rather than improving the educated. Of the modern weekly magazines whose aim is entertainment the oldest is *Punch*, founded in 1841. A popular, fully-illustrated weekly with an enormous circulation, which aims at conveying information in an attractive and easily appreciated way, is *Picture Post*. A few weeklies such as the *Spectator* and the *New Statesman and Nation* adopt a more critical and thoughtful attitude, with a strong, consistent political bias. These have important literary sections and are in the tradition of the great reviews. There are now many children's magazines and also periodicals catering for some special interest, technical or otherwise.

Among the quarterlies, one rather unusual one is the *Countryman*, which writes intelligently and non-technically about anything to do with the English country-side, but is neither literary nor political. Two distinguished literary periodicals have been published in the 20th century. One was the *Criterion* (1922–39), edited by T. S. Eliot, whose emphasis was on the creation of a sensitive, critical, and educated public, which was expected to be small. It published original stories and poetry, and serious critical essays on literature and the arts as practised in all the countries of western Europe. The other was *Horizon* (1939–50), edited by Cyril Connolly and Stephen Spender till 1941, and then by Connolly alone. Its aim was to interpret the 1940's to themselves, and so help to bring about a new and more vigorous literature. It wished also to preserve the best of western European civilization, and bring modern psychology in line with the arts. It published original work and critical essays from European countries and America. It was very pessimistic, advanced in thought, interesting, and difficult.

All the periodicals mentioned have a marked quality of their own, coming from the personality of their editors. It needs a man of strong personality, with decided ideas and sound judgement, to make a periodical successful.

See also ESSAYS.
See also Vol. IV: NEWSPAPERS, HISTORY OF; MAGAZINES AND PERIODICALS.

PERSIAN ART. The Persians have shown a genius for artistic creation from early times, and in spite of foreign invasion and conquest their art has developed continually. Many of their methods of building and of decorating which appear at subsequent periods of their history can be traced to those of their ancestors some 2,500 years ago. Persian art has had a wide influence, for at its height the Persian Empire spread as far as Afghanistan and north-western India (*see* PERSIAN ANCIENT CIVILIZATION, Vol. I).

1. ANCIENT PERSIA. Little beyond a few carved reliefs and rock tombs is known of the art of the earliest people of Persia, or of the Medes who succeeded them. When the Persian ruler CYRUS (q.v. Vol. V) came to power in 550 B.C. Persia became a great empire, reaching its zenith under DARIUS and XERXES (qq.v. Vol. V). The ruins of Persepolis (*see* Vol. I, p. 354) and Susa give a clear idea of the grandeur of the art of this dynasty. At Persepolis a stone stairway of over a hundred steps leads to the portico of the royal palace. The sides of the stairway are decorated with modelling in low relief depicting the great king's soldiers and attendants and a procession of foreign princes offering him tribute. The portico, formed of two great winged bulls with human heads, was the entrance to the columned halls which were the royal audience chambers (*see* Vol. V, p. 494).

Grandeur was the keynote of the architecture of this period; everything was designed to inspire reverence and awe for the king. The Persians inherited many of their artistic ideas from the Assyrians, whose political power in the Near East they had helped to overthrow. The Persians, like the Assyrians, excelled in the portrayal of animals and fabulous monsters such as human-headed bulls and winged lions.

In 330 B.C. ALEXANDER THE GREAT (q.v. Vol. V) conquered Persia and introduced Greek civilization. Under his rule and that of his successors, Greek forms of art were adopted by the Persians. About 150 B.C. the Parthians, a people of nomadic origin, drove out the Greeks and restored the political independence of Persia, but not its artistic traditions.

RUINS OF THE PALACE AT CTESIPHON

Probably built in the reign of Shapur I (A.D. 241–72). All that remains are the left-hand part of the façade and the great vaulted arch which linked the two sides. The material is brick. (From *A Survey of Persian Art*, edited by A. U. Pope and P. Ackerman)

2. THE SASSANIAN PERIOD. The Sassanian rulers, who followed the Parthians in A.D. 224, sought to revive the greatness of ancient Persia. They were great builders, their best-known monument being the palace at Ctesiphon (in what is now Iraq). In this very dignified building the two halves of the façade are joined by a vast vaulted hall open to the front, in which the king held public audiences. The vaulting is a wonderful piece of construction.

Remarkable rock carvings were made to commemorate the triumphs of the king over his enemies or his investiture with the crown by the Persian divinity, Ahura Mazda (*see* ZOROASTRIAN, Vol. I). Fine examples of bronze, silver, and golden vessels have also been found (*see* Vol. I, p. 355).

3. THE MOSLEM PERIOD. The Arab conquest of Persia in the 7th century (*see* ARABS, Vol. I) did not mean the end of Persian art, but rather the reverse. The conquerors had no artistic skill or traditions of their own, and relied on the native artists and craftsmen to provide them with mosques and palaces and all those objects which they thought necessary for civilized life. Sassanian methods of building and decoration, such as brick vaulting and stucco carving, came to be adopted by Moslem craftsmen and spread to remote parts of the Islamic world. At the same time, in accepting the religion of the conquerors, the Persians became members of the wider community of Islam. Yet Persian art, though at this period a branch of ISLAMIC ART (q.v.), retained many of its own traditions, adapting them to the new religion.

In the 9th century independent rulers began to establish kingdoms in Persia, and Turkish tribes began to enter Persia from beyond the River Oxus (Amu Dar'ya). The best-known surviving building of the first of these Turkish settlers is the tomb tower of the ruler Mahmud at Ghazna in Afghanistan. Similar towers were erected by the rulers of another Turkish dynasty, the Seljuks, who conquered Persia in the 11th century and ruled until nearly the end of the 12th century. The Seljuks also introduced the 'cruciform' type of MOSQUE (q.v.) in which each of the four sides of the court has a vast niche. This niche is derived from the vaulted hall in the palace of Ctesiphon. Another type of Seljuk building is the mausoleum, a square tomb building with a door in the centre of each side and surmounted by a dome.

The Seljuks also excelled in the minor arts: in silk weaving, metal-work, and pottery. The artists often painted miniature scenes of a high quality on the pottery. In decoration the Seljuks made much use of the 'arabesque' pattern of interweaving foliage or scrolls, and figures of animals.

In the 13th century Mongol invasions caused havoc in Persia, but when, by the close of the century, the Mongols had established settled government, a fresh impetus was given to the arts. Many mosques and other religious buildings were built, and Persian miniature painting was becoming important. Persia was again invaded at the close of the 14th century, this time by TAMBURLAINE (q.v. Vol. V), a Turk from central Asia; but under his successors Persia enjoyed a renaissance of civilization. The finest examples of the architecture of this period are at Herat in Afghanistan and at Samarkhand and Bokhara in Russian Turkestan (see UZBEKISKAYA, Vol. III). During the period of the Timurid Empire in the 15th century many magnificent mosques were built. These consisted of a square or rectangular court with a

TOMB TOWER OF MAHMUD (d. 1031) AT GHAZNA, AFGHANISTAN

The bricks of which the tower is built are arranged in decorative patterns. (From *A Survey of Persian Art*, edited by A. U. Pope and P. Ackerman)

British Museum

SELJUK DISH, LATE 12TH CENTURY

It is painted in turquoise and outlined in red with touches of gilding

vast niche on each side, and between them two-storeyed arcades. Their great beauty lay in the mosaics formed of coloured tiles, ranging from turquoise and cobalt blue to purple, green, yellow, pink, and dark red, which decorated large parts of the walls and domes and made a wonderful contrast with the desolate landscape of Persia. A fine example of the beautiful Timurid domes is that of the Gur-i-Mir in Samarkhand. This is bulbous-shaped with ribs decorated with black and white ornament on a ground of turquoise tiles.

A SCENE IN A GARDEN. PERSIAN MINIATURE
Illustration to the poems of Khwaju Kirmani, by a painter
of the Baghdad School, 1396

Some idea of the magnificence of Timurid architecture can be seen in the miniature painting and illuminated manuscripts of the period. The great Persian painter Bihzad, who was working at the Timurid court at Herat, gives a wonderful picture of Persian life in his paintings, with their subtle colours, precision of detail, and fine sense of grouping. In such masterpieces as the illustrations to the poems of Nizami, in the British Museum, there are Court and battle scenes, scenes of pastoral life and landscapes, and even pictures of workmen building a mosque (see Colour Plate, Vol. I, opp. p. 352).

From 1587 to 1628 Persia was ruled by Shah Abbas, the greatest of the native Safavid rulers. He built a large part of the city of Isfahan, a fine piece of town-planning. The centre of the town is a public square bounded by trees and a canal. Around this square Shah Abbas built the Royal Mosque and a palace set amidst pleasure gardens. During this great period of Persian art, the finest carpets were woven and

some magnificent illustrated manuscripts and paintings were produced, as well as beautiful pottery. In the 16th and 17th centuries the influence of Chinese art was marked.

After the end of the Safavid dynasty, the arts declined; the attempt to absorb European ideas seemed to stifle native genius.

See also ISLAMIC ART; MOSQUE.
See also Vol. I: PERSIAN ANCIENT CIVILIZATION; PERSIANS.

PERSIAN LITERATURE. The chief work of ancient Persian literature is the *Avesta*, the Zoroastrian scriptures (*see* SACRED BOOKS, Section 5, Vol. I) of which only fragments survive. The date of these is not known, but some parts almost certainly date back to the Prophet himself, perhaps about 700 B.C. From the 3rd to the 7th century A.D., the period of the Sassanid rulers when Persia was a world power, there was considerable literary activity, mainly on religious themes. Particularly important was the *Zend*, a commentary on the *Avesta*.

The Arab conquest in A.D. 651 brought about a decline in Persian literature because of the greater prestige of Arabic, the language of the new rulers. About A.D. 892, however, the native Samanid dynasty established itself in Transoxiana, the land east of the river Oxus, and Persian poetry began to flourish. In those days, there being no large book-buying public, the one way a poet could be sure of making a living was to win the favour of some rich patron. That is why much of classical Persian poetry is full of ridiculous flattery, sometimes of quite minor rulers, and has little appeal for us.

Of all the people who adopted the religion of ISLAM (q.v. Vol. I) the Persians took least kindly to Arab domination, which followed naturally on the Arab military successes and on the fact that the prophet Mohammed was an Arab. Largely for this reason, the most revered name in Persian poetry is Firdawsi (died *c.* 1020), whose *Shahnama* ('King-book') tells the proud legends of Persian kings and warriors from the dawn of time till the coming of the Arab conquerors. Although to European taste it is long and monotonous, it is treasured by Persians as their great national epic.

The most important single influence on the literature of the Persians has been the system of mystical beliefs and practices known as Sufism (*see* DERVISHES, Vol. I), which inspired all their great poets but Firdawsi. Many Persians found consolation in the doctrines of Sufism for the horrors of the Mongol invasion and the reign of Timur (*see* TAMBURLAINE, Vol. V).

Of all the figures of Persian literature, the best-known in England is the 11th-century Omar KHAYYÁM (q.v. Vol. V), although in his own country he is remembered more as a mathematician and astronomer than as a poet. Farid al-Din Attar (*c.* 1200) wrote a number of mystical works, of which the most famous is the *Mantiq al-Tayr* ('The Speech of the Birds'), a lengthy poem recounting the birds' quest for their king, the Phoenix, which was an allegorical description of the Sufis' search for truth. A much-loved Sufi poet, Jalal al-Din Rumi (born 1207), founder of the Mevlevi order of dervishes, wrote the *Masnawi*, an enormously long mystical work in rhymed couplets. Sa'di of Shiraz (died 1291) wrote two delightful dissertations on justice, humility, and the other virtues: the *Bustan* ('Orchard') in verse and the *Gulistan* ('Rose-garden') in alternate prose and verse.

The majority of classical Persian writers chose to express themselves in verse rather than prose. The greatest of them was Hafiz of Shiraz (died 1389), whose sweet songs in praise of love, wine, and good fellowship are regarded by Sufis as allegories of the Divine Love, though he probably meant them literally.

Many great writers of Persian birth, in particular prose writers, wrote in Arabic. Among these was the famous 11th-century philosopher-physician Ibn Sina (Avicenna).

See also ARABIC LITERATURE.
See also Vol. I: PERSIAN ANCIENT CIVILIZATION; DERVISHES.
See also Vol. IV: PERSIAN LANGUAGE.

PERSPECTIVE.

Strictly speaking, perspective is a mathematical system which enables an artist or engineer to make realistic pictures of solid objects such as houses or pieces of machinery (*see* ENGINEERING DRAWING, Vol. VIII). When drawn in perspective objects appear to be solid, and the space between them seems as clear and convincing as if it were really there.

Modern perspective was probably invented in about 1420 by the great Florentine architect, BRUNELLESCHI. The theory of the system, and an explanation of how to use it in painting, was written down in 1435 by his friend ALBERTI (qq.v. Vol. V) in a book *On Painting*, which

British Museum

FIG. I. EGYPTIAN PAINTING FROM 'THE BOOK OF THE DEAD'

helped to shape the ITALIAN ART (q.v.) of the Renaissance. Nowadays, however, the term 'perspective' is often used to describe any attempt to show space and solidity on the flat surface of a picture, even those made before the Renaissance period.

The artists of prehistoric times and those of the ANCIENT CIVILIZATIONS (q.v. Vol. I) were quite uninterested in trying to deceive the on-looker by creating an appearance of space and solidity. The Egyptian artist, for example, showed only one side of the tables and chairs in his pictures (Fig. 1), and as all the receding sides are hidden, we see only a flat picture on a flat surface. The ancient Greeks were the first to try to make some of the things that they painted look solid. They may even have developed a theory of perspective, which was later forgotten (*see* GREEK ART). After the Greeks, attempts were continually being made in various parts of the world to force the flat surfaces of pictures to show space and solidity. Without the help of mathematical theories or systems, artists tried to portray the things they saw with greater accuracy and realism.

A scene painted by the Italian artist Simone Martini, about 80 years before the invention of mathematical perspective, shows how much could be done without the help of science (Fig. 2). The little buildings seem solid, and there is plenty of space in front of them, since the ground is clearly shown, and their sides as well as their fronts are seen, growing smaller as they run into the distance. This is called 'foreshortening'. Artists had observed that things appeared

Anderson

FIG. 2. SCENE FROM THE LIFE OF ST. AUGUSTINE BY SIMONE
MARTINI (1285?–1357?)

National Gallery

FIG. 3. 'THE ANNUNCIATION' BY CARLO CRIVELLI, 15TH
CENTURY

smaller the farther off they were, but had not worked out the exact relation to each other of things in space.

The mathematical perspective invented by Brunelleschi and Alberti defines this relation precisely, and therefore gives a much stronger feeling of orderliness and of deep space than anything that had been done before. This is because the entire construction is based upon the spot from which an imaginary observer is seeing all the things shown in the picture. All the lines and surfaces, whether of ground or ceilings, or the sides or roofs of houses, which are supposed to run straight into the distance, disappear into a single point (marked X on Fig. 3) called a 'vanishing point'. This corresponds exactly to the supposed position of the observer's eye. It may be to left or right, high or low, or in the centre of the picture; or even outside it. Wherever it is, this vanishing point always coincides with the line of the horizon. Of course, all the receding lines and surfaces do not necessarily run straight into the distance. Some recede at an angle to the spectator but their appearance in perspective is still precisely controlled by his fixed viewpoint. Lines parallel to one another but at an angle to the spectator disappear at a vanishing point which is on the horizon but not in the same position as the vanishing point for lines running straight away from the spectator.

In fixing the exact point from which his picture is to be viewed, the artist also decides how far away from the painted scene the onlooker is supposed to be. This distance controls the speed at which objects in the picture grow smaller as they recede into space. It is one of the special advantages of perspective that if one thing is supposed to be twice as far away as another, it also appears to be only half as big; if it is three or four times as far away, then it is only a third or quarter as big, and so on. This makes it possible to tell exactly how far away and how big all the things in the finished picture are in comparison with each other. As a result, even in a picture like the one in Fig. 3, which contains a great many different details, everything seems to be well ordered and clearly placed. Just as in real life, we can measure exactly where everything is in the space the artist has made.

Not only do objects appear to grow less in size the farther away they are, but their colours

National Gallery

FIG. 4. 'A VENETIAN SCENE' BY J. M. W. TURNER (1775–1851)

also appear to diminish. Near things are sharply defined, their colours are strong and their shadows sharp. In the distance their colours appear paler and their outlines less well defined. This 'aerial perspective' cannot be worked out mathematically as can linear perspective, although the two kinds are often used together (Fig. 4).

Besides helping the artist to create realistic space and clearly positioned solid-looking objects, perspective is useful in other ways. The placing of the vanishing point can be used, for instance, to draw our attention towards a particular feature and away from another. Combined with the pattern of lines and colours, it gives the artist increased control over his design.

It is precisely because a picture is not just a geometrical construction, that despite the many refinements in perspective since the Renaissance, and despite its usefulness to engineers and architects, modern painters often ignore it, or only use part of it. For the engineer it is a tool, and for the artist a servant but not a master. It all depends what the artist wants to do.

PHAROS OF ALEXANDRIA, *see* WONDERS OF THE WORLD.

PIERS PLOWMAN, by William Langland, *see* ALLEGORY.

PILGRIM'S PROGRESS. This is an ALLEGORY (q.v.), a story in which a second meaning lies beneath the obvious meaning. The author, John Bunyan, though a man of simple education, had a genius for putting religious truth in this picturesque form. He gives his characters names which make his allegorical meaning clear. The allegorical meaning of *Pilgrim's Progress* is the journey of the Christian soul from earth to heaven. The pilgrim, Christian, sets out on a journey. The road is hard, and there are many pitfalls. Fellow travellers, such as Pliable and Worldly Wiseman, try to entice him back. Others, such as Interpreter, help him on the way. He is hampered by a heavy burden, his sins; but at last he comes to a Cross on a hill, where the burden falls off. Yet his troubles are not over. He has to contend with monstrous enemies, Apollyon in the Valley of Humiliation

'PILGRIM'S PROGRESS'
Frontispiece to the 14th edition, 1695

and Giant Despair in Doubting Castle. Passing through the city of Vanity Fair, where the people spend their lives in pleasure and money-making, his companion Faithful is cruelly killed and he himself barely escapes. From the Delectable Mountains he gains a sight of the Golden City, and then passes through the river of Death to be greeted by saints and angels.

Part II of the book tells the story of Christiana, his wife, and their four children, who follow him later on the same journey. As they are weaker than Christian, a strong protector, Greatheart, helps them through their difficulties. At last, one by one, Christiana and other pilgrims who have joined them are called to their rest. The passing of Valiant-for-Truth (in whose mouth Bunyan puts the well-loved hymn, 'Who would true valour see') is told in singularly moving words.

The religious teaching of *Pilgrim's Progress* is of 17th-century Puritanism. In places it sounds somewhat harsh and forbidding to modern ears, but Bunyan's broad sympathy and deep knowledge of human nature leave much that can be appreciated by men of all creeds. The 17th-century prose style is simple and vivid. The book was immediately popular, 100,000 copies being sold during Bunyan's lifetime. Its appeal has been so wide that it has been translated into more than 100 languages.

See also Vol. V: BUNYAN.

PLAINSONG. This earliest music in the Christian Church is still performed, principally in the Roman Catholic Church. It is always in unison (that is, with all voices singing the same tune, without HARMONY (q.v.)), and it is without a definite series of time values. Its rhythm is free, basically a prose rhythm, for it developed many centuries before harmonized music brought with it 'measured' music (*musica mensurata*). When harmonized music was introduced, the old music was called *cantus planus* (plainsong or plainchant) to distinguish it.

The simplest and oldest form of plainsong lies in the chanting of the psalms. This practice developed not only in the Mass but even more in the singing of various services or 'offices', such as Matins and Vespers, which still are a regular feature of the daily lives of monastic communities. The psalms are sung to eight basic 'modes' or 'tones' (*see* SCALES), each of which is not only completely different from the others but also often has variations itself at the final cadence of each verse. The following quotation from a typical psalm shows the method of chanting (Fig. 1):

FIG. I

The examples quoted here are given in modern notation, but it must be remembered that the time values are only approximate. In Fig. 1, for example, the semibreves (○) merely show the note on which the greater part of the psalm is sung, at an ordinary speaking speed. These are called reciting notes. The quavers are only roughly equal, and the crotchets roughly equal to two quavers.

Another ancient and simple type of plainsong is known as 'syllabic' plainsong, in which each syllable has a separate note of its own or, occasionally, two. This syllabic chant was the important half-way house between what was merely an inflected monotone in the psalms and the very elaborate forms of plainsong which could be described as compositions in our modern sense. Its development from psalm-singing can be seen in the following extract from the *Gloria* of a 10th-century Mass (Fig. 2):

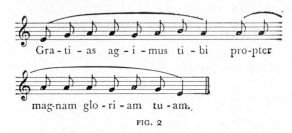

FIG. 2

The Lord's Prayer as it is sung in the Roman Catholic Church by the celebrating priest in the Mass is an example of an independent syllabic chant, one not derived from the psalm tones (Fig. 3):

FIG. 3

The syllabic chant developed into more florid chant in the antiphons, short texts sung before and after the psalms. Originally they consisted of simple syllabic chant closely related to the psalm tones, but in the Mass these antiphons gradually became so elaborate that they tended to displace the psalms around which they were originally constructed. In the Introit, for example, the antiphon sung while the priest approaches the altar to celebrate, only one verse of the psalm and the *Gloria Patri* have survived, with a lengthy antiphon sung before and after them. In the Communion and Offertory antiphons the psalm has completely disappeared, and the antiphons are now sung once only by themselves.

FIG. 4

The more elaborate antiphons have many notes to a syllable. Such chant is called 'melismatic', and is to be found at its most complex in the chants which are sung between the Epistle and the Gospel in the Mass (Fig. 4).

From very early times the execution of these chants was entrusted to specially skilled singers because of the elaborate nature of melismatic chant. Much of the simpler chant, however, was also sung by the congregations.

All the chants we have so far discussed were set to prose texts, but hymns of Greek origin with metrical texts (in which the tunes were repeated exactly for all verses) were introduced supposedly by Bishop Ambrose of Milan (died 397). One of the most famous of plainsong hymns still in use is the 8th-century 'Veni Creator Spiritus', sung on Whit Sunday (Fig. 5).

Pope GREGORY THE GREAT (q.v. Vol. V), who was often depicted writing down the plainsong melodies at the dictation of the Holy Ghost in the form of a dove, established a song-school in Rome. Its members collected and standardized the various chants in use at his time and by sending musical missionaries throughout the Christian world, also achieved a more or less consistent practice. Consequently the great collection of plainsong in the Western Church is often known as Gregorian Chant; but a few slightly different traditions survived locally, such as the 'Ambrosian' chant in Milan and the 'Mozarabic' chant in Spain.

Verse 1. Ven-i Cre-a-tor___ Spir-i-tus,
Verse 2. Qui di-ce-ris Par-a-cli-tus,

Men-tes tu-or-um vis-i-ta:
Alt-iss-i-mi do-num De-i,

Im-ple sup-er-na grat-i-a·
Fons vi-vus, ig-nis car-i-tus,

Quae tu cre-as-ti___ pect-or-a.
Et spir-i-ta-lis___ unct-i-o.

FIG. 5

With the development of *musica mensurata* the traditions and standards of chanting began to decline. In the middle of the 16th century, an attempt was made, among others by the great church composer Palestrina, to revive and revise the old chants. Owing, however, to the loss of an authentic tradition and ignorance of the ancient manuscripts, there was little success. By the 19th century, plainsong had deteriorated into a lifeless and corrupt condition: its ancient flexibility lost, it was forced into exactly measured rhythms and frequently harmonized.

Towards the end of the 19th century the Benedictine monks of Solesmes in France began their great work of restoring plainsong from all the most ancient manuscripts, of preparing performing editions, and, in their own singing, of establishing high standards of performance. When from 1901 to 1921 the monks of Solesmes were exiled from France, they continued their preparation of liturgical books in the Isle of Wight. Their work has been largely responsible for the considerable modern revival of interest in plainsong.

After the Reformation the Gregorian chants dropped out of use in the Church of England, although John Merbecke specially composed some plainsong which was suited to the English words of the new rite (*see* SACRED MUSIC). In recent years, however, various arrangements of the old Gregorian chant itself, set to English words, have been made according to Solesmes principles.

Being essentially sung prayer, plainsong is purely religious in character, and is generally rather restrained and peaceful in expression. But although its scope seems limited compared with that of the large orchestras and choirs of modern music, it is in fact capable of expressing a wide range of emotion and (within the limits of its contemplative spirit) of dramatic representation.

See also SACRED MUSIC; MUSICAL NOTATION; MUSIC, HISTORY OF; SCALES.

PLAYS, *see* DRAMA.

POETRY. The word poetry is derived from the Greek verb *poiein*, 'to make', which was used especially of works of art, and from which came *poiētēs*, 'a poet'. To remember this root of the word is to remind ourselves of an important truth about the nature of poetry: that although it is made with words whose sounds die immediately after they are spoken (and poetry should always be spoken, whether aloud or in the mind's ear), it is a creation, independent of its maker when once he has finished with it, just as a vase is independent of the craftsman who shaped it. Indeed, as long as the language lives in which it was written, a poem is made of less perishable material than a vase.

Words, the material from which poetry is made, influence the result of the poet's labour, just as the shape and quality of a block of stone must influence the sculptor's. Jacob Epstein has said that 'In carving, the suggestion for the form of the work often comes from the shape of the block'. Similarly, a word or phrase, coming to the poet's mind as the direct expression of his thought, will suggest other words and images, by association of meaning or of sound. So the original impulse—of love, awe, joy, sorrow, intellectual curiosity, or whatever it was—which lay at the heart of the poem is transformed by the amassing of sounds and images, growing somewhat as a snowball grows in moving. An example is Shakespeare's Sonnet 140 ('In the old age black was not counted fair'). In this sonnet the whole poem grows from the double meaning of the word 'fair', signifying beautiful as well as blonde.

The sculptor may find a flaw in the block of stone which obliges him to change his plans. The poet has even more difficulty in making words do just what he wants, because his material is common property, and the use of words in everyday speech is constantly making slight alterations in their meaning. New inventions give extensions of meaning—for instance, the participle 'grounded' has acquired a new unfavourable sense since men learnt to fly. Some words move down in the world, or even completely change their meaning, as the centuries go by: for example, if we trace the history of the words 'nice' or 'imprecation', we shall find that they used to have quite different meanings. Some words again become so debased by careless use that they cease to have any precise meaning at all. A poet needs to be conscious of the exact value of the words he uses, for one of his great tasks is to preserve the vitality and expressiveness of his native language, using what is best in the rhythms and diction of contemporary speech.

Both form and content in poetry depend upon words; but for the purpose of criticism we separate the two, abstracting what we think to be the 'content' or meaning of a poem from the form in which it is contained. ('Form' can mean metrical form simply, or the whole body of words—images as well as rhythms—by means of which the meaning is expressed.) For instance, it would be possible to simplify the course of Shakespeare's thought in Sonnet 140, summarizing his theme of dark and fair women, true and false beauty, and to call this the meaning of the poem, expressed in the form of a fourteen-lined rhyming stanza, or sonnet. This might be a useful stage in the process of understanding Shakespeare's poem, but only a stage. It would give us that part of the meaning which can be reduced to logical form, but would leave out that which lies beyond the scope of logic. An attempt to make a paraphrase of Blake's poem beginning

Tyger! Tyger! burning bright
In the forests of the night

makes it obvious that the vision of the primitive tiger, the meaning which we apprehend through our senses when we read the poem, has eluded our mental efforts and is missing from the paraphrase. In Keats's *Ode to Autumn* he makes a personification of plenty; in Hood's ode on the same subject he makes a personification of emptiness and gloom; yet when the two poems are read, the similarity of feeling between them is at least as striking as the difference. To give one more example, the difference between Keats's first version of the first line of *Endymion*

A thing of beauty is a constant joy

and what he afterwards changed it to,

A thing of beauty is a joy for ever

is greater than the difference in meaning alone.

Thus there is no way of giving the full meaning of a poem except in the words of the poem itself: its form and content cannot finally be separated. To give an illustration from another art: there is a story told of Schumann, that when he was asked to give the 'inner meaning' of a piece of music, he said, 'Of course I can explain', and sitting down at the piano, played the piece through once more. It follows that there is no such thing as complete translation of poetry from one language into another: paraphrase is the nearest we can get to it.

The impulse to write poetry springs, as suggested above, from the poet's experience of words as well as from his experience of life. He wants to make something; and he wants to speak to someone—for although a listener may have no part in the original impulse, he is ultimately necessary, for poetry is a means of communication. A great deal of hard work is needed if the poet is to transform his original impulse into a finished poem; and the beginning of every poem must be a step in the dark for its creator, however vivid his inner vision, and however directly (if he is a lyric poet) he attempts to set it down. Perhaps no finished work has ever quite fulfilled the first glimpse that its author had of it, still potential in his mind; though excellences then unseen may have been achieved in the process of writing.

If we turn from the activity of the poet to the word poetry again, we shall see that men have given very different meanings to it at different times. Poetry can have the most exalted or the most humble function: it is, as Wordsworth said (quoting Aristotle), 'the most philosophic of all writing', the most sensuous, the most practical; it is the proper language for oracles and for lullabies, for charms to cure warts and for rites to summon the devil. Whereas some have worshipped the source of their inspiration as a goddess, the Muse, others have thought to find it in their own subconscious minds.

Poetry and music were originally closely allied: we know that the earliest stories were in verse, with musical accompaniment, and that the drama of medieval times developed from the chanted sequences introduced into the Mass for special festivals (*see* MIRACLE PLAYS and MORALITY PLAYS). Our use of the term 'foot' (probably the movement of the foot in beating time) as a unit of measurement in versification is a reminder of the early relationship between poetry and dancing.

The simplest definition of poetry is 'rhythmic speech'. But since much prose could also be so described, we are at once obliged to make a distinction between poetry and prose. Some would make the difference a purely technical one, describing as poetry all forms of speech, or written speech, which deliberately use a rhythmic figure—that is, a pattern of repeating rhythms. Others would use the word 'verse' as the technical opposite to prose, and would keep the word 'poetry' for speech which expresses exalted emotion or thought, whether given a metrical form or not. According to this definition, not only the lyrical parts of the Bible in our Authorized Version, but also a good deal of the prose of writers such as Sir Thomas Browne could be described as poetry. As early as 1581, poetry was defined as 'the expression of beautiful and elevated thought, imagination or feeling, in appropriate language'; and again in the 19th century, John Ruskin in *Modern Painters* calls poetry 'The suggestion, by the imagination, of noble grounds for the noble emotions'. Wordsworth, in his great poem *The Prelude*, took a similarly exalted view of the art; he starts the poem by giving a list of the qualities necessary to his task:

> for I neither seem
> To lack, that first great gift! the vital soul,
> Nor general truths which are themselves a sort
> Of Elements and Agents, Under-Powers,
> Subordinate helpers of the living mind.
> Nor am I naked in external things,
> Forms, images; nor numerous other aids
> Of less regard, though won perhaps with toil,
> And needful to build up a Poet's praise.

If exaltation of thought and language is to be the test of poetry, it follows not only that much writing supposed to be prose is really poetry, but also that much which goes under the name of poetry is not poetry at all. This was, broadly speaking, the view which the 19th century took of the poetry of the 18th. Matthew Arnold writes in *Essays in Criticism*: 'The difference between genuine poetry and the poetry of Dryden, Pope, and all their school, is briefly this: their poetry is conceived and composed in their wits, genuine poetry is conceived and composed in the soul'. In the 18th century, however, Dr. Johnson, who held that 'a definition (of poetry) which shall exclude Pope will not easily be made', came near to denying the name of poet to 17th-century writers such as Donne and Vaughan (*see* METAPHYSICAL POETRY). It is clear, therefore, that the opinion of any age upon the poetry of its predecessors depends upon the canons of taste which are in fashion. In our own century we have reacted against the definitions of the Victorians; we say instead that just as a man is still to be described as a man, whether he is good or bad, so poetry is still poetry, whether it is good or bad, exalted or humble in its aims. Modern critics have given greater recognition to the verbal nature of poetry: Michael Roberts, in his introduction to the *Faber Book of Modern Verse*, defines it as 'primarily . . . an exploration of the possibilities of language'. Some critics, instead of looking to the soul as the sphere of poetry, claim to recognize it by its physical results. In *The Name and Nature of Poetry*, A. E. Housman, who had been asked for a definition, wrote: 'I replied that I could no more define poetry than a terrier can define a rat, but that I thought we both recognized the object by the symptoms which it provokes in us'.

See also EPIC POETRY; LYRIC POETRY; ODE; MODERN POETRY; VERSIFICATION.

POMPEII. This town, in Italy near Naples, was founded by an Italian people called the Oscans and was the most southerly town to come within the sphere of Etruscan civilization. Later the culture of Pompeii was strongly influenced by the Greeks of south Italy. In the 1st century B.C. the town became a Roman colony. In A.D. 63 it was partly destroyed by an earthquake; in A.D. 79 a violent volcanic eruption of Mount VESUVIUS (q.v. Vol. III) buried the town under a rain of ashes and mud and destroyed nearly all its inhabitants. To this catastrophe we owe the astonishing preservation of Pompeii's buildings, statues, furniture, utensils, and even the corpses of some of its inhabitants, which were protected from decay by the thick covering of ashes.

Occasional finds of antiquities from Pompeii

P. Hart

THE HOUSE OF THE FAUN, POMPEII
In the foreground is the courtyard (atrium) and behind, the colonnaded garden (peristyle)

are recorded in the Renaissance, but systematic excavation only began in 1748, and still continues. The excavations are exceptionally important because they have disclosed for the first time an ancient city, with its public and private buildings, shops, streets, fountains, and markets, still standing. Most of the houses open on to small enclosed gardens surrounded by columns. Many show important remains of wall-paintings, which are almost the only evidence we have of this branch of ancient art (*see* Vol. I, p. 334). Their subjects also provide valuable information on ancient religion and everyday life. The quality of many of the paintings is generally not very high, for Pompeii was only a provincial town.

Of particular interest among the public buildings are the amphitheatre (80 B.C.), which is the oldest surviving, and the baths which made use of the volcanic springs in the neighbourhood. Further, there were temples of various gods, covered and open-air theatres, a forum, a basilica, a sports ground, and barracks for gladiators. The town, most of which was laid out on a rectangular street-plan, was surrounded by a wall with many gates.

See also ROMAN ART.

PORCELAIN FIGURES, *see* POTTERY AND PORCELAIN FIGURES.

PORTRAITS. A portrait is a record of an individual person's appearance, carried out either in sculpture or on the flat surface of canvas, wood, paper, or ivory. Many portraits are great works of art, but when a portrait is commissioned the main requisite is that it should be a good likeness. As this is not a purely artistic consideration, portraiture to that extent differs from other forms of art.

The Egyptian, Assyrian, and other early arts included busts which represented actual people. But it is only from the time of the Greeks and Romans that large numbers of portrait busts survive (*see* ROMAN ART). During the Middle Ages people were more interested in men's souls than in their bodies, and there was very little portraiture. But by the 15th century the ideas of the RENAISSANCE (q.v. Vol. I) had turned men's thoughts to an interest in humanity again, and a number of fine portraits were produced both in Italy and Flanders. These early portraits, whether carved or painted, are simple and straightforward, usually showing only the head and shoulders of the sitter and with no

National Gallery

'A MAN PRAYING' BY HANS MEMLINC, 15TH CENTURY

as to make possible broad, sweeping gestures and lordly accessory details, such as a helmet in his hand or a hound at his feet (*see* Vol. V, p. 362). This type of portraiture started with the great Venetian, TITIAN, in the 16th century and culminated in the 17th century in the works of VAN DYCK (qq.v. Vol. V); he carried it to such a length that if, for example, the subject of his portrait had ugly hands he would paint the beautiful hands of someone else in their place.

In sculpture, the great BERNINI (q.v. Vol. V), Van Dyck's contemporary, made a number of portrait busts which seem to have been good likenesses as far as the sitter's features were concerned but which, like Van Dyck's paintings, tend to glorify him by giving him an air of importance which he would have liked to possess but very often did not.

While some 17th-century portraitists were thus flattering their sitters, another form of portraiture was being practised by the two men who are unquestionably the greatest portraitists of all time—the Dutchman REMBRANDT and the Spaniard VELAZQUEZ (qq.v. Vol. V). Neither

attempt to idealize him in any way. We may be sure, in fact, that they were excellent likenesses. In addition to single portraits it was the practice in the 15th century, particularly in Flanders, to include in a religious picture a portrait of the man who had commissioned the picture and often also a portrait of his wife. These are shown being presented to Christ and the Virgin Mary (*see* p. 150).

This straightforward type of portraiture lasted long in the north of Europe and was being practised well into the 16th century by such painters as the German, Lucas Cranach, and by his greater contemporary, Hans HOLBEIN the Younger (q.v. Vol. V) (*see* Colour Plate, Vol. VII, opp. p. 32). But in Venice, where portraiture particularly flourished, something new was demanded. It was expected that when the sitter was of noble birth something of his nobility should be obvious in the portrait. Thus the portrait 'in the grand manner' began, in which the sitter was shown very often at full length, so

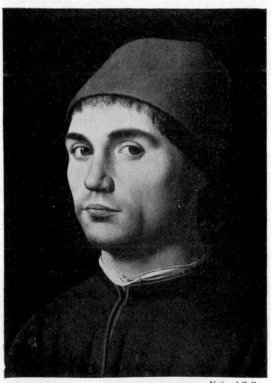

National Gallery

PORTRAIT BY ANTONELLA DA MESSINA (*c.* 1430–79)
This may be a self-portrait

Anderson

THE FAMILY OF CHARLES IV OF SPAIN. PAINTING BY GOYA (1746–1828)

of these men made any attempt to flatter the sitters—which is the more remarkable in the case of Velazquez, since he was Court painter to the Spanish king. Rembrandt preferred painting people for whom he felt sympathy— his family or himself, for example (he painted many self-portraits with the aid of a mirror), or the poor or downtrodden, such as old Jews, and old people in general. But Velazquez was able to paint in the same detached spirit anyone whom he saw, from the king to the Court dwarfs, and to make a masterpiece of the result (*see* Vol. V, p. 456). His detachment and his refusal to regard the king as other than an ordinary man, in spite of the silk clothes and gold trimmings which he painted brilliantly, was developed by his great successor, GOYA (q.v. Vol. V), to the point of satire. Goya, a

passionate and bitter man, despised the weakness and stupidity of the royal family whom it was his duty to paint, and made no attempt to conceal this in his paintings. The king appears to have been so stupid that he did not realize what was happening.

It was during the 18th century that the British school of portraiture came into its own. During the reigns of Queen Elizabeth and James I there had been excellent portraitists in MINIATURE (q.v.), such as Nicholas Hilliard. But throughout the 17th century portraiture in England was largely carried out by foreigners, such as Van Dyck, Lely, or Kneller. In the mid-18th century REYNOLDS and GAINSBOROUGH (qq.v. Vol. V) developed a national school of portraiture of a high class. Much of it, since the sitters were men and women of fashion, was in the 'grand manner', though not to such a degree as Van Dyck's. In particular Reynolds was fond of a type of fancy portrait with men and women portrayed as Roman gods or goddesses, which appealed to the taste of the time. But for beauty and elegance of general effect, combined with a certain restrained dignity which is typically English, this type of portraiture ranks high (*see* Plate 3).

Portrait painting and the portrait groups known as CONVERSATION PIECES (q.v.) continued to show quality in England during the first quarter of the 19th century with such painters as Lawrence. Later during the century its quality declined, and though the 20th century produced one British portrait painter of the first class—Augustus John (*see* Vol. V, pp. 412 and 495)—the development of photography has set up a formidable rival to the portrait painter.

Since the 15th century in Florence the art of portrait sculpture has never been practised so widely as painting, but a certain amount, of a high standard, was done in the 18th century in France, and the 20th-century sculptor, Jacob Epstein, has achieved his best work in this field (*see* Vol. V, p. 437).

A special form of portraiture is CARICATURE (q.v.), in which the features are exaggerated—a man with a large nose, for example, is portrayed with one larger still. The result may recall him better than an entirely truthful portrait. There has been an element of caricature in many portraits painted in the past, and it is often impossible to draw the dividing line between it and serious portraiture.

See also MINIATURES; SILHOUETTES.

POSTER. This form of commercial art, usually a large coloured illustration publicly displayed, is a product of the last 100 years. Posters began to appear when paper became cheap and plentiful, and when modern industry, becoming more and more competitive, sought for ways of making people familiar with proprietary goods.

Advertisements have frequently been used in the past (*see* ADVERTISING AND PUBLICITY, Vol. VII). The Romans displayed public notices on a notice-board known as the *album*, and famous actors employed artists to portray them in favourite parts for exhibition on the *album*. During the Middle Ages and for long afterwards the town-crier was the chief means of advertising. In the 18th century, although paper was rare and expensive and many people could not read, small printed handbills, displayed as posters, announced, for instance, the departure and arrival of stage-coaches; sometimes these bills were decorated with woodcut illustrations. Other small handbills advertised such things as tobacco or tea.

The first posters in the modern sense were produced in Paris in the 1860's. Jules Chéret produced over 1,000 designs and added to the gaiety of the Paris streets with his sparkling, colourful drawings—frequently of pretty girls—advertising theatres, soap, or paraffin lamps. His first poster announced a fairy play in which the great actress Sarah Bernhardt appeared.

Famous painters, such as Manet and Bonnard, occasionally designed posters. Some of the finest were drawn by Toulouse-Lautrec (1864–1902). His posters were simple in design, composed of large areas of flat colour and considerable areas of plain paper; such boldness of design made the picture easy to see and understand across a wide street. He depicted dancers at the Moulin Rouge variety theatre, with legs

Victoria & Albert Museum

POSTER BY TOULOUSE-LAUTREC (1864–1901)

POPE INNOCENT X
PAINTING BY VELAZQUEZ (1599–1660)

PORTRAIT OF THE PAINTER IN OLD AGE
PAINTING BY REMBRANDT (1606–69)

PORTRAIT OF A WOMAN
PAINTING BY FRANS HALS (1580/1–1666)

RIGHT: MRS. ROBINSON ('PERDITA')
PAINTING BY THOMAS GAINSBOROUGH (1727–88)

PLATE 12   POST-IMPRESSIONIST PAINTING

STILL LIFE:
PLATE AND FRUIT DISH
PAINTING BY PAUL CÉZANNE
(1839–1906)

WOMEN OF TAHITI
PAINTING BY PAUL GAUGUIN
(1848–1903)

POSTER BY E. MCKNIGHT KAUFFER

little artistic value. In the 1930's some artists and advertisers were concerned to raise the standard of advertising art, and well designed posters were produced, notably by E. McKnight Kauffer for Shell Petrol, London Passenger Transport Board, and other organizations. McKnight Kauffer's posters attracted attention by their simplified and well planned patterns of pleasant colours; he used good LETTERING (q.v.) and brief texts so that they could be quickly read, and a simple technique which could be printed economically.

Nowadays the artist does not usually draw his work directly on a lithographic stone or plate; he makes his design on prepared cardboard, using a gouache or 'poster-colour', which is opaque water-colour. Poster-colour can be made to lie in flat washes more readily than transparent water-colour; it also photographs better. The artist's original design may be transferred to the plate photographically, or it may be copied by hand.

Other methods besides lithography can be used for printing posters. As well as the more usual methods of printing from metal or wooden blocks (see PROCESS REPRODUCTION, Vol. VII), they may be produced from linocuts or by silk-screen printing, a method used for TEXTILE PRINTING (q.v. Vol. VII).

See also LITHOGRAPHY.
See also Vol. IV: ILLUSTRATION.
See also Vol. VII: ADVERTISING AND PUBLICITY.

POST-IMPRESSIONIST PAINTING. This name is given to the work of painters who, working almost entirely in France at the end of the 19th century and the beginning of the 20th, brought about revolutionary changes in artistic outlook and practice and paved the way for most forms of art which flourish today.

The Post-Impressionists are so called because they came after and broke away from IMPRESSIONIST PAINTING (q.v.). At first their work aroused public scorn and distrust, just as the paintings of their predecessors had done. Nevertheless the Post-Impressionists were making, in some respects, a return to more orthodox principles of painting. However revolutionary in appearance and tendency, they brought back into art a sense of structure and composition on the one hand, and of poetry and self-expression on the other, principles which the Impressionists, in their single-minded pursuit of atmospheric

kicking high from a mass of frilled petticoats; or he showed a top-hatted gentleman, large in the foreground, relishing the pleasures of smoking a cigar and watching the dancing girls. These (as are most posters) were produced by LITHOGRAPHY (q.v.), Toulouse-Lautrec drawing the design himself upon the stone; they were not only efficient advertisements but also works of art.

In England at the end of the 19th century William Nicholson and James Pryde, who chose the professional name of 'the Beggarstaff Brothers', elevated the poster into a fine art. They made their designs by cutting out the shapes from coloured paper, thus ensuring clean, crisp outlines and perfectly flat colour (see Vol. IV, p. 198).

In the 20th century the number of posters increased enormously, many of them having

Rijksmuseum Kröller-Müller

'CYPRESSES WITH A STAR' BY VINCENT VAN GOGH

effects and the appearance of things, had tended to ignore.

Unlike the Impressionists, the Post-Impressionists were not a compact group of artists working towards a common aim in close personal association. The most representative of these painters —CÉZANNE (q.v. Vol. V), Paul Gauguin (1848–1903), and Vincent Van Gogh (1853–90)—were solitary men of very pronounced individuality who discovered and worked out their own artistic problems, not seated at a Paris café table, but away from their fellows. Cézanne worked in southern France, Gauguin in the South Sea Islands, and Van Gogh, an artist of extreme sensibility who came to a tragic end, worked partly in a mental hospital in which he was confined. Gauguin and Van Gogh, it is true, began to work together at Arles in 1888, but the relationship only hastened Van Gogh's insanity and finally his suicide. Cézanne, the most fortunate of the three in having a private income and the only one to reach comparative old age, sacrificed the comforts of a home for the pursuit and conquest of artistic problems.

These three men were convinced that Impressionism was inadequate as an artistic creed, and could not develop further. But, though they shared this belief, they produced works of art which expressed three very different personalities, even when they were painting the same kind of subject.

When Cézanne painted a STILL-LIFE (q.v.), he was intensely interested in the shape of each of the different objects before him, and the way in which these shapes together formed a composition. He painted slowly, because he would only create after analysing the abstract problems which the objects aroused in his inquiring type of mind—the relationship, for example, between the colour and shape of an object; and his interest in these abstract problems made him ignore the purely personal or literary associations which particular objects have for most of us.

Van Gogh, on the other hand, was so keenly alive to these personal associations that, even when he was painting a still-life, the different objects he was painting unfolded a page in his intimate life-history: the old pair of boots, the pipe and tobacco pouch, the book, are all clearly his magic links in a chain of thought or suffering.

Gauguin, less aloof than Cézanne, less personally involved than Van Gogh, drew upon his experiences in the South Sea Islands to create a private dream world of alluring and sometimes sinister appeal. Like Cézanne and Van Gogh, he had been influenced by the Impressionists, but while Cézanne and Van Gogh retained a modified version of the Impressionists' theory of colour in their mature pictures, Gauguin entirely discarded it. He built up his compositions in large areas of colour, symbolic and decorative in function and little related to physical appearances.

While Cézanne and Van Gogh worked, like the Impressionists, directly from nature, Gauguin went back to the earlier practice of artists by painting his pictures in a studio; but all three men were alike in believing that art was distinct from nature—as Cézanne expressed it, art was 'a harmony parallel with nature'. From their different ways of achieving their own peculiar 'harmony' emerged the various forms of painting which we know today—Cubism from Cézanne, EXPRESSIONIST ART (q.v.) from Van Gogh, SURREALISM (q.v.) from Gauguin.

In addition to these three painters, a number of other artists are given the general label of Post-Impressionists. Some painters, called 'Pointillists', pushed to its logical conclusion the

Impressionist theory of colour, building up their pictures in minute dabs of unmixed colour. Seurat used this technique, but his balanced, almost classical, composition is typical of Post-Impressionism. Among the older artists, Degas (*see* p. 333) and Renoir also occupy an intermediate position, combining the Impressionists' interest in the transient effect of light and movement with the Post-Impressionists' study of form and composition (*see* Colour Plate opp. p. 256).

See also MODERN ART.

POTTERY AND PORCELAIN FIGURES.

The practice of making small figures in clay has continued since the very earliest times (*see* TERRACOTTAS), but it was not until about the second half of the 17th century that pottery figures were produced in any quantity in England. The earliest type was made of a material known as salt-glazed STONEWARE (q.v. Vol. VII), so called because salt was used in the firing, giving a surface akin to orange peel, which lent itself very well to enamelling. At about the same time a number of earthenware figures were produced, decorated with mottled

Albert Amor Ltd.

TYROLESE DANCERS. 18TH-CENTURY PORCELAIN GROUP MADE AT MEISSEN, GERMANY

and coloured glazes; it is this technique which was developed by the Staffordshire potters, Astbury and Whieldon, and at a later stage by Ralph Wood and his famous family of potters.

These figures, which were produced largely for the local people, represented and satirized local or national figures, either singly or in groups. The vigour of the modelling and the amusing character of many of the subjects gives Staffordshire figures of the late 17th and early 18th centuries a charm unequalled by the porcelain figures of a later and more sophisticated age (*see* Vol. X, p. 450, and Vol. VI, p. 448).

Although PORCELAIN (q.v. Vol. VII) was invented in China some thousand years ago it was not until the early 18th century that it was produced in Europe at the factory of Meissen in Germany, under the patronage of the Elector of Saxony. Soon other factories sprang up in Italy, France, Germany, and later in England, all making variations of this porcelain. English figures were often copies of those brought from Meissen and other continental factories or show

ST. GEORGE AND THE DRAGON. 18TH-CENTURY POTTERY GROUP BY RALPH WOOD

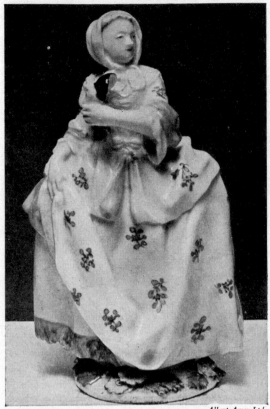

A LADY FROM THE ITALIAN COMEDY. 18TH-CENTURY
PORCELAIN FIGURE MADE AT CHELSEA

Albert Amor Ltd.

with the later productions of all the European factories, became more and more elaborate, with gaudy colours enriched with sumptuous gilding.

The model was first made by a very skilful modeller. This model was then divided up, the head, legs, arms, and other parts being cut from the body and a separate mould made of each piece. Into these moulds the clay was pressed, and when sufficiently dry the pieces were taken from the moulds and joined together by workmen known as 'repairers'. This finished, the figure was placed in a stoneware box called a 'seggar' to be fired in a kiln; when cool it was painted, glazed, and then fired a second time. In the early days flowing draperies and unsupported limbs were kept to the minimum, and figures were usually seated on mounds or standing against tree-trunks. As the modellers and repairers became more skilled, and experiments with the consistency of the clay produced porcelain less likely to warp and crumble in the firing, more ambitious poses were used and complicated groups and combinations of figures were made.

See also TERRACOTTAS.
See also Vol. VII: POTTERY; PORCELAIN; STONEWARE.

their influence, but an unmistakably English character was given even to those figures which were direct copies.

At first porcelain figures were made as table ornaments to take the place of the elaborate scenic arrangements hitherto made of sugar or some equally perishable substance, but later they were made singly or in pairs for mantelpiece ornaments and to decorate candlesticks.

Ideas for figures came from the theatre, mythology, or from the craftsmen and ordinary people of the 18th century. Characters from the Italian stage, and from classical mythology, and figures of cooks, shepherds and shepherdesses, gallants, beggars, and musicians were produced in many of the factories.

The early examples from the factories of Chelsea, Bow, and Derby, the chief producers in England, are exquisite figures and groups, which have typically English faces, softly blended colours, and sparing use of gilding. By the 1760's and 1770's, however, these, in common

PREHISTORIC ART. 1. THE OLD STONE AGE.
The hunting tribes living in parts of western Europe, probably somewhere between 100,000 and 15,000 years ago, were remarkable artists. Engravings and carvings on bone tools and weapons, and statuettes in bone, stone, and clay all show a beauty and skill which demands admiration. With only coloured earths for paints, these peoples covered cave walls with pictures which rank high in the artistic treasures of the world.

We sometimes talk of 'Cave Art', but this is a misleading title if it suggests that the art of the Stone Age is found only in caves. These were only the people's winter shelters; and, though it is true that wall-paintings and engravings are better preserved in deep caves than elsewhere, carvings and engravings on tools and ornaments have been found in other Old Stone Age homes. Being less well preserved, however, the objects are less easy to identify.

Among the small carvings and engravings are stone and ivory figures of women with fat bodies, found from France in the west to Russia in the east (*see* Vol. I, p. 399). These figures may have

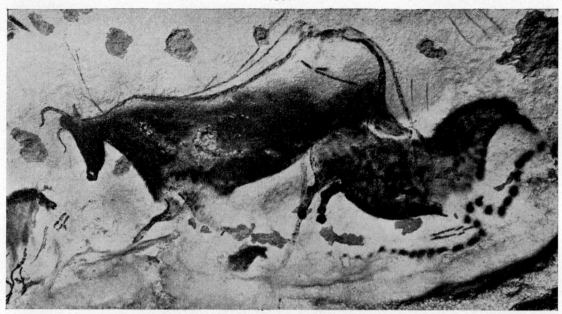

A BULL AND HORSE. PAINTING IN LASCAUX CAVE, FRANCE
From F. Windels, *The Lascaux Cave Paintings*, Faber and Faber

had some religious meaning connected with a cult of a mother goddess of fertility—indeed, in one Stone Age house in Russia several were found placed round the walls as if they were idols of some kind. In western France a remarkable head-and-shoulders portrait of a man wearing a fur cloak has recently been discovered, carved on a slab of stone in low relief and coloured. There are other exquisite small girls' heads carved in bone from France and Czechoslovakia. Animals, too, were carved in the round, often as tool handles but sometimes just as figurines; and engravings on bone, ivory, and flat pieces of stone are common. Occasionally spiral, zig-zag, or other conventional patterns are used. In Britain, only one or two sketchy engravings on bone from Derbyshire are known; but Britain was on the extreme northern edge of the Old Stone Age world.

Paintings and engravings on cave walls were first discovered in Spain, and later more were found in France: one of the most remarkable painted caves, at Lascaux in the Dordogne, was only discovered by accident during the Second World War. Between thirty-five and forty caves are now known in north Spain and western France, with a couple in Italy; but none in Britain. Archaeologists have been able to find out much about the development of the

various styles of engraving and of colouring in outline or in masses. The artists worked with pointed stone gravers, and the colours were red, yellow, and brown earths, with lamp-black or charcoal. The colours were mixed with animal fat and stored in hollow bones, or worked into rough crayons. The animals shown all represent the wild herds or individual beasts of the time —bison, reindeer, other deer, horses, mammoth, woolly rhinoceros, cave bear, boar, wolf, a few fish and birds, and very rarely men or women: one famous representation shows a man dancing, disguised as a fantastic animal with reindeer horns.

Large sculptured reliefs of animals have been found in certain French caves. The animals are practically never grouped to form scenes or tell a story, and often two or three engravings or paintings are superimposed one on top of another. But in some Spanish caves probably of late Old Stone Age date there are vivid scenes such as those of men hunting deer with bows and arrows (*see* Vol. I, p. 381), or a woman gathering honey from a wild bees' nest, with bees as big as pigeons buzzing round her.

It is uncertain why the artists painted their pictures in deep caves, where the only light could have been that of smoky torches or fat lamps. Probably the pictures were in some way

A WOMAN GATHERING WILD HONEY. PAINTING IN A CAVE IN
SPAIN

From Obermaier, *Fossil Man in Spain*, Yale University Press

connected with hunting magic (*see* CAVE MAN, Vol. I).

This ancient art is realistic and easily enjoyed, but it is a primitive form of art, because it simply represents an object and does not try to show ideas, or to bring natural forms into a pattern. Late cave-paintings and engravings do show the use of a sort of shorthand instead of the exact representation of animals (the honey-gathering scene mentioned above is an example). This beginning of artistic conventions shows that men were using their minds in a rather more complicated way; perhaps this went with a more developed form of language for the expression of ideas. This tradition of animal art, more or less conventionalized, continued for long among the hunter-fisher folk of the far north of Europe and Asia, mostly as rock-engravings in the open air but sometimes as stone carvings in the round on tools. This hunters' art turns up again among the Northern Nomads (*see* Section 3).

2. NEW STONE AGE AND BRONZE AGE. After about 3000 B.C. there was practically no naturalistic art in Europe (except in the extreme north), but a great deal of elaborate pattern-making, and sometimes recognizable conventions for the representation of the human figure, and less often of animals. In the western Mediterranean, and along the Atlantic coasts from Spain to Ireland and the Orkneys, we find traces of what must have been the worship of a mother goddess, who is shown carved in low relief on stone, incised on pots, and painted in the old manner in caves or rock-shelters. Very often the designs only show the last remnants of the human face which inspired them, conventionalized into patterns of spirals, circles, and zig-zags. These magic patterns must have had a very real significance to the early agriculturalists who made them, and no doubt were intended to bring them good luck. In Scandinavia, however, there are rock engravings which, while conventionalized, are nevertheless more naturalistic than these mother-goddess patterns; these show spirited scenes of warriors in long ships, men blowing trumpets, or driving in carts and chariots. All these are late in the Bronze Age, from about 1000 B.C. onwards.

In Sardinia, at about the same time, remarkable bronze statuettes were being made of men and women, including warriors armed with round shields and swords or with bows and arrows. These give a vivid idea of what the people actually looked like to their contemporaries.

3. EARLY IRON AGE. The ancient tradition of animal art, preserved in northern Europe and Asia by the nomad hunters and herdsmen of those regions, was transformed into something very rich and strange from about 700 B.C. onwards by various groups of peoples who may be called the Northern Nomads; one group was known to the Greeks as the Scythians (*see* RUSSIANS, Vol. I). Most of the art was devoted to portable objects such as nomadic warriors would use — horse-harness, shield-mounts, or arrow-quivers, and, perhaps because of the necessity of avoiding awkward or fragile projections which might get broken when packing up camp and travelling, the animal figures are worked into most ingenious compact and conventionalized patterns. As a result of the movement of these tribes, there is an extraordinary unity in their art, from the Great Wall of China westwards to Hungary and Germany.

4. CELTIC ART. Round about 450 B.C. there grew up in central Europe a remarkable art, fostered by the Celtic chieftains of that part of the world, who were importing wine from Italy,

ABOVE LEFT: BRONZE-AGE CHALK IDOL FROM FOLKTON, YORKSHIRE, DECORATED WITH A PATTERN DERIVED FROM A FACE (*British Museum*)

ABOVE RIGHT: SCYTHIAN GOLD SHIELD MOUNT IN THE FORM OF A DEER

BELOW LEFT: BRONZE FIGURE OF A WARRIOR FROM SARDINIA (*Supt. of Sardinian Antiquities*)

BELOW CENTRE: CELTIC FLAGON FROM LORRAINE (from Jacobstal, *Early Celtic Art*)

BELOW RIGHT: SCABBARD MOUNT OF A CELTIC SWORD, 1ST CENTURY, A.D. FOUND IN THE RIVER WITHAM (*Warburg Institute*)

and with it bronze and pottery vessels of Greek workmanship and ornament (*see* CELTIC CIVILIZATION, Vol. I). The patterns on these vessels formed, for example, from plant-tendrils intrigued them. At the same time they had some contacts with the art of the Northern Nomads, with its fantastic patterns of animals. Combining these two sources of inspiration with their own ideas of patterns, the Celtic craftsmen brought into being a beautiful and fantastic decorative art known mainly from the metalwork which has survived. It was no doubt also used on such materials as wood and leather and in textiles, which have decayed. This artistic tradition, which continued to invent new methods and ideas, was brought to Britain by Celtic immigrants about 250 B.C., where it lasted right into the Dark Ages, and had its last flowering in the metalwork and manuscript illuminations of north England and Ireland, and in the art of the Picts in Scotland (*see* MEDIEVAL ART, EARLY).

As a result of the import of Greek painted pottery into Spain, a native Iberian style grew up from about 350 B.C., with pottery decorated with conventionalized patterns as well as spirited representations of birds, animals, and people in an individual manner. Here and in the south of France massive stone sculpture in the round was carried out by native artists inspired by Greek models.

One of the most highly developed arts of prehistoric Europe is the Celtic art of the pre-Roman period; in this we have a sum of all the main traditions of prehistoric Europe—the animal art, transmitted from the Arctic hunter-fishers to the nomads and the Scyths; the strong formalization of patterns from the early agriculturalists of the New Stone Age and Bronze Age; and the influence from at least 500 B.C. of the classical tradition of representational art from Greece and Rome, which the barbarians of the north and west turned into a style of their own.

See also PRIMITIVE ART.
See also Vol. I: PREHISTORIC MAN; MEXICAN ANCIENT CIVILIZATION; PERU, ANCIENT.

PREHISTORIC MUSIC, *see* PRIMITIVE MUSIC.

PRE-RAPHAELITES. The Pre-Raphaelite Brotherhood was founded in 1848 by the 20-year-old Dante Gabriel ROSSETTI (q.v. Vol. V), a painter and poet, supported by two young painters, William Holman Hunt and John Everett Millais. There were only four other members, but a number of painters and writers

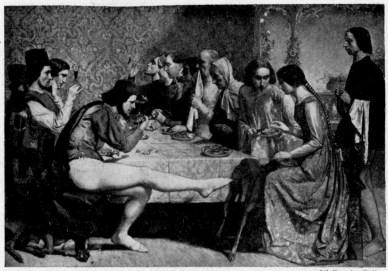

Walker Art Gallery

'LORENZO AND ISABELLA' BY J. E. MILLAIS
This illustrates the first lines of Keats's *Isabella, or the Pot of Basil*

were in sympathy with their aims, including the painter Ford Madox Brown, and the poets Christina Rossetti and Coventry Patmore. The early work of William MORRIS and A. C. SWINBURNE (qq.v. Vol. V) was influenced by the movement.

The title 'Pre-Raphaelite' implies a revolt against the teaching of European ACADEMIES (q.v.) which was held to have become outworn and corrupt in both subject-matter and form since the days of the painter RAPHAEL (q.v. Vol. V), 300 years earlier.

The movement was marked by enthusiasm and high ideals rather than by clear principles. Its sources lay in literature and religious thought, and it shared some of the moral earnestness of Evangelicalism. The medieval and Italian imagery of Keats's poetry influenced the paintings of Hunt and Millais and the poetry of the Rossettis. The medieval flavour of Tennyson's 'Lady of Shalott' set an example to the Pre-Raphaelites. The Brotherhood also went to great trouble to check historical accuracy and realistic detail in their work, a method perhaps inspired by the novels of Sir Walter SCOTT (q.v. Vol. V).

There were few early Italian pictures in London on which the Pre-Raphaelites could base their style. They adopted what they supposed to be the technique of 15th-century Flemish painters (*see* FLEMISH ART), painting in

Lady Lever Collection

'THE SCAPEGOAT' BY W. HOLMAN HUNT

This illustrates Leviticus xvi and symbolically the text 'Surely He hath borne our griefs, and carried our sorrows'

LEFT: 'BEATA BEATRIX' BY DANTE GABRIEL ROSSETTI

Painted in memory of the death of his wife, it illustrates symbolically the death of Dante's Beatrice

Tate Gallery

bright, strong colours with precise details. RUSKIN (q.v. Vol. V), who defended their work against the attacks of critics, had stressed the moral importance of a precise technique, and in his book *Modern Painters* he had given artists a sense of the nobility of their profession. The mixing of moral earnestness with an exact and 'documentary' approach to both subject-matter and technique was the essence of Pre-Raphaelite painting. The idea was followed strictly by Holman Hunt, but Millais interpreted it more freely and later returned to the general fashion of Victorian painting. In the pictures and poetry of D. G. Rossetti and the poetry of his sister Christina the moralizing is absent, and the precise detail is used with great imagination, sometimes creating a dream-like world. In contrast to the vivid light, colour, and realism of the painting of Holman Hunt, Millais, and Madox Brown (*see* Plate 1), Pre-Raphaelite poetry has constant references to solitude, sleep, night, decay, and death. The archaic form of the poetry, however, matches the technique of the painting.

This conflict between a matter-of-fact and an imaginative outlook was the cause of the rapid break-up of the Brotherhood about 1850. The conflict shows itself in such paintings as Holman Hunt's 'The Scapegoat', where spiritual or allegorical subject-matter is treated in terms which belong to 19th-century materialism. The

most valuable works of the movement are those in which matter and method are related, as in the realistic frescoes of scientific subjects painted by Madox Brown in Manchester Town Hall or, conversely, in Rossetti's illustrations to Dante's *Divine Comedy* where both subject and treatment are dream-like and symbolic.

See also BRITISH ART; ROMANTIC MOVEMENT.

PRIMITIVE ART. The term 'primitive' can be applied to art in several different senses. Here we are using it to denote the art of the so-called primitive peoples who were, until recently, and in many cases still are, little affected by the higher civilizations of Europe and Asia. Though their tools were simple, the complexities of modern science and machinery being unknown to them, their art was not necessarily childish or crude. These peoples comprise, broadly speaking, the NEGRO AFRICANS south of the Sahara, the BUSHMEN of South Africa (now almost extinct), the AMERICAN INDIANS or 'redskins', the ESKIMOES, the AUSTRALIAN ABORIGINES and those of Oceania (*see* PACIFIC ISLANDERS), and a number of Asiatic folk, chiefly the SIBERIAN PEOPLES and some INDO-CHINESE (qq.v. Vol. I). One may also include the prehistoric peoples, whose culture was at a similar level (*see* PREHISTORIC ART).

Although materially the lives of primitive people are simple compared with ours, their social organization and religious ideas are often quite complicated. Since they live in close contact with nature by cultivation of the soil, cattle-keeping, or hunting and fishing, they all possess some skill as craftsmen. Almost every man can build his own hut, every woman make her own baskets and pots for domestic use. From artisan to artist is but a small step, and it is often impossible to draw a clear distinction between fine craftwork and what we call art. To such people art is not something separate from ordinary life; it shows itself in the tasteful shapes and decoration of useful objects such as pottery, or, at a higher level, in ritual carvings such as masks and fetish figures, which have a magico-religious purpose. While these objects may possess a beauty of form and colour which we can all admire, we cannot grasp their real meaning without learning something about the part they play in the cultural life of their makers and users. Figures and masks generally represent supernatural beings or spirits of the dead; the latter are intended to be worn with a costume in rites and ceremonies, which are often accompanied by music and dancing (*see* RITUAL, Vol. I). They are thus only one element in a complex setting of movement and pageantry. Other carvings, such as houseposts and doors or the tall totem poles of north-west America, may have a social as well as a religious function (*see* TOTEMISM, Vol. I). Totem poles tell a story of ancestors and clans, and by their size and beauty they may confer social prestige on their owners (*see* Colour Plate, Vol. I, opp. p. 464).

British Museum
PUEBLO INDIAN VASE PAINTED WITH ABSTRACT PATTERNS

Perhaps the artistic impulse in its purest form appears in the decoration of useful objects, for this has no purpose except to please the eye of the user. The attractive designs painted on pottery by the Pueblo Indian women of Arizona and New Mexico (*see* AMERICAN-INDIAN ART) and the intricate scroll patterns carved and burnt on the surface of many kinds of tools and receptacles in New Guinea (*see* OCEANIC ART) are outstanding examples of an innate feeling for beauty which is almost universal among primitive peoples. Each tribe or local group has developed its own distinctive style, so that it is usually easy to tell where an ornamental object comes from. Individual artists often introduce variations of their own; but they all follow the particular conventional idiom, which is understood by all members of the group. In fact, art is a kind of pictorial language and conveys its message by means of visual symbols familiar to the whole community.

Tribal styles vary from naturalistic to more or less conventional renderings of living forms, which sometimes develop into purely abstract geometric patterns. Symbolism is very widespread. Animals such as leopards and elephants are treated as symbols of power or destructiveness, birds may indicate keen vision, while snakes and frogs are commonly connected with rain. Animals often serve as family or clan badges, somewhat after the manner of the heraldic beasts in our coats-of-arms (*see* HERALDRY, Vol. IV). Human and animal subjects rather than plant forms enter largely into primitive art, but they are not usually copied very exactly. Their shapes are modified in various ways; the head, perhaps, being enlarged and other parts of the body being out of proportion. The artist may be striving for greater symmetry or a more compact design, but his rendering is often due to the idea that size indicates importance; thus he may strike a balance between reality and abstract concepts of beauty. Another factor which influences design is the character of the materials used. The shape of a tree-trunk obviously limits the carver's freedom and favours rigid attitudes. In the drawing of figures on flat surfaces there is rarely any attempt to suggest space or volume by the use of perspective. Linear designs tend to be geometric and are often enhanced by the use of colour.

The most realistic art is found among some hunting peoples, whose very existence depended

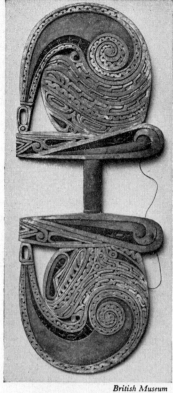

British Museum

LEFT: DANCE PADDLE FROM NEW GUINEA
The pattern is derived from the frigate bird

CENTRE: CARVED HORSEMAN FROM THE
IVORY COAST
The figure, being more important, is
larger than the horse

RIGHT: CARVED WOODEN HEADREST FROM
THE BELGIAN CONGO
The figures are distorted to fit the required
shape

British Museum

British Museum

upon close observation of the animals they hunted. Many of the pictures of animals painted in their caves and rock shelters by the South African Bushmen are astonishingly accurate and true to life, although they must almost always have been done from memory (*see* p. 6). They resemble some of the prehistoric cave-paintings in France and Spain, and were probably inspired by a similar magical purpose. Another race of hunters, the Eskimoes, carved little figures of seals, walruses, and bears in bone and ivory which are masterpieces of realism (*see* p. 12).

In the art of people who lived by agriculture a more formal treatment of nature is characteristic, while the art of wandering herdsmen is generally limited to simple decoration of useful objects.

See also ART; AFRICAN ART; AMERICAN-INDIAN ART; OCEANIC ART; PREHISTORIC ART.

British Museum

WOODEN MASKS OF THE IBIBIO TRIBE, NIGERIA, SHOWING VARYING DEGREES OF DISTORTION

PRIMITIVE MUSIC. When we talk about primitive music we are referring to the music, either in the present or the past, produced by native tribes and races, such as the VEDDA (q.v. Vol. I) of Ceylon and some of the natives of central New Guinea or east Brazil, which have until recently been cut off from contact with the civilized world. These peoples have generally retained musical practices which can only be described as primitive more or less to our own times. Such music has, in fact, been invaluable in helping us to reconstruct the prehistoric music of our ancestors.

The important factor which has always marked the end of the primitive era in the musical history of any people has been the recognition of the octave (*see* SCALES). The different range of men's and women's voices meant that when they sang their elementary musical phrases together they were, in fact, singing an octave apart. That this was not at all the same thing as singing at the same pitch seems to us obvious enough, but nevertheless it was the epoch-making discovery on which all civilized music has depended. When that had been achieved, theorists tackled the problem of subdividing the octave, and of deciding which of these sub-divisions made good resting-points in a melody. But all this comes later. The important thing is that primitive music, ancient and modern, pays no regard to the octave or to set musical intervals: its intervals are usually small, undefined, and variable.

Many theories have been put forward about the origin of melody (*see* MELODY AND RHYTHM): that man attempted to imitate bird songs; that the ordinary sounds of speech gave rise to musical intervals in a kind of sing-song; that speech and singing developed together; that cries of anger, pain, grief, and so on became stabilized into quasi-musical sounds. A combination of the latter two theories seems most likely, but we have to admit that this is all conjecture, for such a rudimentary stage lies countless years behind our first historical knowledge of man's activities, and even before the crude musical conditions which are to be found amongst primitive peoples of our own times.

The earliest melodies consisted of only two or three notes, and of phrases built on these notes continually repeated. Melodies of this kind are still to be found amongst certain modern primitive tribes (Fig. 1). Gradually

FIG. 1. PRIMITIVE MELODIES
a. East Brazil, *b.* Vedda, *c.* Patagonia

other notes were added, and melodies based on four or more notes are to be found in different parts of the world. Fig. 2 is an example from

FIG. 2. MELODY FROM NEW GUINEA

Figs. 1 and 2 after Hornbostel, from Curt Sachs, *The Rise of Music in the Ancient World*, W. W. Norton & Co.

New Guinea. In Bantu Africa and in the western Caroline Islands singing in thirds is to be found. In Bantu Africa we also find examples of a rough counterpoint, that is, the combination of different melodies (*see* HARMONY, Section 2), when a song is shared between a soloist and a chorus and their lines overlap (Fig. 3).

The first stage in the development of rhythm

FIG. 3. BANTU AFRICAN SONG.
From *Musical Year Book*, vol. vii, Hinrichsen Edition

was probably man's recognition of equal beats —the pulsation of regular steps he felt when walking, for example. Perhaps he imitated these pulsations by clapping and stamping, and then applied them to his singing. He strengthened them by crude PERCUSSION INSTRUMENTS (q.v. Vol. IX), such as rattles and drums. Some Indians still use a very simple kind of drumbeating, consisting of a regular series of absolutely equal and undifferentiated beats. The endless sequence of uniform beats was organized into groups of strong and weak, just as a child thinks of the equal beats of a grandfather clock as TICK-tock, TICK-tock. The next step was to play the strong beats on one percussion instrument and the weak on another.

This kind of regular rhythm is most used for dancing. But even within its ordered framework many extraordinarily complex elaborations are to be found in primitive drum-playing in different parts of the world. Indeed, so complex are they that our notation of rhythm is quite inadequate to depict them, just as our notation of pitch gives no idea of the vague intervals of many primitive melodies. In Africa, for example, we find complicated cross rhythms between two and more drums, and different shades of tone and loudness produced by using the fingers in alternation with the palm and so on. Drums are played by hand amongst many primitive peoples, and the basic idea of the familiar tom-tom—a deep, small, leatherheaded drum—is not peculiar to any one race. Where sticks are used for drum-beating, for instance amongst the North American Indians, the upward move of the stick is often regarded by the drummer as the accented beat, so that the stick actually hits the drum on the weak beat. This to a European sounds like SYNCOPATION (q.v.).

Not all drum-playing is concerned with dancing. A kind of 'free recitation' on the drums is used for ceremonial purposes and, amongst medicine men, to dispel evil spirits. Warnings of danger and other messages are often conveyed with great rapidity amongst primitive peoples, especially in Africa, by means of drums. The method employed is not, as is often thought, a kind of crude Morse code. It is, in fact, a method of speaking on the drums, which reproduces as nearly as possible the natives' actual speech. Different pressures are used on the drum-head, different hand-techniques, while

other effects are produced by a knee vibration against the drum.

See also MUSIC; MUSIC, HISTORY OF; PRIMITIVE ART.

PRINTS, *see* ETCHING AND ENGRAVING; LITHOGRAPHY; WOOD-ENGRAVING AND WOODCUTS. *See also* Vol. VII: PRINTING.

PROGRAMME MUSIC. This is music which describes in musical terms stories, places, people, events, and so on, in contrast to 'absolute' or 'abstract' music, which is music for its own sake and which does not attempt to give other than musical impressions. The earliest existing attempts to describe non-musical things in terms of music are 14th-century Italian vocal pieces describing a fire, a hunting scene, street cries, and so on. Clément Jannequin, a 16th-century French composer, wrote descriptive four-part *chansons* (a kind of part-song) such as 'Le Chant des Oyseaux', 'La Chasse', and the 'Battle of Marignano'. Keyboard composers took over the idea, and in the early 17th-century *Fitzwilliam Virginal Book* there are imitations of 'Lightning', 'Thunder', and 'Faire Wether' by John Mundy (died 1630). William Byrd (*c.* 1542–1623) wrote a piece about a battle which consisted of sections, each aiming at reproducing on the keyboard instruments the sounds to which they refer, such as marching horsemen, retreat, and burying the dead. One section, 'The marche of footemen', for instance, is a military march with side-drum accompaniment suggested. In another, 'The trumpetts', we hear typical trumpet tunes; in 'The flute and the droome' a persistent drum figure is maintained throughout; and in 'The buriing of the dead' there is a suggestion of a muffled peal of bells.

A little later Johann Kuhnau (1660–1722), who was one of the most notable composers in Germany before Bach, composed a series of pieces entitled *Biblische Historien* depicting favourite Bible stories—for example, the fight between David and Goliath, in which we can hear the stone flying from the catapult and Goliath falling to the ground. A Frenchman, Jean Philippe Rameau (1683–1764), very realistically imitates the clucking of a hen in his piece 'La Poule'. Keyboard composers down to our own times have continued to describe actual sounds in music. DEBUSSY (q.v. Vol. V), for example, depicted the splashing of rain in his piano composition 'Jardins sous la pluie'.

The orchestra, however, presented an even larger scope. One of the most famous early examples of orchestral descriptive music, the 'Representation of Chaos' by HAYDN (q.v. Vol. V), serves as an introduction to his oratorio *The Creation*. The modern period of orchestral programme music begins with Beethoven's 'Pastoral' Symphony (No. 6, in F major, 1808). BEETHOVEN (q.v. Vol. V) himself said that the symphony was 'more an expression of feeling than painting', and by this he surely meant that although the symphony might suggest country scenes by representing, for instance, the notes of the cuckoo and a thunderstorm, his primary purpose (as in his other symphonies) was to appeal to the emotions of his listeners by the power of music alone, without other associations. Since Beethoven's day much programme music has the qualities of 'abstract' music: the 'programme' may perhaps throw new light on it, but we can understand and enjoy it simply as music even if we do not know the theme on which it is based. This is true, for instance, of the *Symphonie Fantastique* (1832) (*see* SYMPHONY) by BERLIOZ (q.v. Vol. V).

In the 19th century the possibilities of programme music were widened. The early composers attempted only to reproduce sounds in a musical way, as in Byrd's account of a battle. But Berlioz was aiming chiefly at reproducing emotions: it was as though he were to say, 'If you listen to my *Symphonie Fantastique* you will feel what the young man I am telling you about felt'. LISZT (q.v. Vol. V) did the same sort of thing in the large-scale descriptive works for orchestra in one movement which he invented and called symphonic poems. As a rule these were not in any of the conventional MUSICAL FORMS (q.v.). His symphonic poem *Hamlet* begins slowly and rather gloomily, recalling to us Hamlet himself in a melancholy, brooding mood. Later there is a section for wood-wind and solo violin to which he added a note, 'This episode should be kept extremely quiet and should sound like a shadow picture suggesting Ophelia'. The whole work ends 'moderato' and 'funèbre', in a way which is in keeping with the climax of the tragedy itself. Later composers of the ROMANTIC MOVEMENT (q.v.) eagerly seized on Liszt's idea of the symphonic poem. Smetana (1824–84) produced six symphonic poems collectively entitled *Ma Vlast* (My Country). One of these, 'From Bohemia's Woods and Fields', is in a pastoral style, and suggests the feelings of a traveller arriving in the country on a fine summer day, with the birds singing, the sun blazing, and a rustic festival in progress. Borodin (1833–87) described the progress of a native caravan across the vast desert in 'The Steppes of Central Asia'; and TCHAIKOVSKY (q.v. Vol. V) wrote a series of descriptive pieces which he called OVERTURES (q.v.), but which are really symphonic poems, among them *Hamlet, Romeo and Juliet*, and *1812*.

The greatest writer of symphonic poems, however, was undoubtedly Richard STRAUSS (q.v. Vol. V), who enlarged the scope of descriptive music far beyond the limits reached by Liszt without sacrificing the purely musical qualities of his works. Strauss was one of the greatest masters of ORCHESTRATION (q.v.) who have ever lived, and his skill enabled him to write many unusual musical descriptions with great brilliance. He was able vividly to reproduce the sound of things, often quite unexpected things, just as Rameau had given a keyboard impression of a hen in 'La Poule'. Thus his symphonic poems suggested their subjects much more exactly than Liszt's had done. He not only described emotions, but also related stories stage by stage with great realism because of his skill at describing non-musical sounds, characters, and emotions in terms of music. Yet all this he did within the framework of established musical forms. *Don Quixote*, for example, is a 'theme and variations'. The second variation tells how Don Quixote mistakes a cloud of dust for a hostile army: he attacks it only to find he is attacking a flock of sheep, and is rewarded by a crack on the head from the outraged shepherds. The bleating of sheep is very realistically portrayed. His symphonic poems, or 'tone poems' as he called them, such as *Till Eulenspiegel* (1895) and *Ein Heldenleben* (A Hero's Life, 1899), nearly all describe stories as well as characters.

It is not possible to make any real distinction between tone poems and symphonic poems. They are both in one movement but not in any particular form. Liszt, as we have seen, usually used a free form; Strauss used the classic forms that suited him best: *Till Eulenspiegel*, for example, is in rondo form and *Ein Heldenleben* in sonata form. Two more recent examples of programme music, Dukas's *The Sorcerer's Apprentice* and Honegger's *Pacific 231* (a powerful railway engine) are both scherzi. Elgar's *Falstaff*, a more extended work, is not in any easily classifiable form, though it has a musically logical shape of its own. In these works we see the two ambitions of programme music side by side: the ambition to give a musical impression of actual sounds, and the ambition to induce feelings and emotions. In *Falstaff* we are at one moment entertained by a march tune accompanied by a grotesque theme suggesting the marching gait of Falstaff's scarecrow army, at another moved by the feelings which the rejection and death of Falstaff arouse.

See also Music; Musical Form; Symphony; Overture.

PROVERBS. These are short wise sayings, accepted into current speech and writing. Proverbs spring from two sources. Those that convey practical wisdom—such as the hunter's maxim 'A bird in the hand is worth two in the bush'—flow from the people of all nations. Others are the reflections of wise men which, adopted by the people, have attained proverbial usage. 'Hope deferred maketh the heart sick', from the Book of Proverbs, is such a one.

The Book of Proverbs in the Bible is one of the earliest collections of such sayings, many of which have become so much part of ordinary speech that we do not remember their origin.

A soft answer turneth away wrath.

The way of transgressors is hard.

In a multitude of counsellers there is safety.

A living dog is better than a dead lion.

These are well known to many people who have read very little of the Book of Proverbs.

Literature in all ages and all countries abounds in proverbs, some of them very ancient. Some reflect a past way of life: for example, we still use Langland's phrase 'dead as a door-nail', though it is long since we used a wooden beam and door-nail to fasten the door—a common practice in the 14th century when Langland wrote *Piers Plowman*. Some of our proverbs have been borrowed from other languages and literatures: for example, 'A liar is not believed when he speaks the truth' is translated from the Latin of Cicero. The simplest proverbs are capable of the most various applications by metaphor. When Bryce wrote, 'Mr. Gladstone showed in argument the knack of hitting the nail not quite on the head', we do not imagine that Mr. Gladstone argued with a hammer.

Some proverbs flatly contradict others: 'Absence makes the heart grow fonder', for example, is opposite in sense to the more cynical 'Out of sight, out of mind'.

This last proverb occurs—in a slightly different form—in the 13th-century poem *Proverbs of Alfred*. Proverbs were very popular in the Middle Ages: priests used them in homilies, and teachers of rhetoric, poets, and translators used them in their writings. Besides the native saws, there were many translated from the Bible, from Greek and Latin authors, from French romances. The first dated book that Caxton's press published was a translation of a French collection—*Dictes and Sayings of the Philosophers*. The Renaissance added many more. In 1500 Erasmus published his *Adagia*, a vast collection of Greek and Latin proverbs, with anecdotes explaining their origin and meaning; these incidentally added greatly to his many readers' knowledge of the ancient world. The constant travel of scholars and translators made the proverbs of one country known to the next, and many collections were published.

By Elizabeth's reign, proverbs had attained an unparalleled popularity. Their simplicity and familiarity lent themselves to the elaboration, allusion, and play on words which the Elizabethans loved. Politicians, orators, playwrights, as well as the man in the street, all used them.

After this peak, they fell so much from favour in literary circles that in 1741 we find Lord Chesterfield, an arbiter of good taste, advising his son that 'A man of fashion never has recourse to proverbs'. But the proverbs beloved of such writers as Rabelais, Cervantes, and Shakespeare, though rare in 18th-century writers, never vanished from the speech of the people. They reappeared in many 19th-century novels, notably in Dickens, Scott, and Trollope, and have always retained their position in the spoken language.

English is not alone in its wealth of proverbs. All European languages, but especially Spanish, Russian, and German, are rich in them. In Oriental tongues, too, the proverb is familiar; Arabic, Persian, Indian, and Turkish all have a wealth of wise sayings, that often combine poetry with wisdom.

PSALMS, *see* Hymns; Sacred Music.

PUBLIC BUILDINGS

PUBLIC BUILDINGS. The earliest important buildings were the palaces of kings, such as the ancient palace at KNOSSOS (q.v.) in Crete, and religious TEMPLES (q.v. Vol. I), such as those in Egypt and Greece. Little remains of Greek public buildings apart from the ruined groups of temples such as those on the ACROPOLIS (q.v.) at Athens, at Delphi, and elsewhere, and the open-air theatres (*see* Vol. I, p. 206) and stadiums. The Romans had a number of magnificent public buildings, including basilicas or halls of justice, vast public baths, theatres, and various kinds of sports arena. Roman engineers, using the ARCH and VAULT (qq.v.), could build much larger buildings than the Greeks could, and these were decorated with columned porticoes and statues (*see* ROMAN ART). In Rome and other Mediterranean countries the climate allowed public meetings and assemblies to take place in the open air, and consequently the theatres and amphitheatres, such as the COLOSSEUM (q.v.), were not roofed.

In the Middle Ages public meetings often took place in the naves of the parish churches, and apart from churches few other public buildings were erected. Westminster Hall, London, where Parliament first met, was really the great hall of the King's palace. The first separate public buildings were those built by the merchants in market towns as places where the various CRAFT GUILDS (q.v. Vol. VII) could meet, and public business could be discussed. As town life became more highly organized and the dominion of the Church less absolute, these became important civic centres. These guild-halls, moot-halls, or market-halls, often with a meeting-chamber built over a covered market, are found in many English towns, where they and the parish church are usually the only ancient buildings to survive. Architecturally they follow the usual style of late Gothic or Tudor buildings, which was much the same for public buildings as for churches. But in areas where there was no natural building stone (even though stone might be imported for the church) the guild-hall or market was timber-framed, as for instance, at Lavenham in Suffolk, Ledbury in Herefordshire and Thaxted in Essex. Sometimes it was a building of some elaboration, like the stone guild-hall at Cirencester or that at York with its splendid wooden roof. The guild-halls and town halls of Italy, Holland, and Belgium, the focus of pride and mercantile achievement of the CITY-STATES (q.v. Vol. X), were magnificent. The finest in the north are those at Louvain (*see* p. 149) and Brussels (both 15th century) and at Antwerp and Leyden (both 16th century). The most splendid of all, the Cloth Hall at Ypres (14th century), was destroyed by the Germans in the First World War. Many old town halls survive in Italy (*see* Vol. X, p. 87).

From the 17th century onwards, with the increase in trade and in town populations, with improving standards of education and greater popular participation in public affairs, many more public buildings were needed—not

Crown Copyright

LEDBURY MARKET HALL, HEREFORDSHIRE, 1633

only halls, markets, law-courts, and exchanges but also, as each town became a social centre for its immediate neighbourhood, assembly-halls, theatres, and the like. In the 18th century many of these public buildings, such as the assembly-rooms at Bath, built in the accepted classical style (*see* GEORGIAN ARCHITECTURE), were lavishly decorated and painted. Later, when railways and other means of travel allowed people to flock to the big cities for society and entertainment, some of these buildings in the smaller towns fell into disuse. Good examples of the larger public buildings of this period are Liverpool Town Hall, Rochester Corn Exchange, King's Lynn Customs-house and, in London, the Bank of England by Sir John Soane and Somerset House by Sir William Chambers, the latter being the first building (1776–86) designed specially as Government offices. Dublin is famous for its fine array of 18th-century public buildings.

With the growth of LOCAL GOVERNMENT (q.v. Vol. X) in the 19th century, many imposing town halls and municipal offices were built, as well as the commercial exchanges and customs-houses that accompanied the continuing expansion of trade. These buildings, together with the many semi-public buildings, such as hospitals, theatres, railway-stations, museums, public libraries, swimming-baths, and meeting-halls of all kinds, were designed in styles reminiscent of the architecture of every country and climate. Often the style was not suited to the purpose of

Neals

THE GREAT HALL OF THE ASSEMBLY HOUSE, NORWICH
Built by Thomas Ivory (1709–1779)

the building, and a considerable sacrifice of convenience had to be made to achieve the desired pictorial effect. The richest architectural styles were preferred, since cities tried to outrival each other in the splendour of their public buildings, which to them meant wealth and prestige. Nineteenth-century England, however,

Stewart Bale

ST. GEORGE'S HALL, LIVERPOOL, BUILT IN 1839 BY H. L. ELMS

Luce Agency

RAILWAY STATION AT ROME
Built in 1950

produced some public buildings of real nobility and dignity, such as St. George's Hall, Liverpool (1839), by H. L. Elmes; the Houses of Parliament, London (1840–60) (*see* Vol. X, p. 197), by Sir Charles Barry and A. W. Pugin; the British Museum (1823–47), by Sir Robert Smirke; and the Ashmolean Museum, Oxford (1845) by C. R. Cockerell.

During the 20th century some cities have laid out new civic centres, that is, groups of public buildings planned as a whole; but these have not always proved suited to the informal character of the average English city, and tend to become isolated from the life of the city instead of being its true centre. The problem of modern architects is to evolve a style symbolizing, by rich and impressive effects, the dignity and enterprise of a city. The most important English public building erected since the Second World War is the Royal Festival Hall, London (1951), by the architects of the London County Council.

See also ARCHITECTURE.

PYRAMIDS. Egyptian pyramids are stone or brick structures with rectangular bases and sloping sides meeting at an apex. They were the principal feature of a 'tomb complex', or a group of burial buildings, erected by the Pharaohs between about 2800 and 1700 B.C. (*see* EGYPTIAN CIVILIZATION, Vol. I). There was

usually a 'Valley' building (in which the dead king was purified and embalmed) built near the Nile and leading by means of a causeway to a mortuary temple on higher ground. Near this stood the pyramid proper, which contained passages leading to the tomb-chambers. The temple and pyramid were enclosed within a boundary wall. The ruins of about eighty such pyramids can be traced in Egypt.

The earliest pyramid complex was built at Sakkara for the Pharaoh Djeser of the 3rd Dynasty (*c.* 2800 B.C.). It consisted of a number of buildings and courts within an enclosure, dominated by an erection rising in six stages to a height of 200 feet, now known as the 'Step Pyramid'. The first true pyramid appears to have been built by Sneferu of the 4th Dynasty (*c.* 2700 B.C.) at Meydum; but the most famous were the three built by Sneferu's successors, Cheops (Khufu), Chephren (Khafra), and Mycerinus at Giza. These were accounted among the seven WONDERS OF THE WORLD (q.v.). The Pyramid of Cheops, known as the Great Pyramid, is the largest of the three and the most accurately constructed. It is orientated almost exactly to the four compass points, the degree of error in laying out its square base of over 13 acres being less than one in a thousand. This achievement is the more remarkable since the pyramid was built over a rocky mound which made it impossible to check the diagonals. Despite this obstacle, the north-west corner is only half an inch lower than the south-east corner.

The pyramids of succeeding dynasties are very much smaller, less accurately built, and less well preserved. With the rise of the 18th Dynasty (*c.* 1580 B.C.) pyramids ceased to be the fashion for royal burials, rock-hewn tombs taking their place.

The earliest pyramids appear to be elaborations of the earth mounds heaped over primitive tombs. They were built of huge stone blocks which were probably hauled into position up ramps. Each layer of stone was stepped above the one below; the steps were afterwards filled in, and finer stone was applied as a smooth outer casing.

In the earlier pyramids the internal burial chamber was reached by a passage which had its entrance concealed on the north side. Several changes of plan must often have taken place during the actual construction of the superstructure: thus in the Great Pyramid three burial chambers were built at different times, and a passage widened into a remarkable 'Grand Gallery'. Later pyramids often had their entrances ingeniously hidden at a point in the ground well outside the superstructure.

After the interment of the dead king in opulent trappings, the burial chamber was walled up and the passages blocked.

At a later period pyramids were built with a system of inner retaining walls and compartments filled with mud-brick and rubble. Much effort was put into making the internal burial chambers proof against robbery by building them of massive hardstones, by constructing a maze of internal passages with blind corridors, false chambers, and artfully concealed entrances, and by increasing the number of granite portcullises and blocking stones. But in spite of this they were all pillaged.

The chambers and passages of most pyramids were left undecorated, but the internal walls of the causeways, valley temples, and mortuary chapels were embellished with painted reliefs showing the king triumphing over traditional foes, hunting, fowling, and receiving offerings. In the chambers of five later pyramids, however, religious compositions, known today as the Pyramid Texts, were inscribed in hieroglyphs for the use of the dead king. They are among the earliest known religious writings, and parts of them are of very great antiquity.

See also EGYPTIAN ART.
See also Vol. I: EGYPTIAN CIVILIZATION.

RECONSTRUCTION OF THE PYRAMIDS AT ABUSIR
From L. Borchardt, *Das Grabmal des Ne-user-Re*. J. C. Hinrichs Verlag, 1907

Q R

QUARTET, *see* CHAMBER MUSIC.

RECITATIVE, *see* SONG, HISTORY OF, Section 4.

REGENCY ARCHITECTURE. This term is used to describe a style rather than a period. GEORGE IV (q.v. Vol. V) was Prince Regent only between the years 1811 and 1820, and Regency architecture and decoration flourished throughout his subsequent reign as king and that of William IV, until it merged into the early Victorian style around 1840. It is primarily a domestic style; the term is not usually applied to the many large buildings put up during those years, such as Soane's Bank of England, Smirke's British Museum, and Barry's Pall Mall club-houses.

The Regency style developed from GEORGIAN ARCHITECTURE (q.v.) and showed the same respect for rules of proportion, for restraint in external decoration, and for neighbourly submission of the part (such as the individual house) to the whole (such as the square or terrace). New and sometimes exotic fashions were introduced towards the end of the 18th century, the decorative elements coming from many sources —Greek, Gothic, even Hindu and Chinese, as well as from the old Georgian pattern-books. Architects were less interested than hitherto in

National Buildings Record

WOLSEY TERRACE, CHELTENHAM
The classical pilasters, iron railings, and hooded windows are typical of Regency design

reproducing the exact forms of classical buildings, and ornament was therefore more freely and fancifully used.

The vogue, nevertheless, was for simplicity combined with elegance. Regency architecture is notable for the extreme refinement and lightness of its detail—for example, the graceful ironwork balconies and railings which adorned many façades. The façades themselves were simple to the point of severity and often were only broken by slight arched recesses in which doors and windows were set. Window-bars were as slender as possible; roofs were low in pitch and, when not concealed behind a parapet, projected over wide eaves.

The favourite Regency material was stucco, an enduring form of plaster used to cover the brick walls, which were often shoddily built by speculative builders more interested in profit than good work. The stucco was often painted cream or yellow. The years after the Regency, as the depression caused by the Napoleonic Wars moved away, were years of economic expansion and so of great building activity. As means of transport improved, merchants, instead of living over their shops, built for themselves neat stucco villas on the fringes of the towns. Following the fashion set by royalty, sea-bathing and family holidays by the sea became the vogue, and some of the best Regency architecture is to be found in the seaside resorts that grew up at this time (such as Brighton, Ramsgate, and Sidmouth) and in the inland health-resorts (such as Cheltenham, Leamington, and Clifton) where people went to drink the healing waters and enjoy gay society, and which colonial and military officers chose for their retirement.

At Brighton a long sea-front of stucco terraces was laid out, with squares opening off it. Many of the houses had the boldly rounded bay-windows in which Regency seaside architecture specialized. In many other places new districts composed of elegant squares, terraces, and crescents were built with the same special regard for the scenic effect of the whole. A master of this combined art of architecture and town-planning was George IV's architect, John NASH (q.v. Vol. V), to whom the King's interest in architecture gave the opportunity of adding many fine groups of classical stucco buildings to London (see Vol. V, p. 330). Nash also designed the Prince Regent's fantastic Oriental Pavilion at Brighton (see p. 78). Other Regency architects were Decimus Burton, who designed the Piccadilly entrance to Hyde Park, the Athenaeum Club, and seaside terraces at St. Leonards, Brighton, and Hove; George Basevi, who designed Belgrave Square; and J. B. Papworth, who designed much of the best architecture in Cheltenham.

See also ARCHITECTURE.

RENAISSANCE ART, see ITALIAN ART; CLASSICAL ART. See also Vol. I: RENAISSANCE.

REREDOS, see ALTAR.

RESTORATION DRAMA. This is the name given to the plays written during a period of some 40 years after the Restoration of Charles II. During the rule of the Puritans, DRAMA (q.v.) had been at first discouraged and later all but suppressed in England. When the playwrights Sir William Davenant and Thomas Killigrew received permission by royal patent to open two theatres in London in 1660, plays were performed again after a period of nearly 20 years.

The Restoration stage was distinguished by the appearance of actresses for the first time (see ACTING, HISTORY OF, Vol. IX). There were fine actors, notably a pastrycook's son, Thomas Betterton, one of the major tragedians of the English stage. The plays were performed in indoor theatres on a 'picture-frame' stage (see THEATRE, HISTORY OF, Vol. IX) instead of in open theatres as in the time of Elizabeth I. The enthusiasm and ribald excitement of the Elizabethan and Jacobean audiences had died during the long period without a theatre, and the plays were now largely a pastime for the Court and society.

The plays fall into two classes: heroic TRAGEDY and the COMEDY of manners (qq.v.). Heroic tragedy, written as a rule in rhymed couplets, imitated the fashionable French style of CORNEILLE and RACINE. The principal themes were love and honour. John DRYDEN (qq.v. Vol. V), the best-known Restoration dramatist, wrote both tragedies and comedies. In All For Love, he undertook to rewrite Shakespeare's Antony and Cleopatra in blank verse but according to Restoration taste. All was smoothed out, 'refined'. Shakespeare's superb (but, to the Restoration mind, careless) theatrical touches were removed. *All For Love* ends with these lines, typical of Dryden's method:

> Sleep, blest pair,
> Secure from human chance, long ages out,
> While all the storms of fate fly o'er your tomb;
> And fame, to late posterity shall tell,
> No lovers lived so great, or died so well.

Thomas Otway (1652–85), whose plays have genuine pathos, is nearer in spirit to the Elizabethans than any other dramatist of his time. His tragedy, *Venice Preserved*, a vigorous work about a conspiracy to wreck the Venetian state, has some fine verse and sure insight into human nature.

Perhaps the most typical Restoration play was the artificial comedy, the comedy of manners. It has been called the comedy of bad manners because, after the restrictions of Puritanism had been removed, dramatists had licence to say on the stage almost anything they wished. Much Restoration comedy is cheerfully coarse and immoral. It was the work of an odd, elegant, dissolute theatre, where an unconcerned lack of morals went with a flashing of wit. William Congreve (1670–1729), perhaps the most successful of the dramatists, had a brilliant prose style. His plays, full of wits and fops, have uncommonly involved plots about intrigues in London society, which make them sometimes tedious to watch, but the language is unfaltering. Other Restoration dramatists were William Wycherley, the only true satirist of the period, Sir John VANBRUGH (q.v. Vol. V), Sir George Etherege, and George Farquhar. They were all witty writers, whose situations, like Congreve's, concerned the complicated intrigues of brilliant young wits and their equally brilliant, though rarely respectable, ladies.

Though few would now agree with the severity of the moralist Jeremy Collier's attack on the contemporary theatre at the end of the 17th century, called *A Short View of the Immorality and Profaneness of the English Stage* (1698), most critics agree that the merit of the Restoration writers lies less in what they say than the way in which they say it. The characters of Restoration comedy are rarely real people, but are, as Charles Lamb wrote, 'a world of themselves almost as much as fairyland'.

See also AUGUSTAN AGE; DRAMA; COMEDY; TRAGEDY.
See also Vol. V; DRYDEN.

REVIEWS, *see* PERIODICALS.

RHETORIC. This is the art of using language to influence an audience. Schools of rhetoric existed in ancient Greece and Rome, and for long afterwards. They taught oratory and the technique of prose composition—such matters as the structure of composition, prose rhythms, and figures of speech. The poet Gerard Manley Hopkins once referred to rhetoric as the grammar of literature.

Rhetoric was first taught about the 5th century B.C. in Athens to train young men to plead in lawsuits. Skill in devising and arranging plausible argument was at first most emphasized. Then teachers became concerned with public and ceremonial oratory to please and cajole great audiences, and they gradually built up an elaborate system of rules for dividing and subdividing the oration, for employing symmetrical clauses, poetic diction, rhythmic phrases, and figures of speech. ARISTOTLE (q.v. Vol. V) in his *Rhetoric* takes a larger view of the subject. To him rhetoric was more than an eloquent display of skill and ingenuity in arguing; persuasion was part of the art of reasoning itself. The first two books of the *Rhetoric* are largely concerned with arguments and evidence, the third with style. Clearness and appropriateness, he says, are the essentials. He emphasizes that a good orator must be sincere, clearthinking, widely read, and eloquent. Aristotle divided oratory into three classes: political, forensic (that is, of law-courts), and ceremonial. His *Rhetoric*, one of the most influential books ever written on the subject, was used as a textbook for centuries.

While Aristotle was formulating the theory of rhetoric, his contemporary DEMOSTHENES (q.v. Vol. V) was making a name for ever famous in the practice of that art. When he argued in the law-courts, he launched against his opponents not only argument, but irony, sarcasm, and invective. From his speeches against Philip of Macedon, we have inherited the word 'philippic', which describes any bitter invective.

In later times, Greek orators were divided into two opposing groups: those who based their method on the principles of Aristotle, and those who put great emphasis on form, with many mechanical rules and a tendency to ornateness. In Rome, rhetoric was the main

Bavarian National Museums

THE ROOM OF MIRRORS, AMALIENBURG

in the early 17th century; it was on a large scale and used principally for religious buildings. Rococo art started in France in the early 18th century; it was on a miniature scale and used for the interior decoration of private houses.

In the 18th century, when the centre of Court life was shifting from Versailles to Paris, a section of French society, tired of the heavy and overpowering splendours of the Court of Louis XIV at VERSAILLES (q.v.), wanted a style of decoration for their houses which should be light and gay. Indeed, the feeling of the rococo style in general is one of drawing-room intrigue and masked balls, of powder, patches, and candlelight. The French queen, Marie Antoinette, who loved to dress up as a milkmaid or shepherdess and to take part in plays, was in every way a typically rococo figure. Rococo rooms are small, with curved walls, frequently covered with mirrors; ceilings are painted in light colours—pale pink or blue—and are lavishly gilded. There is a profusion of decoration, small in scale and usually not symmetrical in arrangement. In view of the later developments of the style and of the excessively artificial conditions in which it flourished, it is, perhaps, curious that in the early stages it was, to a certain extent, a 'back-to-nature' movement. One sees this very clearly in the works of the only really great rococo painter—Antoine WATTEAU (q.v. Vol. V). His paintings of picnics have a make-believe quality and are peopled by society men and women dressed in beautiful silks and satins; but he had a real feeling for nature and expressed it in the landscape backgrounds of his pictures.

The style became too fantastic and unreal to appeal for very long—even to the French who had invented it. By towards the end of the 18th century French taste was swinging back to a more sober style, first in architecture, and then in painting.

The style, however, took root to a great extent in Bavaria and Austria. The French artist, Cuvilliés, working mainly in Germany in the mid-18th century, created there what is probably the most exquisite and typical monument of rococo art— the Amalienburg, near Munich. The rococo decoration, which had travelled east from France, blended well with the baroque architecture which had travelled north from Italy, and sometimes it is impossible to say exactly where the baroque elements end and the rococo begin.

One other form of rococo art in Germany— the porcelain figures first made near Dresden —is important because similar figures made in England in the factories at Chelsea and elsewhere are, together with the interior decoration of a few theatres, the only rococo art which England produced (*see* PORCELAIN AND POTTERY FIGURES).

ROLAND, SONG OF, *see* CHANSON DE ROLAND.

ROMAN ART. ETRUSCAN ART and the later stage of GREEK ART (qq.v.) were the most important of the various roots from which Roman art sprang. As the Roman Empire expanded, its art was affected to some extent by that of the conquered peoples, especially those of Egypt and the Near East. In spite of the many sources on which it drew, Rome developed a charac-

Mansell

MAISON CARRÉE, NÎMES, FRANCE
A Roman temple built in the 2nd century A.D.

teristic art, the greatest achievements of which lie in the sphere of architecture.

The great advance which Roman architecture shows over Greek is the invention of the Arch and the Vault (qq.v.). While the Greeks built in hewn stone, the typical Roman building-materials were bricks and cement. Arches and vaults were first used in engineering constructions such as bridges, aqueducts, and viaducts (*see* Vol. I, p. 412); but from there it was only a short step to their use in palaces, theatres, and other buildings.

When a Roman architect planned a building containing a number of rooms and

THE INTERIOR OF THE PANTHEON, ROME
Built in the 2nd century A.D.

open spaces, he usually laid them out in such a way that they were symmetrically grouped on either side of an imaginary central line, or axis. We meet the simplest examples of this in Roman houses (best represented at Pompeii (q.v.)), where the entrance hall opens into an internal courtyard (atrium) surrounded by symmetrically grouped rooms, behind which is a colonnaded garden (peristyle), all three parts of the plan being centred on the same axis. The same kind of plan appears in a bigger and more elaborate form in the imperial dwellings such as the Flavian palace on the Palatine hill and Hadrian's villa at Tivoli. The curving walls and vaulted ceilings of the vast halls in these buildings could only be achieved by the use of bricks and concrete.

Symmetrical planning finds its most complete expression in the imperial Fora (*see* Vol. I, p. 411). These were large enclosed squares with a temple forming a focal point in the centre of one of the sides. Such temples, which often abutted directly on to the enclosure wall, stood on high platforms and, unlike Greek temples which were accessible from every side, had a staircase on the front only. The porch was composed of a row of free-standing Greek columns, continued as attached half-columns along the sides of the temple-chamber, which occupied the whole width of the platform. This type of temple is Etruscan in origin.

Another building usually found on the forum is the basilica, a law-court, place of public assembly, or market-hall. It was normally a rectangular structure divided by two rows of columns into a nave and side aisles. The basilica greatly influenced later Christian church architecture (*see* Early Christian Art).

A fundamental difference between Greek and Roman architecture is seen in the treatment of the interior of buildings. The interior of a Greek temple was a small, unlit room with a flat ceiling, only a by-product, so to speak, of its fair outside. Roman architecture on the other hand strove to create vast interiors, often neglecting exterior appearances. The most significant example of this tendency is the Pantheon, a circular building erected by the Emperor Hadrian in honour of all the gods. From outside, the building looks like an enormous undecorated brick drum, with a Greek temple-façade forming a low entrance-porch. The circular interior is decorated with alternating niches and columns and is covered by a coffered dome 129 feet in diameter, in the centre of which is a round opening for light, 30 feet across. The dome is 141 feet high.

Mastery of the technique of vaulting was also indispensable for the construction of the great bathing establishments which the emperors provided for the citizens of Rome. Only vaults could span the vast halls, round which were

THE ARCH OF TITUS, ROME

sloping ground, and the lofty stage-building formed a single unit with the semicircular auditorium, both rising to the same height. The actors performed on a raised stage, the front of which was usually decorated with reliefs. The amphitheatre, which was used for gladiatorial combats, fights of wild beasts, and mock naval engagements, was unknown in Greece. It was probably invented by the Etruscans, but Roman architects gave it monumental form. It was oval in plan, the arena being surrounded by concentric rows of seats. Both in the theatre and in the amphitheatre the outer wall of the auditorium was composed of several storeys, each formed by a row of arches, and decorated with one of the orders of architecture (*see* COLOSSEUM).

The arch found its purest use in the triumphal gateways. In early examples, such as the Arch of Titus, the triumphal arch had only one passage-way and little relief-decoration. But later, in gateways such as the Arch of Constantine in Rome (*see* Vol. V, p. 104), there were three passage-ways and a rich complex of columns and relief sculpture. A particular example of the triumphal arch was the four-sided arch with two passage-ways intersecting at right angles.

Tombs were often elaborate buildings. In those of the Emperors Augustus and Hadrian in Rome we see how Roman architects transformed the simple low-walled mounds of Etruscan cemeteries into funeral monuments of enormous size. Of the tombs of wealthy private families built along the APPIAN WAY (q.v. Vol.

grouped the smaller rooms used for changing, for baths of all kinds, and for games and entertainment. Heating was provided by furnaces from which hot air circulated through hollow floors and walls.

No less important were the achievements of Roman architecture in the design of theatres and amphitheatres. The auditorium of a Greek theatre was often simply a hillside, and lacked any constructional connexion with the low stage-building. The Roman theatre seldom used

Superintendency of Antiquities, Tripoli

RUINS OF A ROMAN THEATRE AT SABRATHA, LIBYA
The stage building can be seen in the background

Alinari

MARBLE HEAD FROM A STATUE OF A ROMAN SACRIFICING
(ABOUT 50 B.C.)

In Greek sculpture gods and men are depicted in a timeless present. The historical relief of the Romans, on the other hand, represents a particular action in a particular moment of time. The earliest example occurs on the victory-monument of Aemilius Paullus at Delphi and shows incidents from the battle of Pydna (168 B.C.). Representations of historical scenes frequently appear on imperial triumphal monuments, such as the arches of Titus, Septimius Severus, and Constantine, and on TRAJAN'S COLUMN (q.v.) and that of Marcus Aurelius. As well as showing actual events in simplified form, Roman reliefs often include personifications and allegorical figures. For instance, the victorious emperor is accompanied by the goddess Roma or is received by the goddess of victory; conquered lands appear in the form of mourning women; rivers and hills are personified as divinities. The result is a curious mixture of reality and symbolism. One of the stone screens enclosing Augustus's Altar of Peace (13–9 B.C.) is carved with a relief of the emperor and his family sacrificing; another shows an allegory of the blessings of peace which his victories and diplomatic skill had restored to

IV), some are circular in plan while others imitate small rectangular temples.

The walls of rooms were often painted with decorative designs and scenes. Mythical scenes were often copied from Greek models, but the representation of landscape and architecture for its own sake is probably a Roman innovation. Patterns and pictures in MOSAIC (q.v.) first appear on floors, but later, also, on walls in place of paintings. Ceilings were often decorated with relief designs in stucco.

Compared with their splendid architectural achievements the sculpture of the Romans seems somewhat weak and derivative. Most of the statues of the Roman period which have survived are mechanically reproduced copies of famous Greek originals, for which the Romans developed a great taste. Their portrait sculptures and historical reliefs were, however, important and independent works of art. Portraiture is one of the most characteristic and important achievements of every period of Roman art. In their observation and rendering of detail, however unflattering it may be, they went far beyond the Greeks, who never abandoned their tendency to idealization.

Anderson

EQUESTRIAN STATUE OF MARCUS AURELIUS IN ROME

Alinari

RELIEF FROM THE ALTAR OF PEACE ERECTED BY THE EMPEROR AUGUSTUS, 13–9 B.C.

the world. Mother Earth is surrounded by her children, cattle, flocks, and harvests; on the right a girl on a sea-dragon symbolizes the water, on the left a girl on a flying swan, the air. Thus the Roman relief aimed not only at pleasing the spectator by its artistic form but also at conveying a meaning to him.

In later Roman art this tendency to communicate directly with the spectator expressed itself in other ways too. On the Altar of Peace the figures were drawn in profile or oblique view, but on a later relief from the Arch of Constantine, which shows the Emperor making a speech from the Rostrum, nearly all the figures are seen from the front as if they had turned outwards in order to engage the spectators' attention. Here instead of attempting to please the spectator by outward beauty, everything is

Anderson

THE EMPEROR CONSTANTINE MAKING A SPEECH
Relief from the Arch of Constantine, Rome

subordinated to the wish to express an inner life. In this last phase of Roman art no small part was played by Christianity, the official recognition of which by Constantine (A.D. 313) marks the beginning of EARLY CHRISTIAN ART (q.v.).

See also MONUMENTS.

ROMANCE LITERATURE.

Courtly romances first appeared in France in the second half of the 12th century. These stories of love and knightly adventure replaced the EPIC (q.v.), which had been till then the chief literary form of feudal society (see FEUDAL SYSTEM, Vol. X). The romance fashion marked a great change in social life and manners as well as in literature; it reflected, for instance, the altered position of women in feudal society. In the epics women hardly appear at all, and when they do, it is only in a very subordinate role. The epics were tales for men, dealing with the feudal relationships between men, and showing these as the highest and most binding of ties. For example, when in the CHANSON DE ROLAND (q.v.) the hero lies dying, he thinks of his Emperor, of his brother-in-arms, Oliver, but never of his betrothed, Alda, though she dies of grief on hearing that he has been slain. In the romances, however, it is of his lady that the knight thinks when he rides into battle; it is her favours that he seeks, for her that he performs knightly deeds. The chief interest in these stories is in the love of a knight for a lady, and no man is a perfect knight and real hero unless he is in love.

In romance literature it is not enough for the hero to be dauntless in battle; he must also be well versed in all the social arts, as indeed must the lady whom he serves. The romance poems give lavish descriptions of dress and jewels, and reveal the new taste for luxury and display in their accounts of feasts and tournaments. They offer an escape from everyday and humdrum reality into a new and exciting world.

To 12th-century people the Golden Age of ancient Greece and Rome seemed a time of wealth and splendour that their own time could not equal; and it was to ancient literature that the romance writers first turned. They took stories from Ovid's *Metamorphoses*; they made romances out of the stories in the *Iliad* (see HOMERIC LITERATURE), and turned the *Aeneid* (see VIRGIL, Vol. V) into a romantic story by adding a long account of the loves of Aeneas and Lavinia. Then they discovered the even

British Museum

THE GARDEN OF LOVE. ILLUMINATION FROM A FLEMISH MANUSCRIPT OF THE 'ROMANCE OF THE ROSE'

more exciting world of Celtic history and legend. The Norman poet Wace first introduced French-speaking audiences to the ARTHURIAN LEGEND (q.v. Vol. I), and this began a fashion for stories with a Celtic background which lasted for many generations. The most famous 12th-century writer of the stories of Arthur and the Knights of the Round Table was Chrétien de Troyes, who wrote for the Countess of Champagne the tales of Erec and Enid, Lancelot and Guinevere, and Perceval and the Grail. Other writers wrote fairy-stories and love stories combined, or told the tragic history of Tristram and Iseult and King Mark of Cornwall.

The romance poems based on classical and Celtic legends had an element of mystery and strangeness which the audiences obviously enjoyed, but the setting was in medieval France. Both Aeneas and Tristram wear medieval armour and fight with medieval weapons, and the ladies wear 12th-century dress. The love stories, too, are concerned with problems of lovers in the feudal society of the 12th century, where both men and women are bound by the etiquette of courtly society and by the obligations of their rank (see CHIVALRY, Vol. X). Romance literature, like most early medieval literature, was written to be read aloud or recited.

The romance writers used ALLEGORY (q.v.) a great deal to show the various states of mind of their characters. They personify feelings and qualities, and make these argue among themselves or debate with the real person whose attributes they represent; so, for instance, the hero may be seen debating with a figure called Reason who is the embodiment of his common sense. The most famous example of the use of allegory is the *Romance of the Rose*, written in the 13th century by Guillaume de Lorris. The different characteristics of the Lady that the lover meets in his wooing are personified—Fair-welcome, Pity, Pride, Anger, and so on. The lady herself never appears in the story at all, but various aspects of her are presented by these allegorical figures. The poem gives a most attractive picture of a courtly wooing. Guillaume, however, died before he had finished, and the romance was continued by Jean de Meung. He was far more interested in philosophy than in courtly love, and used the figure of Reason to expound his views on all kinds of subjects, from the way the universe works to the power of witches.

In the 13th century, romances which gave realistic descriptions of contemporary manners became very popular, though the stories of the Arthurian legend had by no means lost their interest. The earlier romances had been written in octosyllabic rhyming couplets, which were easy for the reciter to remember. In the 13th century, however, more people could read, and more books were available, so people often read the romances for themselves instead of listening to them. Consequently, authors began to write in prose, and the use of verse as the medium for telling a story gradually fell out of use.

By the 14th century many of the French romances had been translated into other European languages: the story of Perceval and the Holy Grail and that of Tristram and Iseult, for example, passed into German, while in England the stories of the Round Table were adapted by Malory (*see* ARTHURIAN LITERATURE), and the *Romance of the Rose* was translated by CHAUCER (q.v. Vol. V). Not only the stories but also the courtly tradition they express continued to exercise an influence, and their conception of chivalry has helped to shape our modern social ideals. The French romances mark the beginning of a type of narrative which led later to the novel of manners (*see* NOVEL).

See also ARTHURIAN LITERATURE.
See also Vol. X: CHIVALRY.

ROMANCE OF THE ROSE, by Guillaume de Lorris, *see* ALLEGORY; ROMANCE LITERATURE.

ROMANESQUE ART. European continental art of the late 11th and the 12th centuries is generally called Romanesque, and that of England, Norman. The builders of this period, instead of drawing their inspiration from early BYZANTINE ART (q.v.) as their predecessors had done, began to study the Roman ruins in their own neighbourhood and to use them as models.

The style probably developed first in southern France, where many Roman buildings and sculptures still survived; and it spread rapidly through France, Spain, and Germany, and the countries on the Rhine and in northern Italy. It was brought by the Normans to England where the traditional skill of English carving was used to enrich it. The style spread rapidly, probably because, just at this time, there was great enthusiasm for building very large monasteries and cathedral churches. New monasteries were being established, and the designs of the new buildings were often influenced by that of the mother-house, which was often far away (*see* MONK, Vol. I).

The masons who worked on these great buildings could not copy Roman models exactly, for they were not suited to their needs. They had not the building skill of the Romans, but their building methods show a great advance on those of their predecessors (*see* MEDIEVAL ART, EARLY). One of their chief problems was how to build stone instead of wooden roofs, for wooden roofs were too easily burnt. The Romans had used several different kinds of stone VAULT (q.v.) for their roofs, but the medieval builders had neither the necessary knowledge nor the mechanical aids to be able to build successfully this way. They tried covering their buildings with solid, semicircular 'barrel' vaults, but they found that although they could use these for roofing over narrow spaces, such as the side aisles of churches, they were too heavy for the wide nave. In the end they invented an ingenious system by which they built a skeleton of stone ribs crossing the nave, and filled in the space between with lighter stones. The nave was roofed with a series of square vaults, supported by alternate pillars of the arcade. The vaults of the side aisles, being half the size of the nave vault, sprang from each of the pillars of the arcade. Measurements now

WEST FRONT OF THE CHURCH AT ST. GILLES, SOUTHERN FRANCE, COMPLETED IN 1142

The whole conception and much of the detail may have been inspired by a Roman triumphal arch, but the treatment, particularly of the recessed doorways and sculptured tympana, is Romanesque

PLATE 14   ROMANESQUE ART

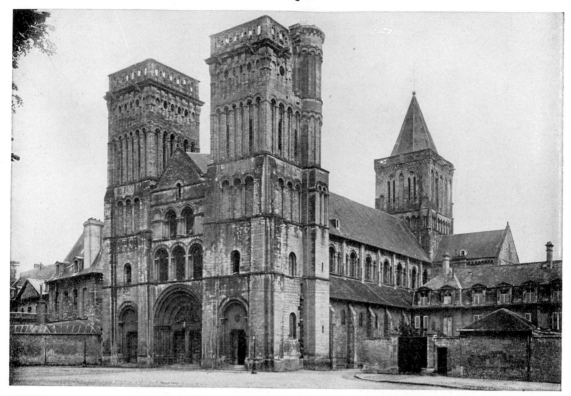

ABOVE:

ABBAYE AUX DAMES, CAEN, FRANCE, FOUNDED BY MATILDA, WIFE OF WILLIAM THE CONQUER-OR, IN 1066

All three towers originally had spires. The very thick walls are strengthened with buttresses

THE NAVE, DURHAM CATHEDRAL, BUILT IN 1130 IN ACCORDANCE WITH THE PLAN OF 1093

This is the first ribbed vault in Europe. The grooving on the immense columns reduces their effect of clumsiness

became more accurate, and this mathematical
relationship of the different parts of the building
to each other made the whole appearance more
dignified and impressive. The walls were
divided vertically by the shafts supporting the
vaults as well as horizontally by two galleries,
the clerestory and the triforium. The walls had
to be very thick and the pillars of the arcades
which supported the vaults had to be very
strong; in English churches these are often of
enormous diameter. It is to the honour of
English builders that the first ribbed vault was
built in Durham Cathedral at the end of the
11th century.

The choir, the eastern part of the church used
by the clergy, was lengthened in Romanesque
churches, and, in order to provide a more dignified setting for the altar, the choir was sometimes raised on a vaulted crypt. In England the
aisles usually ended in separate apses at the east
end, but in France they were often curved round
and joined so that they encircled the choir and
High Altar by a passage called the ambulatory,
from which small chapels radiated.

The outside of Romanesque churches became
more impressive. The size of the towers was
increased; there was usually an enormous
square tower over the part where the transepts
crossed the nave, and this had windows which
brought light into the central part of the building; two further towers were often added at the
west end, and sometimes smaller ones at the
corners of each transept. Further interest was
given to the outside of the building by the
buttresses, used to strengthen the walls at the
points where the thrust of the vaults was most
felt.

Perhaps the most characteristic feature of
Romanesque architecture is the semicircular
arch. It is these arches which make Romanesque
buildings look like those of the Romans, though
the method of construction is quite different.
Ancient Roman arches are flush with the face
of the wall and have enormous and very accurately shaped 'voussoirs' (wedge-shaped stones)
set round the opening. These were temporarily
supported on a wooden centring until the
cement dried. The Romanesque builders had
not the tackle to hoist heavy stones, and their
cement was less good, so they had to use smaller
stones. They began with a comparatively small
arch encircling the opening, and from this they
built out successive rings of stonework until the

Courtauld Institute

DAVID KILLING THE LION. CAPITAL IN THE ABBEY CHURCH
AT VÉZELAY, FRANCE, EARLY 12TH CENTURY

width necessary for supporting the immensely
thick, rubble-filled walls was reached. This
gives beautiful effects of light and shade, especially when the angles of the stonework are
smoothed off into mouldings or elaborately
carved. Each arch is supported by a separate
shaft, which usually has a carved capital. These
new methods invented by Romanesque builders
to meet their difficulties were further developed
by Gothic craftsmen later on (*see* p. 81).

A comparison of the west front of the Cathedral of St. Gilles in southern France with a Roman
triumphal arch, such as that of Constantine (*see*
Vol. V, p. 104), shows how the Romanesque
builders adapted their Roman models. At St.
Gilles the openings are spaced out to give ad-
mittance to the nave and the two aisles, but the
general design with the detached columns on
pedestals is similar. Fragments of Roman carving are used in the cornices, and the columns
and capitals are modelled on Roman columns.
The carved figures are naturalistic and rather
like Roman statues.

In Romanesque times the arts of sculpture
and painting were subordinate to that of

architecture. For the most part carved figures were very simple and were designed with more regard to the part that they played in the pattern of a great composition than to their likeness to living people. The purpose of both sculpture and painting was to emphasize the design of the whole building. The most elaborate sculpture is found on the west doorways of the cathedrals. The heads of the three archways leading into the building were filled in and decorated with great carvings in relief, and the sides of the porches have figures standing either between or against the columns which support the successive rings of the whole arch. The curved space over the door, the 'tympanum', is carved with reliefs; these usually represent Christ, surrounded by the symbols of the Evangelists (a subject drawn from the Book of Revelation), or the Last Judgement, a terrifying scene showing the righteous being received into Heaven and the wicked being driven into Hell by demons.

Inside the churches there was little sculpture, decoration being confined almost entirely to carved capitals. Here the figures and decoration were arranged so as to stress the way in which the capital supports the arches which spring from it and transfers their weight to the columns below. In northern Europe, especially in England, some Romanesque carving is barbaric and seems to reflect the animal art practised in Scandinavia by the Vikings before they came to Normandy. The artists were not usually successful in carving human figures. Some Romanesque churches, in fact, look rather like the grim stone keeps which were taking the place of the earlier wooden fortifications.

Inside the buildings large and impressive wall-paintings covered the wide spaces between the rather small windows, especially on the curved walls of the apse over the High Altar. The figure of Christ would be painted in the centre on the domed ceiling above the altar,

A. G. Ph.

TYMPANUM OVER THE WEST DOOR OF THE CHURCH AT MOISSAC, SOUTH-WEST FRANCE, 1100–15
The composition focuses on Christ in Majesty surrounded by two Angels and the symbols of the Evangelists. Around and beneath are the twenty-four elders of the Apocalypse

Archives Photographiques

THE TOWER OF BABEL. PAINTING IN THE CHURCH AT ST. SAVIN, FRENCH PYRENEES, *c.* 1100
Four tiers of paintings of Old Testament scenes cover the barrel vault of the nave

with rows of saints and apostles below. In other parts of the church the paintings are often less formally arranged and very lively. Some of the finest are on the vaulted roof of the Church of St. Savin in central France.

STAINED GLASS (q.v.) began to be used in the larger churches during the Romanesque period. Like painting and sculpture, it formed, with its rich colours, an integral part of the scheme of decoration. At first the figures were large, the lines of the 'leading' (strips of lead round each piece of glass) accentuating their outlines.

The illuminators, who decorated the manuscripts written in the *scriptoria* of monasteries, did a great deal of painting on a smaller scale. Both artists and scribes were usually monks. The favourite books of this period were very large Bibles which contained both large pictures and elaborate initial letters in the text. Each book of the Bible began with a decorated page, the style of the decoration with its scrolling leaves, fantastic dragons, and unrealistic figures harmonizing well with the fine large script (*see* ILLUMINATED MANUSCRIPTS).

Another art which reached great perfection in the 11th and 12th centuries was that of enamelling, usually on bronze. The technique is especially suited to the formalized figures and bright colours of the period (*see* ENAMEL, Vol. VII).

Towards the middle of the 12th century Romanesque art began to change, especially in the part of France near Paris. A new kind of poetic feeling came into the religious writing of the late 12th century, especially in the works of St. BERNARD (q.v. Vol. V), the founder of the strict Cistercian order of monks. He said that all new Cistercian abbeys should be dedicated to the Virgin, whom he described with love and tenderness. People began to take a greater interest in the more human side of the Gospel story, and artists were commissioned to illustrate the events in the life of Christ, the Virgin, and the saints. This led artists to look for models in Byzantine manuscripts, in which many of these scenes had been illustrated from early times. In copying the arrangement of the figures they also learnt to make the figures more lifelike and the folds of drapery softer. In architecture the builders were experimenting with the possibilities of building higher and lighter churches by the use of ribbed vaults, and discovered how to use pointed arches instead of semicircular ones. This gave them a new freedom and opened the way for the wonderful development of the art of building in the Gothic period (*see* GOTHIC ART).

See also CHURCH ARCHITECTURE, ENGLISH.

ROMAN LITERATURE, *see* LATIN LITERATURE.

Louvre

ALGERIAN WOMEN. PAINTING BY EUGÈNE DELACROIX, 1834
An example of the romantic interest in exotic subjects and brilliant colour

ROMANTIC MOVEMENT. This landmark in literature and the arts of the late 18th and early 19th centuries was closely involved, as was the RENAISSANCE (q.v. Vol. I) of the 15th and 16th centuries, with great social and political upheavals, and with the new ideals of political freedom which were associated with the French Revolution. The movement may be thought of as a tide which swept over Europe, arriving in different countries at different times; in England its beginnings are usually traced back as far as the publication of James Thomson's poems, the *Seasons* (1726–30) (*see* NATURE WRITING), and it was brought to a head by the publication of the *Lyrical Ballads* by WORDSWORTH and COLERIDGE (qq.v. Vol. V) in 1798. In Germany it arrived some decades later; in France and Scandinavia it coincided roughly with the Napoleonic Wars, and after the fall of Napoleon made its way into Italy, Spain, and most other countries, gaining momentum with the spread of French culture. Later still, the influence of French Romanticism carried the movement not only to Russia, where it marked the beginnings of a national literature, but also as far afield as Spanish America and Brazil.

Literature takes its characteristics from the life of its day. The literature of the Renaissance had centred around the great nobles, such as the MEDICI FAMILY (q.v. Vol. V) in Italy and the noble patrons of the Elizabethan poets. Later it centred around the royal Courts, such as the Court of LOUIS XIV (q.v.): poetry and drama were courtly and their subjects and form were taken, as often as not, from the ancient classics (*see* CLASSICAL ART). In the 18th century the influence of monarchs grew less. Historians such as Montesquieu and philosophers such as VOLTAIRE turned searchlights upon the existing institutions of government and religion. The philosopher ROUSSEAU (qq.v. Vol. V), one of the most powerful influences of all, directed men's minds to the value of education and to the simplicities of Nature, from which they had become estranged by a false notion of civilization. Meanwhile science and social studies began to get into their stride.

Writers began to conceive of men as thinking individuals rather than mere wheels in the machinery of Church or State. The social position of writers improved: being no longer dependent on the patronage of Courts, they formed themselves into groups or 'schools of thought' and wrote for a wider public—the ever-growing middle class. What they sought above all was liberty of expression. Old tyrannies had been overthrown, and men were ready to face others courageously; the Church's power to regulate conscience was weakened. Writers were concerned more with the general problems of humanity than with the virtues and vices of the individual; they were boldly asking questions and refusing to accept the conventional answers. The poet in the Romantic period—and later the dramatist and, more and more, the novelist—was out to play a part in the community, to express the feelings and ambitions of his particular class or party. Romanticism was to underlie much of the political progress of the 19th century. BYRON, the perfect example of 'romantic melancholy', took part in the Greek War of Independence. Many were exiled for their views: SHELLEY (qq.v. Vol. V), the reformer, settled in Italy and made human liberty the subject of his *Prometheus Unbound*. Political refugees from the Continent, writers among them, came to live in England.

Another aspect of the Romantic writers' concern with the life around them is their interest in actual people, rather than the conventional types of classical literature. With the study of individuals went an interest in their surroundings. Romantic writers were preoccupied with nature for its own sake; Wordsworth's poetry of the English Lakes

National Gallery

HORSE FRIGHTENED BY LIGHTNING. BY THÉODORE GÉRICAULT (1791–1824)

is an example of what was happening in many lands. Some writers found especial fascination in the strange life and colour of the East. In nature the poet could often find an expression for his feelings about Man, as KEATS did in his 'Ode to a Nightingale', Shelley in his poem on a cloud, or Wordsworth's to a cuckoo. With the desire to study scenes and surroundings went a renewed interest in the romance of history, fed and stimulated by Sir Walter SCOTT (qq.v. Vol. V).

A new interest in historic buildings, fostered by travel, was followed by an enthusiasm for the Middle Ages, which led, in turn, to a cult of the supernatural. 'Thrillers' were very popular among the young ladies in Jane Austen's novels; the writings of Mrs. Radcliffe and M. G. Lewis expressed a 'Gothic gloom', full of mysterious castles, ghosts, and subterranean passages. Mary Shelley's *Frankenstein* might be said to belong to this class, though its theme is based upon deeper thinking and is a warning of the dangers of science. Goethe's mighty FAUST (q.v.) had already explored the supernatural, with its theme of the restless seeker after power who barters away the freedom of the human soul.

The Romantic writers looked far outside their own age and country for inspiration.

They turned to Shakespeare, who had been regarded as something of a barbarian for 200 years; the Bible, too, was a ready source for stories and colour. Poems, said to be written by Ossian, a legendary Celtic bard, but in reality forged by an 18th-century writer named Macpherson, appealed to the romantic taste for wild scenery and northern folk-lore. Turning to Spain, people rediscovered *Don Quixote* (1605) by CERVANTES (q.v. Vol. V) and the 17th-century plays of Calderón; in one of these occurs the 'devil's bargain' theme used by Goethe in *Faust*. As the Romantic Movement spread many of its writers began, themselves, to exercise an influence extending far beyond their own countries.

The artists of the Romantic Movement had the same aims and expressed the same ideas as the writers. The fullest expression to these ideas was given by the French painters of the early 19th century, particularly DELACROIX (q.v. Vol. V) and Géricault (1791–1824). Whereas in Classical art painters are primarily concerned with the balance and proportion of their compositions, in Romantic art we find an interest in depicting emotion; the classical subjects were replaced by unfamiliar subjects taken either from past history or from distant places, and artists were more interested in colour and light and the free handling of paint than the study of form and precise drawing.

In the middle of the 18th century Horace Walpole made his house at Strawberry Hill, Twickenham, 'a little Gothic Castle', and there he wrote the *Castle of Otranto, a Gothic Story*. Both illustrate his yearning to recapture a sense of the past, not as an archaeologist seeks to discover the exact features of an earlier time, but for its romantic remoteness as opposed to the prosaic present. The same spirit led the eccentric William Beckford to build Fonthill, in Wiltshire, a fantastic house in the Gothic style, with gloomy vaulted halls and an immense spire. Structurally unsound and hopelessly inconvenient it fell into ruins soon after his death. The same interest in unfamiliar things led to the importation of works of art from the Far East and their imitation by European craftsmen (*see* CHINOISERIE).

English LANDSCAPE PAINTING (q.v.) of the end of the 18th and beginning of the 19th centuries reflects an interest in nature similar to that of the nature poets, and the study of nature as a background to the thoughts and feelings of man led to an appreciation of landscape for its own sake. This study led to a new vision and a new technique of rendering light and colour in paint which CONSTABLE (q.v. Vol. V) was the first to practise.

In France Géricault and Delacroix revolted against the limitations imposed on art by the classical painters David (1748–1825) and Ingres (1781–1867). Delacroix combined in his work all the elements of romantic art; he often chose subjects from history or foreign countries, his interest was in colour and its emotional quality, and his compositions are full of movement. Géricault showed an even more intense interest in movement in his paintings of horses, and a romantic interest in the morbid which led him to make studies of dead people.

The French landscape painter Corot (1796–1875) painted idealized studies of trees, J. F. Millet (1814–75) found romance in the character and occupations of peasants, and a group of artists who worked at Barbizon, near Fontainbleau, interpreted the moods of nature in their paintings. But later romantic painters began to become stereotyped in their subjects and treatment, and by the middle of the 19th century COURBET (q.v. Vol. V) was leading a reaction to a more direct study of nature.

Romantic music, which flourished at its best in Germany and also in France, had the same character as literature and painting. Much romantic music is concerned with the musical description of scenes and stories (*see* PROGRAMME MUSIC). The songs of SCHUBERT and SCHUMANN, for example, which are set to lyrics by HEINE (qq.v. Vol. V) and others, cover all the moods of Romanticism. Their titles—for example, Schubert's 'The Erl King', 'The Wraith' (supernatural element), 'Hark, hark, the Lark', 'Who is Silvia?' (Shakespeare cult), and Schumann's 'The lovely month of May', 'Ladybird' (nature), 'From out my tears are springing . . .', 'I will not grieve' (romantic melancholy)—show the typical romantic subjects. Among major works Wagner's opera cycle The RING (q.v.) and *Tristan and Isolde* were inspired by northern folk-lore, while VERDI (q.v. Vol. V) used Shakespearian themes for his operas *Otello* and *Falstaff*.

See also CLASSICAL ART.

RONDO FORM, *see* MUSICAL FORM, Section 5.

ROOD SCREENS. The screen which marks the division between the nave and chancel in a church is called a rood screen in England because in medieval times there was always a large carving of the Crucifixion over the entry to the chancel (the Anglo-Saxon word 'rood' means crucifix). In early times, when the chancel arches were small and low, the figures were set against the wall above; but later, when the arches became high and wide, the figures were placed on a beam which ran across the arch high above the floor, often directly over the top of the screen. Since a lamp was usually kept burning in front of the rood and many other candles and tapers were placed on the beam at festivals, it became the practice to build a loft or gallery over the screen, from which the lamps and candles could be reached. Sometimes, as church music became more elaborate and churches began to have fixed organs, this loft seems to have been used as a singers' gallery. Sometimes an altar was placed on it beneath the rood, and it is possible that in the bigger churches and cathedrals the Epistle and Gospel were read from the loft during the celebration of Mass.

The earliest screens, which were of stone, often consisted of an arcade of three arches, also probably filled in with light wooden screen-

F. H. Crossley

ROOD SCREEN IN KENTON CHURCH, DEVON, *c.* 1480
The panels of the screen are painted with figures of saints. The loft and vaulting have been reconstructed from fragments

work. Later a strongly-made wooden screen with doors in the centre ran across the width of the chancel arch. In churches with side aisles the screens were sometimes carried round in front of the piers of the arch and across the aisles. In some churches altars were placed at the sides of the central opening, and the upper part of the screen was filled in to form a reredos, or altar back.

The earliest wooden screens consisted of a simple rectangular framework of vertical posts supporting the horizontal head beam. The lower part had simple boarding between the upright posts, and the upper part was subdivided by slender shafts. The top of the space between these shafts was filled in with a thin board pierced to look like traceried arches, so that the shafts appear to support a little arcade. Later the rood lofts were supported by beautiful fan tracery which was copied from that of the stone VAULT (q.v.) of the period; this was made

to spring from between the arches of the arcade. In Devon and East Anglia the screens were lavishly decorated with carving, colour, and gilded gesso (plaster).

The panels of the lower parts of the screen and also those of the loft gave opportunity for the representation of saints. The saints are often those reverenced by special sections of the community or those who had powers of healing special illnesses, from toothache to the plague. Sometimes there are Annunciation or Nativity scenes which may be connected with MIRACLE PLAYS (q.v.). The possession of a richly decorated screen and rood loft was the ambition of every parish. The accounts kept by the churchwardens show how money was raised for this expensive improvement. Occasionally rich donors came forward, but more often money was raised by village guilds or groups of individuals. The accounts tell of archery competitions held by the young men, Christmas plays, church ales,

The late Rev. F. R. P. Sumner

THE ADORATION OF THE MAGI. PAINTING ON THE ROOD SCREEN IN BUCKLAND-IN-THE-MOOR CHURCH, DEVON, EARLY 16TH CENTURY

The scene, with figures in contemporary costume, may be inspired by a Christmas play acted by the villagers

and organized 'hold-ups' on the roads when every passer-by had to contribute to the funds.

The vast majority of screens which survive are in Norfolk and Suffolk, Devon and Somerset, and on the Welsh border, in which districts a great many churches were rebuilt or radically altered in the 15th century, when the finest screen work was made. The west-country churches were usually built without any chancel arches, so the screen was essential to mark the division between nave and chancel. In East Anglian churches the chancel arches are wide and high, and if the screens have been removed the churches look bare and empty.

Rood lofts were ordered to be taken down by Elizabeth I; some were destroyed and others were erected under the tower to form galleries for the singers. Many others were destroyed both by the Puritans and by church restorers in the 19th century.

Rood screens and rood lofts are found mainly in northern European countries, and are less common on the Continent than in England. There are examples in stone and bronze as well as wood, the stone screens of the greater churches in Belgium being especially fine. Only in Brittany are there wooden screens which can compare with those of England, and there they can be seen complete with their lights and images.

See also WOODCARVING.

ROUNDEL, *see* VERSIFICATION, Section 5.

ROUNDS, *see* SONGS, Section 1.

ROYAL ACADEMY OF ARTS, *see* ACADÉMIES.

RUSSIAN ART. Russian art originated among the Slav-speaking people who settled in the 7th century A.D. in the great central plain contained by the rivers Dnieper and Volga, and who by then were already developing a distinct culture of their own. In the 10th century the Slav rulers adopted Christianity and ruthlessly swept away all vestiges of the earlier civilization.

Russia in the 10th century was a small country centred round the principality of KIEV, the satellite city of NOVGOROD (qq.v. Vol. III), and several minor towns. Christianity in its ORTHODOX EASTERN form (q.v. Vol. I) reached Kiev from Constantinople—the foremost Christian city of its day and the capital of the powerful and intensely creative BYZANTINE EMPIRE (q.v. Vol. I). Christianity formed the core of Byzantine culture, inspiring its art and directing its thought. The people of Kiev acquired from the Byzantines a similar conception of religion and shared the belief that the function of their art lay in service to the Church. They built churches and monasteries and adorned them

A. F. Blunt

ST. SOPHIA, NOVGOROD, 1045–52

There are five domes

Historical Museum, Moscow
HEAD OF THE ANGEL OF THE ANNUNCIATION
Detail from a 12th-century icon of the Kiev School

metal work, carving, and bookbinding, also flourished, and followed the Byzantine style to a greater or lesser degree.

The Mongol occupation of Russia, which lasted from the middle of the 13th century until the end of the 14th century (*see* TARTARS, Vol. I), arrested the normal growth of Russian art; but the Mongols failed to destroy it, and it emerged from the ordeal virile and flourishing. During the 15th century the most important centre of art was Novgorod. Among other architectural innovations was the wooden 'iconostasis' (stand for icons), a screen to separate the altar in the apse from the body of the church. This not only greatly altered the interior appearance of the churches, but also served as an additional incentive to artists, who were called upon to paint icons for its decoration; and throughout the 14th and 15th centuries, religious paintings of outstanding quality were produced. In

with scenes from the Scriptures painted on the interior walls of religious buildings as well as upon individual panels (*see* ICONS).

Although at first Russian painting was indistinguishable from Byzantine, and although it always remained close to it in style, by the close of the 12th century the Russian painters had acquired such mastery of technique that their best work was truly national in character.

In architecture, in which the Russian genius has always seemed happiest, national trends blended with the Byzantine at an even earlier date than in painting. Basically the churches had, like their Byzantine models, three aisles and a dome; but the Russians soon began experimenting with the shape of the dome until, in the 12th century, they had evolved the characteristic onion shape. The more important churches had several domes, although usually not more than three or five, and perhaps as many as five aisles. The walls were built higher and the roofs steeper to allow the snow to fall off. The minor arts necessary to the decoration of a church, such as embroidery,

Russian Museum, Leningrad
ST. BORIS AND ST. GLEB
14th-century icon of two saints of princely birth

Novgorod, the rigid Byzantine style gave place to a gentleness inspired by slight contact with Italian art. The devotional fervour of the age expressed itself in an elongation of the figures, a delicacy yet forcefulness of colour, and a flowing line which gave an emotional quality to the paintings (*see* Colour Plate opp. p. 400).

This ability to create an atmosphere by means of colour and line is a basic characteristic of Russian art, and also gives the work of the craftsman, whether in wood, pottery, or fabric, something of the quality of works of art. Right up to the present century, the Russian country-side was enlivened by the harmonious colours used to offset the splendid carving of door jambs and window surrounds, garden gates and farm carts, domestic utensils, furniture, and toys.

During the Mongol occupation there had been such poverty in Russia that only the Church or ruling princes had enough money to commission works of art. As the Muscovite (Russian) Empire became consolidated, how-ever, in the 16th century, more people grew wealthy, and consequently art entered more into every aspect of life. At the same time con-tacts with the West resulted in a greater varia-tion in style. The Russians' innate decorative sense was given freer rein, and foreign and national forms were combined with remarkable felicity. Fairy-tale palaces, enchanted fortifica-tions, and churches of delightful imaginativeness sprang up throughout the land. Among the most picturesque were those which re-created the native wooden pyramid style of building in stone and wood.

The painting, however, which was still almost entirely religious in character, was less success-

T. Talbot Rice

THE RAZUMOVSKY PALACE, MOSCOW
Built by Kazakov in 1790

ful. A new miniature style of painting was evolved but, excellent as it was, the very minute-ness of the work, verging on the finicky, shows signs of decadence. The medieval style of religious painting came to a sudden end when PETER THE GREAT (q.v. Vol. V) westernized Russia and transferred his capital from Moscow to St. Petersburg (now Leningrad). Though churches continued to be built in the traditional manner throughout the 18th and 19th centuries, and were still decorated in the Russo-Byzantine style, little of this work proved truly inspired.

Since Russian artists could not instantly pro-duce the secular, westernized art Peter desired, foreign artists from Holland, Italy, Germany, and France were employed. As in the 10th century, when a reforming ruler had looked to Byzantium for inspiration, so, in the 18th an alien art was grafted on the national, and in its turn was absorbed and developed. In archi-tecture, buildings of Dutch, Roman, or Grecian form became elongated, flattened, colour-washed, and turned into something which, though Western in the main essentials of the style, was altogether Slav in its proportions, rhythm, and colour. In painting and sculpture, portraits and busts wholly Western in manner were soon permeated by a sincerity and inti-macy of approach which was thoroughly indivi-dual. Crafts, on the other hand, were little

T. Talbot Rice

SILVER AND NIELLO LOVING CUP
Made in Moscow in the 16th century for Tsar Fedor

influenced by Western ideas, but retained their original flamboyance, their intricacy of pattern, and their medieval forms.

Peter the Great, in revolutionizing native traditions, had inadvertently created the revolutionary mind. The French Revolution stimulated its growth and awakened the conscience of Russia's intellectuals, leading inevitably in the 19th century to a turbulent, unhappy period. Artists threw their skill into the social battle, producing numerous paintings, each pointing a moral, few attaining to beauty; and in every field of art, excepting music and literature, the result was disastrous. At the turn of the century, however, a group of artists, known today as 'The World of Art' group, set out to revive artistic quality under the banner of 'Art for Art's Sake'. They succeeded astonishingly well in their aim, creating many paintings of fine quality, and making their influence felt in every branch of art, though perhaps most forcefully on the stage, particularly in BALLET (q.v. Vol. IX), and in the field of book illustration. The Russian genius for architecture is also once again finding expression in a new and contemporary form, and buildings such as power stations, factories, and dams are taking on a beauty entirely their own.

See also BYZANTINE ART; KREMLIN.
See also Vol. I: RUSSIANS.

RUSSIAN LITERATURE. Of all the great nations of Europe Russia was the last to produce a modern literature. Although books were written in Russia from the 11th century onwards, for most non-Russians Russian literature may be said to begin in the 19th century or, at the earliest, in the second half of the 18th. Down to the time of PETER THE GREAT (q.v. Vol. V) the way of life of the Russians was in many respects similar to that of the English in the Middle Ages. In particular, the only section of the population which was interested in books was the clergy; and the written literature of old Russia was made up largely of religious works and of chronicles which are of little interest to the modern reader.

Peter the Great brought his country into the community of European nations and opened it up to influences from the West. It took longer, however, to create a literature than to build an army and a navy, and the first great modern Russian writer, Mikhail Lomonosov (1711–65),

did not appear until after Peter's death. Up to this time books had been written, not in the spoken language of Russia but in Old Slavonic, which stands to Russian more or less as Latin to French and Italian, and Lomonosov's prime task was to create a literary language which could serve as a vehicle for a modern literature. He solved the problem by blending the spoken language with Old Slavonic elements, and his solution was accepted by succeeding generations of Russian writers (see SLAVONIC LANGUAGES, Vol. IV).

Russia in the 18th century produced a number of other writers who are still read, notably the lyric poet Gavrila Derzhavin (1743–1816) and the dramatist Denis Fonvizin, who is remembered chiefly for his satirical comedy, *The Minor*. About this time French influence did much to reform the Russian prose style, which had tended to be heavy and involved. Thanks largely to the work of the historian Nikolai Karamzin (1766–1826), Russian prose, despite the highly inflected character of the language, has become as easy to read as English or French. The other outstanding writer of Karamzin's generation was Ivan Krylov, the greatest Russian author of fables, and one of the most profoundly national of all Russian writers.

The golden age of Russian literature began soon after the close of the Napoleonic Wars, in which Russia played so glorious a part, and extended to about 1880. Until the 1840's the greatest achievement was in the field of poetry, its supreme representative being Alexander PUSHKIN (q.v. Vol. V), whom his countrymen regard as the greatest figure in Russian literature. Mikhail Lermontov and Fyodor Tyutchev rank as lyric poets next to Pushkin. Alexander Griboyedov was the author of the greatest Russian comedy in verse, *The Misfortune of Being Intelligent*. This same period saw the beginnings of the Russian novel. Both Pushkin and Lermontov wrote some prose fiction of very high quality, but they are remembered mainly as poets, and the man who is generally regarded as the first of the great Russian novelists was Nikolai Gogol (1809–52), whose novel *Dead Souls*, despite its title, is one of the world's masterpieces of humour.

It is safe to say that no country has ever possessed a galaxy of novelists as brilliant as that which dominated the next period of Russian literature. The first of them to win recognition in western Europe was Ivan TURGENEV; but the two greatest are now recognized to have been TOLSTOY and DOSTOEVSKY (qq.v. Vol. V), each of whom has his supporters for the title of the greatest novelist in world literature (*see* NOVEL).

Of the writers who arose between the death of Dostoevsky and the Revolution of 1917, the celebrated Anton CHEKHOV (q.v. Vol. V) wrote many inimitable short stories and a few exquisite plays. Among other notable writers of this period were the novelist Maxim Gorky (1868–1936) and the poet Alexander Blok.

Since the Revolution the poet Vladimir Mayakovsky and the Cossack novelist Mikhail Sholokhov are outstanding.

Traditionally, the Russian writer is not merely, or mainly, an entertainer; he has something serious to say, whether the subject be the position of Russia in the world, the relation of man to society, or the nature of the human mind. This is not to say that Russian literature is dreary or pompous. On the contrary, one of its most marked characteristics is its humour, which, it may be said in passing, is more readily appreciated by English people than by other non-Russians. The fact is that Russia for the past 200 years has been faced with a succession of urgent problems, the existence of which has been painfully clear to all educated people in the country, and on which all the great Russian writers have taken up a position one way or the other. Russian literature is rarely frivolous. The writer takes his function more seriously, and, in turn, is taken more seriously by his public, than the writer in other countries. He is regarded as a teacher, with a responsibility to society. So it was in the days of Gogol and of Tolstoy; so it is today.

One of the respects in which Russian fiction differs from that of 19th-century England or France is the lack of concern with plot. The novelist is interested in the state of mind of his character rather than in his adventures, and concentrates his attention on that. This characteristic is tending to disappear, but the native output of adventure stories is still unequal to the demand, and the gap is filled with translations from other languages, particularly English: two of the most popular writers in Russia today are Mark Twain and Jack London.

The first people in western Europe to display intelligent interest in Russian literature were the French, and they were the first to translate the great Russian writers. Prosper Merimée, the author of *Carmen*, himself translated some of Gogol; and Turgenev was saluted as 'master' by Flaubert. In England George Borrow, who spent some time in St. Petersburg in the 1830's, translated a few poems of Pushkin, but they attracted little attention. In 1840 Carlyle could write of Russia as a country without a literature, and Russian literature was not 'discovered' by English readers until towards the end of the 19th century.

The Russian writers who have exercised the greatest influence on English literature are probably Dostoevsky and Chekhov: Dostoevsky through his studies of the contradictory processes of the mind, Chekhov through the technique of his short stories, the interest of which lies not in the unexpected ending, but in the evocation of atmosphere and character. On the whole, however, the influence of Russian literature on English has not been very great, and its charm for the English reader lies to a large extent in the very strangeness of the individuals and the society which it depicts.

See also NOVEL; SHORT STORIES.
See also Vol. I: RUSSIANS.
See also Vol. IV: SLAVONIC LANGUAGES.

S

SACRED MUSIC. Music has always been used in church worship, especially in celebrating the service of the Mass, both as an accompaniment of the RITUAL (q.v. Vol. I) and as a medium through which the congregation could take part in the services. The type of music has followed the development of music in general; but religious forms tend to change slowly, and so old forms of church music have been kept alive. PLAINSONG (q.v.), which was universal in the Middle Ages, is still regularly used in the services of the Roman Catholic Church and occasionally in the Church of England. The Orthodox Eastern Church has resisted any change in its music, which consists mainly of unaccompanied plainsong. It did not officially approve of harmony until the end of the 17th century, and none of its churches has ever had an organ.

The service of the Mass, the central service of the Christian Church, has two elements, the Proper—those parts which vary according to the particular season of the Church, and the Ordinary—those parts which are the same throughout the year. The Proper is usually sung by the choir, the traditional plainsong settings of the early Church being still usually used. The Ordinary, which consists of the *Kyrie*, *Gloria*, *Credo*, *Sanctus*, and *Agnus Dei*, is sung by the choir, and sometimes by the congregation as well. At first the singing was in unison, to simple plainsong settings; but later, as counterpoint and HARMONY (q.v.) developed, the music for the Ordinary became more elaborate.

As it became more elaborate, the music in the Mass and in other church services was often performed more for its own sake than for its part in the ritual of the services. The unaccompanied voice parts were built up around not only plainsong melodies but sometimes also secular melodies. Even the words of these secular melodies were occasionally sung together with those of the sacred text. At last, the Council of Trent, which was set up in 1545 to reform the abuses that had grown up in the Roman Catholic Church, recommended the bishops to ban music of 'an impious or lascivious character' and to discourage the use of music of which the words could not be heard owing to the over-elaborate weaving of the voice parts. The development from plainsong culminated at the end of the 16th century in the Masses of Palestrina in Italy and of Byrd in England.

After the 16th century, Masses modelled on the style of the 'golden age' represented by Palestrina continued to be written. A new direction was taken, however, with the introduction of instruments and of solo singing into church music. This new music followed closely all the developments of secular music, unlike the church music of Palestrina which betrayed no secular influences. Throughout the 17th and 18th centuries many Masses with solo singing and orchestras were written, notably by HAYDN and MOZART (qq.v. Vol. V). These were often performed in the private chapels of wealthy princes and bishops for whom they were composed. The more elaborate settings (such as Bach's Mass in B minor and Beethoven's Mass in D) were too lengthy for use as part of church services. Some of the 17th- and 18th-century Masses were rather cheap and vulgar, being often influenced by the love of solo display which was popular in the OPERA (q.v.) of that time; but many of them were sincere and powerful expressions of religious faith. Their secular influences and elaboration, however, make them distracting and therefore unsuitable for use as part of church services. During the 19th century the demand for public concerts increased, and consequently most of the Masses composed at that time belong to the concert hall rather than to the church; though in the early 20th century attention was turned once more to music for church services.

In Protestant countries greater stress was laid on the part the congregation took in the services and less on the ritual. Martin LUTHER (q.v. Vol. V) encouraged the singing of HYMNS (q.v.) and wrote many himself, and CALVIN (q.v. Vol. V) and his followers in England wrote metrical versions of the psalms which were set to music.

In England the substitution of English for Latin in the church services called for new musical settings, and in 1550 John Merbecke issued his *Book of Common Praier Noted* (that is, set to music). The music he composed for it was a type of late plainsong, the words being set to a simple note-for-syllable plan. His setting of the Communion Service is still widely used in our churches today. The metrical psalms of Luther also formed part of the music of the services, and these were sung to well known hymn-tunes.

The psalms, as they appear in the Book of Common Prayer, are sometimes sung to plainsong, except that English words instead of Latin are used. It is much more common, however, to use a harmonized chant (called Anglican Chant) which has a sustained reciting note, on which most of the words are sung, and a cadence at the half-verse and end of each verse (*see* Fig. 1). The two methods of chanting are similar in principle, but the use of harmony in Anglican Chant makes it easier to give suitable words strong accents; this is very desirable in English, but would be less so in Latin, which has a different kind of verbal accentuation. The way in which the words of English psalms are divided to fit the music of the chant is called 'pointing':

PSALM 95   J. Nares

1. O come, let us | sing un - to the
2. Let us come before his | presence with

Lord: | let us heartily rejoice in the
thanksgiving: | and   show   ourselves

strength of | our   sal - vation.
glad   in | Him with   psalms.

FIG. 1.   ANGLICAN CHANT

many different methods are in use. A few early Anglican Chants were harmonizations of rather cut-about plainsong melodies, but most of them are original compositions. They are either 'single', that is, each verse is sung to the same chant, or 'double', that is, twice as long as single chants and covering two verses of the psalm.

During the Commonwealth period only simple congregational music was allowed in the church services; but after the Restoration English church music was revived and took on a more secular character, in keeping with the style Charles II had introduced from France. Composers such as Blow and PURCELL (q.v. Vol. V) began to set the church canticles—the *Te Deum, Benedictus, Magnificat,* and others—to music of a more modern character. Many ANTHEMS (q.v.) composed during this period were for the first time accompanied by an orchestra, and were sung at the Chapel Royal and cathedral services by the re-established choirs. Many composers, such as Greene, Boyce, and S. S. Wesley, maintained a high standard of dignified cathedral music for choir and organ. In parish churches, however, the main stock of music consisted of metrical psalms, hymns, and a somewhat haphazard chanting of the psalms. Accompaniments varied from church to church. Here and there an organ was provided; in some places a miscellaneous collection of instruments, such as flute, clarinet, bassoon, and string bass, afforded a musical background to the singing of choir and congregation; elsewhere a barrel-organ or harmonium provided the accompaniment. Sometimes there was no accompaniment, the singing being led by a precentor.

In the second half of the 19th century, partly due to the influence of the Oxford Movement, a renaissance of sacred music began in England. Services, anthems, and oratorios were composed by such men as Stanford, Parry, and Vaughan Williams. Vaughan Williams and other composers have also composed music for the Roman Catholic Church in which the voices are unaccompanied in a style akin to that of composers of the 16th century.

See also MUSIC, HISTORY OF; PLAINSONG.

SAGA. The prose narratives composed in Iceland and Norway between the end of the 9th century and the beginning of the 15th century are known as sagas (literally, 'something said'). The sagas, of which there are a great many, vary in length, in literary value, and in historical interest; but they have a common form: each is an historical or biographical narrative, relating some memorable event, or recounting the life and exploits of a great man. They are still read and enjoyed in Iceland, for the language there —unlike the languages of most European countries—has undergone so little change that Icelanders can read with ease their medieval literature.

In the second half of the 9th century, Norway, then consisting of a number of small independent kingdoms, was united by the strong hand of Harald the Fairhaired. Many of the earls who had opposed him fled with their adherents to Iceland, then uninhabited. For the next 50 years colonists poured in, both from Norway and from Norwegian settlements in Britain. These pioneers loved to recount with pride the great men and deeds of their families, their travels and sojourns, their battles and their Viking plunderings. In these stories the sagas have their origin. The descendants of the settlers, themselves adventuring to Baltic lands, to the British Isles, and to Russia, and discovering Greenland and North America, were men whose intellectual curiosity equalled their physical daring, and whose skill in story-telling matched their thirst for knowledge. All over 12th-century Europe there were Icelandic bards (*skalds*) to be found in noble households, and in Iceland saga-telling was the most popular form of entertainment.

For 200 years the sagas were spoken, but in 1117 'it was decreed that our laws should be written in a book'. This quotation is from a book written about 12 years later by Ari Thorgilsson, who is the chief link between the age of the spoken saga and the written, and who set high standards which influenced all his successors. His own chief work, the *Islendigabok* or Book of Icelanders (*c.* 1130), recounts concisely and accurately the settlement and early history of Iceland. For the next two centuries many hands were at work, writing down known sagas and composing new ones. The historical sagas—the most important class—deal with Iceland, Norway, the Orkneys, the Faeroes, and Denmark; but there are also sagas on mythological themes such as the Nordic Nibelung legend, and some with themes deriving from Latin sources.

Of the historical sagas the most notable are contained in two collections:

Heimskringla (literally, 'the round world', from the first words of the manuscript), is by Snorri Sturlason (1178–1241). This recounts the history of the kings of Norway. It begins with a narrative of Odin and other gods, the kings' presumed ancestors (*see* NORSE MYTHS, Vol. I). Then follow the sagas proper, one for each of the kings of Norway till 1177. The saga of Olaf Haraldsson, which comprises more than a quarter of the book, includes an account of his expedition to England to aid Æthelred, and describes a fight at London Bridge.

Sturlunga saga (saga of the House of Sturla) presents a vivid picture of Icelandic life from 1117 to 1262. Its author, Sturla Thordsson (1214–84), was the nephew of Snorri Sturlason. In one saga he described Snorri's assassination by order of King Haakon.

Some sagas are semi-historical: they could be compared with historical novels. Five of these, all relating to early Iceland, are pre-eminent:

The *Eyrbyggya saga* describes life in a district of the west of Iceland between 884 (the settlement period) and 1031. It is a main source of much of our knowledge of Scandinavian religious belief and worship.

The *Egils saga*, after an account of the events which drove Egil's grandfather to Iceland, relates Egil's life in Iceland and abroad, and his death in 982. His adventures included visits to England, where he helped King Athelstan fight against the Scots and where once, at York, he saved his head by composing in one night a poem praising his enemy, Eric Bloodaxe.

The *Laxdaela saga* is more romantic in tone. Its most famous part is the story of the beautiful Gudrun, who, beloved by both Kjartan and his friend Bodli, loves Kjartan, but is tricked into marriage by Bodli. Later, maddened by the scorn that the revelation of his trick produces, Bodli slays Kjartan, and is himself slain by Kjartan's brothers.

The *Grettla* is the story of a famous 11th-century outlaw, Grettir the Strong, whose quarrelsome temper involved him in feuds and killings. The most vivid tale in it is the tale of Glam the shepherd, whose ghost Grettir overcomes; but the ghost's curse condemns him to a lonely hunted life and a miserable death.

The *Njal saga* is, in character-drawing and descriptive power, of the highest excellence. It consists of three parts, the second and main part relating the calamities that Njal's sons brought upon him and themselves till the final disaster, when their enemies surprised and burned them all in their home.

The sagas present a full and detailed picture of the old Scandinavian civilization, its religion, law, customs, and conditions. But they convey not only this background; the vivid stories they tell and the men and women who enact them bring to us not only the civilization but the very life of those times.

See also Vol. I: SAGA; NORSE MYTHS.

ST. PAUL'S CATHEDRAL. The present cathedral, the largest building Sir Christopher WREN (q.v. Vol. V) designed, was built between 1675 and 1710 on Ludgate Hill to replace the Gothic cathedral destroyed in the Great Fire of London in 1666. Its great dome, reaching 365 feet above ground-level, still dominates the City.

Wren made several designs for the cathedral, all with domes, before the design that was finally followed. A large mahogany model of a design on the plan of a Greek cross (that is, with all four arms of equal length) can be seen in the cathedral. The City of London, however, wanted a cathedral more closely resembling the previous building, and so the plan eventually agreed upon is a Latin cross (with one arm longer than the others). St. Paul's is, therefore, somewhat of a compromise: a Renaissance design with the traditional Gothic layout of nave, choir, and transepts (*see* CHURCH ARCHITECTURE, ENGLISH). The dome is over the 'crossing', and at the west end are a bell tower and a clock tower, crowned by turreted spires in the same style as many of Wren's City churches. The clock tower contains a particularly fine circular staircase. The long nave,

National Buildings Record

ST. PAUL'S CATHEDRAL FROM THE SOUTH-EAST

THE HOLY TRINITY. RUSSIAN ICON BY ANDREJ RUBLEV, *c.* 1408

In Russian art the Trinity was represented by the three angels who visited Abraham

terminating in a two-tiered portico, cuts off the full view of the dome from the main approach up Ludgate Hill. Consequently the building as a whole can be seen better from other directions.

Another feature which Wren took over from the Gothic builders was the flying buttress. A row of buttresses occurs on either side of the

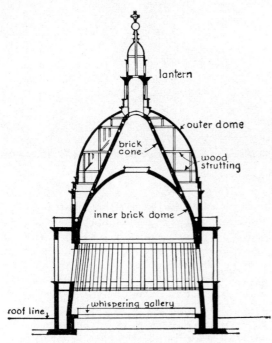

SECTION OF THE DOME OF ST. PAUL'S SHOWING THE CONSTRUCTION

nave and choir to take the thrust from the arches and domes above them. These cannot be seen from outside because the outer walls of the relatively low aisles are carried up as a screen to hide them. The walls are of Portland stone, richly sculptured.

The dome is an ingenious piece of construction. It consists of a cone of brickwork, on top of which rests a heavy stone lantern; the bottom of the cone is surrounded by an iron chain to prevent it from spreading outwards. A timber framework built out from this cone forms the outer dome, which is covered with lead. Inside, the base of the cone is filled by a domed ceiling, round which runs a gallery, called the Whispering Gallery because its circular walls carry the faintest sound from one side to the other. There are also two galleries on the outside of the dome accessible to the public: the Stone Gallery

below the drum from which the dome rises, and the Golden Gallery at the foot of the lantern.

The interior of St. Paul's has some splendid furniture by craftsmen contemporary with Wren, including wrought-iron screens and gates by Jean Tijou and carved choir-stalls by Grinling GIBBONS (q.v. Vol. V). The late-Victorian alabaster reredos, which was damaged by a bomb during the Second World War, is being replaced by a canopy over the High Altar resembling a design made by Wren but never executed. In the crypt are the tombs of Nelson and Wellington, with Wellington's cast-iron funeral car, and in the nave is a monument to Wellington by Alfred Stevens.

See also CHURCH ARCHITECTURE, ENGLISH; DOME.

ST. PETER'S CATHEDRAL. The old cathedral of St. Peter at Rome is supposed to have been built in the 4th century by the Emperor Constantine. It was the grandest example of the early Christian type of basilican church (*see* EARLY CHRISTIAN ART); it had five aisles, flat roofs, and a huge arcaded courtyard. For over 1,000 years this building was the central church in Western Christendom; but by the middle of the 15th century, when the RENAISSANCE (q.v. Vol. I) had changed men's ideas, it was felt that a more modern building should replace it. The first serious rebuilding was begun to the plans of BRAMANTE (q.v. Vol. V), and a start was made inside the old cathedral by building the four arches intended to support the central dome. Only three of these were finished when Bramante died in 1514. New plans were drawn up, but little was done until, in 1547, MICHELANGELO (q.v. Vol. V) was appointed architect. He made yet another new plan, more or less following that of Bramante, for a huge church, centred round the dome and without a long nave; and work proceeded on this plan. After Michelangelo's death, the church authorities insisted on a long nave, and in the early 17th century the architect, Maderno, added this. It was found, however, that the original plan, started from the inside, had overlooked the necessity of providing steps up to the main entrance; consequently the whole floor had to be considerably raised inside. The façade of Maderno's nave, which included a prominent balcony from which the Pope could bless the people (as he still does), looked too wide, and it was proposed to build towers on

Anderson

ST. PETER'S, ROME, AND THE PIAZZA

each side to overcome this. The foundations, however, were not strong enough to carry the towers, and the plan was abandoned. Finally, in the middle of the 17th century, BERNINI (q.v. Vol. V), who had already decorated most of the interior of the building, solved the problem of the façade by constructing colonnades surrounding the piazza in front of the building which, by an optical illusion, make the church look narrower than it is. Thus by the end of the 17th century the new St. Peter's, by far the largest church in the world, was finally finished. During and after the Second World War excavations made under the church revealed what is claimed to be the tomb of St. Peter.

See also ITALIAN ART.

ST. SOPHIA. For more than 1,000 years the Cathedral of St. Sophia at Constantinople (*see* ISTANBUL, Vol. III) was unquestionably the finest church in Christendom. Today, even though the building first became a mosque and is now a museum, St. Sophia still retains a magic of its own.

St. Sophia was built for the Byzantine Emperor JUSTINIAN (q.v. Vol. V) by two architects, Anthemius of Tralles and Isidore of Miletus. The work was begun in the year 532, and progressed so quickly that the cathedral was dedicated with the utmost pomp on Christmas Day, 538. Its great dome, measuring 105 feet in diameter, was the largest that existed, and is still the widest ever built. The first dome collapsed in an earthquake in 558, but a new one was immediately erected, and as an improvement it was raised by 25 feet. Ever since, although the dome has been damaged by several earthquakes, the repairs have always closely followed the lines of the original. Throughout the Middle Ages its size aroused universal wonder; and when Sir Christopher Wren came to design ST. PAUL'S CATHEDRAL (q.v.) he asked the English merchants in Constantinople to send him all available information about it.

Every possible luxury was lavished on the interior of St. Sophia. The finest marble columns with elaborately carved capitals were used for the aisles; the floors and the lower levels of the walls were sheeted with precious marbles, and wonderful MOSAICS (q.v.) shimmered above. The screen was of silver, the golden altar shone from beneath a silver canopy, the pulpit was of silver, ivory, and precious marbles, and the ICONS (q.v.), or sacred pictures, were studded with rare jewels. Russian envoys to Byzantium in 988 said they felt themselves in Paradise when they entered the cathedral, and they advised their monarch to adopt the religion of the Byzantines for the Russian State.

St. Sophia was shamefully looted by the Crusaders in 1204, and at Constantinople's fall in 1453 the Turks converted it into a mosque.

INTERIOR OF ST. SOPHIA

They added minarets to the exterior, and covered the mosaics with whitewash. This is now being removed, and those mosaics which have survived the various earthquakes are again appearing in all their original glory.

See also BYZANTINE ART.
See also Vol. III: ISTANBUL.

SARCOPHAGUS, *see* TOMBS.

SATIRE. This is the only literary form which the Romans invented (*see* LATIN LITERATURE). A Roman satire was a piece of verse, or verse mingled with prose, which aimed at improving society by mocking its follies and vices. It was written in racy language studded with dialogue, and was full of topical reference, ironical wit, and often indecent humour. The 'biting satires' of Juvenal (*c.* 60–130 A.D.) and of his predecessor Lucilius have influenced nearly all the great satirists since, especially those whose fierce indignation and savage mockery have been used for the betterment of mankind. Later satirists did not keep to the Roman form but used any form that suited them—verse or prose, play, travel-tale, epic, romance, or novel.

Hardly any other form of literature has had so powerful an influence on world affairs. For example, Erasmus's satire *In Praise of Folly*, written in Latin in 1509, and directed principally against Church dignitaries and theologians, is generally considered to have played an important part in preparing the way for the REFORMATION (q.v. Vol. I). Similarly Voltaire's satires, such as *Candide*, in which he showed his contempt for authority and institutions, prepared the way for the FRENCH REVOLUTION (q.v. Vol. X).

Two great 16th-century writers, the Frenchman RABELAIS and the Spaniard CERVANTES (qq.v. Vol. V), produced works which burlesqued the romances of chivalry (*see* ROMANCE LITERATURE). Rabelais's *Gargantua* and *Pantagruel* relate the extravagant adventures of these two giant kings, father and son, adventures ludicrously like those of the heroes of the popular romances. In *Gargantua*, a war takes place between Gargantua's father, the easy-going King Grandgousier, and King Picrochole, the tyrannical and ambitious king of Lerne. Most popular romances included wars; but Rabelais uses his war to show how petty causes can lead to devastating calamities. One method of satire is to depict an ideal which by contrast shows up the flaws and defects of the reality. Rabelais uses this method in his description of the founding of the abbey of Theleme, which he depicts as the opposite of all the idle and ignorant monastic communities which he knew and hated. In Theleme there were to be no rules, except 'Do as you like'. As only people who were free, well-born, and well-educated would be received in the honourable company of each other and of great books, such people would be naturally virtuous and industrious and need no rules. Everything in Rabelais's work is on a vast scale: its burlesque and satire, its heroes' preposterous adventures, its coarse language and humour—which have given us the word 'Rabelaisian'—and its heroes' gigantic appetites—which have given us the word 'Gargantuan'.

Cervantes's *Don Quixote de la Mancha* is about a poor and amiable gentleman who has read so many romances that his imagination is disordered, and he thinks that he, too, is a hero of chivalry, whose duty it is to roam the world in search of adventure and fame. In this entertaining and picturesque book, the mock-heroic passages, and the whole design, satirize amusingly the romance. But the book as a whole, which had been planned as a criticism of the romantic interpretation of life, deepened into a criticism of life itself; and Don Quixote, instead of being a mere caricature as Cervantes had planned, wins our tenderness and affection. Incidents and phrases from *Don Quixote* have become proverbial all over Europe, for example: 'There are but two families in the world, as my grandmother used to say, the Haves and the Havenots.'

One of the greatest and bitterest of English prose-satires is *Gulliver's Travels* (1726) by SWIFT (q.v. Vol. V), a book which has been read with delight by generations of children for its story of Gulliver's adventures among the tiny Lilliputians and the giant Brobdingnagians. By transferring to pigmy Lilliputians some of the main concerns of European life—wars of ambition, political and religious quarrels, the pomp and precedence of Courts—Swift makes them all look very silly. In the second part, when Gulliver tells the Brobdingnagians about his country, their king comments, 'I cannot but conclude the bulk of your natives to be the most pernicious race of little odious vermin that nature ever suffered to crawl upon the surface of the earth'.

demands sympathy and curative treatment. His satire is directed against the stupidity and hypocrisy which he saw in family and public life.

The 20th century has produced many interesting satirical novels. Evelyn Waugh, one of whose heroes 'found a peculiar relish in contemplating the victories of barbarism', wrote a brilliant and cruel satire, called *The Loved One*, set in an elaborate American cemetery. In this Waugh ridicules the attitude to death which demands euphemistic terms for 'death', and cosmetics for corpses. George Orwell's *Animal Farm* is a political satire using a method akin to Swift's in the last book of *Gulliver's Travels*. But *Animal Farm* is directed not against all mankind but rather at certain systems of government. At a deeper level, it illustrates how power corrupts its possessors. Aldous Huxley has used the method of imagining a world which is the logical outcome of the world of today. In *Ape and Essence*, for example, civilization as we know it has been destroyed by atomic bombing, and a horrifying decadent system has replaced it.

See also COMEDY.

SCALES. 1. SOUND (q.v. Vol. III) is the result of a series of waves, the 'pitch' (whether the sound is high or low) depending on the speed of the vibration of the wave. Since this speed can vary infinitely there can be an infinite variety of sounds. A random choice of sounds would not make a musical composition any more than random splashes of colours on a canvas would make a painting. The composer selects and arranges his sounds, as the painter selects and arranges his colours, in patterns of MELODY AND RHYTHM and HARMONY (qq.v.) to build up a balanced composition.

Groups of selected sounds arranged in order are called 'scales', from the Latin word *scala* (a staircase or ladder). There are many different types of scale which have been used at different periods or in different places, each with its own character.

Some sounds stand in a definite relationship to each other, the simplest being the notes whose difference in pitch represents an 'octave'; all scales are built up on this basic relationship. The number of vibrations per second (or 'frequency') of a note an octave higher than another

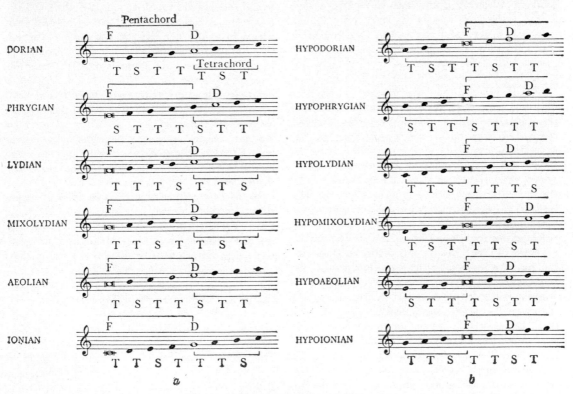

FIG. 1. *a*. AUTHENTIC MODES. *b*. PLAGAL MODES

is twice as great; for instance, the frequency of Middle C on the piano is 256 vibrations per second, and the note with a frequency of 512 per second is exactly an octave above. The Greek philosopher PYTHAGORAS (q.v. Vol. V) made experiments with the stretched string of a musical instrument. He found that a string of a certain length gave one note, and one of half the length (vibrating at twice the speed) gave a note an octave higher. He then divided the octave into eight notes (hence its name), of which the fifth was the sound made by a string two-thirds the length of the original, and the fourth was made by a string three-quarters the length of the original. Between these two notes and the fundamental one the ear recognizes a special relationship, corresponding to their scientific relationship.

The distance between the pitch of one note and another is called an 'interval'. The intervals between the eight notes of the octave are not all equal; some are half as large as others. The larger intervals are called 'tones' and the smaller ones 'semitones'.

2. MODES. The many scales which have been used in Western music are of Greek origin. These scales, or 'modes' as they were called, were taken over and adapted to its own use by the Christian Church. There are six basic modes, called the 'Authentic' modes, each with a particular arrangement of tones and semitones (Fig. 1 a). Each mode might start at any note or pitch, providing the order of the tones and semitones remained unchanged. Fig. 1 shows them each starting on a different note, so that only the white notes of the piano are used. A mode is made up of two groups: one of five notes (pentachord) and one of four (tetrachord), the middle note being common to both. The last note of the tetrachord is the first note of the pentachord repeated an octave higher. If the position of the pentachord and tetrachord is reversed, 'Plagal' modes are produced (Fig. 1 b).

The note on which the melody finished was known as the 'final' (F in Fig. 1 a). The final was the same for both the authentic mode and its corresponding plagal mode. The note a fifth above was the next of most importance and was called the 'dominant' (D in Fig. 1 a). In the early Middle Ages there was no exact MUSICAL NOTATION (q.v.) and it was, therefore, not possible to indicate exact pitch. The final was sung at any pitch which was convenient to the

singers, the other notes of the mode being calculated from it.

Modal melodies lie mostly within one octave. The dominant is, as it were, the hub around which the melody revolves, and it ends on the final. The English folk-song 'It was Hankey the Squire' is in the Dorian mode (Fig. 2).

FIG. 2. 'IT WAS HANKEY THE SQUIRE'

What characterizes a modal scale is its arrangement of tones and semitones, but with the development of harmonized music it was found necessary to alter certain notes of the mode to avoid discords, that is, sounds unpleasant to the ear. If the notes were altered, the arrangement of tones and semitones no longer remained the same, and the particular character of the mode was therefore lost. For example, the interval between the fifth and sixth notes of the Dorian mode is a tone; if this is made a semitone the series becomes identical with the Aeolian mode (see Fig. 1 a). Gradually it was found that only two arrangements proved satisfactory—and these have become our major and minor scales.

3. MAJOR AND MINOR SCALES. The arrangement of the intervals of a major scale is tone, tone, semitone, tone, tone, tone, semitone. Fig. 3 a shows the scale of C major, which only uses the white notes of the piano. If the scale starts

FIG. 3. a. SCALE OF C MAJOR. b. SCALE OF E MAJOR

on any other note, some of the notes will have to be raised or lowered a semitone (sharpened or flattened); that is, some of the black notes of the piano must be used. Fig. 3 *b* shows the major scale starting on E. A musical composition is said to be in the 'key' of the scale on which it is based.

The minor scale varies from the major by having the third note flattened. The sixth and seventh notes may be flat or natural, giving two forms, the 'harmonic' and the 'melodic'; the latter varies according to whether it is ascending or descending (Fig. 4 *a* and *b*).

FIG. 4. MINOR SCALES
a. Harmonic. *b.* Melodic

The first note of the scale, the 'keynote' from which all the others are calculated, is called the 'tonic', the fifth note is the 'dominant', and the others are also named (Fig. 5).

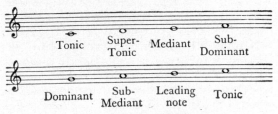

FIG. 5. THE NOTES OF THE SCALE

4. OTHER SCALES. A scale which includes all twelve semitones in the octave is called a chromatic scale (Fig. 6 *a*), and one which uses only tones is called a whole-tone scale (Fig. 6 *b*).

FIG. 6. *a.* CHROMATIC SCALE. *b.* WHOLE-TONE SCALE

Many other scales have been used in music. There are various five-note or 'pentatonic' scales which have been used by, for instance,

FIG. 7. THE SCOTTISH SONG 'YE BANKS AND BRAES', WHICH IS IN A PENTATONIC SCALE

the Scots (Fig. 7), the Chinese, the Japanese, and the Javanese. Some scales are very complicated: an early form of Persian scale consisted of notes corresponding to C, D, E♭, E♮, F, G, A♭, A♮, B, C. Later more semitones were added, and then quarter-tones (having a variation in pitch of only half that between semitones), until the octave was divided into seventeen notes. Hindu scales are even more complicated (*see* ORIENTAL MUSIC).

See also HARMONY; MELODY AND RHYTHM; MUSICAL NOTATION.

SCHOOLS OF ART. The word 'school' used in connexion with art may refer merely to a building in which art is taught, but it is used specially to denote the work of all artists of one region or nation, or of the followers of one great master.

The first of these two special meanings has long been in use. The 18th-century painter, Sir Joshua REYNOLDS (q.v. Vol. V), refers in his writings to the 'Dutch School' and the 'French School'. Such terms are vague when applied to painters of widely differing periods, yet some tendencies recur again and again in the works of artists of the same country. It is natural that the French school should differ from the Dutch, since the forms of government, religion, and climate, and the conditions of artistic life were different in the two countries. But what is astonishing is that in Italy, in the 15th and 16th centuries, there were many schools flourishing at the same time within a few miles of each other. Ferrara, for instance, which was never a very large town, had a school of painting of a high level which was quite distinct from the Venetian school flourishing less than a hundred miles away. The towns of Florence and Siena, where distinctive schools of painting flourished at the same time, are equally close together (*see* FLORENTINE and SIENESE PAINTING).

Artists who live abroad often retain the characteristics of their homeland. The 17th-century French painter Nicolas POUSSIN (q.v. Vol. V) spent all his adult life in Rome, where the style of painting which was being practised all round him was the opposite of his own. Yet he is, perhaps, the most typical representative of the French school.

Such terms as 'School of Rembrandt' and 'School of Rubens' are comparatively modern; they describe paintings by unnamed artists working in the style of the master. The art critic who attempts to find out who painted such works can, in many cases, judge only by style. The pupils in the studio of a famous painter, when they had learnt their craft, were often expected to help him to paint unimportant parts of his picture (such as clothes or backgrounds). Rubens, in particular, of whom so many pictures were demanded that he did not have time to paint them entirely himself, used pupils a great deal in this way. When, therefore, these pupils came to paint pictures of their own it is not surprising that they imitated the peculiarities of the master's style, and that their works, in consequence, are difficult to tell from inferior works of the master himself.

Courtauld Institute

FIGURES ON THE CENTRAL PORCH OF THE WEST FRONT OF CHARTRES CATHEDRAL

The elongated forms with limbs held close to the body fit the shape of the columns against which the figures stand

SCULPTURE. This can mean either the carving of material such as stone or wood, or the modelling of material such as clay or wax. The first is called the 'glyptic' method, the second the 'plastic' method, from two Greek words meaning 'to carve' and 'to mould'. Each reaches the desired result from opposite ends. A carver begins with a block larger than he wants and cuts it away till his forms are realized. A modeller begins with a core and adds piece to piece till he has built up the required forms. There can also be a mixture of the two which entails 'over-modelling' and afterwards 'dressing down'. Sculptors have used marble, stone, wood, and ivory as materials for carving (*see* STONE CARVING, WOODCARVING, IVORY CARVING). Models in clay, a soft material, are sometimes baked to make them permanent. The Greeks and Romans produced TERRACOTTAS by this method, and POTTERY AND PORCELAIN FIGURES (qq.v.) are made in the same manner. Another way to produce a permanent result is to reproduce the clay or wax model by casting

DAVID. MARBLE STATUE BY MICHELANGELO

The figure, carved from a piece of marble so large that other sculptors had not dared use it, is a representation of an ideal human figure

National Buildings Record

BRONZE STATUE OF CHARLES I BY HUBERT LE SUEUR (1595–1650) IN TRAFALGAR SQUARE, LONDON

it in bronze, silver, lead, or concrete (*see* BRONZE SCULPTURE).

At all times sculpture has been used to glorify the gods, to commemorate heroes, and to decorate objects of daily and ceremonial use. Because of the durability of its materials it has often been an important, or even the only, source of information about prehistoric peoples, and has added considerably to the knowledge of civilizations of more recent times. Sculpture has formed an important part of the cultural life of countries ranging from China to Mexico, India to Africa, and also of Greece and Rome and of all countries which have derived their culture from them.

Sculpture is sometimes made 'in the round', sometimes 'in relief'. 'In the round' means that it has full or natural measurement in every direction. 'In relief' means that it has reduced measurement forward and backward, but the

proportions of length and breadth remain as in nature. When the relief is shallow it is called 'bas-relief'; when the projection is nearer the natural it is called 'high relief'. Sculpture in the round can be viewed from any position; that in relief from the front only.

One of the most important uses of sculpture is in collaboration with architecture, and at all times when it has been at its best its association with buildings has been its chief purpose. The pediments (gables) surmounting classical temples were filled with sculptures, usually in the round, which symbolized gods, giants, or heroes (*see* GREEK ART). Relief sculptures depicting scenes such as processions, priests making offerings to the gods, and athletic games were used as decorative bands or friezes round buildings (*see* ELGIN MARBLES). Sometimes parts of buildings were supported by single carved figures, instead of columns; these figures are called 'caryatids'. In the Middle Ages sculpture was used to decorate many parts of buildings both inside and on the outside. The vast range of subjects included figures of Christ, the Madonna and Child, angels, saints and prophets, animals, flowers, and a great variety of natural subjects, some of which taught the Bible stories, while others told of everyday life (*see* GOTHIC ART).

Memorial sculpture, which includes TOMBS (q.v.), is not necessarily associated with architecture. It may consist of a statue of a great man set on a pedestal, or it may be a tablet carved in relief and fixed to a wall. Such memorials include equestrian statues such as those of the Colleoni in Venice, or Charles I in London, and single figures such as that of General Gordon which used to stand in Trafalgar Square.

Free decorative sculpture includes symbolic statues which are not designed as memorials or as architectural features but are carved as artistic expression in forms, just as a sonnet is in words or a sonata in music. There has been a great increase of sculpture of this kind in the 20th century, and at the same time correspondingly less architectural and memorial sculpture has been used. There has also been a greater interest in abstract sculpture (*see* MODERN ART).

The materials used for sculpture have always had a marked influence on the work produced. The hard granite used by the Egyptians led to a simplification of shapes. The marble used by the Greeks, quarried from Mounts Pentelicus and Paros, led to softer forms, while the coarser freestones of the Gothic sculptors led to harder forms. Alabaster, a soft but tough stone used very much by the Nottingham school of carvers in the 14th and 15th centuries, led to considerable intricacy of details. Modern sculptors have given great importance to the materials they have used, striving to keep the stoniness of stone, the woodlike qualities of wood, and the metallic qualities of bronze.

Sculpture until about 400 years ago was generally coloured. There is evidence that the backgrounds of pediments on ancient Greek and Roman buildings were painted, and that decorations were painted on the marble draperies of figures. Gothic sculpture was painted extensively; the Spanish sculptors of this period often made their sculpture startlingly lifelike by their use of naturalistic colour. The appreciation of uncoloured sculpture is a comparatively recent taste.

See also STONE CARVING; BRONZE SCULPTURE; WOOD-CARVING.

SCYTHIAN ART, *see* PREHISTORIC ART, Section 3.

SEALS, *see* Vol. IV: SEALS.

SERMONS. The term 'sermon' is used not only for an address on points of Christian doctrine or conduct delivered by a priest or minister, but also for written works of similar purpose, even if they are never delivered in public. Preaching goes back as far as the Apostles, some of whose sermons are recorded in the Acts. These were simple in style, concentrated mainly on the doctrines of the Redemption and Resurrection, and were aimed to build on the foundation of the accepted ideas of those who heard them. Thus St. Paul, when speaking to the Athenians, gave a philosophical cast to his words.

Preaching is usually at its most vigorous and best in times of acute religious controversy. The doctrinal divisions of the 4th century produced a host of brilliant preachers, such as St. Chrysostom and St. AUGUSTINE (q.v. Vol. V), who wrote the first treatise on the art of preaching. Medieval heresy was partly responsible for the founding of the Order of Preachers, the Dominicans (*see* MONK, Vol. I). In the 13th century both they and the Franciscans provided a nucleus of trained preachers who travelled over wide areas. The Dominicans were concerned mainly with doctrine, the Franciscans with the practice of the Christian life, a distinction which has been preserved in these orders ever since.

The REFORMATION (q.v. Vol. I) produced another flowering of preaching in the 16th century, both from the Catholics and the Protestants. Indeed, some of the reformed Churches gave to the sermon the central position in Christian worship which the Mass occupies in the Catholic Church. John CALVIN (q.v. Vol. V) inaugurated a deeply intellectual and argumentative form of preaching which was accepted by those countries which adopted his religious system, including Holland and Scotland. The 17th century, a period of profound religious divisions in France and England, was a great age of preaching in both, and produced such masters as St. François de Sales and Bossuet in France, and DONNE (q.v. Vol. V), Andrewes, and Jeremy Taylor in England. Their sermons, preached in a most elaborate style, were often magnificently written literary compositions. John Donne, in a sermon on *Eternity*, wrote:

Methusalem, with all his hundreds of years, was but a Mushroom of a night's growth to this Day [Eternity], and all the four Monarchies, with all their thousands of years, and all the powerful Kings and all the beautiful Queens of this world, were but as a bed of flowers, some gathered at six, some at seven, some at eight, all in one morning, in respect of this Day.

John WESLEY (q.v. Vol. V) in 1738 began a long series of missionary journeys throughout England, in the course of which he preached some 40,000 sermons. His style was intensely enthusiastic, often moving his hearers to extraordinary emotion. Such emotional, soul-stirring sermons are still often preached by Nonconformists or by evangelical parsons in the Church of England. The sermons of Cardinal NEWMAN (q.v. Vol. V), who preached first as an Anglican and then as a Roman Catholic, were of high literary merit and very moving:

May He support us all the day long [he preached in a sermon on *Wisdom and Innocence*] till the shades lengthen, and the evening comes, and the busy world is hushed, and the fever of life is over, and our work is done! Then in His mercy may He give us a safe lodging, and a holy rest, and peace at the last.

Wesley and Newman, the two greatest preachers and greatest religious leaders of modern England, were the cause of much violent opposition as well as fervent support.

In the late 18th and 19th centuries many books of sermons were published. Sermons were often read aloud in the family circle; Lady Bertram, for example, in Jane Austen's novel *Mansfield Park*, had 'cried herself to sleep after hearing an affecting sermon'. Modern sermons, however, which are usually short and often colloquial in style, are designed to be listened to rather than to be read.

SHAKESPEARIAN DRAMA. William SHAKE-SPEARE (q.v. Vol. V), the world's greatest dramatic poet, wrote altogether thirty-seven plays. When Shakespeare began to write in 1591, English popular DRAMA (q.v.), strengthened by borrowings from other literatures and by the 'mighty line' of blank verse introduced by Christopher MARLOWE (q.v. Vol. V), was developing fast, free from the restraint of any pedantic theories. The drama was able to appeal to nearly all tastes, for it could present high-sounding poetry, clever wit, or scenes of violent excitement or broad humour. Much of Shakespeare's unique genius lay in his ability to excel in all these styles and to unite them in plays which are full of dramatic contrast and suspense. The plays abound in striking scenes—a bride denounced at the altar, a spy stabbed behind the curtain, murders, love-scenes, and battles; heroines disguised as boys seek out their lovers, and comic clowns, ghosts and fairies, pirates and robbers, all have their place.

The poetry in Shakespeare's plays deepens the obvious interest of these episodes, for the characters speak in verse of incomparable vividness and variety. As the Elizabethan THEATRE (q.v. Vol. IX) had no stage scenery, Shakespeare often describes the imagined setting of the play through the mouths of the characters, as in the lovely lines spoken by Oberon, the Fairy King, in *A Midsummer Night's Dream*:

> I know a bank whereon the wild thyme blows,
> Where oxlips and the nodding violet grows
> Quite over-canopied with luscious woodbine,
> With sweet musk-roses, and with eglantine:
> There sleeps Titania some time of the night,
> Lull'd in these flowers with dances and delight.

Such descriptive poetry is often used to create a special kind of atmosphere, as in the pathos of Queen Gertrude's description of Ophelia's death in *Hamlet*, or the spring-like joyousness of Perdita's flower speech in *The Winter's Tale*:

> daffodils,
> That come before the swallow dares, and take
> The winds of March with beauty;

The way the characters speak describes, also, the kind of persons they are, and they reveal their innermost thoughts and feelings, especially when thinking aloud to themselves in soliloquy. We see, for example, how Macbeth's crimes have withered up his sense of the meaning of life when he says

> Tomorrow, and tomorrow, and tomorrow,
> Creeps in this petty pace from day to day,
> To the last syllable of recorded time;
> And all our yesterdays have lighted fools
> The way to dusty death. Out, out, brief candle!
> Life's but a walking shadow, a poor player
> That struts and frets his hour upon the stage,
> And then is heard no more; it is a tale
> Told by an idiot, full of sound and fury,
> Signifying nothing.

Such soliloquies in the later plays, especially in *Hamlet*, are full of great poetry, giving a deep insight into men's thoughts and moods.

In these various ways Shakespeare's language enriches the bare outlines of the story, giving it greater dramatic force and meaning. In the early plays the poetry is fairly simple, written in blank verse with a regular beat, mixed with many rhyming couplets. In the later plays the verse becomes extremely flexible, with varied length and beat, very few rhymes, and with the sense running on from line to line. The language is occasionally difficult, perhaps because the ideas are subtle and difficult, but also sometimes because the meaning of words has changed since Shakespeare's day or because in writing hastily Shakespeare has left his meaning doubtful.

Shakespeare's plays are usually divided into histories, comedies, tragedies, and romances. The histories are 'chronicle-plays' about the English kings who ruled before the Tudors. The three plays on Henry VI, produced in 1592, were probably the first that Shakespeare wrote, and for these he may have had the help of Marlowe. Like *Richard III*, produced in the same year, they are energetic in speech and action, but the characters have little subtlety. *Richard II* (1595) shows a great advance. We pity the weak king, yet recognize that he has brought his sufferings upon himself; the other

A PERFORMANCE OF 'TITUS ANDRONICUS' IN SHAKESPEARE'S DAY
Drawing from a volume of letters in the possession of the Marquess of Bath

characters are more varied than in the earlier plays, and the verse is less stiff, richer in music and meaning. In *Henry IV, Parts I and II* (1597–8) the verse is strong and flexible, while there is magnificent prose in the humorous scenes. Personal and political themes unite in the adventures of Prince Hal, who worries his dying father, the king, by keeping the low company of fat Sir John Falstaff, a man 'witty himself, and cause of wit in other men'. Falstaff is one of the greatest comic characters in English literature. Eventually the Prince rejects Falstaff, and, in *Henry V* (1599), becomes the great English hero-king. Although Shakespeare often telescoped historical events to suit his dramatic purpose, he kept to the general truth of history as far as it was known to him, and his portrait of Richard II, for example, is still convincing. His patriotic vision of England is nobly expressed by the dying Gaunt in *Richard II*:

This royal throne of kings, this scepter'd isle . . .
This happy breed of men, this little world,
This precious stone set in the silver sea

In Shakespeare's comedy there is humour, either of farcical situation, as in the early *Taming of the Shrew*, or of speech and thought, as in the merry wit of Rosalind in *As You Like It*. (Humour, indeed, is to be found in all the plays—even in the most powerful tragedies Shakespeare uses humorous scenes to relieve yet heighten the tragedy.) In the comedies there is also the interest of a love-story with a happy ending. Such love-stories, combined with humour, form the main plots of his comedies of romance (*see* COMEDY, Section 5), of which the earliest are *The Two Gentlemen of Verona* and *Love's Labour's Lost* (both 1594–5) and the latest *Twelfth Night* (1602). In *The Two Gentlemen of Verona*, however, the amusing clown Launce is so real that by contrast the artificial love-story seems merely silly. But in *A Midsummer Night's Dream* (*c.* 1595) Shakespeare is more successful in combining humour with a love-story; he moves with ease from broad rustic humour to rapid punning or playing on words and to passages of lovely descriptive verse. The humour of the clowns is only connected with the delicate comedy of the lovers because they are all in the same enchanted wood, but the atmosphere of fantasy which wraps the whole scene prevents the humour from spoiling our pleasure in the romance. Later, in *Twelfth Night*, the various elements are superbly combined: we love and respect the heroine Viola and at the same time laugh at the rich humour of Sir Toby Belch and at the absurd posturings of Malvolio. In the romantic comedies the heroines are the most important characters; though they are princesses among women, with strong wills and witty tongues, they remain attractive and light-hearted girls who give the plays a special warm-hearted glow and delight. The third element in the comedies is serious drama, or even melodrama. In *Much Ado About Nothing* (1598) the melodrama of Hero and Claudio runs side by side with the witty romance of Benedick and Beatrice and the comic absurdity of Dogberry and his watchmen; there is a similar division in *The Merchant of Venice* (1596). The so-called 'dark comedies', however, *Troilus and Cressida* (1600), *Measure for Measure*, and *All's Well that Ends Well* (both 1604), are not meant to be amusing. They contain some of Shakespeare's least pleasant characters, and are among the least well-constructed and well-written of his plays.

Shakespeare's tragedies developed from the crude horrors of *Titus Andronicus* (*c.* 1593) and the youthful romantic passion of *Romeo and Juliet* (1594). Though most are based on historical events, Shakespeare seems to have been more interested in the good and evil of the men and women he portrays, their sufferings and their greatness, than in the historical events. The four greatest tragedies are *Hamlet* (1601), *Othello* (1604), *Macbeth*, and *King Lear* (both 1606). These plays are dominated by the heroes, who die at the end; but the sadness of waste and suffering is overcome by a sense of wonder at the greatness of man and a feeling of relief that evil has been conquered, even at the great cost of life itself. Othello's dying words best sum up the nobility and suffering of Shakespeare's tragic heroes:

> When you shall these unlucky deeds relate,
> Speak of me as I am; nothing extenuate,
> Nor set down aught in malice: then, must you speak
> Of one that loved not wisely but too well;
> Of one not easily jealous, but, being wrought,
> Perplex'd in the extreme; of one whose hand
> Like the base Indian, threw a pearl away
> Richer than all his tribe; of one whose subdu'd eyes
> Albeit unusèd to the melting mood,
> Drop tears as fast as the Arabian trees
> Their med'cinable gum.

In *King Lear*, Kent's words suggest both the sadness and the sense of release at Lear's death:

> O! let him pass; he hates him
> That would upon the rack of this tough world
> Stretch him out longer.

Shakespeare also wrote several plays on subjects from Roman history. Political themes and studies of masterful men (*Coriolanus*, for example) provide much of the interest, but the magnificent *Antony and Cleopatra* unites the themes of empire and of tragic love. It contains some of the most glorious verse that Shakespeare ever wrote, as in Cleopatra's praise of Antony:

> His legs bestrid the ocean; his rear'd arm
> Crested the world; his voice was propertied
> As all the tunèd spheres, and that to friends;
> But when he meant to quail and shake the orb,
> He was as rattling thunder. For his bounty,
> There was no winter in't, an autumn 'twas
> That grew the more by reaping;

or in Enobarbus's description of Cleopatra:

> Age cannot wither her, nor custom stale
> Her infinite variety.

In the last few plays of his life, usually called the romances, Shakespeare, instead of stopping at the tragic climax, goes on to show how a tragic crime can be atoned for; and so presents a happy ending. In both *The Winter's Tale* and *The Tempest* the harm done by a wicked deed is healed by the love between the children of the next generation. In these plays Shakespeare is not interested in describing characters or events realistically. He seems to be trying to show deeper truths through interesting but unusual stories which have a fairy-tale quality. Though there is still evil in the world, suffering tests the worthiness of love, and through love 'that which was lost is found'.

Shakespeare took his themes from all manner of sources. The historical plays, for example, are based largely on the chronicles of Holinshed (*see* HISTORIES), and the Roman plays on North's translation of Plutarch's *Lives* (*see* BIOGRAPHIES). *As You Like It* is a dramatization of a popular prose romance, Thomas Lodge's *Rosalynde*; *Twelfth Night* is derived from a popular Italian comedy. But Shakespeare made everything his own. Occasionally he merely put the original prose into verse, but usually he transformed the work entirely. This, for example, is a passage from Holinshed, about Macbeth:

Horsses in Louthian, being of singular beauty and swiftnesse, did eate their owne flesh, and would in no wise taste anie other meate. There was a spar-hawke also strangled by an owle. Neither was it anie less wounder that the sunne . . . was continually couered with clouds for six moneths space. And all men understood that the abhominable murther of King Duffe was the cause hereof.

And this is how Shakespeare transformed it:

ROSS: . . . Thou seest, the heavens, as troubled with
    man's act,
Threaten his bloody stage; by th'clock 'tis day,
And yet dark night strangles the travelling-lamp.
Is't night's predominance, or the day's shame,
That darkness does the face of earth entomb,
When living light should kiss it?

OLD MAN: 'Tis unnatural,
Even like the deed that's done. On Tuesday last,
A falcon, towering in her pride of place,
Was by a mousing owl hawk'd at and kill'd.

ROSS: And Duncan's horses,—a thing most strange and
    certain,—
Beauteous and swift, the minions of their race,
Turn'd wild in nature, broke their stalls, flung out,
Contending 'gainst obedience, as they would
Make war with mankind.

OLD MAN: 'Tis said they eat each other.

But, in the finest passages of his plays, Shakespeare calls only on himself. He has creative power, poetic utterance, a remarkable grasp of human nature, and the knowledge of a man of the theatre. His ability to write dramas which act well is unrivalled, and they should always be thought of as set on the stage. The characters are so alive, and the style so rich, that the more we see or read them the more we find in them. Perhaps Shakespeare's greatest characteristic is his humanity; he seems to have been able to interpret the thoughts and feelings of every kind of person. His thought is the orthodox political and Christian thought of his day, but his poetry so relates it to living experience that we not only seem to live with his characters, but their deeds and sayings throw light on our own lives.

See also DRAMA; TRAGEDY; COMEDY.
See also Vol. V: SHAKESPEARE.

SHANTIES, see FOLK-SONG.

SHORT STORIES. A novel tells a story at length, its characters gradually displaying themselves in a sequence of events. But a short story as a rule describes one episode or situation, and in this single event the characters, necessarily few, must reveal themselves. The 'event' may belong to the world of external reality, or it may exist in the thoughts or emotions of the characters. But it must be such that the characters' reactions to it will light them up, define them for us. The short story, then, differs from the novel in its lack of complexity as well as in

length. It may be paradoxically a long short story such as Conrad's *Heart of Darkness* of 40,000 words. It may be as short as 200 words. A very usual length is 3,000–4,000 words.

The short story as a form of literature hardly existed before the 19th century, when it originated simultaneously in Russia with PUSHKIN (q.v. Vol. V) and Gogol (1809–52), and in America with Edgar Allan Poe (1809–49) and Nathaniel Hawthorne (1804–64). It is thought to have flourished in America because the pace of life demanded a literary form that was uncomplicated and quick to read. Magazines and similar periodicals, popular in the States from the early days of the 19th century onwards, provided a ready and profitable market for short stories. Many of the best-known American short-story writers, such as Bret Harte (1836–1902), were journalists, expert in telling tales of adventure with skill and gusto. The ingenious stories of another journalist, W. S. Porter, whose *nom de plume* was O. Henry (1862–1910), were immensely popular; he was especially fond of using the trick ending, and the beginning that plunges straight into the story without any previous explanations:

So I went to a doctor. 'How long has it been since you took alcohol into your system?' he asked.

He wastes no words in describing scenes or characters, but leaves the reader to supply these from the clues given in the dialogue.

In France, Guy de Maupassant (1850–93) also used the abrupt opening, and occasionally the surprise ending, in his two hundred and more short stories. They are written in a hard, realistic style; their characters are usually drawn from among Norman peasants or from low life; they convey to the reader Maupassant's vision of human life as hateful and sordid, relieved only by bursts of comedy. He inspires little sympathy for the people whom he so vividly brings to life. In his most famous story, *The Necklace*, a young woman loses the diamond necklace which a friend has lent her for an evening party. She and her husband condemn themselves to years of grinding poverty in order to pay for a second necklace to return to the friend, only to learn, too late, that the original diamonds were, in fact, worthless paste. The reader is left with an awareness of life's irony rather than any pity for the unfortunate couple.

Russia has produced some of the world's

Foto Marburg

THE SHRINE OF THE THREE KINGS IN COLOGNE CATHEDRAL, *c.* 1200

life would make a story at all; Maupassant might have described her brilliantly but contemptuously. Chekhov leaves the reader with feelings of tenderness and wonder at the diversity of human nature. This sympathetic attitude towards human frailties and sufferings is a characteristic of the Russians; and in relating simple events in the lives of simple people the great Russian writers were able to imply universal human conflicts and values.

There is no English short-story writer as pre-eminent as the two great masters of the form, de Maupassant and Chekhov. But there are great numbers of English short stories of the most varied kinds—tales of adventure like Rudyard KIPLING's stories of the East, studies in mystery and detection like Conan DOYLE's famous tales of Sherlock Holmes, H. G. WELLS's scientific fantasies (qq.v. Vol. V), and those greater short stories such as Katherine Mansfield's, greater because they illumine aspects of human nature by communicating the deepest experiences of others to the reader.

Katherine Mansfield (1888–1923) is one of the few English writers—A. E. Coppard is another—whose talent found its best expression in the short story. Many modern writers who are best known either as novelists or dramatists have been notable short-story writers as well. There is scarcely a major novelist of the last 100 years who has not also written short stories. Some of the most eminent of these masters of two forms are Joseph CONRAD, Robert Louis STEVENSON, Henry James, James JOYCE, and D. H. LAWRENCE (qq.v. Vol. V).

See also NOVEL; DETECTIVE STORIES.

greatest short-story writers. Gogol and Pushkin were succeeded by TOLSTOY, TURGENEV, CHEKHOV (qq.v. Vol. V), and later Gorky (1868–1936). These and other Russian writers have had a great influence on the development of the short story. They are, broadly speaking, not interested in tales of action, complicated plots, or dramatic incidents, but concern themselves rather with threading the mazes of the human mind and soul. There is often only a slight anecdote or an emotion to form the basis of the story; sometimes it consists of an apparently formless piece cut out of life. The lack of incident may make the pace slow to some readers; but at its best the Russian short story is a revelation of and a commentary on the whole of human nature. For example, one of Chekhov's stories, *The Darling*, is about a dull woman in a small Russian town. Olenka has no individuality of her own; all her thoughts and opinions derive in turn from her two successive husbands, her admirer, and finally her admirer's son. Tolstoy wept when he read this story because, he said, it sprang from a great heart. Bret Harte or O. Henry might not have thought that Olenka's

SHRINES. In the early and medieval church the bones of saints were so venerated that magnificent shrines were made to contain them. Shrines consisted, as a rule, of an inner rectangular wooden box with straight sides, a good deal

EDWARD THE CONFESSOR'S SHRINE IN WESTMINSTER ABBEY, 1268

The base is decorated with a mosaic pattern, called 'Cosmati work' after the Italian makers

smaller than a coffin, and an outer rectangular casing with a gabled top. The shrines of the more famous saints were made of precious metal, gold, silver, or silver-gilt, sometimes studded with jewels; the sides and top of this outer metal box were often decorated with figures or scenes in relief. Miniature shrines, called reliquaries, were made to hold relics of saints; these were also usually made of metal, though sometimes of wood or leather, and they were decorated with enamels and semi-precious stones.

In the earliest days of Christian churches the shrine was kept in the crypt. Later, as it was an object of PILGRIMAGE (q.v. Vol. I), it was placed behind the High Altar so as to be more easily accessible to the public. The shrine itself was raised on a very high base so that it was visible above the altar.

In England no gold or silver shrines have survived, for they were destroyed at the Reformation, but the original wooden coffin into which St. Cuthbert's body was put in 698 is still at Durham. It is fitted inside with a tray, like a

trunk, for the purpose of holding some of the more precious offerings made at St. Cuthbert's shrine; some of its contents were probably added about 240 years after St. Cuthbert's death, when King Athelstan went to Durham. There are in England a number of shrine bases, the most famous of which is the lower part of the shrine of Edward the Confessor in Westminster Abbey. It is of marble and mosaic, made by Italian workmen who were specially brought to the country by Henry III. The bases also remain of the shrine of St. Alban in the Cathedral of St. Albans, and of the Canteloupe shrine in Hereford Cathedral.

In Germany and the Low Countries there are a number of medieval shrines which are still complete with their outer coverings of precious metals, as for instance at Cologne, Aachen, and Xanten.

In later times elaborate figure sculpture was used for shrines, as in the case of the great 17th-century silver shrine of St. John Nepomuk at Prague. This is a silver tomb with life-sized silver angels at each end.

See also TOMBS.

SIENESE PAINTING. The city of Siena is only some 60 miles from Florence, and the Sienese and Florentine schools of painting flourished at the same time; but it is hard to imagine two centres more different in every way. Siena is built on hills, Florence in a valley. The Florentine painters devoted all their energy to mastering the art of representing nature in their paintings by studying perspective, anatomy, and light and shade; while the Sienese paid little attention to these things and had quite different aims. The sum of these differences is that while FLORENTINE PAINTING (q.v.) of the Renaissance looks to us comparatively modern, Sienese painting at its greatest period seems to belong to the Middle Ages.

Duccio, the first of the great Sienese painters, worked at the end of the 13th and beginning of the 14th centuries. The chief influence on his art was the type of painting which had flourished throughout the Middle Ages at Constantinople (see BYZANTINE ART). His most famous painting is a large altar-piece, the 'Maesta', with the Virgin and Child and saints on the front and scenes from the New Testament on the back. In this, though the figures appear flat and unlifelike, the lines of the draperies make up a

Anderson

THE 'MAESTA'—THE VIRGIN AND CHILD IN MAJESTY SURROUNDED BY SAINTS. PAINTING BY DUCCIO (*c.* 1260–*c.* 1320)

Anderson

THE ANNUNCIATION. PAINTING BY SIMONE MARTINI (?1285–?1357) AND LIPPO MEMMI (d. 1347?)

pattern of astonishing beauty, enhanced by the lavish use of gold and painstaking treatment of the details.

The other three important Sienese painters—Simone Martini and Pietro and Ambrogio Lorenzetti—all lived later in the 14th century, at a time when there were no really first-class painters working in Florence. At this time, therefore, the Sienese school of painting was the foremost in Italy, and even, for a short time, influenced painting at Florence.

National Gallery

ST. JOHN RETIRING TO THE DESERT. PANEL OF AN ALTARPIECE BY GIOVANNI DA PAOLO (1403–1482)

Simone Martini was perhaps the most typical of all the Sienese. He was inspired more by GOTHIC ART (q.v.) than by the Byzantine influences of Duccio. But like Duccio he concentrated on grace and beauty of line and richness of effect obtained through exquisite painting of details. Like Duccio, too, he seems to have preferred easel pictures, which give scope for detail, to wall paintings which require breadth of effect. In his most characteristic picture, 'The Annunciation' in the Uffizi Gallery at Florence, the whole of the background is gold; this gives a rich effect, though it corresponds with nothing to be seen in nature. The pattern of the folds of the drapery is of the greatest delicacy; the details, such as the angel's wings and the flowers, are painted in minute and loving detail; and the whole is blended admirably with the elaborate Gothic frame. Simone Martini ended his life at the Court of the exiled Popes at Avignon in the south of France, and he may not have felt out of his element in such an atmosphere where Gothic art flourished all round him.

The Lorenzetti brothers were painters of great power who combined the decorative qualities of Sienese painting with the grandeur and greater simplicity of the Florentine artist GIOTTO (q.v. Vol. V). Consequently their figures are both more human and more monumental than Simone's. The most characteristic Sienese painters of the 15th century, such as Sassetta (*see* Vol. I, p. 331) or Giovanni di Paolo, were far closer to the spirit of Simone Martini than

to the Lorenzetti. In the 16th century Siena still produced painters, one of whom, Peruzzi (1481–1537), was an artist of originality. But all that is most typical in Sienese painting was opposed to the ideas of the RENAISSANCE (q.v. Vol. I), and the style did not develop any further.

See also ITALIAN ART.

SILHOUETTES. These are shadow-pictures, generally portraits. They can be made in their simplest form by placing the sitter in profile between a bright light and a wall, so that his shadow falls sharply on a sheet of paper on the wall; the shadow of the head is then outlined, and filled in with black.

Between about 1770 and 1840 silhouette portraits of miniature size had a great fashion all over Europe. They were known as 'the poor man's miniature', for they were cheap (between a shilling and a guinea) and sittings were very quick, often taking only a minute or so. Until the 19th century they were known in England as 'shades' or 'profiles'; the word 'silhouette' comes from de Silhouette, a finance minister of France, who was said to be so mean that he decorated his house with cut-paper pictures because they cost him nothing.

There were several techniques; some painted the silhouette in black on to a white card or plaster, or on to a glass mounted over a white background; others cut out the portrait from black paper and mounted it on white (or vice versa). This method was used by the most famous silhouette artist of the 19th century, Augustin Edouart (1789–1861), a Frenchman who worked mainly in England and America. Machines were also patented which produced silhouette portraits automatically. The 18th-century silhouettes show generally the head only, always in profile, though later Edouart and others produced whole-length figures with an attempt at an illusion of movement; group portraits are rare. Coloured silhouettes, sometimes with the face alone left black, were also made. The silhouette, like the MINIATURE (q.v.), fell out of fashion when the photograph became established in about 1840–50.

See also PORTRAITS.

Victoria & Albert Museum
SILHOUETTE OF A BOY BY AUGUSTIN EDOUART

SILVER WORK, *see* Vol. VII: GOLD AND SILVER WORK.

SIMILE, *see* FIGURES OF SPEECH, Section 1.

SINGING, *see* SONG, HISTORY OF. *See also* Vol. IX: SINGING.

SISTINE CHAPEL, *see* VATICAN.

SISTINE MADONNA, *see* Vol. V: RAPHAEL.

SKYSCRAPER. Tall buildings of many storeys, especially the office-buildings erected in American cities since the 1880's, are called skyscrapers. They were made possible by the invention of steel-frame construction, which allowed walls of great height to be built without a corresponding increase in thickness (*see* BUILDING CONSTRUCTION, Vol. VIII), and they were made practical by the invention of the electric LIFT (q.v. Vol. IV).

The first skyscraper was a ten-storey insurance office built in 1885 at Chicago, the home of many pioneers of steel-frame construction. Further skyscrapers appeared in Chicago and then in other American cities where expensive and restricted sites encouraged growth in an upward direction. The skyscrapers of New York, responsible for the city's romantic skyline, are particularly famous (*see* Vol. III, p. 311). Their foundations rest on solid rock; in London skyscrapers would not be practicable because the clay soil could not carry such heavy loads. Beyond a certain height skyscrapers are not economical because too much of the floor-space has to be taken up by additional lifts. This limit has probably been reached in some of the tallest American skyscrapers, which were erected as much for their publicity value as for their utility.

The earliest Chicago skyscrapers were simple and severe in design and made no attempt to disguise their frame construction; but later the frame was used to support an outer clothing of masonry dressed up in some ornamental period style. The Woolworth Buildings (1913) in New York with sixty storeys in all and the Tribune Tower in Chicago (1922) both have elaborate Gothic-style embellishments. After about 1930 architects began to realize that simplicity was both more appropriate and more effective, and that interest should depend on the dramatic lines of the structure and the pattern made by the hundreds of windows. One of the best, as well as the first, examples of this change of outlook was the Philadelphia Savings Building (1929). Outstanding recent skyscrapers are the United Nations' Secretariat, New York (1951), and the Lever Building, New York (1952). Both these are of the flat 'slab' type, a change from the

Gottscho-Schleisner

NEW YORK SKYSCRAPERS. LEFT, CHRYSLER BUILDING
RIGHT, DAILY NEWS BUILDING

older square-tower type; the sides are faced almost wholly with glass.

At Rockefeller Centre, New York (1950), a group of fourteen skyscrapers, designed as a whole, covers several city blocks. In the centre is the R.C.A. Building of seventy storeys. The tallest skyscraper of all is the Empire State Building, also in New York (1931), which has eighty-five main storeys, and a total of 102.

See also MODERN ARCHITECTURE.
See also Vol. III: NEW YORK.

SONATA. At first the word 'sonata' was used to distinguish instrumental compositions from CANTATAS (q.v.), which were sung compositions, and, in the broadest sense, a sonata is simply a piece of music which is played by an instrument or instruments, and not sung by voices. Many fine works of different types have been called sonatas by their composers. About 1600, for example, Giovanni Gabrieli wrote a *Sonata pian' e forte* (meaning sonata soft and loud) for two choruses of brass instruments; Domenico Scarlatti (1685–1757) left some 600 pieces for harpsichord entitled sonatas, which are mostly quite short and usually in a simple binary form (*see* MUSICAL FORM, Section 2). His great contemporary, J. S. BACH (q.v. Vol. V), wrote many exceedingly different works for different instruments, all called sonatas. Some were violin sonatas, others were entitled 'Sonatas or Suites', that is, collections of dance movements, and in a few cases the instrumental introductions to church cantatas were also called sonatas. There were also six Trio Sonatas for organ.

The structure of the classical sonatas of Haydn, Mozart, Beethoven, and their successors, however, has recognizably consistent characteristics. It can be traced back to the early 17th century, when it was often the custom to accompany madrigals with instruments (*see* SONGS, Section 2); as the madrigals became more difficult to sing, this practice became more frequent. Later the madrigals were often performed solely as instrumental pieces, and then purely instrumental pieces (called *canzonas*) were composed in imitation of them. Other sources of the classical sonata include dance movements and instrumental introductions and interludes from OPERAS (q.v.). The classical sonata consisted of several contrasted pieces or movements played together as one work. The suite was simply a collection of dance movements (*see* DANCE MUSIC): the sonata might or might not include dance movements but it was not based on these, and the first movement at least was usually of a much more intricate nature. There was no measure of agreement upon the number of movements in a sonata, but there was a practical agreement that the movements should be contrasted as regards speed (quick, slow, and so on) and as regards their general style (for example, fugal, dance, or free movements). Because of their origin in the instrumental *canzonas*, sonatas at first were usually composed for several instruments; but the development of KEYBOARD INSTRUMENTS (q.v. Vol. IX), which were capable of providing all the necessary harmonies alone, tended to reduce the number of instruments.

Trio sonatas for two solo instruments accompanied by a keyboard instrument became a very popular form of musical composition in the 17th and 18th centuries. Trio sonatas for organ or pedal harpsichord were in three parts: one played by the left hand, one by the right, and one by the feet. The so-called *Sonata da Chiesa* (Church Sonata) consisted of two contrasted pairs of slow and quick movements in severe and formal style, and the *Sonata da Camera* (Chamber Sonata) consisted mainly of dance movements, and was more like a suite. Corelli (1653–1713) composed such sonatas and also solo sonatas for violin, accompanied by a keyboard instrument. He was a very great violinist himself, and he founded a school of famous violinist composers in Italy who not only aided the development of the sonata there but also had great influence on the sonatas of composers elsewhere, such as PURCELL (q.v. Vol. V) in England and, later, J. S. Bach in Germany.

It was left to the period after J. S. Bach and largely to that great composer's own sons (particularly C. P. E. Bach) to arrange the classical sonata in the form we know it: that is, a work for one or two solo instruments, usually in three or four movements. C. P. E. Bach established the 'sonata form' (*see* MUSICAL FORM, Section 4) which, because the first movements of sonatas are almost invariably written in this form, is sometimes called 'first movement form'.

HAYDN (q.v. Vol. V) was the first really great composer to write classical sonatas. In a long life he made clearer the outlines of the sonata form and of the sonata as a whole. He introduced the minuet and trio, and was the first to use the rondo frequently. MOZART (q.v. Vol. V) took no great part in the fashioning or developing of the sonata; but his sonatas, though they do not radically differ in structure from Haydn's maturer sonatas, are stamped with his personal qualities and stature as a composer. BEETHOVEN (q.v. Vol. V) made the sonata much more dramatic and expressive. Some sections of the sonata had consisted merely of padding—scale-work, arpeggios, and so on. Beethoven had no use for padding and filled out all such sections with really important musical material. This meant that his movements as a whole were much more closely knit and that their outlines were not so clearly discernible.

Many 19th-century composers, such as Weber, SCHUBERT, SCHUMANN, and BRAHMS (qq.v. Vol. V), continued to write sonatas along these lines, generally for piano or violin and piano. In general the demands upon the performers' technique became more and more severe. LISZT (q.v. Vol. V), one of the greatest pianists who have ever lived and also a considerable composer, wrote a fine Piano Sonata in B minor which is exceptionally difficult to play. It is unusual in that it only has one movement, but it is nevertheless a true sonata in the way it develops and discusses musical ideas and in the balance between its contrasts.

An essential feature of 'first movement form' is the contrast in character between the two principal subjects. But contrast between one movement and another plays an even larger part. The second movement, for example, is often a slow lyrical movement, a kind of instrumental song. This balances the more energetic first movement which is concerned rather to discuss and argue musical ideas than to sing a lovely melody. The third movement is probably a dance movement—a minuet and trio, or, after Beethoven, a scherzo (a quickened form of minuet) and trio. The last movement is often even quicker, and usually more intricate in design: often it is in sonata form (or some modification of sonata form) or in rondo form (*see* MUSICAL FORM, Section 5).

A sonata never rigidly follows any hard and fast outlines, and Liszt's Sonata shows how the form is always subject to the demands of the musical material. This, though always true, became increasingly so when Beethoven constantly modified musical forms to enable him to express what he had to say more perfectly and directly. In our own times composers often write sonatas with the broad outlines of the classical sonata, but they do not hesitate to make use of recent musical developments; typical is Constant Lambert's Piano Sonata, which shows the influence of JAZZ (q.v.). On the other hand, modern sonatas are often only sonatas in the broader sense of 'music which is played'. They show, however, the essentials of sonatas in the sense in which the word has been used since C. P. E. Bach: they have a large-scale musical form of some kind; they present balanced contrasts as regards speed and the character of the music; and they present and seriously develop musical ideas in purely musical terms—that is, they are not, for example, primarily concerned with telling stories, as PROGRAMME MUSIC (q.v.) is.

See also CHAMBER MUSIC; MUSICAL FORM; MUSIC.

SONG, HISTORY OF. 1. A song is a short composition, the meaning of which is conveyed by the union of words and melody; thus it

ar torte departille en mannt ettur dotus.   rpriftrent contre por teefte achrison.
u leftone durat fort fu et vigrous.   a mort curent une par mult gnt traison.
ardi e conquerant e engnnus.   ne ancient mande par menite nation.

Larousse

14TH-CENTURY MINSTRELS
From a French manuscript of 'The Romance of Alexander' (*Bibl. Nat. MS. Fr. 24364*)

belongs equally to poetry and music. Indeed, many forms of poetry were first composed as songs. In ancient Greek drama LYRICS were sung by the chorus and ODES (qq.v.) were originally intended to be sung. Singing, either accompanied or unaccompanied, has always played a large part in music.

2. TROUBADOURS. During the Middle Ages music was provided in the castles and houses of the rich by MINSTRELS (q.v. Vol. IX) who were employed by a wealthy lord or who wandered from place to place. Their songs were often composed by poet-musicians, mostly of noble birth, who wrote love-songs and songs in praise of princes and of their noble deeds. The most famous of these were the Troubadours, who flourished in Provence from the end of the 11th century for about 200 years. In northern France similar composers of courtly songs were called *Trouvères* and in Germany *Minnesingers* (*minne* means love). The poems were written in stanzas, each stanza being sung to the same melody. The music was founded on the modes of PLAINSONG (q.v.), but the melodies were adapted to fit the regular metre of the verses. The Ionian mode (*see* SCALES), though discouraged by the Church, was most commonly used for secular songs, and, as this is similar to the modern major scale, some of these early tunes sound more familiar to our ears than the contemporary church music.

The refined and polished songs of the troubadours appealed mainly to the Courts and nobles. The songs of the people were simpler and dealt with familiar incidents of everyday life, especially of daily work (*see* FOLK-SONG).

By the end of the 15th century the minstrels who carried their songs in their memory had mostly disappeared. The invention of printing hastened their departure, and they were replaced by the pedlar, travelling the countryside with his penny books of BALLADS (q.v.) and his songs, ready made, on broadsheets. One of the last songs of the minstrel period was the 'Agincourt Song', written to commemorate Henry V's victory in 1415.

3. RENAISSANCE SONGS. The period between 1450 and 1600 was a time of great activity in the field of song composition all over Europe, and not least in England, where both Henry VI and Henry VIII, in particular, were accounted composers of merit. The modern system of scales and keys was gradually replacing the old modes: some of the songs were harmonized by the addition of one or more voice parts or were accompanied by instruments. Many Elizabethan plays, especially Shakespeare's plays, contain songs, either Court songs such as 'Oh Mistress Mine' sung by the Court minstrel to the Duke in *Twelfth Night*, or country songs such as those sung by the pedlar Autolycus in *The Winter's Tale*. Some of the finest poetry of the period was set to music and, as often as not, the music matched the excellence of the words.

The well-to-do people of the 17th century often sang madrigals (*see* SONGS, Section 2) in their homes, and would entertain their guests to musical evenings, all taking part as they sat round a table. If there were not enough voices, one or more of the parts might be played on the viol.

The most fashionable form of entertainment in the 16th and 17th centuries was the MASQUE (q.v. Vol. IX), in which acting was accompanied by songs and instrumental music. In these the actor wanted a tune, and the poet wanted his lines to be clearly heard; this was difficult in the madrigal where the part-singers were often singing different words at the same time. Henry Lawes (died 1662) saw that he could satisfy both by making the music fit exactly the metrical accents of the lines and by keeping strict time. In this way he was able to set Milton's *Comus* successfully to music.

4. RECITATIVE AND ARIA. The appearance of opera in Italy at the beginning of the 17th century created something of a revolution in the art of song because of the very great demands it made on singers. With opera the song came into its own as a means of displaying the power and technique of the solo voice. At first the singing was entirely in a form called recitative which, moving as rapidly as speech, provided an excellent test of the singer's diction. If accompanied by occasional chords from the harpsichord, it was called *recitativo secco* or dry recitative; if the words were accompanied by a combination of instruments, it was called *recitativo stromento*, or recitative with instruments.

The aria (or air) was introduced at the end of the 17th century as a contrast to the recitative. There were many kinds of aria, but most of them had orchestral accompaniment and were cast in the same pattern—a first section, a contrasting section, and the first one again. The quality of voice required for singing arias was described as *bel canto* (beautiful singing). Singers often vied with one another in embellishing the melodies which the composers had written. The words did not seem to matter very much so long as the music gave the singer full scope for ornamentation. PURCELL (q.v. Vol. V), avoiding the exaggerated tendencies of many European composers and setting words to music with a fitness which has never been surpassed, brought the art of song to the highest pitch of excellence.

5. NATIONAL SONGS. During the 18th century in many countries, and especially in England, as a reaction against the artificialities of much contemporary music, attention was turned to the traditional songs of the people. For the first time popular songs were composed by educated musicians, many of which, by reason of their enduring qualities, have survived and are called National Songs. They are usually melodious, with a marked rhythm and simple accompaniment, and all the verses are sung to the same tune. Often the songs record contemporary events, such as 'The Vicar of Bray' or 'Admiral Benbow'.

6. LIEDER. In the 19th century the song came to be treated as an independent composition and not, as usually hitherto, as a part of a dramatic performance. The ROMANTIC MOVEMENT (q.v.) led to the composition of music which expressed emotion or told a story, a type of music especially suitable for song. SCHUBERT (q.v. Vol. V) was the first great composer to express in his music the feeling of the poem to which it was set. He set music to the words of the most famous poets of his day, notably SCHILLER and GOETHE (qq.v. Vol. V), and varied his treatment according to their several styles. In *The Trout*, for instance, the accompaniment suggests the flow of water while the voice moves with swift flashes like a fish. Composed chiefly by German musicians, this type of song is called *Lied*, German for 'song'. SCHUMANN (q.v. Vol. V) studied the normal accents of the words, and fitted his music to them, instead of making the words fit the music. Other composers, including BRAHMS (q.v. Vol. V), developed the *Lieder*, making use of the vastly improved pianofortes to write more descriptive accompaniments than had previously been possible. MENDELSSOHN (q.v. Vol. V), in his 'Songs without Words', used the form of the song and its descriptive quality for piano compositions.

Modern song composers owe much to the *Lieder* writers, both in the character of their musical settings, which reflect the spirit of the poems, and in the function of the accompaniment. Originally this had merely supplied to the voice a scanty background on the harpsichord or early pianoforte; with the *Lieder* writers the accompanist became a partner on equal terms with the singer, the composer often demanding from him not only great technical skill but artistic ability as well.

SONGS. Songs may be written for a single voice, for solo voices singing in harmony, or for a choir singing either in unison or in harmony.

SINGING (q.v. Vol. IX) has not only played an important part in SACRED MUSIC (q.v.) and in formal musical entertainment as, for example, in OPERA (q.v. Vol. IX), but it has also been important in the lives of ordinary people, both at their work and at their recreation (*see* FOLKSONG). This article describes some of the different kinds of songs which people have sung for their entertainment.

1. ROUNDS AND CATCHES. These are short 'canons', that is, compositions where the phrases are taken up and repeated exactly by the different parts (*see* MUSICAL FORM, Section 8). They are sung unaccompanied. The first singer leads off, the second joins in at the first phrase when the first singer has reached the second phrase, and so on. 'Three Blind Mice' is one of the best-known rounds. Rounds are an early form of song: the Reading Rota (or round), 'Sumer is Icumen In', for four upper voices and two bass parts, was written in the 13th century, probably by a monk of Reading Abbey. Rounds were especially popular in the 16th century.

Catches are rounds which contain some humorous point in the words: for example, the catch in *Twelfth Night*, 'Hold thy Peace', for three voices, or the 17th-century catch for four voices:

MY DAME HATH A LAME TAME CRANE
4 voices

My dame hath a lame tame crane, My

dame hath a crane that is lame.

Pray gen-tle Jane let my dame's lame tame crane

Feed and come home a - gain.

A CATCH
The voices, all singing the same tune, enter one after another at the star

British Museum
FIRST PAGE OF THE MANUSCRIPT OF 'SUMER IS ICUMEN IN'
A 13th-century English round for six voices

2. MADRIGAL. This type of song for two or more voices originated in north Italy in the 14th century, and was revived in the 16th century, when it became popular throughout western Europe. It seems that the word was first used for poetry of a rustic character, written in the mother tongue; but later it was applied to the musical settings of such poetry, much as the word 'hymn' is applied either to the words or to the tune to which they are set.

Madrigals became known in England through a collection which was brought from Italy towards the end of the 16th century; and for the next hundred years English composers, such as William Byrd, composed madrigals which are as fine as any of the Italian or Flemish ones. The poems, which include compositions by Sir Philip SIDNEY, Sir Walter RALEIGH, and John DONNE (qq.v. Vol. V), are some of the loveliest short lyrics of the period. Many composers wrote their own words. Early in the 17th century *The Triumphs of Oriana*, a collection of madrigals in praise of Elizabeth I by English composers, was published.

Flemish and Italian composers of the 16th century first produced madrigals for four unaccompanied male voices, the upper part having the chief melody, and the three lower parts merely filling in the harmonies; but later five-

Meade Collection

LADIES AND GENTLEMEN SINGING AIRS
Frontispiece to *A Pocket Companion for Ladies and Gentlemen, being a Collection of Songs, c.* 1740

and six-part madrigals appeared, in which the parts were given much greater freedom and were consequently more interesting to sing. Each line of the poem was introduced by one of the voices with a new musical phrase, which was taken up by another voice soon afterwards. Apart from this there were no further repetitions of the music, each line being linked to a fresh musical phrase: for example, 'I will no more come to thee', by Thomas Morley. If one of the voice parts was missing, it could be filled in by a viol—or, indeed, the whole composition could be played by these instruments.

The other types of madrigal are called the 'ayre' (air) and the 'ballett'. The ayre came from Spain and reached its zenith in England in the works of Dowland, whose first book of ayres appeared in 1597. The soprano voice was the most important, the other voices (sometimes replaced by lutes) being in the form of an accompaniment; the melody was repeated for each verse. The ballett was similar to the ayre but with a dance-like rhythm and '*fa-la*' refrains; indeed it was often danced by the singers.

3. GLEE. In the 18th century the madrigal was superseded by the glee. This was set for male voices and sung unaccompanied. It was primarily for solo male voices, the highest part being sung by a male alto, the other voices forming an accompaniment to it. The music was the same for each verse. The glee, which was peculiar to England, was fostered by the many glee clubs which grew up all over the country during the late 18th century.

4. PART-SONGS. It would seem reasonable to describe any song for several voices as a part-song, but in practice the term has a special meaning. It differs from the glee in that it may be sung by any number of mixed, male, or female voices. At first it most closely resembled the ayre, with its chief melody given to the highest voice, the other parts forming the accompaniment; but in recent years the lower parts have been given more importance and independence, so that its form has become more akin to that of the madrigal. Often a separate accompaniment is now added, either for pianoforte or orchestra.

The part-song is again almost exclusively a British production, and is especially popular with choral societies.

See also SONG, HISTORY OF.
See also Vol. IX: SINGING.

SONNET. This is a poem of emotional or reflective character with a definite form, the main features of which are:

(*a*) It has 14 lines; in England each line consists of 10 syllables (5 iambs); in Italy, 11 syllables; and in France, usually 12.

(*b*) Its rhyme-scheme follows one of two main patterns, called Petrarchan or Shakespearian. The Petrarchan sonnet rhymes either

a b b a a b b a ; c d c d c d

or

a b b a a b b a ; c d e c d e.

The last 6 lines, the 'sestet', are sometimes rhymed according to other patterns. This scheme emphasizes the unity of the first 8 lines, the 'octet'. The Shakespearian sonnet rhymes

a b a b c d c d ; e f e f g g.

(c) There is a pause after the octet, so that within the unity of the sonnet octet and sestet are clearly defined. The theme of the sestet is new, but arising out of, or developing from or against, the theme of the octet.

The sonnet form—and its name—originated in 13th-century Italy, where it achieved immediate esteem and excellence. Among early Italian masters of the form are notably DANTE, BOCCACCIO, and PETRARCH (qq.v. Vol. V), each of whom wrote a series of sonnets recounting his devotion to 'the glorious lady of his mind'— Beatrice, Fiammetta, Laura—and mourning that she had died, young and fair. Many of these sonnets have been translated into English, particularly by Rossetti. Dante's sonnets are interspersed in a prose narrative of incidents of his early life, *La Vita Nuova*. Petrarch's sonnet-sequence was published under the title *Rime in Vita e Morte di Madonna Laura*. Petrarch's influence on European poets is immeasurable. By the 16th century the sonnet was a favourite form in all European countries, and, except during the 18th century, it has remained so since.

Wyatt and Surrey, who wrote the first English sonnets, published in *Tottel's Miscellany* in 1557, diverged from the Petrarchan model by closing every sonnet with a rhymed couplet; and SPENSER (q.v. Vol. V) followed their example. This caused the English sonnet to lose the clear balance of octet-sestet, and to resolve itself into three quatrains and a couplet, all independently rhymed. This is the form used by Sir Philip SIDNEY in his sequence *Astrophel and Stella* (1591); SHAKESPEARE (qq.v. Vol. V) also used this form, which is now known by his name.

From the beginning poets used the sonnet to express a mood, a moment, a rapture, a despair. From this naturally evolved the sonnet-sequence —a succession of sonnets each complete but all related, a record of the weather of the soul. And since external events are powerful to alter thoughts and emotions, a sonnet-sequence often contained reference to the external events of the writer's life. Shakespeare's sonnets, poems of incomparable beauty and power, have this extra interest, that they refer to events in his life, sometimes explicitly, sometimes enigmatically; as a document, his sonnet-sequence is of compelling interest. 'With this key Shakespeare unlocked his heart', wrote Wordsworth. The date of their composition is uncertain.

We know that some of them were written before 1598, and that they were first published in 1609. Of the 154 sonnets, 126 express the poet's passionate devotion to a young noble patron. Sonnets 127–154 describe his love for a dark lady, beautiful and inconstant, who betrays him with his friend. From the dedication of the sonnets to Mr. W. H. and other evidence, it seems likely that the patron was either William, Lord Herbert, afterwards Earl of Pembroke, or Henry Wriothesley, Earl of Southampton. Although his identity be uncertain, his immortality is assured by such poems as this (Sonnet XVIII):

Shall I compare thee to a Summer's day?
Thou art more lovely and more temperate:
Rough winds do shake the darling buds of May,
And Summer's lease hath all too short a date;
Sometime too hot the eye of heaven shines,
And often is his gold complexion dimm'd;
And every fair from fair sometime declines
By chance, or nature's changing course untrimm'd;
But thy eternal Summer shall not fade,
Nor lose possession of that fair thou ow'st,
Nor shall Death brag thou wander'st in his shade,
When in eternal lines to time thou growest;
  So long as men can breathe, or eyes can see,
  So long lives this, and this gives life to thee.

Since Shakespeare, KEATS is the only great English poet who has used the Shakespearian form. MILTON's formal master was Petrarch, but his sonnets owe much in substance and spirit to the odes of the Latin poet, HORACE (qq.v. Vol. V). Though he wrote only twenty-three sonnets—and five of those in Italian—his influence over his successors of the 19th century was very great. They followed him in writing not sonnet-sequences but single sonnets; in abandoning the Shakespearian form for the Petrarchan; and in using the sonnet for august themes and great occasions. Milton's sonnet 'On the Late Massacre in Piedmont', for example, can be compared with WORDSWORTH's 'On the Extinction of the Venetian Republic' (q.v. Vol. V).

Wordsworth, indeed, affirms that his first sonnets were written one afternoon after reading Milton's—'I took fire', he says. He wrote some 400 sonnets, of unequal merit; but the best of them, by the greatness of their felt thought, the sweep of their harmonies, above all by the immense variety of their themes, enlarged the sonnet's power. He showed that any theme that was a subject for poetry was a subject for a sonnet:

The world is too much with us; late and soon,
Getting and spending, we lay waste our powers:
Little we see in Nature that is ours;
We have given our hearts away, a sordid boon!
This sea that bares her bosom to the moon;
The winds that will be howling at all hours,
And are up-gathered now like sleeping flowers;
For this, for everything, we are out of tune;
It moves us not.—Great God! I'd rather be
A Pagan suckled in a creed outworn
So might I, standing on this pleasant lea,
Have glimpses that would make me less forlorn;
Have sight of Proteus rising from the sea;
Or hear old Triton blow his wreathèd horn.

John Keats's earliest published poem is a sonnet, as is his last poem. His most notable sonnets are those inspired by ancient Greece—the sonnets 'To Homer', 'On Seeing the Elgin Marbles', and 'On First Looking into Chapman's Homer'—and those inspired by nature. Keats wrote equally fine sonnets in the Petrarchan and the Shakespearian forms.

In 1850 Elizabeth Barrett BROWNING published a sonnet-sequence called *Sonnets from the Portuguese*, celebrating her love and devotion to her husband, the poet Robert BROWNING (qq.v.

Vol. V). The title derives from the 16th-century Portuguese poet Camoens, with whose sonnets, addressed to Catarina, Elizabeth Barrett Browning was familiar.

Another notable book of sonnets, *The Trophies*, written by José Maria de Hérédia (1842–1905), was published in France in 1893. Each sonnet crystallized some moment or event of western European history—from ancient Greece till the Renaissance. Very different from these polished, classical sonnets are those of de Hérédia's English contemporary, Gerard Manley Hopkins, who, in vivid, passionate language, with 'sprung' rhythms, compound words, alliteration, repetitions, and compressions, sings earth's beauty, God's grandeur, and the soul's loneliness and despair.

See also POETRY; VERSIFICATION.

SPANISH ART. There is an old saying that Europe ends at the Pyrenees. Indeed, it is true that Spain, both because of her geographical position and the impact of ISLAM on her history (q.v. Vol. I), stands somewhat apart from the main European tradition. For 7 centuries she was the battle-ground of Christian and Moor, and this long crusade left a legacy of religious fervour that colours the whole of Spanish culture. It sharpened, too, the Spaniards' sense of independence and individualism, so that even today they find compromise and tolerance difficult (*see* SPANIARDS, Vol. I). Mysticism and realism, then, are the mainsprings of the Spanish character. Don Quixote, the visionary, and Sancho Panza, the realist, are the two sides of the same coin (*see* SPANISH LITERATURE).

From Europe Spain derived the great Western styles, such as ROMANESQUE and GOTHIC ART (qq.v.), and adapted them to suit her own peculiar conditions. Though less dominant, the influence of MOORISH ART (q.v.) is equally evident. The Moors who remained under Christian rule continued to

Mas

COURTYARD IN THE ROYAL ALCAZAR, SEVILLE
This courtyard was built in the early 16th century by *Mudejar* craftsmen

practise their traditional crafts, creating a blend of European and Oriental elements called the *mudejar* style. They were particularly skilled in the use of brick and stucco, and as makers of pottery and tiles they were unsurpassed. Moreover, it was from Moorish examples that the Spaniards seem to have acquired their characteristic passion for lavish ornamentation.

In keeping with the Spanish character, Spain's art tends to swing between extremes—extreme realism or fantasy, extreme austerity or exuberance. Philip II's bleak palace, the Escorial near Madrid, is as authentically Spanish as the extravagantly decorated sacristy of the Carthusian monastery at Granada, a late but masterly example of the fusion of European and Moorish elements. In painting, too, the ecstasies of El Greco are matched by the realism of José de Ribera, while in Goya fantasy and realism go hand in hand.

When the canons of Seville decided to build their cathedral in 1400, they determined to make it so vast that men should think they were mad. So today Seville boasts the world's largest Gothic cathedral, while those of Toledo, Burgos, and Gerona are scarcely less huge. This passion for extremes explains why the ideal of CLASSICAL ART (q.v.)—balanced, serene, and restrained—never took deep root in Spain. Strictly speaking, she had no RENAISSANCE (q.v. Vol. I) as other European countries had. In architecture she took over the classical forms and decoration and applied them profusely to Gothic structures, producing a style known as 'plateresque' from its similarity to silversmiths' work (*platera* means silverwork). Similarly in painting, classical mythology was either parodied or reduced to the terms of everyday life, as in Velazquez's 'Topers'. Spanish artists avoided the nude. Yet, it would be wrong to suppose that VELAZQUEZ (q.v. Vol. V), who twice visited Italy, or his contemporaries such as the sculptor Martínez Montañés were entirely unaffected by the classical ideal; its influence is visible, not in their themes, but in the clarity, balance, and sense of proportion with which they handled them.

Though Spanish painting has a long history, going back to the prehistoric drawings in the Cave of Altamira (*see* PREHISTORIC ART), until the late 16th century Spanish and Portuguese artists followed the lead of other countries, especially of Italy and Flanders. The realism

Mas

ST. BRUNO. DETAIL FROM A PAINTED WOODEN FIGURE BY MANUEL PEREYRA (DIED 1667), IN THE MONASTERY OF MIRAFLORES, BURGOS

The Saint, gazing in ecstasy at the Cross, is an example of the realism combined with religious fervour found in Spanish art

of Flemish painters had a great influence on them, as is shown in the altar-piece consisting of six panels by the Portuguese painter Nuño Gonçalves. In the 15th and 16th centuries Spanish seamen and explorers were building up her Empire and bringing wealth and prosperity. In 1492 Granada, the last Moorish stronghold, fell, and Spain, now mistress of her own country and with all the wealth of the New World soon to further her political and artistic enterprises, was set to become a great power. The next century saw the emergence of a specifically Spanish school of painting. Its first great figure, however, was a foreigner from Crete, known as El GRECO (the Greek) (q.v. Vol. V).

El Greco introduced from Italy a style of painting distinguished by its love of the unreal, of distortion, elongation, and strident colouring. He used this style so expressively that he made it the means of capturing on canvas the intensely religious spirit of contemporary Spain, thereby creating an art that is unmistakably Spanish. Later 17th-century painters, such as Ribera, Zurbarán, Valdés Leal, and Velazquez (in his early days), used a realistic treatment for their subjects, however lowly or gruesome, heightened by extreme contrasts of light and shade. Velazquez enriched this realistic style with the poetry of light, colour, and atmosphere. Unlike most of his fellow artists, he painted few religious pictures. As the Court painter, he had to paint subjects chosen by the king; he was not dependent for his livelihood on commissions from the Church, like his great contemporary, Zurbarán, for instance, who is best known for his paintings of austere monks and friars.

El Greco interpreted the mystical element in the Catholic religion, while Zurbarán excelled as the interpreter of the ascetic element; Murillo (1617–82) was the perfect devotional painter. At first Murillo painted naturalistic subjects, groups of Spanish gipsies and beggar children, for example; but later he was influenced by the BAROQUE ART (q.v.) of Italy, with its fondness for heavenly visions bathed in light, for ecstatic expressions, flying angels, and expansive gestures. His pictures, in spite of their theatrical effects and self-conscious expressions, are far more lively and varied than those of the more single-minded Zurbarán. Baroque art survived in Spain until the very end of the 18th century, the last great work of Spanish Baroque painting being the early paintings of GOYA (q.v. Vol. V) in the church of San Antonio de la Florida at Madrid. But Goya developed a realism and intensity of feeling which enabled him to comment on the characters and events of his time with great originality (*see* p. 351).

As with painting, Spanish sculpture of the Middle Ages was strongly influenced by other countries, particularly France. One of the great masterpieces of medieval sculpture in Spain is the Portico de la Gloria, the richly carved door of the Cathedral of Compostella. Because, according to tradition, the body of the Apostle St. James was buried there, it was one of the most important places of PILGRIMAGE (q.v. Vol. I) in medieval Europe. A distinctively Spanish style of sculpture did not evolve, however, until the 16th century, with the appearance of the sculptor Alonso Berruguete. Subjects were invariably religious, and the artists worked chiefly in wood. Statues were coloured so as to make them as lifelike as possible. Sometimes real hair and clothing were used, particularly for those made to be carried in religious processions.

Wood-carving was not confined to figure-sculpture. No Gothic cathedral, no Baroque church lacks its great carved altar-piece in gilded or painted wood. Sometimes whole interiors are sheathed in gilding. Organ-casings, pulpits, and choirstalls of unbelievable richness dazzle the eye. Especially magnificent are the elaborate geometrical ceilings carved by *mudejar* craftsmen, particularly between 1350 and 1500.

The Spaniards' skill in metalwork was outstanding. No other country possesses anything to compare with the immense wrought-iron screens in her great cathedrals and monastic churches. No less impressive are the huge silver monstrances used for exposing the Sacrament and carrying it in procession, as well as the chalices, candlesticks, censers, altar-lamps, and other items of church plate. Yet, by contrast, there is little domestic silver. In fact, the domestic crafts were rather neglected in Spain. Even the arts of embroidery and needlework were devoted largely to the production of vestments and church draperies. Though it shows the immense importance of the Church as a patron of the arts in Spain, this one-sidedness is one of the limitations of Spanish art. Yet to the Spaniard it would not have seemed amiss, since for him art could have no higher purpose than to serve the cause of religion.

See also MOORISH ART.

SPANISH LITERATURE. Castilian Spanish, the literary language of Spain and now spoken in twenty different countries, began to take shape before the year 900 among restless, wandering shepherds in a corner of Old Castile in north-eastern Spain. It was a countrified form of the everyday Latin once brought to the peninsula by Roman soldiers, traders, mining engineers, and officials, but became greatly altered by the natives of the country (*see* SPANISH LANGUAGE, Vol. IV). The Castilians were forceful, determined people who drove a wedge down among the farmers and fruit-growers in the south, and eventually reached the Mediterranean coast. Their speech was clear and emphatic; while the southern peoples had softer and less distinct forms of everyday Latin, mixed with many words picked up from the Arabic-speaking invaders who had first

WROUGHT-IRON SCREEN IN THE CHAPEL OF THE CATHOLIC KINGS, GRANADA, BY BARTOLOMÉ DE JAÉN, 1520

It is in the 'Plateresque' style. The details, such as the ornament, are Renaissance but the character of the whole is Gothic

PLATE 16   SPANISH ART

ABOVE:

LEFT: PANEL OF THE POLYPTYCH
OF ST. VINCENT
PAINTING BY NUÑO GONÇALVES
(MID-15TH CENTURY)

RIGHT: ST. FRANCIS
PAINTING BY MURILLO
(1617–82)

THE TOPERS
PAINTING BY VELAZQUEZ
(1599–1660)

arrived in the year 711. The Castilians, also, adopted many Arabic words for things and occupations which they had not got themselves.

In the south the earliest Spanish poetry, little songs sung by women, although Spanish in language was not written in a Latin hand-writing but in the characteristic scripts of Arabic and Hebrew, written from right to left and leaving out most of the vowels. The Castilians, on the other hand, wrote long EPICS (q.v.). The first great poem in Spanish, by an unknown author, is the *Poem of my Cid*—a dashing military leader of the 11th century (*see* CID, THE, Vol. V). He was a Christian, but his title, *Cid* ('lord'), is Arabic, and he is addressed in the poem as *Ya* ('Oh') *mio Cid*—much as a modern French soldier will say *Mon général*. This poem is vividly written: there are graphic descriptions, for instance, of a small town waking up, with the Cid and his men hiding outside ready to rush in the moment the gates are open. Yet even the grim warriors in chain-armour notice how lovely the rising sun looks, darting its rays from behind a hill.

Spanish literature is greater than perhaps any other literature in the number and excellence of its BALLADS (q.v.). The ballads succeeded the epic when the minstrels who sang the epics could no longer collect an audience. Indeed a few of the ballads seem like broken pieces of longer epics—probably the popular pieces which the audience liked to hear again. There are many ballads about the Cid, and also about other heroes—ancient kings of Castile, with royal ladies such as Doña Urraca ('Lady Magpie'); great lords and their retainers, gentle and simple; Homeric Greeks and noble Romans; King Arthur and the Knights of the Round Table (*see* ARTHURIAN LITERATURE); the Emperor CHARLEMAGNE (q.v. Vol. V) with his paladins and their ladies; tales of mystery and adventure, and many more which are sheer fairy-tale. Ballads were not chanted by professional ballad-singers, but by everyone—by men on long rides or women putting a baby to sleep, for example. Because everyone kept them in their memories, the long ballads tended to be shortened to a length that could easily be remembered; this improved them as poetry, since the great moments remained while the rest was forgotten.

About the middle of the 16th century Spanish ballads began to be printed. Then the famous Spanish infantry soldiers, the terror of the Netherlands and of all Europe, sometimes carried little books of poetry in their pockets. These either contained ballads, or the beautiful sonnets, eclogues, and elegies of Garcilaso de la Vega, himself a dashing Spanish infantry officer who was killed in action in the south of France.

When in the 16th and 17th centuries drama became popular in Spain, many plays were made from the ballad stories. Drama became one of the greatest of Spanish achievements; public theatres were opened in Madrid—and also in Mexico and Peru—almost as soon as they were in London. Because the plays followed so closely the familiar ballads of the people, being indeed mostly written in ballad verse which the people knew by heart, the Spanish theatre grew up as a 'people's theatre'. The greatest Spanish dramatists were Lope de Vega (died 1635) and Calderón (died 1681) (*see* DRAMA).

Spain's most famous writer and best known outside his own country is Miguel de CERVANTES Saavedra (q.v. Vol. V), who is supposed to have begun his great *Don Quixote* when in prison in Seville in 1597. *Don Quixote* was a completely original work which stands by itself; but Cervantes' twelve short 'novels', published in 1613, would of themselves have established his name. He also wrote poetic romances and many plays, few of which have survived.

After Cervantes, de Vega, and Calderón, there were no outstanding Spanish writers until the second half of the 19th century. From the Spanish American colonies, however, came some fine prose writing: the letters of CORTÉS (q.v. Vol. V) to the Emperor Charles V, for example, and the vivid *History of the Conquest of New Spain* by Bernal Díaz del Castillo, whose work is full of accounts of what he had seen with his own eyes in the conquest of Mexico.

After the Spanish dominions had won their independence from Spain at the beginning of the 19th century, they produced very little literature for nearly 100 years, though Argentina has a *gaucho* (cowboy) epic. The great Spanish poet Rubén Darío (1867–1916), however, came from one of the smallest of the Spanish-speaking American republics, Nicaragua. He was followed, in Spain, by several important poets, including García Lorca who returned to the writing of ballads—not copies of the old ones, but new and exciting poems which he used to read aloud in a warm, friendly voice. There have been several Basque writers, including Pío Baroja, who wrote in the twelve or more volumes of *Memoirs of a Man of Action* the adventures which were supposed to have happened to his uncle, Aviraneta.

The modern novel began in Spain in the 1870's with Juan Valera and Pérez Galdós. Other novelists, including Pérez de Ayala, were reaching maturity when the disaster of the civil war of 1936–9 put a temporary end to Spanish literature. The best writing in Spanish is now coming from South America.

SPECTATOR, THE, *see* PERIODICALS.

SPEECHES, *see* RHETORIC.

SPHINX. This name, which means 'strangler', was given by the ancient Greeks to a FABULOUS CREATURE (q.v. Vol. I). The most famous sphinx, which had the head and bust of a woman, the body of a lion, and the wings of a bird, laid waste the region around Boeotian Thebes. The Muses had taught her a riddle which the The-

bans had to solve on pain of having one of their number periodically devoured by her. The riddle was: 'What is it that has four legs, three legs, and two legs, and when it has most is weakest?' The answer is 'man', who as a child crawls on all fours and in old age walks with a stick—a sort of third leg. Oedipus correctly guessed the answer and so liberated Thebes.

The sphinx appears to have originated in Egypt as a form of the sun god with whom the Pharaoh was identified. The Egyptian sphinx is usually represented as a lion with the head of the king wearing his characteristic wig-cover, though rare representations exist of sphinxes with the heads and coiffures of queens. Occasionally a type of sphinx or griffin having the body of a lion and the wings and head of a hawk is represented, and ram-headed sphinxes are also known as aspects of the god Amun. The most famous Egyptian sphinx is the Giant Sphinx of Giza (240 feet long) which was carved for King Chephren (Khafra) about 2600 B.C. out of a knoll of rock left in the quarry from whence the stone was taken for the Great PYRAMID (q.v.). This sphinx, whose head is a

Griffith Institute

THE SPHINX AT GIZA
In the background is the pyramid of Chephren

portrait of Chephren, was regarded by the ancients as the guardian of the Giza cemeteries.

Representations of such mythical creatures were taken over by the Syrians and Phoenicians who, however, commonly represent the sphinx as feminine and winged. It is probably from this source that the Greek conception of the sphinx is derived.

See also EGYPTIAN ART.
See also Vol. I: FABULOUS CREATURES.

STAGE DESIGN, *see* Vol. IX: STAGE DESIGN.

STAINED GLASS. A stained-glass window consists of numerous small pieces of coloured glass, which are held together by grooved strips of lead; the whole forms a design when daylight is seen through it. The finest stained-glass windows were made in the Middle Ages, and many can still be seen in churches.

1. TECHNIQUE. The great traditions of the craft are based, not on the painting of colour on glass, but on the cutting and assembling of small pieces, each of which already has a distinctive colour. The colour was produced by mixing metals with the molten glass before this was poured out in sheets to harden (*see* GLASS-MAKING, Vol. VII); thus the glass was stained right through. There was one exception to this rule: the red colour known as 'ruby', made by the addition of gold to the molten glass, would be too expensive and too deep in colour if the glass were stained right through; it was therefore 'flashed', that is, a thin skin of red glass was fused on to a pane of plain glass.

Although colour was never painted on the glass, details were added by brush to give black lines or grey shadows. Thus, on a piece of flesh-coloured glass, the craftsman would draw an eye, a mouth, or the lines between the fingers, or on pieces of coloured glass representing the clothing of sacred figures he would add lines and shadows to suggest the folds of drapery. Lettering on scrolls was also painted on. The pigment was generally an oxide (such as iron rust) mixed with powdered glass. After painting, the glass was fired in a kiln to fuse the pigment on to the glass. White glass could also be painted with 'silver stain' (silver nitrate) which, reacting chemically, coloured the glass yellow.

In modern stained glass, many colours other than ruby are 'flashed' on plain glass. Artists may also paint pictures on glass with thin

Victoria & Albert Museum

THE SOWER. PART OF A 12TH-CENTURY STAINED-GLASS WINDOW IN CANTERBURY CATHEDRAL

coloured ENAMEL (q.v. Vol. VII), which is a form of coloured glass.

The strips of lead which hold together the fragments of glass in a window have a sectional shape like that of the letter H lying on its side, thus ⊥. The pieces of glass are fitted into the grooves on either side of the thick middle bar. Where strips of lead meet at a corner, they are soldered together. To give added strength, a large window is supported by an iron frame.

In the Middle Ages the craftsman broke up his sheet of glass by passing a hot piece of iron across it and then cold water, which caused the glass to break along the line taken by the hot iron. He repeated this process until the piece of glass roughly approached the required shape. Finally he chipped away the edges of the glass to its exact size by breaking off small fragments with a notched tool called a 'grousing iron'. Later, a diamond was used for cutting, but nowadays the glass is cut with a tool bearing a tiny wheel of toughened steel which makes a groove; if the glass is then bent or tapped, it breaks along the line of the cut.

2. DESIGN. The earliest existing stained-glass windows are in Augsburg Cathedral, Germany, and date from the 11th century. By that date the craft was completely formed; but although there are references to coloured windows in early manuscripts, we know almost nothing of the growth of the craft in its early stages.

Little stained glass remains which is earlier than the 12th century, and hardly any in England of that date. In Canterbury Cathedral there are 12th- and 13th-century windows which show how bright and pure the colours of this early glass were, though the range of colours was limited. Many colours, such as 'ruby', were named after precious stones—there was a popular belief that precious stones were actually used in making glass. Other colours were a bright blue, a brownish pink, a fresh green, a yellowish green, and a golden straw yellow. These were used in about equal quantities with white glass of a slightly greenish tint. The design generally consisted of a single human figure, filling the whole window (or 'light', as a window was often called). Sometimes a window consisted of a number of simple geometrical shapes, called medallions, one above each other, each medallion containing scenes, and the surrounding part filled with patterns such as leaf scrolls. When the increasing size of the windows made it necessary to support the glass with iron bars, these were designed in geometrical shapes to emphasize the medallions. The grandest series of early windows is at CHARTRES CATHEDRAL (q.v.).

In the 14th century colours became more varied and not so bright, and there were more shades of each colour. In addition to the dark pigment used for drawing details on the glass, patterns were painted on white glass with 'silver stain'. The designs at this time were lighter and yet more elaborate—just like the architecture of the period, which was often imitated. The subjects were usually standing figures which were designed to look like statues in a niche. In the 13th century this niche had been a simple arch above the head, but in the 14th century the arch grew into an elaborate canopy, and later into a picture of a great steeple, full of pinnacles, flying buttresses, and niches, which quite dwarfed the figures or scene beneath it. The simple forms of Perpendicular architecture set off to advantage these elaborate windows (see GOTHIC ART). Fourteenth-century glass remains in Tewkesbury Abbey, Gloucester Cathedral, and many Gloucestershire churches.

In the 15th century figures were still placed under canopies; but they are not so overpowering either in size or colour, for a great deal of white glass was used, enriched with yellow stain. Indeed, there is often little colour in English 15th-century stained glass—only a few jewels of red and blue set in surroundings of silvery white. This was partly a matter of artistic choice and partly economic—the result of wars and the Black Death—for the coloured glass, being mostly made on the Continent, had to be imported, while the white glass was made in England. The Minster and many of the churches in York have fine 15th-century windows, as well as earlier glass (see Colour Plate opp. p. 80).

A medieval glass-worker would probably have a number of standard designs to hand, which may have been derived from the pictures in ILLUMINATED MANUSCRIPTS (q.v.), and he would use these designs as the basis of many subjects. For example, the main lines of a design showing the visit of the Three Kings to Bethlehem would also do for the visit of the Queen of Sheba to Solomon, or for any other subject where one figure kneels before another; and one saint could easily be changed into another by altering the emblem he or she held. From the sketch a 'cartoon' or full-sized drawing was made from which the exact shape of each piece of glass could be traced.

Throughout the Middle Ages the designs were always in accord with the purpose and material of the windows. No attempt was made to suggest depth, which would be unsuitable in glass; the compositions were suited to the shapes they filled, and the leading which held the pieces of glass together was made to form part of the design. But at the end of the 15th century, with the growing interest in perspective and realism of RENAISSANCE ART (q.v.), windows became more like glass pictures, the figures being made to appear solid and round. In France the spirit of stained-glass work was never quite lost, in spite of the new tendency, and in England, especially in the north, the medieval tradition continued for some time. Windows in the new style were imported from the Netherlands or made under Flemish masters brought over to teach the London craftsmen. In the church at Fairford, Gloucestershire, for example, the windows were filled with glass made about 1485 either abroad or in this country under Flemish direction. These windows just manage to keep the balance between the two ideas—stained glass as a pattern of pieces and as a picture painted on glass.

Soon the medieval tradition was completely

THE CRUCIFIXION. PART OF THE WEST WINDOW IN FAIRFORD CHURCH, *c.* 1485

lost. In the 16th century the windows of large houses were decorated with medallions, often imported from Germany, which were not stained glass but white glass painted in colours. The practice of painting glass continued until the 19th century, when there was a revival of interest in medieval art. Now stained-glass windows are made in almost precisely the same way as in the Middle Ages.

Much of the stained glass which once filled the windows of our churches has been destroyed, but it is often still possible to see fragments of early glass in the upper parts or 'heads' of the windows.

See also CHURCH ARCHITECTURE, ENGLISH; GOTHIC ART. See also Vol. VII: GLASS-MAKING.

STANZA, *see* VERSIFICATION, Section 4.

STATUE, *see* SCULPTURE; MONUMENTS; STONE CARVING; BRONZE SCULPTURE; WOODCARVING.

STILL-LIFE PAINTING. This term describes paintings of collections of objects, usually small and arranged on a table. Collections of glasses, jugs, flowers, fruit, vegetables, dead game, and so on are the subjects most usually painted in pictures of this type.

It is, by its nature, a humble and homely type of painting, calculated to appeal to the tastes of ordinary people. From the painter's point of view it has many advantages, chief of which, perhaps, is that the painter may work quietly in his studio and spend as long over a picture as he likes, for there are no figures to move about, or problems, as with landscape, of changing lights. This factor is very important for timid or temperamental painters, such as CÉZANNE (q.v. Vol. V) who had a particular fondness for still life.

In many 15th-century pictures, both Flemish and Italian, there are delicate and detailed paintings of fruit and flowers in the background of figure pictures; but still life, as a re-

National Gallery

FLOWER PIECE BY THE DUTCH PAINTER JAN VAN HUYSUM (1682–1749)

Archives Photographiques

MENU DE MAIGRE. STILL-LIFE BY J.-B.-S. CHARDIN (1699–1779)

cognized branch of painting, did not become common until the 17th century. Then it was practised by a great many Dutch and Flemish painters who are now known as 'minor masters'. Some Dutch and Flemish artists specialized in flower-pieces, which they painted with astonishing skill and delight in minute detail.

The French 18th-century artist, Chardin, who painted many still-life pictures, is, perhaps, the greatest of all masters of this type of work. He painted with more breadth and less minute precision than the 17th-century Dutch and Flemish painters, but he noted everything— the bloom on a peach, the glint of light on a glass—and he painted in rich and glowing colours.

There were other painters of still life in the 18th century in France, but after them it was nearly 100 years before any fine still-life pictures were again produced. Then the artist who is now regarded as the most important exponent of POST-IMPRESSIONIST PAINTING (q.v.)—Paul Cézanne—devoted much of his life to it. He hated being disturbed, and so enjoyed the peaceful nature of still-life painting. What interested him was not the play of light on the apples and jugs which he painted, but their solidity and firmness. Cézanne's Dutch contemporary, Vincent Van Gogh, painted still life from a different and abnormal point of view: the kitchen chairs or flower vases in his pictures seem almost alive and moving.

Since Cézanne, many artists have painted still life, though the way they have treated it has varied greatly. Some painters have become more interested in the patterns made by the arrangement of the objects on a table than in the objects themselves. Such painters as the Cubists looked at an apple, not as a piece of fruit, but as a sphere which, placed beside an object of different shape, such as the cube of a loaf of bread, would make an interesting pattern. These cubist painters, particularly Braque and Léger, have concentrated especially on still

Rijksmuseum, Amsterdam

'STILL LIFE WITH ONIONS' BY VINCENT VAN GOGH (1853–90)

life, though they also interpret other subjects in the same way (*see* MODERN ART).

STONE CARVING. Many primitive peoples have carved in stone. Some 15,000 or more years ago men of the Stone Age scratched figures or symbols with a sharp flint tool on the rocky walls of caves (*see* PREHISTORIC ART).

Egyptian sculptors seem to have been the first to attain sufficient skill in stone carving to be able to make grand stone images. A 6-foot statue of the god of fertility, Min of Captos, dates from before 3000 B.C. It is carved out of fossiliferous limestone, the surface carefully 'dressed' with hammer blows, and with the human form only roughly suggested. After 3000 B.C. Egyptian sculpture is closely connected with architecture, and both serve the gods and the pharaohs (*see* EGYPTIAN ART). Many statues were made as symbols of the after-life, at first of pharaohs only, later also of great and wealthy nobles; one Egyptian expression for sculptor means 'He-Who-Keeps-Alive'.

Limestone, which is fine-grained and comparatively soft, was generally used. The stone was frequently painted in natural colours, but sometimes it was covered with plaster, in which the finer details were worked, and then painted.

Cairo Mus.

BLACK GRANITE SPHINX OF AMENEMHET III, MIDDLE KINGDOM

The general shape is simple and compact and the details of hair and inscriptions finely incised

Anderson

LAOCOÖN AND HIS SONS BEING KILLED BY SERPENTS

Greek Hellenistic marble group, *c.* 25 B.C. Great technical skill is needed to carve such a complicated group with unsupported limbs

Other stones used were black, grey, and green granite, black basalt, and dark grey diorite—harder stone with a fine grain and capable of delicate carving, though the hardness of the stone enforced a simplicity of shape. Coarser-grained red granite was used for colossal statues. The carving was done with metal tools.

Egyptian sculptors often decorated the walls of temples and tombs with reliefs, which were usually incised in low relief and were originally painted; but from the Middle Kingdom onwards (after about 2150 B.C.) there are also hollow or sunk reliefs (*see* p. 125).

Mesopotamian stone sculpture was not nearly so fine as the best Egyptian sculpture of the Old and Middle Kingdoms (*see* SUMERIAN, ASSYRIAN, and BABYLONIAN ART). This is, perhaps, to some extent because stone was scarce in Mesopotamia and had to be brought long distances by perilous journeys. However, diorite and black granite from Arabic countries and basalt and clunch (a chalky stone) from Asia Minor and from farther north were procured, though such expensive material was only used for the royal houses and religious ceremonial. Monuments were almost always cut in very low relief to match the incised lettering which covered the figures and told their story. Statues were also occasionally made; there is a diorite statue of the priest-king Gudea enthroned with a kind of turban on his head, his enormous hands folded and exposing an extremely muscular right arm. All shapes of the head and body were as far as possible reduced to those of sphere and cylinder, and the surface treatment, including the lettering, was of great precision and highly polished (*see* Vol. I, p. 457).

Greek and Roman sculptors used marble, which is very hard to cut but in which the most precise contours and finest details of drapery and features can be carved. The Greek marble, quarried at Pentelicus and Paros, is very enduring and has a beautiful texture and, often, colour. The Roman marble from Carrara is white.

Greek and Roman carvers used various types of chisels with smooth or tooled edges, and often files for finishing; the drill for making deep holes did not come into use until late Roman times. Greek marbles were rarely polished, but they were sometimes painted. Before carving the marble the Greeks probably made a small model, but we cannot be sure of this because they would have made it in perishable materials such as wax, clay, or plaster. Half-finished statues which have been excavated suggest that Greek sculptors worked directly on the block. First, they cut round the outline of the front and the back, giving the figure something of the character of a plank, and then they rounded the forms. Although works of sculpture are discussed in Greek literature, and sculptors are often highly praised, they do not seem to have enjoyed a very high social standing (*see* GREEK ART).

The special contribution of Roman sculptors, who first learned from Greek colonists and slaves, is their highly realistic and individual portrait sculpture and their grand historical reliefs with which they decorated triumphal arches, columns, and tombs. In these they introduced the illusion of space and depth (*see* ROMAN ART).

In the Middle Ages, stone sculpture was used predominantly in church architecture and religious monuments and effigies (*see* TOMBS). The medieval stone-mason carved architectural mouldings, capitals, and window tracery, as well as figures and decorative work. Building stone, such as limestone and grey and yellow sandstone, was used almost exclusively for sculpture. Harder stones were used for special types of work: smaller objects, such as the font in Winchester Cathedral (see p. 157), were carved in black marble from Tournai in Belgium, and dark marble from the Isle of Purbeck was often used for tombs.

The medieval carver did not make a model, as far as we know, but a drawing. He worked the stone with chisel and hammer (the earlier sculptors probably also used an axe for the rough cutting). The carved figure was usually finished with gesso (plaster) and colour, which protected the stone from the weather. Considerable traces of this treatment can often be seen on medieval carvings. Very early in the Middle Ages, capitals and minor ornamental work were sometimes carved after having been

National Buildings Record

THE MURDER OF THOMAS BECKET. VAULT BOSS IN EXETER CATHEDRAL, 14TH CENTURY

Though high up in the roof the details are finely carved. Remains of painting can be seen

put into position. Later, the carver invariably worked on the floor of the workshop, and then hoisted the completed figure into its place (*see* GOTHIC ART).

The technique of the sculptors of the Italian Renaissance is much better known to us than that of earlier periods. At that time artists were conscious that they were helping to create a civilization by reviving some of the ideals of the ancients (*see* ITALIAN ART). They discussed their problems in great detail, for they believed that the artist must work with his brain as well as his hand. ALBERTI (q.v. Vol. V) expressed their faith when he wrote: 'The arts are learned by reason and method; they are mastered by practice'. The intellectual and social status of artists rose; the master craftsmen of the past, who usually remained unnamed, were replaced by known personalities, the equals of philosophers and poets. Marble, once used by the ancients, was again the chief material, and great attention was paid to the perfecting of technique.

DONATELLO (q.v. Vol. V) and his contemporaries worked from small models, but by the mid-16th century it was usual to create a full-size model in clay or wax. MICHELANGELO (q.v. Vol. V), however, always preferred to make small and probably fairly rough models. He believed that the sculptor should reveal the figures seen by his mind's eye within the stone

Alinari

THE PROPHET JEREMIAH. MARBLE STATUE BY DONATELLO
ON THE CAMPANILE, FLORENCE

The strong modelling of the features and drapery enables
the details to be seen from below

by cutting direct into the block from the surface. He took enormous care in selecting his marble block for a piece of work. Other sculptors normally transferred the measurements from the full-size models to the block with the aid of mechanical devices. First they used compasses of varying sizes, then a special apparatus—probably some kind of frame—which was fixed above the head of the model and from which plumb-lines descended to various important points on the figure; this made it possible to measure the height and projection of the outlines of the model. By placing a similar apparatus above the block of stone the sculptor's assistants could cut down the block until the points measured by the plumb-lines were reached. Then the master himself would complete the figure by carving and polishing its surface.

In the early 19th century, a more exact machine was devised to transfer the measurements of the model to the block. The model was placed on a pedestal bearing a number of measurement marks. A block of stone was placed on a similar pedestal bearing similar marks. A 'pointing machine'—an apparatus consisting of long, movable metal arms—was then arranged so that one arm touched a point on the model while another arm touched a mark on the pedestal below. The arms were locked and moved across to the other pedestal, and an appropriate measurement marked on the block of stone. A hole was drilled into the stone at this point until it reached a depth corresponding to the required point on the model. This process was repeated until the stone had been drilled at a number of places. An assistant then cut away the stone to the bottom of all the holes, and the result was a block of stone shaped roughly like the model. The pointing machine was applied again with finer measurements until the work was completed.

Such mechanical methods had little connexion with true carving, and modern sculptors no longer employ them. Many people believe that the pointing machine was responsible for much that is lifeless in 19th-century sculpture. In England, sculptors such as Eric Gill and Henry Moore have returned to direct sculpture, working the stone itself rather than the machine (*see* MODERN ART).

See also SCULPTURE; BRONZE SCULPTURE; WOOD-CARVING.

British Museum

THE OLDEST COPPER RELIEF IN THE WORLD. FROM A TEMPLE AT AL 'OBEID, IRAQ, *c.* 3000 B.C.

STONEHENGE, *see* Vol. I: STONEHENGE.

SUITE, MUSICAL, *see* DANCE MUSIC.

SUMERIAN ART. Nearly 4,000 years B.C., earlier than the Babylonians or Assyrians, the SUMERIANS (q.v. Vol. I) were established in the land between the rivers Tigris and Euphrates at the head of the Persian Gulf. They had a splendid civilization which flourished especially from about 2800 to 2300 B.C., and then again from about 2100 to 1800 B.C. The art of these

centuries was the basis on which the succeeding BABYLONIAN ART and ASSYRIAN ART (qq.v.) were developed. Most of our knowledge of Sumerian art is derived from the excavation of their cities, such as Ur and Erech (mentioned in the Old Testament), Lagash and Nippur.

The dominant feature of the larger Sumerian cities was a temple-tower (*ziggurat*) built in from three to seven tiers or stages. The *ziggurat* was built of clay bricks, mainly kiln-baked and bonded with bitumen mortar. The bricks were probably brightly coloured, white, black, purple,

British Museum

MOSAIC 'STANDARD' FROM UR
A chief, shown by his greater size, feasts with his followers

PART OF A FOUR-STRING NECKLACE IN GOLD LEAF AND
PRECIOUS STONES, FOUND IN THE ROYAL GRAVES AT UR

made models of animals in copper, sometimes hammered over a bitumen core; but the main use of copper and bronze was for making war weapons—daggers, lances, and arrow-heads. The archaeologist Sir Leonard Woolley found the finest of these small objects in the royal tombs at Ur.

The Sumerian craftsmen made pottery on a wheel, and sometimes coloured their pots deep purple in geometric and other designs. Using tools such as a copper chisel and a drill spun by a bowstring, they were able to hollow stone vessels and to carve reliefs. The stone had to be brought from some distance, and was so valuable that most stone objects were dedicated to one of the temples, the subject of the sculpture being of religious significance. Delicate and careful as was the craftsmanship, Sumerian figures, especially human ones, appear stiff and lifeless. Men are depicted with shaven heads and, like the women, wear short sheepskin skirts or combed woollen tunics, leaving the right shoulder bare (see Vol. I, p. 457).

The Sumerians, who knew the art of writing from 3300 B.C. or earlier, made seals for use on the clay tablets which were their writing materials (see CUNEIFORM WRITING, Vol. IV). These seals were cylindrical engraved stones which, when rolled over the damp clay before it was hardened, left in it an impression of the engraving (see Vol. I, p. 61). The seals were carved with a scene from some religious myth or with a picture of the owner's protecting god, and were also worn as charms. The engraving was often very fine, and the seals are the commonest and the finest witness to the high standard of craftsmanship of these ancient people.

Wood, as well as stone, had to be carried from a distance, and was therefore used, like ivory, only for valuables such as musical and toilet instruments, or for essential purposes such as furniture and the sledges and wheeled vehicles which the Sumerians were the first to use.

See also ASSYRIAN ART; BABYLONIAN ART.
See also Vol. I: SUMERIANS.

dark blue, red, silver, or gold, each stage of the building being a different colour; but few traces of the glazed bricks have survived. A brick stairway led to the summit of this artificial mountain, on top of which stood a small temple. The Tower of Babel (Babylon) was probably a building such as this, and the trees and gardens planted on the high terraces may have later given rise to the name 'Hanging Gardens' (see WONDERS OF THE WORLD). The main temples and buildings of the city clustered round the foot of the *ziggurat*. These buildings had wooden beams, which sometimes supported vaulted roofs, and they also used the arch and dome. Sumerian private houses were generally built so that all the rooms and the staircase faced into an inner court, which was only partly roofed to catch the infrequent rains. The Sumerians decorated their façades with columns and bands of bitumen, into which were inlaid lapis lazuli, shell, and mother-of-pearl. They also made fine MOSAICS (q.v.) by setting variously coloured cones into clay or bitumen.

Inlay work similar to the mosaics is found on many smaller objects such as boxes, lyres, and gaming boards. The Sumerians made jewellery of the most delicate silver and gold work. They

SURREALIST ART. This movement in art and literature appeared in the period between the First and Second World Wars. Its principles were derived from the theories of the psychologist Sigmund FREUD (q.v. Vol. V), who taught that human behaviour and emotion are governed not only by the thoughts and desires of which we are conscious, but also by hidden, 'uncivilized' impulses, which a sort of 'censor' in our minds does not allow to become conscious. These thoughts and desires push themselves forward in a disguised, symbolic form in dreams, daydreams, and in creative art.

The artists and poets of the Surrealist movement believed that art was valuable only in so far as it gave expression to these unconscious wishes. This being so, the real source of the poem or work of art is the unconscious part of the mind, the working of which should not be interfered with by any conscious control. Poets discovered that, simply by letting words and phrases follow one another without conscious effort or control, they could write poems which, although they did not make ordinary sense, yet had a strange and rather disturbing fascination. 'Automatic writing' of this sort never really worked in painting or sculpture, because the technique of these arts requires too much planning; but the German Surrealist painter Max Ernst achieved a dreamlike quality by sticking pictures from old magazines and catalogues on to his pictures in an order dictated by the same random method. Others painted real things and human beings, but combined them in a strange way, so that the feeling of a nightmare resulted. The Spaniard Joàn Mirò painted strange shapes which were almost, but not quite, human or animal.

The aim of the Surrealists was to free the artist's imagination from the 'restraint' of reason, so that he need not describe reality but could express by symbols the subconscious desires of men, which they believed to be on a higher plane than the everyday world ('surrealism' means 'above realism'). The most famous Surrealist, Salvador Dali, a Spaniard, went so far as to imitate the state of insanity known as paranoia, in which the most ordinary objects are regarded by the madman as symbols with hidden meanings. The Surrealists claimed as predecessors all artists in whose

Roland Penrose

L'INQUIÉTUDE DU POÈTE. PAINTING BY GIORGIO DE CHIRICO, 1913

The contrast between the statue and bananas, and the exaggerated perspective effect of the empty background have the disquieting effect which is the aim of Surrealism

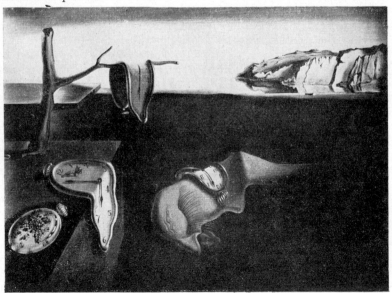

Museum of Modern Art, N.Y.

THE PERSISTENCE OF MEMORY. PAINTING BY SALVADOR DALI, 1931

Surrealist painters distort ordinary objects so that the spectator is made to feel that the everyday world is trivial. The melting watches seem to discredit ordinary ideas of time

work fantasy has been allowed to pass the bounds of common sense—Lewis Carroll and the non-sense poet Edward Lear, for instance (*see* COMIC VERSE and CHILDREN'S BOOKS). In particular they claimed one painter, Giorgio de Chirico, who had painted strangely empty town squares and streets, to which he gave a dreamlike un-reality by over-emphasized perspective and shadows.

Surrealist sculpture obeyed similar principles to those of Surrealist painting and poetry. Sur-realist 'objects'—such as a horrifying tea-set (cup, saucer, and spoon) made of fur—were made largely with the purpose of giving the spectator the disturbing feeling that the world is not all that it seems. Many artists who did not join the movement profited by the way in which it allowed the artist to depart from logical realism, to let the imagination roam freely, and to show things in a new light by placing them in strange surroundings.

See also ART; MODERN ART; MODERN POETRY.
See also Vol. XI: PSYCHOLOGY.

SYMPHONY. The word symphony (or *sin-fonia* in Italian) originally meant simply a piece of music that was played by instruments and not sung by voices. Many short instrumental inter-ludes in 17th-century OPERAS (q.v.) were called symphonies; and much later, in Handel's orato-rio *Messiah* (1742), there is a short instrumental piece in the middle which is generally called 'Pastoral Symphony'.

Composers in the early 18th century, such as Stamitz (1717–57), C. P. E. Bach (1714–88), and Sammartini (1704–75), began to write in-dependent symphonies for concert performance. They had many problems: in particular they had to design movements that would hold the attention of an audience for a considerable time; and they had to organize the available instru-ments into a group that would give them the finest and best-blended sound. They had to learn also to write music that sounded full and harmonious without the co-operation of a key-board instrument, which had hitherto been con-sidered indispensable in music of symphonic character and had been known as the 'continuo' instrument (*see* ORCHESTRATION). Many com-posers contributed to this development, using the experience that they had gained in writing CON-CERTOS and SONATAS (qq.v.); but pre-eminent was Haydn, who during his long life saw and

was largely responsible for the development of the symphony from a short-winded and some-times trivial piece into a great organization of noble sound and wide emotional range.

Many orchestral works which were called symphonies in the time before HAYDN (q.v. Vol. V), and many of the early symphonies of that master, are modest works of slight dimen-sions. The later symphonies of Haydn, and also those of MOZART (q.v. Vol. V), however, are very different in range and style from their early works and contain much of their most profound and spacious music. Haydn wrote about 104 symphonies and Mozart nearly 50. It was against this background that BEETHOVEN (q.v. Vol. V) saw the problems of writing sym-phonic music. He himself did not tackle a symphony till he was 30 years old and already the successful composer of many large-scale works. During the rest of his career he used the symphony for the expression of many great conceptions, and the grandeur of his nine symphonies made it impossible for the name ever to be associated again with music of a light or occasional kind. A composer does not nowadays embark on a symphony unless he is prepared to put into his work his whole powers, and feels that he has something really important to say. This explains the remark, attributed to Brahms, that 'it's no joke to write a symphony nowadays'. Brahms himself wrote only four.

Since the maturer works of Haydn, sympho-nies have been fairly regular in their general form, number, and contrast of movements (*see* chart). They might be defined as pieces of music composed on a large scale for full orchestra, and having one or more movements—a kind of grandiose SONATA (q.v.) for orchestra, in fact. Most symphonies have four movements, but there is no hard and fast rule about this. When a work for orchestra has six or seven movements of a fairly light character it can be called a divertimento or serenade or suite. A miniature symphony is often known as a 'sinfonietta'.

Since Beethoven's time the principal changes in symphonic style have come from the desire of composers to link together all the movements of a symphony by the use of some master-theme, and also from their attempts to associate symphonic form with stories, places, and literary ideas in general (*see* PROGRAMME MUSIC). This tendency was already apparent in Beethoven's 'Eroica' and 'Pastoral' Symphonies (Nos. 3 and

	MOZART SYMPHONY NO. 40 IN G MINOR (1788)	BEETHOVEN SYMPHONY NO. 7 IN A MAJOR (1812)	MENDELSSOHN 'ITALIAN' SYMPHONY (1833)	SIBELIUS SYMPHONY NO. 4 IN A MINOR (1913)
FIRST MOVEMENT	Fairly quick movement in G minor (sonata form)	Slow introduction leading in to a quick movement in A major (sonata form)	Quick movement in A major (sonata form)	Slow movement in A minor (sonata form)
SECOND MOVEMENT	Slow movement in E♭ major (sonata form)	Slow movement in A minor	Slow movement in D minor	Quick movement (scherzo) in F major
THIRD MOVEMENT	Minuet in G minor	Quick movement (scherzo) in F major	Minuet in A major	Slow movement in C♯ minor
FOURTH MOVEMENT	Quick, cheerful movement in G minor (sonata form)	Contrasted quick movement in A major (sonata form)	Saltarello (a quick Italian dance) in A minor	Quick movement in A major-minor

ANALYSIS OF SYMPHONIES OF DIFFERENT PERIODS

This chart shows how the essential outlines of the symphony—the contrast of key, speed, and style of the movements, and the use of sonata form—have not changed

6), and it was much emphasized by Romantic composers of the later 19th century. Berlioz's *Symphonie Fantastique*, for example, is described as 'an episode in the life of an artist', and it illustrates the reveries of a young artist, disappointed in love, who has taken an overdose of opium. It is in five movements. The first tells of his longing for the woman he loves, the second depicts a ball in which he catches fleeting glimpses of her amongst the dancers. In the third movement, 'In the Fields', he wanders aimlessly in a general atmosphere of melancholy, broken by moments of serenity. Then he dreams he has killed his beloved, and the fourth movement is a 'March to the Scaffold'. The last movement depicts his final debasement in a witches' dance. In all these movements, the beloved is represented by one theme, which undergoes many transformations.

The more usual and classical style of symphony, however, has been continued right up to our own times by many composers such as SCHUBERT, MENDELSSOHN, SCHUMANN, DVOŘÁK, BRAHMS, TCHAIKOVSKY, SIBELIUS, ELGAR (qq.v. Vol. V), Mahler, Bruckner, Vaughan Williams, and Walton.

See also MUSIC, HISTORY OF; SONATA; CONCERTO; OVERTURE; PROGRAMME MUSIC.

SYNCOPATION. The music of modern Western civilization, as well as that of many primitive peoples, derives its movement and vitality from regularly recurring patterns of beats or pulses (*see* MELODY AND RHYTHM). These patterns are roughly shown by the division of the music into bars (*see* MUSICAL NOTATION). The first beat of the bar is usually felt to be the strongest, though there may be other accented beats. In a bar of three there is one strong beat; in a bar of four the strongest beat is the first, with a subsidiary emphasis on the third. The other beats are weak.

Syncopation is any interference with this pattern of weak and strong beats, any method by which normally weak beats are made strong or strong weak. Weak beats may be strengthened by such signs as > or ∧ or *sf* (*sforzando*); strong beats may be weakened by tying them to the previous beat so that there is no fresh sound of the note on the strong beat. Or, of course, there simply may not be any notes on the strong beats. A few examples of possible methods of syncopation will make this clear (Fig. 1).

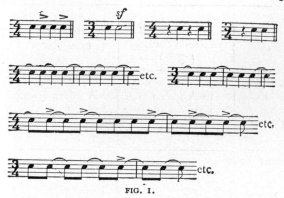

FIG. 1.

To feel the effect of syncopation, however, we have either to remember or to be reminded of the normal pattern of beats. That is why we often find that syncopation is used together with the ordinary accents. In the opening of the last movement of Beethoven's Fifth Piano Concerto (the 'Emperor'), for example, the ordinary pattern of the beats is marked by the left-hand part on the lower stave while the right-hand part on the upper stave is highly syncopated (Fig. 2). Sometimes whole chords are sustained from a weak beat to a strong to produce the effect of syncopation (Fig. 3 a). If this method is employed for too long the listener

may forget where the strong beats really are, and the effect of syncopation will be lost (Fig. 3 b).

As we may see from the above examples, syncopation is no discovery of modern JAZZ (q.v.), although jazz has used it considerably. The madrigal music of the 16th and 17th centuries was often far more rhythmically complicated, although this arose not from the disturbance of regular patterns of beats but from the complete independence of each part and from the reliance of each part on the words for

Coleridge Taylor

FIG. 3.

its accents rather than on beat patterns. Syncopation, in the correct sense, may be said to have grown up in the period immediately before Bach and Handel, the period which saw the fixing of the rigid patterns of strong and weak beats on which syncopation is dependent.

See also MUSIC HISTORY OF.

BEETHOVEN PIANO CONCERTO NO. 5.

FIG. 2.

STONEHENGE. WATER-COLOUR BY JOHN CONSTABLE, 1776–1837

T

TAJ MAHAL. This is a mausoleum or tomb built by the Mogul Emperor of India, Shah Jahan, to contain the body of his wife, Mumtaz Mahal, who died in 1632. It was the practice in Moslem countries to build tombs for saints and famous men and women. The Taj Mahal is a splendid example and perhaps the finest achievement of the Mogul architects. It was built, at a vast cost, by architects and craftsmen assembled from various parts of the Mogul Empire and the Islamic World (*see* INDIAN CIVILIZATION, Vol. I).

The Taj Mahal stands in a garden on the right bank of the River Jumna at Agra, south of Delhi. The approach is by a great portal, through the archway of which is the finest view

Dorien Leigh

THE TAJ MAHAL, AGRA

of the Taj. An artificial canal flanked by tall cypresses leads to the building, which is erected on a plinth. The Taj is built of a translucent white marble. The design of the façade is repeated on each of the four sides. Inside and under the dome is an octagonal vaulted chamber, in the centre of which is the sarcophagus of Mumtaz Mahal and by its side that of Shah Jahan; both are surrounded by a beautiful carved marble screen.

See also INDIAN ART; ISLAMIC ART.

TAPESTRY, *see* Vol. VII: TAPESTRY.

TATLER, THE, *see* PERIODICALS.

TEMPERA PAINTING, *see* PAINTING METHODS, Section 3.

TERRACOTTAS. This is an Italian word meaning baked earth. Terracotta is made from fine clay which is moulded into shape and then baked, like a very refined form of brick. It is generally reddish in colour but varies almost as much as brick does. It was extensively used in early classical Greece both for architectural decoration and for small human figures and household gods. Such figures have been found in large numbers in cemeteries and are usually known by the name of Tanagra, this being the place where the first important discovery of these statuettes was made. Terracotta was used on buildings principally for the decoration of roofs, including figures on the gable ends and decorative tiles and gutters; later these features were carried out in marble. In pre-Roman Italy, where Greek influence was strong, terracotta was used in similar ways (*see* ETRUSCAN ART). These early terracottas were nearly always painted in bright colours.

Terracotta remained a traditional technique in the Mediterranean countries, particularly in Italy. In northern Europe from the Middle Ages till the 17th century it was little used, and then only as a rule to imitate Italian examples. The borderline between terracotta sculpture and very refined moulded brick is, however, so narrow that it cannot be said for certain that the late medieval brick-makers in north Germany, the Low Countries, and eastern England, did not develop, unprompted, something similar to terracotta architectural decoration. Nevertheless, the best-known English terracotta work, of the time of Henry VIII, is strongly Italian in character and in some cases known to have been executed by Italians. The most notable examples are at Hampton Court and at Layer Marney in Essex. At Hampton Court medallions of heads of Roman Emperors and the coat of arms of Cardinal Wolsey are known to be by Italian workmen. At Layer Marney the terracotta work, which is of about the same date, consists of the traceried windows of the house, a cresting of dolphins round the top of the towers, and also a fine canopied monument in the church. All this English terracotta is of a pinkish-cream colour and was originally gilded.

Following Italian practice, terracotta was extensively used throughout western Europe until the 19th century for the making of sketches for sculpture and also for models (*see* Vol. V, p. 207) for BRONZE SCULPTURE and STONE CARVING (qq.v.). From the 16th to the 19th centuries life-size terracotta busts were made

Victoria & Albert Museum

THE ANNUNCIATION TO THE SHEPHERDS. COLOURED TERRACOTTA PLAQUE BY LUCA DELLA ROBBIA (1400–82)

The late Rev. F. R. P. Sumner

TERRACOTTA DECORATION ON THE CHURCH OF THE
CERTOSA, PAVIA

(*see* Vol. V, p. 288). The early examples, such as the bust of Henry VIII, were painted in naturalistic colours, but by the 18th century these busts were usually made only as models, which were then cut in marble.

The real home of terracotta is in northern Italy where, since the 14th century, very expert terracotta architectural decoration and sculpture has been practised. The elaborate decoration of doorways and windows, the capitals of columns, and the mouldings round arches were all carried out in this material. The most remarkable examples are at Certosa di Pavia, a great monastic church of the late 14th and early 15th century, the church itself, the cloisters, and other parts being elaborately decorated with terracotta. The best-known examples of terracotta work are, however, probably the works of the Florentine family of della Robbia. These are coloured and glazed like pottery and include architectural decoration on a big scale, such as the medallion of the arms of René of Anjou (now in the Victoria and Albert Museum), originally set high up on the wall of a palace in Florence, and individual coloured relief pictures and sculptural groups.

See also SCULPTURE; POTTERY AND PORCELAIN FIGURES.

THEATRE, *see* DRAMA. *See also* Vol. IX: THEATRE, HISTORY OF.

TILES, *see* Vol. VII: TILES, ORNAMENTAL.

TOMBS. In ancient times there were three kinds of tomb, the stele, the mausoleum, and the sarcophagus. The stele, which dates from at least the 6th century B.C. and was common in ancient Greece, is an upright gravestone on which is a carving in low relief. The large majority of those found in the Greek territories and islands have either a full-length relief portrait of the deceased or else pleasant scenes of family life.

The tomb at Halicarnassus of Mausolus, who died in 353 B.C. (*see* WONDERS OF THE WORLD), became so famous that the name 'mausoleum' was given to large buildings erected to commemorate the dead. The Nereid monument, another large monument, perhaps dating from 100 years earlier, is now in the British Museum. This is in the form of a small temple standing on a high base. Sculptured friezes decorate the base and surround the temple above the columns. Figures of nereids (sea-nymphs) stand between the columns, and the pediments (gables) are filled with statues.

The third type of antique monument is the sarcophagus, an oblong marble or stone box with carved reliefs on the sides and lid. The lids of sarcophagi are mostly pointed or gabled like a roof, but those found in Etruria and Rome have flat lids on which there is often a recumbent effigy of the deceased (*see* ETRUSCAN ART). The most famous is the Alexander Sarcophagus, found in the royal tomb at Sidon, though of Greek workmanship and dating from the 4th century B.C. All Greek sculpture was painted, and the Alexander Sarcophagus still shows traces of its naturalistic colouring. Antique sarcophagi continued in use into the early Christian era.

After the decline of Rome few sculptured memorials to the dead were made for a considerable time. The form of the sarcophagus with the pointed lid was soon adapted by the Christians on a smaller scale for the purpose of SHRINES (q.v.) and reliquaries. Standing stone CROSSES (q.v.) were also used occasionally to mark the grave of a saint or high ecclesiastic; otherwise almost the earliest form of memorial, and one which continued throughout the Middle Ages, was the flat stone on which a recumbent figure of the deceased was shown. These early figures were usually either incised (an outline cut in the flat stone) or carved in low relief. A few grander tombs are found in England probably dating from the 8th century. At Bakewell in Derbyshire there is a Saxon coffin lid, gabled in shape, on which beasts and symbols are carved. The Hedda Stone at Peterborough is a solid block in the form of a chest with figures carved along the sides, and birds and interlacing ornament on the gable-shaped roof. A very early and unusual example dating from the early Dark Ages is a figure in mosaic on a stone slab found at Tarragona in Spain. A later, coloured enamel figure on a flat slab, at Le Mans in France, dates from the 12th century and represents the father of Henry II.

As the new ideas and designs of GOTHIC ART (q.v.) spread from central and northern France over western Europe in the late 12th and 13th centuries, more sculptured tombs were made

Alinari

GREEK MARBLE MONUMENT (STELE),
c. 500 B.C.

Stelæ were erected to mark graves, often by the roads leading out of a city

F. H. Crossley

PURBECK MARBLE TOMB OF A BISHOP, PROBABLY ISCARUS, c. 1180, IN EXETER CATHEDRAL

Much of the sculpture has been destroyed, especially in France, the Low Countries, Germany, and northern Italy, which have suffered the devastation of wars and revolutions. These countries, however, together with England, were engaged in prosperous trade in the Middle Ages, and consequently were rich and able to develop and spend money on their arts; and it is in these that the finest monuments are found. England and a large part of Italy have, for geographical reasons, been spared the continental wars, and consequently their arts have suffered less destruction. A far larger proportion of medieval tombs have survived in England than in any other country.

In the second half of the 12th century many English tombs were made of the dark grey Purbeck marble from the Isle of Purbeck in Dorset. On the grander monuments the figure of the deceased was carved in relief, though the tombs were still floor slabs. All those that survive represent ecclesiastics, usually bishops with crozier and mitre. The carving is still primitive and very formalized, but the figures, lying stiffly on their backs on the floor, are the first attempts to transfer to permanent stone or marble the dead figure as it had lain in state.

In the Gothic period the sculptured tomb was very similar in all the western European countries, though the art of each country had its own characteristic way of handling the details (see GOTHIC ART). The majority of effigies were stone, but wooden effigies were also made. Metals such as Limoges ENAMELS (q.v. Vol. VII)

and latten (a kind of brass) were imported to England, and the latten gave rise to two new types of monument—the flat engraved plate (see BRASSES) and the bronze effigy. The earliest bronze figures were those of Queen Eleanor, wife of Edward I, and Henry III in Westminster Abbey (see BRONZE SCULPTURE).

Not only high ecclesiastics but also kings and queens and wealthy nobles and knights and their ladies were given sculptured tombs. As the skill of the carvers and masons developed, so the tombs grew more elaborate. The recumbent figure cut in low relief gave way to an effigy cut in the round, a portrait in stone, marble, or gilded bronze of the deceased lying in state, dressed in ecclesiastical robes, robes of state, or armour. At first the figures were idealized, but at least as early as the second half of the 14th century individual features were portrayed, based on the death-mask which had been used on the effigy of the deceased as it lay on the coffin. The folds of the drapery were more deeply and freely cut, the armour on the knights was very detailed and realistic, and the ladies' clothes illustrate the fashions of the day. The tombs themselves, from being mere floor slabs, became raised, the effigy lying at approximately table-height, on what is commonly called a table tomb, the sides of which were carved with figures of saints or mourners, called 'weepers'. Above the tomb there was often a carved stone canopy, generally decorated with the coat of arms of the family. These monuments were elaborately painted and picked out

Crown Copyright   *Anderson*

LEFT: TOMB OF EDMUND CROUCHBACK, EARL OF LANCASTER, DIED 1296, IN WESTMINSTER ABBEY
The tomb was originally richly gilt and painted, and decorated with coloured glass. Along the side of the tomb-chest
are 'weepers'

RIGHT: BRONZE MONUMENT TO POPE INNOCENT VIII BY POLLAIUOLO, IN ST. PETER'S, ROME, 1498
The Pope is shown twice: below, he is dead on his sarcophagus; above, seated on his throne indicating triumph over death

in coloured enamels and glass. In England Purbeck marble gave place to stone and alabaster which were more suitable for painting. Some tombs were free-standing, others were placed in wall recesses.

The pose of the figures became gradually less stiff: the head was raised on a cushion; knights in armour lay with one leg crossed over the other, and sometimes an arm also was taken across the body and the hand grasped the hilt of the sword; husbands and wives lying side by side held hands. Though the majority of tombs had recumbent figures until the end of the 16th century, these were, in some cases, replaced by kneeling figures; a very early example is the tomb of Lord Despencer in Tewkesbury Abbey, about 1375; here the effigy kneels on top of the canopy of his tomb. By the 16th century many painted wall monuments were being erected with husband and wife kneeling facing each other, one each side of a prayer desk, their children kneeling in rows behind them.

Sometimes a pet dog was also included on a monument.

In Italy there was little Gothic art, and there the table tomb with mourners was never general. In the 12th century sarcophagi made of porphyry stone, and copied from antique examples, were erected to commemorate the kings of Sicily, and then became fashionable. The tomb was often surmounted by the effigy and placed in a wall embrasure. The grander these tombs became, the higher they were raised; such tombs may be seen in Rome and also in Florence, where they were made by DONATELLO (q.v. Vol. V) and his contemporaries in the 15th century.

In 15th-century Venice, and even more in 16th-century Milan, the design of the wall monument became a more or less flat representa-tion of the Roman triumphal arch, with the main figure set in the space of the arch. This produced a far more architectural effect than the Gothic canopy. The early sculptures had represented the deceased as a stiff, recumbent figure; but gradually more natural, interesting poses were sought, offering greater scope to the sculptor, until the statue represented the deceased no longer as a dead but as a living man. In the bronze monument erected at the end of the 15th century to Pope Innocent VIII in St. Peter's at Rome, the Pope is shown twice— below lying dead on his sarcophagus, and above sitting on his Papal Throne, his right hand raised in blessing. In England it is not uncommon to see an alabaster or marble nobleman lying dressed in his robes of state as in life, while underneath him lies his marble skeleton

MONUMENT TO LORENZO DE MEDICI BY MICHELANGELO IN THE MEDICI CHAPEL, FLORENCE, WHICH MICHEL-ANGELO BUILT 1520–34

Lorenzo's face in shadow adds to the effect of the brooding figure. On the austere sarcophagus below are figures of Dusk on the left and Dawn on the right, implying the passing of the days. The monument to Giuliano, with figures of Night and Day, is on the opposite side of the chapel.

Anderson

or shrouded corpse. In the 17th century and later, the effigy on the tomb was usually a standing, sitting, or kneeling figure, or lying reclining on one elbow. Life-sized portrait busts were also common. The symbolism on the tombs also changed with the Renaissance— saints and mourners being replaced by the classical heroes and personified virtues, and angels by cherubs. It might seem that the medieval tomb with the figure lying in state was more religious than the later monuments, but this was not the intention. The artists, it is true, with their increased technical skill, did demand more freedom for their art, but the representation of a live instead of a dead man implied to them the Resurrection and triumph over death. In his great monuments to Lorenzo and Giuliano Medici in the Medici Chapel in Florence (1520–34), MICHELANGELO (q.v. Vol. V) used with genius and originality a number of classical themes, some of them not necessarily connected with tomb sculpture. Michelangelo's knowledge of antiquity was based on Rome, not Greece, and he had only a very limited knowledge of Roman art at that. At that time it was thought that antique sculpture was in plain, unpainted marbles—not painted, as we now know it to have been; consequently Italian sculptors replaced coloured monuments by white marble figures, often set against a grey or dark marble background.

The classical restraint of the Renaissance monument gave place in its turn to the Baroque monument, the essence of which is movement and a dramatic free composition (see BAROQUE ART). BERNINI (q.v. Vol. V), the greatest Baroque sculptor, created an entirely free pictorial and theatrical type of sculpture on his tombs (see Vol. V, p. 443). Bernini's influence, though it was very widespread, naturally varied according to the temperament of the people and sculptors concerned. In France and Germany he had a considerable following; the theme, for instance, of the skeleton representing Death rising out of the tomb to slay the person commemorated, which Bernini had used on his monument to Pope Alexander VII, was several times copied—in England by Roubilliac (1695–1762) on the monument to Nightingale in Westminster Abbey. England was, however, less affected than the continental countries by Bernini, for the 18th-century sculptors used more restrained classical figures and draperies.

National Buildings Record

MONUMENT TO JOSEPH WARTON IN WINCHESTER CATHEDRAL BY JOHN FLAXMAN (1755–1826)

The figure was often clothed in Roman costume to imply that it represented a hero (see Vol. V, p. 338). Towards the end of the 18th century the increased knowledge of Greek antiquities led to the use of Greek, in preference to Roman, decoration. The great exponents of this neo-classicism on the Continent were the Italian sculptor Canova and the Dane Thorvaldsen, and in England John Flaxman, who had a European reputation.

See also SCULPTURE; SHRINE.

TONE POEM, see PROGRAMME MUSIC.

TONIC SOL-FA. This is a method of indicating musical notes which can be read by singers who may not know the ordinary system of MUSICAL NOTATION (q.v.). Early in the 11th century, a learned monk named Guido d'Arezzo devised a method for teaching sight-singing. At this time there was no musical notation which indicated the exact pitch of a note, and music had to be learnt by ear. Guido noticed that each line of a certain hymn-tune began one

Ut que-ant lax - is   Re -so -na -re fi-bris

Mi - ra ges -to-rum   Fa-mu-li tu - or-um

Sol - ve pol-lu-t i   La-bi-i re-a - tum

Sanc-te Jo-annes

FIG. 1. HYMN FROM WHICH THE SOL-FA NAMES WERE TAKEN

note higher than the previous line and named these notes from the first word or syllable of each line—Ut, Re, Mi, Fa, Sol, La (Fig. 1). He believed that if a singer knew the hymn tune he would be able to sing any one of these notes at the correct pitch, and so could learn to read other tunes, if the notes were written with the sol-fa names. At a later stage Ut was changed to the Italian form of it—Doh—because it was an easier sound to sing, and Te was added later to complete the eight-note scale. The system spread all over Europe, being used mainly in cathedrals and monasteries, where sight-singing was a necessary part of the training of the choir. The system had its limitations, for the names applied to particular notes, and when the modern SCALES (q.v.) were developed it fell into disuse, mainly because no provision had been made for naming the various sharpened and flattened notes which these scales require. None the less, it was used during the 17th and 18th centuries by Italian singers as a vocal exercise under the name *Solfeggio*.

In the 19th century the system was revived and revised by a Congregational minister, John Curwen (1816–80), who wished to teach his flock to read music at sight. Using the old sol-fa names, he invented the 'movable doh' system, whereby the names were applied, not to particular notes, but to the relative positions of the notes in the scale, whatever its key. Thus, given the keynote, doh, the pitch of the other notes can at once be recalled.

See also MUSICAL NOTATION.

TOWN HALL, *see* PUBLIC BUILDINGS.

TOWNS, *see* Vol. XI: TOWNS, HISTORY OF.

TRAGEDY. Tragedy, the noblest form of drama, tells in dignified language a moving story which usually ends in death. Its purpose is to give pleasure to the audience, not by delighting them as in COMEDY (q.v.), but by moving them to deep spiritual experience, by releasing in them a storm of pity and terror that will expend itself and be succeeded by a 'calm of mind, all passion spent'.

Tragedy has its origins in the religious festivals of the Greek god Dionysus (*see* GREEK DRAMA), and, though it was not an act of worship, Greek tragedy dealt with problems of human destiny, with the relation of man and the gods. The three great tragedians of Greece—AESCHYLUS, SOPHOCLES, and EURIPIDES (qq.v. Vol. V)—used as plots stories from GREEK MYTHS (q.v. Vol. I), which had already proved themselves powerful and moving. Their characters are always men of high moral quality and courage, of intellectual power, and of noble family. They are virtuous, but usually some fatal flaw in their character, matching with fateful circumstances in the story, brings them to disaster. This fateful circumstance is often the doom upon a family, as in the *Oedipus Tyrannus* of Sophocles. Oedipus unknowingly slays his father and marries his mother; but the fatal flaw in his character is his obstinate pride which impels him towards the terrible and foredoomed crisis. These three dramatists differ greatly in their presentation of character: the men and women of Aeschylus's plays are not so much individuals as types, embodying a passion or principle; Sophocles' characters, on the other hand, are real persons, but always noble and remote; Euripides' men and women are more human in their living and suffering.

The Greek dramatists fixed the character and features of tragedy, and the Greek philosopher ARISTOTLE (q.v. Vol. V) analysed and defined its nature. 'Tragedy', he said, 'is essentially an imitation not of persons, but of action and life, of happiness and misery'. Its elements are plot, character, thought, diction, melody, and spectacle; plot being the most important of these. The drama should have unity of action—that is, there should be a single plot, without side-plots, with a beginning, middle, and end; and it should have 'magnitude'. Indeed, everything should match the plot in this quality of grandeur.

Arch. Museum, Istanbul

EURIPIDES HANDING A TRAGIC MASK TO AN IDEAL REPRESEN-
TATION OF THE STAGE BEFORE THE STATUE OF DIONYSUS.
GREEK RELIEF, 1ST CENTURY B.C.

From the 5th century B.C. no great tragedy was written for some 2,000 years. The Romans, who imitated all the Greek art-forms, were not successful tragedians; though it was largely from the unactable, blood-and-thunder dramas of Seneca that the Renaissance writers derived their knowledge of tragedy. The tragic dramatists of Italy, in the 16th century, produced horrific dramas of ruthless tyrants, with bloody murders enacted on the stage—not, as in Greek drama, reported by a messenger. In England, Kyd's *The Spanish Tragedy* (1592), a violent drama of revenge in the Italian style, revelled in atrocities. Kyd's contemporary, Christopher MARLOWE (q.v. Vol. V), not only brought into English tragic drama the power and richness of his blank verse, but also a new emphasis on greatness of personality, as in *Tamburlaine the Great* (1587), and on development of character, as in *Dr. Faustus* (1588).

These were the forerunners of Shakespeare, supreme among dramatists, and at his greatest in drama's noblest form. In the four greatest tragedies of SHAKESPEARIAN DRAMA (q.v.), *Hamlet*, *Othello*, *King Lear*, and *Macbeth*, character and event interact with each other to fuse eventually in disaster. Macbeth and Lady Macbeth, for example, are impelled by ambition to kill their king. Their crime hardens them, making them capable of new crimes. Action, therefore, springs from character, and character produces new actions till the final catastrophe. The weakness or 'fatal flaw' of Shakespeare's tragic heroes may be bad, like Macbeth's 'vaulting ambition', or it may be good, like Hamlet's reluctance to kill, even when he is prompted to revenge 'by

heaven and by hell'. Shakespeare's tragedies excel in their human drama, in grandeur and truth of imagination, in sublime poetry, and in design. Shakespeare took from classical or Renaissance drama all that he wanted, but he did not confine himself to classical practice or theory. His emphasis was on the development of human character rather than on human fate He presented calamities on stage or off, and ignored at his discretion the unities of time, place, and action, which Aristotle had established (*see* DRAMA), transcending them by the unity of feeling which integrates each of his plays. His men and women talk in character, not necessarily in elevated language.

Though other notable tragedies were produced by Shakespeare's near contemporaries—among them the learned and dignified tragedies of Rome (*Sejanus* and *Catiline*) by Ben JONSON, and the revenge tragedies (*The Duchess of Malfi* and *The White Devil*) by WEBSTER (qq.v. Vol. V), a greater poet than dramatist—English tragic drama never again approached its Shakespearian peak. Later in the 17th century, the 'heroic tragedies' of RESTORATION DRAMA (q.v.) by John Dryden and others were pale reflections of the glories that Marlowe and Shakespeare had achieved.

In France, in the second half of the 17th century, the great dramatists CORNEILLE and RACINE (qq.v. Vol. V) consciously imitated Greco-Roman forms in their tragedies, observing the rules of unity built up from the dictates of Aristotle. In spite of these restrictions, however, or because of the tension and concentration they gave, Corneille and Racine wrote tragedies which are matched in power only by the greatest Greek and Shakespearian dramas. The four most celebrated of Corneille's thirty tragedies are *Le Cid* (1636), *Horace* (1639), *Polyeucte* (1640), and *Rodogune* (1644). Corneille's favourite theme was the conflict between love and duty; he did not try so much to interest audiences in the fate of his characters as to impress them by the dignity with which the characters endured their fate. This dignity is equalled by the grandeur of the language and by Corneille's power to move his audience to admiration and terror.

Racine's characters are more moving, more human and impassioned than Corneille's, and, in spite of their classical or Biblical names and settings, they reflect the loves and intrigues of his contemporaries. Three of his eight tragedies take their themes from Euripides—*Andromaque* (1667), *Iphigénie* (1674), and *Phèdre* (1677); three have themes from ancient history—*Britannicus* (1669), *Bérénice* (1670), and *Mithridate* (1673); and two from the Old Testament—*Esther* (1689) and *Athalie* (1690). Except for the last two plays, all have a love-interest as the main theme, and in most of them the tragic interest is concentrated on a heroine rather than a hero. Racine's exquisite, precise poetry, his sure insight, and his austere tragic sense have made him the most notable tragedian since Shakespeare.

At the end of the 19th century the tragic prose-dramas of the Norwegian Henrik IBSEN (q.v. Vol. V), which show man in conflict with social and economic problems, lack tragedy's customary grandeur. Ibsen's dialogue, too, is very near to the conversation of real life. But by following the practice of Racine and Corneille in the strict observance of the dramatic unities he achieved a remarkable intensity and concentration in his dramas. In the present century, the most notable tragedies in the English language have been J. M. SYNGE's (q.v. Vol. V) *Riders to the Sea* (1904) and *Deirdre of the Sorrows* (1910); the American Eugene O'Neill's trilogy, *Mourning Becomes Electra* (1931), in which a Greek story is re-enacted in New England; and T. S. Eliot's poetic dramas, among them *Murder in the Cathedral* (1935), whose Christian theme is expressed in a dramatic form closely resembling that of Aeschylus.

See also DRAMA; GREEK DRAMA; SHAKESPEARIAN DRAMA.

TRAJAN'S COLUMN. This column, 112 feet high, which stands in the forum of Trajan at Rome between the Basilica Ulpia and two library buildings, was dedicated in A.D. 113. The column rises on a rectangular pedestal decorated in relief with trophies and figures representing victories. The victories hold an inscription not yet satisfactorily interpreted. The interior of the pedestal served as a sepulchre for TRAJAN (q.v. Vol. V) and his wife Plotina, the Emperor's ashes being deposited there in a golden urn by his successor Hadrian in A.D. 117. Originally the column was built to commemorate two victorious campaigns waged by Trajan against the barbarian tribes of Dacia, the present Roumania.

The huge shaft, which contains a staircase, is decorated with a spiral band of relief sculpture representing incidents from the Dacian wars and

TRAJAN'S COLUMN, ROME

including about 2,500 figures. The lower part shows events of the first campaign (A.D. 101–2). Beginning with the mighty figure of the river-god Danuvius (Danube) there follow scenes of Roman soldiers loading equipment, building camps and bridges, and on the march. Then come sacrifices, the Emperor exhorting his army, battles with the barbarians, parleys and prisoners, marches and journeys (*see* Vol. X, p. 36). Half-way up the column appears a figure of victory personifying the successful end of the first campaign. The peace treaty of A.D. 102 was broken by the barbarians, and the upper part of the column represents the second campaign (A.D. 105–6). A striking passage shows the barbarians, their water-supply having failed, burning their capital and fleeing. The representation closes with a figure of mourning Dacia. The column is crowned by a platform which originally carried a hemisphere surmounted by an eagle; later a figure of Trajan replaced the eagle. Today a figure of St. Peter stands there.

See also ROMAN ART; MONUMENTS.

TRANSLATIONS. 1. The turning of literary works from one language into another has been of immense importance to writers and their readers, to language and to literature. Translation has been recognized for centuries as a useful exercise for developing students' powers of writing and for enriching their language. To readers, translations reveal other realms of thought and literature. Keats expressed this in his sonnet 'On First Looking into Chapman's Homer' (a translation of the *Iliad* and the *Odyssey* made between 1598 and 1615) when he wrote:

> Then felt I like some watcher of the skies
> When a new planet swims into his ken.

By translations words of one language have become naturalized in another: for example, many Greek and Latin words came into the modern languages of Europe in this way, especially into French, English, and Spanish in the late Middle Ages and early Renaissance.

Translations are not often great literary works in themselves; though they often help great literary works to be created. For example, North's translations of Plutarch's *Lives* gave Shakespeare the themes for *Coriolanus* and *Julius Caesar*, and Wyatt's translations from Italian gave to English verse two of its greatest modes, the blank-verse line (*see* VERSIFICATION) and the SONNET form (q.v.). Sometimes a technique of writing, developed in one country, spreads to other countries through translations: for example, the great Russian novelists of the 19th century, TOLSTOY, DOSTOEVSKY, TURGENEV (qq.v. Vol. V), have had an immense influence on English novelists, most of whom read the Russian masters in the English versions of translators such as Constance Garnett (*see* NOVEL).

2. BIBLE TRANSLATION. The BIBLE (q.v. Vol. 1) has been translated more than any book in the world. The earliest Hebrew manuscript of the Old Testament dates only from the 9th

century A.D., though its text, the Massoretic text, is considered to be of the 1st century A.D. The most notable early translation is the Septuagint, a 3rd-century Greek version made for the Jews in Alexandria.

The earliest manuscripts of the New Testament are in Greek, and there exist early Latin, Syriac, and Coptic translations from the Greek. One of the most important versions of the Bible is the Latin translation completed by St. Jerome in A.D. 405, and known as the Vulgate. It contains the Old Testament freshly translated from the Hebrew by St. Jerome, and the New Testament in a revised version of an older Latin translation. The Vulgate was, from the beginning of the 5th century till the 16th, the Bible of the Western world. It is still the authorized text of the Roman Catholic Church. The Douai Version (1582–1610) is an English translation of it, and so is the English New Testament which Ronald Knox produced in 1945.

The Venerable BEDE (q.v. Vol. V) translated into English the Gospel of St. John from the Vulgate in the 8th century (he is said to have finished it on his death-bed), but this translation has not survived. There were some 9th- and 10th-century translations of the Psalms and Gospels, the most famous of which is the 10th-century word-for-word version of the four Gospels written between the lines of Latin (called a 'gloss') in the magnificent 7th-century illuminated manuscript, the Lindisfarne Gospels. At the end of the 10th century Ælfric translated the Old Testament into English. Little more translating was done till the 14th century, when WYCLIFFE (q.v. Vol. V) and his followers produced the first complete English Bible (1382–8). With the Renaissance came not only the invention of printing but also a renewed interest in Greek and Hebrew studies. Consequently a Hebrew Old Testament (1488) and a Greek New Testament (1516) were published. William Tyndale, a leader of the Reformation movement, first translated the New Testament direct from Greek into English, and much of the Old Testament from Hebrew. (He was later burnt at the stake for heresy.) A complete English Bible incorporating Tyndale's translations and completing them was produced in 1535 by Miles Coverdale. The 1539 revision of this is known as the Great Bible. The edition of this, printed at Geneva and issued in convenient sizes with division into verses, was called the

Geneva Bible. In 1604, the first year of James I's reign, the Hampton Court conference proposed that scholars should undertake a new revision of the Bible: hence came in 1611 the Authorized Version. The beauty of its language and rhythms has made the Authorized Version of the Bible the most powerful force in English literature. It proves that a translation can be a magnificent literary work. The Revised Version (1881–5), made because better Greek texts than those previously used had become available, has never displaced the Authorized Version as the accepted English Bible.

3. MEDIEVAL AND RENAISSANCE TRANSLATIONS. The first known translation of a purely literary work was made in 250 B.C. when Livius Andronicus turned Homer's *Odyssey* into a Latin paraphrase. From this time Greek was taught in Roman schools as an essential part of education, and translation and imitation of Greek texts were regularly practised.

During the Middle Ages the study and translation of other languages was carried on mainly in the monasteries. In the monastery of Whitby in the 7th century, for example, the illiterate poet Caedmon made his *Song of the Creation* from passages of the Vulgate which the monks translated to him. King Alfred, wishing to revive literature and education in England, had four Latin books on religion, history, geography, and philosophy translated into the language of his country, Anglo-Saxon. In the preface to the book on religion Alfred expressed his wish to rebuild the mind of England by such translations. The growth of intellectual activity in Europe which characterized the 12th and 13th centuries showed itself, among other ways, in the frequent translations from Latin into the native languages.

The Renaissance of art and letters in the 14th, 15th, and 16th centuries, and the rediscovery of Greek, stimulated much translation of the Greek manuscripts brought to Europe by refugees from Constantinople, as well as the forgotten Latin texts unearthed in neglected libraries. The Renaissance, therefore, was the great age of classical translation. Translations were made all over Europe of the poetry of Homer, Virgil, Ovid, and Horace; of the histories of Herodotus, Thucydides, Plutarch, Caesar, and Tacitus; of the philosophical works of Plato and Aristotle; and of many other works, among them plays, orations, and romances.

4. LATER TRANSLATIONS. Since the Renaissance, not only classical works, but works from all languages have been translated; some great works have been translated again and again, in particular, works of poetry—which is the most difficult literary form to render in another language. Opinion is divided about how to translate poetry. Some people think that the translator's first aim must be to produce a poem; others that the translator's duty is to produce a word-for-word version of the original, that he should be, as Robert Browning said, 'literal at every cost save that of absolute violence to the language.' Edward Fitzgerald, translator of the *Rubáiyát* of the Persian poet, Omar KHAYYÁM (q.v. Vol. V), belonged to the first school of thought. One much-quoted stanza of the Fitzgerald translation runs—

> A Book of Verses underneath the Bough,
> A Jug of Wine, a Loaf of Bread—and Thou
> Beside me singing in the Wilderness—
> Oh, Wilderness were Paradise enow!

but the literal, word-for-word translation of this same stanza is—

If by good fortune you have a loaf of the kernel of wheat,
A gourd of wine, a leg of mutton,
[To be] sitting with a tulip-cheeked [girl] in the wilderness,
That is pleasure, beyond the reach of any sultan.

The translator changes the poem into that of a cultured Victorian; but fashions change, and though the cultured Victorian might have thought a book of verses preferable to a leg of mutton in the circumstances, it is doubtful whether lovers or poets of today would endorse his view.

Other 19th-century Englishmen produced notable translations from Eastern literatures, such as the ARABIAN NIGHTS (q.v.) and certain Oriental religious classics. In this century many excellent translators, among them Arthur Waley, have made versions of Chinese and Japanese poems, and in thus interpreting another art have influenced a number of contemporary poets. C. K. Scott-Moncrieff made an English version of Proust's great French novel, *Remembrance of Things Past*, so excellent that some French intellectuals have said they prefer it to Proust's original. Professor Gilbert Murray has made new versions of Greek plays. The poets

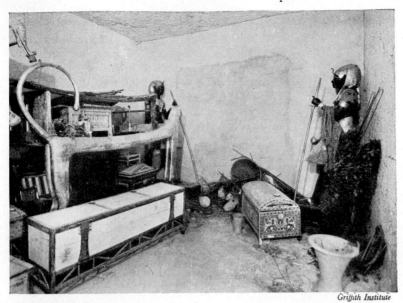

Griffith Institute

THE ANTE-CHAMBER OF TUTANKHAMEN'S TOMB AS IT WAS WHEN FOUND
The two figures guard the entrance to the burial chamber

father-in-law AKHNATEN (q.v. Vol. V), the king who imposed disastrous new ideas upon the age-old culture of Egypt. The young king, led by his advisers, had the task of restoring order and prosperity, but after a reign of 9 years he died at the age of 18 and was buried in the Valley of the Kings at Thebes. In 1922 Howard Carter, excavating for Lord Carnarvon, uncovered the tomb with most of its magnificent equipment intact. This small tomb was crammed with objects in some confusion, since it had been ransacked by plunderers and only perfunctorily cleared up by inspectors soon after the king's interment. The body of Tutankhamen had not, however, been molested. The tomb consisted of an ante-chamber, with a small annexe at one end, and at the other, behind a sealed doorway, the burial chamber with a 'treasury' adjoining. In the burial chamber four carved and gilded wooden shrines surrounded the stone sarcophagus which contained three coffins, the innermost of inlaid gold (see Vol. I, p. 156) and the outer ones of gilded and inlaid wood. There were also objects specially provided for the burial of the king, such as wines, oils, and preserved food, and others used in the funeral ceremonies, such as three large couches with animal heads, ritual implements, and wreaths and bouquets; finally there were things which the king had used in his lifetime, such as thrones, beds, chests, clothing, jewellery (see Vol. I, p. 158), toys, walking-sticks, sceptres, chariots, weapons, and the like. All these specimens in fine woods, ivory, silver, gold, bronze, pottery, glass, and semi-precious stones reflect the wealth and high artistic and technical ability of the Egyptians at that period.

See also EGYPTIAN ART.
See also Vol. I: EGYPTIAN CIVILIZATION.

C. Day Lewis and Louis MacNeice are producing for this generation translations of such world-famous poetry as Virgil's *Aeneid* and Goethe's *Faust*

Classical, modern European, and Oriental literatures, therefore, can now be read in the English language and heard in English broadcast programmes, and their plays seen in English theatres. The great works of English literature are in the same way available in other languages, often in excellent translations. One of the best poets of the U.S.S.R., Boris Pasternak, for example, has devoted himself to translating Shakespeare into Russian.

TRIO, *see* CHAMBER MUSIC; SONATA.

TROUBADOURS, *see* SONG, HISTORY OF, Section 2.

TURKISH ART, *see* ISLAMIC ART.

TUTANKHAMEN'S TOMB. Tutankhamen was a Pharaoh who ruled from about 1357 to 1349 B.C., when Egypt was a wealthy imperial power He came to the throne on the death of his

V

VATICAN. This is the palace of the Popes, adjoining St. Peter's Cathedral (q.v.) in Rome. Since 1929 the palace, the cathedral, the palace gardens, and certain other buildings have been known as the Vatican City, an independent sovereign State, geographically within Italy but subject only to the Pope and not to the Italian Government. The Vatican has its own postal service, wireless transmitter, and newspaper (see Roman Catholic Church, Vol. I). The palace is one of the largest in the world. It is unique in having no main façade; the upper parts of one side of it are visible from the forecourt of St. Peter's, but the bulk of it lies behind high walls and is only in places visible from the street.

The palace in its present form was started in the middle of the 15th century. It then consisted of two parts—a main block near St. Peter's and a pavilion (known as the Belvedere) several hundred yards to the north. In the narrow space between the main block and the cathedral a chapel for the private use of the Pope was built in 1473 by Pope Sixtus IV, and called, after him, the Sistine Chapel. Artists from Tuscany and Umbria, among them Botticelli (q.v. Vol. V), Ghirlandaio, and Perugino, painted on the walls scenes from the life of Moses and also of Christ. The Florentine painter Fra Angelico had earlier decorated a small chapel in the Vatican, and the Paduan painter Mantegna (qq.v. Vol. V) had likewise worked there, though his frescoes no longer survive. The notorious Pope, Alexander VI (see Borgia Family, Vol. V), occupied a suite of rooms on the ground floor of the main block, which were gorgeously decorated for his use by the Umbrian painter, Pintoricchio.

Under Pope Julius II (1503–13) great changes were made. He commissioned Bramante (q.v. Vol. V) to link the main block with the Belvedere by means of gigantic connecting wings, and to rebuild the cathedral. He also ordered what subsequently became the two most famous series of paintings in the whole of Italy—firstly, the decoration of the ceiling of the Sistine Chapel by Michelangelo (q.v. Vol. V) with frescoes of the Creation (see Vol. I, p. 221), the story of Noah, and many figures of prophets, sibyls, and the ancestors of Christ; and secondly, the paintings in the suite of rooms on the top floor of the main block (the Stanze) (see Vol. I, pp. 215, 402) by Raphael (q.v. Vol. V). Finally under Julius's successor, Leo X, two further works were commissioned from Raphael, the designs for tapestry hangings to be woven in Flanders and to decorate the lower part of the walls of the Sistine Chapel (these, known as the Raphael Cartoons, are now in the Victoria and Albert Museum (see Vol. I, p. 320); and the frescoes, designed by Raphael but executed by his pupils, round the open balconies (*Loggie*) of the courtyard. Later, in 1536, Michelangelo returned to the Sistine Chapel to decorate the whole of the wall behind the altar with a huge fresco of the Last Judgement. Six years later he painted his last frescoes in the so-called

Anderson

THE 'SCALA REGIA' IN THE VATICAN

Pauline Chapel in the short wing which links the Vatican to the front of St. Peter's.

In the 17th century the sculptor and architect BERNINI (q.v. Vol. V) constructed the main staircase (*Scala Regia*) leading from the fore-court of St. Peter's up to the Sistine Chapel. As there was no room between the walls of the old building to lay out the staircase symmetrically, Bernini was forced to use an ingenious theatrical trick of false perspective (similar to that which he used in the forecourt to St. Peter's) whereby the canted walls of the staircase are made to appear regular. Bernini also adapted other parts of the Vatican.

The Pope lives in a relatively small portion of the Vatican palace, most of the rest being now open to the public as a vast museum of antique sculpture, coins, manuscripts, and books. There is also a separate picture gallery, which is one of the finest in Italy.

See also ITALIAN ART.
See also Vol. I: ROMAN CATHOLIC CHURCH.
See also Vol. IV: VATICAN LIBRARY.

VAULT. The method of roofing over a space in a building by a series of arches is known as 'vaulting'. This, made of stone or brick, usually takes the form of a ceiling: that is, the vault does not show externally but supports a roof or upper floor. Vaults are very strong, they give greater protection against fire than wooden roofs, and they can be used to span large spaces. Their ingenious use had a great effect on the development of building from the time of the Romans.

The barrel-vault was most commonly used by the Romans. It was semicircular with an unbroken under-surface (Fig. 1 *a*). Its construction is an extension of the ARCH (q.v.), for it is built up, as it were, of a series of arches placed side by side and supported on the side walls of the building. These walls had to be so strong to support the great weight of the vault that windows could only be inserted in the end walls.

If two barrel-vaults are made to intersect at right angles a cross-vault is formed, which can be supported on piers at the four corners (Fig. 1 *b*). The method of cross-vaulting gives an architect freedom to design a rectangular building of almost any shape, for a number of cross-vaults can be placed side by side indefinitely. Large cross-vaults were used in this way to cover the Roman baths, and sometimes a single unit covered a square space up to 100 feet across.

Romanesque builders used the cross-vault to cover their churches, but the smaller stones and poorer quality of cement which they had to use made their vaulting less successful. The edges, crossing diagonally from corner to corner where the two vaults met, were the weakest points, and were strengthened by ribs or groins forming diagonal arches (Fig. 1 *c*). The groined vault had a number of disadvantages; it was built on the round arch, the height of which is always exactly half its width; and, as the sides of a vault must always be the same height, the widths had also to be the same, with the result that the vault was always square. Nor was it possible to make a very large vault, for the diagonal groins, being wider than the side arches, were flattened, a shape which is structurally weak. The heavy vault also needed immensely strong walls to support it.

a   b   c

FIG. 1. ROMANESQUE VAULTS: *a.* BARREL, *b.* CROSS, *c.* GROINED

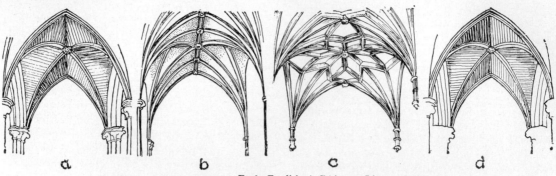

FIG. 2. GOTHIC VAULTS: *a.* Early English, *b.* Ridge, *c.* Lierne, *d.* French

The Gothic builders overcame the difficulty by using pointed arches which could be made the same height though the widths might vary. This made it possible to vault an oblong compartment and allowed great flexibility in the design of buildings. The structure of Gothic vaults was quite different from that of the Roman and Romanesque vaults. The arches at the side and the diagonal groins became the structural skeleton which supported a light skin of stone; the weight of the vault was therefore concentrated at the springing of the arches (the point at which the arch rested on a pillar or wall); at this point buttresses and flying buttresses were built out from the walls to support the thrust of the vaults (*see* p. 79). The walls, being relieved of much weight, could then have large windows.

In the Early English period a simple quadripartite vault, that is, of four compartments divided by diagonal and transverse ribs (Fig. 2 *a*) was usual, as in the naves of Durham, Salisbury, and Gloucester Cathedrals; but later the vault was elaborated by the addition of ridge ribs, as in Westminster Abbey (Fig. 2 *b.*). In England in the Decorated period more ribs, called lierne ribs, were added, making a star-shaped pattern, as at Canterbury, Wells, and Winchester (Fig. 2 *c*). The ribs were enriched with carved bosses covering the points where the ribs crossed (*see* p. 441). In France the vaults were usually simpler, without ridge or lierne ribs, the ridge line often rising in a curve instead of being level. The stones that filled in the vaults were laid in rows parallel to the ridge, whereas in England they were laid at right angles to a line bisecting each panel (Fig. 2 *d*).

The final development of the vault at the end of the Middle Ages was the fan vault, which was only used in England. Groups of ribs sprang upwards in the shape of a fan and spread outwards in a circle till they met the ribs springing from the opposite side (Fig. 3). Sometimes the centre of each circle hung downwards in the form of a pendant. The multiplication of the ribs made the panels between them so small that the same piece of stone could form both the rib and the space between, thus reverting from the skeleton construction of the early Gothic vault to the continuous stone construction of

FIG. 3. FAN VAULT IN KING'S COLLEGE CHAPEL, CAMBRIDGE

the Roman vault. The first fan vault was built over the cloisters of Gloucester Cathedral in 1381–1412, and the grandest examples are those which cover the chapels built by royal patronage at the end of the Gothic period—Henry VII's chapel in Westminster Abbey, St. George's Chapel, Windsor, and King's College Chapel, Cambridge.

Vaulting played only a small part in Renaissance and later buildings.

See also GOTHIC ART; CHURCH ARCHITECTURE, ENGLISH.

VENETIAN PAINTING. The city of VENICE (q.v. Vol. III) is built on mud banks in a lagoon on the north-east coast of Italy. From the time of the Middle Ages the Venetians traded with the East and were thus enabled to enrich their city with many-coloured marbles and costly damask draperies. Worldly magnificence is strongly marked in most Venetian painting, though the religious character of the Venetian Republic (see CITY-STATE, Vol. X) is also apparent in its art. In the great council chamber, for instance, in the palace of the Doge—a room which, by its nature, was not intended or used for religious ceremonies—the place of

honour is occupied by a huge picture of Paradise. Throughout the palace, too, the various State officials are painted together with Christ or the Virgin Mary in a way which is not found in the other Italian States of the Renaissance.

The combination at Venice of Eastern colour and splendour and a romantic site resulted in a type of painting, much of which is romantic in feeling and reveals the particular qualities of the painter—richness and warmth of colour and tone, and delight in the handling of paint—as opposed to those of the draughtsman or sculptor. It was therefore natural that the Venetians should have developed at an early stage the art of oil painting, which gave the greatest scope for those qualities (see PAINTING METHODS). The earliest of the great Venetian painters, Giovanni BELLINI (q.v. Vol. V), was, in fact, using an oil technique well before the end of the 15th century.

As Venice was linked more closely to the East than to the rest of Italy, Renaissance art did not penetrate till late (see ITALIAN ART, Section 4). The early painting is similar in character to BYZANTINE ART (q.v.), and not till the mid-15th century did the Renaissance artists Gentile and

National Gallery

THE AGONY IN THE GARDEN. PAINTING BY GIOVANNI BELLINI (*c.* 1430–1516)

Anzan

DETAIL OF A WALL PAINTING BY PAUL VERONESE (1528–88)
IN THE VILLA GIACOMELLI, MASER, NEAR VENICE
The figures and architectural details are painted to give
an illusion of reality

character, combined it with a vivid interest in nature.

Other 15th-century painters, such as Crivelli, while adopting Renaissance motives and showing great interest in perspective, retain something of Byzantine magnificence and lack of movement which makes their work little more than rich decoration (*see* p. 342).

By the beginning of the 16th century another typically Venetian quality—the romantic—was coming to the fore in the paintings of a young genius called GIORGIONE (q.v. Vol. V). His picture known as 'The Tempest' sums up his qualities and his novelty. There is no central figure; the landscape is almost more important than the people, and the picture has a romantic, poetic atmosphere which inspired a host of imitators in the early 16th century (*see* Vol. V, p. 190)

This romantic quality, which was made possible only by increased skill in the handling of oil-paint, did not reappear in Venetian painting until the 18th century. In the meantime the greatest Venetian painter, TITIAN (q.v. Vol. V), though strongly influenced by Giorgione at the beginning of his career and learning much from him, soon developed a more robust style of his own. Titian's life nearly spans the 16th century, and his influence on later painters was perhaps greater, and lasted longer, than that of any other master. He was supreme alike in religious and mythological pictures and in portraiture,

Giovanni Bellini, who studied under their father Jacopo in Padua introduce the new ideas into Venice. Bellini's works which, apart from a few portraits of high quality, are almost exclusively religious, express in the most beautiful and sincere way the religious side of the Venetian

and no painter has equalled the splendour of his colours and few the accomplishment of his brushwork (*see* Colour Plate opp. p. 336).

During the middle and at end of the 16th century two more great painters were active in Venice, each representing different aspects of Venetian life and character, though both basing themselves on Titian to a large extent. Paul Veronese was a great decorator of palaces, and TINTORETTO (q.v. Vol. V) was perhaps the greatest religious decorator of all time. The courtly refinement of Veronese's style, expressed in

National Gallery

FÊTE ON THE PIAZZA, VENICE. PAINTING BY GUARDI (1712–93)

exquisite, silvery tones, reflected the magnificence of Venetian life, while Tintoretto's darker, glowing colours and his inexhaustible invention expressed a religious feeling quite as intense as Giovanni Bellini's.

In the 18th century, at a time when painting in the rest of Italy was dead, Venice produced her last great painters, who were more light-hearted and romantic in character than any since Giorgione. The most characteristic at this time were the great decorator, Tiepolo, and the painters of romantic views of Venice, Guardi and Canaletto (*see* Vol. IX, opp. p. 208). Both artists painted in a spirit of gaiety and intrigue, like that of a masked ball, and when they died Venetian art, which has been the chief inspiration of much later painting, died too.

See also ITALIAN ART.

VENUS DE MILO. This famous marble statue of the Goddess of Love (known to the Greeks as Aphrodite and to the Romans as Venus) is in the Louvre Museum in Paris. It was found in 1820 in the ruins of an ancient theatre on the Greek island of Melos (in modern Greek, Milo).

The Venus was made about 150 B.C. by a Greek from Asia Minor. The goddess is slightly larger than life-size. The pose is twisted to make the statue look interesting from all angles, and is one of the most successful of ancient statues in this respect. The arms are now missing; originally the figure's right arm hung down in front, the hand holding up the drapery, and the left arm rested on a tall column, the hand holding an apple (the heraldic device of Melos). The head is based on a 5th-century original and is carved with the serenity of that age. The body follows a 4th-century model but is given a more violent twist.

See GREEK ART.

VERSAILLES. This town in France, some 10 miles from the centre of Paris, is famous in art and history for the colossal palace built there by LOUIS XIV (q.v. Vol. V) in the late 17th century. In the centre of the site which it now occupies there was a small hunting-box built by Louis XIII. Louis XIV is said to have chosen the place for his chief residence because of the natural disadvantages of the site: his vanity was such that he wished to show that he could make something out of nothing. He did not destroy his father's little building, but commanded that the vast

Alinari

THE VENUS DE MILO

new palace be built round the small chateau, and all his life he retained his bedroom in the old building, not in the grand new additions.

The palace and gardens of Versailles were largely the creation of four artists—the architects Le Vau and J. H. Mansart, the painter Lebrun, who supervised the interior decoration, and the garden architect Le Nôtre. During some 50 years, about 1660–1710, work proceeded at Versailles at such a speed that it is very remarkable that the workmanship throughout should have been so excellent. Vast sums of money were spent on enlarging the palace till it became one of the largest in the world, on replanning the town of Versailles and constructing great avenues radiating from the palace, and on

Archives Photographiques

THE GARDEN FRONT OF VERSAILLES PALACE

setting up artificial terraces in the gardens and every variety of costly fountain and garden statuary. Versailles was intended to be a background magnificent enough to show off appropriately the most spectacular and powerful monarch in Christendom, and, in spite of its piecemeal character, the splendour of the house and gardens is still undimmed after two centuries (*see* Vol. X, p. 273). In the middle of the 18th century Louis XV built for Madame Dubarry the exquisite house called Petit Trianon in the park of Versailles, and this later became famous as the favourite residence of Queen Marie Antoinette.

VERSE, *see* POETRY; VERSIFICATION, Section 4.

VERSIFICATION. 1. METRE. Poetry sounds different from prose chiefly because its rhythms are more definite and more regular. Rhythms depend upon the arrangement of syllables. In classical languages the rules of versification were based on 'quantity' (the time taken to utter a syllable). Certain vowels were spoken as long sounds and others as short—though there were numerous and complicated exceptions. The rules were first made by the Greeks and copied by the Romans, and the Greek names for the various kinds of rhythm are still used today. The classical 'quantities', however, cannot be applied exactly to modern European languages, since in languages such as English the vowels

have no fixed quantity, but can be either long or short as the rhythm and meaning demand. It is easier, therefore, to speak of stressed or unstressed syllables.

Syllables are arranged into fixed patterns which we call 'feet'; for convenience a short syllable is indicated by ◡, and a long by —. The commonest feet in English verse are the 2-syllable iamb (◡—), trochee (—◡), and spondee (— —); and the 3-syllable anapaest, (◡◡—). Coleridge wrote for his sons a verse in which each line explains and illustrates a metric foot:

Trochee | trips from | long to | short;
From long to long in solemn sort
Slow Spon | dee stalks; | strong foot! | yet ill able
Ever to | come up with | Dactyl tri | syllable.
Iam | bics march | from short | to long;
With a leap | and a bound | the swift An |apaests throng;
One sylla | ble long, with | one short at | each side;
Amphibra | chys hastes with | a stately | stride;
First and last being long, middle short, Amphimacer
Strikes his thun | dering hoofs | like a proud | high-bred Racer.

In Latin and Greek two of the commonest metres were the 6-foot dactylic line (hexameter), and the 5-foot or equivalent 5-foot dactylic line (pentameter). A spondee (— —) might often be substituted for a dactyl (—◡◡), on the principle that a long syllable was roughly equivalent to two short. In English, substitution of one foot for another is very free; in particular trochees, anapaests, and iambics are interchangeable. A monosyllabic foot, too, often substitutes for another. Such substitutions, however, should not be so frequent as to disguise the basic metre, and the ear should always approve. Here is a stanza of 'The Cloud' by Shelley, with basic anapaestic metre and frequent substitutions.

Line number		rhyme-scheme
1.	I sift | the snow ‖ on the moun | tains below,	aa
2.	And their great | pines groan ‖ aghast;	b
3.	And all | the night ‖ 'tis my pil | low white,	cc
4.	While I sleep ‖ in the arms | of the blast.	b
5.	Sublime | on the towers ‖ of my ski | ey bowers,	dd
6.	Light | ning ‖ my pi|lot sits;	e
7.	In a cav | ern un | der ‖ is fet | tered the thunder,	ff
8.	It strug | gles and howls ‖ at fits;	e
9.	Over earth | and o | cean, ‖ with gen | tle motion,	gg
10.	This pi | lot is gui | ding me, ‖	h
11.	Lured | by the love ‖ of the gen | ii that move	ii
12.	In the depths ‖ of the pur | ple sea;	h
13.	O | ver the rills, ‖ and the crags, | and the hills,	jj
14.	O | ver the lakes ‖ and the plains,	k
15.	Where | ver he dream ‖, under moun | tain or stream,	ll
16.	The Spi | rit he loves ‖ remains;	k
17.	And I | all the while ‖ bask in Hea | ven's blue smile,	mm
18.	Whilst he ‖ is dissol | ving in rains.	k

The basic metre is four anapaest feet to every odd line, three to every even. The feet which substitute for anapaests are usually iambs, for example, the first 2 feet of the stanza; but sometimes, as in the first foot of lines 6 and 11, a monosyllabic foot substitutes. Such a foot of one long syllable usually substitutes for the first or last foot of a line, or at a pause in the line. Another recognized metrical irregularity occurs at the end of line 7, where there is an extra syllable—the -*der* of thunder—after the last foot.

In this stanza the sign ‖ indicates the pause (in Latin verse, *caesura*). In every 4-foot line here—that is, in every odd line—the pause is a true regular middle pause, at the end of the second foot; moreover it is accentuated by internal rhyme: (line 1) snow–below, (line 3) night–white, and so for every odd line. In the 3-foot lines—that is, the even lines—more variation appears; the pause comes after the first foot or the second, or (line 6) in the middle of the second foot, or (line 10) at the end of the line. In English poetry the pause is, after foot-substitution, the most important variable. In very long lines the pause tends to occur in the middle of the line, or sometimes the line is divided into three by two equidistant pauses. Sometimes lines (and some couplets and even stanzas) do not pause at the end, but run straight on to the next line; this is called 'over-run' or 'enjambment'. The lines 11–12 above, for example, have no pause after 'move'. This flexibility in the use of the pause is the source of great variety in the rhythms of English poetry, and most particularly in blank verse.

2. RHYME. The 18 lines of Shelley's stanza are grouped into three units of 4 lines each, and a fourth of 6 lines; and this arrangement is emphasized by rhyme (the rhyme-scheme is indicated by the letters on the right). Rhyme is used most frequently at the end of lines, but, as here, it can be used internally too, to bind and isolate groups of lines and to add its music to the poetry. Rhyme is the correspondence of vowel-sounds, and of any following consonant-sounds, in words. Thus *sea* rhymes with *me* because the vowel-sounds correspond; and *night* with *white* because the vowel and following consonantal sounds correspond. 'Identical' rhymes, that is, rhymes such as *night* and *knight* where there is a correspondence between the consonant-sounds which precede the vowel, are used rarely and with discretion. A 'double' rhyme is when both of two consecutive syllables rhyme, as ocean–motion, under–thunder. 'Triple' and more than triple rhymes, though rarely used in serious verse, are effective in comic verse, as in this stanza of Edward Lear's—

> His mind is concrete and fast*idious*,
>   His nose is remarkably big;
> His visage is more or less *hideous*,
>   His beard it resembles a wig.

Poets may occasionally use words—as Shelley in line 11 of his stanza uses *love* and *move*—which do not rhyme to the ear but only to the eye.

Rhyme dates only from the 11th century. Old English poetry had no rhyme, and the basis of its structure was 'alliteration', that is, using in close connexion syllables—particularly stressed syllables—which begin with the same letter (*see* BEOWULF). Alliteration in modern English poetry is not structurally necessary, as it was in Old English, but it can be an additional strength and grace. Two late 19th-century poets used alliteration with great success: Swinburne used it to make the sound echo the sense, as in—

With lisp of leaves and ripple of rain.

Gerard Manley Hopkins's alliteration is forceful, passionate, complex—

Oh let them be left, wildness and wet,
Long live the weeds and the wilderness yet.

These two lines illustrate 'assonance' as well as alliteration: that is, the repetition of the same vowel-sound, particularly in accented syllables —let, left, wet, yet. In Old French and Spanish verse, assonance was often used as rhyme is now.
Something harder to define than assonance has been called vowel-music. It eludes analysis as a musical theme does: the sequence of vowel-sounds, like a sequence of notes, can be observed and charted; but the music can only be heard and felt. Shakespeare is a supreme master of this—

Under the greenwood tree,
Who loves to lie with me
And turn his merry note
Unto the sweet bird's throat,
Come hither, come hither, come hither:
    Here shall he see
    No enemy
But winter and rough weather.
                            (*As You Like It.*)

3. LINE. In theory, a line of poetry may be of any length; but in practice some lines are more successful than others, more apt to particular languages and to particular purposes. Some are named according to the number of feet they contain, like the 'hexameter', the great 6-foot metre of Greek and Latin EPIC POETRY (q.v.); some according to the number of syllables in the line, for example, the 11-syllable 'hendeca-syllabic' line which is the staple of Italian verse; or the English 'fourteener', which Chapman used in his translation of the *Iliad*, and whose 7 iambic feet are the original of the ballad-measure (*see* BALLAD). The most notable

line of English verse is the 'decasyllabic', the 10-syllable line of blank verse, sonnet, and heroic couplet. Some have more individual names, such as the French 'Alexandrine', the 6-foot iambic line probably named from the old French poem on Alexander, which is the metre of Corneille's and Racine's plays and is unrivalled in French verse.
Lines are usually grouped into 'stanzas' or verses, the equivalent in poetry of paragraphs. An exception to this is blank verse, the greatest, freest, most flexible metre of English, the metre of Shakespeare's plays, of Milton's *Paradise Lost*, of Keats's *Hyperion*. The rhythms of its lines— normally of 5 iambic feet—without the discipline of rhyme or stanza, are modulated by foot-substitution, variable pause, and enjambment.

4. STANZAS. A stanza may consist of any number of lines; even in the same poem the stanzas can vary in length (the 18-line stanza of Shelley's 'The Cloud' quoted above is preceded by a 12-line stanza, and followed by a 14-line one). Most usually, however, poems are arranged in equal stanzas. The shortest, simplest stanza form is the 'couplet', and the most important English couplet is the 'heroic couplet', with two rhyming lines of 5 iambs each. Chaucer, who first brought order and form to modern English prosody, established the heroic couplet in English, and used it with great skill in the Prologue to the CANTERBURY TALES (q.v.); since then, its popular name has been, aptly, 'riding rhyme'. The second and third of the following three lines is the couplet:

And Frensh she spak ful faire and fetisly,
After the scole of Stratford atte Bowe,
For Frensh of Paris was to hir unknowe.

A 'triplet' or 'tercet' is a group of 3 lines, usually rhymed together. The tercet of the Italian *terza rima* is a triplet in which the first and third lines rhyme, while the second commonly rhymes with the first and third of the next group. Such tercets are very familiar in the 'sestet' (the last 6 lines) of the SONNET (q.v.). *Terza rima* is a magnificent Italian measure, and Dante its greatest exponent.
The stanza of 4 lines, the 'quatrain', is a universal measure, used by the Greeks in lyric metres and adapted by the Romans, notably Horace, and used by many poets since. The ballad-stanza was an early English form of rhyming quatrain. The English 'decasyllabic

quatrain' has a long and honourable history as an independent stanza form in lyric and dramatic poetry. Some poets have varied it by altering the length of its lines, some by modifying its rhyme-scheme from a b a b to a b b a. And quatrain is often extended to quintet (5-line stanza).

The two most notable 6-line metres of English are 'Burns metre' and 'romance-six', both originally French metres. The former was used in English miracle plays and then survived in Scotland, where Burns found and revived it. Here is Burns's metre, in a stanza of his to a mouse whose nest was destroyed by his plough:

> But, Mousie, thou art no thy lane,   (alone)
> In proving foresight may be vain:
> The best laid schemes o' mice an' men
>   Gang aft a-gley,   (go oft awry)
> An' lea'e us nought but grief an' pain
>   For promis'd joy.

Romance-six, as its name implies, was often used in medieval English romances, such as *Sir Eglamour* and *Sir Thopas*; but English lyricists have adopted it for their own. Lines 1, 2, 4, and 5 are 4-feet lines; 3 and 6 are 3-feet. The rhyme-scheme varies: *Sir Thopas*, for example, rhymes a a b c c b. Here is a stanza by a modern poet, Dylan Thomas, in this metre, with a rhyme-scheme a b c a b c:

> Dry as a tomb, your coloured lids
> Shall not be latched while magic glides
> Sage on the earth and sky;
> There shall be corals in your beds,
> There shall be serpents in your tides,
> Till all our sea-faiths die.

The most successful 7-line stanza is 'rhyme-royal'. It can have either 7 decasyllabic lines, or 5 decasyllabic followed by a hendeca-syllabic couplet; its rhyme-scheme is a b a b b c c. Originally a French metre, it was introduced into English by Chaucer, and became a favourite 15th-century metre. Chaucer used it in *Troilus and Criseyde*, from which this stanza is quoted:

> For of fortune's sharp adversitee
> The worste kynde of infortune is this,
> A man to han ben in prosperitee,
> And it remembren, whan it passed is.
> Th'art wis ynough, forthido nat amys:
> Be naught to rakel, theigh thow sitte warme;
>   (not too rash)
> For if thow be, certeyn, it wol the harme.

One of the two principal 'octave' (8-line) stanzas, the form that rhymes a b a b b c b c, was also used by Chaucer. The other, derived from the Italian *ottava rima* and rhymed a b a b a b c c, though it appeared later in English, has been used more: Byron, for example, used it for *Don Juan*—

> 'Tis sweet to win, no matter how, one's laurels,
>   By blood or ink; 'tis sweet to put an end
> To strife; 'tis sometimes sweet to have our quarrels,
>   Particularly with a tiresome friend:
> Sweet is old wine in bottles, ale in barrels;
>   Dear is the helpless creature we defend
> Against the world, and dear the schoolboy spot
> We ne'er forget, though there we are forgot.

Spenser added an Alexandrine to Chaucer's octave, thus forming the 'Spenserian stanza' of 9 lines, rhyming a b a b b c b c c, the metre of *The Faerie Queene* The invention of this beautiful stanza was only one of Spenser's many contributions to versification. Because of changing pronunciation in the 15th century, Chaucer's measures had been misunderstood, and it fell to Spenser to re-establish harmonious form in English poetry.

5. SHORT POEM FORMS. There are other forms where the structural unit is not the stanza, but the whole poem—for example, the sonnet. In such forms, usually both the number and kind of lines and the rhyme-scheme are fixed. The 'ballade' usually consists of three 8-line stanzas followed by a 4-line envoy, all on three rhymes only in the same order in each stanza, and with the same line ending each stanza and the envoy. A longer and more elaborate ballade, with five stanzas of 11 lines each and an envoy of from 5 to 8 lines, is called 'Chant Royale', and, like the ballade, is of French origin. The 'rondeau' is another kind of verse-form, with its variants, 'rondeau of Villon', 'rondel', and 'roundel'. In all of these forms the ending re-echoes the opening—hence the name 'round'; and all the rhymes re-echo the first two.

> A roundel is wrought as a ring or a starbright sphere,
> With craft of delight and with cunning of sound un-
>   sought,
> That the heart of the hearer may smile if to pleasure
>   his ear
>   A roundel is wrought.
>
> Its jewel of music is carven of all or of aught—
> Love, laughter, or mourning—remembrance of
>   rapture or fear—
> That fancy may fashion to hang in the ear of thought.

As a bird's quick song runs round, and the hearts in us
    hear
Pause answer to pause, and again the same strain
    caught,
So moves the device whence, round as a pearl or tear
        A roundel is wrought.

              (Swinburne.)

The 'triolet' is an 8-line verse in which the first line occurs three times (lines 1, 4, 7); and the second line twice (lines 2, 8); the other lines rhyme with these two. Here is Gerard Manley Hopkins's triolet protesting against Wordsworth's paradox, which he quotes in the first line:

'The child is father to the man.'
How can he be? The words are wild.
Suck any sense from that who can:
'The child is father to the man'.
No; what the poet did write ran,
'The man is father to the child.'
'The child is father to the man!'
How *can* he be? The words are wild.

See also POETRY.

VICTORY OF SAMOTHRACE. This colossal marble statue was found on the Greek island of Samothrace, and is now in the Louvre Museum in Paris. It portrays the Goddess of Victory in the form of a winged woman, flying down from the skies to alight on the bow of a war-galley. It has been put together again from many fragments which were discovered in 1863 and shortly after. In 1950 a few more fragments were excavated, and the statue was proved to have been made about 200 B.C.

Although the head and most of both arms are still missing, enough has been preserved to show one of the finest Greek sculptures which we possess of the Hellenistic period (*see* GREEK ART). The drapery clings to the body in front and is blown out behind, as the goddess floats gently down to the ship. The enormous wings,

Alinari

THE VICTORY OF SAMOTHRACE

stretched out behind her, balance the forward-tilting body. Originally the head was thrown back, the left arm was stretched downwards, and the right arm was raised up in a gesture of leadership.

This statue must have been made to celebrate a victory at sea. It was set up on the heights not far from the sea, overlooking the magnificent religious buildings of Samothrace, and must have appeared to be sailing out of harbour against the enemy. In front and below it was a large basin filled with water and framed partly by marble steps and partly by boulders.

See also GREEK ART.

W

WATER-COLOURS. For many centuries painters have used water as a means of making their colours fluid (*see* PAINTING METHODS). In the Middle Ages ILLUMINATED MANUSCRIPTS were painted in water-colours, and the medium has normally been used for portraits in MINIATURE (qq.v.). The fresco method of wall-painting is merely a special form of water-colour painting on plaster. Furthermore, early artists, such as DÜRER (q.v. Vol. V), sometimes used water-colours to emphasize their pen drawings of plants or animals, and washes of grey or black have long been used to finish off architectural drawings. Nevertheless, water-colour painting as an independent and honoured form of art was little practised before the middle of the 18th century.

Water-colour pictures are usually painted on paper and are normally considerably smaller than the average oil-painting on canvas. The white of the paper tends to show through the thin colours, and, although this can be used to give a luminous or sparkling effect, it means that dark tints are difficult to obtain. The thinness of the paint, again, and the fact that it dries quickly makes correcting—which is easy when the painter is using thick oil-colour—difficult or impossible. For all these reasons water-colour paintings tend to be more delicate in effect than oils. They are also more delicate to preserve, since, unlike oils, water-colours fade quickly in the sun.

The medium has been found specially suited to landscape subjects, with their soft atmospheric effects and their quickly changing light and colour. It is therefore not surprising that water-colour painting, although practised in other countries such as Holland, is particularly associated with the British school, which has specialized in all forms of LANDSCAPE PAINTING (q.v.). In the middle of the 18th century, when Richard Wilson was laying the foundations of the great British school of landscape in oil, artists such as Paul Sandby and Alexander Cozens were doing the same in water-colours. They were followed by the most distinguished of all the British landscape painters in water-colours—J. R. Cozens (the son of Alexander), Thomas Girtin, J. S. Cotman, and Peter de Wint.

With the work of these painters the art of water-colour painting was able for the first time to stand comparison with the finest oils of similar subjects. J. R. Cozens was a friend of the rich and eccentric William Beckford and, like him, took part in the beginning of the ROMANTIC MOVEMENT (q.v.), in which poets and painters rebelled against the rigid rules of earlier 18th-century art and looked for their inspiration to the wilder aspects of Nature. 'Sublime' and 'awful' became fashionable words for describing scenery, and J. R. Cozens's fame rests largely on his dramatic pictures of the Alps painted in this vein. He used a very restricted palette, largely confined to grey and blue. Girtin, who

Victoria & Albert Museum

THE LAKE OF NEMI. WATER-COLOUR BY J. R. COZENS (1752–97)

Victoria & Albert Museum
DURHAM. WATER-COLOUR BY THOMAS GIRTIN (1775–1802)

colours other than preliminary sketches for oil paintings, though one of his finished water-colours—of Stonehenge—is among the finest ever painted. Two painters roughly contemporary with the landscape school—the satirical cartoonist Rowlandson and the religious visionary William BLAKE (q.v. Vol. V)—used water-colours in preference to oils in depicting figure subjects, which is exceptional (*see* Colour Plates opp. pp. 448 and 288).

Since the death of Turner, in 1851, water-colour painting has declined somewhat, though certain famous painters, such as Cézanne, have used it from time to time as an alternative to oils, and some still use it. At the present time water-colour is still one of the media most favoured by amateurs. It is also normally used for designs for fashion-plates and for theatrical scenery and costumes, though these, as well as POSTERS (q.v.), are often painted in opaque 'poster colours' or gouache rather than the transparent pigments used for landscapes.

See also DRAWING; PAINTING METHODS; LANDSCAPE PAINTING.

died when only 27, also avoided bright, vivid colours and favoured a brownish tone. He frequently produced a romantic effect in his pictures by painting ruins towering dramatically in a landscape. With Cotman the choice of the subject becomes less important. He saw the landscape round him as a well-ordered pattern, and his representations of it are astonishingly precise and delicate (*see* Colour Plate, Vol. VII, opp. p. 384). Contemporary with these artists was J. M. W. TURNER (q.v. Vol. V), probably the greatest landscape painter who has ever lived, who, unlike the others, was equally successful in oils and water-colours. Constable, Turner's rival in oils, made relatively few water-

WONDERS OF THE WORLD. The Greeks of the age following the death of Alexander the Great (about 320–100 B.C.) were great sightseers, and a number of guide-books were compiled for their use. In some such guide-book a list must have been drawn up of the seven works of art considered most worth seeing. This list, which has come down to us in several versions, is usually known as the 'Seven Wonders of the World'. The original Seven Wonders are in all probability the following:

1. *The* PYRAMIDS (q.v.) *of Egypt.*
2. *The Hanging Gardens of Babylon.* These were probably gardens planted on the terraced stages of the massive Babylonian temple-towers or *ziggurats* (*see* SUMERIAN ART). The Walls of Babylon, which are found on some lists, are probably connected with these.
3. *The Temple of Artemis at Ephesus.* A magni-

British Museum
GRETA BRIDGE. WATER-COLOUR BY J. S. COTMAN (1782–1842)

ficent Greek temple was built outside the city of Ephesus, in Asia Minor, between 350 and 300 B.C. to replace an earlier one which had been burnt down. It was unusually large, and had 127 columns, many of which were sculptured in relief; some of these sculptures are in the British Museum.

4. *The Statue of Zeus at Olympia.* The Athenian sculptor Phidias made this, probably about 450 B.C., of gold and ivory for the temple of Zeus at OLYMPIA (q.v.). The statue has perished, but some idea of its appearance can be gained from the detailed descriptions which have come down to us, and from its representation on coins. It was a seated figure, nearly 40 feet high.

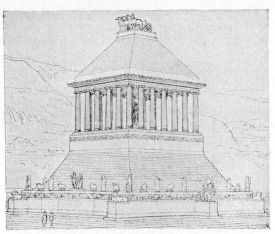

RECONSTRUCTION OF THE MAUSOLEUM OF HALICARNASSUS
From the *Journal of Hellenic Studies, vol. lix*

6. *The Colossus of Rhodes.* This enormous bronze statue of the sun-god Helios was made by the Greek sculptor Chares in 250 B.C. It stood about 100 feet high, and was probably situated by the harbour, but not (as was once thought) astride it. It was knocked down by an earthquake in 224 B.C., and nothing remains of it.

STATUE OF ZEUS AT OLYMPIA
From A. B. Cook, *Zeus*, C.U.P.

5. *The Mausoleum at Halicarnassus.* This was the tomb of Mausolus, ruler of Caria in Asia Minor, built about 350 B.C. Its form is not certain, but it must have been somewhat like the sketch shown here. The tomb was surmounted by a statue of Mausolus and decorated with sculptures, of which those that survive are in the British Museum.

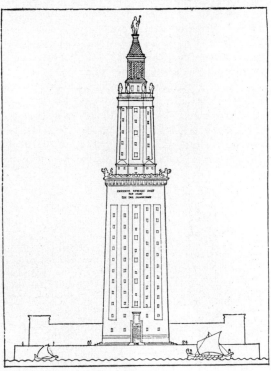

RECONSTRUCTION OF THE PHAROS OF ALEXANDRIA
From T. Fyfe, *Hellenistic Architecture*, C.U.P.

7. *The Pharos of Alexandria.* This was a lighthouse, the first of its kind, built on the island of Pharos at the entrance to the harbour at Alexandria by Ptolemy Philadelphus, the ruler of Egypt (285–246 B.C.). It stood about 400 feet high.

WOODCARVING.

Wood has been carved from earliest times, for few countries are short of wood and many possess it in abundance. Wood, however, is a more perishable material than baked clay, or stone, or some metals. Being a living substance, unless it is very carefully protected, it may rot, warp, or split and crack. It may be attacked by insects, worms, and in hot countries, ants; the beetle is a familiar enemy of old English oak.

To enable wood to survive for more than a few centuries, special conditions are necessary. For instance, wooden animals carved about 2,500 years ago, which have been found in a number of graves in Siberia, owe their preservation to having been long buried in a layer of soil which was completely frozen. In Egypt the dry atmosphere has caused a few carved wooden figures to survive in hermetically sealed tombs from a still more remote antiquity. An oak figure-head (or possibly stern-post) from a Viking ship of the early 9th century, nearly 5 feet long, recovered with a ship's timbers from the Scheldt, survived because it had settled down into the thick mud of the river-bed. On the other hand, none has survived of the hundreds of wooden statues described by the Greek geographer and historian Pausanias in his detailed account of his travels through Greece in the 2nd century A.D.

The principal soft woods used for carving are those of the conifers—pine, fir, and cedarwood. Being easier to work, they are for some purposes more suitable than hard woods, but pine is uneven in grain, often knotty, and very liable

British Museum

Griffith Institute

F. H. Crossley

LEFT: VIKING SHIP'S FIGUREHEAD FOUND IN THE RIVER SCHELDT, PROBABLY 9TH CENTURY

CENTRE: SHEIKH-EL-BELED. EGYPTIAN WOODCARVING, *c.* 2800 B.C.

RIGHT: BENCH-END IN SOUTH BRENT CHURCH, SOMERSET, 15TH CENTURY
A fox, dressed as an abbot, is preaching to geese

to splinter. The hard woods include oak, beech, walnut, lime, sycamore, mahogany, teak, ebony, box, cherry, apple, pear-wood, and a variety of others. They are very attractive materials, with their varied graining, texture, and colour, but they are often difficult to carve on account of their much closer grain.

The carver's principal tools are chisels of various sizes; with hard wood a mallet may be needed to force the chisel into the wood. Other tools are a gouge for the preliminary roughing-out and a rasp for smoothing off the rough edges. Sometimes the rough edges are left, and in some circumstances can be very attractive. When, however, a smooth wooden surface is required, it is rubbed with fine sandpaper; the finished surface is then sometimes waxed or oiled to help to preserve it. Wood darkens with age, and oiling helps to darken it more quickly; indeed, one of the delights of wood is that, if properly cared for, it grows more and more beautiful with age.

The carver must respect the particular qualities of his material: in fact, to a considerable extent he may allow the material itself to determine the form. Just as a large ivory statuette often follows the curving form of an elephant's tusk, so also in wood sculpture the tree form is often implicit in the composition itself. This is apparent, for example, in the Viking figurehead mentioned earlier.

AFRICAN ART (q.v.) includes some of the finest works carved in wood. The African Negroes, before contact with Europeans, had a particularly vivid feeling for the character of wood. Some of their figures were intended to embody the spirits of things which in their lives they found fearful. This explains the distortions and the highly conventional, frequently semi-abstract, character of much Negro art (*see* p. 363).

The peoples of the Nile Valley, on the other hand, were concerned mainly with naturalistic representation. The so-called Sheikh-el-Beled statue, for example, as we now see it, presents, in the face at least, an almost life-like portrait. The wood, however, of such statues was not originally left bare, nor were the joints visible. It was either tightly bound with strips of linen, brightly coloured, or covered with gesso (fine plaster mixed with glue) and painted. Furthermore, the eyes were represented by pieces of rock-crystal (for the iris) and ebony (for the pupil), while the head was covered with a wig of actual hair.

Victoria & Albert Museum
KUAN YIN (DEITY OF COMPASSION)
Chinese woodcarving, 12th or 13th century

The Chinese and Japanese have always been enthusiastic woodcarvers. They too coated the wood with gesso, which was coloured and gilded. The richly decorated Buddhist figure illustrated achieves a balance and a poise which are as pleasing as its generous and kindly spirit.

In Europe the art of woodcarving has flourished, especially during the 15th to 18th centuries. In Germany in the 15th and 16th centuries many altar-pieces were carved with figures in high relief as well as free-standing figures (*see* ALTAR). The technical skill of the woodcarvers was so great that they often sacrificed the quality of the material in their attempts to render biblical scenes with naturalism and feeling.

In England there is a great natural wealth of oak, and woodcarving, particularly in oak, has always been important, especially in the Middle Ages and in the 16th and 17th centuries. At these times oak was the chief material for furniture and was much used in buildings, being frequently enriched by ornamental carving. Not much domestic furniture of the Middle Ages has survived; but in many churches, often in quite small villages, especially in the eastern counties and in the south-west, innumerable examples of 15th- and 16th-century woodcarving can be seen in roofs, screens, stalls, bench-ends, font-covers, pulpits, chests, and so on. Sometimes the decoration follows architectural forms, as in the carved tracery on ROOD SCREENS (q.v.) and on the canopies of stalls; sometimes intertwined leaves or animals enrich the surfaces. Figure subjects may be used decoratively, as in the angels with spread wings on the roofs of a number of churches in East Anglia, or they may tell a story, as in some of the MISERICORDS (q.v.) beneath the seats in choir stalls. There is rich variety in the decoration of bench-ends, which were cut from oak planks 3 to 4 inches thick, sawn vertically from the tree-trunk. Some were designed with square heads, others with 'poppy-heads' (from the Latin *puppis*, meaning the curved poop, or sometimes figurehead, of a ship).

Little medieval woodcarving on a large scale remains, though there are some wooden tomb effigies similar in style to stone figures (*see* TOMBS), which were originally covered with a thin coat of gesso, and painted and gilded. A wood figure commemorating William de Valence (died 1296) in Westminster Abbey is covered with plates of copper, enriched with gilding, enamels, and originally, also, with jewels.

The furniture, staircases, and fireplaces of the 16th and 17th centuries were lavishly carved in bold relief. In the late 17th century the quality of the carving became more refined; in England the most intricate and delicate work was done by Grinling GIBBONS (q.v. Vol. V) and his followers.

See also Vol. VII: HARDWOODS; SOFTWOODS.
See also Vol. XI: FURNITURE, HISTORY OF.

WOOD-ENGRAVING AND WOODCUTS.

The oldest form of printed picture was made by cutting the face of a block of wood until the shape of the picture stood out in relief, and then dabbing or rolling with ink the part in relief and pressing it on the printing surface. This is still the principle on which the two kindred crafts of wood-engraving and woodcutting are based. They are both forms of relief printing (*see* PRINTING, Section 1, Vol. VII). The word 'engraving', when used alone, refers to engraving on metal, which is not a form of relief printing (*see* ETCHING AND ENGRAVING).

Woodcutting differs from wood-engraving in the tools used and the wood employed. For woodcuts, the tree (usually pear or cherry) is cut into planks along the grain of the trunk or branch; the surface is known as 'plank-grain'. For wood-engravings a harder wood is necessary (almost always boxwood), and this is cut into slices across the grain of the trunk or branch, so that the print is cut on the 'end grain'.

The chief tool for making woodcuts is a sharp knife; this is used to outline the shapes and to cut down below the surface parts not intended to print. Large pieces are removed with a gouge; but fine white lines are produced by making two cuts side by side with the knife held at different angles so that the cuts meet below the surface of the wood and a triangular shaving of wood is removed. In woodcutting it is almost impossible to obtain very fine white lines, though the astonishing skill of 15th- and 16th-century craftsmen overcame this difficulty to some extent; the technique is better suited to a bold, simple design with strong contrasts of black and white.

Wood-engraving is done with a graver or burin, which is triangular in section and cuts out a V-shaped piece of wood. A single stroke

British Museum

'ARS MORIENDI' (THE ART OF DYING)
Woodcut from a Block Book, c. 1450

Bodleian Library

WOODCUT FROM 'THE DREAM OF POLYPHILO' BY FRANCESCO
DE COLONNA, 1499

of the graver on the end-grain of boxwood will remove a thin, triangular shaving of wood that would need at least two and probably four cuts with the knife on the plank-grain. Very fine lines can be obtained in wood-engraving, and these can be cut close together to give the effect of a grey tone.

Woodcutting is by far the older of the methods. It was being used by the Chinese in the 9th century A.D. In Europe, in the late 14th century, woodcuts were used to make playing cards and images of saints, and also for printing fabrics, but it was not until the 15th century that woodcuts became widespread.

The first printed books were block-books, in which the text as well as the illustration was cut in a piece of wood. A popular block-book in Europe, in the 15th century, was the *Biblia Pauperum* (Poor Man's Bible) in which the Bible stories were told in a series of pictures with short explanations beside them. When movable types came into use in the middle of the 15th century, woodcuts were used for the illustrations and also for decorated initials and ornamental borders. This medium is particularly suited for book illustration because the woodcuts can be printed at the same time as the text. One of the finest illustrated books, *The Dream of Polyphilo*, published in Venice in 1499, was illustrated with magnificent woodcuts by an unknown artist.

In the 15th century many important artists designed woodcuts, especially in Germany, the actual cutting usually being done, not by the artists, but by expert craftsmen. In the following years the two greatest producers of woodcuts,

Albrecht DÜRER and Hans HOLBEIN (qq.v. Vol. V), both designed series of pictures with religious or moral themes: for example, Dürer's scenes from the Life and Passion of Christ (*see* Vol. IV, p. 196) and Holbein's 'Dance of Death', in which men and women of all ranks are shown with Death always at their elbow. Such series of illustrations were produced in great numbers in woodcut and also in etching and engraving.

Some of the earliest woodcuts were coloured, either by hand or with stencils, and some have had colours printed by superimposing additional blocks, each printing a separate colour. In the 16th century the 'chiaroscuro' woodcut was used. This was made with two or more blocks: one, printed in black, reproduced the outline

British Museum

SOLDIERS AND A WOMAN, DEATH IN A TREE. WOOD-
ENGRAVING BY URS GRAF, 1524

of the design, while the second was printed in a neutral grey or brown tint. This added tone and richness to the picture.

After the magnificent work of the early 16th century the woodcut gradually declined in excellence and popularity. Cuts illustrating herbals (books about medicinal plants) in the 17th century were sometimes very decorative but often crude, and during the 18th century woodcuts were mostly decorative head- and tail-pieces for books.

In Japan, during the late 18th and early 19th centuries, cheap woodcuts, exquisitely printed in colour, were produced in large numbers, mostly by quite humble craftsmen. They were mainly landscapes, pictures of actors and actresses, and scenes from everyday life, and the design was so good and strong that many great European artists were influenced by them (see JAPANESE ART).

Metal engravings replaced woodcuts for the illustration of books at the end of the 17th century, for in these the lines could be much finer and minute detail was possible. At the end of the 18th century the method of engraving on the end grain of wood was invented, and this could give results as fine as metal engraving, though, since boxwood branches are small, the size of the blocks was limited.

Towards the end of the 18th century an English engraver, Thomas Bewick (1753–1828), raised the art of wood-engraving to a level of excellence that has not been surpassed. Triumphing over the limitations of the material Bewick managed to suggest on a few square inches of wood wide landscapes with figures, and animals and birds portrayed with astonishing detail. In earlier woodcuts the wood was usu-ally cut away, leaving the lines of the composition on the surface of the block so that these printed black. Bewick used the cuts to indicate the main lines of his designs so that they printed white against a black background. His technique was, therefore, closer to drawing direct on the block in white on black, using the graver instead of a pencil. He illustrated books on birds and animals and also children's books and fables.

During the 19th century, before the invention of PROCESS REPRODUCTION (q.v. Vol. VII), wood-engraving became a mere trade for the reproduction of drawings. An artist would make his original drawing on a wooden block, and then an engraver, or sometimes a team of engravers, cut away the wood round the lines of the drawing—the engraver's object (which was not always successful) being to retain the individual style of each artist. Even newspapers were illustrated with wood-engravings. But this kind of reproductive engraving soon became so dull and uninspired that, at the end of the 19th century, William MORRIS (q.v. Vol. V) led a movement to recapture the spirit that had produced the beautiful books of the 15th century. Artists again began to design and cut their own wood-engravings, and wood-engravings of a high artistic quality resulted.

In the 20th century wood-engraving has again become popular for book illustrations. Artists have studied not only the way to achieve fine effects within the limitations of the material, but also have designed blocks which look well in relation to the type in which the book is printed.

See also ETCHING AND ENGRAVING; LITHOGRAPHY.
See also Vol. IV: BOOKS, HISTORY OF; ILLUSTRATION.
See also Vol. VII: PROCESS REPRODUCTION.

British Museum

HANGING OUT WASHING
WOOD-ENGRAVING BY BEWICK, 1827